Caring for Your Baby and Young Child

This invaluable volume was prepared under the editorial direction of distinguished pediatricians Tanya Altmann, MD, FAAP, and David L. Hill, MD, FAAP, and draws on the contributions and practical wisdom of more than 100 pediatric experts and an editorial review board. Written in a warm, accessible style and illustrated with more than 300 helpful drawings and diagrams, this book gives you the information you need to safeguard your child's most precious asset: his or her health.

In *Caring for Your Baby and Young Child* you'll find:

- A month-by-month guide to your baby's first year that lets you know what to expect in terms of growth, behavior, and development
- A yearly guide to ages one through five, with practical advice for dealing with sleeping, toilet training, and temper tantrums
- "Health Watch" features that alert you to potential medical problems at each stage
- "Safety Check" reminders for home, outdoors, and car travel
- A discussion of family issues—from grandparents and siblings to single parenting and stepfamilies

Plus reliable information on:

- All common infectious diseases, from chickenpox and measles to flu and ear infections
- Developmental disabilities, such as congenital abnormalities, cerebral palsy, hearing loss, autism, and intellectual disability
- Skin problems, from birthmarks to head lice and sunburn
- Emergencies, including bites, poisoning, choking, and CPR
- Feeding and nutrition
- Car safety seats

The seventh edition of this book includes current AAP policy information and updated content on developmental disabilities, early brain development, breastfeeding and nutrition, obesity, and safety standards, as well as updated content on the effects of media and technology on children.

Additional Parenting Books from the American Academy of Pediatrics

COMMON CONDITIONS

Allergies and Asthma: What Every Parent Needs to Know

The Big Book of Symptoms: A–Z Guide to Your Child's Health

My Child Is Sick! Expert Advice for Managing Common Illnesses and Injuries

Sleep: What Every Parent Needs to Know

Waking Up Dry: A Guide to Help Children Overcome Bedwetting

DEVELOPMENTAL, BEHAVIORAL, AND PSYCHOSOCIAL INFORMATION

ADHD: What Every Parent Needs to Know

Autism Spectrum Disorder: What Every Parent Needs to Know

NEWBORNS, INFANTS, AND TODDLERS

Baby and Toddler Basics: Expert Answers to Parents' Top 150 Questions

Baby Care Anywhere: A Quick Guide to Parenting on the Go

Dad to Dad: Parenting Like a Pro

Guide to Toilet Training*

Heading Home With Your Newborn: From Birth to Reality

New Mother's Guide to Breastfeeding

Raising Twins: Parenting Multiples From Pregnancy Through the School Years

Retro Baby: Cut Back on All the Gear and Boost Your Baby's Development with More Than 100 Time-Tested Activities

Retro Toddler: More Than 100 Old-School Activities to Boost Development

* This book is also available in Spanish.

Understanding the NICU: What Parents of Preemies and
Other Hospitalized Newborns Need to Know

Your Baby's First Year*

NUTRITION AND FITNESS

Achieving a Healthy Weight for Your Child: An Action Plan for Families

Food Fights: Winning the Nutritional Challenges of Parenthood Armed
With Insight, Humor, and a Bottle of Ketchup

Nutrition: What Every Parent Needs to Know

SCHOOL-AGE CHILDREN AND ADOLESCENTS

Building Resilience in Children and Teens: Giving Kids Roots and Wings

Caring for Your School-Age Child: Ages 5 to 12

Parenting Through Puberty: Mood Swings, Acne, and Growing Pains

Raising Kids to Thrive: Balancing Love with
Expectations and Protection with Trust

———————————

FOR ADDITIONAL PARENTING RESOURCES,

VISIT THE HEALTHYCHILDREN BOOKSTORE AT

SHOP.AAP.ORG/FOR-PARENTS/.

* This book is also available in Spanish.

Caring for Your Baby and Young Child

Tanya Altmann, MD, FAAP

EDITOR-IN-CHIEF

Pediatrician and Founder, Calabasas Pediatrics Wellness Center
Calabasas, California

Assistant Clinical Professor of Pediatrics, UCLA Mattel Children's Hospital
Los Angeles, California

David L. Hill, MD, FAAP

ASSOCIATE MEDICAL EDITOR

Goldsboro Pediatrics
Goldsboro, North Carolina

Adjunct Assistant Professor of Pediatrics
University of North Carolina School of Medicine, Chapel Hill, North Carolina

Steven P. Shelov, MD, MS, FAAP

FOUNDING EDITOR, EMERITUS

Founding Dean
Professor of Pediatrics
NYU Long Island School of Medicine

Robert E. Hannemann, MD, FAAP

ASSOCIATE MEDICAL EDITOR, EMERITUS

Visiting Professor, Child Psychology, Biomedical and Chemical Engineering
Purdue University

BANTAM BOOKS
New York

2019 Bantam Books Trade Paperback Edition

Published in the United States by Bantam Books, an imprint of Random House, a division of Penguin Random House LLC, New York.

BANTAM BOOKS and the HOUSE colophon are registered trademarks of Penguin Random House LLC.

Originally published in the United States in hardcover in 1991 and in revised paperback editions in 1993, 1998, 2004, 2009, and 2014 by Bantam Books, an imprint of Random House, a division of Penguin Random House LLC.

ISBN 978-1-9848-1770-9

Printed in the United States of America on acid-free paper

randomhousebooks.com

2 4 6 8 9 7 5 3 1

Reviewers and Contributors

Section on Oral Health
Section on Orthopedic Surgery
Section on Otolaryngology—Head and
   Neck Surgery
Section on Pediatric Pulmonology and
   Sleep Medicine
Section on Plastic Surgery
Section on Rheumatology
Section on Surgery
Section on Tobacco Control
Section on Uniformed Services
Section on Urology
Subcommittee on Bronchiolitis

Subcommittee on Children and
   Adolescents with Attention-Deficit/
   Hyperactivity Disorder
Subcommittee on Type 2 Diabetes
Subcommittee on Febrile Infants
Subcommittee on Hyperbilirubinemia
Subcommittee on the Management of
   Infantile Hemangioma
Subcommittee on Screening and
   Management of High Blood Pressure in
   Children
Subcommittee on Urinary Tract Infection
Task Force on SIDS

Acknowledgments

We thank Founding Editor Emeritus, Steven P. Shelov, MD, MS, FAAP, and Associate Medical Editor Emeritus, Robert E. Hannemann, MD, FAAP, and the countless contributors and reviewers for their work on the first six editions of Caring for Your Baby and Young Child: Birth to Age 5. *Special thanks to Marc Weissbluth, MD, FAAP, for his review and consultation on the "Sleep" chapter and the "How to Tell a Nightmare from a Night Terror" chart, and to Alain Park for his dedicated work on this current edition.*

Illustrators:
Wendy Wray/Morgan Gaynin, Inc.
Alex Grey

Please Note

The information contained in this book is intended to complement, not substitute for, the advice of your child's pediatrician. Before starting any medical treatment or medical program, you should consult with your child's pediatrician, who can discuss your child's individual needs and counsel you about symptoms and treatment. If you have questions regarding how the information in this book applies to your child, speak to your child's pediatrician.

Products mentioned in this book are for informational purposes only. Inclusion in this publication does not constitute or imply a guarantee or an endorsement by the American Academy of Pediatrics.

The information and advice in this book apply equally to children of both sexes (except where noted). To indicate this, we have chosen to alternate between masculine and feminine pronouns throughout the book. Best efforts were made to use people first language, and as such, certain phrasing may not read as familiar. For example, "an overweight child" now reads as "a child with overweight" or "a child has overweight."

~ ~ ~

The American Academy of Pediatrics constantly monitors new scientific evidence and makes appropriate adjustments in its recommendations. For example, future research and the development of new childhood vaccines may alter the regimen for the administration of existing vaccines. Therefore, the schedule for immunizations outlined in this book is subject to change. These and other potential situations serve to emphasize the importance of always checking with your child's pediatrician for the latest information concerning the health of your child. For additional information on caring for your child and their health and well-being, visit HealthyChildren.org.

*This book is dedicated to all the people
who recognize that children are our greatest inspiration
in the present and our greatest hope for the future.*

Contents

Introduction.................................... xxi

PART 1

1 Preparing for a New Baby 3
Giving Your Baby a Healthy Start.................. 4
Getting the Best Prenatal Care..................... 10
Nutrition 11
Eating for Two.. 11
Exercise 11
History of Preterm Birth 12
Tests During Pregnancy 12
Preparing for Delivery 15
Choosing a Pediatric Healthcare
  Provider... 19
  A Pediatrician's Training 19
  Finding a Pediatrician......................... 20
Issues to Discuss with Your
  Pediatrician 26
  *When Should the Baby Leave the
    Hospital?*.. 26
  Should the Baby Be Circumcised? 28
  The Importance of Breastfeeding............ 30
  *Should I Store My Newborn's
    Cord Blood?*.. 31
Preparing Your Home and Family
  for the Baby's Arrival 32
  *Choosing Baby Clothing and
    Accessories*... 32
  *Buying Furniture and Baby
    Equipment*.. 33
  *Preparing Your Other Children for
    the Baby's Arrival* 38
  Finally—Delivery Day! 42

2 Birth and the First Moments
After 45
Routine Vaginal Delivery 45
Delivery by Cesarean Section.................. 48
Delivery Room Procedures
  Following a Normal Vaginal Birth 51
Leaving the Delivery Area....................... 53
Reflecting on Your Baby's Arrival............... 54
If Your Baby Is Premature 54

3 Basic Infant Care 61
Day to Day 62
  Responding to Your Baby's Cries 62
  Helping Your Baby Sleep...................... 64
  Positioning for Sleep.......................... 66
  Diapers.. 68
  Urination 72
  Bowel Movements................................ 73
  Bathing.. 75
  Skin and Nail Care.............................. 78
  Clothing 80
Your Baby's Basic Healthcare....................... 82
  Taking a Rectal Temperature................ 82
  Visiting the Pediatrician 83
  Immunizations.................................... 85

4 Feeding Your Baby......................... 87
Breastfeeding... 89
  *Getting Started: Preparing for
    Lactation*... 92
  Letting Down and Latching On............ 94
  When Your Milk Supply Increases........ 101
  How Often and How Long?.................. 105
  What About Bottles?............................ 109
  Milk Expression and Storage 110

Possible Nursing Concerns and Questions 114
Bottle-Feeding 120
Why Formula Instead of Cow's Milk? 120
Choosing a Formula 121
Feeding and Oral Health 124
Preparing, Sterilizing, and Storing Formula 124
The Feeding Process 127
Amount and Schedule of Formula Feedings 128
Supplementation for Breastfed and Bottle-Fed Infants 131
Vitamin Supplements 131
Iron Supplements 132
Water and Juice 132
Fluoride Supplements 133
Burping, Hiccups, and Spitting Up 134
Burping 134
Hiccups 134
Spitting Up 134

5 Your Baby's First Days 139
Your Newborn's First Days 140
How Your Newborn Looks 140
Your Baby's Birth Weight and Measurements 145
How Your Newborn Behaves 147
Going Home 148
Parenting Issues 149
Mother's Feelings 149
Partner's Feelings 152
Siblings' Feelings 152
Health Watch 153

6 The First Month 159
Growth and Development 159
Physical Appearance and Growth 159
Reflexes 161
Crying and Colic 167
The First Smile 170
Movement 171
Vision 172

Hearing 174
Smell and Touch 175
Temperament 175
Basic Care 178
Bowel Movements 178
Carrying Your Baby 178
Pacifiers 178
Going Outside 180
Finding Help at Home 181
Traveling with Your Baby 183
The Family 184
A Special Message to Mothers 184
A Special Message to Fathers 185
A Special Message to Grandparents 187
Health Watch 190
Safety Check 196
Car Safety Seats 196
Bathing 197
Changing Surfaces 197
Suffocation Prevention 197
Fire and Burn Prevention 198
Supervision 198
Necklaces and Cords 198
Head Support 199

7 Age One Month Through Three Months 201
Growth and Development 202
Physical Appearance and Growth 202
Movement 203
Vision 206
Hearing and Making Sounds 208
Emotional and Social Development 210
Basic Care 215
Feeding 215
Sleeping 217
Siblings 217
Health Watch 220
Immunization Update 224
Safety Check 225
Falls 225
Burns 225
Choking 226

8 Age Four Months Through Seven Months.................227

Growth and Development...........................229
  Physical Appearance and Growth...........................229
  Movement...229
  Vision...233
  Language Development.....................235
  Cognitive Development....................236
  Emotional Development....................238
Basic Care..241
  Introducing Solid Foods..................241
  Dietary Supplements.......................245
  Sleeping...246
  Teething and Dental Care...............246
  Swings and Play Yards.....................247
Behavior...249
  Discipline...249
  Siblings..252
Health Watch...253
Immunization Update..............................255
Safety Check..256
  Car Safety Seats..............................256
  Drowning...257
  Falls...257
  Burns..257
  Choking..257

9 Age Eight Months Through Twelve Months..............259

Growth and Development...........................260
  Physical Appearance and Growth........260
  Movement...261
  Hand and Finger Skills.....................265
  Language Development.....................267
  Cognitive Development....................269
  Brain Development...........................271
  Emotional Development....................274
Basic Care..281
  Feeding..281
  Introducing a Cup............................284
  Sleeping...286
  Teeth..286
Behavior...287
  Discipline...287

Siblings...289
Grandparents.......................................290
Immunization Update..............................291
Safety Check..292
  Car Safety Seats..............................292
  Falls...292
  Burns..293
  Drowning...293
  Poisoning and Choking....................293

10 Your One-Year-Old.....................295

Growth and Development...........................296
  Physical Appearance and Growth........296
  Movement...297
  Hand and Finger Skills.....................299
  Language Development.....................300
  Cognitive Development....................302
  Social Development..........................304
  Emotional Development....................307
Basic Care..309
  Feeding and Nutrition......................309
  Getting Ready for Toilet Training...........321
  Sleeping...322
Behavior...323
  Discipline...323
  Coping with Temper Tantrums.............326
  Family Relationships........................330
Immunization Update..............................330
Blood Tests...331
Safety Check..331
  Sleep Safety....................................331
  Toy Safety..332
  Water Safety....................................333
  Auto Safety......................................333
  Home Safety....................................334
  Outdoor Safety................................335

11 Your Two-Year-Old.....................337

Growth and Development...........................338
  Physical Appearance and Growth........338
  Movement...339
  Hand and Finger Skills.....................340
  Language Development.....................342
  Cognitive Development....................344
  Social Development..........................346
  Emotional Development....................350

Basic Care 353
   Feeding and Nutrition 353
   Teething and Dental Hygiene 355
   Toilet Training 357
   Sleeping 360
   Discipline 363
Family Relationships 366
   A New Baby 366
   Hero Worship 368
Visit to the Pediatrician 371
Immunization Update 371
Safety Check 372
   Falls 372
   Burns 372
   Poisoning 372
   Car Safety 373

12 Your Three-Year-Old 375
Growth and Development 376
   Physical Appearance and
      Growth 376
   Movement 377
   Hand and Finger Skills 379
   Language Development 381
   Cognitive Development 384
   Social Development 385
   Emotional Development 389
Basic Care 392
   Feeding and Nutrition 392
   Beyond Toilet Training 393
   Bed-Wetting 394
   Sleeping 395
   Discipline 396
   Preparing for School 397
   Traveling with Your Preschooler 400
Visit to the Pediatrician 402
Immunization Update 403
Safety Check 403
   Falls 403
   Burns 403
   Car Safety 404
   Drowning 404
   Poisoning and Choking 405

**13 Your Four- and
Five-Year-Old** 407
Development 408
   Movement 408
   Hand and Finger Skills 409
   Language Development 411
   Cognitive Development 413
   Social Development 414
   Emotional Development 416
Basic Care 419
   Healthy Lifestyle 419
   Feeding and Nutrition 420
   Sleeping 425
   Discipline 427
   Preparing for Kindergarten 429
Visit to the Pediatrician 432
Safety Check 433
Traveling with Your Child 434

**14 Early Education and
Childcare** 437
What to Look for in a Care Provider:
   Guidelines for the Toddler and
   Preschool Child 438
Choices in Care 440
   In-home Care/Nanny 441
   Family Childcare 443
   Childcare Centers 447
Selecting a Childcare Center 449
Building a Relationship with Your
   Child's Care Providers 455
Resolving Conflicts 457
What to Do When Your Child
   Is Sick 458
Controlling Infectious Diseases 460
   Colds 462
   Cytomegalovirus (CMV) and
      Parvovirus Infection 462
   Diarrheal Diseases 462
   Eye and Skin Infections 463
   Head Lice 463
   Hepatitis A Virus 463
   Hepatitis B Virus 463

Human Immunodeficiency Virus
(HIV)/AIDS 464
Ringworm 464
Preventing Injuries and Promoting
Car Safety 464
Care for Children with Special
Needs 466

15 Keeping Your Child Safe 473
Why Children Get Injured 474
Safety Inside Your Home 476
Room to Room 476
Nursery 477
Kitchen 481
Laundry Room 482
Bathroom 482
Garage and Basement 484
All Rooms 484
Baby Equipment 488
High Chairs 488
Infant Seats and Bouncers 489
Play Yards 490
Walkers 491
Pacifiers 491
Toy Boxes and Toy Chests 492
Toys 493
Safety Outside the Home 495
Car Safety Seats 495
Choosing a Car Safety Seat 496
Types of Car Safety Seats 498
Installing a Car Safety Seat 499
Using the Car Safety Seat 501
Airbag Safety 503
Kids Around Cars 506
Baby Carriers: Backpacks, Front
Packs, and Slings 507
Strollers 508
Shopping Cart Safety 509
Bicycles and Tricycles 509
Playgrounds 511
Your Backyard 513
Water Safety 514
Safety Around Animals 517

In the Community and
Neighborhood 518

PART 2

16 Abdominal/Gastrointestinal
Tract 527
Abdominal Pain 527
Abdominal Pain in Infants 528
Abdominal Pain in Older Children 529
Appendicitis 531
Celiac Disease 533
Constipation 534
Diarrhea 537
Food Poisoning and Food
Contamination 544
Hepatitis 549
Inguinal Hernia 552
Communicating Hydrocele 552
Malabsorption 554
Reye Syndrome 555
Vomiting 555

17 Asthma and Allergies 561
Asthma 561
Eczema 568
Food Allergy 571
Nasal Allergy/Allergic Rhinitis 573
Hives 576
Insect Bites and Stings 577

18 Behavior 581
Anger, Aggression, and Biting 581
Behaviors Raising Concerns About
Abuse or Neglect 585
Coping with Disasters and Violence 586
Death of a Loved One 588
Teeth Grinding (Bruxism) 589
Hyperactivity and the Easily
Distractible Child 590

Pacifier, Thumb, and Finger Sucking 594
Temper Tantrums 596
Tics and Stereotypies 599

19 Chest and Lungs 603
Bronchiolitis 603
Cough 605
Croup 608
Influenza (Flu) 609
Pneumonia 612
Tuberculosis 614
Whooping Cough (Pertussis) 616

20 Chronic Health Conditions and Diseases 619
Coping with Chronic (Long-Term)
    Health Problems 619
Anemia 627
Cystic Fibrosis 630
Diabetes Mellitus 632
HIV Infection and AIDS 634
Sickle Cell Disease 637

21 Developmental Disabilities 641
Autism Spectrum Disorder 643
Cerebral Palsy 648
    Associated Problems 651
Congenital Abnormalities 652
    *When Your Child Has a Congenital
    Disorder* 654
    Congenital Conditions 654
Hearing Loss (Hearing Impairment) 659
Intellectual Disability 663

22 Ears, Nose, and Throat 667
Colds/Upper Respiratory Infection 667
Middle Ear Infections 670
Sinusitis 675
Epiglottitis 677
Herpes Simplex 678
Nosebleeds 679
Sore Throat (Strep Throat,
    Tonsillitis) 681

Tonsils and Adenoid 683
Swimmer's Ear (External Otitis) 685
Swollen Glands 687

23 Emergencies 691
Bites 694
Burns 697
Cardiopulmonary Resuscitation
    (CPR) and Mouth-to-Mouth
    Resuscitation 699
Choking 700
Cuts and Scrapes 701
Drowning 705
Electric Shock 706
Fingertip Injuries 707
Fractures/Broken Bones 708
Head Injury/Concussion 711
Poisoning 713

24 Environmental Health 719
Air Pollution 719
Asbestos 720
Carbon Monoxide 721
Drinking Water 722
Fish 726
Lead Poisoning 727
Pesticides/Herbicides 730
Radon 732
Smoke Exposure 733

25 Eyes 735
Amblyopia 738
Cataracts 739
Eye Infections 739
Eye Injuries 740
Eyelid Problems 742
Glaucoma 743
Strabismus 744
Tear (or Lacrimal) Production
    Problems 745
Vision Difficulties Requiring
    Corrective Lenses 746

26 Family Issues.................................749
Adoption..749
Child Abuse and Neglect 751
Divorce 755
Grief Reactions.................................760
Sibling Rivalry..................................764
Single-Parent Families.....................766
Stepfamilies 769
Multiples..771

27 Fever 775

**28 Genital and Urinary
Systems** 783
Blood in the Urine (Hematuria).................783
Proteinuria 785
Circumcision.....................................785
Hypospadias and Chordee 786
Meatal Stenosis................................787
Labial Adhesions 787
Posterior Urethral Valve..................788
Undescended Testicles
   (Cryptorchidism)..........................789
Urinary Tract Infections 790
Wetting Problems or Enuresis 792

**29 Head, Neck, and Nervous
System**..797
Meningitis..797
Motion Sickness 800
Mumps 801
Seizures, Convulsions, and Epilepsy.........803
Head Tilt (Torticollis)......................805

30 Heart...807
Arrhythmias.......................................807
Heart Murmur....................................809
Hypertension/High Blood Pressure..........811
Kawasaki Disease 814

31 Immunizations.............................817
Important and Safe..........................818
What Shots Does Your Child Need?.........821

32 Media..827
Development and Learning..............827
Childhood Obesity 830
Sleep...830
Monitoring Technology Use............831
Guidelines for Media Use...............832
A Message to Parents......................832

33 Musculoskeletal Problems......835
Arthritis..835
Bowlegs and Knock-Knees..............840
Elbow Injuries...................................840
Flat Feet/Fallen Arches...................842
Limp 843
Pigeon Toes (Intoeing)....................844
Sprains..846

34 Skin...847
Birthmarks and Hemangiomas 847
Chickenpox (Varicella).....................850
Cradle Cap and Seborrheic
   Dermatitis......................................852
Fifth Disease (Erythema
   Infectiosum) 853
Hair Loss (Alopecia)........................854
Head Lice 855
Impetigo...857
Measles 857
Molluscum Contagiosum 860
Mosquito-Borne Illnesses (Zika and
   West Nile) 860
MRSA Infections...............................862
Pinworms...863
Poison Ivy, Poison Oak, and Poison
   Sumac...864
Ringworm (Tinea).............................865
Roseola Infantum.............................866
Rubella (German Measles)..............867
Scabies..868
Scarlet Fever.....................................870
Sunburn..870
Warts...872

35 Your Child's Sleep................................873

How Much Sleep Does My Baby
  Need?..873
    Getting Sleep in Sync............................875
Sleep Routines and Dealing with
  Crying..877
Sharing the Bedtime Routine....................878
Parent Sleep Deprivation..........................878

Daytime Nap Evolution.............................881
Getting the Most Out of Sleep..................882
Dealing with Other Sleep Concerns.........885
Putting Sleep in Perspective.....................885

Appendix..887

Index...905

Introduction

CONGRATULATIONS! YOU ARE LIKELY reading this book because you are pregnant, have a newborn, or care for a child birth to age five. No matter what the reason, this book will provide you with everything you need to know to raise a healthy, happy, and resilient child. Whether you choose to read it from cover to cover, read the chapter for your child's current age to discover what she will be doing next month, or you just want to flip to the specific symptoms, illness, or issue that your child has, you will find a wealth of information vetted by an organization comprised of more than 67,000 pediatricians. That's a lot of brain power and advice!

Most of your newborn's needs are the same as generations ago, while others have changed due to modern-day busy lifestyles. Babies always need love, nutritious food, good health, secure surroundings, skills to build self-esteem and resilience, and plenty of one-on-one time together with you reading books and having fun. They don't need distractions or electronics (please put your phone down).

For you, becoming a parent is one of the greatest gifts, and you will learn, grow, and smile every day in ways you didn't even know were possible. There will be good days and some not so good days, but that's normal life. Don't beat yourself up if the diaper doesn't get put on correctly or if you're late getting out the door with baby in tow. As long as everyone is safe and healthy, take each day in stride and enjoy every minute that you can.

It's also important to know when you need to ask for help. If you're over-tired or overstressed, ask your partner, a relative, or a friend to lend a hand. Whether you need help breastfeeding, cooking, potty training, or taking your preschooler to the zoo, you can't do it all every day, and that's okay. Reach out to your support team, which should also include your pediatrician. Your pediatrician can help advise you on feeding, sleeping, and behavior in addition to seeing your child for complete well-child exams and sick visits.

The days and years pass quickly, so take a few photos or journal along the way, because before you know it your baby will be going off to kindergarten! That's a lot of ground to tackle in the following chapters, but rest assured it's all there, from caring for your newborn and young child, to helping with nutrition, sleep, and behavior, to building resilience and good self-esteem, to fevers, tummy aches, and other illness symptoms or concerns that come up along the way. Of course, if you have any questions about what you have read, have a specific concern, or are worried about anything, please contact your pediatrician. After all, that is what we are here for, even in the middle of the night!

~ PART 1 ~

~ 1 ~

Preparing for a New Baby

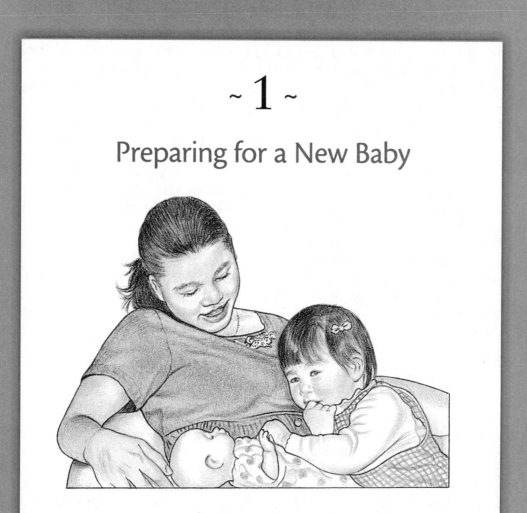

PREGNANCY IS A TIME of anticipation, excitement, and, for many new parents, uncertainty. You dream of a baby who will be strong, healthy, and bright—and you make plans to ensure her success. You probably also have fears and questions, especially if this is your first child, or if there have been problems with this or a previous pregnancy. What if something goes wrong during the pregnancy? What if labor and delivery are difficult? What if your expectations of being a parent aren't met? These are perfectly normal feelings and fears. The nine months of pregnancy will give you time to answer questions, calm fears, and prepare for the realities of parenthood.

Some of your initial concerns may already have been addressed if you had difficulty becoming pregnant, particularly if you sought fertility treatment. But now that you're pregnant, preparations for your new baby can begin. The best way to help your baby is to take care of yourself. Regular medical and dental attention and good nutrition directly benefit both you and your baby's health. Plenty of rest and moderate exercise will help ease the physical stresses of pregnancy. Talk to your physician about your health and your baby's health, including prenatal vitamins, and avoid smoking, alcohol, using drugs (including marijuana), and eating fish containing high levels of mercury. If you are taking any medications, check with your obstetrician about their safety during pregnancy.

As pregnancy progresses, you're confronted with a long list of decisions, from planning for the delivery to decorating the nursery. Many decisions may already have happened, but others may have been postponed because your baby doesn't seem "real." However, the more actively you prepare for your baby's arrival, the more real that child will seem.

You may find yourself constantly thinking about this baby-to-be. This preoccupation is perfectly normal and actually may help prepare you emotionally for the challenge of parenthood. After all, you'll be making decisions about your child for the next two decades—at least! Now is a perfect time to start.

Giving Your Baby a Healthy Start

Virtually everything you consume or inhale while pregnant will be passed through to the fetus. This process begins as soon as you conceive. In fact, the embryo is most vulnerable during the first two months, when the major body parts (arms, legs, hands, feet, liver, heart, genitalia, eyes, and brain) are just starting to form. The chemical substances in cigarettes, alcohol, illegal drugs, and certain medications can interfere with the developmental process, and some can even cause congenital abnormalities. For instance, if you smoke cigarettes during pregnancy, your baby's birth weight may be decreased. Even breathing in smoke from the cigarettes of others (passive smoking) can affect your baby. Stay away from smoking areas and ask smokers not to light up around you. If you're a smoker, this is the time to stop—not just until you give birth, but forever. Children who grow up in a home where someone smokes have a greater risk of sudden infant death syndrome (SIDS), more ear infections and more respiratory problems during infancy and early childhood, and even an increased risk of childhood obesity. They also have been shown to be more likely to smoke when they grow up.

Alcohol consumption during pregnancy is also a concern and increases the risk for a condition called fetal alcohol syndrome (FAS), which is responsible for birth defects, low birth weight, and below-average intelligence. Fetal alcohol syndrome is the leading cause of intellectual disability in newborns. Alco-

WHERE WE STAND

THE AMERICAN ACADEMY OF PEDIATRICS' message is clear—don't smoke when pregnant; protect yourself and your children from secondhand tobacco smoke. Many studies have shown that if a woman smokes or is exposed to secondhand smoke during pregnancy, her child may be born too early (prematurely) or be smaller than normal. Other effects of smoking during pregnancy may include sudden infant death syndrome (SIDS), depressed breathing movements while in the uterus, learning problems, respiratory disorders, and heart disease as an adult.

After birth, children exposed to secondhand tobacco smoke have more respiratory infections, bronchitis, pneumonia, poor lung function, and asthma than children who aren't exposed. Smoke exposure is most dangerous for younger children because they have immature lungs and spend more time with parents or other smokers.

If you smoke, quit. Ask your child's pediatrician or your primary care doctor for free help, or call 1-800-QUIT-NOW. If you can't quit, don't expose your child to smoke—make your home and car completely smoke-free. The Academy supports legislation that would prohibit smoking in public places, including outdoor public places that children frequent.

hol consumption during pregnancy also increases the likelihood of a miscarriage or preterm delivery. There is evidence that the more alcohol consumed, the greater the risk to the fetus. It is safest not to drink any alcoholic beverages during pregnancy.

Chemicals from marijuana, either smoked or from edibles, can be passed to your developing baby during pregnancy. Studies are limited, but the data suggest that use of marijuana may interfere with the baby's brain development, cause intellectual disabilities, or cause behavioral problems later in life. Marijuana smoke also poses risks similar to tobacco smoke.

No illicit drug is safe to use during pregnancy. Stimulants like cocaine and methamphetamine can cause elevated maternal blood pressure, low birth weight, and premature delivery. Opioids like OxyContin and heroin cause withdrawal symptoms in newborns that can keep them hospitalized for weeks or more. If you become pregnant while using drugs, inform your obstetrician so that she can help you find safe, appropriate care.

WHERE WE STAND

DRINKING ALCOHOL DURING pregnancy is one of the leading preventable causes of birth defects, intellectual disability, and other developmental disorders in newborns. There is no known safe amount of alcohol consumption during pregnancy. For that reason, the American Academy of Pediatrics recommends that women who are pregnant, or who are planning to become pregnant, abstain from drinking alcoholic beverages of any kind.

When preparing for your baby, you may decide to paint and add new furniture to the nursery. It's important to have good ventilation in spaces you're painting, to avoid inhaling large amounts of fumes. New furniture can harbor chemicals and should be allowed to ventilate before placing your baby in or near it. Exposures do not only happen in the home; workplaces may have chemicals in use that, when inhaled, can result in harm to you and your baby. Your employer should provide you with personal protective equipment or other task assignments if you are exposed to chemicals or dust in the workplace.

You should avoid all medications and supplements except those your physician has specifically recommended. This includes not only prescription drugs you're already taking, but also nonprescription or over-the-counter products such as aspirin, cold medications, and antihistamines. Even vitamins can be dangerous if taken in high doses. (For example, excessive amounts of vitamin A have been known to cause congenital abnormalities.) Consult with your physician before taking drugs or supplements of any kind during pregnancy, even those labeled "natural."

WHERE WE STAND

MARIJUANA USE HAS been legalized in a number of states, which may lead some women to believe that the drug is safe or even beneficial in pregnancy. Research on the effects of marijuana exposure in the womb or through breast milk is limited, but what we do know suggests that marijuana use by mothers may be dangerous to the baby's developing brain. Women who are pregnant, planning to become pregnant, or nursing should avoid marijuana use. If you are using marijuana to treat nausea, talk to your doctor about safer alternatives.

Fish and shellfish contain high-quality protein and other essential nutrients, are low in saturated fat, and contain omega-3 fatty acids. They can be an essential part of a balanced diet for pregnant women.

However, you should be aware of the possible health risks from eating fish while pregnant. Avoid raw fish, as it may contain parasites such as flukes or worms. Cooking and freezing are the most effective ways to kill the parasites. For safety reasons, the US Food and Drug Administration (FDA) recommends cooking fish to an internal temperature of 140 degrees Fahrenheit (60 degrees Celsius). Certain types of cooked sushi such as eel and California rolls are safe to eat when pregnant.

The most worrisome contaminant in fish is mercury (or more specifically, methylmercury). Mercury has been shown to be damaging to the fetus's brain and nervous system development. The FDA advises pregnant women, women who may become pregnant,

nursing mothers, and young children to avoid eating shark, swordfish, king mackerel, and tilefish (from the Gulf of Mexico) due to high levels of mercury in these fish. According to the FDA, pregnant women can safely eat an average of 8–12 ounces (two to three average servings) of a variety of other types of cooked fish each week. Five commonly eaten fish low in mercury are shrimp, canned or packaged light tuna, salmon, pollock, and catfish. Albacore tuna can be high in mercury, so canned chunk light tuna is a better choice. If there are no local health advisories about fish caught in your area, you can eat up to 6 ounces (one average meal) per week of local fish, but don't consume any other fish during that week.

While no adverse effects from minimal caffeine intake (1 to 2 cups of caffeinated coffee per day, or about 200 mg of caffeine) have yet been proven, you may want to limit caffeine to the minimum needed when you are pregnant. Remember, caffeine is also found in many soft drinks and foods such as chocolate.

Another cause of congenital abnormalities is illness during pregnancy. Take precautions against these dangerous viral infections:

German measles (rubella) can cause intellectual disability, heart abnormalities, cataracts, and deafness, with the highest risk occurring in the first twenty weeks of pregnancy. Fortunately, this illness can be prevented by immunization, *although you must not get immunized against rubella during pregnancy.* If you are unsure whether you're immune, your obstetrician can order a blood test. In the unlikely event that you're not immune, you must do your best to avoid sick children, especially during the first three months of pregnancy. It is then recommended you get immunized after giving birth to prevent this same concern in the future.

Chickenpox (varicella) is particularly dangerous if contracted shortly before delivery. If you have not already had chickenpox, avoid anyone with the disease or anyone recently exposed to the disease. You also should receive the preventive vaccine when you are not pregnant.

Herpes is an infection that newborns can get at the time of birth. Most often, it occurs as the infant moves through the birth canal of a mother infected with genital herpes. Babies who get a herpes viral infection may develop fluid-filled blisters on the skin that can break and then crust over. A more seri-

Tdap/DTaP Vaccine: Protection for You (Tdap) and Baby (DTaP)

In their first four to six months after birth, babies are more prone to infections because their immune systems are not fully developed. It is important that moms are protected against many things, including three serious diseases: tetanus, diphtheria, and pertussis (covered by the Tdap or DTap vaccine).

- *Diphtheria.* A severe throat infection that causes difficulty breathing. This can affect the heart and nervous system and lead to death.

- *Tetanus*, also called lockjaw. A painful tightening of the muscles, including the jaw, which gets "locked" shut, making it impossible to open the mouth or swallow. This can lead to death.

- *Pertussis*, also called whooping cough. In adults, causes severe coughing and vomiting, and may cause trouble sleeping for months. In infants, this infection can be much more serious: it causes severe coughing and trouble breathing that lasts for months and can even lead to brain damage or death. There has been a recent rise in the cases of pertussis in the United States, as well as infant deaths due to pertussis. For this reason, it is recommended that everyone around your baby (grandparents, parents, and children) make sure they are current on pertussis vaccines.

Bacteria cause all these diseases, and infection can be prevented with vaccines. Diphtheria and pertussis are spread from person to person. Tetanus enters the body through cuts, scratches, or wounds.

Since newborns haven't received their first few doses of the vaccine that protects them from these diseases, mothers who were never immunized or who may have waning immunity could become ill with these diseases and pass them on to their babies.

Tdap is recommended for every pregnant woman and during each and every pregnancy to protect herself and her baby against pertussis. After a pregnant woman is immunized, she passes her protection across the placenta to her baby. This helps protect the baby from pertussis until he or she is old enough to get vaccinated. The ideal time for a pregnant mom to be vaccinated is between the twenty-seventh and thirty-sixth weeks. If the vaccine is not given during pregnancy, it should be given to the mom immediately after delivery. It is recommended that anyone in close contact with your baby should be vaccinated as well. This includes dads, grandparents, other relatives, and childcare providers, regardless of age. Make sure other children in the family are up to date on their Tdap immunizations also.

ous form of the disease can progress into a severe and potentially fatal inflammation of the brain called encephalitis. When a herpes infection occurs, it is often treated with an antiviral medication called acyclovir. For the last month of pregnancy, your doctor may advise taking preventive medications like acyclovir or valacyclovir to reduce the risk of an outbreak. If you have an outbreak or feel symptoms of one coming on during your delivery time, you should notify your obstetrician, and a Cesarean section (or C-section) may be recommended to decrease the risk of exposure to the baby.

Toxoplasmosis may be a danger for cat owners. This illness can be caused by a parasitic infection common in cats, but it is much more often found in uncooked meat and fish. Take care that meat is cooked thoroughly prior to consumption, and avoid tasting undercooked meat like beef tartare or carpaccio. Wash all cutting boards and knives thoroughly with hot soapy water after each use. Wash and/or peel all fruits and vegetables before eating them. Outdoor cats are far more likely to contract toxoplasmosis and excrete a form of the parasite in their stools. People who come in contact with the infected stools could become infected themselves. Someone who is healthy and not pregnant should change the cat's litter box daily; if this is not possible, gloves should be worn and hands washed well with soap and water afterward. Also, wash your hands with soap and water after *any* exposure to soil, sand, raw meat, or unwashed vegetables. There have been no documented cases of animal-transmitted toxoplasmosis in the United States in recent years.

Zika virus can infect pregnant women through the bite of an infected mosquito or via sexual intercourse with an infected partner, even if that partner has no symptoms. The Centers for Disease Control and Prevention (cdc.gov) can help you learn what regions host these mosquitoes, such as the tropics and the far southern portions of the United States. Pregnant women who travel to areas where Zika is present should take precautions to avoid mosquito bites, such as using DEET, wearing long sleeves and long pants, and avoiding being outside at dawn and dusk. They should also use protection during sexual intercourse if their partner has been in such areas. Zika virus can cause severe defects of the developing baby's brain and eyes. At this time, there is no vaccine against the virus.

Listeria is a bacteria that can be transmitted from raw or undercooked dairy products and meat or seafood. It causes flu-like symptoms, such as fever, muscle aches, and diarrhea, and pregnant women are more susceptible. To decrease the risk, avoid unpasteurized milk; soft cheeses made from unpasteurized milk, like feta, queso blanco, queso fresco, Camembert, Brie, or blue-veined cheeses; hot dogs, lunch meat, and cold cuts (unless heated to high temperature before consuming); and smoked seafood. Also, avoid handling raw or undercooked eggs, meat, and seafood. Wash hands frequently while cooking.

Flu. Infants under six months of age are at high risk if they acquire influenza, or the flu. One way to protect your newborn from the flu is to get the flu vaccine yourself if you are pregnant during flu season. This is especially important because pregnancy puts you at higher risk of complications from getting the flu. Adults and all children over six months of age should be immunized during flu season, typically from early fall to late spring, to prevent passing this deadly respiratory illness to young infants.

Getting the Best Prenatal Care

Throughout your pregnancy, you should work closely with your obstetrician or American Midwifery Certification Board–certified nurse midwife to make sure that you stay as healthy as possible. Regular visits up until the birth of your baby can significantly improve your likelihood of having a healthy newborn. During each visit, you will be weighed, your blood pressure checked, and the size of your uterus estimated to evaluate the size of your growing fetus.

During your pregnancy, do not forget about your oral health. Mothers can unintentionally pass cavity-causing bacteria to their newborn baby, which can increase a child's risk for tooth decay. Preventive dental work while pregnant is essential to avoid oral infections such as gum disease, which has been linked to preterm labor and low birth weight. Dental cleanings, X-rays, fillings, and annual check-ups during pregnancy are safe and important.

Nutrition

Follow your obstetrician's advice on prenatal vitamins. You should take vitamins only in the doses recommended by your doctor. Perhaps more than any other single vitamin, make sure you have an adequate intake of folic acid (generally 400 mcg a day), a B vitamin that can reduce the risk of certain birth defects, such as spina bifida, or abnormalities of your baby's spine. Your obstetrician may recommend a daily prenatal vitamin pill, which includes not only folic acid and other vitamins, but also iron, calcium, and other minerals, and the fatty acids docosahexaenoic acid (DHA) and arachidonic acid (ARA). DHA and ARA are "good" fats, and DHA in particular accumulates in the brain and eyes of the fetus, especially during the last trimester of pregnancy. These fatty acids are also found in breast milk (also known as *human milk*). Make sure your doctor knows about any other supplements you may be taking, including herbal remedies.

Eating for Two

When it comes to your diet, plan balanced meals. They should contain protein, carbohydrates, fats, vitamins, and minerals. This is not the time for fad or low-calorie dieting. In fact, as a general rule, you need to consume about 350–450 more calories per day during your second and third trimesters of pregnancy compared to what you needed prior to becoming pregnant. You need these extra calories and nutrients so your baby can grow normally. If you have morning sickness and are vomiting frequently, rinse your mouth with a teaspoon of baking soda mixed with water to stop stomach acid from attacking your teeth.

Exercise

Physical activity is just as important when you're pregnant as at any other time of life. Discuss a fitness program with your doctor, including fitness videos or online programs. If you haven't been exercising regularly, your doctor may suggest a moderate walking or swimming regimen, prenatal yoga, or a Pilates class. Take it slowly during the first few workouts—even just five to ten minutes a day is beneficial and a good place to start. Drink plenty of water while working out, and avoid activity with jumping or jarring movements. If you are already physically active, certainly maintain the level of activity you're comfortable with, but also listen to your body, and be willing to slow down when you need to.

History of Preterm Birth

If you have had a previous premature birth and are pregnant with a single fetus, weekly 17P injections, beginning between sixteen and twenty-one weeks, can reduce your risk of having another preterm delivery by 33 percent. Talk to your obstetrician if you think this may apply to you.

Tests During Pregnancy

Whether your pregnancy is progressing normally or concerns are present, your obstetrician may recommend some of the following tests.

- An *ultrasound* exam is a safe procedure and common test performed on pregnant women. It monitors your fetus's growth and the well-being of his internal organs by taking sonograms (images made from sound waves). It can ensure your baby is developing normally and will help determine any problems or fetal abnormality. It also can be used close to the time of delivery if your doctor suspects your baby is in the breech position (positioned so that his buttocks or feet would move first through the birth canal, before the baby's head). Because of the risk of head entrapment, breech deliveries are not advised in developed countries such as the United States except in very rare circumstances. Even when a new mother is fully dilated, if the baby is found to be breech, the recently revised recommendations are to always perform a C-section. (For further discussion of breech babies and Cesarean births, see *Delivery by Cesarean Section* in Chapter 2, pages 48–49.)

- A *nuchal translucency scan* is an ultrasound performed at 11–12 weeks to look for signs of genetic problems like Trisomy 13, Trisomy 18, and Trisomy 21 (Down syndrome). This test is often combined with two blood tests, PAPP-A and beta-HCG, to create a risk score called the First

Trimester Combined Test or "triple test." In the second trimester the obstetrician may check a dimeric inhibin A (DIA) level, combining it with the triple test to produce a "quad test."

■ A *nonstress* test electronically monitors the fetus's heart rate and movements. In this test, a belt is positioned around your abdomen. In a nonstress test no medications are used to stimulate movement in your unborn baby or trigger contractions of the uterus.

■ A *contraction stress test* is another means of checking the fetus's heart rate, but in this case it is measured in response to mild contractions of the uterus that are stimulated (for example, by an infusion of the hormone oxytocin). By monitoring your baby's heart rate during the contractions, your doctor may be able to determine how your baby will react to the contractions of delivery; if your baby is not responding favorably during these contractions, the delivery of your baby (perhaps by Cesarean section) might be scheduled prior to your due date.

■ A *biophysical profile* uses a nonstress test and an ultrasound. It evaluates the movement and breathing of the unborn baby, as well as the volume of amniotic fluid. A collective score will help determine whether there is a need for an early delivery.

Other tests may be recommended, depending on your physical health and personal and family history. For example, for women with a family history of genetic problems or for those who are age thirty-five or older, your obstetrician may advise genetic tests. The most common genetic tests are *amniocentesis* and *chorionic villus sampling,* which are described in the box *Detecting Genetic Abnormalities* on page 14.

Many states have standard programs to screen for chromosomal abnormalities (such as Down syndrome) and other birth defects.

Other screening tests are available for conditions such as:

■ *Neural tube defects* (an incomplete closure of the fetal spine)

■ *Abdominal wall defects*

■ *Heart defects* (in which the chambers of the heart are not well developed)

■ *Trisomy 18* (a chromosomal abnormality that causes birth defects)

Also see the box *Detecting Genetic Abnormalities* on page 14.

Detecting Genetic Abnormalities

Some tests can detect genetic abnormalities before birth. By learning about these problems before birth, you can plan your child's healthcare in advance, and in some cases even treat the disorder while the baby is still in the womb.

■ With *amniocentesis*, a thin needle is inserted through the abdominal wall and into the uterus, where a small sample of amniotic fluid is withdrawn from the sac surrounding the fetus. The test can indicate (or rule out) serious genetic and chromosomal disorders, including Down syndrome and some cases of spina bifida. Amniocentesis is usually performed during the second trimester (between the fifteenth and twentieth weeks), although it may be done later (typically after the thirty-sixth week) to test whether the baby's lungs are developed enough for birth. Results of most amniocentesis tests are available in about two weeks.

■ With *chorionic villus sampling (CVS)*, a long, slender needle is inserted through the abdomen to remove a small sample of cells (called chorionic villi) from the placenta, or a catheter (a thin plastic tube) is inserted through the cervix to withdraw cells from the placenta. CVS is usually performed earlier than amniocentesis, most often between the tenth and twelfth weeks of pregnancy, and the test results are available within one to two weeks. It can be used to detect various genetic and chromosomal conditions, including Down syndrome, Tay-Sachs disease, and (especially in African American families) red blood cell disorders, such as sickle cell disease and thalassemia (see pages 647–50).

Both amniocentesis and CVS are considered accurate and safe procedures for prenatal diagnosis, although they pose a small risk of miscarriage and other complications. You should discuss both the benefits and risks with your doctor and, in some cases, a genetic counselor.

Your doctor may recommend other screening tests:

■ *Glucose screening* can check for high blood sugar levels, which could be an indication of gestational diabetes. To conduct the test, usually performed between the twenty-fourth and twenty-eighth weeks, you need to drink a sugar solution and then a blood sample is collected. If a high level of glucose is detected, then additional testing should be done. This will determine if you might have gestational diabetes, which is associated with an increased likelihood of pregnancy complications.

- *Group B streptococcus (GBS) screening,* which will determine the presence of a bacteria that can cause a serious infection (such as meningitis or a blood infection) in your baby. This is usually a urine sample test. While GBS bacteria are common and may be found in the mother's vagina or rectum—and are harmless in healthy adults—they can cause illness in a newborn if transmitted during childbirth. If GBS is detected in a pregnant woman, antibiotics are given intravenously during the birthing process; once the baby is born, she may be observed for a longer time in the hospital nursery. The GBS screening test is usually performed between the thirty-fifth and thirty-seventh weeks of pregnancy.

- *HIV (human immunodeficiency virus) testing* is now commonly done in pregnant women, preferably early in their pregnancy. HIV is the virus that causes AIDS, and when a pregnant woman is infected with the virus, it can be passed to her baby during pregnancy, during delivery, or during breastfeeding. Early diagnosis can lead to treatment to decrease the risk of infection in the baby. It is important to know the pregnant woman's HIV status so that appropriate medications can be administered during pregnancy and labor. Babies born to HIV-positive mothers also receive preventive medications after delivery.

Preparing for Delivery

As the months pass leading up to your delivery date, you're probably eagerly planning for the new arrival, and adjusting to the changes in your own body. During the third trimester, many changes may affect how you feel:

- You'll gain weight, typically at a rate averaging about 1 pound a week during the last trimester.

- As your baby grows and places pressure on nearby organs, you may experience episodes of shortness of breath and back pain.

- You may urinate more frequently from pressure on your bladder, and you might have episodes of incontinence (leaking of urine).

- You may find it harder to get comfortable, and sleep may become difficult. You may prefer to sleep on your side.

- You could experience more fatigue than usual.

■ You may have heartburn, swelling in your feet and ankles, back pain, and hemorrhoids.

■ You may have "false labor" contractions, known as Braxton-Hicks contractions. These Braxton-Hicks contractions begin to soften and thin the cervix, preparing it for the delivery of the baby. But unlike true labor contractions, they are irregular, do not increase in frequency, and do not become stronger or more intense.

While you're pregnant, you and your spouse/partner may participate in childbirth education classes, which provide you with information about labor and birth and the chance to meet other parents-to-be. Several types of classes are available in many communities. The Lamaze method, for example, includes focused breathing, massage, and labor support that can be used during the actual childbirth process. The Bradley method emphasizes natural childbirth, and relies heavily on deep-breathing techniques. Many childbirth education classes discuss a combination of methods to teach about the birth process and ways to make the delivery successful, comfortable, and enjoyable. Some obstetricians are now offering group options for prenatal care visits, which gives mothers more time to talk not only to their doctors but to other expectant mothers as well.

Whatever class you're considering, ask in advance about the topics and methods of childbirth that will be emphasized, and whether the classes are primarily lectures or also involve active participation. What is the instructor's philosophy about pregnancy and birth? Is he or she certified? Will you learn proper methods for breathing and relaxation? What will the classes cost? Is there a limit on class size?

At the same time, consider signing up for other classes to prepare you for the parenting challenges ahead. Ask your doctor for referrals to breastfeeding classes, infant care programs, or instructional courses on cardiopulmonary resuscitation (CPR).

Some education classes encourage or help their participants to develop a birth plan. The birth plan is usually a written document for you and your doctor to record your preferences for labor and delivery. For example:

■ Where will you be delivering your baby?

■ Based on your doctor's instructions, will you go directly to the hospital when labor begins, or will you call the office first? What arrangements have you made for transportation to the hospital or birthing center? Do you have a doula or want to participate in a doula program? (A doula provides various forms of nonmedical support in the childbirth process.)

- Whom would you like to deliver your baby: an obstetrician or an American Midwifery Certification Board–certified nurse midwife?

- Whom do you want to be present to support you during the childbirth experience?

- What position would you prefer to be in during delivery?

- What are your preferences for pain medication (if any is going to be used)?

- What options would you consider if unexpected circumstances develop (e.g., the need for an episiotomy or a Cesarean section)?

- If you deliver prematurely, does the facility have adequate resources to take care of your prematurely born infant?

Not only should you talk about and share this document and all of your birth plans with your provider, but also let your family members and friends know of your decisions. (Also see the *Last-Minute Activities* checklist below for other ideas of what to include in your birth plan.)

Last-Minute Activities

If you do have the time, consider these activities before delivery. For example:

- Make a list of people to receive birth announcements. If you're ordering print announcements, select the style and address the envelopes. Likewise, gather email addresses or phone numbers.

- Cook a number of meals and freeze them.

- Look for childcare and/or housekeeping help if you can afford it, and interview candidates. (See *Finding Help at Home,* page 181.) You can also take advantage of friends and family members who are available. Even if you don't think you'll need extra help, you should have a list of names to call in case the situation changes.

Before your ninth month, make last-minute preparations for delivery. Your checklist should include the following:

(continues on next page)

- Name, address, and phone number of the hospital.

- Name, address, and phone number of the doctor or American Midwifery Certification Board–certified nurse midwife who will deliver your baby, and of the person who covers the practice when your doctor is not available.

- The quickest and easiest route to the hospital or birthing center.

- The location of the hospital entrance you should use when labor begins.

- The phone number of an ambulance service, in case of an emergency.

- The phone number of the person who will take you to the hospital (if that individual does not live with you).

- A bag packed with essentials for labor and for the rest of your hospital stay, including toiletries, clothing, addresses and phone numbers of friends and relatives, reading material, a receiving blanket, and clothes for the baby to wear home.

- A car safety seat for the vehicle so you can take your baby home safely. Make sure the seat is approved for use by a baby at typical newborn weights, or for babies less than 5 pounds if you are having multiples or anticipate an early birth. The lower and upper weight limits can be found on the label and in the manual. Read and follow the manufacturer's instructions carefully. Install it in the backseat, facing the rear, and ideally in the middle of the backseat. (*Never* place a rear-facing car safety seat in front of an airbag.) **All infants and toddlers should ride in a rear-facing car safety seat as long as possible, or until they reach the highest weight or height allowed by their car safety seat's manufacturer.**

- Don't forget to have your car safety seat checked by a trained professional. Proper use and installation is key to protecting your little one during a crash. (See *Car Safety Seats*, page 495, for complete details.) Also, remember that the car seat must be installed properly for every use.

- If you plan to breastfeed, find out if you can order an electric breast pump in advance. Some insurance companies will allow this, and the Women, Infants, and Children (WIC) supplemental nutrition program will usually supply a pump after your baby is born. (See Chapter 4.)

- If you have other children, arrange for their care during the time you will be at the hospital.

Choosing a Pediatric Healthcare Provider

Sometime in the last trimester of pregnancy, you will choose a care provider for your baby. It is important to know that infants and young children have many more doctor's visits than most adults.

The person chosen to be your child's healthcare provider may be a pediatrician, family physician, physician assistant, or nurse practitioner. This is a personal decision for families, and you should consider what is most important to your family before choosing your baby's healthcare provider.

- *Pediatricians* are physicians with specialized training in the care of infants, children, and teenagers—all of whom have different healthcare needs, both medical and emotional, from adults. Pediatricians have special, focused training to prevent and manage these health concerns. Pediatricians build a relationship with children and their families, often over many years, creating bonds of trust and familiarity to enhance medical care. (For more information, see *A Pediatrician's Training* below.)

- *Family physicians* have broad experience in caring for patients of all ages, from newborns to senior citizens, and in many cases are able to treat the entire family.

- A *nurse practitioner* is a nurse with advanced training. Nurse practitioners focus on wellness, disease prevention, health education, typical development, and counseling. They can also evaluate children with acute illnesses. Nurse practitioners may be generalists or may receive special training in family medicine (FNP-C) or pediatrics (PNP-C). Some nurse practitioners go on to earn PhDs and the title "Doctor," but they do not have the same training as medical doctors (MDs).

- A *physician assistant (PA)* is a specialist who has earned a certificate or degree from an accredited master's-level educational program. PAs provide medical care under the direction and supervision of a physician and support the concept of physician-directed, team-based care. A PA may also receive specialized training in pediatrics.

A Pediatrician's Training

Pediatricians graduate from medical school and then receive specialized training in pediatrics for three or more years during their residency. Here the pediatrician-in-training acquires the knowledge and skills necessary to treat a broad range of conditions, from the mildest childhood illnesses to the most serious diseases.

After completing residency training, the pediatrician is eligible to take a written exam given by the American Board of Pediatrics, and if she passes she will receive a certificate, which you may see hanging on the office wall. If the initials "FAAP" appear after a pediatrician's name, it means she has passed her board exam and is now a full Fellow of the American Academy of Pediatrics, the highest status of membership in this professional organization.

Following their residency, some pediatricians elect an additional one to three years of training in a subspecialty, such as neonatology (the care of sick and premature newborns) or pediatric cardiology (the diagnosis and treatment of heart problems in children). General pediatricians often consult pediatric subspecialists when a patient develops uncommon or special problems. If a subspecialist is needed, your primary care pediatrician will help you find the right one for your child's problem.

In selecting a pediatrician, you are finding your child a medical home. A medical home is centered on the needs of the patient and family. It involves not just a doctor or other provider but the entire team, from every member of the office staff to consultants whose expertise may be needed. It's comprehensive, meaning the team addresses not only current medical needs but also prevention of future disease to emotional health and social stressors that contribute to disease. Your medical home should be accessible to you at convenient times, and people should be able to explain what they are doing to ensure that their quality of care is excellent and always improving.

Finding a Pediatrician

The best way to start looking for a pediatrician is by asking other parents you know and trust. They are likely to know you, your style, and your needs. You might also ask your obstetrician for advice. She will know respected pediatricians within the medical community. If you're new to the community, you may decide to contact a nearby hospital, medical school, or county medical society for a list of local pediatricians. If you are a member of a managed care plan, you probably will be required to choose a pediatrician from their approved network of doctors. (For more information about managed care, see *Managed Care Plans: Getting Good Care for Your Child* on pages 27–28.)

Once you have several pediatricians you wish to consider, start by arranging a personal interview with each during the final months of your pregnancy. Many pediatricians are happy to fit such preliminary interviews into their schedules. Before meeting with the pediatrician, the office staff should be able to answer some of your more basic questions:

■ Is the pediatrician accepting new patients with my insurance or managed care plan? Is she in network or out of network? Are there any additional fees?

■ What are the office hours? Do they include weekends and holidays?

■ What is the best time to call with routine questions?

■ Do the doctors answer secure email or other HIPPA-compliant electronic communications?

■ Who answers the phone if my baby has an issue after the office is closed?

■ How does the office handle billing and insurance claims? Is payment due at time of visit?

Both parents should attend the interviews with pediatricians, if possible, to be sure you both agree with the pediatrician's policies and philosophy about child rearing. Don't be afraid or embarrassed to ask any questions. Here are a few suggestions.

■ *How soon after birth will the pediatrician see your baby?*
Most hospitals ask for the name of your pediatrician when you're admitted to deliver your baby. Some hospitals have their own pediatricians on staff to see newborns. The pediatrician or her associate on call is contacted as soon as your baby is born. If you had any complications during your pregnancy or delivery, your baby should be examined at birth. This exam may be conducted by a staff pediatrician or neonatologist at the hospital if your pediatrician is not there at the time of delivery. Otherwise, the routine newborn examination can take place anytime during the first twenty-four hours after birth. Ask the pediatrician if you can be present during that initial examination. This will give you an opportunity to learn more about your baby and get answers to any questions you may have. Your baby will undergo routine newborn tests for hearing and jaundice levels as well as congenital heart disease and thyroid and other metabolic disorders.
Other tests may be needed if your baby develops problems after birth or to follow up on findings from your prenatal sonograms.

■ *When will your baby's next exams take place?*
Pediatricians routinely examine newborns and talk with parents before the babies are discharged from the hospital. Many pediatricians will

check the baby daily in the hospital, and then conduct a thorough exam on the day of discharge. During these exams, the doctor identifies any problems, while also giving parents a chance to ask questions. Your pediatrician also will convey when to schedule the first office visit and how to reach her if a medical problem develops before then.

All babies should begin their immunizations before leaving the hospital. The first and most important "immunization" is breastfeeding your baby as soon as possible after birth. This provides some early disease protection for your baby. The second recommended immunization is the first dose of the hepatitis B vaccine, which is given as a shot in the baby's thigh. Your baby will receive the next series of vaccinations when he is eight weeks old, including the second dose of hepatitis B. (The American Academy of Pediatrics' immunization schedule appears in the Appendix on page 892.)

■ *When is the doctor available by phone? Email?*

Some pediatricians have specific call-in periods each day for questions, while others return calls as they come in. If office staff routinely answer these calls, consider asking what their training is. Also ask your pediatrician for guidelines to help you determine which questions can be resolved via phone and which require an office visit. Some pediatricians prefer using secure electronic messaging, usually through an online portal, which you both may find more convenient and which helps foster a relationship with the doctor. Some doctors even offer electronic visits via telemedicine.

Telehealth Services for Children

What is a telehealth visit?

■ Telehealth is a tool that can help connect your child to many different types of healthcare services using various types of technology, such as live, interactive audio and video and special diagnostic tools. These services can be used in place of, or in addition to, a traditional face-to-face visit with a pediatrician or other pediatric healthcare provider.

■ Telehealth also provides healthcare services at times and places where children may not usually be able to get those services. For example, pediatric specialists practicing in large cities can use telehealth to see children who live hundreds of miles away. Some pediatric providers can also examine your child through your home computer or a computer in your child's school or childcare setting. Telehealth providers should be trained to treat children. Children are not small adults. Telehealth providers should have the experience and training needed to know how to safely and correctly diagnose and treat your child's condition.

What makes a good telehealth service for children?

- Good telehealth services work *with* your pediatrician. Your pediatrician may be the one seeing your child using telehealth, or he or she may have referred your child for a telehealth service, such as a subspecialist's opinion or child psychiatrist's consultation. Unfortunately, telehealth services not connected to your pediatrician may disrupt your child's care by substituting a provider who does not know your child's history or ensure necessary follow-up. Check with your pediatrician to be sure that a telehealth service you are considering is a good one.

- When connecting with your telehealth provider, the connection must be secure. Both the patient and the telehealth provider should be in a private area, so that people who aren't supposed to be a part of the visit cannot see or hear private information.

- A responsible adult such as a parent, legal guardian, school nurse, pediatrician, or other healthcare provider should always be with your child during the telehealth service.

- After the telehealth visit is over, the telehealth provider should send your pediatrician information about the visit, including any necessary follow-up. If you are unsure whether the telehealth provider has your pediatrician's fax number or other contact information, you should have that information available and request that documentation about the visit be sent promptly to your pediatrician.

- Telehealth providers should perform needed tests and examinations. Many telehealth tools are available to allow for a detailed examination of your child from a distance. These tools, such as otoscopes to look in your child's ear, blood pressure cuffs, and pulse oximeters, can be used in a variety of settings—including the home—but these tools should be the correct size for your child, and their appropriate use requires training and practice.

(continues on next page)

- Before a telehealth provider who has never examined your child gives your child antibiotics for an ear infection, he or she should use an otoscope to look in your child's ear—just as the provider would in an in-person visit.

- Before the telehealth provider treats your child for a urinary tract infection, your child's urine should be tested—as it would be in person.

- Using telehealth should not keep your child from receiving all the right tests and examinations before treatment.

- Telehealth providers should give clear guidance on when a virtual visit should be converted to a face-to-face visit. Sometimes a telehealth provider may determine that your child needs a more thorough examination, or is too sick to be cared for through telehealth, after the telehealth visit has already started. In that case, telehealth providers should know when and how to refer your child to the most appropriate healthcare facility.

How can I make sure I'm using telehealth wisely for my child?

- Always talk to your pediatric healthcare provider about any telehealth service you use. If the interaction is only through the telephone, your first phone call should be to your pediatrician's office or, during off hours, to the on-call service.

- Make sure you get information about how the telehealth visit works before it happens. Except in certain emergencies, the telehealth provider should get your consent for the telehealth service before the visit.

- Be very careful about using a smartphone or mobile device for telehealth. These devices can be lost or stolen, and keeping private health information secure is harder.

- Talk to your pediatric healthcare provider about any prescriptions that you get through telehealth, to make sure the medication is appropriate, necessary, and safe for your child. If you have any questions about appropriate care for your child, please discuss them with your pediatric healthcare provider.

Source: Section on Telehealth Care (Copyright © 2017 American Academy of Pediatrics).

■ *What hospital does the doctor prefer to use?*

Ask the pediatrician where to go if your child becomes seriously ill or is injured. If the hospital is a teaching hospital with interns and residents, find out who would actually care for your child if he is admitted.

■ *What happens if there is an after-hours (nighttime or weekend) concern or emergency?*

Find out if the pediatrician takes emergency calls at night. If not, how are such calls handled? Also, ask if the pediatrician takes office visits after hours, or if you must use the emergency department or urgent care center. When possible, it's easier and more efficient to see the doctor in her office, because hospitals often require lengthy paperwork and extended waits. However, serious medical problems are usually better handled at an emergency department, where staff and medical equipment are always available.

■ *Who covers the practice when your pediatrician is unavailable?*

If your physician is in a group practice, it's wise to meet the other doctors in the practice, since they may treat your child in your pediatrician's absence. If your pediatrician practices alone, she probably will have an arrangement for coverage with other doctors in the community. Usually your pediatrician's answering service will refer you to the doctor on call, but it's a good idea to know the names and phone numbers of all the doctors who take these calls—just in case you have trouble getting through to your own physician.

If your child is seen by another doctor at night or on the weekend, you should check in with your own pediatrician the next morning (or first thing Monday, after the weekend). Your doctor will probably already know the situation, but this contact will give you a chance to bring her up to date and let her reassure you that everything is being handled as she would recommend.

■ *How often will the pediatrician see your baby for checkups and immunizations?*

The American Academy of Pediatrics recommends a checkup within forty-eight to seventy-two hours after your newborn is discharged from the hospital. This is especially important in breastfed babies to evaluate feeding, weight gain, and any yellow discoloration of skin (jaundice). Your pediatrician may adjust this schedule, particularly in the first weeks after birth, depending on how your newborn is doing.

During your baby's first year after birth, additional visits should take place at about two to four weeks of age, and then at two, four, six, nine, and twelve months of age as well. During your baby's second year after birth, she should be seen by your pediatrician at ages fifteen, eighteen, twenty-four, and thirty months, followed by annual visits from three to five years of age. If the doctor routinely schedules examinations more or less frequently than the Academy's guidelines, discuss the differences with her. Additional appointments can be scheduled anytime you have a concern or if your child is ill.

■ *What are the costs of care?*

Your pediatrician should have a standard fee structure for hospital and office visits as well as after-hours visits and home visits (if she makes them). Find out if the charges for routine visits include immunizations. Be sure to familiarize yourself with the scope of your insurance coverage before you actually need services.

After these interviews, ask yourself if you are comfortable with the pediatrician's philosophy, policies, and practice. You must feel able to trust her and that your questions will be answered and your concerns handled compassionately. You also should feel comfortable with the staff and general atmosphere of the office.

Once your baby arrives, the most important test for the pediatrician is how she cares for your child and responds to your concerns. If you are unhappy with any aspect of the treatment you and your child are receiving, you should talk to the pediatrician directly about the problem. If the response does not address your concerns, or if the problem simply cannot be resolved, seek out another physician.

Issues to Discuss with Your Pediatrician

Once you have found a pediatrician with whom you feel comfortable, let her help you plan for your child's basic care. Certain decisions and preparations should be made before the baby arrives. Your pediatrician can advise you on issues such as the following.

When Should the Baby Leave the Hospital?

Each mother and baby should be evaluated individually to determine the best time of discharge. The timing of the discharge should be the decision of you and the physician caring for the infant, not the insurance company.

Managed Care Plans:
Getting Good Care for Your Child

Many Americans are part of managed care plans. These plans, typically offered by employers and state Medicaid programs, provide services through health maintenance organizations (HMOs) or preferred provider organizations (PPOs). The plans have their own networks of pediatricians and other physicians, and if your managed care plan changes, you may find that your pediatrician is not part of the new network. Once you have a pediatrician whom you like, ask what plans she is in. You may be able to switch from one HMO or PPO to another.

If you are choosing a managed care plan, go beyond comparing just the various plans' premiums. Be sure to also look at each plan's Summary of Benefits and Coverage. This lets you more easily compare how much you'll pay in other ways, such as in deductibles and copayments, for your household's health needs. For any plan, carefully read the other materials provided by the plans, often called Certificates of Coverage.

Managed care plans attempt to reduce their costs by having doctors refer patients to certain healthcare services. Your pediatrician may act as a "gate-keeper," needing to give approval before your child can see a pediatric subspecialist. This is important since your primary care provider should be aware of all medical issues you are concerned about, and then your provider can help coordinate care and work with specialists. Without this approval, you'll have to pay for part or all of these services out of pocket.

To help you maneuver effectively through your managed care plan, here are some points to keep in mind:

- To determine what care is provided in your managed care plan, carefully read the materials provided by the plan (often called a certificate of coverage). If you have questions, talk to a plan representative or your employer's benefits manager. All plans limit some services (e.g., mental healthcare, home healthcare), so find out what's covered and what's not.

- Know what your benefits coverage and out-of-pocket expenses will be. When you're part of a managed care plan, primary and preventive care visits are usually covered, including well-child checkups, treatment for illnesses or injuries, and immunizations. Your plan may require you to pay money out of pocket for certain types of visits, so research your policy carefully and budget for these expenses.

(continues on next page)

- Once you've chosen a pediatrician, it's best to stay with her. But if you feel the need to switch, all plans allow you to select another doctor from their network. The plan administrator can give you information on how to do this.

- If you feel your child needs to see a pediatric subspecialist, work with your pediatrician to find one who is part of your plan, and obtain approval to schedule an appointment. Check your plan contract about whether your insurer will pay at least a portion of these costs. Also, if hospital care is needed, use your pediatrician's guidance in selecting a hospital in your plan that specializes in the care of children. (Most hospital procedures and surgeries require prior approval.)

- Know in advance what emergency services are covered, since you won't always have time to contact your pediatrician. Most managed care plans will pay for emergency room care in a true emergency, so in a life-threatening situation, go immediately to the nearest hospital. In general, follow-up care (e.g., removing stitches) should be done in your pediatrician's office.

- To file a complaint—for example, if coverage of certain procedures is denied—start by expressing your concern to your pediatrician. If she is unable to resolve the problem, contact your plan's member service representative or employee benefits manager about filing a complaint. If a claim has been denied, you typically have fifteen to thirty days to file an appeal, and you should receive a decision within thirty to ninety days of the appeal. If you still are dissatisfied, you may decide to seek help from your state insurance commissioner's office, or you can take legal action.

Should the Baby Be Circumcised?

At birth, most boys have skin that completely covers, or almost covers, the end of the penis. Circumcision removes some of this foreskin so that the tip of the penis (glans) and the opening of the urethra are exposed to air. Routine circumcisions are performed in the hospital within a few days of birth. When done by an experienced physician, circumcision takes only a few minutes and complications are rare. After consultation with you, local anesthesia (numbing medicine) is provided during the procedure; the doctor should inform you in advance about the type of anesthesia she recommends.

If you have a boy, you'll need to decide whether to have him circumcised. It's a good idea to make a decision about circumcision ahead of time, so you don't have to struggle with it amid the fatigue and excitement following delivery. We recommend you talk with your obstetrician or pediatrician early in pregnancy about the pros and cons of circumcision.

Circumcision has been practiced as a religious rite for thousands of years. In the United States, most boys are circumcised for religious or social reasons. Studies have concluded that circumcised infants have a slightly lower risk of urinary tract infections during the first year after birth. Neonatal circumcision also provides some protection from penile cancer, a very rare condition, even in uncircumcised men.

Some research also suggests a reduced likelihood of developing sexually transmitted infections and HIV in circumcised men, and possibly a reduced risk for cervical cancer in female partners of circumcised men. However, while there are medical benefits to circumcision, data are not sufficient to recommend routine neonatal circumcision. (See *Where We Stand* box, below.)

Circumcision does pose certain risks, such as infection and bleeding. A small percentage of circumcised boys develop a condition called meatal stenosis, in which the urethral opening gets scarred or narrowed. This can cause deviation of the urinary stream as well as straining to urinate, or in extreme cases, urinary tract infection or inability to urinate. Some boys can develop scarring of the shaft skin to the head of the penis, called a skin bridge, which requires another procedure to fix. Although the evidence is clear that infants

WHERE WE STAND

THE AMERICAN ACADEMY OF PEDIATRICS believes that circumcision has potential medical benefits and advantages, as well as risks. Evaluation of current evidence indicates that the health benefits of newborn male circumcision outweigh the risks and that the procedure's benefits justify access to this procedure for families who choose it; however, existing scientific evidence is not sufficient to recommend routine circumcision. Therefore, because the procedure is not essential to a child's current well-being, we recommend that the decision to circumcise is one best made by parents in consultation with their pediatrician, taking into account what is in the best interests of the child, including medical, religious, cultural, and ethnic traditions. Your pediatrician (or your obstetrician, if he or she would be performing the circumcision) should discuss the benefits and risks of circumcision with you and the forms of analgesia that are available.

experience pain with circumcision, there are several safe and effective ways to reduce this pain. If the baby is born prematurely, has an illness at birth, or has congenital abnormalities or blood problems, he should not be circumcised immediately. For example, if a condition called *hypospadias* (see page 786) is present, in which the infant's urinary opening has not formed normally, your doctor will probably not recommend circumcision at birth. In fact, circumcision should be performed only on stable, healthy infants.

The Importance of Breastfeeding

The American Academy of Pediatrics recommends breastfeeding as the optimal form of infant feeding. Even though formula-feeding is not identical to breastfeeding, formulas do provide appropriate nutrition. Both approaches are safe and healthy for your baby, and each has its advantages.

The most practical benefits of breastfeeding are convenience and cost, but there are real medical benefits, too. Breast milk provides your baby with natural antibodies that help her resist some infections (including ear, respiratory, and intestinal infections). Breastfed babies have lower risk of dying from SIDS. Breastfed babies are also less likely to suffer from allergies that occasionally occur in babies fed cow's milk formulas. Breastfed infants may also be less likely to develop asthma and diabetes, or have overweight, than those who are bottle-fed. Certain types of childhood cancer occur less frequently in children who were breastfed.

Mothers who nurse their babies benefit from many emotional rewards. Once the milk supply is established and the baby is nursing well, both mother and infant experience a tremendous sense of closeness and comfort, a bond that continues throughout infancy. The first week or two can be challenging for some, but most pediatricians can offer guidance or refer you to a certified lactation consultant if needed.

The American Academy of Pediatrics recommends exclusive breastfeeding for about the first six months after birth, with continued breastfeeding after introduction of complementary pureed, solid foods six months after birth. Breastfeeding should continue for at least the first year after birth, and beyond, if mother and baby desire. Breastfeeding should start soon after birth and continue regularly, about eight to twelve times a day in the beginning. A

The American Academy of Pediatrics recommends breastfeeding as the optimal form of infant feeding.

trained professional should evaluate how well breastfeeding is going before discharge from the hospital. An early follow-up office visit is important to ensure the mother's milk supply and adequate milk transfer during feedings.

If there is a medical reason you cannot breastfeed or you choose not to do so, you still can achieve similar feelings of closeness during bottle-feedings. Rocking, cuddling, stroking, and gazing into your baby's eyes will enhance the experience for both of you, regardless of milk source.

Chapter 4 more thoroughly explains the advantages and disadvantages of breastfeeding and bottle-feeding. There are breastfeeding classes available in many communities to help you plan for breastfeeding and get your questions about it answered. Ask your doctor for a referral.

Should I Store My Newborn's Cord Blood?

Umbilical cord blood has been used successfully to treat a number of genetic, blood, and cancer conditions in children, such as leukemia and immune disorders. Some parents choose to store their baby's cord blood for possible future use. However, there are no accurate statistics on the likelihood of children someday needing their own stored cells. In response, the American Academy of Pediatrics discourages storing cord blood at private banks for later personal or family use as a general "insurance policy." Rather, they encourage families to donate their newborn's cord blood, which is normally discarded at birth, to cord blood banks (if accessible in their area) for other individuals in need. (You should be aware, though, that your baby's donated cord blood would not be available as a stem cell source if your child developed leukemia later in life.)

Storing your child's cord blood is an issue that you and your partner should discuss with your obstetrician or pediatrician before your baby is born, not during the stressful time of delivery. She may refer you to cord blood banks in your community. You will need to register ahead of time so a collection kit can be sent to be used at your delivery. Many states now mandate that obstetricians and pediatricians discuss cord blood collection with their patients. An informed consent form must be signed prior to the onset of active labor and before the cord blood collection.

Keep in mind that because cord blood is collected after the baby is born and the umbilical cord is clamped and cut, it does not affect the baby or the birth experience. The cord blood stem cell collection process should not alter the routine practice for the timing of umbilical cord clamping.

Once the cord blood is collected, it is typed and screened for infectious diseases and hereditary hematologic diseases. If donation meets all the required standards, it will be cryogenically stored for potential transplantation if a match is found, or it might be used for quality improvement and research.

Preparing Your Home and Family for the Baby's Arrival

Choosing Baby Clothing and Accessories

As your due date nears, this is a suggested list of baby clothes and accessories for your newborn's first few weeks:

3 or 4 sleepwear sets

6 to 8 T-shirts

3 newborn sleep sacks

2 sweaters

2 caps/hats

4 pairs of socks or booties

4 to 6 receiving/swaddle blankets

1 set of baby washcloths and towels (look for towels with hoods)

3 to 4 dozen newborn-size diapers

3 to 4 onesies/T-shirts with snaps between legs

For more help on selecting items you may need, see *Guidelines on Clothing Choices* on page 34.

Buying Furniture and Baby Equipment

Walk into any baby store and you may be overwhelmed by the available selection of equipment. A few items are essential, but most things, while enticing, are not necessary. In fact, some are not even useful. To help sort the options, here is a list of basic necessities you should have when your baby arrives.

- A *crib* that meets the current safety standard (see *Safety Alert: Cribs,* page 35). New cribs sold today must meet this standard and are the best choice. If you're looking at used cribs, check them carefully to make sure they were originally sold after June 28, 2011, and have not been recalled. Cribs purchased before June 2011 probably do not meet the current safety standard and are illegal to sell, even privately; they should be taken apart and discarded. Your baby may outgrow a bassinet in just a few weeks, but if you use one, check for a label indicating it meets safety standard F2194.

- *Bedding for the crib,* including a cotton flannel waterproof mattress cover and snug fitted sheets. No other bedding products should be used in the crib. This means there should be no pillows, loose blankets, quilts, comforters, pillow-like toys, positioning devices, or bumper pads in the crib.

- A *changing table* that meets all safety specifications (see *Changing Tables,* page 479). It should be placed on a carpet or padded mat and against a wall, not a window, so there is no danger of your child falling out the window. Put shelves or tables to hold diapers, wipes, and other changing equipment within your reach (but away from the baby's reach), so you will not have to step away from the table—even for a second—to get anything.

- A *diaper pail.* Keep the pail securely closed. If you are going to wash your own diapers, you'll need a second pail so you can separate wet diapers from soiled ones.

- A *large plastic washtub* for bathing the baby. As an alternative to the washtub, you can use the kitchen sink to bathe your newborn, provided the faucet swings out of the way and the dishwasher is off. (The water from the dishwasher could dump into the sink, resulting in scalding.) After the first month, it's safer to switch to a separate tub, because the baby will be able to reach and turn on the faucet from the sink. Always make sure the bathing area is clean before starting. Also, be sure the hottest temperature at the faucet is no more than 120 degrees Fahrenheit (48.9 degrees Celsius) to avoid burns; in most cases, you can adjust your water heater. Never leave your baby unattended during a bath. Prepare all of your supplies beforehand and have a towel within your reach.

Everything in the nursery should be kept clean and dust-free. (See Chapter 15 for safety specifications.) All surfaces, including window and floor coverings, should be washable. Although stuffed animals are cute (they seem to be a favorite shower gift), they tend to collect dust and may contribute to stuffy noses. Since your baby won't actively play with them for many months, you might consider storing them until she's ready for them.

Guidelines on Clothing Choices

- Buy big. Unless your baby is born prematurely or is very small, she will probably outgrow newborn sizes in days—if she ever fits into them at all! Even three-month sizes may be outgrown within the first month. Your baby won't mind roomier clothes for a while.

- To avoid injury from a garment that catches fire, all children should wear flame-retardant sleepwear and clothing. Make sure the label indicates this. These garments should be washed in laundry detergents, not soap, because soap washes out the flame retardant. Check garment labels and product information to determine which detergents to use.

- Make sure the diaper area of clothing has snaps or access to be able to change diapers.

- Avoid any clothing that pulls tightly around the neck, arms, or legs, or has ties or cords. These clothes not only are safety hazards, but are also uncomfortable.

- Check washing instructions. Clothing for all children should be washable and require little or no ironing.

- Do *not* put shoes on a newborn's feet. Shoes are not necessary until after she starts to walk. Take care that socks are not too tight around your baby's feet and ankles.

Safety Alert: Cribs

To reduce the risk of SIDS, the AAP recommends that new babies sleep in the parents' room, with the baby on a separate sleep surface, such as a safety-approved bassinet or infant crib, for at least the first six months, and ideally for the first year. The crib should be a totally safe environment. You can prevent serious injuries by using a safe crib with no soft objects or loose bedding, placing it away from windows, and keeping cords and other objects well out of reach. Falls can be prevented by lowering the crib mattress as your baby grows; it should be in its lowest position before the baby can stand. Remember that the safest position for a baby to sleep is on her back (see *Positioning for Sleep*, page 66).

A new mandatory crib safety standard was implemented in 2011. This new standard prohibits the manufacture or sale of cribs with a drop-side rail and implements requirements for stronger parts, hardware, and safety testing. **It is strongly recommended to use a crib that meets the current safety standard.** All cribs sold since June 28, 2011, must meet this standard. Check to see if an older crib has been recalled at cpsc.gov.

All cribs should be inspected carefully for the following features:

- Slats should be no more than 2⅜ inches (6 cm) apart so a child's head cannot become trapped between them.

- There should be no cutouts in the headboard or footboard, as your child's head could become trapped in them.

- Corner posts should be flush with the end panels or very, very tall (such as posts on a canopy bed). Loose clothing can become snagged on these and choke your baby.

You can prevent other crib hazards by observing the following guidelines:

1. If you purchase a new mattress, remove and destroy all plastic wrapping material that comes with it, because it can suffocate a child. The mattress should be firm, not soft.

2. As soon as your baby can sit, lower the crib mattress to the level where she cannot fall out either by leaning against the side or by pulling herself over it. Set the mattress at its lowest position before your child can stand (typically between six and nine months of age). The most com-

(continues on next page)

mon falls occur when a baby tries to climb out, so move your child to another bed when she is 35 inches (88.9 cm) tall, or the height of the side rail is at or below her nipple line while standing.

3. The top of the crib's side rail should be at least 4 inches (10.16 cm) above the mattress, even when the mattress is set at its highest position.

4. The mattress should fit snugly so your child cannot slip between it and the crib side. If you can insert two fingers between the mattress and the sides or ends of the crib, replace the mattress with one that fits snugly.

5. Periodically check the crib to be sure all hardware is tight, there are no rough edges or sharp points on the metal parts, and there are no splinters or cracks in the wood.

6. Bumper pads and other products that attach to crib slats should not be used. There is no evidence that they prevent injuries and there is the potential for suffocation, entrapment, and strangulation.

7. There should be no soft objects or loose bedding in the crib. This includes pillows, quilts, comforters, sheepskins, and stuffed toys. Dress your baby in a wearable blanket, warm sleeper, or layers of clothing as an alternative to a blanket.

8. If you use a mobile or crib gym, securely attach it to the side rails. Hang it high enough so your baby cannot reach it to pull it down, and remove it when he starts to push up on his hands and knees or when he reaches five months, whichever comes first. Even before pushing up, some infants roll on their side and reach up to grab the mobile.

9. Keep baby monitors and other products well out of reach. Your baby may be able to reach the cord before you realize it, which can lead to strangulation. Cords from window coverings should be far out of reach as well; it is best to use cordless window products, if possible.

10. To prevent the most serious falls, don't place a crib—or any other child's bed—beside a window. Do not hang pictures or shelves above the child's bed; they can fall onto your child.

Safety Alert: Bassinets and Cradles

Many parents prefer to use a bassinet or cradle for the first few weeks, because it's portable and allows the newborn to sleep in the parents' room. To get the longest and safest possible use from your baby's first bed, check the following before buying:

1. The bassinet should meet the current safety standard. This means it is safest to buy a new one, but if you receive a secondhand bassinet, check that it was manufactured recently.

2. The bottom of the cradle or bassinet should be well supported so it cannot possibly collapse.

3. The bassinet or cradle should have a wide base so it cannot tip over. If the bassinet or cradle has folding legs, they should be locked straight whenever in use. Your baby should graduate to a crib around the end of the first month or by the time she weighs 10 pounds (4.5 kg).

A "sidecar" arrangement—the crib placed next to the parents' bed—may be more comfortable and will be safer than bed sharing. For most families, a crib in the parents' room allows plenty of togetherness with fewer interruptions to sleep. The AAP recommends that new babies sleep in the room with their parents, ideally through the first year after birth. The baby should be on a separate sleep surface, such as a crib, bassinet, or play yard. Infants should always be placed to sleep flat on the back without pillows, loose blankets, stuffed animals, or other bedding. Offering a pacifier also reduces the risk of SIDS. In breastfed infants, the pacifier may be delayed until breastfeeding is well established.

If the air in the nursery is extremely dry, your pediatrician may recommend using a cool mist humidifier or vaporizer. This also may help clear your child's stuffy nose when she has a cold. If you do use a humidifier or vaporizer, clean it frequently as directed in the manual and empty it when not in use. Otherwise, bacteria and molds may grow in the still water.

One object your baby may enjoy is a mobile. Look for one with bright colors (the first color she'll see is red) and varied shapes. Some also play music. When shopping for a mobile, look at it from below so that you'll know how it appears to your baby. Make sure you remove the mobile at five months of age or as soon as your baby can sit up, because that's when she'll be able to pull it down and risk injury.

Other useful additions may include a rocking chair or glider. The rocking motion of the chair will increase the soothing effect your baby feels when you hold her. Playing soft music or white noise may comfort her and help her fall asleep.

You will want to keep lights in the bedroom soft and leave a nightlight on after dark. The nightlight will allow you to check on the baby more easily, and as she gets older, it will reassure her when she awakens at night. Make sure all lights and cords are kept safely out of the baby's reach.

Preparing Your Other Children for the Baby's Arrival

If you have other children, you'll need to plan how and when to tell them about the new baby. A child who is four or older should be told as soon as you start telling friends and relatives. She should have a basic sense of how she is related to her new brother or sister. Fables about storks and such may seem cute, but they won't help her understand and accept the situation. Using one of the picture books published on the subject may help you to explain "where babies come from." Too much detail can be scary. For young children it's usually enough to say, "Like you, this baby was made from a little bit of Mommy and a little bit of Daddy." Older children may have more questions, and you should answer those in simple and age-appropriate ways.

If your child is younger than four when you become pregnant, you can wait a while before telling her. At this age, it may be difficult to understand an abstract concept like an unborn baby. But once you start furnishing the nursery, putting a crib or bassinet in the nursery, and making or buying baby clothes, you should share the news about the new baby. Picture books about babies or about becoming a big sister or brother can be useful with very young children, too, as well as sharing ultrasound pictures. Even if she doesn't ask any questions, start talking to your older child about the baby by the last few months of pregnancy. If your hospital offers a sibling preparation class, take her so she

Take advantage of any questions your child may ask about Mom's growing "stomach" to explain what's happening.

can see where the baby will be born and where she can visit. Point out other newborns and their older siblings, and tell her how she's going to be a big sister soon.

Don't promise things will be the same after the baby comes, because they won't be, no matter how hard you try. But reassure your child that you will love her just as much, and help her understand the positive side of having a baby sibling.

Picture books can be helpful with very young children.

Breaking the news is most difficult if your child is between two and three. At this age, she's extremely attached to you and doesn't yet understand the concept of sharing time, possessions, or your affection with anyone else. She's also very sensitive to change and may feel threatened by the idea of a new family member. The best way to minimize jealousy is to include her as much as possible in the preparations for the new baby. Let her shop with you for baby clothing and nursery equipment. Show her pictures of herself as a newborn, and if you're reusing previous baby equipment, let her play with it before setting it up for the newcomer.

If you can, try to make any major changes in your preschooler's routine, such as toilet training, switching from a crib to a bed, changing bedrooms, or starting a new preschool, before the baby arrives. If that's not possible, put them off until after the baby is settled at home. Otherwise, your older child may feel overwhelmed when the baby's arrival is added to the stress of her own adjustments.

Help your child with the impending birth of a new sibling. Don't be alarmed if the news—or, later, the baby's arrival—prompts your older child's behavior to regress a little. She may demand a bottle, ask to wear diapers again, cry for no apparent reason, or refuse to leave your side. This is her way of demanding your love and attention and reassuring herself that she still has it. Instead of resisting, simply grant her requests, and don't get upset about it. A three-year-old toilet-trained child who demands a diaper for a few days, or the five-year-old who wants her outgrown (you thought long-forgotten) security blanket for a week, will soon return to her normal routine when she realizes that she still

Make sure you reserve some special time each day just for you and your older child.

has just as important a place in the family as her new sibling. Similarly, an older sibling who wants to try nursing again will quickly lose interest.

Though you may be preoccupied with your new arrival, make sure you reserve special time each day for you and your older child. Read, play games, listen to music, or simply talk. Show her you're interested in what she's doing, thinking, and feeling—not only in relation to the baby, but about everything else in her life. It takes only five or ten minutes a day of protected time—time when the baby is asleep or being cared for by another adult—to make your older child feel special.

For both parents, once your baby finally arrives, all the waiting and discomforts of pregnancy will seem like minor inconveniences. Suddenly you'll meet this new person who's been so close and yet so mysterious all these months. The rest of this book is about the child she will become and the job that awaits you as a parent.

There's only so much preparation you can do before you start any journey. We have discussed the supplies you may need as well as many do's and don'ts. Ultimately, your role as a parent is determined more by the way you prepare yourself emotionally than by what color you choose for the nursery. Only you know how you respond to stress and change. Try to prepare yourself for parenthood in a way that feels most comfortable to you. Some parents find support groups helpful; others prefer to meditate, sketch, or write.

Preparing Dad for Delivery

If you're the father-to-be, you have an enormous role in preparing for the baby's arrival. At the same time, you'll be making your own adjustments, which are challenging, too. At times you've felt excited; other times, fearful, exhausted, and perhaps just anxious for the baby to arrive. There probably have been moments when you've been an emotional anchor for your partner, from periods of extreme fatigue to morning sickness.

When you attend prenatal visits, discuss what role you'll play in the delivery room. Be sure to get all questions answered about what will take place and how you can be most supportive. If you can do advance planning to take off a few days or weeks from work once the baby arrives, make those arrangements now. And, of course, be ready to play a very active role in your child's life, not only in the first few days after her birth, but for the rest of your lives together. (For a further discussion about the unique role of fathers—and grandparents—in the birth of their baby, see Chapter 6, pages 185–88.)

Preparing yourself might be more difficult for some soon-to-be parents than others, especially if you are the kind of person who likes spontaneity, but preparation is important, since it gives rise to greater confidence. It takes a stunning amount of confidence for a child to begin to walk. You will need that same type of confidence to take your own first steps into parenting.

Finally—Delivery Day!

Most pregnancies last between thirty-seven and forty-two weeks. Labor contractions are the clearest indication that your body is getting ready to deliver your baby. When labor starts, your cervix (the lower end of the uterus) will open, and the uterus will begin contracting (or squeezing). The cervix must be thinned out in order for the baby's head to move into the birth canal. Each time a contraction occurs, your uterus and abdomen will become tighter and firmer. Between contractions, the uterus will soften, and you can relax for a short time while awaiting the next contraction.

Although most women know when they are nearing labor or when labor has started, it isn't always easy to tell when this process has begun. That's because "false labor" can occur, in which contractions are sporadic and relatively weak. Even so, don't be embarrassed to call your doctor or go to the hospital if you're uncertain whether this is the real thing!

With actual labor, you will experience:

- Repeated contractions, cramps, and increases in pain levels corresponding to the opening (dilating) of your cervix and the baby's descent through the birth canal

- A slightly bloody, pink, or clear vaginal discharge that is the mucus plug at the cervix

- A breaking of your water, which is really a rupture in the amniotic sac that contains watery fluid that surrounds and protects your baby

As labor progresses, the contractions will become stronger, they'll occur more often, and they'll continue for about thirty to seventy seconds each. The pain of the contractions will tend to start in your back and then move forward to the lower abdomen.

When should you call your doctor or go to the hospital? Hopefully you've already discussed this with your doctor. In general, you should head for the hospital or phone your doctor if your water breaks (even if you aren't having contractions yet), you're experiencing vaginal bleeding, or the pain is severe and persistent even between contractions.

The doctor may induce labor before you go into labor on your own. This induction may be chosen if your doctor determines that your health or the health of your baby is at risk. Perhaps you have a chronic disease such as diabetes or high blood pressure that may pose risks to you or your child. Or your doctor may recommend inducing labor if tests indicate that your baby's growth is unusual. With certain medications (such as oxytocin or prostaglandin drugs that may be given intravenously in the hospital), the mother will have contractions and her cervix will start to dilate and thin. The doctor can also intentionally rupture the membranes that surround the fetus or use other means to get labor started.

What About the Pain?

Pain levels during delivery vary from one woman to another. For some, the process can be very painful, but women can often turn to relaxation and breathing techniques (taught in their childbirth classes) to help deal with the discomfort. Massage on the lower back by a spouse or other labor coach often eases discomfort as well, as does taking a bath or shower (if allowed) or applying ice packs to the back.

Trained labor coaches, such as doulas, can help mothers deal with the pain and anxiety of delivery. Doulas provide emotional support, massage, and recommendations about positioning, which may make labor shorter and decrease the chance of having a Cesarean section. Mothers should research doulas before delivery and make sure that they are encouraged by the delivery hospital.

If an episiotomy (surgical incision in the vaginal area) is needed to ease the baby's head through the birth canal, a local anesthetic is used. Local anesthetics given in this manner almost never negatively affect the baby.

As labor progresses, many women decide to have medication to ease the pain of contractions. These include:

- *Narcotic (opioid) medications given as a shot or through an intravenous catheter.* These medications make the labor pains more tolerable but can slow the baby's breathing if given very close to delivery.

- *Numbing medicines given in the spinal region to reduce the intensity of the contractions.* This is generally referred to as epidural analgesia or an epi-

(continues on next page)

dural block. A small catheter is placed into the epidural space, an area just outside the spinal cord region, as a delivery method for the medication. This decreases the feeling in your abdomen and makes the contractions less painful. Relief generally begins within ten to twenty minutes. Often these medications are given in small enough doses so that you are still alert, are aware of the contractions (though they do not feel as painful), and still have enough strength to push the baby down the birth canal. Side effects or complications are rare, but may include headaches or a drop in your blood pressure.

If your doctor decides that a Cesarean section is necessary, there are three options for pain relief/anesthesia:

■ *Additional numbing medicine can be given through an epidural catheter to make your entire lower body numb (from below your rib cage to your toes).* If you already had an epidural catheter placed to ease the labor pain, then extra medicine can be given through this catheter. The advantage of this type of anesthesia is that the baby will not be as sleepy and you can be awake when the baby is born.

■ *If you are having a scheduled Cesarean section, your doctor may recommend a spinal block.* This is a single injection into the fluid surrounding the spinal cord. Spinal blocks are very quick and easy to perform and generally make you even more numb than an epidural block. Pain relief begins immediately. One difference between a spinal and an epidural block is that a spinal is a one-time shot of pain medication that wears off on its own in several hours, instead of being administered continuously through a catheter. Side effects or complications are rare, but are similar to an epidural.

■ *If the surgery needs to be performed as an emergency or you have a medical issue that would make an epidural or spinal block dangerous for you, medicines can be given that will make you lose consciousness or be deeply "asleep" (general anesthesia).* This can make the baby very sleepy when he is born and affects the baby's breathing. When general anesthesia is given, the baby must be delivered very quickly in order to decrease these effects, so epidural or spinal blocks are preferred when possible.

(For more detailed information about routine vaginal deliveries and Cesarean sections, including procedures in hospital delivery rooms upon the birth of your baby, see Chapter 2, *Birth and the First Moments After.*)

~ 2 ~

Birth and the First Moments After

IT'S HARD TO IMAGINE any life event that matches childbirth for the anticipation, excitement, and anxiety involved. It's inevitable that you will enter into this moment with expectations borne of stories from relatives, books, television, and movies, and even your own prior experiences. It is also inevitable that each birth will be unique, and that no one can predict exactly what will happen.

Routine Vaginal Delivery

In the weeks leading up to the birth of your baby, you'll probably feel some apprehension along with your excitement. Then, usually between the thirty-seventh and forty-second weeks, you'll go into labor.

Although no one knows for certain what triggers this process, shifts in hormone levels appear to play a role. Your amniotic sac will rupture, commonly referred to as "breaking your water." As you proceed through labor, your uterus will contract rhythmically, or squeeze, which moves your baby down the birth canal. At the same time, these contractions will open, or dilate, your cervix to about 10 centimeters (4 in).

In a routine vaginal delivery, your first view of your child may be the top, or crown, of his/her head, which may be seen in a mirror if you choose. After delivery of the head, there is usually one last pause before the push that sends your baby's body into the doctor's or nurse midwife's arms. Sometimes a vacuum or forceps, special supplies used by obstetricians, are used to help pull the baby out.

For well-appearing infants, it is now common to wait at least thirty seconds to one minute to cut the umbilical cord (also called delayed cord clamping or timed cord clamping), during which time the obstetrician or nurse midwife may place the baby on your lower abdomen. Once the pulsing stops, the cord will be clamped and cut (there are no nerves in the cord; the baby will feel no pain). The clamp remains in place for twenty-four to forty-eight hours, or until the cord is dry and no longer bleeds. The stump that remains will fall off between one and three weeks.

Most of the time, immediately after delivery, your baby will be placed directly on your chest, belly down, for skin-to-skin care. Your provider will dry your baby, put a hat on your baby, and cover your baby with a warm blanket while your newborn settles on your chest. This first hour of skin-to-skin contact allows you and your baby to get to know each other and has other important health benefits. Sometimes babies need to be evaluated and brought to a warmer immediately after birth. If that happens, when your infant is stabilized he/she can be brought to you for skin-to-skin care.

Even if you've seen pictures of newborns, you're bound to be amazed by the first sight of your own. When she opens her eyes, they will meet yours with curiosity. All the activity of birth may make her alert and responsive to your touch, voice, and warmth. Take advantage of this attentiveness, which may last for a few hours. Watch how the baby moves toward your breast, seeking that first feeding. These moments are magical for you and your baby. They should be allowed to happen. Attendants should not wash you or the baby or otherwise interfere. The smell and feel of the moment will guide the baby to her first feeding. As with many moms, you may find that putting your baby to your breast creates an intense emotional bond between you and your newborn.

Fresh from birth, your child may be covered with a white cheesy substance called vernix. This protective coating is produced toward the end of pregnancy by the sebaceous (oil-producing) glands in her skin. She'll also be wet with amniotic fluid. If there was tearing of tissue in the vaginal area, she may have some of your blood on her. Her skin, especially on the face, may be quite wrinkled from the wetness and pressure of birth.

Nursing After Delivery

We recommend that you plan to breastfeed your baby. Today, most hospitals encourage immediate breastfeeding within the first hour following routine delivery, while the baby is held skin-to-skin, unless the baby is having difficulty breathing, which may require monitoring. (See page 52 for detailed information on Apgars.)

Breastfeeding right away benefits the mother by causing the uterus to contract, reducing the amount of uterine bleeding, and it benefits the newborn by giving immediate protection against infections. (The same hormone that stimulates the milk ejection reflex, or let-down response, triggers uterine contractions.)

The first hour or so after birth is the ideal time to begin breastfeeding. Your baby is alert and eager. When put to the breast she may first lick it. Then, with a little help, she'll latch on to the areola (not the nipple) and suck vigorously for several minutes. If you wait until later, she may be sleepier and have more difficulty latching effectively.

For the first two to five days after delivery, your body produces colostrum, a thin, yellowish fluid that contains protein and antibodies that protect her from infection. Colostrum provides all the nutrients and fluids your baby needs in those first few days after birth. (For a complete discussion of breastfeeding, see Chapter 4.) Many hospitals have lactation consultants (professional experts to help mothers with breastfeeding); ask for their help if you are having any difficulty in establishing successful breastfeeding, especially if this is your first baby.

When babies are born, the head shape may be elongated due to pushing through the birth canal. The head was able to adapt to the contours of the passageway as it was pushed through, squeezing to fit. The head shape may also be elongated if a vacuum was used to assist in the delivery. Now free, the baby's head may take several days to revert to its oval shape. Your baby's skin color may be a little blue at first but gradually will turn pinker as her breathing becomes regular. Her hands and feet may be slightly blue and feel cool, and may remain so, on and off, for several weeks until her body is better able to adjust to the temperature around her.

You also may notice that your newborn's breathing is irregular and very rapid. While an adult will normally take twelve to fourteen breaths per minute, your newborn may take as many as forty to sixty breaths per minute. An occasional deep breath may alternate with bursts of short, shallow breaths, followed by pauses. This is typical for the initial days after birth.

Delivery by Cesarean Section

About one-third of births occur by Cesarean section in the United States (also called C-section or simply section). In a C-section, surgery is performed, with an incision made in the mother's abdomen and uterus. The baby is taken directly from the uterus instead of traveling through the birth canal.

Cesarean sections are done most often when:

- The mother has had a previous baby by Cesarean delivery

- The baby is in a breech or "head-up" position

- The cervix does not adequately dilate to the 10 centimeters necessary to start pushing or the baby does not descend through the birth canal despite an adequate pushing effort

- The obstetrician feels that the baby's health might suffer if born vaginally

- The fetus's heartbeat slows abnormally or becomes irregular (in which case the obstetrician will perform an emergency C-section instead of taking the chance of allowing labor to progress)

While most babies are in a head-down position in the mother's uterus, about three in one hundred newborns have their buttocks, feet, or both positioned to come out first during birth (a breech presentation). If your baby has assumed a breech position, your obstetrician will recommend a Cesarean section as the best means of delivery. Breech babies are more difficult to deliver vaginally, and complications are more likely to occur with a vaginally delivered breech baby. A doctor can determine the baby's position by feeling the mother's lower abdomen; the physician may decide to confirm the breech position by ordering an ultrasound.

The birth experience with a Cesarean section is different from that of a vaginal delivery. Typically, the whole operation takes no more than an hour, and—depending on circumstances—you may not experience any labor. Another important difference is the use of medication that affects the mother and may affect the baby. If given a choice, most women prefer to have a regional anesthesia—where a tiny tube (catheter) is placed near your spinal cord and anesthetic drips in to numb your spinal nerves—such as an epidural or a spinal. Administration of a regional anesthesia numbs the body from the waist down, has relatively few side effects, and allows you to witness the delivery. Rarely, a general anesthetic must be used, especially for an emergency C-section, in which case you are not conscious. Your obstetrician and the anesthesiologist will advise you which approach they think best, based on the medical circumstances.

The obstetrician performing a Cesarean delivery may ask a pediatrician or an advanced practice provider such as a nurse practitioner or physician assistant to be in the delivery room with you in case the baby has any complications. The pediatric provider can also work with the obstetrician to determine if delayed cord clamping can safely be permitted. Ask ahead of time about the hospital's policies on skin-to skin care in the delivery room. Today, many hospitals encourage immediate skin-to-skin care if the infant is stable after delivery, whereas other hospitals wait until your baby has been examined and proclaimed healthy or until you are brought to the recovery room. In circumstances where both mom and baby are doing well immediately after delivery, some hospitals allow a brief period of skin-to-skin bonding while the C-section is completed. The newborn should then be kept continuously with you, allowing you to breastfeed, while the hospital staff continue to observe.

Bonding

If you deliver without complications, you'll be able to spend the first hour or so with your baby. Because babies are usually alert and very responsive during this time, researchers have labeled this the sensitive period.

The first exchanges of eye contact, sounds, and touches between the two of you are all part of a bonding process, which helps lay the foundation for your relationship as parent and child. Although it will take months to learn your child's temperament and personality, many of the core emotions you feel may begin to develop immediately after birth.

It's also quite normal if you do not immediately have tremendously warm feelings for your baby. Labor is a demanding experience, and your first reaction may well be a sense of relief that it's over. If you're exhausted and emotionally drained, you may simply want to rest. That's perfectly normal. Give yourself some time, until the strain of labor fades, and then request your baby. Bonding has no time limit.

Also, if your baby is taken immediately to the nursery for medical attention, or if you were sedated during delivery, don't despair. You needn't worry your relationship might be harmed because bonding didn't occur in this first hour. You can and will love your baby just as much, even if you couldn't watch her birth or hold her immediately afterward. Your baby will also be just as loving and connected to you.

If general anesthesia was used during delivery, you may not wake up for a few hours. When you do, you may feel groggy and confused. You'll probably also experience pain where the incision was made. But you'll soon be able to hold, provide skin-to-skin care for, and breastfeed your baby, and make up for lost time.

As mentioned, some obstetricians believe that a previous C-section warrants subsequent births to be delivered the same way, citing higher rates of complications with vaginal deliveries after previously having a C-section. However, most women are candidates for a trial of labor after Cesarean (TOLAC). A decision to do this depends on a number of factors and should be made with your doctor.

Fathers, doulas, or other birth support personnel may still have a role in the delivery room during a Cesarean birth, especially if you are not under general anesthesia. Talk to your partner and your obstetrician about options while you're making your birth plan so that everyone knows what to expect ahead of time.

Delivery Room Procedures Following a Normal Vaginal Birth

As described previously, your baby should be placed skin-to-skin, held by you, and breastfed during the first hour after birth. Apgar scores can be assigned while you hold your baby. After the first hour, your baby will be weighed, measured, examined, and given medication. She will receive a dose of vitamin K, since all newborns have slightly low levels of this vitamin, which is needed for normal blood clotting. The most important thing is to maximize the skin-to-skin contact between you and your baby as much as possible the first hour. Skin-to-skin care helps stabilize blood sugar concentrations and newborn body temperature, can prevent hypothermia, decreases crying, and provides stable blood flow and breathing, especially for late preterm newborns. For mothers, it decreases maternal stress. Breastfeeding within thirty minutes after birth may also reduce postpartum hemorrhage.

Because bacteria in the birth canal can infect a baby's eyes, your baby will be given antibiotic ointment (erythromycin ointment is commonly used), soon after delivery or later, to prevent a potentially serious eye infection.

Lastly and importantly, both you and a support person of your choosing

Vitamin K

Vitamin K plays a critical role in preventing serious, life-threatening bleeding in your newborn. Newborns often do not have enough vitamin K in their bodies because they lack the bacteria that help make this nutrient. All newborns should receive an injection of 0.5 to 1 mg of vitamin K shortly after birth. Those who don't receive this injection are at much higher risk of brain damage and even death occurring as late as two to six months after delivery. Vitamin K has been proven to be safe and effective for decades.

will receive matching labels bearing the newborn's name. After you verify the accuracy, these labels will be attached to your, your partner's, and your baby's wrist (and often her ankle as well). Each time the child is taken from or returned to you while in the hospital, the nurse will check these bracelets. Many hospitals also footprint newborns as an added precaution and attach a small security device to the baby's ankle or umbilical clamp.

Apgar Scores

As soon as your baby is born, a member of the birth team will set a timer for one minute and another for five minutes. When each of these times is up, your baby is given her first tests, called Apgars.

The Apgar scoring system helps the physician estimate your baby's general condition at birth. The test measures your baby's heart rate, breathing, muscle tone, reflex response, and color. It cannot predict how she will develop, nor does it indicate how bright she is or what her personality is like. But it does alert the hospital staff to the need for assistance as she adapts to her new world.

Each characteristic is scored, two points for each category if all is completely well. For example, if your baby has a heart rate of more than 100, cries lustily, moves actively, and grimaces and responds to rubbing and stimulation by the hospital providers, but is blue, her one-minute Apgar score would be 8—two points off because she is blue and not pink. Most newborn infants have Apgar scores greater than 7. Because hands and feet remain blue until they are quite warm, few score a perfect 10.

If your baby is having difficulty breathing, moving, or crying at birth, hospital providers specially trained in evaluation and resuscitation of newborns will evaluate and treat the baby accordingly. This may include drying her vigorously and/or using a special device on the nose and mouth to give breaths of air, called positive pressure ventilation. This intervention usually leads to improvements in breathing, movement, and color. If these strategies do not help, a tube can be placed into her lungs to help breathing, and fluids and medications administered through her umbilical cord to strengthen her heartbeat. If her Apgar scores remain low after these treatments, she may be taken to the special care nursery or neonatal intensive care unit (NICU) for observation or more intensive medical attention.

APGAR SCORING SYSTEM

Score	0	1	2
Heart rate	Absent	Less than 100 beats per minute	More than 100 beats per minute
Respiration	Absent	Slow, irregular; weak cry	Good; strong cry
Muscle tone	Limp	Some flexing of arms and legs	Active motion
Reflex*	Absent	Grimace	Grimace and cough or sneeze
Color	Blue or pale	Body pink; hands and feet blue	Completely pink

* Reflex judged by placing a catheter or bulb syringe in the infant's nose and watching her response.

Leaving the Delivery Area

If you delivered in a birthing room or alternative birth center, you probably won't be moved right away. But if you delivered in a conventional delivery room, you'll be taken to a recovery area where you can be watched for problems such as excessive bleeding. Once again, unless your infant requires urgent medical attention, insist that you not be separated from your infant. Your infant should receive her first medical examination by your side. This exam will measure her vital signs: temperature, respiration, and pulse rate. She will be checked from head to toe, paying specific attention to her color, activity level, and breathing pattern. If she didn't receive vitamin K and eye drops earlier, they will be administered now. Depending on hospital routine, once she's warm, she may be given her first bath, and the stump of her cord will be kept dry or cleaned with alcohol to prevent infection. Then she'll be wrapped in a blanket and, if you wish, returned to you. All medically stable newborns weighing 4 pounds 6½ ounces (2 kg) or more should receive their first dose of the hepatitis B vaccine within the first twenty-four hours after birth. You will be asked to sign a consent form for this vaccine.

Reflecting on Your Baby's Arrival

After all of this activity during her first few hours after birth, your baby probably will fall into a deep sleep, giving you time to rest and process what has just happened. If your baby is with you, you may stare at her in wonder that you could possibly have produced such a miracle. Such emotions may wipe away physical exhaustion temporarily, but once you are rested, gather your strength for the exciting job ahead of you.

If Your Baby Is Premature

Premature birth occurs in about 10 percent of pregnancies in the United States. Almost 60 percent of twins, triplets, and other multiple deliveries result in preterm births. A birth is considered preterm when a child is born before completing thirty-seven weeks of pregnancy. Other categories of newborns include late preterm (thirty-four to thirty-six weeks), moderately preterm (thirty-two to thirty-six weeks), and very preterm (less than thirty-two weeks).

If your baby is born prematurely, she may neither look nor behave like a full-term infant. While the average full-term newborn weighs about 7 pounds (3.17 kg), a premature newborn might weigh 5 pounds (2.26 kg) or even considerably less. Moderately to late preterm (those born before thirty-seven weeks) and very preterm infants (those born before thirty-two weeks gestation) often require medical care in the neonatal intensive care unit or special care nursery

Your premature baby will be placed immediately after birth in an enclosed bed to keep her warm.

because they are not fully developed at birth. The length of time they require care varies tremendously, but many times they need to be hospitalized until the approximate due date. Preterm infants can have a variety of short- and long-term medical problems.

The earlier your baby arrives, the smaller she will be, the larger her head will seem in relation to her body, and the less fat she will have. With so little fat, her skin will seem thinner and more transparent, allowing the blood vessels beneath to show. She also may have fine hair, called lanugo, on her back and shoulders. Her features will appear sharper and less rounded than they would at term, and she probably won't have any of the white, cheesy vernix that would otherwise protect her at term birth. Don't worry—in time she'll look like a typical newborn.

Because she has less fat, your premature baby will get cold at normal room temperatures. Immediately after birth she'll be placed in an incubator (often called an isolette) or under a special heating device called a radiant warmer. Here the temperature can be adjusted to keep her warm. Your baby will be moved to a special-care nursery, often called a neonatal intensive care unit (NICU). In some hospitals you will be able to join her there once you are medically stable. Special care nurseries feature equipment and specially trained staff to assist in the care of preterm or ill newborns.

You may also notice that your premature baby will cry only softly, if at all, and may have trouble breathing. Her respiratory system is still immature. If she's more than two months early, her breathing difficulties can cause serious health problems. Doctors will keep her under close observation, watching her breathing and heart rate with a cardiorespiratory monitor. If she needs help breathing, she may be given a ventilator or another breathing assistance technique called CPAP (continuous positive airway pressure). As important as this care is for your baby's survival, her move to the special-care nursery may be wrenching for you. On top of all the health worries, you may miss the experience of holding, breastfeeding, and bonding with her after delivery.

To deal with this stress, ask to see your baby as soon as possible after delivery, and become as active as you can in her care. Spend as much time with her in the special-care nursery as your condition—and hers—permits. Your special care nursery will encourage you to do skin-to-skin as soon as her medical needs allow.

You can also feed her as soon as your doctor says it's OK. The nurses will instruct on either breast- or bottle-feeding techniques, whichever is appropriate for the baby's needs and your desires. Some premature babies initially require intravenous or feeding tube fluids. But your breast milk is the best nutrition and provides antibodies and other substances that enhance immune response and help resist infection. Breast milk holds special advantages for preterm infants; most important of all is preventing a complication called necrotizing enterocolitis (NEC). If it's too difficult for your premature baby to nurse, you can pump breast milk for feeding through a tube or bottle. Ask your nurse or lactation consultant for help in pumping your milk by hand and with a breast pump. It is important to initiate pumping as soon as possible after delivery and to continue pumping every two to three hours, or eight times per day, to keep up your milk supply. Once breastfeeding directly, your baby should nurse frequently to increase your milk supply. Even so, mothers of premature babies sometimes continue pumping in addition to frequent breastfeeding to maintain a good milk supply. If your own milk is not available, pasteurized donor breast milk is also available specifically for preterm infants depending on hospital policy. You can inquire about it, and if your baby qualifies for donor breast milk you will need to sign a consent form. Donated breast milk does not provide full protection against disease in the environment, since it must be heat-treated to destroy any potentially dangerous bacteria, viruses, or other infectious particles, but it does provide some of the immune benefits and many of the nutrients that formula does not contain.

Using another mother's milk that has *not* been pasteurized, or purchasing milk from another source, whether the mother is known or not, does pose potential risks of infection for the infant. In addition, that mother may not have pumped or stored the milk under the most hygienic conditions. Milk purchased over the Internet has been shown to be contaminated with bacteria, altered with other milk or formula, and not kept frozen throughout the shipping process. This milk should not be fed to infants.

Newborn Screening Tests

Shortly after birth, and before being discharged, your baby will be given a number of screening tests to detect a variety of congenital conditions (genetic blood spot test, pulse oximetry screening test, newborn hearing screen). These tests are designed for early detection to enable prompt treatment, prevent disabilities, and save lives. While laws mandate some tests, tests often differ from state to state (and change periodically). Before your baby is born, talk to your pediatrician about which screening tests your baby will undergo, including benefits and risks, and whether consent is necessary. Ask when test results will be available and what they mean, especially if out of the normal range (that may not necessarily indicate a congenital or genetic condition, so inquire if retesting will be done). Also, double-check to make certain the tests are actually performed prior to discharge.

You may be ready to return home before your newborn, which can be very difficult. Remember that your baby is in good hands, and you can visit her as often as you'd like. More hospitals are allowing mothers to stay with their premature infants until ready to go home together. If this option is not available to you, your time away will allow for some needed rest. Prepare your home and family for your baby's homecoming. Read a book or two on caring for preterm babies, and connect online with support groups. When you have plenty of contact with your infant during this time and participate in her recovery, you'll feel better about the situation and will find it easier to care for her when she leaves the special-care nursery. As soon as your doctor allows it, gently touch, hold, and cradle your newborn.

Your own pediatrician may participate in, or be informed about, your infant's immediate care. He will be able to answer most of your questions. Your baby will be ready to come home once she's breathing on her own, capable of maintaining body temperature, feeding by breast or bottle, and gaining weight steadily. The American Academy of Pediatrics recommends a car safety seat test, or car safety seat challenge, for all babies born before thirty-seven weeks gestation. The car seat test makes sure that premature babies are able to sit in a car seat safely, without any episodes of desaturation (low oxygen), apnea (stopping breathing), or bradycardia (low heart rate).

(For more resources and information on premature birth, contact the March of Dimes [marchofdimes.org; 1-888-663-4637] or the American College of Obstetricians and Gynecologists [acog.org; 1-888-673-8444]).

Health Issues of Premature Babies

Because premature babies are born before they are physically ready to leave the womb, they often have health problems. These newborns have higher rates of disabilities (such as cerebral palsy) and even death. African Americans and Native Americans have the highest neonatal death rate associated with prematurity. In general, male premature infants have poorer health outcomes than female infants.

Premature babies are given extra medical attention and assistance immediately after delivery. Depending on how premature your baby is, your pediatrician or obstetrician may call in a neonatologist (a pediatrician who specializes in the care of premature or very ill babies) to help determine what, if any, spe-

(continues on next page)

cial treatment is needed. Here are some of the most common conditions that occur in premature infants:

- *Respiratory distress syndrome* is a breathing disorder related to the baby's immature lungs. It occurs because the lungs often lack surfactant, a liquid substance that allows the lungs to remain expanded. Artificial surfactants can be used to treat these babies, along with a ventilator or CPAP machine to help them breathe better and maintain adequate oxygen levels in their blood. Sometimes extremely preterm babies may need long-term oxygen treatment and occasionally may go home on supportive oxygen therapy.

- *Bronchopulmonary dysplasia*, or chronic lung disease, is a term used to describe babies who require oxygen for several weeks or months. They tend to outgrow this uncommon condition, which varies in severity, as their lungs grow and mature.

- *Apnea* is a temporary pause (more than twenty seconds) in breathing common in preterm infants. It often is associated with a decline in the heart rate, called bradycardia, and desaturation, a decline in the amount of oxygen in the blood. Apnea, bradycardia, and desaturations are monitored on cardiorespiratory monitors and by pulse oximetry. Most infants outgrow the condition by the time they leave the hospital.

- *Retinopathy of prematurity (ROP)* is an eye disease featuring underdeveloped retinas. Most cases resolve without treatment, although serious cases may need treatment, including laser surgery and/or injections of medication. Your infant may be examined by a pediatric ophthalmologist or retina specialist to diagnose any problems and, if needed, recommend treatment.

- *Intraventricular hemorrhage (IVH)* is bleeding inside or around the ventricles, the spaces in the brain containing the cerebrospinal fluid. Intraventricular hemorrhage is most common in premature babies, especially very-low-birth-weight babies—those weighing less than 3 pounds, 5 ounces (1,500 g). Bleeding can occur because blood vessels in a premature baby's brain are very fragile and immature and rupture easily. Nearly all IVH occurs within the first week after birth. It is diagnosed by doing an ultrasound of the head. Grades 1 and 2 are most common, and often there are no further complications. Grades 3 and 4 are the most serious and may result in long-term brain injury to the baby. Hydrocephalus (too much cerebral spinal fluid in the brain) may develop after severe IVH. There is no specific treatment for IVH, except to treat any other health problems that may worsen the condition. Although care of sick and premature babies has advanced greatly, it is not possible to prevent IVH from occurring in some babies.

■ *Necrotizing enterocolitis (NEC)* is the most common and serious intestinal disease among premature babies. It happens when tissue in the small or large intestine is injured or inflamed. This can lead to death of intestinal tissue and, in rare cases, a hole (perforation) in the intestinal wall. Most cases of necrotizing enterocolitis occur in babies born before thirty-two weeks gestation. Babies with NEC usually develop it within the first two to four weeks after birth. It is diagnosed with signs of feeding intolerance or belly distension and confirmed with X-rays. Treatment involves stopping feedings for five to seven days and giving antibiotics. If it is severe, a consultation with a pediatric surgeon to discuss surgery may be needed. Breast milk feeding is the single most effective means to prevent NEC in preterm infants.

■ *Jaundice* happens when a chemical called bilirubin builds up in the baby's blood. As a result, the skin may develop a yellowish color. Jaundice can occur in babies of any race or color. Treatment involves placing the undressed baby under special lights (while her eyes are covered). (For additional information about jaundice, see pages 155–57.)

■ Other conditions sometimes seen in preterm babies include *anemia of prematurity* (a low red blood cell count) and *heart murmurs*. (For additional information on heart murmurs, see pages 809–11.)

~ 3 ~

Basic Infant Care

AFTER ALL THE ANTICIPATION and planning, the arrival of your new baby is a big transition. Routine tasks such as diapering and dressing her can fill you with anxiety—especially if you haven't spent much time around babies. But it doesn't take long to develop the confidence of an experienced parent, and you'll have help. While in the hospital, the nursery staff and your pediatrician will give you instructions and support. Family and friends can be helpful; don't be bashful about asking for assistance. Start to identify positive resources for you and your partner. Your baby will give you the most important information—how she likes to be treated, talked to, held, and comforted. She'll bring out parental instincts that will guide you to many of the right responses, almost as soon as she's born.

The following sections address the most common questions and concerns during the first months after birth.

Day to Day

Responding to Your Baby's Cries

Crying is common for babies. Crying serves several useful purposes for your baby. It allows her to call for help when she's hungry or uncomfortable. It shuts out sights, sounds, and other sensations too intense to suit her. And it helps her release tension.

You may notice your baby has fussy periods, even when she's not hungry, uncomfortable, or tired. At times it may seem like nothing can console her. Right after these spells, she may seem more alert than before, and then may sleep more deeply than usual. This kind of fussy crying seems to help babies get rid of excess energy to allow for a more contented state. As you get to know your infant's crying patterns, you may feel as if you can identify specific needs by the way she cries. Is she hungry? Angry? Distressed or in pain? Sleepy? Each baby will use her voice differently.

Sometimes different types of cries overlap. Newborns generally wake up hungry and crying for food. If you're not quick to respond, your baby's hunger cry may turn to a wail of rage. You'll hear the difference. As your baby matures, her cries will become stronger, louder, and more insistent. They'll also begin to vary more, as if to convey different needs and desires. The best way to

Respond promptly to your infant whenever she cries during her first few months. You cannot spoil a young baby by giving her attention.

handle crying is to respond promptly during her first few months. You cannot spoil a young baby with attention, and if you answer her calls for help, she'll cry less overall.

When responding to your child's cries, try to meet her most pressing need first. If she's cold and hungry and her diaper is wet, warm her up, change her diaper, and then feed her. If there's a shrieking or panicked quality to the cry, consider if a piece of clothing or something else is making her uncomfortable. Perhaps a strand of hair is caught around a finger or toe. If she's warm, dry, and well fed but the crying won't stop, try the following consoling techniques. Find the ones that work best for your baby:

- Rocking, either in a rocking chair or in your arms as you sway from side to side

- Gently stroking her head or patting her back or chest

- Safe swaddling (wrapping her snugly in a receiving blanket)

- Singing or talking

- Playing soft music

- Walking her in your arms, a stroller, or a carriage

- Rhythmic white noise and vibration

- Burping her to relieve any trapped gas bubbles

- Warm baths (*most* babies like this, but not all)

Sometimes, if all else fails, the best approach is simply to leave the baby alone in a safe location such as a crib. Many babies cannot fall asleep without crying and will fall asleep quicker if left to cry. The crying shouldn't last long if the child is truly tired. If the crying does not stop, but intensifies and persists throughout the day or night, it may be caused by colic. Unfortunately, there is no definite explanation for why this happens. Most often, colic means simply that the child is unusually sensitive to stimulation or cannot self-console or regulate her nervous system. As she matures, this inability to self-console—marked by constant crying—will improve. In breastfeeding babies, sometimes colic is a sign of sensitivity to a food in the mother's diet. Colic drops are expensive, and

Enjoy all those wondrous moments with your child.

studies suggest that they're not effective. You can look into more non-medication options such as reevaluating your diet, slow feeding, and ensuring appropriate burping to help. If your baby is inconsolable, she may be sick. Check her temperature (see *Taking a Rectal Temperature*, page 82). If you take it rectally and it is 100.4 degrees Fahrenheit (38 degrees Celsius) or higher, she could have an infection. Contact your pediatrician.

The more relaxed you remain, the easier it will be to console your child. Even very young babies are sensitive to tension and react to it by crying. Hearing a wailing newborn can be agonizing, but letting your frustration turn to anger or panic will only intensify your infant's screams. If you start to feel you can't handle the situation, set the baby down in a safe location and get help from a family member or friend. This will give you needed relief, and a new face can sometimes calm your baby. No matter how impatient or angry you feel, *do not* shake or hit the baby. Shaking an infant hard can cause blindness, brain damage, or even death. It's important to share this information on crying with anyone else who cares for your baby, including your spouse, partner, or babysitter.

Above all, don't take your newborn's crying personally. She's not crying because you're a bad parent or because she doesn't like you. All babies cry, often without any apparent cause. Newborns routinely cry one to four hours a day. It's part of adjusting to this strange new life outside the womb.

No parent can console his or her child *every* time she cries, so don't expect to be a miracle worker. Instead, take a realistic approach. Line up some help, get plenty of rest, and enjoy all those wondrous moments with your child.

Helping Your Baby Sleep

Initially your infant doesn't know day from night. Her stomach holds only enough to satisfy her for three or four hours, regardless of the time. (Bottle-fed infants may sleep slightly longer.) There's no escaping the round-the-clock waking and feeding those first few months. But even at this age, you can begin to teach her that nighttime is for sleeping and daytime for play. Keep nighttime feedings as subdued as possible. Don't turn up the lights or prolong diaper changes. Instead of playing, put her right back down after feeding and changing her. If she's napping longer than three or four hours, particularly in late afternoon, wake her up and play with her. This will train her to save extra sleeping for nighttime. Also, begin to develop a routine before bedtime. Experiencing a strong sensation (like a sponge bath), followed by soothing time (like applying a bit of moisturizing lotion and reading or singing), and then a final feeding followed by a short bedtime story, can help signal to your baby that the longer nap is coming.

How Your Baby Sleeps

Even before birth your baby had periods of sleep and wakefulness. By the eighth month of pregnancy, her sleep periods had the same distinct phases we all experience:

1. Rapid eye movement (REM, "active") sleep, the times she does her active dreaming. Her eyes will move beneath her lids, almost as if she were watching a dream take place. She also may seem to startle, smile, twitch her face, and make jerking motions with her hands and feet. All are normal signs of REM sleep.

2. Non-REM (or quiet) sleep, which consists of four phases: drowsiness, light sleep, deep sleep, and very deep sleep. In newborns, however, non-REM sleep is undifferentiated, with well-defined stages appearing by six months of age. During the progression from drowsiness to deepest sleep, your baby becomes less and less active, and her breathing slows and becomes very quiet. In deepest sleep she is virtually motionless. She may also make suckling movements. Very little, if any, dreaming occurs during non-REM sleep.

At first your newborn will probably sleep about sixteen hours a day, divided into three- or four-hour naps evenly spaced between feedings.

Each of these sleep periods will include relatively equal amounts of REM and non-REM sleep, organized in this order: drowsiness, REM sleep, light sleep, deep sleep, and very deep sleep.

After about two to three months the order will change. As she grows older, she will cycle through all the non-REM phases before entering REM sleep. This pattern remains through adulthood. Young children achieve non-REM deep sleep fairly quickly upon sleep onset and it is difficult to wake them from it. With age, the amount of REM sleep decreases, and her sleep will generally become calmer. By the age of three, children spend one-third or less of total sleep time in REM sleep.

Positioning for Sleep

The American Academy of Pediatrics recommends that healthy infants be placed on their backs for sleep, as this is the safest position for an infant to sleep. **Putting your baby to sleep on her back decreases her chance of sudden infant death syndrome (SIDS),** which is responsible for more infant deaths in the United States than any other cause during the first year (beyond the newborn period).

In addition, recent findings suggest that certain regions of the brain may be underdeveloped in babies who die from SIDS. When these sleeping babies encounter a situation challenging to their well-being, they may fail to wake up to remove themselves from danger. Babies who sleep on their stomachs sleep more deeply, and so it is harder for them to wake up; this is probably why stomach sleeping is so dangerous. Since it is impossible to identify which babies may not arouse normally, and because the relationship between SIDS and sleep position is so strong, the Academy recommends that all infants be placed to sleep on their backs. Some doctors once thought that sleeping on the side might be a reasonable alternative to back positioning, but we now know that side sleeping is just as dangerous as stomach sleeping for babies. Babies placed to sleep on their sides can roll onto their stomachs, which increases the risk of SIDS. Do not use a positioning device, like a wedge or blanket roll, to keep your baby on her back. These can lead to suffocation. It is enough just to put your baby on her back. All healthy babies, including those with gastroesophageal reflux, should sleep on their backs. Your pediatrician will tell you if your baby has one of the rare medical conditions that requires her to sleep in a different position. Once the infant can roll both back to front and front to back, you may let her stay in the sleep position she chooses.

It is also important to avoid placing your baby to sleep with or on soft surfaces such as pillows, quilts, comforters, bumper pads, or bean bags—even stuffed toys—in the infant sleep area, which may block her airway if she burrows her face into them. Also avoid having her sleep on an adult's chest because of the risk of the adult falling asleep while holding the baby. Waterbeds, sofas, and soft mattresses are also especially unsafe sleep environments for babies. Car safety seats, strollers, swings, infant carriers, and slings are not recommended for routine sleep, especially in infants under four months of age. An infant this young may not be able to reposition herself to breathe safely. A flat, firm (hard) crib mattress (in a safety-approved crib or bassinet) covered by a fitted sheet is the safest bedding. Do not pad the mattress with pillows or blankets to make it softer; this will make it more dangerous. Keep all soft toys and stuffed animals out of your child's crib throughout the first year. Keep the temperature in your baby's room comfortable. Use sleep clothing (such as a one-piece sleeper) with no other covering, instead of blankets. If you are worried that your baby will be cold, you can use layers of clothing, a wearable blanket sleeper, or sleep sack as safe alternatives.

WHERE WE STAND

BASED ON AN evaluation of current sudden infant death syndrome (SIDS) data, the American Academy of Pediatrics recommends that healthy infants always be placed for sleep on their backs—whether for nap time or nighttime. Despite common beliefs, there is no evidence that choking is more frequent among infants lying on their backs (the supine position) when compared to other positions, nor is there evidence that sleeping on the back is harmful to healthy babies. Babies with gastroesophageal reflux (excessive spitting up) should still be placed on their backs. In some very rare circumstances (for instance, if your baby has just had back surgery), your infant may need to be on the stomach for sleep. Discuss your individual circumstances with your pediatrician.

Since 1992, when the American Academy of Pediatrics began recommending this sleep position, the annual SIDS rate has declined more than 50 percent. However, there has also been an increase in accidental suffocation deaths. A safe sleep environment (baby on his back in a crib close to the parents' bed without any bedding or soft objects) is important to protect your baby from SIDS or an accidental suffocation death.

Many parents have felt the temptation to keep their babies in bed with them, especially when they are exhausted and the babies are fussy. Bed-sharing, however, raises the risk of infant death. Instead, place the baby's bassinet or crib in your room, where you can monitor her and comfort her as needed, always returning her to a safe sleep environment. Your baby is safest sleeping in your room on her own separate sleep surface, ideally for the first year.

Pacifiers may also help reduce the risk of SIDS. However, if your baby doesn't want the pacifier or it falls out of her mouth, don't force it. If you are breastfeeding, wait until breastfeeding is well established, usually around three or four weeks of age, before using a pacifier. If you are formula-feeding or giving expressed breast milk, you can start the pacifier at any time. Pacifiers should not have strings, ties, or stuffed animals attached to them, since they can pose a strangulation risk.

Swaddling can help calm your baby, but it must be done safely. Swaddling should allow ample room for hip and knee movement in order to allow for proper leg development. Your baby has a very sensitive hip joint that can be harmed by too much pressure or stress from abnormal hip positions or restricted motion, potentially causing lifelong problems like arthritis. Swaddling should be snug around the infant's chest, leaving enough space so that the caregiver's hand can fit between the blanket and the baby's chest. If the swaddle becomes loose, it can result in suffocation or strangulation. Always lay your swaddled infant on her back. When an infant exhibits signs of attempting to roll, it's time to stop swaddling, since a swaddled infant in the prone position is at high risk for SIDS and suffocation.

While sleeping on the back is important, your baby should also spend time on her stomach *when awake and being observed*. This will help to develop her shoulder muscles and head control and avoid flat spots on the back of her head. No one can say how much tummy time babies need, but be sure to spend part of her alert time every day playing with her in this position.

As her stomach grows, your baby will go longer between feedings. In fact, you'll be encouraged to know that while the average longest sleep period for infants from birth to five months is 5.7 hours, this increases to 8.3 hours by six to twenty-four months of age. Many infants can last for as long as 6 hours between feedings when they reach 12 or 13 pounds (5.44–5.89 kg). Larger babies may begin sleeping for longer periods at a time a little sooner. As encouraging as this sounds, don't expect the sleep struggle to end all at once. Most children swing back and forth, sleeping beautifully for a few weeks, even months, then returning abruptly to a late-night wake-up schedule. This may be due to growth spurts, when babies need more food; later, teething or developmental changes can cause increased awakenings.

From time to time, you will need to help your baby fall asleep or go back to sleep. Especially as a newborn, she will probably doze off most easily if given gentle continuous stimulation. Some infants are helped by rocking, walking, patting on the back, or with a pacifier. That said, if you always rock your baby to sleep, she may not learn to fall asleep on her own. Practice putting her to bed while she is sleepy but not fully asleep so that she can build this skill. For others, music can be very soothing if played quietly.

Diapers

Since disposable diapers were introduced about eighty years ago, they have been meeting the needs and expectations of most parents; however, diaper choice is a decision every new parent faces. Ideally, you should make the choice between cloth and disposable diapers before the baby arrives, in order to stock up or make delivery arrangements. In planning, be aware that most newborns use about ten diapers a day.

How to Diaper Your Baby

Before you start, make sure you have all the necessary supplies within arm's reach. Never leave your baby alone on the changing table—not even for a second. Babies wiggle and squirm and can easily fall off a changing table. In addition, it won't be long before she can turn over, and if she does when your attention is diverted, a serious injury could result.

When changing a newborn, you will need:

- A clean diaper (plus fasteners if a cloth diaper is used)

- Unscented diaper wipes, or a small basin (or a mug or bowl) with luke-warm water and a washcloth; soft paper towels or cotton can also be used

- Diaper ointment or petroleum jelly

- *Do not* use baby powder, since babies can breathe the dust from powder, potentially irritating the lungs

This is how you proceed:

1. Remove the dirty diaper and use the lukewarm water and cotton ball, soft paper towel, or unscented diaper wipe to gently wipe your baby clean. (Remember to wipe front to back on female infants.)

2. Use the diaper ointment recommended by your pediatrician if needed. Make sure the diaper area is completely dry before applying.

DISPOSABLE DIAPERS. Most disposable diapers consist of an inner liner designed to help keep wetness away from the skin, an absorbent core, and an outer waterproof covering. Over the years, they have become thinner and lighter, while continuing to meet the needs for containment, comfort, ease of use, and skin care. When changing a soiled diaper, dump stool into a toilet. Do not flush the diaper, as it can block plumbing. Wrap the diaper in its outer cover and discard in a waste receptacle. Some diapers now have a stripe that turns color to indicate wetness.

CLOTH DIAPERS. Like disposable diapers, reusable cloth diapers have improved over the years, and are available in a variety of absorbencies and textures. If you want to use a diaper service, shop around; ideally, a diaper service should pick up dirty diapers and drop off clean ones twice a week. If you choose to wash diapers yourself, keep them separate from other clothes. After you dump stool into the toilet, rinse the diapers in cold water, then soak in a mild detergent solution with bleach. Wring them out, then wash in hot water with mild detergent. Some newer diaper types offer a disposable cloth liner with a reusable outer cover.

DIAPER CHOICE. Diaper choice has been complicated in recent years by the debate on the environmental effects of diapers, mostly centered on disposable diapers and landfill space. Actually, a number of scientific studies have found that both cloth and disposable diapers have environmental effects, including raw material and energy usage, air and water pollution, and waste disposal. Disposable diapers add to municipal solid waste, while cloth diapers use more energy and water in laundering and contribute to air and water pollution. In the end, you must make your own decision about diaper type based on your concerns and needs.

There are health aspects to consider as well. Excessively wet skin and contact with urine and stool can cause diaper rash. Because cloth diapers can't keep wetness away from your baby's skin as effectively as disposables, it's especially important to change cloth diapers quickly after they become wet or soiled.

Diaper Rash

Diaper rash describes a rash or irritation in the area covered by the diaper. The first sign of diaper rash is usually redness or small bumps on the lower abdomen, buttocks, genitals, and thigh folds—surfaces in direct contact with a wet or soiled diaper. This type of diaper rash is rarely serious and usually clears in three or four days with appropriate care. The most common causes of diaper rash include:

- Leaving a wet diaper on too long. The moisture makes the skin susceptible to chafing. Over time, the urine in the diaper decomposes, forming chemicals that can further irritate the skin.

- Leaving a stool-soiled diaper on too long. Digestive agents in the stool then attack the skin, making it more susceptible to a rash.

Regardless of how the rash begins, once the skin surface is damaged, it becomes even more vulnerable to irritation by urine and stool and susceptible to subsequent infection with bacteria or yeast. Yeast infections are common in this area and often appear as a rash on the thighs, genitals, and lower abdomen, but they almost never appear on the buttocks.

Although most babies develop diaper rash at some point, it happens less often in babies who are breastfed. Diaper rash occurs more often at particular ages and under certain conditions:

- Among babies eight to ten months old

- If babies are not kept clean and dry

- When babies have diarrhea

- When a baby starts to eat solid food (probably due to changes in the digestive process caused by the new variety of foods)

- When a baby is taking antibiotics (because these drugs encourage the growth of yeast organisms that can infect the skin)

To reduce your baby's risk of diaper rash, make these steps part of your diapering routine:

1. Change the diaper as soon as possible after a bowel movement. Cleanse the diaper area with a diaper wipe or soft cloth and water after each bowel movement.

(continues on next page)

2. Change wet diapers frequently to reduce skin exposure to moisture.

3. Expose the baby's bottom to air whenever feasible. When using diaper covers or disposable diapers with tight gathers around the abdomen and legs, make sure air can circulate inside the diaper.

If a diaper rash develops in spite of your efforts, begin using a diaper rash ointment as a barrier to prevent further irritation and to allow the skin to heal. The rash should improve noticeably within two to three days. If it doesn't improve or it gets worse (or if you see pimple-like pustules) consult your pediatrician.

Urination

Your baby may urinate as often as every one to three hours or as infrequently as four to six times a day. If she's ill or feverish, or when the weather is extremely hot, her usual output of urine may drop by half and still be normal. Urination should never be painful. If you notice any signs of distress while your infant is urinating, notify your pediatrician. This could be a sign of infection or another problem in the urinary tract.

In a healthy child, urine is light to dark yellow in color. (The darker the color, the more concentrated the urine; the urine will be more concentrated when your child is not drinking a lot of liquid.) In the first week after birth, you may see a pink or brick-red stain on the diaper, often mistaken for blood. In fact, this stain is usually a sign of highly concentrated urine, which has a pinkish color. As long as the baby is wetting at least four diapers a day, there is probably no cause for concern. If the pinkish staining persists, consult your pediatrician.

Newborn girls may have a small spot of blood in the diaper, also usually in the first week after birth; this blood is caused by her mother's hormones affecting the baby's uterus. After that time, however, the presence of actual blood in the urine or a bloody spot on the diaper is never normal, and your pediatrician should be notified. It may be due to nothing more serious than a diaper rash sore, but it also could be a more serious problem. If this bleeding is accompanied by other symptoms, such as abdominal pain, poor feeding, vomiting, fever, or bleeding in other areas, seek medical attention immediately.

Bowel Movements

For the first few days after birth, your baby's first bowel movements will be a substance known as meconium. This thick black or dark green substance filled her intestines before birth, and once passed, the stools turn yellow-green.

Baby stools vary in color and consistency due to their immature digestive system. If your baby is breastfed, her stools should be yellow liquid mixed with some particles. Until she starts to eat solid foods, the consistency of the stools may range from very soft to loose and runny. If she's formula-fed, her stools will usually be tan or yellow in color. They will be firmer than a breastfed baby's but should be no firmer than soft clay. Green stools are not unusual, either, and they should not cause you alarm.

Whether your baby is breast- or bottle-fed, hard or very dry stools may be a sign she is not getting enough fluid or losing too much fluid due to illness, fever, or heat. Once solids are introduced, hard stools might indicate she's eating too many constipating foods, such as cereal or cow's milk, before her system can handle them. (Whole cow's milk is not recommended for babies under twelve months.)

Here are some other important points to keep in mind about bowel movements:

- Occasional variations in color and consistency of the stools are normal. For example, if the digestive process slows down because of foods requiring more effort to digest (e.g., large amounts of cereal), the stools may become green, or if the baby is given supplemental iron, the stools may turn dark brown. If there is a minor irritation of the anus, streaks of blood may appear on the outside of the stools. However, if there are large amounts of blood, mucus, or water in the stool, call your pediatrician immediately. These symptoms may warrant attention from your doctor.

- Because an infant's stools are normally soft and a little runny, it's not always easy to tell when a young baby has mild diarrhea. The telltale signs are a sudden increase in frequency (to more than one bowel movement per feeding) and unusually high liquid content in the stool. Diarrhea may be a sign of intestinal infection, or it may be caused by a change in the baby's diet. If the baby is breastfeeding, diarrhea can develop due to a change in the mother's diet.

- The main concern with diarrhea is the possibility of dehydration. If fever is also present and your infant is less than three months old, call your pediatrician. If your baby is over three months and the fever lasts more than a day, check her urine output and rectal temperature; then report your findings to your doctor for consideration. Make sure your baby continues to feed frequently. As much as anything else, if she simply looks sick, let your doctor know.

The frequency of bowel movements varies widely among babies. Many pass a stool soon after each feeding, a result of the gastrocolic reflex, which causes the digestive system to become active whenever the stomach is filled with food.

By three to six weeks of age, some breastfed babies have only one bowel movement a week and still are normal. Breast milk leaves very little solid waste to be eliminated from the child's digestive system. Thus, infrequent stools are not a sign of constipation and should not be considered a problem as long as the stools are soft and your infant is otherwise normal, gaining weight steadily, and nursing regularly. Babies with this breastfed stool variant usually have a large volume of stool if it has been a few days (so you should be prepared with lots of wipes to clean up).

If your baby is formula-fed, she should have at least one bowel movement a day. If she has fewer than this and appears to be straining, she may be constipated. Check with your pediatrician for advice on how to handle this problem. (See *Constipation*, page 529.)

Baby towels with built-in hoods are a very effective (and cute) way to keep your baby's head warm when she's wet.

Bathing

Your infant doesn't need much bathing if you wipe or wash the diaper area thoroughly during diaper changes. A short bath with a mild cleanser three times a week to once a day during her first year may be enough. More frequent bathing may dry out her skin, particularly if drying or irritating soaps are used or moisture is allowed to evaporate from the skin. Patting her dry and applying a fragrance-free, hypoallergenic moisturizer immediately after bathing can help prevent eczema (see page 570).

In a warm room, lay the baby anywhere that's flat and comfortable for both of you—a changing table, bed, floor, or counter next to the sink will do. Pad hard surfaces with a blanket or fluffy towel. If the baby is on a surface above the floor, use a safety strap or keep one hand on her *at all times* to make sure she doesn't fall.

Have a basin of water, a damp, double-rinsed washcloth (with no soap residue), and a supply of mild baby cleanser within reach before you begin. Keep your baby wrapped in a towel, and expose only the parts of her body you are washing. Use the dampened cloth with no soap to wash her face. Then use the soapy water to wash the remainder of her body ending with the diaper area. Pay special attention to creases under the arms, behind the ears, around the neck, and, especially with a girl, the genital area. For boys, if uncircumcised, the foreskin should never be retracted forcefully for cleaning. The foreskin may take several years to retract completely, and forcible retraction can cause inflammation and scarring. The skin on the genitals can be gently cleaned with soap and water on the outside and under the foreskin only if it easily retracts. For circumcised boys, the genital skin, including the head of the penis, can be cleaned with regular cleanser and water.

Once the umbilical area is healed, you can try placing your baby directly in the water. Her first baths should be as gentle and brief as possible. She will probably protest; if she seems miserable, go back to sponge baths for a week or two, then try again. She will make it clear when she's ready.

Most parents find it easiest to bathe a newborn in a small bathtub, sink, or plastic tub lined with a clean towel. Fill the basin with 2 inches (5 cm) of water that feels warm—not hot—to the inside of your wrist or elbow. If you're filling the basin from the tap, turn the cold water on first (and off last) to avoid scalding yourself or your child. The hottest temperature at the faucet should be no more than 120 degrees Fahrenheit (48.9 degrees Celsius) to avoid burns. In many cases you can adjust your water heater.

Supplies should be at hand and the room warm before undressing the baby because babies lose body heat easily. You'll need the same supplies you used for sponge bathing, but also a cup for rinsing with clear water. When your child has hair, you'll need baby shampoo, too.

Bathing Your Baby

Once you've undressed your baby, place her in the warm water immediately so she doesn't get chilled. Use one hand to support her head and the other to guide her in, feet first. Speak encouragingly, and gently lower her body until she's in the tub. Most of her body and face should be well above the water level for safety, so you'll need to pour warm water over her body frequently to keep her warm.

If you've forgotten something or need to step away, *you must take the baby with you*, so keep a dry towel within reach. *Never leave a baby alone in the bath, even for an instant.*

If your baby enjoys her bath, give her extra time to splash and explore the water. The more fun your child has, the less she'll be afraid of the water. As she gets older, bath time will lengthen until most of it is play. Bathing should be a relaxing and soothing experience, so don't rush unless she's unhappy.

Use a soft cloth to wash her face and hair, cleansing once or twice a week. Massage her entire scalp gently, including over her fontanelles (soft spots). When you rinse the soap or baby shampoo from her head, cup your hand across her forehead so that the suds run toward the sides, not into her eyes. Should you get some cleanser in her eyes, simply take the wet washcloth and liberally wipe her closed eyes with plain, lukewarm water until the cleanser is gone, and she will open her eyes again. Wash the rest of her body from the top down.

Bath toys are not needed for very young babies. The stimulation of water and washing is exciting enough. Once a baby is old enough for the bathtub, however, toys become a fun addition. Containers, cups, age-appropriate toys, and even waterproof books make wonderful distractions as you cleanse your baby. Remember that bath toys can grow mold if they stay wet, so expel any retained water and give them a chance to dry between uses.

Baby towels with built-in hoods are the most effective way to keep your baby's head warm when the bath is over. Bathing a baby of any age is wet work, so be prepared to keep yourself dry.

A bath is a relaxing way to prepare her for sleep and should be given at a time that's convenient for you.

Skin and Nail Care

Your newborn's skin may be susceptible to irritation from chemicals found in new clothing and from soap residue on washed clothes. Double-rinse all baby clothes, bedding, blankets, and other washable items before exposing the child to them. For the first few months, do your infant's wash separately. It is com-

In the early weeks, your baby's fingers are so small and her nails grow so quickly you may have to trim them twice a week.

mon for a baby's skin to peel in the first few weeks, as her body is clearing away the extra skin cells from being in amniotic fluid.

Babies don't routinely need skin moisturizer, especially if you avoid bathing them too often. If you do feel as if your baby's skin is too dry, you may use an oil, lotion, cream, or ointment that contains no scents or coloring agents. If your baby has a persistent bumpy or dry rash, ask her pediatrician if she may have eczema (see page 578).

Your child's nails only require trimming. You can use a soft emery board, baby nail clippers, or blunt-nosed toenail scissors, but be very careful when using clippers or scissors. A good time to trim nails is after a bath if your baby will lie quietly, but you may find it easiest when she's asleep. Keep her finger-

Dressing and Undressing Your Baby

Support your baby on your lap and stretch the garment's neckline to pull it over your baby's head. Use your fingers to keep it from catching on her face or ears.

Don't try to push your baby's arm through the sleeve. Instead, put your hand into the sleeve from the outside, grasp your baby's hand, and pull it through.

When undressing, take off the sleeves one at a time while you support your baby's back and head.

Then stretch the neckline, lifting it free of your baby's chin and face as you gently slip it off.

nails as short and smoothly trimmed as possible to help her avoid scratching herself (or you). In the early weeks, her fingers are so small and her nails grow so quickly you may have to trim them twice a week. Avoid the temptation to bite your child's nails as a way of trimming them, as this habit can lead to a skin infection.

By contrast, your baby's toenails grow much more slowly and are usually soft and pliable. They needn't be kept as short as fingernails, so they may only have to be trimmed once or twice a month. Because they are so soft, they sometimes look ingrown, but there's no cause for concern unless the skin alongside the nail gets red, inflamed, or hard, or you see an area of pus. As your baby gets older, her toenails will become harder and better defined.

Clothing

Unless the temperature is hot (over 75 degrees Fahrenheit [24 degrees Celsius]), your newborn will need several layers of clothing to keep warm. It's generally

Swaddling

During the first few weeks, your baby may like to be wrapped in a receiving blanket. Not only does this keep her warm, but the slight pressure around the body seems to give some newborns a sense of security. To swaddle, spread the blanket out flat, with one corner folded over. Lay the baby face-up on the blanket, with her head at the folded corner.

Wrap the left corner over her body and tuck it beneath her. Bring the bottom corner up over her feet, and then wrap the other corner around her, leaving only her head and neck exposed. As an option, you can keep her hands close to her chin, so that she can still self-soothe or display hunger cues. It is important that the hips and legs are allowed to move freely within the blanket. Tight swaddling of the hips could lead to dysplasia or even dislocation. Never place your swaddled baby in any position other than on the back. Stop swaddling as soon as your baby starts trying to roll over (even when she is not swaddled), usually around two to three months of age, because being on her stomach while swaddled can be dangerous. Babies born early may need to be swaddled for longer. (For more information on swaddling, visit HealthyChildren.org/swaddling.)

best to use an undershirt and diaper, covered by pajamas, and then wrapped in a receiving blanket. If your baby is premature, she may need still another layer of clothing until her weight increases and her body is better able to adjust to the temperature. In hot weather you can reduce clothing to a single layer. A good rule of thumb is to dress the baby in one more layer of clothing than you are wearing.

If you've never taken care of a newborn before, the first few clothing changes can be quite frustrating. Not only is it a struggle to get that tiny little arm through the sleeve, but your infant may shriek in protest through the whole process. She doesn't like the rush of air against her skin, nor does she enjoy being pushed and pulled through garments. It may be easier to hold her on your lap while changing the upper half of her body, then lay her on a bed or changing table while doing the lower half. When dressing her in one-piece pajamas, pull them over her legs before putting on the sleeves. Pull T-shirts over her head first, then guide one arm at a time through the sleeves. Use this opportunity to ask, "Where's the baby's hand?" As she gets older this will turn into a game, with her pushing her arm through just to hear you say, "*There's* the baby's hand!"

Certain clothing features can make dressing much easier. Look for garments that

- Snap or zip all the way down the front, instead of the back

- Snap or zip down both legs to make diaper changes easier

- Have loose-fitting sleeves so your hand fits to gently pull the baby's arm through

- Have no ribbons or strings to knot up, unravel, or wrap around the neck (which could cause choking)

- Are made of soft stretchy fabric (avoid tight bindings around arms, legs, or neck)

Your Baby's Basic Healthcare
Taking a Rectal Temperature

Very few babies get through infancy without a fever, usually a sign of infection. A fever often indicates that the immune system is actively fighting viruses or bacteria, so—in this respect—it is a positive sign the body is protecting itself.

Because young babies give very few signs when ill, any child younger than three months with a fever needs an urgent evaluation by a physician to determine the cause; if it is due to a minor viral infection, it will usually resolve on its own, while a bacterial infection or more serious viral infection (e.g., herpes) will usually require immediate treatment with medications and frequently, in infants under two months of age, hospitalization.

An infant or toddler cannot hold a thermometer steady in her mouth for an oral temperature, and "fever strips" that are placed on the child's forehead are not accurate. While temporal artery thermometers (electronic devices that measure the skin temperature of the forehead) can be reliable, tympanic thermometers (devices that fit inside the ear canal) are unreliable in infants, especially under six months of age. The best way to measure fever in a young child is rectally. Once you know how to take a rectal temperature, it is quite simple, but it's best to learn the steps in advance so you're not nervous about them when your child is actually sick. For a complete description of taking a rectal temperature properly, or other means of properly taking temperatures in infants and children, see Chapter 27, *Fever*.

Visiting the Pediatrician

You will probably see more of your pediatrician in your baby's first year than at any other time. The baby's first examination takes place immediately after birth. The schedules on pages 888 and 889 list the minimum routine checkups from infancy through adolescence. Your pediatrician may want to see your child more often.

Ideally, both parents (or other regular caregivers) should attend these early visits. These appointments give you and your pediatrician a chance to get to know each other and exchange questions and answers. Don't restrict yourself to medical questions; your pediatrician is also an expert on general childcare issues and a valuable resource if you're looking for childcare help, parent support groups, or other outside assistance. Many pediatricians offer information that covers common concerns, but it is a good idea to make a list of questions before each visit.

If only one parent or caregiver can attend, try to get a friend or a relative to join the parent who does. It's much easier to concentrate on your discussions with the doctor if you have a little help dressing and undressing the baby and gathering all of her things. As you're getting used to outings, an extra adult can help carry the diaper bag and hold doors.

The purpose of these early checkups is to make sure your child is growing and developing properly and has no serious abnormalities. Specifically, the doctor will check the following areas.

GROWTH. You will undress your baby to be weighed on an infant scale. Her length may be measured on a flat table and her head size measured with a special tape. These measurements should be plotted in order to determine her growth curve from one visit to the next. (You can plot your baby's growth curve in the same way using the charts on pages 894–901.) This is the most reliable way to judge whether she's growing normally, and it will show you her position on the growth curve in relation to other children her age. If you are unsure about your breast milk supply, going into the office for additional weight checks may be reassuring.

HEAD. The soft spots (fontanelles, normal skin-covered openings in the skull) should be open and flat for the first few months. By two to three months of age, the spot in the back should be closed. The front soft spot should close before two years (around eighteen months of age).

EARS. The doctor will look inside both ear canals and at the eardrums with an otoscope. This detects any evidence of fluid or infection in the ear. You'll also be asked if the child responds normally to sounds. Formal hearing tests are done in the newborn nursery and later if a problem is suspected.

EYES. The doctor will catch your baby's attention and track her eye movements. She also may look inside the baby's eyes with a lighted instrument called an ophthalmoscope—repeating the internal eye examination first done in the hospital nursery. This is particularly helpful in detecting cataracts (clouding of the lens of the eye). (See *Cataracts*, page 739.)

MOUTH. The mouth is checked for signs of infection and, later, for teething progress. The doctor may feel the roof of the mouth to look for a cleft palate, a condition where the bones or soft tissue do not close completely during development.

HEART AND LUNGS. The pediatrician will use a stethoscope on the front and back of your baby's chest to listen to the heart and lungs. This examination determines whether there are any abnormal heart rhythms, sounds, or breathing difficulties.

ABDOMEN. By placing her hand on the child's abdomen and gently pressing, the doctor is checking for enlarged organs or unusual masses or tenderness.

GENITALIA. The genitalia are examined at each visit for any unusual lumps, tenderness, or signs of infection. In the first exam or two, the doctor pays special attention to a boy's circumcised penis to make sure it's healing properly.

Pediatricians also check all boys to make certain both testes are down in the scrotum.

HIPS AND LEGS. The pediatrician will check for problems with the hip joints. The movements your pediatrician will perform with your baby's legs are designed to detect dislocation or dysplasia. Doing this is important, as early detection can lead to proper referral and correction. Later, after the baby starts to walk, the doctor will watch her take a few steps to make sure the legs and feet are properly aligned and move normally.

DEVELOPMENTAL MILESTONES. The pediatrician also asks about the baby's general development. Among other things, he'll observe and discuss when the baby starts to smile, roll over, sit up, and walk, and how she uses her hands and arms. During the exam, the pediatrician will test reflexes and general muscle tone. (See Appendix and Chapters 5 through 13 for details of normal development.)

Immunizations

Your child should receive most childhood immunizations before her second birthday. These will protect her against thirteen major diseases: hepatitis B, diphtheria, tetanus, pertussis (whooping cough), polio, *Haemophilus influenzae* type b (Hib) infections, pneumococcal infections, rotavirus, measles, mumps, rubella, chickenpox, and hepatitis A. In addition, after six months of age your baby will receive a yearly flu vaccine. (See Chapter 31, *Immunizations*, for more information on each of these diseases, and see the Appendix for the immunization schedule recommended by the American Academy of Pediatrics.)

This chapter has dealt with basic infant care. However, your baby is a unique individual. Questions specific to her and her alone are best answered by your own pediatrician.

~ 4 ~

Feeding Your Baby

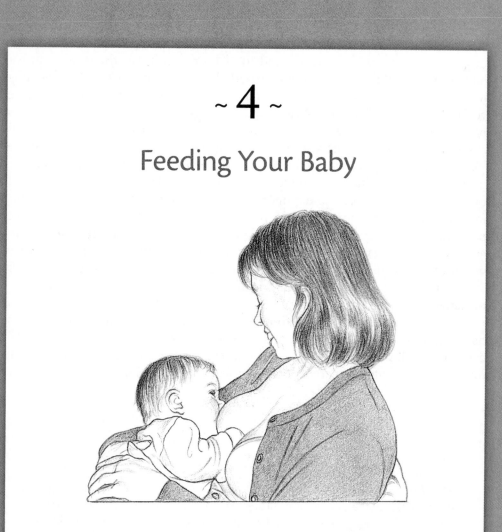

YOUR BABY'S NUTRITIONAL NEEDS during the rapid-growth period of infancy are greater than at any other time in his life. He will approximately triple his birth weight during his first year.

Feeding your infant provides more than just good nutrition. It also allows you to hold your newborn close, cuddle him, and make eye contact. These are relaxing and enjoyable moments for you both, bringing you closer together.

Before your baby arrives, you should consider how you are going to feed him. All major medical groups worldwide agree that breastfeeding is best for mother and baby. This chapter will provide the basic information on infant feeding so you can feel comfortable with your feeding decision.

Because of its nutritional composition and health-promoting

properties, breast milk (also referred to as human milk) is the ideal food for human infants. Babies who are not breastfed are at an increased risk of acquiring ear infections, eczema, asthma, and gastrointestinal infections that cause vomiting and diarrhea, and of developing allergic reactions. Breastfeeding has been associated with reduced risk of sudden infant death syndrome (SIDS) and childhood leukemia. Furthermore, formula-fed babies are 75 percent more likely to need hospitalization for respiratory problems and have a 70 percent increased risk of dying from sudden infant death syndrome. The advantages of breastfeeding are magnified exponentially for premature babies. Recent information indicates that breastfeeding plays a significant role in the prevention of overweight and diabetes, both in childhood and later on. In addition, for mothers, there is some evidence that breastfeeding helps to return to pre-pregnancy weight, prevents diabetes, and reduces the incidence of certain types of cancers later in life. As a result, most pediatricians urge expectant and new mothers to breastfeed.

Some women are uncertain about breastfeeding for various reasons. If you have questions about breastfeeding, ask your prenatal care provider, pediatrician, or a lactation consultant—someone knowledgeable with whom you can discuss your specific concerns, doubts, or fears. With support, most women are

WHERE WE STAND

THE AMERICAN ACADEMY OF PEDIATRICS believes that breastfeeding is the optimal source of nutrition through the first year. We recommend exclusively breastfeeding for about the first six months, and then gradually adding solid foods while continuing breastfeeding for at least the first year. Thereafter, breastfeeding can continue for as long as both mother and baby desire it.

Breastfeeding should begin as soon as possible after birth, usually within the first hour. Newborns should nurse whenever they show signs of hunger—approximately eight to twelve times every twenty-four hours. The amount of time and frequency for each feeding vary widely for each mother-baby pair. It is important to recognize signs that the baby is latching on to the breast and getting milk. The amount of milk a baby will get during each breastfeeding attempt is small during the first day (about 1 teaspoon) and increases on the second and third days. Before going home it is important to identify the signs that your baby is getting milk during breastfeeding. (See *Is Your Baby Eating Enough?* on page 108.)

able to successfully breastfeed their babies. If you are unable to breastfeed, infant formula is an acceptable and nutritious alternative to breast milk. But you should thoughtfully weigh the many benefits of breastfeeding before making the choice to formula-feed. It's important to give it serious consideration before your baby arrives, since starting with formula and then switching to breast milk can be difficult if you wait too long. The production of milk (called lactation) is most successful if breastfeeding begins immediately after delivery.

The American Academy of Pediatrics, the World Health Organization (WHO), and many other experts encourage women to breastfeed as long as possible, one year or longer, with a recommendation of six months of exclusive breastfeeding (see *Where We Stand* on page 88). Breast milk provides optimal nutrition and protection against infections. One recent survey found that 80 to 90 percent of pregnant women wanted to breastfeed. Of infants born in 2015, 83 percent were breastfed at birth and 58 percent at six months of age (see the CDC's breastfeeding report card at cdc.gov/breastfeeding/data/reportcard.htm). Because most women want to breastfeed, and start out breastfeeding, national efforts have shifted to building a better support system for maintaining breastfeeding. The longer your baby is breastfed, the greater the benefits.

Breastfeeding

Breast milk (also referred to as *human milk*) is the best possible food for any infant. Its major ingredients are water, sugar (lactose), easily digestible protein (whey and casein), and fat (digestible fatty acids)—all properly balanced and enhanced to protect against such conditions as ear infections (otitis media), allergies, vomiting, diarrhea, pneumonia, wheezing, bronchiolitis, and meningitis. In addition, breast milk contains minerals and vitamins, as well as enzymes that aid the digestive and absorptive process. Formulas only approximate these nutrients and don't provide all the enzymes, nor the antibodies, growth-promoting factors, and many other valuable components.

There are many practical reasons to breastfeed your baby. Breast milk is relatively low in cost—a slight increase in your caloric intake costs much less than what you would spend on formula. Also, breast milk needs no preparation and is instantly available, wherever you may be. Breastfeeding uses about 500 calories a day to produce the milk and may make it easier for some women to get back into shape after giving birth. At the same time, it's especially important that mothers continue to eat a healthy, balanced diet while nursing to avoid nutritional deficiencies. Breastfeeding also helps the uterus tighten and return to its normal size more quickly.

The psychological and emotional advantages of breastfeeding are just as compelling, for both mother and child. Nursing provides skin-to-skin contact, which is soothing for your baby and pleasant for you. The same hormones that stimulate milk production and release also may promote feelings that enhance bonding. Almost all nursing mothers find that the experience of breastfeeding makes them feel more attached and protective toward their babies and more confident about their own abilities to nurture and care for their children. When breastfeeding is going well, it has no known disadvantages for the baby. The breastfeeding mother may feel an increased demand on her time. Studies, however, show that breastfeeding and formula-feeding take about the same amount of time. Bottle-feeding requires more time for shopping and cleaning feeding utensils. Time spent with the baby is important for infant nurturing and development and can be pleasurable to the mother. Other family members can assist by covering household tasks, especially during the first few weeks, when the mother needs extra rest and the baby demands frequent feeding.

The Health Benefits of Breastfeeding

Studies show there are numerous health benefits for breastfed babies. Compared to formula-fed babies, those who are breastfed have lower rates of:

- Ear infections
- Gastrointestinal infections that cause vomiting and diarrhea
- Septicemia and bacterial meningitis
- Urinary tract infections
- Eczema, asthma, and food allergies
- Respiratory diseases, including pneumonia
- Diabetes (types 1 and 2)
- Obesity in adolescence and adulthood
- Inflammatory bowel disease
- Childhood leukemia and lymphoma
- Sudden infant death syndrome (SIDS)

Source: Adapted from American Academy of Pediatrics, *New Mother's Guide to Breastfeeding*, ed. J. Y. Meek, 3rd ed. (New York: Bantam Books, 2017).

Other family members can actively share in all aspects of baby care even though they do not directly feed her milk. Remain sensitive to the needs of fathers, partners, and siblings. A partner's nonnutritive cuddling with the baby plays an important role, as does the comforting of the mother and baby when needed. A partner can hold, burp, diaper, bathe, and walk with the baby. After breastfeeding is well established (about three to four weeks of age), the partner may feed expressed milk with a bottle.

Considering Special Circumstances

In rare medical circumstances, breastfeeding may not be recommended. An extremely ill mother may not have the energy to breastfeed without interfering with her own recovery. She also may be taking certain medications that would pass into her milk and be dangerous to her infant. Most medications, however, are safe for breastfeeding. If you're taking medications for any reason (prescription or over-the-counter), let your pediatrician know before you start breastfeeding. She can advise whether anything you are taking can pass through breast milk and cause problems. Sometimes medicines can be switched to safer ones while you are nursing. Also, be aware that just because something is labeled as a "dietary supplement" or "all natural" does not mean it can't harm your baby when excreted in breast milk. (To get more information you can visit LactMed, a database of drugs and dietary supplements that may affect breastfeeding [toxnet.nlm.nih.gov/newtoxnet/lactmed.htm]. It includes information on the levels of such substances in breast milk and infant blood, and possible adverse effects in the nursing infant. It is also available as a free app in Android or iOS.)

It's best for parents to discuss feeding issues openly to make sure everyone understands and supports the choices made before the baby arrives. Parents and care providers want a child to receive the best possible nutrition from the start, and without question, that is mother's milk. If breastfeeding is well established (usually between three and four weeks of age) and the mother needs to be away from the baby for a period (e.g., she is returning to work, or she is taking some personal time), she can continue to provide her milk by pumping and collecting breast milk for feeding from a bottle.

Some mothers may experience mild discomfort during early breastfeeding. But significant discomfort is *not* normal. If you experience pain, have difficulty getting the baby to latch on and feed well, or would like further support with nursing, seek help from an experienced health professional (pediatrician, nurse, or lactation specialist). All babies should be seen by a pediatrician, nurse, or lactation consultant within two to three days of hospital discharge to check on how breastfeeding is going.

Self-confidence is important for breastfeeding, but there are a number of common problems that may arise. Seeking help from an expert early is a good way to overcome problems and maintain the confidence necessary to continue breastfeeding. Occasionally some mothers have breastfeeding problems that lead to untimely weaning (before the mother had intended). Many women feel disappointed when breastfeeding does not work out as planned. Still, you should not feel you have failed. Sometimes, despite your best attempts and with all available support, it just doesn't work. (Also see *Bottle-Feeding* on page 120.)

Getting Started: Preparing for Lactation

Your body starts preparing to breastfeed as soon as you become pregnant. The area surrounding the nipples—the areola—becomes darker. The breasts enlarge as milk manufacturing cells multiply and the milk-carrying ducts develop. The increase in breast size is normal and a sign that your breasts are preparing to produce milk. Meanwhile, your body starts storing excess fat to provide the extra energy needed for pregnancy and lactation.

As early as the sixteenth week of pregnancy, the breasts are ready to produce milk as soon as the infant is born. Early milk, called colostrum, is a rich, slightly thick-appearing, orange-yellow substance produced for several days after delivery. Colostrum contains more protein, salt, antibodies, and other protective properties than later breast milk, but it has less fat and calories. Colostrum helps your baby establish his immune system. Your body produces colostrum for several days after delivery, and then the colostrum gradually changes into transitional and then mature milk. The nutritional qualities of breast milk adjust to match the changing needs of your growing infant and will continue to do so for the duration of breastfeeding. This is a characteristic that infant formula cannot duplicate.

As your body naturally prepares for breastfeeding, there is little you need to do. Your nipples do not need to be "toughened up" to withstand your baby's sucking. Tactics such as stretching, pulling, rolling, or buffing the nipples may interfere with normal lactation by harming the tiny glands in the areola that secrete a milky fluid that lubricates the nipples in preparation for breastfeeding. In short, it could make your nipples more likely to develop soreness and irritation.

Normal bathing and gentle drying is the best way to care for your breasts during pregnancy. Although many women use lotions and ointments on their breasts, these are not necessary and may even clog skin pores. Salves, particularly those containing vitamins or hormones, are unnecessary and could cause problems for your baby if used while breastfeeding. On the other hand, some women find purified lanolin is helpful in soothing sore or irritated nipples. If lanolin makes nipple pain worse, it may be an indication of allergy to even the purified form of lanolin.

Some women start wearing nursing bras during pregnancy. They are more adjustable and roomier than normal bras and are more comfortable as the breast size increases. Nursing bras also have flaps that can be opened for breastfeeding or expressing milk. Pads may be inserted into the nursing bra to absorb leaking

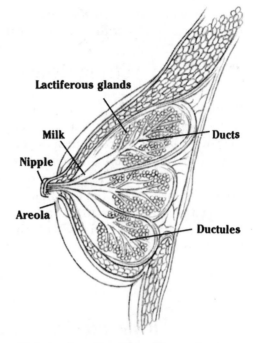

Milk is produced by the lactiferous glands. The milk then passes through the ductules into the ducts and out the nipple.

Nursing bras have flaps that allow easy access to the breast. If you wear a nursing bra, make sure it fits properly and is not too tight or constricting.

milk. Be aware that some mothers are allergic to some of these pads, so it is important to speak with your doctor if you develop a nipple rash or pain.

Letting Down and Latching On

By the time your baby is born, your breasts are already producing colostrum. As he nurses, your infant's actions let your body know when to start and stop the flow of milk. The placement of your baby on your chest in the first moments after birth allows your baby to move up your chest and latch on during the first minutes after giving birth. If the baby is uninterrupted, the first feeding will usually happen within the first hour after birth. Latching begins with the baby finding and attaching onto a good portion of the areola (*not* just on the nipple) and starting to suckle. He will do this latching on instinctively as soon as he feels the breast against his mouth and the nipple against his nose.

Inverted Nipples and Breastfeeding

Normally, when you press the areola between two fingers, the nipple protrudes and becomes erect. If the nipple seems to pull inward and disappear instead, it is "inverted" or "tied." Inverted nipples are a normal variation. They may begin to move out more as the pregnancy progresses. If you have questions about your nipples, discuss the issue with your prenatal professional or with a lactation specialist.

Normal nipple   Inverted nipple

At times, inverted nipples are noticed only at delivery. In this case, the postpartum staff will assist you with early feedings. Working with a lactation consultant is often helpful, and they may recommend pumping briefly before nursing to help bring out the nipple, or temporarily using a nursing shield to help latch on.

If you are having a vaginal delivery or a planned Cesarean, you will need to talk to your prenatal healthcare provider about skin-to-skin contact and breastfeeding immediately after birth. While on your chest, your baby will begin to move toward your breast and latch on to one of your breasts. If there are complications with delivery, or if your newborn needs immediate medical attention, you may have to wait a few hours. If the first feeding takes place within the first day or two, you should have no physical difficulty nursing. If nursing must be delayed beyond the first few hours after birth, the nursing staff will assist you with pumping or hand expression.

When you begin breastfeeding, you may start by reclining and placing your baby on your chest between your breasts without your bra. Just like in the delivery room, your baby will begin to move toward one of your breasts and latch on. You may also start by positioning your baby so that he squarely faces the breast and then stroking his lower lip or cheek with the nipple or touching his chin to your breast. Doing this causes him to search for the nipple with his mouth (the rooting reflex). The infant opens his mouth widely and moves toward the breast. Using your hand to express a few drops of milk will also help your baby root and latch on to your breast, as the smell and taste will stimulate the latching reflex. The hospital staff or your birth attendant will show you how to hand-express your milk.

As your baby takes the breast into his mouth, his jaws should open wide and a good portion of the areola (not just the nipple) should be in his mouth. His lips will pull back and look like fish lips on your skin, the gums encircling the areola. His tongue will form a trough around the nipple and, in a wavelike motion, compress the milk reservoirs and empty the milk ducts. Putting your baby to the breast in the first hour after delivery will establish a good breast-feeding pattern at a time when infants are usually alert and vigorous. Later in the first day, he may be sleepy, but if he begins nursing in the first hour, he is more likely to successfully breastfeed.

When your baby suckles effectively at the breast, his movements will stimulate the breast and start milk flowing through the milk ducts. This is known as the let-down reflex; it is associated with the release of a pituitary hormone, oxytocin. In turn, the release of the hormone prolactin from the pituitary gland and the removal of milk from the breast cause the breasts to make more milk.

Oxytocin causes many wonderful things to happen. It gives a feeling of euphoria and diminishes pain immediately after birth. It enhances the feeling of love between you and your baby. It also causes the uterine muscles to contract, and so in the first days or weeks you may feel afterpains, or cramping of the uterus, each time you nurse. Although this may be annoying and occasionally painful, it helps the uterus return to its normal size and condition and reduces postpartum blood loss. These cramps are a good indicator that your baby is feeding effectively. Use some deep-breathing techniques or pain medication (ibuprofen is commonly prescribed after delivery) to ease the pain.

Once lactation has begun, it usually takes only a brief period of sucking before the milk lets down (begins to flow). Just hearing your baby cry may be enough to trigger milk flow. Signs of let-down vary from woman to woman and change with the volume of milk the baby demands. Some women feel a subtle tingling, while others experience a pressure that feels as if their breasts are overfull—all sensations that are quickly relieved as the milk starts to flow. Some women never feel these sensations even though the infant is getting plenty of milk. The way the milk flows also varies widely. It may spray, gush, trickle, or flow. Some women have leakage with let-down or between feedings and others don't; either case is normal. Flow or leakage also may be quite different in each breast—even gushing on one side and trickling on the other. There are slight differences in the ducts on either side, and this is no cause for concern as long as the baby is getting adequate milk.

When you nurse in the days right after birth, you might find it comfortable to lie on your side, with the baby facing you, opposite the breast. If you'd rather sit, use pillows to support your arms and cradle the baby slightly below breast level, making sure his entire body, not just his head, is facing your body.

The baby has latched on to the breast correctly. The nose, lips, and chin are all close to the breast, allowing for effective breastfeeding.

Most of the areola and nipple are in his mouth.

Cradle or Madonna hold

Following a Cesarean delivery, the most comfortable position may be a side hold, also called a football hold, in which you sit and the baby lies at your side facing you. Curl your arm underneath him and support his head at your breast. This position keeps the baby's weight off your abdomen, but the infant must squarely face the breast for the proper grasp.

If you stroke your newborn's lip with the nipple, he'll instinctively open wide, latch on, and begin to suck. He's been practicing this for some time in utero by sucking his hand, fingers, and possibly even his feet. (Some babies actually are born with blisters on their fingers from this sucking in the womb.) It takes little encouragement to get him to nurse, but you may need to help him properly grasp the areola. You can hold the breast with your thumb above the areola and your fingers and palm underneath it. Some gentle compression may be helpful to form a surface for latch-on. Then, when the baby opens his mouth very wide, pull him onto the breast. It is important to keep the nipple level or pointed slightly up, and to keep your fingers clear of the areola so the baby can grasp it. Be sure your fingers are no closer than 2 inches from the base of the nipple. Let your baby nurse on one side as long as he wishes, then put him on the other side if he is still interested in feeding. It is more important to complete a feeding on one breast than to have brief feedings from both. With each feeding, the earlier milk is more carbohydrate-packed, and as your baby consumes more, the hindmilk (later milk) becomes fattier and calorie-rich. Let-down, uterine cramping, swallowing sounds, and return to sound sleep by the baby are all signs of successful breastfeeding. In the beginning, it may take a couple of minutes for letdown to occur. Within a week or

Football or clutch hold

Whichever position you choose, make sure his entire body, not just his head, is facing your body.

so, let-down will take place more rapidly and your milk supply will increase dramatically.

If you are not sure a let-down is happening, just watch your baby. Following a let-down, he should be swallowing after every few sucks. After five or ten minutes, he may switch to a more relaxed nonnutritive sucking that provides emotional comfort along with small amounts of creamier, fat-rich hindmilk. Other signs of let-down vary from woman to woman: uterine cramps the first days after delivery, let-down sensations, milk leakage from the opposite breast, the breast feeling full before and soft after feeding, or milk in or around the baby's mouth after feeding. The more relaxed and confident you feel, the quicker your milk will let down.

The first feedings may be difficult. Breastfeeding should not cause sustained pain in the nipple, areola, or breast. If pain remains after the initial moments of breastfeeding, ask your doctor, nurse, or lactation specialist to evaluate the breastfeeding and suggest changes. Ask the hospital staff for help; they are usually very experienced at assisting nursing mothers and babies. In some cases, an infant will have trouble latching on. Suckling from the breast is different from sucking the nipple on a bottle or pacifier, and some infants are sensitive to the difference. These babies may simply lick,

If you stroke your newborn's cheek or lip with your finger or with the nipple, he'll instinctively turn, latch on, and begin to suck. You may need to help him properly grasp the areola.

You may continue to provide some breast support while the baby is feeding, especially if the breasts are large.

You can slide your finger into the corner of your baby's mouth if you need to interrupt the feeding before the baby is finished.

nibble, or chew with their jaws instead of using the tongue. Others may show frustration by pulling away or crying. Researchers are still uncertain if artificial nipples are the cause of breastfeeding problems or are just a response to a breastfeeding problem that already existed. *Some experts recommend that you avoid bottles and pacifiers for the first several weeks until you feel that breastfeeding is going well.* During that time, if the baby seems to need more sucking, offer the breast again, or help him to find his own hand or fingers to soothe himself. If your baby has trouble latching on after you leave the hospital, you should call your baby's doctor for help or for a referral if needed.

Once home, try the following suggestions to help the let-down reflex.

- Apply moist heat (e.g., warm, wet washcloths) to the breast for several minutes before starting the feeding.

- Sit in a comfortable chair, with good support for your back and arms. (Many nursing mothers recommend rocking chairs or gliders, while others do best in a straight-back chair using propping pillows.) At night, when it is common to fall asleep during breastfeeding, it is best to breastfeed in bed instead of a sofa or chair, then return the baby to a separate sleep surface for sleep once the feeding is complete.

- Make sure the baby is positioned so he squarely faces the breast and is well latched on, as described earlier.

- Use some relaxation techniques, such as deep breathing or visual imagery.

- Listen to soothing music. Sip a nutritious drink, or drink water and have a nutritious snack during feedings.

- If your household is very busy, find a quiet corner or room where you won't be disturbed during feedings.

- Do not smoke, and avoid secondhand smoke. Do not use marijuana or illegal drugs (cocaine, heroin, ecstasy, etc.), as all contain substances that can interfere with let-down, affect the content of breast milk, and be harmful to the baby. Check with your obstetrician or pediatrician about any prescription or nonprescription drugs, as well as any herbal supplements, you may be taking. If you do drink alcohol, limit your consumption to one serving of alcohol a day, ideally two hours prior to nursing.

If you still are not letting down after trying these suggestions, contact your pediatrician for additional help. If you continue to have difficulties, ask to be referred to a lactation expert.

When Your Milk Supply Increases

For the first days after delivery, your breasts will be soft. But as the blood supply increases and milk-producing cells start to function more efficiently, the breasts will become firmer. By the second to fifth day following delivery, your breasts should be producing transitional milk (milk that follows colostrum) and may feel very full. At the end of the baby's first week, you will see creamy white breast milk. After ten to fourteen days, the milk at the beginning of a feeding may look like skim milk, and as the feeding continues, the amount of fat in the milk will increase and the milk will look creamier. This is normal. Nursing your baby frequently and massaging your breasts prior to and during feeding may help minimize the fullness.

Engorgement occurs when the breasts become overfilled with milk and excess body fluids. This can be very uncomfortable and at times painful. The best solution is to nurse your baby whenever she is hungry, feeding at both breasts about eight to twelve times per day or before your breasts get swollen, firm, or painful. Sometimes the breasts are so engorged the baby has trouble latching on. If that happens, apply moist heat to soften the breasts, and if necessary, manually express some milk or use a mechanical breast pump before you start to nurse. Doing this may help the baby to get a better grasp and nurse more efficiently. (See page 110 regarding milk expression.) You also can try several techniques to ease the pain of engorgement, such as:

- Take a warm shower or use a warm washcloth. These techniques, when used just before breastfeeding or expressing milk, will encourage milk flow.

- Warmth may not help cases of severe engorgement, especially if no milk is flowing. In this case, you may want to use cool compresses in between or just after feeding.

- Express milk or pump just enough milk for comfort's sake.

- Try feeding your baby in more than one position. Begin by sitting up, then feed lying down. This changes the segments of the breast that are drained most at each feeding.

■ Gently massage your breasts from under the arm and down the nipple. This will help reduce soreness and ease milk flow.

■ The use of ibuprofen has been shown to be safe and effective for the treatment of engorgement. Take the dosage recommended by your doctor. Do not take any other medications without your doctor's approval.

Is Your Baby Nursing Correctly? A Breastfeeding Checklist

SIGNS OF OPTIMAL NURSING

■ Your baby's mouth is open wide with lips turned out.

■ His chin and nose are resting against the breast.

■ He is suckling rhythmically and deeply, in short bursts separated by pauses.

■ You can hear him swallowing regularly.

■ Your nipple is comfortable after the first few suckles.

SIGNS OF SUBOPTIMAL NURSING

■ Your baby's head is not in line with his body.

■ He is sucking on the nipple only, instead of suckling on the areola with the nipple far back in his mouth.

■ He is sucking in a light, quick, fluttery manner rather than taking deep, regular sucks.

■ His cheeks are puckered inward or you hear clicking noises.

■ You don't hear him swallow regularly after your milk production has increased.

■ You experience pain throughout the feed or have signs of nipple injury (such as cracking or bleeding).

Source: American Academy of Pediatrics, *New Mother's Guide to Breastfeeding,* ed. J. Y. Meek, 3rd ed. (New York: Bantam Books, 2017).

What About Vitamins for Breastfed Babies?

Your breast milk provides your baby with all the vitamins he needs, except for vitamin D. Even though breast milk (also known as *human milk*) provides small amounts of vitamin D, it is not enough to prevent rickets (softening of the bones). The current American Academy of Pediatrics recommendation is that all infants and children should have a minimum intake of 400 IU (10 mcg) of vitamin D per day beginning soon after birth, with 600 IU (15 mcg) per day in children over age one. Prepared formula has vitamin D added to it. If your baby is drinking only formula and takes about 32 ounces per day, he will get the same about of vitamin D as a supplement of 400 IU (10 mcg) per day. If you are breastfeeding and supplementing with formula, your baby will still require a vitamin D supplement. Some maternal vitamin D can make it into the breast milk. A mother needs to take 6,400 IU (160 mcg) of vitamin D per day for the baby to receive 400 IU (10 mcg).

Your baby also may need vitamin or iron supplements if he was born prematurely or has certain other medical problems. Discuss the need for supplements of vitamins or minerals with your doctor.

If you are a vegan (that is, you eat a diet that excludes all foods of animal origin), talk about your nutritional needs with your pediatrician. A vegan diet lacks not only vitamin D but also vitamin B_{12}. A deficiency in B_{12} in babies can lead to anemia and nervous system abnormalities.

(For more information about vitamin D and other supplements, see pages 131–33.)

Engorgement lasts only a few days while lactation is getting established. However, your breasts can still get firm or overfilled anytime feedings are skipped and the breast is not emptied. The volume of milk produced increases dramatically over the first week. Your baby may take as little as 1 teaspoon (5 ml) at each feeding the first couple of days, and up to 1 ounce (30 ml) at each feeding by the fourth or fifth day. By the end of the week—depending on the size and appetite of the baby and length of feedings—you may be producing 2 to 6 ounces (60–180 ml) at each feeding. By the end of the first month, your infant should be consuming an average of 24 ounces (720 ml) of milk. (See pages 108–9 and 113 for information on how to tell if your baby is getting enough.)

Breastfeeding Twins

Twins present a unique challenge to the nursing mother. At first it may be easier to feed them one at a time, but after lactation is established, often it's more convenient and time-saving to feed them simultaneously. Feeding them together can also increase your milk supply. You can do this using the football hold to position one at each side, or cradle them both in front of you with their bodies crossing each other.

(For more information about raising multiples, seek support groups like La Leche League or consider books such as *Raising Twins: Parenting Multiples From Pregnancy Through the School Years* by Shelly Vaziri Flais, MD, FAAP, published by the American Academy of Pediatrics [2020]).

How Often and How Long?

Breastfed newborns vary greatly in their feeding behaviors. They generally eat more frequently than formula-fed infants, eight to twelve (or more) times per twenty-four hours. As they get older, with enlarged stomach capacity and mother's increased milk production, some can go longer between feedings. Others continue to prefer frequent, smaller feeds.

The best feeding schedule for a breastfed baby is the one he designs himself. Your baby lets you know he's hungry by waking and looking alert, putting hands toward his mouth, making sucking motions, whimpering, flexing arms and hands, becoming more active, and nuzzling against your breast (he can smell its location even through your clothing). It is best to nurse your baby before he starts crying, a late sign of hunger. Whenever possible, use these signals rather than the clock to decide when to nurse. This way, you'll ensure he's hungry. In the process, he'll stimulate the breast more efficiently to produce milk.

As stated earlier, breastfeeding is generally most successful when started immediately after delivery (in the first hour). Keep the baby with you as much as possible (rooming with him in the hospital) and respond promptly to hunger cues (a practice called *demand feeding*). A baby may have one or two 4-hour periods of not feeding, but then will feed frequently in the intervening hours. It is best to tally the feeds over the course of the day to make sure there are a minimum of eight feeds per twenty-four-hour period. At night, breastfeeding babies will typically need to feed, and not sleep through the night; keeping the baby in the same room with you at night for at least the first six months will both facilitate cue-based feeding as well as promote safe sleep to decrease the risk of sudden infant death syndrome. Long stretches of uninterrupted sleep are not typical for a breastfeeding baby until he is about four months old and generally over twelve pounds. Your pediatrician will monitor his growth until he has regained his birth weight.

Allow your baby to nurse on the first breast as long as desired. When he stops for a prolonged period or withdraws from the breast, burp him. If he seems sleepy after the first breast, you

Your baby will generally feed for about ten to fifteen minutes on the first breast. Then your baby can be burped and offered the other breast.

may want to wake him up by changing his diaper or playing with him a little before switching him to the second side. Since your infant suckles more efficiently on the first breast he uses, you should alternate which breast you offer him first from feeding to feeding. You might consider placing a safety pin or other marker on your clothing on the side last nursed as a reminder. Or you can start on the breast that feels fuller.

Initially your newborn will probably nurse every couple of hours, regardless of whether it's day or night. By six to eight weeks of age, many newborns have one sleep period of four to five hours. Establish nighttime sleep patterns by keeping the room dark, warm, and quiet. Don't use a bright light for nighttime feedings. If his diaper is soiled or wet, change it quickly and without fanfare before feeding and put him right back to sleep afterward. By four months, many—but not all—babies are sleeping six hours or more at night without awakening. However, some breastfed babies may continue to awaken more frequently for night feedings. (See *Helping Your Baby Sleep*, page 64.)

Getting to Know Your Baby's Feeding Patterns

Each baby has a particular style of feeding. Years ago researchers at Yale University playfully attached names to five common eating patterns. See if you recognize your baby's dining behavior among them.

Barracudas get right down to business. As soon as they're put to the breast, they grasp the areola and suck energetically for ten to twenty minutes. They usually become less eager as time goes on.

Excited ineffectives become frantic at the sight of the breast. In a frenzied cycle they grasp it, lose it, and start screaming in frustration. They must be calmed down several times during each feeding. The key to nourishing this type of baby is to feed him as soon as he wakes up, before he gets desperately hungry. Also, if the milk tends to spray from the breast as the baby struggles, it may help to manually express a few drops first to slow the stream.

Procrastinators can't be bothered with nursing until the milk supply increases, commonly referred to as "coming in." These babies shouldn't be given bottles of water or formula, as feeding them bottles may make it more difficult to get them to nurse at the breast. You should continue to put them to the breast regularly, whenever they appear alert or make mouthing movements. Reluctant nursers sometimes benefit from being placed naked on the reclining mother's bare abdomen and chest for a period of time. They may spontaneously move toward the breast, or they can be placed on the breast after a time. You may find advice on improved positioning and attachment from a lactation specialist helpful. For a baby who resists nursing for the first few days, you can use an electric pump between feedings to stimulate milk production. (See pages 111–12.) Just don't give up! Contact your pediatrician's office for assistance or referral to a lactation specialist.

Gourmets or *mouthers* insist on playing with the nipple, tasting the milk first and smacking their lips before digging in. If hurried or prodded, they become furious and scream in protest. The best solution is tolerance. After a few minutes of playing, they do settle down and nurse well. Just be sure the lips and gums are on the areola and not on the nipple.

Resters prefer to nurse for a few minutes, rest a few minutes, and resume nursing. Some fall asleep on the breast, nap for half an hour or so, and then awaken ready for dessert. This pattern can be confusing, but these babies cannot be hurried. The solution? It's best just to schedule extra time for feedings and remain as flexible as possible.

Learning your own baby's eating patterns is one of your biggest challenges in the weeks after delivery. Once you understand his patterns, you'll find it much easier to determine when he's hungry, when he's had enough, how often he needs to eat, and how much time is required for feedings. It is generally best to initiate a feeding at the earliest signs of hunger, before the baby cries. Babies also have unique positions that they prefer and will even show preference for one breast over the other.

You'll also find that your infant may require long feedings at certain times and be satisfied quickly at others. She'll let you know when she's finished by letting go or drifting off to sleep between spurts of nonnutritive sucking. A few babies want to nurse around the clock. If your baby falls into this category, check with your pediatrician's office. You may be referred to a lactation specialist. There are several reasons why infants behave this way, and the sooner the situation is evaluated, the easier it is to address the cause.

Is Your Baby Eating Enough?

In the first week after birth, doctors will check your newborn to ensure that weight loss is not excessive (more than 10 percent of the birth weight), there is no excessive jaundice, and your baby is producing at least a few wet diapers and stools per day. Wet diapers and stooling are reliable signs of feeding two days after birth. There should be four to eight wet diapers, and three to four loose, seedy stools per day by the third day. Given that wet diapers and stooling patterns during the first two days can be unreliable indicators of feeding adequacy, it is important to schedule a follow-up visit with your pediatrician within forty-eight hours of going home. This visit will help to ensure that your milk supply is increasing and that your baby is getting milk from breastfeeding. By the end of the second week, your baby should be back to birth weight or have gained some weight. If you've breastfed other children, lactation will probably be established more quickly this time, so the new baby may lose little weight and return to birth weight within days.

During the first month, after your milk supply increases, an adequate diet should produce six or more wet diapers a day and generally three to four or more bowel movements (often one little one after each feeding). Later, he may have less frequent bowel movements, and there may even be a day or more between them. If bowel movements are soft and your baby is otherwise thriving, this is typical. Another clue about intake is whether you can hear your baby swallow, usually after several sucks. Appearing satisfied for a couple of hours after a feeding is also a sign. On the other hand, a baby who is not getting enough to eat over several days may become very sleepy and seem "easy" to care for. In the early weeks, a baby who is excessively sleepy or feeds less frequently than eight times in a twenty-four-hour period should be seen by the pediatrician to make sure he is gaining weight as expected.

Once your milk supply is established, your baby should gain between ½ and 1 ounce (14–28 g) a day during his first three months. Between three and six months, weight gain will taper off to about ½ ounce (14 g) a day, and after six months, weight gains each day will be even less. Your pediatrician will weigh the baby at every visit. If you have concerns between visits, call to schedule an appointment; don't depend on a home scale, as they are not very reliable for young infants.

What About Bottles?

Newborns are usually best breastfed around the clock, something made easier by rooming in with your baby in your hospital room. You might be tempted to have your baby sleep in the nursery for one night so you can get an uninterrupted night's sleep. But most hospitals now provide mother-infant care, so you can sleep in the same room while your newborn is being safely cared for by his nurse. Research shows that mothers actually sleep better when their newborns are cared for in the same room as opposed to a nursery setting. Hospitals are shifting away from the traditional nursery model and instead using their nurseries for procedures and sick newborns. Furthermore, if your newborn is rooming in, you can respond to early feeding cues and avoid unnecessary water or formula supplementation, which may interfere with a successful breastfeeding experience. Even in the hospital, however, it's important to follow safe sleep guidelines. Make sure that your newborn is placed on her back in a bassinet and not in your bed.

If circumstances keep you away from your baby, you will need to express breast milk, manually or mechanically, in order to stimulate continued milk production. The hospital staff will work with you to express your milk in a way that enables transitioning back to the breast, including using feeding techniques that avoid bottles and teats. These techniques may include syringe or cup feeding, paced bottle-feeding, or feeding through a supplemented nursing system. Always check with your pediatrician or other expert before you stop giving your breast milk to your baby or begin supplementing with formula.

Once the milk supply is established, usually three or four weeks after delivery, you may decide to use a bottle for expressed milk, so you can be away during some feedings. Expressing breast milk in advance and storing it allows your baby to receive the benefits of your milk by bottle. In addition, using expressed breast milk will maintain your body's full milk production. An occasional bottle at this stage probably won't interfere with your baby's nursing habits, but it may cause another problem with engorgement if the milk isn't expressed in a timely manner. Milk you express while you're away from your baby should be stored, so that you can replace the breast milk used by other caregivers while you are away. Wearing nursing pads will help you manage leakage. (Some women wear nursing pads constantly during the first month or two to avoid milk stains.) It is important to either breastfeed or express your milk regularly throughout the day to avoid engorgement and potential problems from milk stasis, which may lead to decreased milk production or clogged ducts.

Milk Expression and Storage

Milk can be expressed either by hand or by manual or electric pump. In any case, you must have the let-down reflex for the milk to flow. Manual or hand expression is easier to learn visually, rather than just reading about it, and can be quick and effective once learned, though it requires practice. Many hospitals teach mothers hand expression before leaving the hospital. Breast pumps may seem easier than learning hand expression, but the quality of pumps varies widely. Luckily there are many quality pumps available at various price points. A poor-quality breast pump will not remove milk effectively, resulting in engorgement or a gradually lower milk supply over time. Poor-quality breast pumps also may irritate the nipples or be painful.

Hand Expression

If you choose to hand-express, wash your hands and use a clean container to collect the milk. Place your thumb above the areola and your fingers underneath. Gently but firmly roll the thumb and fingers toward each other while compressing the breast tissue and pushing toward the chest wall. Do not slide your fingers toward your nipple, as this can cause soreness. Transfer the milk to a clean bottle, rigid plastic container, or specially made plastic bag for storage in the freezer. (See page 112.) If your baby is hospitalized, the hospital may give you specific and detailed information about milk collection and storage, and may lend you a hospital-grade breast pump.

Breast Pump

While manual breast pumps are available and may be easy to use while out and about, good-quality electric pumps are a wonderful option and can stimulate the breast more effectively than manual expression. These pumps have regulated pressures and are self-cycling for efficient milk removal. They are used primarily to induce or maintain lactation when a mother is unable to breastfeed directly for several days or more, such as with a hospitalized infant, or

Expressing milk is easier if you stimulate the breast first by massaging it gently.

To use hand expression, hold the breast with the thumb and index finger at the edge of the areola on opposite sides of the breast, then press toward the chest wall with a rhythmic motion. Rotate position of fingers so all parts of the breast are emptied.

when the mother returns to work or school. Electric pumps are efficient but can be costly, ranging in price from $50 to $300 and up. If you need a pump temporarily, you can rent one from a medical supply store, hospital, or lactation rental agency.

In many states, you can obtain a good-quality pump through your insurance or your state's Women, Infants, and Children (WIC) program. Sometimes you can also upgrade the insurance-supplied pump. Ask your obstetrician or pediatrician for a prescription and talk to your insurance provider to find out where to purchase a covered pump. The costs related to breastfeeding supplies, such as pumps, may also be a deductible item if you participate in a flexible spending plan.

When shopping for an electric pump, make sure it creates a steady milking action with variable pressure, not simply suction. You may also consider a double electric pump that expresses both breasts at the same time; such a pump will increase your milk volume as well as save time. There are also bras and tops available to help hold both cones in place at once. Make sure that all parts of the pump that come in contact with the skin or milk can be removed for proper cleaning. Sterilization is not required for pumps and containers for a healthy baby; simply washing well with hot soapy water is fine, as is using the dishwasher. Talk to your pediatrician or lactation consultant for advice on which type of pump may be best. And remember to wash your hands immediately before pumping.

As with manually expressed breast milk, pumped milk should be stored in clean containers, preferably glass or rigid plastic, or special plastic bags. Baby bottle insert bags are not sufficiently strong or thick enough to protect the milk from contamination. Expressed breast milk can be stored safely at room temperature for three to five hours, in the refrigerator up to three to five days, or in a freezer (0 degrees Fahrenheit [-20 degrees Celsius]) up to nine months. Store frozen breast milk in the back of the freezer, where it's coldest. Write the date on each container and use the oldest milk first. It's useful to freeze milk in the amount needed for a single feeding, about 3 to 4 ounces (90–120 ml). You also can freeze some 1- to 2-ounce portions (30–60 ml), which come in handy if the baby wants a little extra at any feeding.

When it's time to use stored milk, keep in mind that your baby is accustomed to breast milk at body temperature, so the milk may need to be heated to at least room temperature (68–72 degrees Fahrenheit [20–22 degrees Celsius]). Frozen milk may be thawed in the refrigerator, under warm running water, or immersed in

Hand pumps are available at most drug and baby stores.

a container of warm water. Don't use the microwave to warm milk, as this leads to uneven heating and risk of scalding. Once milk is thawed, its fat may separate, but this has no effect on quality. Swirl the container gently until the milk returns to a uniform consistency. Stored breast milk may have an altered smell or taste due to breakdown of fat. This is not harmful to the baby. Thawed milk should be refrigerated and used within twenty-four hours. Never refreeze. If the infant does not finish all the thawed breast milk in the bottle, it should be consumed within one to two hours or discarded.

"Is My Baby Getting Enough Nourishment?"

If you're breastfeeding, you've probably wondered whether your baby is getting enough to eat. After all, there's really no way to determine exactly how much breast milk he's getting.

If this is a concern, here are some guidelines that can help ensure your baby is getting the nourishment he needs. Your well-fed newborn should:

■ Lose no more than 10 percent of his birth weight in the first few days after birth before he starts to gain weight again.

■ Have one or two bowel movements per day in the first two days after birth, with blackish, tarry stools, and at least two stools appearing greenish to yellow in days three and four. By days five to seven, stools should be yellow and loose, with small curds, and should number at least three to four per day. When your milk production increases, your baby will often have a bowel movement with each feeding during the first month after birth.

■ Have six or more wet diapers per day, with urine that is nearly colorless or pale yellow, by days five to seven.

■ Appear content and happy for an average of one to three hours between feedings.

■ Nurse at least eight to twelve times during every twenty-four-hour period.

Source: Adapted from the American Academy of Pediatrics, *New Mother's Guide to Breastfeeding*, ed. J. Y. Meek, 3rd ed. (New York: Bantam Books, 2017).

Do not heat breast milk, formula, or bottles in a microwave oven. Microwaving overheats the milk in the center of the container. Even if the bottle feels comfortably warm, the superheated milk in the center can scald your baby's mouth. In fact, the bottle itself can explode if left in the microwave too long. Heat can also destroy some of the anti-infective, nutritious, and protective properties of breast milk.

Not all breastfed babies react to the bottle the same way. Some accept it easily, regardless of when it is introduced. Others take an occasional bottle, but not from the mother or when the mother is present. You can increase the likelihood your baby will first accept a bottle if someone other than the mother offers it and she is out of sight at the time. Once familiar with the bottle, he may take it in his mother's presence, possibly even from his mother. If your breastfed baby refuses a bottle, try a cup or sippy cup instead. Even premature newborns are able to cup-feed. Some breastfed babies go from breast to cup without ever using a bottle.

Possible Nursing Concerns and Questions

For some, nursing goes well from the start and there are never problems. But breastfeeding can have its ups and downs, especially in the beginning. Fortunately, many common difficulties can be prevented with proper positioning and latch-on along with frequent feedings. Problems may resolve quickly if you seek advice right away. Don't hesitate to ask your pediatrician or office nurse for help with the following problems.

SORE AND CRACKED NIPPLES. Breastfeeding may produce initial mild soreness, especially with latch-on in the first week or so. Breastfeeding should not cause sustained pain, discomfort, or open cracks. Proper latch-on is the most important factor in preventing sore and cracked nipples. If your nipples or other areas of the breast are painful, seek advice from your lactation expert.

During bathing, wash your breasts with mild soap, taking care to use only water on the nipple. Creams, lotions, and more vigorous rubbing are not necessary and may actually aggravate a problem. Also, try varying the baby's position at each feeding to help with nipple irritation.

You may use purified lanolin on cracked or dry nipples to protect and allow them to heal. If this does not solve the problem, consult your doctor or lactation consultant for further advice; you might have a yeast or bacterial infection of the nipple, or may have a skin condition such as dermatitis that requires treatment.

ENGORGEMENT. As already mentioned, your breasts can become severely engorged if your baby doesn't nurse often or efficiently during the first few days after your milk comes in. While some engorgement is to be expected when lactation starts, extreme engorgement causes swelling of the milk ducts and of blood vessels across the entire chest area. The best treatment is to breastfeed frequently; express milk between feedings, either manually or with a pump; and offer both breasts at every feeding. If the baby feeds from only one side, it may help to manually express milk from the other side. Since warmth encourages milk flow, standing in a warm shower as you manually express may help. You also may get relief with warm compresses during nursing and cool compresses between nursing. If engorgement persists, it may lead to a decrease in milk production. This happens because breasts have a mechanism to turn off milk production when milk is not removed from the breast. To avoid problems with breast milk supply, it is important to relieve engorgement as soon as it is recognized.

MASTITIS. Mastitis is an infection of the breast tissue caused by bacteria. Mastitis causes flu-like symptoms of fever, chills, headache, nausea, dizziness, and lack of energy. These general symptoms occur along with localized symptoms of redness, tenderness, swelling, heat, and pain in and around the breast. If you experience any of these symptoms, call your doctor at once. The infection is treated with milk removal (by feeding or pumping), rest, fluids, antibiotics, and pain medicine if needed. Your doctor will prescribe an antibiotic that is safe during breastfeeding. Be sure to take all the antibiotics even if you feel better. Do not stop nursing; doing so will worsen the mastitis and cause increased pain. The milk itself is *not* infected. Your baby will not be harmed by nursing during mastitis, and mastitis or the antibiotics will not change milk composition.

Mastitis may be a sign your body's immune defenses are down. Bed rest, sleep, and decreased activity will help recover your stamina. Rarely, you may find it's too painful to nurse on the infected breast; in that case, let the milk flow from the painful breast onto a clean towel or absorbent cloth, relieving the pressure as you nurse from the opposite side. Then your baby can finish feeding on the infected side with less discomfort. Some women with severe pain find it is more comfortable to pump the breast than to feed the baby directly, even if just for a few feedings. The pumped milk can be stored or fed to the baby immediately after.

A mother's return to work is a peak time for the development of mastitis. It is important to express milk regularly, approximately on the same schedule as the baby would feed, to try to prevent the infection.

Supplemental Nurser (Infant Feeding Device)

The amount of milk your breasts produce depends on the amount of milk removed from them. If you miss too many feedings, your body will decrease milk production. This can occur even if you express milk during missed feedings, since pumps do not stimulate or empty the breasts nearly as efficiently as your baby's sucking.

If your milk supply is not meeting the needs of your baby, if you miss a number of feedings because of illness, or if your baby is unable to nurse for some reason, you may be able to reestablish your milk supply by nursing more frequently (every hour for twenty-four hours) or by using a supplemental nurser (also known as a supplementer tube, infant feeding device, or nursing trainer). Unlike a bottle, which trains the baby away from the breast, this device provides supplemental expressed milk or formula while the infant is at the breast.

The supplemental nurser is also used for premature infants or to train babies with feeding problems. It even can help stimulate lactation in adoptive mothers, or in mothers who stopped breastfeeding for a prolonged period and wish to start again.

Hung from your neck, the container holding the formula or expressed milk has a thin flexible tube aligned along the breast with its tip adjacent to the nipple and placed in the corner of the baby's mouth as she sucks. Her suction draws the formula or breast milk from the container, so even if you aren't producing much milk, she will still get a full feeding. This reinforces her desire to nurse at the breast. At the same time, her sucking stimulates your body to step up milk production.

Supplemental nursers are available from lactation specialists, medical supply stores, some pharmacies, or online. If possible, purchase the device from someone who can show you how to use and clean it. Most mothers and babies need a few days of practice to get comfortable with the device. Using a supplemental nurser requires commitment and dedication, as it may take weeks or months to rebuild the milk supply and the breastfeeding relationship.

INFANT FUSSINESS. Sometimes babies, even breastfed babies, can be unusually fussy. Reasons for fussiness can range from normal personality variations to serious illness. Although most fussy babies do not have a serious medical problem, their constant crying can become extremely difficult for parents. The fussy baby wears on a parent's energy, time, and enjoyment of their young infant. Here are some general causes and suggestions for excessive crying in the breast-fed baby.

- *Hunger.* If your newborn feeds constantly and is never satisfied after feeding, your breastfeeding needs to be evaluated by an experienced healthcare provider. He will weigh and examine your baby, examine your breast and nipples, and observe an entire breastfeeding session. The solution may be as simple as improving the baby's positioning and latch-on, or it may be more complicated, particularly if the baby has lost too much weight or is not gaining well.

- *Growth spurt.* A rapid growth phase often happens at two to three weeks of age, again around six weeks, and again at about three months. During these spurts, babies will want to nurse *constantly.* Many women think this is because the baby is not getting enough to eat (which is correct) and are tempted to give supplemental bottles. However, the baby is doing what is right. When you nurse constantly or every hour or so for several days, your breasts will make more milk. Remember, this is normal, and only temporary; keep breastfeeding frequently, and do not give your baby other liquids. If this frequent feeding does not return to a more regular pattern after four to five days, or if you are tempted to start bottles, call your pediatrician's office for assistance. He should see the baby, check her weight, and evaluate the feeding process (or refer you to a lactation specialist if needed).

- *Hyperalert or high-needs infants.* These babies require more of everything, except sleep. They seem to cry around the clock. They are irregular in their eating, sleeping, and reactions to others. They need lots of holding, carrying, and usually motion, such as rocking. Sometimes swaddling in a blanket helps them; other times it makes them worse. They tend to "snack" at the breast frequently and sleep in catnaps, brief fifteen- to thirty-minute naps while someone is holding or carrying them. Slings or other baby carriers, as well as swings, are good to help calm these babies. In spite of fussiness, they should be gaining weight normally.

- *Colic.* Colic begins after four weeks of age. Colicky babies generally have at least one period each day when they appear to be in pain, crying hard, turning red, and drawing their legs up. They may act hungry, but then pull back and refuse the breast. Your baby's doctor can provide suggestions for managing colic. (For more on colic, see pages 168–69.)

- *Oversupply or overactive let-down of breast milk.* This could begin at any time in the first month. Your breasts will feel very full, and you may experience lots of leaking and spraying. Your baby will be gulping down milk very fast, sometimes pulling away to catch his breath or coughing or sputtering milk. As a result, the baby swallows lots of air and milk. Later, gas bubbles form, causing discomfort. Your pediatrician may guide you to a lactation consultant to assist with this problem. (Also see *Engorgement*, page 115.)

- *Reflux (also called gastroesophageal reflux).* Most newborns spit up after feeding. This is normal and requires no treatment. When spitting up results in problems such as fussiness, becomes more like vomiting (much larger amounts), or is associated with weight loss, your baby should be evaluated by your pediatrician. Physiological reflux is normal in all infants till twelve months of age and may be more prominent in preterm infants. Medication (antacid) is not required as long as your infant is gaining normal weight. (See page 221.)

- *Food sensitivities.* Occasionally a particular food you're consuming (including caffeinated beverages) may cause problems in your breastfed baby. If you suspect a food, avoid it for one week to see if the symptoms go away. Then you may try the food again carefully to see if the symptoms return.

- *Allergies.* Although infant crying is often blamed on food allergies, such allergies are less common than some other reasons for fussiness. Allergies occur more often in babies from families where the mother, father, or siblings are affected by asthma, eczema, or other allergic diseases. In the breastfed baby, the mother's diet may be the source. It can be difficult to pinpoint the precise food, however, and allergic symptoms can linger for more than a week after the food has been removed from the mother's diet. Sometimes food allergies, such as to milk protein, can result in blood in the stool. If blood in the stool is the only symptom, then generally no treatment is necessary. However, food allergies can be very serious, sometimes causing wheezing, hives, or shock (collapse). Severe food allergies definitely require the attention of your pediatrician.

- *Other serious illnesses.* Illnesses not related to feeding may cause babies to cry endlessly, unable to be comforted. If this occurs suddenly or seems unusually severe, call your pediatrician or seek emergency care immediately.

THE CANCER QUESTION. Most studies indicate breastfeeding offers some protection against breast cancer, perhaps because nursing lowers the total number of menstrual cycles during a woman's lifetime (see cancer.org). If a woman has been diagnosed with cancer or has had a malignant tumor removed but is no longer on chemo or radiation therapy, breastfeeding should be safe (check with your physician). Breastfeeding is also safe after a woman has had a benign (noncancerous) lump or cyst removed.

BREASTFEEDING AFTER PLASTIC SURGERY ON THE BREASTS. Plastic surgery to enlarge the breasts usually does not interfere with breastfeeding—provided the breasts were previously normal, the nipples were not moved, and no ducts were cut. Breastfeeding after breast reduction surgery is highly individual. Surgery to reduce breast size typically involves at least some disruption of breast tissue and often movement of the entire nipple and areola. Each mother-baby pair must be helped and followed individually. Your baby's weight should be checked more frequently, at least twice a week, for the first few weeks, until the baby is gaining well. You can still breastfeed and supplement with formula if you aren't able to produce enough breast milk. This will provide your baby with some of the benefits of receiving breast milk. Make sure you discuss all concerns with your doctor. Your baby's pediatrician needs to be aware of previous breast surgery you've had so your infant can be followed closely.

Bottle-Feeding

Even with tremendous effort and plenty of support, breastfeeding does not always go well for every mother-infant pair. In other cases, parents who recognize the benefits of breastfeeding may still prefer bottle-feeding. Some believe bottle-feeding provides more freedom and time for activities. Dad, grandparents, sitters, and even older siblings can feed an infant breast milk or formula in a bottle. This may give some mothers more flexibility. There are other reasons some feel more comfortable with bottle-feeding, such as knowing exactly how much food the baby is getting. Others prefer formula-feeding for reasons such as not needing to worry about the mother's diet or medications that might affect the milk.

Even so, it is impossible for formula manufacturers to reproduce the components that make breast milk from mothers so unique. Although formula does provide the basic nutrients for an infant, it lacks the antibodies, some of the specific components and sugars that feed good bacteria in a baby's gut, and many of the other components found in breast milk. Formula-feeding is also costly and may be inconvenient for some families. The formula must be bought and prepared or otherwise managed, and you'll need a reliable source of clean water for mixing the formula. This means trips to the kitchen in the middle of the night, as well as extra bottles, nipples, and other equipment.

If you have decided to bottle-feed your baby, you'll start by selecting a formula. Your pediatrician will help you pick one based on your baby's needs. Today there are several varieties and brands of commercial formulas from which to choose, all of which are equally safe and nutritious. The American Academy of Pediatrics does not recommend homemade baby formulas, since they can be deficient in vitamins and other important nutrients and may be contaminated with potentially harmful bacteria.

Why Formula Instead of Cow's Milk?

Many parents ask why they can't feed their baby cow's milk. The answer is simple: infants cannot digest cow's milk as completely or easily as they do formula. Also, cow's milk contains high concentrations of protein and minerals, which can stress a newborn's immature kidneys and cause severe illness at times of heat stress, fever, or diarrhea. In addition, cow's milk lacks the proper amounts of iron, vitamin C, and other nutrients infants need. It may even cause iron-deficiency anemia, since cow's milk protein can irritate the lining of the stomach and intestine, leading to loss of blood in the stools. Cow's milk also does not contain the healthiest types of fat for growing babies. Your baby should not receive any cow's milk (or other non-human animal milk or milk substitute) for the first twelve months after birth.

Once over one year old, your baby may consume whole cow's milk or reduced-fat (2 percent) milk, provided he has a balanced diet of solid foods (cereals, vegetables, fruits, and meats). His intake should be limited to 2 cups (approximately 16 ounces) per day or less. More than 24 ounces a day has been associated with iron deficiency if toddlers aren't getting enough other healthy iron-rich foods. If your baby is not yet eating a broad range of solids, talk to your pediatrician about the best nutrition for him.

At this age, children still need a higher fat content, which is why whole vitamin D–fortified milk is recommended for most infants after one year of age. If your child is or is at risk for having overweight, or if there is a family history of obesity, high blood pressure, or heart disease, your pediatrician may recommend 2 percent (reduced-fat) milk. Do not give your baby 1 percent (low-fat) or nonfat (skim) milk before his second birthday, as it does not contain enough fat for brain development. After two years of age, you should discuss your child's nutritional needs, including choice of milk products, with your pediatrician.

Choosing a Formula

To maintain safety standards, US law and the Food and Drug Administration (FDA) govern the contents and safe production and distribution of all infant formulas. When shopping for infant formula, you'll find several basic types.

Cow's milk–based formulas account for about 80 percent of formula sold. Although cow's milk is the basis for such formulas, the milk has been changed dramatically to make it safe for infants. It is treated by heating and other methods to make the protein more digestible. More milk sugar (lactose) is added to make the concentration equal to that found in breast milk, and the butterfat is removed and replaced with vegetable oils and other fats that infants can more easily digest and that are better for infant growth.

Cow's milk formulas have additional iron added. These iron-fortified formulas have dramatically reduced the rate of iron-deficiency anemia in infancy in recent decades. Some infants do not have enough natural reserves of iron, a mineral necessary for normal human growth and development. For that reason, the American Academy of Pediatrics currently recommends that iron-fortified formula be used for all infants who are not breastfed, or who are only partially breastfed, from birth to one year of age. Additional iron is available in many foods (including baby food), especially in meats, egg yolks, and iron-fortified cereals. Low-iron formulas should not be used. Some mothers worry about iron causing constipation, but the amount of iron in infant formula does not contribute to constipation. Most formulas also have docosahexaenoic acid (DHA) and arachidonic acid (ARA) added to them, fatty acids believed to be important for the development of a baby's brain and eyes.

Some formulas also are fortified with probiotics, types of "friendly" bacteria. Others are now fortified with prebiotics, in the form of manufactured oligosaccharides, in an attempt to mimic the natural breast milk oligosaccharides, which are substances that promote a healthy intestinal lining. (For more information on probiotics, see opposite.)

Another type of formula is *extensively hydrolyzed formula*, which often is called "predigested," since the protein content has already been broken down into smaller proteins that can be digested more easily. Ask your pediatrician to recommend a brand of hypoallergenic formula if one is needed for allergies or other conditions. However, these extensively hydrolyzed formulas tend to be costlier than regular formulas.

Soy formulas contain a protein (soy) and carbohydrate (either glucose or sucrose) different from milk-based formulas. They are sometimes recommended for babies unable to digest lactose, the main carbohydrate in cow's milk formula, although lactose-free cow's milk–based formula is also available. Many infants have brief periods when they cannot digest lactose, particularly following bouts of diarrhea, which can damage the digestive enzymes in the intestine linings. This is usually only a temporary problem and does not require a change in your baby's diet. It is extremely rare for babies to have a significant problem digesting and absorbing lactose (although it tends to occur in older children and adults). While lactose-free formulas are fine sources of nutrition, check with your pediatrician before starting your baby on a lactose-free formula, since whatever problem she may be having is likely due to something else.

With a true milk allergy causing colic, failure to thrive, and even bloody diarrhea, the allergy is to the protein in the cow's milk formula. In this case soy formulas may seem like a good alternative. However, up to half the infants who have a milk allergy are also sensitive to soy protein, and thus must be given specialized formula (such as amino acid–based or elemental) or breast milk.

Some strict vegetarian and vegan parents choose to use soy formula because it contains no animal products. Remember that breastfeeding is the best option for vegetarian and vegan families. And while some parents believe a soy formula might prevent or ease the symptoms of colic or fussiness, there is no evidence to support this.

The American Academy of Pediatrics believes there are few circumstances when soy formula should be chosen instead of cow's milk–based formula. However, one situation is for infants with a rare disorder called galactosemia; children with this condition have an intolerance to galactose, one of the two sugars in lactose, and cannot tolerate breast milk and must be fed a lactose-free formula. All states include a blood test for galactosemia in routine newborn screening after birth.

There are specialized formulas for infants with specific disorders or diseases, including for premature babies. If your pediatrician recommends a specialized formula, follow his guidance about feeding requirements (amounts, scheduling, special preparations), since these may be different from regular formulas.

Probiotics

"Probiotics" (meaning "for life") is a word you may see when shopping for infant formula and supplements. Some formulas are fortified with these probiotics, which are types of live bacteria. Doctors may also recommend probiotic drops or powders for breastfed infants. These are "good" or "friendly" bacteria already present at high levels in the digestive system of breastfed babies. In formula-fed babies, probiotics in formulas promote a balance of bacteria in your baby's intestines, and offset the growth of "unfriendly" organisms that could cause infections and inflammation. Increasingly, parents can find probiotic supplements outside of formula, including for breastfed infants. Research on the benefits of probiotics is ongoing, with some pediatricians embracing their use for infants delivered by C-section or those whose mothers are given antibiotics during labor.

The most common types of probiotics are strains of bifidobacteria and lactobacilli. Some research has shown these probiotics may prevent or treat disorders such as infectious diarrhea and atopic dermatitis (eczema) in children (see pages 537 and 568). Other possible health benefits are being studied as well, including the possibility of reduced risk of food-related allergies and asthma, prevention of urinary tract infections, and relief of symptoms of infant colic.

With many of these health conditions, the evidence confirming any positive effects of probiotic use is limited and more research is needed. At this time, benefits appear to occur only as long as probiotics are being taken. Once your baby stops consuming probiotic-fortified formula, intestinal bacteria levels return to previous levels. This is different from in breastfed infants, where the bacteria in the gut resulting from breastfeeding are more resilient and set the stage for healthier outcomes.

Before giving your child infant formula fortified with probiotics, discuss the issue with your pediatrician. (For more information about probiotics, see page 543.)

Feeding and Oral Health

As the number one chronic disease in US children, dental caries (cavities) should be a concern for all parents. Research has shown that diet and hygiene practices in the first twenty-four months after birth play a significant role in the risk of cavities as the child becomes older. While much more beneficial than cow's milk or formula, breast milk contains lactose. Breastfeeding until up to twelve months of age decreases the risk of dental caries by half, most likely due to other immune modulating effects and a protective microbiome, despite the lactose sugar in breast milk. If infants breastfeed to sleep, the gums and erupting teeth should be wiped to minimize risk of caries.

Preparing, Sterilizing, and Storing Formula

Most infant formulas are available in ready-to-feed liquid forms, concentrates, and powders. Although ready-to-feed formulas are very convenient, they are also the most expensive. Formula from concentrate is prepared by adding water as the manufacturer directs. Unused concentrate may be covered and refriger-

Preparing Formula from Concentrate (One Bottle at a Time)

Wash hands and measure concentrate.

Pour in an equal amount of water. Shake and use promptly. Unused concentrate may be covered and refrigerated for no more than forty-eight hours.

ated for no more than forty-eight hours. Powder, the least expensive, comes either in premeasured packets or in a larger can. Most powdered formula requires one level scoop of powder for every 2 ounces (60 ml) of water. Mix thoroughly to ensure that there are no clumps of undissolved powder. Always read the label instructions for mixing the formula properly.

Aside from the price, powder is also light and portable. The powder will not spoil, even if it stays in the bottle several days before adding water. If you choose a formula requiring preparation, be sure to follow the manufacturer's directions exactly. Too much water and your baby won't get the calories and nutrients needed for proper growth; too little and the extra-concentrated formula could cause diarrhea or dehydration and will give your infant more calories than needed.

If you use well water or are concerned about the safety of your tap water, boil it for approximately one minute before adding it to the formula, making sure to let it return to room temperature before feeding. (If there is any concern, it may be a good idea to have your well water tested for bacteria or other contaminants.) You also can use bottled water.

Powdered infant formula is not commercially sterile and has been associated with a severe illness attributed to *Cronobacter* bacteria. However, the illness is very rare and the World Health Organization (WHO) has issued guidelines to improve the safety of powdered infant formula. The CDC and other US organizations recommend heating the water to *at least* 158 degrees Fahrenheit (70 degrees Celsius) before mixing with powder to reduce the possibility of infection with this bacteria. These instructions may be found at: cdc.gov/features/cronobacter.

Make sure all bottles, nipples, and other utensils used in preparation and feeding are clean. If your home has chlorinated water, a dishwasher or hot tap water with dishwashing detergent can be used. Rinse in hot tap water. For nonchlorinated water, boil the utensils for five to ten minutes.

Store formula prepared in advance in the refrigerator to discourage bacterial growth. Unused refrigerated formula should be discarded after twenty-four hours. Refrigerated formula doesn't necessarily have to be warmed, but most infants prefer it at least at room temperature. To warm it, you can either leave the bottle out for an hour or warm it in a pan of hot water (again, do not use a microwave). If you warm it, test it in advance to make sure it's not too hot by shaking a few drops onto the inside of your wrist.

Be sure to test the temperature of warmed formula before feeding it to your child.

Preparing Formula from Powder

Wash your hands and then add powder.

Measure water and stir to mix thoroughly.

Fill clean bottles and place in refrigerator.

Bottles may be glass or plastic and may have a soft plastic liner. These inner liners are convenient and may limit the amount of air your baby swallows when feeding, but they are also more expensive. As your baby begins holding the bottle herself, avoid using breakable glass bottles. Also, bottles designed to promote self-feeding are not recommended, as they may contribute to early childhood caries (ECC, formerly known as baby bottle tooth decay) by promoting constant feeding and overexposing the teeth to sugars. When milk or any other sugar-containing liquid sits in contact with tooth enamel over a prolonged period of time, bacterial overgrowth and acid production occurs. ECC is most commonly seen in children six months and older who bottle or breastfeed to fall asleep or demand at-will feedings throughout the night. Also, self-feeding while lying on the back has been shown to contribute occasionally to ear infections. (See *Middle Ear Infections,* page 670.) A bottle should not be given to suck on overnight. If you give your infant a bedtime feeding, take away the bottle and brush his teeth before he falls asleep to prevent ECC.

You may need to try several nipples before finding the one your baby prefers. There are standard silicone or rubber nipples, orthodontic ones, and special designs for premature infants and babies with cleft palates. Whichever type used, always check the size of the hole. If the hole is too small, your baby may suck so hard that he'll swallow too much air; if it's too big, the formula may flow so fast he might choke. Ideally, formula should flow from an upended bottle at a rate of one drop per second and stop dripping after a few seconds.

The Feeding Process

Feeding times should be relaxing, comforting, and enjoyable. They provide opportunities to show your love and to get to know each other. If you are calm and content, your infant will respond in kind. If you are nervous or uninterested, he may sense these negative feelings and a feeding problem can result.

You will probably be most comfortable in a chair with arms or with pillows that let you prop up your arms as you feed your infant. Cradle your baby in a semi-upright position and support his head. Don't feed him when he's lying down flat as this will increase the risk of choking and may also cause formula to flow into the middle ear, leading to possible infection.

Hold the bottle so that formula fills the neck of the bottle and fills the nipple. This will prevent your baby from swallowing air as he sucks. To get him to open his mouth and grasp the nipple, stimulate his rooting reflex by stroking the nipple against the lower lip or cheek. Once the nipple is in his mouth, he will begin to suck and swallow naturally.

Amount and Schedule of Formula Feedings

Paced feedings are recommended to avoid overfeeding, a problem commonly seen with bottle-fed babies. In the first week after birth, babies should be eating no more than 1 to 2 ounces (30–60 ml) per feed. This volume increases gradually over the first month until babies take 3 to 4 ounces (90–120 ml) per feed, resulting in about 32 ounces per day. Formula-fed babies typically feed on a more regular schedule, such as every three to four hours. This happens because all of the nutrients in formula are always exactly the same. Breast milk components vary over the twenty-four-hour period and result in more irregular feeding patterns. Breastfed infants also take smaller, more frequent feedings than formula-fed infants. During the first few weeks, if your baby sleeps longer than four to five hours and starts missing feedings, wake her up and offer a bottle.

By the end of her first month, she'll be up to at least 3 to 4 ounces (120 ml) per feeding, with a fairly predictable schedule of feedings about every three to four hours. By six months, your baby will consume 6 to 8 ounces (180–240 ml) at each of four or five feedings in twenty-four hours.

On average, your baby should consume about 2½ ounces (75 ml) of formula a day for every pound (453 g) of body weight. But he probably will regulate his intake from day to day to meet his own specific needs, so let him tell you when he's had enough. If he becomes fidgety or easily distracted during a feeding, he's probably finished. If he drains the bottle and continues smacking his lips, he might still be hungry. There are high and low limits, however. If your baby consistently seems to want more or less, discuss this with your pediatrician. Your baby should usually drink no more than an average of about 36 ounces (960 ml) of formula in twenty-four hours, although this is not a strict maximum. Some babies have higher needs for sucking and may just want to suck on a pacifier after feeding.

Initially it is best to offer formula-fed newborns a bottle on demand, or whenever they cry with hunger. As time passes, your baby will begin to develop a fairly regular timetable of his own. As you become familiar with his signals and needs, you'll be able to schedule his feedings around his routine.

Between two and four months of age (or when they weigh more than 12 pounds [5.4 kg]), most babies no longer need middle-of-the-night feedings. They're consuming more during the day, and their sleeping patterns have become more regular (although this varies considerably from baby to baby). Their stomach capacity has increased, too, which means they may go longer between daytime feedings—occasionally up to four or five hours. If your baby still seems to feed frequently or consume larger amounts, try distracting him with play or

WHERE WE STAND

THE AMERICAN ACADEMY OF PEDIATRICS believes that healthy children receiving a normal, well-balanced diet do not need vitamin supplementation over and above the recommended dietary allowances, which includes 400 IU (10 mcg) of vitamin D a day for infants less than one year of age and 600 IU (15 mcg) a day for children over one year of age. Megadoses of vitamins—for example, large amounts of vitamins A, C, or D—can produce toxic symptoms, ranging from nausea to rashes to headaches and sometimes even more severe effects. Talk with your pediatrician before giving vitamin supplements to your child.

TOO MUCH FEEDING

Some signs that your baby may be overfeeding:

- If bottle-fed, the baby is consuming more than 4 to 6 ounces (120 to 180 ml) per feeding.

- She vomits most or all of the food after a complete feeding.

- Her stools are loose and very watery, and occur eight or more times a day. (Keep in mind that breastfed babies normally tend to have much more frequent and looser stools.)

TOO LITTLE FEEDING

Some signs that your baby may be underfeeding:

- If breastfed, the baby falls asleep while feeding after a short time, and does not seem satisfied after the feeding.

- She wets fewer than four diapers per day; particularly if she has begun sleeping through the night, she may be feeding inadequately (since most babies feed at least once during the night), and may urinate less often and become mildly dehydrated.

- She has infrequent or very hard stools in the first month.

- She appears hungry, searching for something to suck shortly after feedings.

- She becomes more yellow, instead of less, during the first week.

- She seems excessively sleepy or lethargic.

FEEDING ALLERGY OR DIGESTIVE DISTURBANCE

Signs of a feeding allergy or problem with digestion:

- Your baby vomits most or all food after a complete feeding.

- She produces loose and very watery stools eight or more times a day or has blood in the stools.

- She has a severe skin rash.

a pacifier. Sometimes patterns of obesity begin during infancy, so it is important not to overfeed your baby.

The most important thing to remember, whether you breastfeed or bottle-feed, is that your baby's feeding needs are unique. No book can tell you precisely how much or often he needs to be fed or exactly how you should handle him during feedings. You will discover these things as you and your baby get to know each other.

Supplementation for Breastfed and Bottle-Fed Infants
Vitamin Supplements

Breast milk (also known as *human milk*) contains a natural balance of vitamins, especially C, E, and the B vitamins, so if you and your baby are both healthy, and you are well nourished, your child may not require any supplements of these vitamins.

Breastfed infants need supplemental vitamin D. This vitamin is naturally manufactured by the skin when exposed to sunlight. However, the American Academy of Pediatrics feels strongly that all children should be kept out of the direct sun as much as possible and wear sunscreen while in the sun to avoid the long-term risks of sun exposure, which may contribute to skin cancer. Sunscreen keeps the skin from manufacturing vitamin D. Talk to your pediatrician about supplemental vitamin D drops. The current Academy recommendation is that all infants and children should have a minimum intake of 400 IU (10 mcg) of vitamin D per day beginning soon after birth, with 600 IU (15 mcg) per day in children over age one. Prepared formula has vitamin D added to it, so if your baby is drinking formula, vitamin D supplementation is usually not needed. Your baby may need vitamin supplements if born prematurely or if he has certain other medical problems. Discuss the need for supplements of vitamins or minerals with your doctor.

A regular, well-balanced diet should provide all the vitamins necessary for both nursing mothers and their babies. However, pediatricians recommend that mothers continue taking a daily multivitamin supplement to ensure the proper nutritional balance. If you are on a strict vegetarian diet, you need to take an extra B-complex supplement, since certain B vitamins are available only from meat, poultry, or fish products. If your baby is on infant formula, he generally will receive adequate vitamins because formula has added vitamins.

Iron Supplements

Most babies are born with sufficient reserves of iron to protect them from anemia. If your baby is breastfed, weighs more than approximately 5½ pounds (2.5 kg) at birth, and is not receiving medical care as a newborn in a NICU, then there is sufficient, well-absorbed iron and no additional supplement is necessary until four months of age. Premature or low-birth-weight infants have lower iron stores and usually begin supplementation within two weeks after birth. The AAP recommends beginning iron supplementation at four months of age for breastfeeding infants (formula contains extra iron). When she is about six months old, you should be starting your breastfed infant on baby foods with supplemental iron (cereals, meats, green vegetables), further guaranteeing sufficient iron for proper growth. The best way to prevent iron deficiency during infancy is to allow the umbilical cord time to pulsate after birth for at least thirty to sixty seconds before clamping and cutting. You should speak with your obstetrician about this practice before delivery.

If bottle-feeding, it is recommended that you use iron-fortified formula (containing from 4 to 12 mg per liter of iron) from birth through the entire first year. Premature babies have fewer iron stores, so they often need additional iron beyond what's found in breast milk or formula and should be started on iron supplementation by two weeks of age.

Water and Juice

Until your baby starts eating solid foods, he'll get all the water he needs from breast milk or formula. In the first six months, additional water or juice is not needed for breastfed or bottle-fed infants. After six months, you may offer small amounts of water in a cup, but don't force it or worry if he rejects it. He may prefer to get the extra liquid from more frequent feedings. Juice is not recommended for babies in the first year. It is much healthier for infants to eat fruit and drink water instead of drinking juice.

Once your baby is eating solid foods, his need for liquid will increase. Getting your infant used to the taste of water is a healthy habit that will last a lifetime. When infants become used to drinking juice instead of water, they may want only sweet drinks as they get older, which has been associated with overweight and obesity.

Your baby may need extra fluids when ill, especially when a fever, vomiting, or diarrhea is present. The best fluid for a breastfed infant who is ill is breast milk. Ask your pediatrician what liquids are best and how much to give at these times.

WHERE WE STAND

THE AMERICAN ACADEMY OF PEDIATRICS recommends fruit juice not be given to infants under twelve months of age, since it offers no nutritional benefit in this age group and may increase risk of tooth decay while causing preference for sweeter flavors instead of plain water. For children older than twelve months, fruit juice offers no nutritional benefits over whole fruit, but 4 ounces of juice per day given as part of a meal may be a reasonable option. Whole fruits also provide fiber and other nutrients. Children should not be given fruit juice at bedtime, nor as a treatment for dehydration or management of diarrhea. For children ages one to six years old, limit fruit juice consumption to 4 to 6 ounces (120–180 ml) each day.

Fluoride Supplements

Fluoride is a naturally occurring mineral that strengthens your child's enamel and prevents tooth decay. Babies under six months should *not* receive fluoride supplementation. After that time, breastfed and formula-fed infants need appropriate fluoride supplementation if local drinking water contains less than 0.3 parts per million (ppm) of fluoride. If you have well water, have the well tested to determine the amount of natural fluoride in the water. If your baby consumes bottled water or your home has a municipal water supply, check to see if the water is fluoridated. If your family prefers bottled water, you should consider purchasing water marketed for babies with fluoride added (sometimes called "nursery water"). It is available in the baby food aisle and can be used when mixing formula.

Your pediatrician or pediatric dentist can advise you on whether there is a need for fluoride drops and prescribe the appropriate dosage. Formula-fed infants receive some fluoride from their formula if the drinking water is fluoridated. The American Academy of Pediatrics recommends that you check with your pediatrician or pediatric dentist to find out if any additional fluoride supplements are necessary.

Remember, appropriate fluoride supplementation is based on each child's unique needs. A supplement should be considered by you and your doctor until all of a child's permanent teeth are present in the mouth.

Burping, Hiccups, and Spitting Up

Burping

Young babies naturally fuss and get cranky when they swallow air during feedings. Although this occurs in both breastfed and bottle-fed infants, it's seen more often with the bottle. When it happens, it may be helpful to stop the feeding rather than letting your infant fuss and feed at the same time. Continued fussing will cause her to swallow even more air, which only increases her discomfort and may make her spit up.

One thing you can try is to burp her frequently, even if she shows no discomfort. The pause and the change of position alone will slow her gulping and reduce the amount of swallowed air. If she's bottle-feeding, burp her after every 2 to 3 ounces (60–90 ml). If she's nursing, burp her when she switches breasts. Some breastfed babies don't swallow very much air and therefore they may not need to burp.

Hiccups

Most babies hiccup from time to time. Usually this bothers parents more than the infant, but if hiccups occur during a feeding, change his position, try to get him to burp, or help him relax. Wait until the hiccups are gone to resume feeding. If they don't disappear in five to ten minutes, try to resume feeding for a few minutes. Doing this usually stops them. If your baby gets hiccups often, try to feed him when he's calm and before he's extremely hungry. This will usually reduce the likelihood of hiccups occurring during the feeding.

Spitting Up

Spitting up is another common occurrence during infancy. Sometimes it means your baby has eaten more than her stomach can hold; sometimes she spits up while burping or drooling. Although it may be a bit messy, it's usually no cause for concern. It almost never involves choking, coughing, discomfort, or danger to your child, even if it occurs while she's sleeping. Know that even if your baby has frequent spit-ups, the best position for sleep is on her back and with the mattress flat, not elevated.

Some babies spit up more than others, but most are out of this phase by the time they are sitting. A few heavy spitters will continue until they start to walk or are weaned to a cup. Some may continue throughout their first year.

How Do You Burp a Baby?

Here are a few tried-and-true techniques. After a little experimentation, you'll find which ones work best for your child.

- Hold the baby upright with his head on your shoulder to support his head and back while you gently pat his back with your other hand.

- Sit the baby on your lap, supporting his chest and head with one hand while patting his back with your other hand.

- Lay the baby on your lap with his back up. Support his head so it is higher than his chest, and gently pat or rotate your hand on his back.

If he still hasn't burped after several minutes, continue feeding him and don't worry; no baby burps every time. When he's finished, burp him again and keep him in an upright position for ten to fifteen minutes so he doesn't spit up.

It is important to know the difference between spitting up and true vomiting. Unlike spitting up, which most babies don't even seem to notice, vomiting is forceful and usually causes great distress and discomfort for your child. It generally occurs soon after a meal and produces a much greater volume than spitting up. If your baby vomits on a regular basis (one or more times a day) or if you notice blood or a bright green color in your baby's vomit, consult your pediatrician. (See *Vomiting*, page 555.)

Developing the Right Attitude

You can do it! This should be your attitude about breastfeeding from the beginning. There's plenty of help available, and you should take advantage of expert advice, counseling, classes, and group meetings available. For example, you can:

■ Talk to your obstetrician and pediatrician. They can provide not only medical information but also encouragement and support when you need it most.

■ Talk to your prenatal instructors and attend a breastfeeding class; invite your partner to come with you.

■ Watch online videos and talk to women who have breastfed or are breastfeeding successfully and ask their advice. Sisters, sisters-in-law, cousins, office mates, yoga instructors, and fellow congregants at your place of worship are precious resources.

■ Talk to members of La Leche League or other mother-to-mother support groups in your community. La Leche League is a worldwide organization dedicated to helping families learn about and enjoy the experience of breastfeeding. Information and support for parents is available at llli.org.

■ See if there is a Baby Café in your area. Find out at babycafeusa.org/your -nearest-baby-cafe.html.

■ Read about breastfeeding. A recommended book is the American Academy of Pediatrics' *New Mother's Guide to Breastfeeding*, ed. J. Y. Meek, 3rd ed. (New York: Bantam Books, 2017).

(For more information on breastfeeding, visit healthychildren.org.)

While it is practically impossible to prevent all spitting up, the following tips will help you decrease the frequency and amount of spit-up.

■ Make each feeding calm, quiet, and leisurely.

■ Avoid interruptions, sudden noises, bright lights, and other distractions during feedings.

- Burp your bottle-fed baby at least every three to five minutes during feedings.

- Avoid feeding while your infant is lying down.

- Hold the baby in an upright position for twenty to thirty minutes after each feeding.

- Do not jostle or play vigorously with the baby immediately after feeding.

- Try to feed her before she gets frantically hungry.

- If bottle-feeding, make sure the hole in the nipple is neither too big (which lets the formula flow too fast) nor too small (which frustrates your baby and causes her to gulp air). If the hole is the proper size, a few drops should come out when you invert the bottle, and then stop.

As you can tell from the length and detail of this chapter, feeding your baby is one of the most important and, at times, confusing challenges you'll face as a parent. The recommendations in this section apply to infants in general. Please remember that your child is unique and may have special needs. If you have questions that these pages have not answered to your satisfaction, ask your pediatrician to help you find the answers that apply specifically to you and your infant.

~ 5 ~

Your Baby's First Days

AFTER MONTHS OF PREGNANCY, you may believe you already know your baby. You've felt her kicks, monitored her quiet and active periods, and run your hands over your abdomen as she nestled in the womb. Although all of this brought you closer to her, nothing can prepare you for the sight of her face and the grip of her fingers around yours.

For the first few days after her birth, you may not be able to take your eyes off her. Watching her, you may see hints of yourself or other family members. But despite any distinct resemblance, she is uniquely special—unlike anyone else. And she'll have a personality all her own that may start making itself known immediately.

Some babies waste no time protesting wet diapers from day one and complain loudly until they are changed, fed, and rocked back to sleep. Infants who behave like this not only tend to spend more time awake than other babies, but also may cry and eat more. Other newborns won't seem to notice when their diapers are dirty and may be more likely to object to an exposed bottom during changes. These babies tend to sleep more and eat less frequently than their more sensitive counterparts. These kinds of differences are normal and can serve as hints of your child's personality.

Some mothers say that after so many months in their wombs, it is difficult to view their baby as a separate human being, with thoughts, emotions, and desires of her own. Making this adjustment and respecting their baby's individuality, however, are important parts of being a parent. If parents identify their child's uniqueness, they'll have a much easier time accepting the person she will become in the years ahead.

Your Newborn's First Days

How Your Newborn Looks

As you relax with your baby, unwrap her blankets and examine her from head to toe. You'll notice many details that may have escaped you in the moments after birth—eye color, for instance. While many Caucasian newborns have blue eyes, this may change over the first year. If a baby's eyes are going to turn brown, they'll probably become "muddy"-looking during the first six months;

however, if they're still blue at that time, they'll probably remain so. In contrast, infants with dark-skinned heritage generally have brown eyes at birth, and tend to retain that color throughout life.

You may notice a blood-red spot in the whites of one or both of your newborn's eyes. This spot, as well as the general puffiness of a newborn's face, is most commonly caused by pressures exerted during labor. Although you might find them a bit worrisome, both tend to fade in a few days. If your baby was delivered by C-section, she may not have this puffiness and the whites of her eyes likely will not have any red spots.

At birth your baby's skin will seem very delicate. Whether your child is born early, late, or on time, peeling skin is normal and usually requires no treatment. All babies, including those with a dark-skinned heritage, have lighter-appearing skin at birth. This gradually darkens as they become older.

As you examine your baby's shoulders and back, you may notice fine hair, called lanugo. This hair is produced toward the end of pregnancy; however, it's usually shed before birth or soon thereafter. If your baby was born before her due date, she is more likely to still have this hair, and it may take a couple of weeks to disappear.

You also may notice various spots and marks on your baby's skin. Some, like those appearing around the diaper edges, may be due to pressure. Mottled or blotchy-looking patches are commonly caused by exposure to cool air and will disappear quickly if you cover her again. If you find scratches, particularly on your baby's face, it's a good reminder it's time to trim her fingernails. For some new parents, this can be a nerve-racking task, so don't hesitate to ask advice from a nurse at the hospital nursery, your pediatrician's office, or anyone else with experience trimming babies' nails.

The following are the most common skin markings in newborns:

SALMON PATCHES OR "STORK BITES." Distributed over areas where a stork supposedly would carry a baby in its beak, "stork bites" are patches, light to deep pink in color, most commonly located on the bridge of the nose, lower forehead, upper eyelids, back of the head, and/or the neck. They are the most common birthmark, especially in light-skinned babies. Also called "angel kisses," they typically fade over the first few months to years but may become apparent later in life with flushing.

SLATE GRAY MACULES. These birthmarks vary considerably in size, but all are flat areas of skin containing extra pigment, causing a brown, gray, or even blue (like a bruise) appearance. Most often located on the back or buttocks, these spots are very common, especially in dark-skinned babies. They usually disappear before school age and are of no medical significance.

PUSTULAR MELANOSIS. These are small blisters that typically appear at birth, then peel and dry up within a couple of days, leaving dark spots like freckles that usually disappear over several weeks. Some newborns may have only the spots, indicating they had the rash before birth. While pustular melanosis is common (particularly in babies with darker skin) and is a harmless newborn rash, it is always important to have all blister-like rashes evaluated by your baby's doctor to rule out infection.

MILIA. These tiny white bumps or yellow spots are found on the cheeks, on the chin, or across the tip of the nose, and are caused by skin gland secretion. This common newborn rash generally disappears on its own within the first two to three weeks after birth.

MILIARIA. Often referred to as "heat rash" or "prickly heat," miliaria most often occurs in hot, humid climates or when babies are too bundled up. The rash can contain tiny sweat blisters and/or small red bumps. It shows up most often in skin folds and covered areas, and usually goes away within a few days.

ERYTHEMA TOXICUM. Often called "E. tox" for short, this rash is very common and usually appears within the first few days after birth. It consists of multiple red splotches with yellowish white bumps in the center, which come and go days after birth and completely resolve in a week or so.

CAPILLARY HEMANGIOMAS. These raised red spots are caused by a strawberry-like collection of blood vessels in the skin. For the first week or so, they may appear white or pale, then turn red and raised later. While they often enlarge during the first year, most shrink and many disappear by school age.

PORT WINE STAIN. These large, flat, and irregularly shaped dark red or purple areas are caused by extra blood vessels under the skin. Port wine stains are usually located on the face or neck but, unlike hemangiomas, don't disappear without treatment. These birthmarks can be treated, sometimes with laser surgery, by either a plastic surgeon or a pediatric dermatologist. (See also *Birthmarks and Hemangiomas*, page 847.)

When born, babies may have an elongated shape of their head, and may also have scalp swelling in the area pushed out first during birth. If you press gently on this area, your finger may even leave a small indentation. This swelling (called "caput") is not serious and should disappear in a few days.

Sometimes there may be swelling under a newborn's scalp, present on one or both sides, which is firm or springs right back after it is gently pressed. This type of swelling is likely a *cephalohematoma*, and is caused by the intense pressure on the head during labor. While not serious, it represents some bleeding along the outer side of the skull bones—(not inside the brain) and usually takes six to ten weeks to disappear.

All babies have two soft spots, or fontanelles, on the head. These are the areas where the immature bones of the skull are still growing together. The larger opening is toward the front; a smaller one is at the back. Parents needn't be afraid to touch these areas gently, as there is a thick, durable membrane that protects the brain.

Babies are born with hair, but the amount, texture, and color vary from one newborn to another. Most, if not all, "baby hair" falls out during the first six months and is replaced by mature hair. The color and texture of the mature hair may be different from the hair the baby was born with.

In the first few weeks following birth, babies can be affected by their mother's hormones they were exposed to during pregnancy. As a result, babies' breasts may be enlarged temporarily, and they might even secrete a few drops of milk. This is normal. It may occur in boys and girls, and normally lasts less than a week, although it can last longer. It is best not to press or squeeze a baby's breasts, since this won't reduce swelling and could cause irritation. In infant girls, there could be a discharge from the vagina, often white mucus and sometimes containing a little blood. Although disconcerting to some new parents, this so-called pseudomenses is harmless.

Your baby's abdomen may seem prominent, and you may even notice a small area that seems to bulge during crying spells. This bulge is called a hernia. Small hernias are most commonly seen around the umbilical cord (belly button) but may also appear in a line down the center of the abdomen. (For more information, see *Umbilical Hernia* on page 158 of this chapter.)

The genitals of newborn babies can be reddish and seem large for bodies so small. The scrotum of a baby boy may be small and smooth, or it might be large and wrinkled. The testicles can appear to move in and out of the scrotum, and sometimes will move as far up as the base of the penis or even to the crease between the thigh and belly. As long as the testicles are located in the scrotum most of the time, the fact that they move around is normal.

Some boys have a buildup of fluid in a sac called a hydrocele (see page 552) inside the scrotum. This buildup will shrink gradually without treatment over several months as the fluid is reabsorbed by the body. If the scrotum swells suddenly or gets larger when he cries, notify your pediatrician; this could be a sign of an inguinal hernia, which requires treatment.

At birth, a baby boy's foreskin is attached to the head, or glans, of the penis, and cannot be pushed back as it can in older boys and men. There is a small opening at the tip through which urine flows. If the baby is circumcised, the connections between the foreskin and the glans are separated and the foreskin is removed, leaving the head of the penis visible. Without a circumcision, the foreskin will separate from the glans naturally during the first few years. (For a detailed description of circumcision, see *Should the Baby Be Circumcised?* on page 28.)

Care of the Penis

Circumcised Penis: The circumcision procedure usually will be performed in the hospital prior to discharge, but it may be done after discharge during the first weeks at the discretion of your pediatrician (see *Should the Baby Be Circumcised?* on page 28). Ritual circumcisions for religious reasons are usually performed in the second week. After the procedure, a light dressing with petroleum jelly may be placed over the head of the penis. Some pediatricians recommend keeping a clean dressing over the area until the penis is fully healed, while others advise leaving it off. The important thing is to keep the area clean. If stool gets on the penis, wipe it gently with soap and water.

The tip of the penis may look red for the first few days, and you may notice a yellow secretion. Both indicate that the area is healing normally. The redness and secretion disappear gradually within a week. If the redness persists or there are swelling or crusted yellow sores, there may be an infection. This does not happen often, but if you suspect an infection, consult your pediatrician.

After the circumcision has healed, usually the penis requires no additional care. Occasionally a small piece of foreskin remains. You should pull back this skin gently each time the child is bathed. Examine the groove around the head of the penis and make sure it's clean.

If circumcision is desired but is not performed within the baby's first two weeks (perhaps for medical reasons), it is usually put off for several weeks or months. The follow-up care is the same whenever it is done. Should circumcision become necessary after the newborn period, general anesthesia is often used and requires a more formal surgical procedure with control of bleeding and suturing of skin edges.

Uncircumcised Penis: In the first few months, you should simply clean and bathe your baby's uncircumcised penis with soap and water, like the rest of the diaper area. Initially, the foreskin is connected by tissue to the glans, or head, of the penis, so you shouldn't try to retract it. No cleansing with cotton swabs or antiseptics is necessary.

The doctor will tell you when the foreskin has separated and can be retracted safely. This will not be for several months or years, and should never be forced; if you force the foreskin to retract before it is ready, you could cause painful bleeding and tears in the skin. After natural separation occurs, retract the foreskin regularly to gently cleanse the end of the penis.

As your son gets older, you'll need to teach him what he must do in order to urinate and wash his penis. Teach him to clean his foreskin by:

■ Gently pulling it back away from the head of the penis.

■ Rinsing the head of the penis and inside fold of the foreskin with soap and warm water.

■ Pulling the foreskin back over the head of the penis.

Your Baby's Birth Weight and Measurements

What makes a baby big or small? The following are some of the most common causes:

LARGE BABIES. A baby may be born large for a number of reasons, including:

■ Being born to large parents

■ Excessive maternal weight gain during pregnancy

■ A pregnancy that lasts longer than forty-two weeks

■ Overstimulation of the fetus's growth in the uterus

■ Fetal chromosomal abnormalities

■ The mother's ethnicity

■ Diabetes in the mother before or during pregnancy

■ The mother has given birth to other children, often each baby weighs more than the one before it

Large babies may have metabolic abnormalities (such as low blood sugar and calcium), traumatic birth injuries, higher hemoglobin levels, jaundice, or various congenital abnormalities. Almost one-third of large babies initially have feeding difficulties. Your pediatrician will keep a close watch on these issues.

SMALL BABIES. A baby may be born small for a number of reasons, including:

- Being born early (preterm)

- Being born to small parents

- The mother's ethnicity

- Fetal chromosomal abnormalities

- Inadequate weight gain in pregnancy

- The mother's chronic diseases such as high blood pressure, or heart or kidney disease

- Placental issues leading the baby to be undernourished

- The mother's alcohol or substance use during pregnancy

- The mother's smoking during pregnancy

A small baby may need to have temperature, blood glucose, and hemoglobin level closely monitored. After birth, the pediatrician will thoroughly evaluate a small infant and decide when she is ready to go home.

To compare your baby's measurements with those of other babies born after the same length of pregnancy, your pediatrician will use growth charts (see Appendix).

As illustrated in the first two growth charts, eighty of one hundred babies born at forty weeks of pregnancy (full term) weigh between 5 pounds 11½ ounces (2.6 kg) and 8 pounds 5¾ ounces (3.8 kg). This is a healthy average. Those above the 90th percentile are considered large, those below the 10th percentile small. Keep in mind that these early weight designations (large or small) do not predict a child's size as an adult, but they do help determine whether she needs extra attention during the first few days after birth. Head circumference and length will also be measured and compared to growth charts.

At every physical exam, the pediatrician will measure the baby's length, weight, and head circumference and will plot them on growth charts similar to the ones in the Appendix. In a healthy, well-nourished infant, these three measurements should increase at a predictable rate. Any interruption in this rate can help the doctor detect and address any feeding, developmental, or medical issues.

How Your Newborn Behaves

Lying in your arms or in the crib beside you, your newborn makes a tight little bundle. Just as she did in the womb, she'll keep her arms and legs close to her body and her fists tightly clenched, although you should be able to gently straighten them. Her feet will naturally curve inward. It may take several weeks for her body to unfold from this preferred fetal position.

You'll have to wait even longer to hear the cooing or babbling we think of as "baby talk." However, from the beginning she'll be very noisy. Besides crying when something is wrong, she'll have a wide variety of grunts, squeaks, sighs, sneezes, and hiccups. (You may even remember the hiccups from pregnancy!) Many of these sounds, just like her sudden movements, are reactions to disturbances around her; a shrill sound or strong odor may be all it takes to make her jump or cry.

These reactions, as well as more subtle ones, are signs of how your baby's senses are functioning. After months in the womb, she'll quickly recognize her mother's voice (and possibly her father's as well). If you play soothing music, she may become quiet as she listens, or she may move gently in time with it.

By using smell and taste, your newborn is able to distinguish breast milk from other liquids. Breast milk is naturally sweet and will appeal to a baby's sweet tooth.

Your baby's vision will be best within an 8- to 12-inch (20.3–30.5 cm) range, which means she can see your face as you hold and feed her. When you are farther away, her eyes may wander, giving her a cross-eyed appearance. Don't worry about this in the first couple of months. Between two and three months of age, her eye muscles will mature, her vision will improve, and both eyes will remain focused on the same thing more of the time. If this does not happen, bring it to the attention of your baby's pediatrician.

Able to distinguish light from dark at birth and see bright colors, your infant will not yet see the full range of colors. While young infants who are shown a pattern of black and white or sharply contrasting colors may study them with interest, they are not likely to respond at all to a picture with closely related colors.

Perhaps the newborn's most important sense is touch. After months in the womb, your baby is now exposed to all sorts of new sensations—some harsh, some comforting. While she may cringe at a sudden gust of cold air, she loves the feel of being skin-to-skin with her parents, a soft blanket, and the warmth of your arms around her. Holding your baby gives her as much pleasure as it does you. It gives her a sense of security and comfort, and it tells her she is loved. Research shows that close emotional bonding actually promotes her growth and development.

Going Home

Most hospitals discharge you and your baby within forty-eight hours if you delivered vaginally. If you undergo a Cesarean section, you may stay at the facility for three or more days. If your baby is born in an alternative birthing center, you may go home within twenty-four hours. Nevertheless, just because a full-term, healthy infant *could* be discharged in less than forty-eight hours doesn't mean it should necessarily occur. The American Academy of Pediatrics believes that the health and well-being of the mother and her child are paramount. Since every child is different, the decision to discharge a newborn should be made on a case-by-case basis.

If a newborn does leave the hospital early, she should still receive all the appropriate newborn tests and measures, such as a hearing screen, newborn metabolic tests, vitamin K administration, antibiotic eye ointment, heart screening, and hepatitis B vaccine (see *Newborn Screening Tests*, page 56), and be seen by the pediatrician twenty-four to forty-eight hours after discharge. The doctor should be called sooner if a newborn appears listless or is feverish, is vomiting, or has difficulty feeding, or if her skin develops a yellow color (jaundice).

Before you leave the hospital, your home and car should be equipped with at least the bare essentials. Make sure you have a federally approved car safety seat appropriate for your baby's size, and that it's correctly installed, rear-facing in the backseat of your vehicle. It is extremely important to follow the car safety seat manufacturer's instructions on installation and proper use. If possible, get your car safety seat installation checked by a certified child passenger safety technician to ensure you've gotten it right. (For more information on the choice and proper use of car safety seats, see pages 495–507.)

At home you'll need a safe place (crib, bassinet, or portable crib) for the baby to sleep, plenty of diapers, and enough clothing and blankets to keep her warm and protected.

WHERE WE STAND

THE TIMING OF newborn hospital discharge should be a mutual decision between the parents and the physician caring for the infant. The American Academy of Pediatrics believes that the health and well-being of the mother and her baby should take precedence over financial considerations. Academy policy has established minimum criteria for discharge before forty-eight hours after birth: these include term delivery, appropriate growth, and normal physical examination. It often takes forty-eight hours for all of these criteria to be met. The Academy supports state and federal legislation based on AAP guidelines as long as physicians, in consultation with parents, have the final authority in determining when to discharge the patient.

Parenting Issues
Mother's Feelings

If you find your first few days with your baby to be a mixture of delight, pain, utter exhaustion, and—especially if this is your first child—some apprehension about your capabilities, take comfort: you are not alone.

You may be so excited about your new arrival that you don't even notice how tired and sore you are. In spite of the fatigue, it still may be difficult to fall asleep. If you deliver in a hospital and your baby is healthy, she will usually sleep in a hospital-supplied bassinet in your room. You should maximize your time breastfeeding and enjoying skin-to-skin care with your baby, but be careful not to fall asleep with her in your bed or in a chair.

When you or your partner are tired or going to sleep, put your baby back in the bassinet on her back. Swaddling or putting her in a sleep wrap may encourage sleeping apart from you. You may also ask the nursery staff to keep an eye on your baby while you rest or tend to personal care. Take advantage of your time in the hospital to rest, learn from the trained professionals, and let your body recover. If and when your anxiety levels peak, it can be difficult to believe you'll ever be an expert on baby care. However, once new parents have a few days to get used to routine baby care and get home, things usually start

You have just given birth to a wonderful new being, but also to a new awesome responsibility.

to fall into place. Remember you can rely on friends, family members, and your pediatrician for help and advice. (For more information about postpartum blues and depression, see the description on pages 151–52.)

If this is not your first child, there may be some questions on your mind, such as:

- *Will this new baby come between you and an older child?*
  This needn't happen, especially if you make a point of including your older child(ren) in your new routine. Toddlers are usually quite happy to retrieve a clean diaper, and older children often take pride in checking for hazards (e.g., stray toys) and making sure all visitors wash their hands before touching the new baby. As you become more comfortable with your daily routine, be sure to include special times with your older child.

- *Will you be able to give the same intensity of love to the new child?*
  In fact, each child is special and will draw out different responses and feelings from you. Even the birth order may influence the way you relate to each other. It is often helpful to think that "new" isn't "better" or "worse," but usually just . . . different. This concept is important for both you and your child(ren) to remember.

On a practical note, the prospect of taking care of multiple children may worry you. This only makes sense, but as greater time demands and fears of sibling rivalry loom, don't get overwhelmed. Given time and patience, every family member will settle into new roles.

If the newness, fatigue, and seemingly unanswerable questions push you to tears, don't feel bad. You won't be the first new mother to cry—or the last. The hormonal changes you experienced as an adolescent or during your menstrual cycles are minor compared to the hormonal shifts associated with birth. So blame it on hormones!

The emotional changes can sometimes lead mothers to experience sadness, fear, irritability, anxiety, or even anger toward their baby—feelings doctors call postpartum blues or baby blues. About three out of four new mothers experience this a few days after birth. Fortunately, these feelings tend to subside as quickly as they develop, typically lasting no more than several days.

Some new mothers, however, have such severe sadness, emptiness, apathy, and even despair that doctors categorize this as *postpartum depression*. They also may experience feelings of inadequacy and may begin to withdraw from family and friends. This may develop a few weeks after birth and affects about one out of ten new mothers. The symptoms can last many months (or even more than a year), worsen with time, and become so intense that these mothers may feel helpless and incapable of caring for their baby and other children; they may even worry about harming themselves or their baby. Even though they didn't give birth, fathers can also suffer from postpartum depression; they, too, should be alert to the signs and seek help early on.

Discuss your feelings with your partner, your extended family, and close friends. Allow them to relieve you of being the primary caregiver and try to

Do not be afraid to ask for help if your concerns seem too great to handle.

reduce your stress and anxiety by exercising and getting as much rest as possible. If this doesn't help and these feelings are severe and haven't subsided in about two weeks, talk to your obstetrician or pediatrician, or seek help from a mental health professional; counseling and/or antidepressant medications may be recommended (check in with your pediatrician if you're breastfeeding). Many pediatricians now screen for postpartum depression with a questionnaire at each well-child visit in the first six months.

Partner's Feelings

As a partner in parenting, your role is no less complicated than the mother's. No, you didn't carry the baby, but you did make adjustments physically and emotionally as the due date approached and preparations for the baby became all-important. On one hand, you may feel as if you had nothing to do with the birth; but on the other, this is your baby, too.

When the baby finally arrived, you may have been relieved as well as excited and awed. In witnessing your baby's birth, feelings of commitment and love that you had worried might never happen may have surfaced after all. You may also have experienced a greater admiration and love for the birth mother than ever before. At the same time, contemplating the responsibility of caring for this child for the next twenty years or longer may feel more than a little unnerving.

Depending on the hospital and your own schedule, you may have been able to room in with mother and/or child until it was time to go home. This helps you feel less like a bystander and more like a key participant, allowing you to get to know your baby right from the start. It also allows you to share an intense emotional experience with Mom.

If conflicting emotions persist, how should you deal with them? The best approach is to become actively involved in parenting. Once the entire family is home, you can—and should—help feed (if bottle-fed), diaper, bathe, and comfort your baby. Doing these jobs helps you to bond with your child and they are wonderful opportunities for the entire family to get to know, love, and welcome this new member home.

Siblings' Feelings

Older children may greet a new baby with open arms, closed minds, or a mixture of both. Their reaction will depend largely on their age and developmental level. For instance, there's little you can do to prepare a toddler for the changes that will come with a new sibling. To begin with, she may have been confused by the sudden disappearance of her parents when the baby was born. Visiting the hospital, she may have been frightened by the sight of her mother in bed, perhaps attached to intravenous tubing.

She may also be jealous that her parents are holding someone else instead of her, and she may misbehave or begin acting younger (insisting on wearing diapers or suddenly having accidents several months after being toilet trained). These are normal responses to stress and change, and the best way to respond is simply to give extra love and reassurance rather than to punish her. Also, try very hard to catch her "being good," so she gets attention for appropriate behaviors. Praise her for "acting like the big sister," letting her know that she, too, has an important new role to play. Tell her that there's plenty of room in your heart to love both her

and the new baby. Over time, her attachment to the baby will build. You'll want to supervise her with the baby at all times so she can learn how to behave safely around her new sibling.

If your older child is a preschooler, she will better understand what's happening. If you prepared her during pregnancy, you may have helped ease her confusion, if not her jealousy. She would have been able to understand the basic facts of the situation ("The baby is in Mommy's tummy"; "The baby will sleep in your old crib"), and she was probably very curious about this mysterious person.

If school-age, your child still needs to adapt to a new role. At the same time, she was probably fascinated by the process of pregnancy and childbirth and eager to meet the new baby. Once the infant arrives, she may become very proud and protective. Let her help take care of the little one at times, but don't forget she still needs time and attention herself.

Health Watch

Some physical conditions are common during the first couple of weeks after birth. If you notice any of the following in your baby, contact your pediatrician.

Let the older siblings know frequently that there's enough room and love in your heart for both children.

ABDOMINAL DISTENSION. Most babies' bellies normally stick out, especially after a large feeding. Between feedings, however, they should feel soft. If your child's abdomen feels swollen and hard, and if she has not had a bowel movement for more than one or two days or is vomiting, call your pediatrician. Most likely the problem is due to gas or constipation, but it also could signal a more serious intestinal problem.

BIRTH INJURIES. Babies can be injured during birth, especially if labor is long or difficult, or when babies are very large. While newborns recover quickly from some of these injuries, others persist. Occasionally a broken collarbone occurs, which will heal quickly. After a few weeks a small lump may form at the fracture site, but don't be alarmed; this is a sign that new bone is forming to mend the injury, and it will soon be as good as new.

Muscle weakness is another common birth injury during labor, caused by pressure or stretching of the nerves attached to the muscles. These muscles, usually weakened on one side of the face or one shoulder or arm, generally return to normal after several weeks. In the meantime, ask your pediatrician to show you how to nurse and hold the baby to promote healing.

BLUE BABY. Babies may have mildly blue or purple hands and feet, which is usually normal. If their hands and feet turn slightly blue from cold, they should return to pink as soon as they are warm. Occasionally the face, tongue, and lips may turn a little blue when the newborn is crying hard, but once she is calm, her color should quickly return to normal. However, persistently blue skin coloring is a sign the heart or lungs are not operating properly and the baby is not getting enough oxygen in the blood. Immediate medical attention is essential.

BOWEL MOVEMENTS. After birth, the staff will watch for your baby's first urination and bowel movement to make sure she has no problem with these important tasks. It may be delayed twenty-four hours or more. The first bowel movement or two will be black or dark green and very slimy. It is meconium, a substance that fills the infant's intestines before she is born. If your baby does not pass meconium in the first forty-eight hours, further evaluation is required to make sure that no problems exist in the lower bowel. On occasion, newborns have a little blood in their bowel movements. If it occurs during the first few days, it usually means the infant has a little crack in the anus from stooling. This is generally harmless, but even so, let your pediatrician know about any signs of blood to confirm the reason, since there are other causes that require further evaluation and treatment.

COUGHING. If the baby drinks very fast, she may cough and sputter; but this type of coughing should stop as soon as her feeding routine becomes familiar. This may also be related to how strongly or fast a breastfeeding mom's milk comes down. If she coughs persistently or routinely gags during feedings, consult the pediatrician. These symptoms could indicate an underlying problem in the lungs or digestive tract.

EXCESSIVE CRYING. All newborns cry, often for no apparent reason. If you've made sure that your baby is fed, burped, warm, and dressed in a clean diaper, the best tactic is probably to hold her and talk or sing to her until she stops. You cannot spoil a baby this age by giving her too much attention. If this doesn't work, wrap her snugly in a blanket or try some of the approaches listed on pages 168–69.

You'll become accustomed to your baby's patterns of crying. If it ever sounds peculiar—such as shrieks of pain—or if it persists for an unusual length of time, it could mean a medical problem. Call the pediatrician and ask for advice.

FORCEPS MARKS. When forceps are used during delivery, they can leave red marks or even superficial scrapes on a newborn's face and head. These generally disappear within a few days. Sometimes a firm, flat lump develops in one of these areas because of minor damage to the tissue under the skin, but this, too, will usually go away within two months.

JAUNDICE. Many normal, healthy newborns have a yellowish tinge to their skin, which is known as jaundice. It is caused by a buildup of bilirubin in the child's blood. Mild jaundice is harmless. However, if the bilirubin level continues to rise and is not treated, it can lead to brain injury. Jaundice tends to be more common in breastfed newborns, most often in those not nursing well; breastfeeding mothers should nurse at least eight to twelve times per day, which will produce enough milk and keep bilirubin levels low.

Phototherapy—or light treatment—can be delivered through different light sources , such as special lights or on a specialized light blanket with eyes covered for protection.

Jaundice first appears on the face, then the chest and abdomen, and finally the arms and legs in some instances. The whites of the eyes may also be yellow. Most hospitals now routinely screen newborns for jaundice twenty-four hours after birth using a painless handheld light meter. If the pediatrician suspects jaundice may be present—based on skin color as well as the baby's age and other factors—she may order a skin or blood test to definitively diagnose the condition. If jaundice develops before the baby is twenty-four hours old, a bilirubin test is *always* needed to make an accurate diagnosis. If you notice a sudden increase in jaundice when your baby is at home, contact your pediatrician. At three to five days old, newborns should be checked by a doctor or nurse, since this is the time bilirubin levels are highest; for that reason, infants discharged before they are seventy-two hours old should be seen by a pediatrician within two days of discharge. Some newborns need to be seen even sooner, including:

■ Those with a high bilirubin level before leaving the hospital

■ Those born early (more than two weeks before the due date)

■ Those who are not breastfeeding well

■ Those with considerable bruising and bleeding under the scalp, associated with labor and delivery

■ Those who have a parent or sibling who had high bilirubin levels and underwent treatment for it

An elevated bilirubin level can be treated with phototherapy, or light treatment. At either the hospital or home, an undressed infant is placed under special lights or on a specialized light blanket with eyes covered for protection. This kind of treatment can prevent the harmful effects of jaundice. In breastfed babies, jaundice may last for more than two to three weeks; in formula-fed babies, most cases go away by two weeks of age.

LETHARGY AND SLEEPINESS. Every newborn spends most of her time sleeping. As long as she wakes every few hours, eats well, seems content, and is alert part of the day, it's perfectly normal to sleep the rest of the time. But if she's rarely alert, does not wake up on her own for feedings, or seems too tired or uninterested to eat, you should consult your pediatrician. This lethargy—especially if it's a sudden change in her usual pattern—may be a symptom of a serious illness.

RESPIRATORY DISTRESS. It may take your baby a few hours after birth to form a normal breathing pattern, but then she should have no further difficulties. If she seems to be breathing in an unusual manner, it is most often due to blocked nasal passages. Using saline nasal drops, followed by suctioning the mucus from the nose with a bulb syringe, may fix the problem; both are available over the counter.

However, if your newborn shows any of the following warning signs, notify your pediatrician immediately:

■ Fast breathing (more than sixty breaths in one minute), although keep in mind that babies normally breathe more rapidly than adults

■ Retractions (sucking in the muscles between the ribs with each breath, so that her ribs stick out)

■ Flaring of her nose

■ Grunting while breathing

■ Persistent blue skin coloring

UMBILICAL CORD. You'll need to keep the stump of the umbilical cord clean and dry as it shrivels and eventually falls off. There is no need to use alcohol on the cord; just keep it clean. Meanwhile, a quick submersion bath is fine before the cord falls off, just dry the stump afterward. Also, keep the diaper folded below the cord to keep urine from soaking it. You may notice a few drops of blood on the diaper around the time the stump falls off; this is normal. But if the cord actively bleeds, call your baby's doctor immediately. If the stump becomes infected, it will require medical treatment. Although cord infections are uncommon, you should contact your doctor if you notice any of the following:

■ Foul-smelling yellowish discharge from the cord

■ Red skin around the base of the cord

■ Crying when you touch the cord or the skin next to it

The umbilical cord stump should dry and fall off by the time your baby is three weeks old. If it persists beyond that time, a doctor's visit is needed.

UMBILICAL GRANULOMA. Sometimes instead of completely drying, the cord will form a granuloma or a small reddened mass of scar tissue that stays on the belly button after the umbilical cord has fallen off. This granuloma will drain a light-yellowish fluid. This condition will usually go away in about a week, but if not, your pediatrician may need to burn off (cauterize) the granulomatous tissue.

UMBILICAL HERNIA. If your baby's umbilical cord area seems to push outward when she cries, she may have an umbilical hernia—a small hole in the muscular part of the abdominal wall that allows the tissue to bulge out when there is increased abdominal pressure (i.e., crying). This is not a serious condition, and it usually heals by itself in the first twelve to eighteen months. (For unknown reasons it often takes longer to heal in African American babies.) In the unlikely event it doesn't heal by three to five years of age, the hole may need surgery. Don't put tape or a coin on the navel. It will not help the hernia, and it may cause a skin rash.

~ 6 ~

The First Month

Growth and Development

AT FIRST IT MAY seem your baby does nothing but eat, sleep, cry, and fill his diapers. By the end of the first month, he'll be much more alert and responsive. Gradually his movements will be smoother and more coordinated—especially in getting his hand to his mouth. You'll realize he listens when you speak, watches as you hold him, and occasionally moves in response to you or to attract your attention. But before we explore his expanding capabilities, let's look at the physical changes during the first month.

Physical Appearance and Growth

At birth, your baby's weight included excess body fluid. This fluid was lost during his first few days. Babies may lose up to one-tenth of their birth weight during the first seven days. Beginning on about the fifth day after birth they should start gaining steadily, and by about two weeks of age they should have returned to their original birth weight. You can plot your baby's growth on the charts in the Appendix.

Most babies gain weight very rapidly, especially during growth spurts, which occur at around seven to ten days and again between three and six weeks. The average newborn gains weight at a rate of ⅔ ounce (20–30 g) per day and by one month weighs about 10 pounds (4.5 kg), but these numbers can vary dramatically from one baby to the next. He grows between 1½ and 2 inches (4.5–5 cm) during this month. Boys tend to weigh slightly more than girls (by less than 1 pound [approximately 350 g]). They also tend to be slightly longer than girls at this age (by about ½ inch [1.25 cm]).

Your pediatrician will pay attention to your child's head growth, a reflection of brain growth. The bones in your baby's skull are growing faster during the first four months than at any other time in his life. The average newborn's head circumference measures about 13¾ inches (35 cm), growing to about 15 inches (38 cm) by one month. Boys' heads tend to be larger, though the average difference is less than ½ inch (1 cm).

During these first weeks your baby's body will straighten from the tightly curled position he held inside the uterus. He'll stretch his arms and legs and may arch his back from time to time. His legs and feet may continue to rotate inward, giving him a bowlegged look. This condition will usually correct itself over the first year. If the bowlegged appearance is severe or associated with pronounced curving of the front part of the foot, your pediatrician may suggest a splint or cast to correct it, though these circumstances are extremely unusual. (See *Bowlegs and Knock-Knees*, page 840; *Pigeon Toes [Intoeing]*, page 844.)

If your baby's skull appeared misshapen at birth, it will soon resume its normal shape. Any scalp bruising or eyelid swelling that occurred during birth will be gone by the end of the first week or two. Any red spots in the eyes will disappear in about three weeks.

You may discover that the fine hair that covered your child's head at birth begins falling out. He may develop a temporary bald spot on the back of his head from sleeping on his back, even if the rest of his hair remains. This loss is not medically significant. The bare spots will be covered with new hair in a few months.

Another normal development is baby "acne"—pimples that break out on the face, usually during the third to fifth week. Doctors once thought this was due to maternal hormones stimulating glands in babies' skin, but they now think it may be a normal response to bacteria on the skin, and it has been renamed neonatal cephalic pustulosis. If your baby does have baby acne, place a soft, clean receiving blanket under his head while he's awake and wash his face gently once a day with a mild baby soap to remove milk or detergent residue. In severe cases your pediatrician may prescribe a face cream.

Your newborn's skin may also look blotchy, ranging in color from pink to blue. His hands and feet in particular may be colder and bluer than the rest of his body, the blood vessels being more sensitive to temperature changes and tending to shrink in response to cold. If you move his arms and legs, however, they quickly turn pink again.

Your baby's internal "thermostat," which causes him to sweat or shiver, won't be working properly for some time. Also, in these early weeks, he'll lack the insulating layer of fat to help protect him from sudden temperature shifts. It's important to dress him properly—warmly in cool weather and lightly when hot. A general rule of thumb is to dress him in one more layer of clothing than you would wear in the same weather conditions. Don't automatically bundle him up because he's a baby.

Between ten days and three weeks after birth, the stump from the umbilical cord should have dried and fallen off, leaving behind a clean, well-healed area. Occasionally a raw spot is left, and it may even ooze a little blood-tinged fluid. Just keep it dry and clean and it will heal by itself. If it is not completely healed and dry after three weeks, consult your pediatrician.

Reflexes

Much of your baby's activity in his first weeks is reflexive, meaning that it is involuntary or happens without his intending it. If you put your finger in his mouth, he sucks reflexively. He will shut his eyes tightly to a bright light. Some reflexes remain with him for months, while others vanish in weeks.

In some cases, reflexes change into voluntary behavior. For example, your baby is born with a rooting reflex that prompts him to turn his head toward your hand if you stroke his cheek or mouth. This helps him find the nipple at feeding time. At first, he'll root from side to side, turning his head toward the nipple and then away in decreasing arcs. He'll simply move his head and mouth into position to suck.

Sucking is another survival reflex present even before birth. If you had an ultrasound during pregnancy, you may have seen your baby sucking his thumb. After birth, when a nipple and areola are placed deeply in your baby's mouth, he automatically begins to suck. This motion actually has two stages. First, he places his lips around the areola with the nipple far back in the mouth, pointed to the junction of the hard and soft palate, and compresses the breast between his tongue and palate (called "expression," this action forces the milk out). In the second phase, or milking action, the tongue moves from the areola to the nipple. This whole process is helped by the suction that secures the breast to the baby's mouth.

Coordinating these rhythmic sucking movements with breathing and swallowing is a relatively complicated task for a newborn. So even though this is a reflexive action, not all babies suck efficiently at first. With practice, however, the reflex becomes a skill that they all manage well.

Rooting, sucking, and bringing his hand to his mouth are considered feeding cues in the first weeks after birth. Later on, after breastfeeding is well established, your baby will start to use these movements to console himself, and may also be comforted by a pacifier or when you help him find his thumb or fingers.

A dramatic reflex during these first few weeks is the Moro reflex. If your baby's head shifts position abruptly or falls backward, or if he is startled by something loud or abrupt, he will extend his arms and legs and neck, then rapidly bring his arms together. He may even cry loudly. The Moro reflex, which is present in varying degrees in different babies, peaks during the first month and then disappears after two months.

A more interesting automatic response is the tonic neck reflex, or the fencing posture. You may notice that when your baby's head turns to one side, his corresponding arm will straighten, with the opposite arm bent, as if he's fencing. You may not see this response, however, since it is subtle, and if your baby is disturbed or crying, he may not perform it. It disappears at five to seven months of age.

Moro reflex

Both the Moro and tonic neck reflexes should be present equally on both sides of the body. If you note that the reflex seems different on one side, or that the baby moves one side of the body better than the other, tell your pediatrician.

Tonic neck reflex

Newborn Reflexes

The following are some normal inborn reflexes you will see during the first weeks. Not all infants acquire and lose these reflexes at exactly the same time, but this table will give you a general idea of what to expect.

Reflex	Age When Reflex Appears	Age When Reflex Disappears
Stepping	Birth	2 months
Rooting	Birth	4 months
Palmar grasp	Birth	5–6 months
Moro reflex	Birth	5–7 months
Tonic neck reflex	Birth	5–7 months
Plantar grasp	Birth	9–12 months

You'll see still another reflex when you stroke your baby's palm and watch him immediately grip your finger, or stroke the sole of his foot and watch his toes curl tightly. In the first few days after birth, your baby's grasp will be so strong it may seem he can hold his own weight—but don't try it. He has no control over this response and may let go suddenly.

Aside from strength, your baby's other special talent is stepping. He can't support his weight, of course, but if you hold him under the arms (being careful to support his head as well) and let his soles touch a flat surface, he'll place one foot in front of the other and "walk." This reflex will help a newborn crawl to the breast immediately after delivery when lying on his mother's abdomen. This reflex will disappear after two months, then recur toward the end of the first year as the learned behavior of walking.

Although you may think of babies as utterly defenseless, they actually have several protective reflexes. For instance, he'll turn his head and try to squirm out of the way of an incoming object. (Amazingly, if the object is on a near-miss path instead of a collision course, he will calmly watch it approach without flinching.)

Walking/stepping
reflex

Early Brain Development

As a parent, you know your actions affect your child. You laugh, he laughs. You frown at his misbehavior, he saddens. At six to eight weeks, he begins demonstrating social smiles. You are the center of your child's universe, and as your connection with him intensifies, his language and even the effects of your discipline increase.

Research shows during the first three years of a baby's life the brain grows and develops significantly. Holding your baby skin-to-skin in the early weeks is especially important for these early brain connections. Patterns of thinking and responding are established. This means you have a special opportunity to help your baby develop appropriately and thrive socially, physically, and cognitively throughout his life. The first years last forever.

For years, people mistakenly believed the baby's genetic code was an exact replica of the parents'—if, say, the mother is a good artist, then the baby has more potential to possess the same artistic skills when he grows up. While genetics do play a role in determining your child's skills and abilities, new research highlights the equally significant role of environment. Recently, neuroscientists realized that the experiences of a baby's first days, months, and years have a great impact on how the brain develops. Nature and nurture work hand in hand.

Studies have shown that children need certain elements in the early stages to grow and develop to their full potential:

- A child needs to feel special, loved, and valued.

- He needs to feel safe.

- He needs to feel confident about what to expect from his environment.

- He needs guidance.

- He needs a balanced experience of freedom and limits.

- He needs to be exposed to a diverse environment filled with language, play, exploration, books, music, and appropriate toys.

While it may seem that a baby's brain activity would be relatively simple compared to an adult's, in fact a baby's brain is twice as active as an adult's. Seven hundred new connections or synapses form every second. During the first three years, a time neuroscientists have identified as especially important, the human brain has the greatest potential for learning. Not only is learning occurring rapidly, but basic ways of thinking, responding, and solving problems are being established. For example, notice how easy it is for a child to pick up words in a foreign language. How difficult is that same task for an adult?

This means you and the environment you create will influence the way your baby deals with his emotions, the way he interacts with people, the way he thinks, and the way he grows physically. By creating an appropriate environment, you are allowing normal brain development to take place. An appropriate environment is one that is child-centered and provides learning opportunities geared to your child's development, interests, and personality. Fortunately, components of a good environment include basic things that many parents want to provide: proper nutrition; a warm, responsive, and loving family and other care providers; fun playtime; consistent positive reinforcement; engaging conversation; good books to read and to listen to; music to stimulate brain activities; and the freedom to explore and learn from his surroundings.

Review the following elements of children's health and how each one contributes to a child's brain development:

- *Language.* Direct face-to-face communication between parents (and other caregivers) and their young children supports language development, as does reading to them beginning in early infancy.

(continues on next page)

- *Early identification of developmental problems.* Many developmental and medical problems can be treated if detected early. Children with disabilities and other special healthcare needs also can greatly benefit from close monitoring of early brain development.

- *Positive parenting.* Raising a child in a loving, supportive, and respectful environment enhances self-esteem and self-confidence, and has a great impact on the child's development. Your parental nurturing and your responsiveness to your infant will play a critical role in shaping your baby's future.

- *Stimulating environment.* Exploring and problem-solving in a variety of safe places promote learning.

More and more behavioral researchers are discovering how much environment plays a role in shaping a baby's life. This new science helps us understand exactly how significant our role is in a child's brain development.

To build a positive environment for your baby in your home and in your community, follow these suggestions:

- *Get good prenatal care.* Since brain development begins in the womb, good prenatal care can help ensure the healthy development of your child's brain. Start prenatal care early, see your doctor regularly, and be sure to follow his instructions. Eating a balanced, healthy diet, taking prenatal vitamins, and avoiding drugs, alcohol, and tobacco are just a few steps you can take to contribute to your child's future health.

- *Try to create a "village" around you.* Since it's hard to raise a child on your own, seek support from your family, friends, and community. Talk to your pediatrician about parent support groups and activities.

- *Interact with your child as much as possible.* Talk with your child, read, listen to music, draw pictures, and play together. These kinds of activities allow you to spend time focused on your child's thoughts and interests, making your child feel special and important. You also can teach the language of communication that your child will use to form healthy relationships over a lifetime.

- *Give your child plenty of love and attention.* A warm and loving environment helps children feel safe, competent, and cared for, and it allows them to develop concern for others. Such attention cannot spoil a child.

- *Provide consistent routines.* Be sure you and other care providers are working with the same routines. Also, be sure your own guidelines are consistent while taking into account your child's growing competency. Consistency helps children feel confident about what to expect from their environment.

Your Baby's States of Consciousness

State	Description	What Your Baby Does
State 1	Deep sleep	Lies quietly without moving
State 2	Light sleep	Moves while sleeping; startles at noises
State 3	Drowsiness	Eyes start to close; may doze
State 4	Quiet alert	Eyes open wide; face is bright; body is quiet
State 5	Active alert	Face and body move actively
State 6	Crying	Cries, perhaps screams; body moves in very disorganized ways

Crying and Colic

From about two weeks on, infants cry. Some parents hesitate to pick up a crying baby, believing they'll spoil their child. But babies can't be spoiled, and their needs should be met as best as you can.

There are great variations in the crying patterns and temperaments of babies. Sometimes babies cry for no apparent reason, and it can be difficult to figure out what's behind the tears. As the crying persists, parents can understandably become upset and stressed out.

Does your baby have a regular fussy period each day when it seems nothing will comfort her? This is quite common, particularly between 6:00 p.m. and midnight—just when you, too, are feeling tired from the day. These periods of crankiness may feel like torture, especially if you have other demanding children or work to do, but fortunately they don't last long. The length of this fussing usually peaks at about three hours a day by six weeks and then declines to one or two hours a day by three to four months. As long as the baby calms within a few hours and is relatively peaceful the rest of the day, there's no reason for alarm.

However, if the crying intensifies and persists, it may be caused by colic. About one-fifth of all babies develop colic, usually between the second and fourth weeks. It may occur even after changing your baby's diaper, feeding her, or soothing her by cuddling, rocking, or walking. Colicky children cry inconsolably, often screaming, extending or pulling up their legs, and passing gas. The crying spells can occur around the clock, although they often become worse in the early evening.

Unfortunately, there is no definite explanation. Most often, colic means simply that the child is unusually sensitive to stimulation or cannot self-console or regulate his nervous system (also known as an immature nervous system). As he matures, this inability to self-console—marked by constant crying—will improve. Generally, colicky crying stops by three to four months, but it can last until six months. Sometimes, in breastfeeding babies, colic is a sign of food sensitivity in the mother's diet. The discomfort is caused only rarely by sensitivity to milk protein in formula. Colicky behavior also may signal a medical problem, such as a hernia or some type of illness.

Although you may simply have to wait it out, several things might be worth trying. First, of course, consult your pediatrician to make sure that the crying is not related to any serious medical condition that may require treatment. Then ask him which of the following would be most helpful.

- If you're nursing, you can try to eliminate milk products, soy, eggs, onions, cabbage, and any other potentially irritating foods from your own diet. This is a good thing to discuss first with your pediatrician, as a trial of elimination in your diet should be complete (checking all food products for the substance you are eliminating) and needs to be done for about two weeks before you can expect to see any changes. Be sure to eliminate only one thing at a time. If you're feeding formula to your baby, talk with your pediatrician about a protein hydrolysate formula. Less than 5 percent of colicky crying is due to food sensitivity, but in rare cases a change may help within a few days.

- Do not overfeed your baby, which could make him uncomfortable. In general, try to wait at least two to two and a half hours from the start of one feeding to the next. If you are breastfeeding and have a lot of milk, sometimes babies can get fussy. In these cases, if your baby can be satisfied by feeding on one breast only, it will help to regulate your milk supply and decrease gassiness in the baby (see page 115 for information on engorgement).

- Walk your baby in a baby carrier. The motion and body contact will re-assure her, even if her discomfort persists.

- Rock him, run the vacuum in the next room, or place him where he can hear the clothes dryer, a fan, or a white-noise machine. Steady rhythmic motion and a calming sound may help him fall asleep. However, never place your child *on top* of the washer/dryer.

- Introduce a pacifier. While some breastfed babies will actively refuse a pacifier, it will provide instant relief for others. (See page 178.)

- Lay your baby tummy down across your knees and gently rub his back. The pressure against his belly may help comfort him. If he falls asleep this way, you will want to place him in his crib on his back.

- Swaddle her in a large, thin blanket so that she feels secure and warm.

- When you're feeling tense and anxious, have a family member or a friend look after the baby—and get out of the house. Even an hour or two away will help you maintain a positive attitude. If no other adult is available to help, it's OK to lay the baby on his back in the crib or another safe place and leave the room for a few minutes. No matter how impatient or angry you become, a baby should *never* be shaken or hit. Shaking an infant hard can cause blindness, brain damage, or even death (see the box *Abusive Head Trauma: Shaken Baby Syndrome*). Let your own doctor know if you are depressed or are having trouble dealing with your emotions, as she can recommend ways to help.

Abusive Head Trauma: Shaken Baby Syndrome

Shaking a baby is a serious form of child abuse occurring mostly in infants in the first year. The act of severely or violently shaking a baby—which may also include striking the baby's head—is often the result of a parent's or caregiver's frustration or anger in response to a baby's or toddler's constant crying or irritability. Shaking or striking a baby's head can cause serious physical and mental damage, even death.

(continues on next page)

Serious injuries associated with abusive head trauma may include blindness or eye injuries, brain damage, damage to the spinal cord, and delay in normal development. Signs and symptoms may include irritability, lethargy (difficulty staying awake), tremors (shakiness), vomiting, seizures, difficulty breathing, and coma.

The American Academy of Pediatrics feels strongly that it is *never* OK to shake your baby. If you suspect that a care provider has shaken or hurt your baby—or if you or your spouse has done so in a moment of frustration—take your baby to the pediatrician or an emergency room immediately. Any brain damage that might have occurred will only get worse without treatment. Don't let embarrassment or fear keep you from getting treatment for your baby.

If you feel as if you might lose control when caring for your baby:

- Take a deep breath and count to ten.

- Put your baby in his crib or another safe place, leave the room, and let him cry alone for a few minutes.

- Call a friend or relative for emotional support.

- Give your pediatrician a call. Perhaps there's a medical reason your baby is crying.

The First Smile

A few of the most important developments during this month are your baby's first smiles and giggles. These start during sleep, for reasons not understood. They may signal that the baby feels aroused or is responding to some internal impulse. While it's great fun to watch a newborn smile his way through a nap, the real joy comes near the end of this month when he begins to grin back at you during his alert periods.

Those first loving smiles will help you tune in even more closely, and you'll soon discover you can predict a smile, a look, a sound, and, equally important, a pause from play. Gradually you'll recognize each other's patterns of responsiveness, so play becomes a kind of dance in which you take turns leading and following. By identifying and responding to your child's subtle signals, even at this young age, you are telling him that his thoughts and feelings are important and that he can affect the world around him. These messages are vital to his developing self-esteem and sense of fun.

Movement

For the first week or two, your baby's movements will be very jerky. His chin may quiver and his hands may tremble. He'll startle easily, when moved suddenly or from a loud sound, and the startling may lead to crying. If he appears overly sensitive to stimulation, he may be comforted if you hold him close or swaddle him tightly. There are even special blankets for swaddling small babies who are particularly difficult to console. (Babies should not be swaddled tightly when laid down to sleep, however.) But by the end of the first month, as his nervous system matures and his muscle control improves, these shakes and quivers give way to smoother arm and leg movements that can look like he's riding a bicycle. Lay him on his stomach now and he will make crawling motions with his legs and may even push up on his arms.

Movement Milestones for Your One-Month-Old

- Makes jerky, quivering arm thrusts
- Brings hands within range of eyes and mouth
- Moves head from side to side while lying on stomach
- Head flops backward if unsupported
- Keeps hands in tight fists
- Strong reflex movements

Your baby's neck muscles also will develop rapidly, giving him more control over his head movements. Lying on his stomach, he may lift his head and turn it from side to side. However, he won't be able to hold his head up independently until about three months, so make sure you support it when holding him.

Your baby's hands, a source of endless fascination throughout much of this first year, will probably catch his eyes during these weeks. His finger movements are limited, since his hands are likely clenched fists most of the time. But he can flex his arms and bring his hands to his mouth or into his line of vision. While he can't control his hands precisely, he'll watch them closely as long as they're in view.

Vision

Your baby's vision will go through many changes this first month. He was born with better peripheral vision (the ability to see to the sides) than central vision, but he'll gradually be able to focus on a single point in the center of his visual field. He likes to look at objects held about 8 to 12 inches (20.3–30.4 cm) in front of him, but by one month he'll focus briefly on things as far away as 3 feet (91 cm).

At the same time, he'll learn to follow, or track, moving objects. To help him practice, play tracking games with him. Move your head slowly from side to side as he faces you, or pass a patterned object up and down or side to side in front of him (making sure it's within his range of focus). At first, he may only

Your baby likes to look at objects held about 8 to 12 inches (20.3 to 30.4 cm) in front of him.

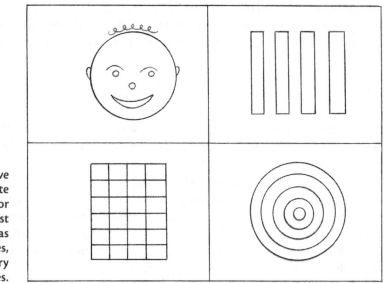

He is most attentive to black-and-white pictures or high-contrast patterns, such as stripes, bull's-eyes, checks, and very simple faces.

be able to follow large objects moving slowly through an extremely limited range, but soon he'll be tracking smaller, speedier movements.

At birth your baby was extremely sensitive to bright light, and his pupils were constricted. At two weeks, his pupils will begin to enlarge, allowing him to react to light. As his retinas develop, his ability to see and recognize patterns will also improve. Extremely sensitive babies will also cry when exposed to a very bright light. The more contrast in a pattern, the more it will attract a baby's attention, which is why babies are most attentive to black-and-white pictures or high-contrast patterns, such as stripes, bull's-eyes, checks, and very simple faces.

If you show your infant three identical toys, one blue, one yellow, and one red, he will probably look longest at the red one, although no one yet under-

Visual Milestones for Your One-Month-Old

- Focuses 8 to 12 inches (20.3–30.4 cm) away
- Eyes wander and occasionally cross
- Prefers black-and-white or high-contrast patterns
- Prefers the human face to all other patterns

stands why. Is it the color red itself? Or its brightness? We do know color vision doesn't fully mature until about four months, so if you show your baby related colors, such as green and turquoise, he probably can't tell the difference.

Hearing

Your baby should have had a hearing screen shortly after birth; in fact, the American Academy of Pediatrics recommends that newborn hearing screenings occur prior to discharge from the hospital, and parents should ask for the results. (See *Hearing Loss*, pages 659–63.)

Infants with normal hearing abilities will pay close attention to human voices during the first month, especially high-pitched ones speaking "baby talk." When you talk to him, he'll turn his head to search for you and listen closely. Watch carefully and you may even see him make subtle movements of his arms and legs in time with your speech.

Your infant also will be sensitive to noise levels. If you make a loud clicking sound in his ear or bring him into a noisy, crowded room, he may shut down, becoming as unresponsive as if he had heard nothing. Or he may be so sensitive that he startles, erupts into crying, and turns his entire body away from the noise. Substitute a soft rattle or quiet music and he'll become alert and turn to locate the source of this interesting sound.

Not only does your baby hear well, but he'll remember some of the sounds. As some research supports, some mothers who repeatedly read a story aloud late in their pregnancy have found that their babies seem to recognize the story when it is read to them again after birth—the babies became quiet and looked more attentive. Try reading your favorite children's story aloud for several days in a row when your baby is alert and attentive. Then wait a day or two before reading it again. Does he seem to recognize it?

Hearing Milestones for Your One-Month-Old

- Hearing is fully mature
- Recognizes some sounds
- May turn toward familiar sounds and voices

Smell and Touch

As with patterns and sounds, babies are also particular about tastes and smells. They will breathe deeply to catch a whiff of milk, vanilla, banana, or sugar, but will turn up their nose at the smell of alcohol or vinegar. By the end of their first week, if they're nursing, they'll turn toward their mother's breast but will ignore the breasts of other nursing mothers. This radar-like system directs them toward the source of food and warns them of substances that could harm them.

Babies are equally sensitive to touch and the way they're handled. They'll nestle into a soft piece of flannel but pull away from scratchy burlap. When they are stroked gently with a palm, they'll relax and become quiet. If picked up roughly, they'll probably take offense and start to cry. If rocked slowly, they'll become quiet and attentive. Holding, stroking, rocking, and cuddling will calm them when they're upset and make them more alert when they're drowsy. It also sends a clear message of a parent's love and affection. Long before they understand a word parents say, they'll understand parental moods and feelings from their touch.

Smell and Touch Milestones for Your One-Month-Old

- Prefers sweet smells
- Avoids bitter or acidic smells
- Recognizes the scent of his own mother's breast milk
- Prefers soft to coarse sensations
- Dislikes rough or abrupt handling

Temperament

Consider these two babies, both from the same family, both boys:

- The first baby is calm and quiet, happy to play by himself. He watches everything around him but rarely demands attention himself. Left on his own, he sleeps for long periods and eats infrequently.

■ The second baby is fussy and startles easily. He thrashes his arms and legs, moving almost constantly whether awake or asleep. While most newborns sleep fourteen hours a day, he sleeps only ten, and wakens to the slightest nearby activity. He seems in a hurry to do everything at once and even eats in a rush, gulping his feedings and swallowing so much air that he needs frequent burping.

Both these babies are absolutely normal and healthy. One is no "better" than the other, but because their personalities are so far apart, the two will be treated very differently from birth.

Your baby will demonstrate many unique personality traits from the earliest weeks after birth. Discovering these traits is one of the most exciting parts of having a baby. Is he active and intense, or slow-going? Is he timid when faced with a new situation, such as the first bath, or does he enjoy it? You'll find clues to his personality in everything he does, from falling asleep to crying. The more you pay attention and respond appropriately to his unique personality, the calmer and more predictable your life will be in the months to come.

While most of these early character traits are built into the newborn's hereditary makeup, their appearance may be delayed in babies born prematurely. Premature babies don't express their needs—such as hunger, fatigue, or discomfort—as clearly as other newborns. They may be extra sensitive to light, sound, and touch, and these stimuli may cause them to become fussy and look away. When this happens, it's up to the parent to stop and wait until the baby is alert and ready for more attention. Eventually most of these early reactions will fade away, and the baby's natural character traits will become more evident. Neonatal intensive care units are now using developmental care that promotes attachment, taking into account a newborn's states of alertness and responsiveness to hearing his mother's voice, and providing kangaroo care when the baby's condition is stable enough to do so safely.

Low-birth-weight babies—those who weigh less than 5½ pounds (2.5 kg) at birth—even if full-term, may also be less responsive than other newborns. At first, they may be very sleepy and not seem very alert. After a few weeks, they seem to wake up, eating eagerly but still remain restless and hypersensitive to stimulation between feedings. This sensitivity may last until they grow and mature further.

From the beginning, your baby's temperament will influence the way you treat him and feel about him. If you had specific ideas about child rearing, re-evaluate them now to see if they're in tune with his character. The same goes for expert advice—from books, articles, and especially from well-meaning relatives and friends about the "right way" to raise a child. The truth is, there is no single way that works for every child. You have to create your own guide-

Developmental Health Watch

If during the second, third, or fourth weeks after birth your baby shows any of the following signs, notify your pediatrician.

- Sucks poorly and feeds slowly

- Doesn't blink when shown a bright light

- Doesn't focus and follow a nearby object moving side to side

- Rarely moves arms and legs; seems stiff

- Seems excessively loose in the limbs or floppy

- Lower jaw trembles constantly, even when not crying or excited

- Doesn't respond to loud sounds

Toys Appropriate for Your One-Month-Old

- Mobile with highly contrasting colors and patterns

- Music players with soft music

- Soft, brightly colored, and patterned toys that make gentle sounds

lines based on your child's unique personality, your own beliefs, and the circumstances of your family life. The important thing is to remain responsive to your baby's individuality. Don't try to box him into some previously set mold or pattern. Your baby's uniqueness is his strength, and respecting that strength from the start will lay the best possible foundation for his self-esteem and for loving relationships with others.

Basic Care
Bowel Movements

You do not necessarily need to be concerned if your newborn has a bowel movement either every time he feeds or only once a week. However, two exceptions exist: (1) if your baby is having bowel movements that are like hard marbles or rocks, he should be checked by his pediatrician, and (2) if a breastfed infant who is less than one month of age does not have at least four bowel movements a day, it can be a sign that he is not getting enough breast milk, so call your baby's pediatrician for a weight check. If your infant is otherwise feeding normally, there is a wide range of acceptable bowel patterns.

While we often refer to normal newborn stool as being yellow, soft, and seedy, normal stool colors also vary widely, from light tan to forest green. The only colors that should prompt concern are white, which can indicate liver or gallbladder disease, and red or tarry black (the first day or two after birth), which can be a sign of bleeding within the stomach or intestines.

Carrying Your Baby

A newborn has almost no head control and needs to be carried in a way that protects his head from flopping from side to side or snapping from front to back. This is done by cradling the head when carrying the baby in a lying position and supporting the head and neck with your hand when carrying upright.

Pacifiers

Many babies soothe themselves by sucking. If after breast- or bottle-feeding your baby still wants to suck, a pacifier can satisfy that need (for nursing infants, introduce it only after breastfeeding is well established, at about one month of age). A pacifier is meant to satisfy your baby's non-eating sucking needs, not to replace or delay meals. Only offer a pacifier to your baby after or between feedings, when you are sure he is not hungry. If you offer a pacifier when he is hungry, he may become angry, which may interfere with feeding and his getting enough to eat. The pacifier is for your baby's benefit, not your convenience. Let him decide whether and when to use it.

Offering a pacifier when your baby is going to sleep may help reduce the risk of SIDS (sudden infant death syndrome). If you are breastfeeding, wait until your baby is consistently nursing well before using a pacifier. However, if

A very young infant who has not developed head control needs to be carried in a way that keeps his head from flopping from side to side or snapping from front to back.

your baby doesn't want it or if it falls from his mouth, don't force it. If your baby does use a pacifier to fall asleep, he may wake up when it falls from his mouth and cry for you to put it back. Babies who suck their fingers or hands have an advantage, since hands are always available. Once older, your baby will have the hand coordination to find and replace it himself.

Look for a pacifier model that is age-appropriate for your baby, has a soft nipple, and does not have any pieces that could break off and become a choking hazard (avoid models that break into two pieces). It should be dishwasher-safe, and you should clean the pacifier by boiling it or running it through the dishwasher frequently, so he's not exposed to any increased risk of infection, as his immune system is still maturing. When he is older, the likelihood of picking up an infection via the pacifier is minimal, and soap and water are sufficient.

Pacifiers are available in a variety of shapes and sizes. Once you find which your baby prefers, buy extras. Pacifiers have a way of disappearing or falling to the ground when you need them most. However, never try to solve this problem by fastening the pacifier with a cord. Babies can choke or strangle on cords, strings, ribbons, and fasteners attached to pacifiers. Also, for safety reasons, it's never a good idea to make pacifiers out of bottle nipples. Babies have pulled the nipple out of such homemade pacifiers and choked on them. Babies also can choke on a pacifier that's not the right size for their age, so again, be sure that the one you choose is age-appropriate, following the recommended age range on the packaging.

Going Outside

Fresh air and a change of surroundings are good for both you and your baby, even in his first month, so take him out for walks when the weather is nice. Be sure to dress him properly for outings, since his internal temperature control isn't fully mature yet. As stated before, follow the one-layer-more-than-yourself rule.

Here are a few suggestions for those outings with your baby:

- Your infant's skin is extremely susceptible to sunburn during the first six months, so keep him out of direct sunlight and remember that water, snow, sand, and concrete can reflect enough sunlight to cause a sunburn. If you must take him out in the sun, dress him in lightweight and light-colored clothing, with a hat to shade his face. If you'll be staying in one place, make sure the spot is shady, and adjust his position as the sun moves. Sunscreen can be used on exposed areas if protective clothing, hats, and shade are not available. Apply it only on small areas such as the face and the backs of the hands as needed, testing ahead of time his sensitivity to it on a small patch on his back. Although sunscreen can be applied to all areas that the sun can reach, be careful to avoid the eyes.

- In hot-weather months, do not let baby equipment (such as car safety seats and strollers) sit in the sun for long periods. The plastic and metal parts can get hot enough to burn. Check the surface temperature of such equipment before allowing your baby to come in contact with it, and throw a blanket or towel over the car safety seat when the car is parked to keep it out of direct sunlight.

- In uncomfortably cold or rainy weather, keep your baby inside as much as possible. If you have to go out, bundle him up and use a warm hat to cover his head and ears. You can shield his face with a blanket when you're outside. If you need to drive, remember to remove thick coats and bulky clothes before strapping him into his car safety seat.

- To check whether he's clothed appropriately, feel his hands and feet and the skin on his chest. His hands and feet should be slightly cooler than his body, but not cold. His chest should feel warm. If his hands, feet, and chest feel cold, take him to a warm room, unwrap him, and feed him something warm or hold him close so the heat from your body warms him. Until his temperature is back to normal, extra layers of clothing will just trap the cold, so use these other methods to warm him before wrapping him in additional blankets or clothing.

Finding Help at Home

Many families need in-home help with a new baby. If your partner is able to take off from work, this will help a lot. If not, one option is to ask a close relative or friend. Some families hire a professional baby nurse to help out. If you think you'll need the extra help, especially of a baby nurse, it is wise to make these arrangements in advance rather than waiting until after delivery.

Some communities have a visiting nurse or housekeeping service. This will not solve middle-of-the-night problems, but it will provide an hour or two during the day to catch up on work or simply rest. These arrangements, too, should be made in advance.

Be selective about the help you seek. Look for assistance from those who will really support you. Your goal is to reduce the stress level in your home, not add to it.

Before you start interviewing or asking friends or family for assistance, decide exactly what kind of help you need. Ask yourself the following questions:

- Do you want someone to help tend to the baby, or do the housework, or cook meals—or a little bit of everything?

- During what hours do you want help?

- Do you need someone who can drive (to pick up other children at school, shop for groceries, run errands, and the like)?

Once you know what you need, make sure the person you choose understands and agrees to meet those needs. Explain your expectations clearly, and if this is an employment situation, put those expectations in writing. This person should be someone you trust. If employing help, be certain a background check has been performed and the person has basic life-support training. If the person will be driving, his or her driving record should be checked. Regardless of whether this is a relative, friend, or employee, ask this person to notify you if he or she becomes ill so that infections aren't passed to your baby.

YOUR BABY'S FIRST SITTER. Sometime in the first month or two, you may need to leave your baby for the first time. The more confidence you have in your babysitter, the easier this experience will be. Therefore, you may want your first sitter to be someone very close and trusted—a grandparent, close friend, or relative who's familiar with both you and the child.

After your first separation, you may want to look for a regular babysitter. Ask your friends, neighbors, and coworkers for recommendations, or see if your pediatrician or nurse practitioner can refer you to someone. Local child-care agencies or referral services are great resources. You might also contact the placement services at local colleges for a listing of child development or early education students who babysit. A number of online services can help you find a sitter and will even perform background checks and provide references, often for a small fee. *It is absolutely essential you check references, inquiring about the sitter's responsibility, maturity, and ability to adhere to instructions—particularly for someone you've only recently met or don't know well.*

Interview every candidate in person with your baby present. You should be looking for someone who is affectionate, is capable, and supports your views about childcare. If you feel comfortable with the individual after talking, let her hold the baby so you can see how she handles the infant. Ask if she's had experience caring for babies. Although experience, references, and good health are very important, the best way to judge a babysitter is by doing a trial run while you're home. It will give your baby and the babysitter a chance to get to know each other before they're alone, and it will give you an opportunity to make sure you feel comfortable with the sitter.

Whenever leaving your child with a sitter, provide a list of all emergency phone numbers, including those where you or other family members can be reached; the sitter should know where you'll be and how to reach you at all times. Establish clear guidelines about what to do in an emergency, and reinforce that the sitter should call 911 for emergency help. Show the sitter where all exits to your home are located, as well as smoke detectors and fire extinguishers. Make sure your sitter has taken an approved CPR class (from the American Red Cross, for example) and has learned how to respond when a child is choking or not breathing. (See *Cardiopulmonary Resuscitation [CPR] and Mouth-to-Mouth Resuscitation*, page 899; *Choking*, page 700.) Some local YMCAs or American Red Cross chapters can provide a list of babysitters who have taken CPR or babysitting safety courses. Give your sitter any other guidelines you feel are important (e.g., never open the door to strangers, including delivery people) and stress that the sitter can call you or a trusted neighbor if he or she is having difficulty with the baby and is getting frustrated. Let friends and neighbors know about your arrangement so they can help if there's an emergency, and ask them to tell you if they suspect any problems in your absence.

Traveling with Your Baby

The key to traveling with your baby during this time is to maintain normal patterns as much as possible. Long trips involving a change of time zones can disturb your baby's sleep schedule. (See *Traveling with Your Preschooler*, page 401.) Do your best to plan according to your child's schedule, and allow several days to adjust to a time change. If he awakens very early in the morning, plan to start your own activities earlier. Be ready to stop earlier, too, because your little one might be getting tired and cranky long before the clock says it's time to go to bed. Always perform a safety inspection of any crib or play yard provided by a hotel for your baby to sleep in. (See *Cribs*, page 477.)

If you remain in a new time zone for more than two or three days, your baby's internal time clock will gradually shift to coincide with the new time zone. You'll have to adjust mealtimes to when he is hungry. Mom and Dad—and even older children—may be able to postpone meals to fit the new time zone, but a baby can't make those adjustments as easily.

Here are some other suggestions when traveling:

- Your baby will adapt to his new environment more quickly if you bring familiar things from home. A favorite rattle and toy will provide comfort and reassurance. Use his regular soap and a familiar towel, and bring along one of his tub toys to make him more at ease during baths.

- When packing for a trip with your baby, it's usually best to use a separate bag for his things. This makes it easier to find items quickly and reduces the chance you'll forget something important. You'll also need a large diaper bag for bottles, formula if formula-feeding, pacifier, a changing pad, diapers, diaper ointment, and baby wipes. Keep this bag with you at all times.

- When traveling by car, make sure your child is safely strapped into his car safety seat. (For more information on car safety seats, see pages 495–503.) The backseat is the safest place for children to ride. Rear-facing seats should never be placed in the front seat with a passenger-side airbag. At this age a baby should always ride in the rear-facing position. The same car seat safety rules apply in rental cars, taxis, and any other vehicle your baby rides in.

- It is safest to use a car safety seat on planes, instead of holding him on your lap. This means your baby ideally needs his own seat on the plane. Besides protecting him from injuries in severe turbulence, riding in his familiar car safety seat may help keep your baby calm and quiet during the flight. If you're not sure how to secure your baby safely on a plane, ask a flight attendant to help you.

■ If your baby is nursing and you are concerned about privacy on a plane or train, bring a nursing cover or ask for blankets to use as a screen. If your baby is bottle-fed, bring extra formula in case delays occur.

■ Breastfeeding (or a bottle or pacifier) may have other benefits when traveling by plane. The rapid air pressure changes can cause discomfort in the baby's middle ear. Babies cannot intentionally "pop" their ears like adults, but relief may occur when they breastfeed, or suck on a bottle or pacifier. To reduce the risk, feed your baby during takeoff and landing.

The Family

A Special Message to Mothers

The first month can be especially difficult because you are still recovering physically from pregnancy and delivery. It may take weeks before your body is back to normal, your incisions (if you had an episiotomy or C-section) have healed, and you're able to resume everyday activities. You may also experience strong mood swings due to changes in hormones. These changes can prompt sudden crying episodes for no apparent reason or feelings of mild depression. These emotions may be intensified by the exhaustion that comes with waking up every two or three hours at night to feed and change the baby.

The postpartum blues may make you feel a little "crazy," embarrassed, or even that you're a "bad mother." Difficult as it may be, try to keep these emotions in perspective by reminding yourself they're normal after pregnancy and delivery. Fathers can also feel sad and unusually emotional after a new baby arrives. To keep the blues from dominating your life—and enjoyment of your new baby—avoid isolating yourself in these early weeks. Try to nap when your baby does, so you don't get overtired. If these feelings persist past a few weeks or become severe, consult your pediatrician or your own physician about getting extra help. (For more information about the postpartum blues and postpartum depression, see also Chapter 5, pages 151–52.)

Visitors often help combat the blues by celebrating the baby's arrival with you. They may bring gifts for the baby or—even better during these early weeks—offer food or household help. But they also can be exhausting for you and overwhelming for the baby, and may expose him to infection. It is wise to strictly limit the number of visitors during the first couple of weeks, and keep anyone with a cough, cold, or contagious disease away from your newborn.

Ask all visitors to call in advance, wash their hands before holding the baby, and keep their visits brief until you're back to a regular schedule. If the baby seems unsettled by the attention, don't let anyone not close to you hold him.

If you become overwhelmed with phone calls, emails, and text messages, consider leaving an automated message with information about your new baby, such as sex, name, birthdate, time, weight, and length. State that you are spending time with your family and will return the call when you have a moment. Then turn off your devices and return messages on your own schedule without feeling stressed or guilty every time someone tries to contact you. With a new baby, constant visitors, an aching body, unpredictable mood swings, and in some cases other children demanding attention, it's no wonder many routine activities will get neglected. Resign yourself ahead of time to the fact that this will happen. What's important is recuperating and enjoying your new baby. Allow extended family and friends to lend a hand with tasks now and then. This is not a sign of weakness; it shows that your priorities are in the right place. And it also allows loved ones to care for you and feel like they, too, are a part of this new child's life.

A Special Message to Fathers

During pregnancy, a lot of attention is naturally paid to mothers. It's easy to feel your involvement doesn't matter. Nothing, however, could be further from the truth. The presence of an involved father during pregnancy reduces rates of premature birth and infant mortality. Mothers-to-be with involved fathers are 50 percent more likely to receive appropriate medical care during pregnancy, and mothers-to-be who were smokers when they became pregnant are 36 percent more likely to quit smoking when fathers are supportive.

While waiting for the baby to arrive, there's plenty to do beyond shopping for cribs and car safety seats. Dads and partners can take an active role in touring the birth hospital, choosing a pediatrician, helping the mother-to-be make a birth plan, and accompanying the mother-to-be to birthing and breastfeeding classes. The father can be a great birth coach, helping the mother-to-be with breathing and positioning during labor while paying attention to the signals she's giving about how much help she wants from moment to moment.

As soon as the baby is born, fathers and partners can play an important role in skin-to-skin "kangaroo care" for the newborn. Ideally, the baby will go to its mother's chest as soon as possible to begin nursing. But not all situations are ideal, and if the mother requires medical attention, the father's may be the first chest the baby feels. Compared to newborns in bassinets in the first two hours after birth, a baby placed on their father's chest cries less, falls asleep sooner, and displays less agitation. But whatever the situation, the mother will need care, and fathers have a chance to enjoy the closeness of their new baby while skin-to-skin.

In the event the newborn is in the neonatal intensive care unit (NICU), the father's role may become even more important. Among preterm infants in the NICU, babies with more involved fathers had better development at three years of age.

While fathers/partners are not able to breastfeed, their involvement makes a huge difference in the success of nursing. Be available to bring the baby to the mother and help her with positioning. Pro tip: Nursing a baby makes mothers very thirsty, so bringing her a glass of water will make the father her hero. When the feeding is complete, change the baby's diaper and ensure he returns safely to his crib or bassinet.

Sleep deprivation is inevitable with a new baby, but fathers and partners can help here, too. Take shifts with diaper changes, feedings (if bottle-feeding), and rocking and calming the newborn. Even just a few extra hours in bed can help parents cope better with the stresses of new parenthood.

In the weeks and months after the baby is born, pay attention to the household moods. Fathers and partners are in an excellent position to notice signs of a mother's postpartum depression and guide her to help. Fathers, however, can also suffer from postpartum depression. We now know that fathers undergo hormonal changes, too, and sharing in the stress and sleep deprivation can further affect mood. A father's depression can affect outcomes for mother and baby, so be proactive about seeking help if you feel unusually down.

Putting effort into helping the mother adjust to having a baby will help both

Become as involved as possible in caring for and playing with your new baby. You'll get just as emotionally attached to him as his mother will.

parents overcome the stress and fatigue of this enormous life change. Make time for cuddling, snuggling, massage, and activities that contribute to a strong and loving bond. Most obstetricians recommend women wait a minimum of six weeks after giving birth before resuming vaginal intercourse.

Many employers in the United States have been slow to adopt generous paternity leave policies, but that trend is changing. Taking time off in the first weeks or months can help lay a foundation for the baby's health and development for years to come. Fathers should ask their employer about taking time for their baby's medical care. Fathers' involvement in their children's healthcare has been linked to children's improved compliance with treatment, better psychological adjustment, and superior overall health status.

As children grow and develop, a father's strengths often complement the mother's. Fathers can be just as good as mothers at adjusting to a child's emotional states, but playtime with the father tends to be more intense and exploratory. The stimulating, vigorous activity fathers encourage can help children build independence, where mothers may provide a sense of safety and balance. Children with involved fathers develop better language skills and enjoy overall better mental health than children whose fathers are less involved.

Having a baby is arguably the biggest challenge for anyone, but also the most rewarding. No one feels quite ready for it, and no one is ever truly sure they're doing it right. But a father should never think he does not matter. This baby needs his father now and for his whole life. For a unique perspective on fatherhood, see the book *Dad to Dad: Parenting Like a Pro*, by pediatrician David L. Hill, published by the American Academy of Pediatrics.

A Special Message to Grandparents

The first time you gaze into the eyes of your new grandchild, you may be overwhelmed by feelings: love, wonder, amazement, and joy, among others. You might find yourself reflecting back to when your own children were born and feel enormous pride that your own child is now raising a family.

Regardless of your individual circumstances, you can and should play as active a role as possible in the life of the new baby. Research shows that children who have grandparents participating in their lives fare better throughout childhood and later in life. You have plenty of love and lots of hugs to give, and they can make a difference. As you spend time with your grandchild, you'll form a lasting bond and become an invaluable source of nurturing guidance.

If you live close to your new grandchild, make frequent visits, as directed by your adult child. (Don't show up uninvited, and, of course, know when to leave.) At the same time, encourage visits to your home. (Make sure your home is childproofed in the ways recommended in this book.) Minimize the advice and certainly the criticism you offer; instead, give the parents support, respect their opinions, and be patient. They may have approaches to child rearing somewhat different from yours, but remember they're the parents now. If they should ask, "What do you think I should do about . . . ?," then, of course, provide input. Share your point of view, but don't try to impose your beliefs.

It's been a while since you raised your own babies, and although much may be the same, much has changed. Ask how to support the child-rearing process, and take leads from your child on how, when, and how often to get involved. You might focus on basic baby care, including feeding and changing diapers, but don't try to take over. Also, offer the parents a break from time to time by giving them a night out (or, at some point, perhaps a weekend away). Make regular phone calls or video chats a staple, not only during your grandchild's infancy but also in the upcoming years when you're able to have conversations with him.

As your grandchild grows, tell him about what his own mother or father was like during childhood. (Sharing family history and teaching family values are important contributions you can make as your grandchild grows.) In the meantime, consider keeping a scrapbook of photos and mementos you can share with him someday; as part of this, create a family tree to which the entire family can contribute. Make holiday get-togethers a priority, attend birthday parties, and, later on, go to as many soccer matches, Little League games, and piano recitals as possible.

If you live hundreds of miles away, you still can be an excellent long-distance grandparent. Technology offers numerous ways to be present today that were not available to prior generations. Share photos, follow your family on social media, and make time for video chats by phone or computer.

Keeping Siblings Happy

Once your new baby arrives, you can expect your older child to be very proud and protective.

With all the excitement over the new baby's arrival, siblings might feel neglected. They may be upset over their mother's hospitalization, especially if this was their first prolonged separation from her. Even after Mom returns, they may have trouble understanding she's tired and cannot play as much as they're used to. Compound this with the attention she's now devoting to the baby—attention that just a couple of weeks ago belonged to them!—and it's no wonder they may feel jealous and left out. It's up to both parents to find ways to reassure the siblings they're still loved and valued, and to help them come to terms with their new "competition."

Here are some suggestions to help soothe your older children and make them feel more involved during the first month home with your new baby.

- If possible, have the siblings visit mother and baby in the hospital.

- When Mom comes home from the hospital, bring each sibling a special gift to celebrate.

- Set aside a special time to spend alone with each sibling every day. Make sure that both parents have time with each child, individually and together.

(continues on next page)

- While you're taking pictures of the new baby, take some of the older children—alone and with the baby.

- Ask the grandparents or other close relatives to take the older children on a special outing—to the zoo, a movie, or just dinner. This special attention may help them through moments when they feel abandoned.

- Have some small gifts for the older child and present them when friends come with gifts for the baby.

- Especially during the first month, when the baby needs to eat so often, older children can get jealous of the intimacy you have with the baby during feedings. Show them you can share this intimacy by turning feeding times into story times. Reading stories that specifically deal with issues of jealousy encourages a toddler or preschooler to voice his feelings so that you can help him become more accepting. There are also a number of books about nursing a new baby geared to the older sibling that are fun for story time.

Health Watch

The following medical problems are of particular concern to parents during the first month. (For problems that occur generally throughout childhood, check the listings in Part 2.)

BREATHING DIFFICULTIES. Normally, your baby should take twenty to forty breaths per minute. This pattern is most regular when he is asleep and healthy. When awake, occasionally he may breathe rapidly for a short period, then take a brief pause (less than ten seconds) before returning to normal breathing. This is called periodic breathing. A runny nose may interfere with breathing because your baby's nasal passages are narrow and fill easily. This condition can be eased by using a cool-mist humidifier and gently suctioning the nose with a bulb syringe (ordinarily given to you by the hospital; for its use, see page 224). Read and follow the cleaning instructions for humidifiers and bulb syringes carefully. Occasionally, mild salt-solution nose drops are used to help thin the mucus and clear the nasal passages. If your baby has a fever, his breathing may become faster, increasing by about two breaths per minute for each degree of temperature elevation. When the number of breaths exceeds sixty per minute, or if the baby's chest muscles are retracting, his nose is flaring, or he is coughing a lot, be sure to contact your pediatrician. A fever with a rectal temperature of 100.4 degrees Fahrenheit (38 degrees Celsius) or higher in a one-month-old baby may be serious, and you should call the doctor.

In the first month after birth, a baby with otherwise normal breathing at birth may develop stridor. Stridor is a high-pitched noise usually heard during inspiration (breathing in). Stridor results from rapid airflow across a narrowing, primarily at the level of the larynx (voice box) or trachea (windpipe). The most common cause of inspiratory stridor is called laryngomalacia, which may worsen during feeds, while lying on the back, or during crying. Most babies with inspiratory stridor from laryngomalacia are able to gain weight well and do not need any change in feeding pattern. Difficulty with feeding (coughing, choking, sputtering), inability to gain weight or maintain weight, or respiratory symptoms such as retractions, sleep difficulty, or changes in color warrant urgent evaluation by a pediatrician and/or a pediatric otolaryngologist.

DIARRHEA. After feedings in the first month after birth, healthy and thriving breastfed babies may have frequent watery stools that some people mistake for diarrhea. However, a formula-fed baby has diarrhea if he produces loose, very watery stools more than six to eight times a day. Diarrhea is usually caused by a viral infection. The danger, especially at this young age, is fluid loss and becoming dehydrated. The first signs of dehydration are dry mouth and a significant decrease in the number of wet diapers. But don't wait for dehydration to occur. Call your pediatrician if the stools are very loose or occur more often than after each feeding (six to eight per day).

CONSTIPATION. A breastfed baby will have more stools each day for the first few days, and by day five at least four stools per day. If stools are not increasing for a breastfed baby, it may be a sign your baby isn't getting enough to eat. A formula-fed baby should be producing a stool at least once a day the first week after birth. If you have concerns about your baby's stooling frequency, call your pediatrician. After the first few weeks, a breastfed baby may slow down the number of stools he produces and even skip days without having a stool. For a formula-fed baby, after a few weeks of age your baby's pattern will become more predictable, demonstrating that he is eating and pooping well.

EXCESSIVE SLEEPINESS. Since each baby requires a different amount of sleep, it's difficult to tell when a baby is excessively drowsy. If your infant starts sleeping much more than usual, it might indicate an infection, so notify your pediatrician. Also, if you are nursing and your baby sleeps more than five hours without a feeding in the first month, you must consider whether he is getting enough milk. Bottle-fed babies may also be sleepy from inadequate feeding. Another possible cause of sleepiness is herbal medication administered by parents.

EYE INFECTIONS/TEAR PRODUCTION PROBLEMS. Some babies are born with one or both tear ducts partially or totally blocked. They typically open by about two weeks, when tear production begins. If they don't, the blockage may cause watery or mucous tearing. In this case, the tears will back up and flow over the eyelids instead of draining through the nose. This is not harmful, and the ducts will generally open without treatment, usually by nine months. You may also help open them by gently massaging the inner corner of the eye and down the side of the nose. However, do this only at the direction of your pediatrician.

If the ducts remain blocked, the blockage will keep the tears from draining properly. Although this will produce mucus, it does not mean your baby has an infection. You may see a greenish yellow or white discharge in the corner of the eye, and the eyelashes may be stuck together when your baby wakes in the morning. But since this discharge does not indicate infection, it is not usually treated with an antibiotic. (See Tear [or Lacrimal] Production Problems, page 745.)

On the other hand, if an infection is suspected, it will usually be treated with special drops or an ointment prescribed after examining the eye. But in many cases, only a gentle cleansing with water is needed. When lashes are sticky, dip a cotton ball or soft washcloth in water, and gently wipe the lid from the nose to the outside. Clean in one motion from inside to outside (avoid going back and forth). Use a new washcloth or cotton ball each time.

Although this type of mild discharge may recur several times, it will not damage the eye and he will probably outgrow it, even without intensive treatment. In rare cases blocked tear ducts require surgical care when they don't open by one year of age.

If the eye itself is bloodshot or pinkish, or has excessive discharge, your infant could have conjunctivitis or "pinkeye," and you should notify your pediatrician (see *Eye Infections*, page 739).

FEVER. Whenever your child is unusually cranky or feels warm, take his temperature. (See *Taking a Rectal Temperature*, page 82.) If his rectal temperature reads 100.4 degrees Fahrenheit (38 degrees Celsius) or higher on two separate readings, and he's not overly bundled up, call your pediatrician at once. Fever in these first few weeks can signal infection, and babies this age can become seriously ill quickly.

FLOPPINESS. Newborn infants all seem somewhat floppy because their muscles are still developing, but if your baby feels exceptionally loose or floppy, it could be a sign of a more serious problem, such as an infection. Consult your pediatrician immediately.

Sudden Infant Death Syndrome (SIDS) and Other Sleep-Related Infant Deaths

Approximately one newborn out of every two thousand dies during sleep, for no apparent reason, usually between one and four months. These babies are generally well cared for and show no obvious symptoms of illness. Their autopsies offer no identifiable cause of death, so the term "sudden infant death syndrome" (SIDS) is used.

The risk factor most clearly associated with SIDS is stomach-sleeping. Therefore, unless your pediatrician has advised otherwise, **your baby should be placed for sleep on his back.** Babies of mothers who smoke and those who sleep in adult beds with other family members (including their parents) are also at increased risk. Soft or loose bedding, pillows, crib bumpers, and stuffed toys are also risk factors and should be kept out of the baby's sleeping environment. Babies who sleep in their own bassinet or crib (particularly when the crib is in the parents' room), breastfed babies, and those who use a pacifier when going to sleep have lower incidences of SIDS.

There are many theories about the cause of SIDS. Infection, milk allergy, pneumonia, and immunizations do not cause SIDS. The most plausible theory at this time is that there is a delay in the maturation of the arousal centers in the brains of certain babies, which means that they do not wake up in response to situations when they are not getting enough oxygen. This is probably why stomach sleeping is so dangerous; babies who sleep on their stomach sleep more deeply and are harder to wake up. Following safe sleep recommendations will not only protect your baby from SIDS but also decrease the chance of death from suffocation or strangulation. So keep your baby on his back, in a bare crib (no pillows, blankets, or bumper pads), next to your bed. If you are worried your baby may be cold, put another layer of clothing on him or use a wearable blanket. You can also use fleece sleepers and other warm pajamas for babies that will keep them warm without blankets.

Along with normal feelings of grief and depression, many parents who lose a child to SIDS feel guilty and become extremely protective of older siblings or any babies born afterward. Help for parents is available through local groups or through the national organization First Candle (firstcandle.org; 1-800-221-7437). Ask your pediatrician about other resources in your area.

Can SIDS Be Prevented?

At this time, the best measures to prevent SIDS are to place your baby to sleep on his back, in a crib close to your bed in a smoke-free environment, without any bedding. Since 1992, the American Academy of Pediatrics has recommended that babies always be placed on their backs. Before this recommendation, more than 5,000 babies died from SIDS every year in the United States. Now, with the decrease in the number of babies sleeping on their stomach, the deaths from SIDS have declined to about 2,300 per year. Each of these deaths is tragic, and campaigns continue to promote a back-to-sleep message for babies. Between the ages of four and seven months, however, you may notice your infant beginning to roll over when placed to sleep on his back. Fortunately, SIDS decreases markedly after six months of age, so while it is important to continue to place your infant to sleep on his back, if your baby can comfortably roll from stomach to back and vice versa, you should not stay up all night constantly flipping him onto his back. You should also double-check that there is no bedding close to the baby that he could get stuck in if he rolls over.

HEARING. Pay attention to how your baby responds to sounds even if he passed his newborn hearing screening. Does he startle at loud or sudden noises? Does he become quiet or turn toward you when you talk to him? If he does not respond normally to sounds around him, ask your pediatrician about formal hearing testing. (See *Hearing Loss*, pages 659–63.) Testing is recommended if your infant was extremely premature, if he was deprived of oxygen or had a severe infection at birth, or if your family has a history of hearing loss in early childhood. If there is any suspicion of hearing loss, your infant should be tested as early as possible, as a delay in diagnosis and treatment is likely to interfere with normal language development.

JAUNDICE. Jaundice, the yellow skin color often appearing shortly after birth, sometimes lasts for more than two to three weeks in breastfed babies. In formula-fed babies, most jaundice goes away within two weeks. If your baby is jaundiced for more than three weeks or the jaundice seems to be increasing, see your pediatrician. (For additional information about jaundice, see Chapter 5, page 155.)

JITTERS. Many newborns have quivery chins and shaky hands, but if your baby's whole body seems to be shaking, it could be a sign of low blood sugar or calcium levels, or some type of seizure disorder. Notify your pediatrician so he can determine the cause.

RASHES AND INFECTIONS. Common newborn rashes include the following:

- *Cradle cap (seborrheic dermatitis)* appears as scaly patches on the scalp. Washing the hair and brushing out the scales daily helps with control. It usually disappears on its own within the first few months but may need treatment with a special shampoo. (See *Cradle Cap and Seborrheic Dermatitis*, page 852.)

- *Fingernail or toenail infections* will appear as redness around the edge of the toenail or fingernail, which may seem to hurt when touched. These infections may respond to warm compresses, but at this age they should be taken seriously and be examined by a doctor, as they may require medication.

- *Umbilical infections* are rare, but if one occurs it often appears as redness around the umbilical stump. There's usually pus and often tenderness. Babies with these infections should be examined by your pediatrician. If your baby is also running a fever, see your pediatrician right away, as he may need antibiotics or hospitalization. It is normal, however, to have a small amount of clear oozing, drops of blood, and a scab around the umbilical stump without any redness or fever. If this is the case, watch it for a few days; if it doesn't heal on its own, see your pediatrician.

- *Diaper rash.* See instructions for handling this problem on pages 71–72.

THRUSH. White patches in the mouth may indicate that your baby has thrush, a common yeast infection. This condition is often treated with an oral antifungal medication prescribed by your pediatrician, but milder cases may resolve without treatment. If Mom is nursing and the baby has thrush, she should let her obstetrician know if she is having symptoms of nipple tenderness.

VISION. Watch how your baby looks at you when alert. When you're 8 to 15 inches (20.3 to 38.1 cm) from his face, do his eyes follow you? Will he follow a light or small object at the same distance? At this age, the eyes may appear crossed, or one occasionally may drift inward or outward. This is because the muscle coordination controlling eye movement is still developing. Both eyes should be able to move equally and together in all directions, however, and he should be able to track slowly moving objects at close range. If he can't, or if he was born premature (less than thirty-two weeks into the pregnancy), or if he needed oxygen as a newborn, your pediatrician may refer you to an eye specialist for further examination.

VOMITING. Although spitting up small amounts after feedings is very common, if your baby starts forcefully vomiting (shooting out several inches rather than dribbling from the mouth), contact your pediatrician at once to make sure he does not have an obstruction of the valve between the stomach and the small intestine (pyloric stenosis; see page 556). Any vomiting that persists for more than eight hours or two to three feedings, or is accompanied by diarrhea or fever, also should be evaluated by your pediatrician.

WEIGHT GAIN. Your baby should be gaining weight rapidly (⅔–1 ounce per day [20–30 g]) after the first few days after birth. If he isn't, your pediatrician will want to make sure that he's getting adequate calories in his feedings and that he is absorbing them properly. Be prepared to answer these questions:

- How often does the baby eat?

- How much does he eat at a feeding, if bottle-feeding? How long does he nurse, if breastfeeding?

- How many bowel movements does the baby have each day?

- What is the amount and thinness or thickness of the stools?

- How often does the baby urinate?

If your baby is eating well and the contents of his diapers are normal in amount and consistency, there is probably no cause for alarm. Your baby may be getting off to a slow start, or his weight could have been inaccurately measured. Your pediatrician may want to schedule another office visit in two or three days to reevaluate the situation.

Safety Check
Car Safety Seats

- Your baby should ride in a properly installed, federally approved car safety seat *every time* he rides in the car. If you are carrying your baby to the car in the car safety seat, make sure he is strapped in securely. Do not use it as a place for him to nap in the house. At this age, he should ride only in the backseat in the car safety seat in the rear-facing position. Never place a baby in the front seat of a car, as the passenger-side airbag can cause serious life-threatening injury. Car safety seats have an expiration date, so if you are using an older car safety seat, check to see if it is still within date. If your car was manufactured after 2002, you should use the included LATCH system to attach the car safety seat.

Bathing

- It is best to bathe your baby in a separate baby bathtub. Fill it and test the water temperature before you put your child in the tub. Always hold your baby under the arms while bathing him. If you are bathing your baby in the sink, seat him on a washcloth or bath mat to prevent slipping and hold him under the arms. Never leave the faucet running while your baby is in the sink; instead, fill the sink first, test the temperature, and then put the baby in the water. The water should feel just slightly warm to the touch. Never run the dishwasher while bathing in the sink; otherwise, you risk scald burns from the dishwasher's hot water.

- Adjust the maximum temperature of your water heater to 120 degrees Fahrenheit (48.9 degrees Celsius) or lower so hot water can't scald her. Any modern water heater should indicate where this setting is, so check your manual or call your plumber if you're unsure.

- Never leave your baby unsupervised in the water, even for just a brief amount of time.

Changing Surfaces

- Never leave your baby unattended on any surface (such as changing tables, chairs, tables, sofas, beds, and countertops) above the floor. Always keep a hand on your baby if he is on a raised surface. Even at this young age, babies can wiggle and move and push against things, and these movements can result in a fall. Place your baby in a safe place such as a crib or play yard when you cannot be with him.

Suffocation Prevention

- Keep the crib free of all objects. Make sure the mattress fits tightly, and use a fitted sheet only.

■ Never leave plastic bags or wrappings where your baby can wiggle or roll into them.

■ Don't have your baby sleep in your own bed next to you. Keep him in his crib or bassinet next to your bed.

■ Do not cover your baby in loose blankets or comforters that he could get tangled in or suffocate under. Instead, dress him in appropriate-weight sleepwear (like a wearable blanket or sleep sack).

■ Don't allow your baby to sleep on his stomach. Nor should he sleep on a soft comforter or pillow. Place him to sleep only on his back on a firm surface.

Fire and Burn Prevention

■ Do not carry your baby and hot liquids like coffee, tea, or soup at the same time. Also, do not hold or cradle your baby near hot liquids on the stove or tabletops. Even a small splash could scald your baby.

■ Install smoke and carbon monoxide detectors in the proper places throughout your home and check them regularly to be sure they are working.

Supervision

■ Never leave your baby unattended in the bathtub, house, yard, or car. Place your baby in a crib or play yard if he is unattended.

Necklaces and Cords

■ Don't let strings or cords (e.g., from a window shade) dangle in or anywhere near the crib or around your baby. Keep cribs away from windows and blind or curtain cords.

■ Don't attach pacifiers, medallions, or other objects to the crib or to your baby with a cord.

- Don't place a string or necklace around the baby's neck.

- Don't use clothing with drawstrings.

Head Support

- Do not jerk or shake the baby. Cradle and rock him gently.

- Always support the baby's head and neck when holding or moving his body.

~ 7 ~

Age One Month
Through Three Months

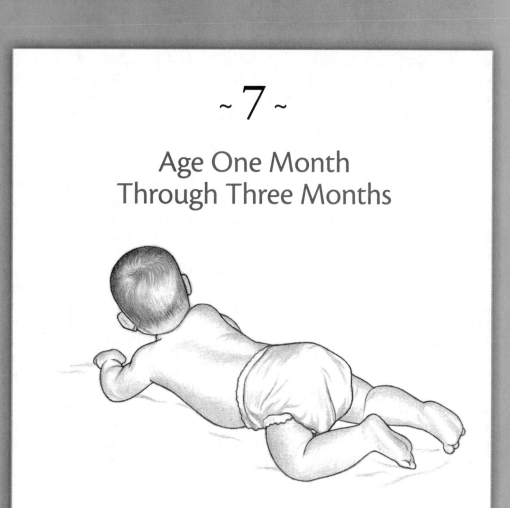

BY THE BEGINNING OF the second month, much of the awe, exhaustion, and uncertainty you may have felt has likely given way to self-confidence. You have hopefully settled into a fairly routine (if still demanding) schedule around her feedings and naps. You've adjusted to having a new family member and are beginning to understand her general temperament. And you probably have already received the crowning reward that makes all the sacrifice worthwhile: her first true smile. This smile is just a glimmer of the delights in store over the next three months.

You may also be returning to work and need to find infant-centered daycare. Chapter 14 will help you select the proper type of childcare depending on your circumstances. The need to be back at work might create a sense of sadness or separation. This is normal and expected. Try to find a setting that allows you frequent check-in visits, but in ways that are not intrusive on the childcare providers. Establishing their sense of attachment and commitment to your child is important, and if your presence appears to question their ability, it needs to be avoided.

Between one and four months, your baby will undergo a dramatic transformation from a totally dependent newborn to an active and responsive infant. She'll lose many of her newborn reflexes while acquiring control of her body. You'll find her inspecting her hands and watching their movements. She'll also become increasingly interested in her surroundings, especially people close to her. She'll often smile when she sees or hears you. Sometime during her second or third month, she'll begin "talking" back in gentle but intentional coos and gurgles. With each new discovery, you'll see a new part of your child's personality.

Occasionally there will be moments when your baby's development seems to lag, usually followed by a spurt in progress. She may seem to be stretching out her nighttime feedings for several weeks, but then begin waking up again to feed more frequently. What should you make of this? It's probably a sign she's about to take a major developmental leap forward. In a week or two (although this varies from child to child), she'll probably be sleeping longer at night again and maybe take fewer naps, although each nap may be longer. In addition, she'll have longer periods during the day where she will be considerably more alert and responsive to people and events. Many other types of developmental progress, including physical growth, may occur in spurts and pauses, with periods of setback or lag. As challenging as this may be, you'll soon learn to read the signals, anticipate these periods of change, and appreciate them.

Growth and Development

Physical Appearance and Growth

From months one through four, your baby will continue growing at the same rate established during her first few weeks. In general, babies gain between 1½ and 2 pounds (0.7–0.9 kg) and grow 1 to 1½ inches (2.5–4 cm) each month during this period. Her head size will increase in circumference by about ½ inch (1.25 cm) each month. These figures are only averages, so keep track of your child's development as it compares to the growth charts in the Appendix.

At two months, the soft spots on your baby's head should still be open and flat, but by three months, the one at the back should be closed. Also, her head is more likely to be proportionately larger compared to her body, since it grows faster. This is normal; her body will soon catch up.

At two months, your baby will look round and chubby, but as she starts using her arms and legs more actively, muscles will develop. Her bones will grow rapidly, and as her limbs loosen up, she'll seem to stretch out, appearing taller and leaner.

Movement

Many of your baby's movements will still be reflexive at the beginning of this period. She may assume a "fencing" position every time her head turns (tonic neck reflex; see page 162) or extend her arms if she hears a loud noise or feels that she's falling (Moro reflex; see page 162). But, as mentioned, most of these common newborn reflexes will begin to fade by the second or third month. She may temporarily seem less active after the reflexes have diminished, but now her movements, however subtle, are intentional and will build steadily toward mature activity.

One of the most important developments of these early months will be your baby's increasing neck strength. Starting at birth, take a few opportunities every day to let her play with you on her tummy (tummy time). Before two months, she'll struggle to raise her head to look around. Even if she succeeds for a second or two, she'll have a slightly different view of the world. These small exercises will strengthen the muscles at the back of her neck so that, by around four months, she'll be able to hold her head and chest up on her elbows. This is a major accomplishment, giving her freedom and control to look around at will.

For you, it's also welcome because you no longer have to support her head as much when carrying her (although sudden movements or force will still require head support). If you use a front or back carrier, she'll now be able to hold her head up and look around as you walk.

A baby's control over the front neck and abdominal muscles develops more gradually, so it will take longer for your baby to raise her head lying on her back. At one month, if you gently pull your baby by the arms to a sitting position, her head will flop backward; by four months, however, she'll hold it steady in all directions.

By four months, your baby will be able to hold up her head and chest as she supports herself on her elbows.

Your child's legs also will become stronger and more active. During the second month, they'll start to straighten from their inward-curving newborn position. Although her kicks will remain mostly reflexive, they'll quickly gather force, and by the end of the third month she might even kick herself over from front to back. (She probably won't roll from back to front until around six months old.) Since you cannot predict when she'll begin rolling over, you'll need to be especially careful whenever she's on the changing table or any other surface above floor level.

Another newborn reflex, the stepping reflex (described in Chapter 6, page 163), allows her to take steps when she is held under her arms and her feet touch the floor. This reflex will disappear at about six weeks, and you may not see your baby step again until she's ready to walk. By three or four months, however, she'll flex and straighten her legs at will. Lift her upright with her feet on the floor and she'll push down and straighten her legs so that she's virtually standing by herself (except for the balance you're providing). Then she'll try bending her knees and will discover she can bounce. Although parents are often concerned that this kind of bouncing is harmful, it is perfectly healthy and safe.

Your baby's hand and arm movements will also develop rapidly during these months. In the beginning, her hands are tightly clenched fists with her thumb inside; if

At one month, your baby's head will flop backward if you gently pull her to a sitting position (so always support your baby's head when picking her up).

you uncoil the fingers, she'll grasp objects automatically, yet she won't be able to move or bring them to her mouth. She'll gaze at her hands with interest when they are in view, but she probably won't be able to bring them to her face on her own.

By four months, however, she will be able to hold her head steady in all directions.

Movement Milestones for Your One- to Three-Month-Old

- Raises head and chest when lying on stomach
- Supports upper body with arms when lying on stomach
- Stretches legs out and kicks when lying on stomach or back
- Opens and shuts hands
- Pushes down on legs when feet are placed on a firm surface
- Brings hands to mouth
- Takes swipes at dangling objects with hands
- Grasps and shakes hand toys

Many changes continue to occur within a month or two. Your baby's hands will relax and her arms will open outward. During the third month, her hands will be half open most of the time, and you'll notice her carefully opening and shutting them. She'll now bring objects to her mouth and drop them only after exploring them fully. (The more lightweight the toy, the better she can control it.) She'll never seem to tire of her hands themselves; just staring at her fingers will amuse her for stretches of time.

At first, your baby's attempts to bring her hands to her mouth will be in vain—even if her fingers occasionally reach their destination, they'll quickly fall away. By four months, however, she'll probably have finally mastered this game (which is also an important developmental skill) and be able to get her thumb to her mouth and keep it there whenever she wishes. She'll clench objects tightly now, shake them, mouth them, and maybe even transfer them from hand to hand.

Your baby will also be able to reach accurately and quickly—not only with hands but with her entire body. Hang a toy overhead and she'll reach eagerly with arms and legs to bat and grab for it, her face will show concentration, and she may even lift her head toward her target. It's as if every part of her body shares in her excitement as she masters these new skills.

Vision

At one month, your baby still can't see clearly beyond 15 inches (38 cm) or so, but she'll closely study anything within this range: the crib corner or the mobile dangling above the crib. The human face is her favorite image, however. As you hold her, she is drawn automatically to your face, particularly your eyes. Often the mere sight of your eyes will make her smile. Gradually her visual span will broaden and she will take in your whole face. As this happens, she'll be much more responsive to facial expressions involving your mouth, jaw, and cheeks. She'll also love flirting with herself in the mirror.

In her early weeks, your baby will have a hard time following an object moving in front of her face. If you wave an object quickly in front of her, she'll seem to stare through it, or if you shake your head, she'll lose your eyes. But this will change dramatically by two months, when her eyes are more coordinated and can work together. Soon she'll be able to track an object moving through an entire half circle in front of her. This increased visual coordination will give her the depth perception needed to track objects as they move toward and away from her. By three months, she'll also have the arm and hand control needed to bat at objects as they move close to her; her aim won't be very good yet, but the practice will help her develop hand-eye coordination. If you think

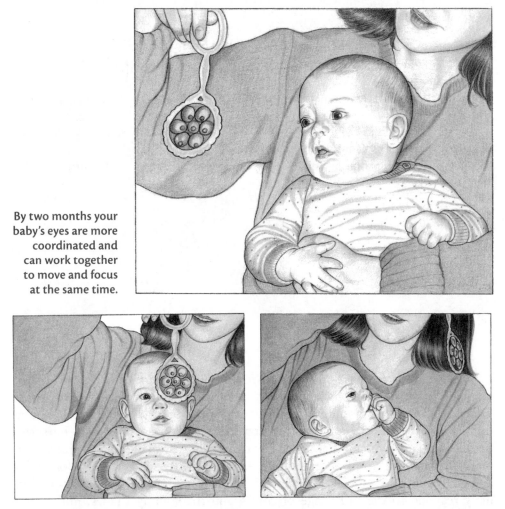

By two months your baby's eyes are more coordinated and can work together to move and focus at the same time.

Soon she'll be able to track an object moving through an entire half-circle in front of her.

your baby's eyes may not be tracking together by three months of age, talk with your pediatrician.

Your baby's distance vision also is developing at this time. At three months, you may notice her smiling at you halfway across the room or studying a toy several feet away. By four months, you'll catch her staring at the distant wall hanging or looking out the window. These are clues to normal development.

Visual Milestones for Your One- to Three-Month-Old

- Watches faces intently
- Follows moving objects
- Recognizes familiar objects and people at a distance
- Starts using hands and eyes in coordination

Your infant's color vision will mature at about the same rate. At one month, she'll be sensitive to the brightness or intensity of color; consequently, she'll prefer bold patterns in sharply contrasting colors or black and white. Young infants do not appreciate the soothing pastels usually associated with nurseries because of their limited color vision. By three months, she'll be more interested in circular patterns (bull's-eyes, spirals)—one of the reasons faces, full of circles and curves, are so appealing to her. By about four months, your baby will finally respond to the full range of colors and their many shades, and as her eyesight develops, your infant will naturally seek out more stimulating things to see.

Hearing and Making Sounds

Just as your baby naturally prefers the human face over other visual patterns, she also prefers the human voice to other sounds. She will recognize and respond to those voices she hears most. She associates them with warmth, food, and comfort. Babies like high-pitched voices in general—a fact that most adults seem to understand intuitively and respond to accordingly, without even realizing it.

Hearing and Speech Milestones for Your One- to Three-Month-Old

- Smiles at the sound of your voice

- Begins to babble

- Begins to imitate some sounds

- Turns head toward direction of sound

Listen to yourself the next time you talk to your baby. You'll probably notice that you raise your pitch, slow your speech, exaggerate syllables, and widen your eyes and mouth more than normal. This dramatic approach is guaranteed to capture almost any baby's attention—and usually make her smile.

By listening to you and others, your baby will discover the importance of speech long before she understands or repeats specific words. By one month, she'll be able to identify you by voice, even if you're in another room. As you talk to her, she'll be reassured, comforted, and entertained. When she smiles and gurgles at you, she'll see the delight on your face and realize talk goes both ways. These first conversations teach her many of the subtle rules of communication, such as turn-taking, vocal tone, imitation, pacing, and speed of verbal interaction.

At about two months, your infant may begin cooing and repeating some vowel sounds (ah-ah-ah, ooh-ooh-ooh). Over the first four to six months, imitate her cooing, while adding simple words and phrases to your "conversations." It's easy to fall into a habit of baby talk, but you should try mixing your conversations with adult language and eventually phase out the baby talk. During early infancy, you should also read to your baby, even if you think she doesn't comprehend.

By four months, your infant will babble routinely, often amusing herself for long periods by producing strange new sounds (muh-muh, bah-bah). She'll also be more sensitive to your tone of voice and the emphasis you put on words or phrases. As you move through each day together, she'll learn from your voice when you're going to feed her, change her diapers, go for a walk, or put her down to sleep. The way you talk shows her much about your mood and personality, and the way she responds shows you a lot about her. If you speak in an upbeat or comforting way, she may smile or coo. Yell or talk angrily, and she'll probably startle or cry.

Emotional and Social Development

By the second month, your baby will spend much of each day watching and listening to the people around her. She learns that they will entertain and soothe her, feed her, and make her comfortable. During her first month, she'll experiment with primitive grins and grimaces. Then, during the second month, these movements will turn to genuine signals of pleasure and friendliness.

If you've experienced her first true smile, then you know it's a major turning point for both of you. All the sleepless nights and erratic days of these first weeks suddenly seem worthwhile, and you'll do everything in your power to keep those smiles coming. For her part, your baby will suddenly discover that just by moving her lips she can have "conversations" with you. Smiling will also give her another way besides crying to express her needs and exert control over what happens to her. The more engaged she is with you and your smiles and the rest of the world around her, the more her brain development advances, and the more she'll be distracted from internal sensations (hunger, gas, fatigue) that once strongly influenced her behavior. Her increasing socialization is further proof she enjoys and appreciates these new experiences. Expanding her world with these experiences is fun for both of you and important to her overall development.

At first your baby may seem to smile past you without meeting your gaze, but don't let this disturb you. Looking away from you gives her some control and protects her from being overwhelmed. It's her way of taking in the total picture without being "caught" by your eyes. In this way, she can pay equal

attention to your facial expressions, your voice, your body warmth, and the way you're holding her. As you get to know each other, she'll gradually hold your gaze for longer and longer periods, and you'll find ways to increase her tolerance—perhaps by holding her at certain distances, adjusting your voice level, or modifying your expressions.

By three months, your baby will be a master of "smile talk." Sometimes she'll start a "conversation" with a broad smile and gurgling to catch your attention. Other times she'll lie in wait, watching your face

Emotional/Social Milestones for Your One- to Three-Month-Old

- Begins to develop a social smile

- Enjoys playing with other people and may cry when playing stops

- Becomes more communicative and expressive with face and body

- Imitates some movements and facial expressions

until you give the first smile before beaming back her enthusiastic response. Her whole body will participate. Her hands will open wide, one or both arms will lift, and her limbs will move in time with your speech. Her facial movements also may mirror yours, especially if you stick out your tongue!

Like adults, your infant will prefer certain people. And her favorites, naturally, will be her parents. Grandparents or familiar sitters may receive a hesitant smile at first, followed by coos and body talk. By contrast, strangers may receive no more than a curious stare or fleeting smile. This selective behavior shows she's starting to sort out who's who in her life. At about three or four months, she'll become intrigued by other children. If she has brothers or sisters, you'll see her beaming as they talk to her. This fascination with children will increase as she gets older.

These early exchanges play an important part in her social and emotional development. By responding quickly and enthusiastically to her smiles and engaging her in these "conversations," you'll let her know she's important to you, can trust you, and has a certain amount of control in her life. By recognizing her cues when she's "talking," you'll also show you are interested in and value her. This contributes to her developing self-esteem.

As your baby grows, communication will vary with her needs and desires. On a day-to-day basis you'll find she has three general levels of need, each of which shows a different side of her personality:

1. When her needs are urgent—hunger or pain, for instance—she'll let you know, perhaps by screaming, whimpering, or using desperate body language. In time you'll learn to recognize these signals so quickly you usually can satisfy her almost before she knows what she wants.

2. When your baby is peacefully asleep, or alert and entertaining herself, feel reassured you've met all her needs for the moment. This is a welcome opportunity to rest or take care of other business. Playing by herself provides you with wonderful opportunities to observe—from a distance—how she is developing important new skills such as reaching, tracking objects, or manipulating her hands. These activities set the stage for self-soothing, which will help her settle down and ultimately sleep through the night. These are especially important skills to learn for more colicky or difficult-to-console babies.

3. Each day there will be periods when your baby's obvious needs are met but she's still fussy or fitful. She may whine, have agitated movements, or exhibit spurts of aimless activity between moments of calm. She probably won't even know what she wants, and any of several responses might help calm her. Playing, talking, singing, rocking, and walking may work. Simply repositioning her or letting her fuss it out may also be a successful strategy. You might also find that while a particular response works momentarily, she'll soon become even fussier and demand more attention. This cycle may continue until you either let her cry a few minutes or distract her with something different—for example, taking her outside. As trying as these spells can be, you'll both learn about each other because of them. You'll discover how your baby likes to be rocked, what funny faces or voices she most enjoys, and what she most likes to look at. She'll find out what to do to elicit your response, how hard you'll try to please her, and where your limits lie.

There may be times, however, when you feel frustrated, even angry, when your baby will not stop crying. The best thing to do here is gently place her back in the crib and take a little break for yourself. It is most important you resist any temptation to shake or strike your baby in any way. The danger from shaking your baby is great and can cause serious damage to your baby. "Shaken baby" situations are one form of child abuse that continues to be a problem around the world. If crying difficulties remain an issue, discuss this in detail with your pediatrician, who will give you other ideas for how to get through these episodes. Be sure you share these new techniques for quieting your infant with your childcare provider, who may feel similar frustrations with inconsolable crying.

Developmental Health Watch

Although each baby develops in her own way and at her own rate, failure to reach certain milestones may signal medical or developmental problems requiring special attention. If you notice any of the following warning signs in your infant, discuss them with your pediatrician.

- Still has Moro reflex after four months

- Doesn't seem to respond to loud sounds

- Doesn't notice her hands by two months

- Doesn't smile at the sound of your voice by two months

- Doesn't follow moving objects with her eyes by two to three months

- Doesn't grasp and hold objects by three months

- Doesn't smile at people by three months

- Cannot support her head well at three months

- Doesn't reach for and grasp toys by three to four months

- Doesn't babble by three to four months

- Doesn't bring objects to her mouth by four months

- Begins babbling, but doesn't try to imitate any of your sounds by four months

- Doesn't push down with her legs when her feet are placed on a firm surface by four months

- Has trouble moving one or both eyes in all directions

- Crosses her eyes most of the time (occasional crossing of the eyes is normal in these first months)

- Doesn't pay attention to new faces, or seems very frightened by new faces or surroundings

- Still has the tonic neck reflex at four to five months

For the Grandparents

As a grandparent, your role is especially important in the lives of your newborn grandchild, her parents, and also the other children in the family. Make sure you pay plenty of attention to the older children, who might feel neglected with all the attention showered on the baby. You can serve as a pinch hitter when the parents are adjusting to their new infant by planning special activities just for you and the baby's older brother(s) or sister(s). For example, make time for the sibling(s) with:

- Trips to the store or movie theater

- Car rides

- Appropriate stimulating times with music or reading stories

- Sleepovers at Grandma's/Grandpa's house

As we've suggested elsewhere in the book (see pages 193 and 289–90), there are other ways to help your daughter or son adjust to the new addition. Help with cleaning, shopping, and other errands. At the same time, without being overly intrusive, pass along your own wisdom and reassurances—perhaps explaining the normalness of crying, color of bowel movements, little rashes or changes in skin color, and a host of other occurrences in the early months. There will be times of frustration for the new parents, especially when the baby is crying inconsolably. Provide support and encouragement—and give them a breather, if possible, by taking the baby out for a stroll. The insights and assistance of both grandfathers and grandmothers can have a calming and lifesaving effect on new parents.

Over time your baby's periods of acute need will decrease, and she'll be able to entertain herself for longer stretches. In part this is because you're learning to anticipate care for many of her problems. But also her nervous system will be maturing, and as a result, she'll be better at coping with everyday stresses. With greater bodily control, she'll amuse and console herself and experience fewer frustrations. The periods when she seems most difficult to satisfy probably won't disappear for a few years, but as she becomes more active, it will be easier to distract her. Ultimately, she should learn to overcome these spells on her own.

During these early months, don't worry about spoiling your baby. Observe her closely and respond promptly when needed. You may not calm her every time, but it never hurts to show how much you care. In fact, the more you promptly and consistently comfort your fussing baby in the first six months, the less demanding she's likely to be when older. At this age, she needs frequent reassurance to feel secure about herself and you. By helping her establish this sense of security now, you're laying a foundation for the confidence and trust that will allow her to gradually separate from you and become a strong, independent person.

Basic Care

Feeding

Ideally, your baby will continue nursing or bottle-feeding until four to six months of age. The best way to monitor whether your baby is getting enough is by monitoring her growth. Your doctor will measure her weight, length, and head at each visit. Most breastfed babies will continue to feed on demand throughout the day and night. Pay attention to your baby's cues for hunger and fullness when deciding how much to feed; these are even more important than the amount of breast milk or formula your baby consumes.

For infants fed formula or expressed breast milk in a bottle, your infant will usually increase the amount of formula or breast milk from 2–4 ounces per feeding to 4–6 ounces per feeding by four months of age. When babies are solely breastfeeding, they will continue to feed eight to twelve times in each twenty-four-hour period. At times a breastfed infant may start demanding to eat more often, such as every ninety minutes to two hours. This is your baby's way of telling you that she is having a growth spurt and needs more milk. The more frequent feedings will send messages to your brain to make more hormones that produce breast milk, your milk supply will increase, and your baby will then return to feeding less frequently. It usually takes two to three days for the milk supply to increase. If your baby still seems persistently hungry after four to five days, call your pediatrician for a weight check appointment. If a breastfeeding infant is not gaining weight, your milk supply may have decreased. This can be associated with Mom's return to work without adequate pumping, increased stress for the mother, longer sleeping for the baby, or a variety of other factors. Your pediatrician can help determine the cause of your decreased milk supply and suggest techniques to increase your milk supply and the baby's intake. This may include increasing the feeding frequency and using a breast pump between or after feedings to increase milk production.

Frequent or repeated coughing during feeds is not normal and should be brought to the attention of the pediatrician. Frequent pauses during feeds or color changes that require the child to pull off the breast or bottle to breathe may indicate that your baby is having a hard time breathing; these should be brought to the attention of your pediatrician.

Even without any additions to your baby's diet, you'll probably notice a change in her bowel movements. Her intestines can hold more and absorb a greater amount of nutrients, so her stools may be more solid than they were during the first month. The gastrocolic reflex (see *Bowel Movements*, page 73) is also diminishing, so she should no longer have bowel movements after each feeding. In fact, between two and three months, stool frequency in both breastfed and formula-fed babies may decrease dramatically; some breastfed babies have only one movement every three or four days, and a few perfectly healthy breastfed infants have one a week. As long as your baby is eating well, gaining weight, and her stools are not too hard or dry, there's no reason to be alarmed by this decrease in stool frequency. If you are worried about stool changes, call your pediatrician.

Some breastfed infants who are getting close to four months of age may begin to sleep more than five hours at a stretch during the night. These babies may feed more often during the day, and these fortunate mothers usually appreciate a longer stretch of sleep at night. At this stage, there is no need to wake a breastfed baby during the night to feed.

As mentioned earlier, some mothers will need to return to work between three and six months after giving birth. This can be more stressful for the breastfeeding mother than the baby. For mothers who will be returning to work, begin offering expressed breast milk in a bottle occasionally by the time your infant is one month of age. This will allow the mother to get used to breast milk expression and the baby to get used to sucking from a bottle. This also will allow a breastfed baby to feed if the mother is away for a period of time. A mother can get information from her baby's pediatrician, a lactation consultant, and in many cases WIC on choosing a breast pump and learning how to use it. In the month before returning to work, many mothers will start expressing breast milk regularly once or twice a day between feedings and freezing the milk to get a supply of frozen breast milk for the daycare or caregiver. It is important for a mother returning to work to discuss her return and need to express milk during work hours with the appropriate work management before her actual return date. Returning to work part-time rather than full-time can make it easier to express breast milk and continue breastfeeding. A new mother may want to ask her manager if she can return on reduced hours for the first one to two months of work. Mothers may notice a decrease in milk supply when they return to work, possibly from the stress of returning to work. Mothers also will need to discuss with the baby's daycare or caregiver that they will be supplying expressed breast milk. Mothers returning to work need to realize that it is more than a full-time job to work and care for a household and themselves, so they need to ask for and accept help with jobs that can be done by others. Some mothers may decide that they will wean their baby gradually from breast milk to formula when they return to work.

Your child should be placed on her back when going to sleep.

Sleeping

By two months, your baby will be more alert and social and spending more time awake during the day. Meanwhile, her stomach capacity will be growing, and she'll need fewer feedings; she may start skipping one night feeding. Around three months, most (but not all) infants consistently sleep through the night (six to eight hours without disruption).

Remember, at this age, your child should be placed to sleep on her back. (See Chapter 35 for detailed information on sleep.)

Siblings

By the second month, although you may be used to having a new baby, your older children still may be adjusting. Especially if the baby is your second child, your first may be saddened by not being the primary focus.

Sometimes older children might display frustration by talking back, doing something known to be forbidden, or literally shouting for attention. A child might also regress, suddenly wetting the bed or having daytime accidents even though she's been toilet trained for months. To a child there is no such thing as negative attention. She would rather be punished for bad behavior than be ignored. This can quickly escalate into a vicious cycle of inappropriate behavior associated with receiving more and more attention. One important way to re-

Invite older siblings to play with the baby.

Set clear and consistent rules, such as never picking up the baby without permission.

verse this frustrating cycle is to actively catch her being good. Giving her praise for playing by herself or reading a book makes those activities more likely to occur the next time she's looking for attention. Having each parent spend some time with her alone each day may also help. You may also need to pick your battles. If your child is doing something to get your attention that is not harmful or dangerous (whining, for example), ignoring that behavior means that she will likely find another way to get your attention.

However, you'll need to take more direct action if your older child takes out her frustration on the baby—pulling away her bottle or even hitting her. Sit down and talk with her. Be prepared to hear things like "I wish that baby had never come here." Try to keep this and her other feelings in mind as you confront her. Reassure her you still love her very much, but explain firmly she must

Toys and Activities Appropriate for Your One- to Three-Month-Old

- Images or books with high-contrast patterns
- Bright, varied mobile
- Rattles (sturdy enough not to break)
- Singing to your baby
- Playing soft music on low volume

not hurt the baby. Make an extra effort to include her in all family activities, and encourage her to interact with the newborn. Make her feel like an important "big kid" by giving her specific baby-related jobs, such as carrying the diaper bag, putting away toys, helping dress the baby, or being in charge of making sure visitors and others wash their hands before they hold "her" baby.

Stimulating Infant Brain Growth: Age One Month Through Three Months

- Provide healthy nutrition as your baby grows; have periodic checkups and timely immunizations from a regular source of medical care.

- Give consistent, warm, physical contact—hugging, skin-to-skin, body-to-body contact—to establish your infant's sense of security and well-being. Talk, read, and sing to your baby during dressing, bathing, feeding, playing, walking, and driving. Use simple, lively phrases and address your baby by name. Respond to her gestures, as well as to the faces and the sounds she makes.

- Read to your baby every day, starting at birth. This time provides close physical contact, helps her learn your voice, and develops a wonderful lifelong habit.

- Be attentive to your baby's rhythms and moods. Learn to read her cues and respond to her when she is upset as well as when she is happy. Babies cannot be spoiled.

- Provide colorful objects of different shapes, sizes, and textures that she can play with. Show her children's picture books and family photographs.

- Your face is by far the most interesting visual object at this age. Play peekaboo with your baby.

- If you speak a foreign language, use it at home.

- Avoid subjecting your baby to stressful or traumatic experiences, physical or psychological.

- Make sure other people who provide care and supervision for your baby understand the importance of forming a loving and comforting relationship with your child and also provide consistent care.

Health Watch

Newborns can get very sick very quickly, so if your infant is under three months and has a rectal temperature of 100.4 degrees Fahrenheit (38 degrees Celsius) or higher, call your pediatrician. The following medical problems are common between the ages of two and four months. If you are concerned your baby has any of these conditions while younger than two months, contact your pediatrician. Check Part 2 of this book for other illnesses and conditions that occur throughout childhood.

DIARRHEA (see also *Diarrhea*, page 537). If your baby has a vomiting spell followed a day or two later by diarrhea, she probably has a viral infection in her intestinal tract. If you're breastfeeding, your pediatrician will probably suggest you continue nursing as usual. If you're formula-feeding, in most cases you can continue to do so. If diarrhea persists, you may be advised to use a lactose-free formula for a while before returning to the original formula. In some instances your pediatrician may advise you to limit your baby's intake to a solution containing electrolytes (e.g., salt and potassium) and sugar, since diarrhea can sometimes "wash out" the enzymes needed to properly and effectively digest the sugar in cow's milk–based formulas.

EAR INFECTIONS (see also *Middle Ear Infections*, page 670). Although ear infections are more common in older babies, occasionally they occur in infants under three months. Babies are prone to ear infections because the tube that connects the nasal passages to the middle ear (the Eustachian tube) is very short and may not function well at this age, allowing fluid to collect in the middle ear and making it easy for a cold virus in the nasal passages to spread to the ear. A middle ear viral infection can then be made worse with a bacterial infection on top of it, becoming a true middle ear infection.

The first sign of an ear infection is usually irritability, especially at night. The infection may also produce a fever. If your pediatrician's ear examination confirms an infection is present, the doctor may recommend giving liquid acetaminophen to your baby. (Do *not* give her aspirin; it can cause a serious brain disorder called Reye syndrome. See page 555.) Your pediatrician also may prescribe antibiotics—either drops, oral liquids, or both—although if your child has no fever or is not severely ill, antibiotics may not be necessary. While ear infections can be caused by bacteria or viruses, antibiotics treat only bacterial infections, and may not be recommended if the pediatrician isn't convinced a bacterial infection is present.

Many parents get concerned about cleaning wax (cerumen) from their babies' ears. Ear wax is normal and healthy, and ears clean themselves. Babies' ears need nothing more than a quick pass of a soft washcloth to stay clean. Discharge from the ear other than wax, such as pus, warrants a visit to the pediatrician.

EYE INFECTIONS (see *Eye Infections*, page 739). Any signs of eye infection, such as eye swelling, redness, or discharge, during the first few weeks after birth can be potentially serious, but certainly not always. For example, if a tear duct is blocked, there can be discharge and tearing, but generally without redness.

SPITTING UP (GASTROESOPHAGEAL REFLUX) (see page 556). This condition occurs when stomach contents make their way back into the esophagus. This reflux takes place when the sphincter (the muscle that keeps the stomach contents from coming back up into the esophagus) relaxes at the wrong time, or, less commonly, is too weak, allowing food or liquid to flow upward. Because of this sphincter immaturity, all babies reflux to some degree, although levels decrease over time with most children. In some cases, reflux can be a sign of overfeeding. If you think this may be the case, remember to use your baby's cues of hunger and fullness to decide how much to feed her, rather than the amount of breast milk or formula in the bottle. If your baby seems to have severe reflux or reflux causes problems with feeds, inform your pediatrician.

Recent research shows that chronic gastroesophageal reflux is more common in children than previously believed, and can begin as early as infancy. An infant with this condition may vomit not long after eating, have periods of coughing, become irritable, have difficulty swallowing, and arch her back; she may also be underweight. Spitting up or vomiting is common in infants less than six months of age, with about half doing this at times; it's seen in about 5 percent of infants at twelve months. To minimize the problem, burp your baby several times during a feed, as well as afterward. Because the condition can worsen when your infant is lying flat, try keeping her in an upright position for about half an hour following each feeding. Because of concerns about SIDS (sudden infant death syndrome), do not place her on her stomach for sleep in an attempt to help relieve her reflux symptoms, unless recommended by a specialist for babies with very severe reflux. The safest way for your baby to sleep is always on her back. Remember: "back to sleep."

In some cases, your doctor may recommend thickening your baby's formula or breast milk to reduce the amount of reflux. She might also suggest switching to a protein hydrolysate formula (ask your doctor what kind to buy) and then see if symptoms improve in the next week or two. If your infant has an allergy to cow's milk, this switch in formulas may help. In cases where your baby isn't keeping enough down to gain weight properly, or if she is very uncomfortable, medications may be prescribed.

Some cases of vomiting in the first few months may be caused by *pyloric stenosis,* a condition where the opening connecting the stomach to the small intestine narrows, causing forceful vomiting and a change in bowel movement patterns. If your pediatrician is concerned your baby may have pyloric stenosis, an ultrasound is ordered, and, if needed, a referral for further treatment. (See also *Vomiting,* page 555.)

RASHES AND SKIN CONDITIONS. Many rashes seen in the first month may persist through the second or third month. In addition, eczema may occur anytime after one month of age. Eczema, or atopic dermatitis, is a skin condition resulting in dry, scaly skin, and often red patches, usually on the face, in the bends of the elbows, and behind the knees. In young infants, it's most common on the elbows and knees. The patches can range from small and mild to extremely itchy, which may make a baby irritable. Ask your pediatrician to recommend treatment, which may vary depending on the condition's severity, and could include either over-the-counter or prescription lotions, creams, or ointments (use the over-the-counter products only if your doctor specifically recommends them, since she can guide you toward those products that are most effective). For babies who have only occasional and mild eczema (small patches), no treatment may be necessary.

To prevent a recurrence, use only mild unscented soaps to wash your baby and her clothes, and dress her only in soft clothing (no wool or rough weaves). Bathe her no more than three times a week, since frequent baths may further dry her skin. (If your doctor believes certain foods may trigger the eczema, particularly once your baby is taking solid foods, she may recommend avoiding these foods.) (For more information about eczema, see pages 568–80.)

RESPIRATORY SYNCYTIAL VIRUS (RSV) INFECTIONS. RSV is the most common cause of lower respiratory tract infections in infants and young children, and is one of many cold-causing viruses in children. Infecting the lungs and breathing passages, it is frequently responsible for bronchiolitis and pneumonia in children under age one. In fact, the highest incidence of RSV illness occurs in infants from two months to eight months. RSV is also the most common reason infants under one year are hospitalized.

RSV is a highly contagious infection, occurring most often during the fall through spring. It causes symptoms like a runny or stuffy nose with or without an accompanying sore throat, mild cough, and sometimes fever. The infection can remain in the nose or involve the ears and can spread to the lower respiratory tract, causing bronchiolitis. The symptoms of bronchiolitis include abnormally rapid breathing and wheezing.

If your baby was born prematurely or has chronic lung disease, she has a higher risk of a serious RSV infection. Premature babies frequently have underdeveloped lungs and may not have received enough antibodies from their mothers to help combat RSV if encountered.

You can reduce your infant's chances of developing a more serious RSV infection in several ways:

■ Have people wash their hands with warm water and soap before picking up and holding your baby.

■ Reduce close contact with people who have runny noses or other sicknesses. Continue to breastfeed when you have a cold, however, since doing so will supply the baby with nourishment and protective antibodies.

■ As much as possible, limit your baby's siblings from spending time with your infant when they have a cold (and make sure they wash their hands frequently).

■ Keep your baby away from crowded areas, such as shopping malls and elevators, where she'll have close contact with people who may be sick.

■ Don't smoke around your baby, and prohibit smoking near her, since secondhand smoke could increase her susceptibility to a serious RSV infection.

If your pediatrician determines that your baby has bronchiolitis or another RSV infection, she may recommend symptomatic treatment, such as easing nasal stuffiness with a nasal aspirator or mild salt-solution nasal drops. Severe pneumonia or bronchiolitis may require hospitalization to administer humidified oxygen and medications to help your child breathe more easily. (For more information about RSV infections, see *Bronchiolitis*, page 603.)

UPPER RESPIRATORY INFECTIONS (URI) (see also *Colds/Upper Respiratory Infection*, page 667). Many babies have their first cold during these months. Breastfeeding provides some immunity, but it is not complete protection by any means, especially if another family member has a respiratory illness. The infection spreads easily through respiratory droplets in the air or by hand contact. (Exposure to cold temperatures or drafts, on the other hand—contrary to popular opinion—does not cause colds.) Washing hands, sneezing or coughing into the crook of your elbow, and refraining from kissing when you have a cold will decrease the spread of the virus; at the same time, keep in mind you won't be able to avoid all colds, since people can spread most viruses before they develop symptoms.

Most respiratory infections in young babies are mild, producing a cough, runny nose, and slightly elevated temperature, but rarely a high fever. A runny nose, however, can be troublesome for an infant. She cannot blow her nose, so the mucus blocks the nasal passages. Before three or four months, an infant doesn't breathe well through her mouth, so this nose blockage causes more discomfort than for older children. A congested nose also often disturbs sleep and causes babies to wake when not able to breathe well. It can interfere with feeding, too, since infants must interrupt sucking to breathe through their mouth.

If congestion does occur and interferes with your baby's ability to feed and breathe comfortably, try using a bulb syringe to suction the mucus from her nose, especially before feedings or when it's obviously blocked. A few drops of normal saline (prescribed by your pediatrician) into her nose will thin the mucus, making it easier to suction. Squeeze the bulb first; then insert the tip *gently* into the nostril and slowly release the bulb. (Caution: Too vigorous or frequent suctioning may cause increased swelling of delicate nasal tissues.) Although acetaminophen will lower an elevated temperature and calm her if she's irritable, you should give it to a baby this young *only* on your pediatrician's advice. *Do not use aspirin.* (See *Reye Syndrome*, page 555; *Medication*, page 779.) Fortunately, for most common colds and upper respiratory infections, babies don't need to see the doctor. You should, however, call if any of the following occurs:

■ A persistent cough

■ Loss of appetite and refuses several feedings

■ Fever: **Contact your pediatrician any time a baby under three months of age has a rectal temperature of 100.4 degrees Fahrenheit (38 degrees Celsius) or higher.**

■ Excessive irritability

■ Unusual sleepiness or hard to awaken

Immunization Update

Your baby should receive the hepatitis B vaccine soon after birth and before she is discharged from the hospital, and again at least four weeks after the first dose.

At two months, and again at four months, your baby should receive:

- DTaP vaccine

- Inactivated polio vaccine

- Hib vaccine

- Pneumococcal vaccine

- Rotavirus vaccine

- Hepatitis B vaccine (if not given at one month of age)

(For detailed information, see page 85 and Chapter 31, *Immunizations*.)

Safety Check
Falls

- Never place the baby in an infant seat on a table, chair, or any other surface above floor level.

- Never leave your baby unattended on a bed, couch, changing table, or chair. When purchasing a changing table, look for one with 2-inch (or higher) guardrails. To avoid a serious fall, don't place it near a window. (For more information about changing tables, see page 479.)

- On all kinds of gear, always use the safety straps.

Burns

- Never hold your baby while smoking, drinking a hot liquid, or cooking by a hot stove or oven.

- Never allow anyone to smoke around your baby.

- Before placing your baby in the bath, always test the water temperature with the inside of your wrist or forearm. Also, fill the bathing tub (or sink) with water—and then test its temperature—*before* placing your baby in the water. To prevent scalding, the hottest temperature at the faucet should be no more than 120 degrees Fahrenheit (48.9 degrees Celsius).

■ Never heat your baby's milk (or, later on, food) in a microwave oven. Mix it well and test the temperature before serving.

Choking

■ Routinely check all toys for small parts that could be pulled or broken off. Also look for sharp edges, which can pose a danger.

■ For this age group, do not attach a toy to the crib, since the baby could pull it down or become entangled in it.

~ 8 ~

Age Four Months
Through Seven Months

THESE ARE GLORIOUS MONTHS for you and your baby. As his personality emerges, his laughter, giggles, and joy of being with you and all he sees are a wonder every day. Each day for him has new surprises and new accomplishments, and for you there is a growing sense of just how special the experience is.

By your infant's four-month birthday, you'll probably have more of a daily routine for his feeding, napping, bathing, and sleeping at night. This routine helps your baby feel secure while allowing you to budget time and activities. The schedule should be flexible, though. During a growth spurt, your baby will eat more frequently; if he's ill, he may have trouble sleeping. And sometimes you might want to have some spur-of-the-moment fun. Short strolls when the sun finally appears on a dreary day, an unexpected lunch visit from grandparents, or a family excursion to the zoo are all wonderful excuses to break the routine. Being open to life events and impulse will make life together more enjoyable and help your baby learn to adapt to the changes in his life ahead. Many parents will be going back to work during this time, and this can cause added stress during the first year.

For the time being, the most important changes are internal. In this period, he'll learn to coordinate his emerging perceptive abilities (vision, touch, and hearing) and his increasing motor abilities to develop skills like grasping, rolling over, sitting up, and possibly even crawling. The control evident in his budding motor skills will extend to every part of his life. Instead of reacting primarily by reflex, he'll now choose what he will and won't do. As a newborn, he sucked on almost anything placed in his mouth, but now he has definite favorites. Before, he merely looked at a strange new toy, but now he mouths, manipulates, and explores all its qualities.

Your baby will better communicate his emotions and desires now, and he'll voice them frequently. He'll cry not only when he's hungry or uncomfortable, but also when he wants a different toy or a change in activity.

You may find that your five- or six-month-old occasionally cries when you leave the room or when he's confronted by a stranger. He's developing a strong attachment to those who regularly care for him. He now associates you with his own well-being and can distinguish you from other people. Even if he doesn't cry out for you, he shows this new awareness by curiously and carefully studying a stranger's face. By eight or nine months, he may openly object to strangers who come too close. This is a normal developmental stage known as stranger anxiety.

However, in the months before stranger anxiety, your child will probably go through a period of delightful showmanship, smiling and playing with everyone he meets. His personality will be coming out in full bloom, and even people first meeting him will notice his many unique character traits. Take advantage of his sociability and acquaint him with people who will care for him in the future, such as babysitters, relatives, or childcare workers. This may help smooth the waters later when your baby hits the stranger-anxiety period.

If you haven't already, you'll learn there is no exact formula for raising an ideal child. You and your baby are each unique, and your relationship is unique as well. What works for one baby may not work for another. You have to discover what succeeds for you through trial and error. While your neighbor's child may fall asleep easily and sleep through the night, your baby may need some extra holding and cuddling. This can be frustrating and cause stress during the first year. While your first child might have needed a lot of hugging and comforting, your second might prefer more time alone. These individual differences don't indicate that your parenting is "right" or "wrong," only that each baby is unique.

Over time, you will get to know your child's individual traits, and you'll develop patterns of interaction designed especially for him. If you remain flexible and open to his special traits, he'll help steer your actions as a parent in the right direction. (Also see the discussion of *temperament* on page 238 in this chapter.)

Growth and Development
Physical Appearance and Growth

Between four and seven months, your baby will gain approximately 1 to 1¼ pounds (0.45–0.56 kg) a month. (By his eight-month birthday, he will probably weigh about two and a half times his birth weight.) His bones also grow at a rapid rate. During these months his length will increase by about 2 inches (5 cm) and his head circumference by about 1 inch (2.5 cm).

Your child's specific weight and height are not as important as his growth rate. By now you should have established his position on the growth curve in the Appendix. Continue to plot his measurements at regular intervals to make sure he maintains his growth rate. If you find he starts following a different curve or gains weight or height unusually slowly, discuss it with your pediatrician.

Movement

Previously, your baby established the muscle control needed to move both his eyes and head, so he could follow objects. He'll now take on an even greater challenge: sitting up. He'll accomplish this as his back and neck muscles gradually strengthen and he develops better balance in his trunk, head, and neck. First he'll raise his head and hold it up while lying on his stomach. Encourage this by placing him on his stomach and extending his arms forward when he is awake; then get his attention with an attractive toy and coax him to hold his head up and look at you. This also is a good way to check his hearing and vision.

Once able to lift his head, your baby will start pushing up on his arms and arching his back to lift his chest. This strengthens his upper body, essential to remaining steady and upright when sitting. At the same time, he may rock on his stomach, kick his legs, and "swim" with his arms. These abilities, which usually appear at about five months, are necessary for rolling over and crawling. By the end of this period, he'll probably be able to roll over in both directions, although the time frame varies for different babies. Most children roll from stomach to back before the opposite direction, although doing it in reverse is perfectly normal.

Once your baby can raise his chest, help him practice sitting up. Hold him up or support his back with pillows as he learns to balance herself. He'll soon learn to "tripod," leaning forward as he extends his arms to balance. Interesting toys in front of him will give him a focus as he gains his balance. It will be some time before he can maneuver himself to sitting without your assistance, but by six to eight months, if you position him upright, he'll remain sitting without leaning forward on his arms. Then he can discover all the wonderful things the world has to offer from this new vantage point.

By the fourth month, your baby can easily bring interesting objects to his mouth. During his next four months, he'll begin to use his fingers and thumbs in a mitten- or claw-like grip or raking motion, and he'll manage to pick up many things. He won't develop the pincer grasp with index finger and thumb until he's about nine months old, but by the sixth to eighth month, he'll learn to transfer objects from hand to hand, and turn and twist them. Remove any objects from his environment that he could choke on or injure himself with.

Movement Milestones for Your Four- to Seven-Month-Old

- Rolls both ways (front to back, back to front)

- Sits with, and then without, support of his hands

- Supports his whole weight on his legs

- Reaches with one hand

- Transfers object from hand to hand

- Uses raking grasp (not pincer)

As his physical coordination improves, your baby will discover new parts of his body. Lying on his back, he can now grab his feet and toes and bring them to his mouth. While being diapered, he may reach down to touch his genitals. When sitting up, he may slap his knee or thigh. Through these explorations he'll discover many new and interesting sensations. He'll start to understand the function of body

Toys Appropriate for Your Four- to Seven-Month-Old

- Unbreakable plastic or mylar mirror
- Soft balls, including some that make soft, pleasant sounds
- Textured toys that make sounds
- Toys that have fingerholds
- Musical toys, such as bells, maracas, tambourines (make sure none of the parts can become loose)
- See-through rattles that show the pieces making the noise
- Old magazines with bright pictures for you to show him
- Baby books with board, cloth, or vinyl pages

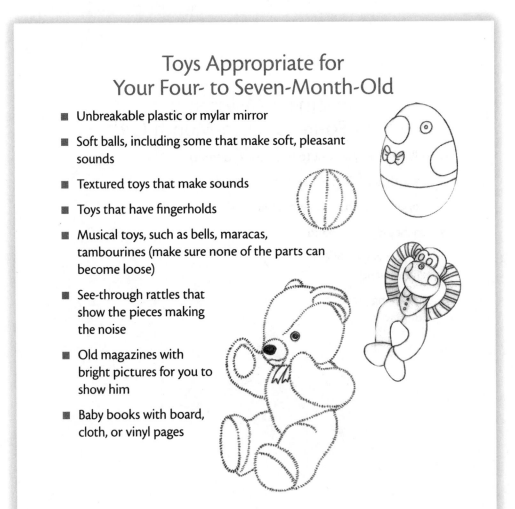

parts. When you place his feet on the floor, he may curl his toes and stroke the surface, use his feet and legs to practice "walking," or bounce up and down. Watch out! These are all preparations for the next major milestones: crawling and standing.

Vision

As your baby works on his motor skills, have you noticed how closely he watches everything he's doing? His concentration reaching for a toy may remind you of a scientist engrossed in research. It's obvious his good vision is playing a key role in his early motor and cognitive development. Conveniently, his eyes become fully functional just when he needs them most.

Although your baby could see at birth, his total visual ability has taken months to develop. Only now can he distinguish subtle shades of reds, blues, and yellows. Don't be surprised if you notice he prefers red or blue to other colors; these seem to be favorites among many infants this age. Most babies also like increasingly complex patterns and shapes as they get older—something to keep in mind when shopping for picture books or posters for your child's nursery.

By four months, your baby's visual range has increased to several yards or more, and it will continue to expand. (See Chapter 25, *Eyes*, for more information on eye maturity.) At the same time, he'll follow faster and faster movements with his eyes. In the early months, if you rolled a ball across the room, he couldn't track it, but now he'll follow moving objects easily. As his hand-eye coordination improves, he'll grab these objects as well.

By four months, your baby will begin noticing not only the way you talk but the individual sounds you make.

A mobile over the crib or in front of an infant's bouncy seat is an ideal way to stimulate a young baby's vision. However, by about five months, your baby will quickly get bored and search for other things. Also, by this age, he may be sitting up and might pull down or tangle herself in a mobile. *For this reason, remove mobiles from cribs or play yards as soon as your baby is able to pull or hold himself upright.* Hold your baby's visual interest by also keeping him moving—around the home, down the block, to the store, or on special excursions. Help him find things he's never seen before, and name each one out loud for him.

A mirror is another source of endless fascination for babies this age. The reflected image is constantly changing, and, even more important, it responds directly to your child's movements. This is a clue the person in the mirror is actually himself. It may take a while to come to this realization, but it will probably register during this period.

Your child's visual awareness should clearly increase during these four months. Watch how he responds when introduced to new shapes, colors, and objects. If he is not interested in looking at new things, or if one or both eyes turn in or out, inform your pediatrician.

Vision Milestones for Your Four- to Seven-Month-Old

- Develops full color vision
- Distance vision matures
- Ability to track moving objects improves

Language Development

Your baby learns language in stages. From birth, he receives information about language by hearing people make sounds and watching them communicate. At first, he is most interested in the pitch and level of your voice. When you talk in a soothing way, he'll stop crying because he hears you want to comfort him. By contrast, if you shout out in anger, he will probably cry and show signs of being frightened because your voice is telling him something is wrong. By four months, he'll notice not only the way you talk, but the individual sounds you make. He'll listen to the vowels and consonants and begin to notice how these combine into syllables, words, and sentences.

Besides hearing sounds, your baby has also been producing them from the very beginning, first as cries and then coos. At about four months, he'll start to babble, using many rhythms and characteristics of his native language. Although it may sound like gibberish, if you listen closely, you'll hear him raise and drop his voice as if he were making a statement or asking a question. Encourage him by talking to him throughout the day. When you recognize a syllable, repeat it back and then say some simple words that contain that sound. If his sound of the day is "bah," introduce "bottle," "box," "bonnet," "baa, baa, black sheep," and so on.

Participation in your child's language development becomes even more important after six or seven months, when he begins actively imitating the sounds of speech. Up till then, he might repeat one sound for a whole day or several days at a stretch before trying another. Now he'll become much more responsive to the sounds he hears you make, and he'll try to follow. Introduce him to simple syllables and words: "baby," "cat," "dog," "go," "hot," "cold," and "walk," as well as "Mama" and "Dada." Although it may be up to a year or more before you can interpret his babbling, your baby can understand many words well before his first birthday.

If he doesn't babble or imitate sounds by his seventh month, it could mean a hearing or speech development problem. A baby with partial hearing loss can still be startled by loud noises or will turn his head in their direction, and he may even respond to your voice. However, he will have difficulty imitating speech. If your child does not babble or produce a variety of sounds by about six months, alert your pediatrician. If he had frequent ear infections, he might have fluid trapped in the middle ear space, which could interfere with hearing. A particularly important group of infants who need audiology follow-up at this age are those who were in the neonatal intensive care unit for any period of time. Usually they have a screening hearing test at birth and a recommendation to have a behavioral hearing test by six months of age. You can discuss this with your primary care pediatrician, since oftentimes there is an audiologist your doctor works with closely.

Language Milestones for Your Four- to Seven-Month-Old

- Responds to own name
- Begins to respond to "no"
- Distinguishes emotions by tone of voice
- Responds to sound by making sounds
- Uses voice to express joy and displeasure
- Babbles chains of consonants

Special equipment is used to check a very young baby's hearing. All newborns should be tested for hearing loss. In addition, your observations are the early warning system for whether further testing is needed. If you suspect a problem, you might ask your pediatrician for a referral to a children's hearing specialist.

Cognitive Development

Previously, you might have wondered if your baby really understood what was happening around him. This reaction is not surprising. After all, although you knew when he was comfortable or not, signs of actually thinking were likely few. But studies show from the minute he's born, your baby is learning about the world around him. Now, as his memory and attention span increase, you'll see evidence he's not only absorbing information but also applying it to his day-to-day activities.

During this period, he'll refine his concept of cause and effect. He'll probably stumble on this notion somewhere between four and five months. Perhaps while kicking his mattress, he'll notice the crib shaking. Or maybe he'll realize his rattle makes a noise when hit. Once he understands he can cause these interesting reactions, he'll continue to experiment.

Your baby will quickly discover that some things, such as bells and keys, make interesting sounds when moved or shaken. Before long, he'll begin dropping things intentionally to see you pick them up, and start a chain of responses from his audience, including funny faces, groans, and laughter. As annoying as

When he bangs certain things on the table or drops them on the floor, he'll start a chain of responses from his audience.

this may be, it's a way for him to learn about cause and effect and his ability to influence his environment.

It's important to give your child what he needs for these experiments and encourage him to test his "theories." Make sure everything you give is unbreakable, lightweight, and large enough that he can't swallow it. If he loses interest in the usual toys, plastic or wooden spoons, unbreakable cups, jar or bowl lids, and boxes are endlessly entertaining and inexpensive.

Cognitive Milestones for Your Four- to Seven-Month-Old

- Finds partially hidden objects
- Explores with hands and mouth
- Struggles to get objects that are out of reach

Another major discovery your baby makes toward the end of this period is that objects continue to exist when out of his sight—a principle called object permanence. During his first few months, he probably thought the world consisted only of things he could see. When you hid a toy under a cloth, he thought it was gone for good, and so he wouldn't bother looking for it. But sometime after four months he'll begin to realize the world is more permanent. You're the same person who greets him every morning. The block you hid under the can did not vanish after all. Playing hiding games like peekaboo and observing the people and things around him, your baby will continue to learn about object permanence for many months to come.

Emotional Development

Between four and seven months, your baby may undergo a dramatic change in personality. At the beginning of this period, he may seem relatively passive and preoccupied with getting enough food, sleep, and affection. But as he learns to sit up, use his hands, and move about, he's likely to become increasingly assertive and more attentive to the world outside. He'll be eager to reach out and touch everything, and if he can't manage, he'll demand your help by yelling, banging, or dropping the nearest object at hand. Once you've come to his rescue, he'll probably forget what he was doing and concentrate on you—smiling, laughing, babbling, and imitating you. While he'll quickly get bored with even the most engaging toy, he'll never tire of your attention.

The subtle aspects of your baby's personality are determined largely by his temperament. Is he rambunctious or gentle? Easygoing or easily upset? Headstrong or compliant? To a large extent, these are inborn character traits. Just like their sizes and shapes, infants' temperaments differ as well and include their activity levels, persistence, and adaptability to the world around them. These traits will become increasingly apparent during these months. You won't necessarily find all of his personal characteristics enjoyable all the time—especially not when your determined six-month-old screams in frustration as he lunges for the family cat. But in the long run, adapting to his natural personality is best. It is real and directly affects you and the rest of the family, so it's important to understand him as completely as possible.

Your child's behavioral style will affect how you parent and sometimes even your feelings toward yourself. An agreeable, even-tempered child, for example, is more likely to make you feel competent as a parent than one who is constantly irritable. As you've probably discovered already, some infants of this age are "easy," calm, and predictable, while others are more difficult. Strongwilled and high-strung babies require an extra dose of patience and gentle guidance. They often don't adapt to changing surroundings easily and will become increasingly upset if pushed to perform before they're ready. You'll fare better and reduce stress by recognizing and accommodating his temperament rather than resisting and trying to change it.

Talking and cuddling sometimes will do wonders to calm the nerves of an irritable child. Distracting him can refocus his energy. If he screams because you won't retrieve the toy he dropped for the tenth time, move him to the floor so he can reach it himself.

The shy or sensitive child also requires special attention, particularly if you have more boisterous children who overshadow him. When a baby is quiet and undemanding, it's easy to assume he's content. If he doesn't laugh or smile a lot, you may not play with him as much. But this baby often needs personal contact even more than others. He may be overwhelmed easily and needs you to show him how to be assertive and become involved. Give him plenty of time to warm up to any situation, and make sure other people approach him slowly. Let him sit on the sidelines before attempting to involve him directly. Once he feels secure, gradually he'll become more responsive to the people around him.

Developmental Health Watch

Because each baby develops in his own manner, it's impossible to tell exactly when or how your child will perfect a given skill. The developmental milestones listed in this book will give you a general idea of the changes you can expect, but don't be alarmed if your baby's development takes a slightly different course. Alert your pediatrician, however, if your baby displays any of the following signs of possible developmental delay for this age range.

- Seems very stiff, with tight muscles
- Seems very floppy, like a rag doll
- Head still flops back when body is pulled up to a sitting position
- Reaches with one hand only
- Refuses to cuddle
- Shows no affection for the person who cares for him
- Doesn't seem to enjoy being around people
- One or both eyes consistently turn in or out
- Persistent tearing, eye drainage, or sensitivity to light
- Does not respond to sounds around him
- Does not turn his head to locate sounds by four months
- Has difficulty getting objects to his mouth

(continues on next page)

- Doesn't roll over in either direction (front to back or back to front) by five to seven months
- Seems inconsolable at night after five months
- Doesn't smile spontaneously by five months
- Cannot sit with help by six months
- Does not laugh or make squealing sounds by six months
- Does not actively reach for objects by six to seven months
- Doesn't follow objects with both eyes at near (1 foot [30 cm]) and far (6 feet [180 cm]) ranges by seven months
- Does not bear some weight on legs by seven months
- Does not try to attract attention through actions by seven months
- Does not babble by eight months
- Shows no interest in games of peekaboo by eight months

Also let your pediatrician know if you have concerns about your baby's emotional development. Your pediatrician can help, but such concerns can often be difficult to detect in a routine office visit. That's why it's important to call the doctor's attention to your concerns and describe your day-to-day observations. Write them down so you don't forget. And take comfort in the fact that with time and patience, some of his personality traits you wish you could change will evolve. In the meantime, enjoy him as he is.

Social/Emotional Milestones for Your Four- to Seven-Month-Old

- Enjoys social play
- Interested in mirror images
- Responds to other people's expressions of emotion and appears joyful often

Basic Care
Introducing Solid Foods

Exclusive breastfeeding is recommended until around six months of age. At four to six months, you can begin adding solid foods. Introducing peanut products to infants between four and six months of age may prevent a developing peanut allergy. If your child has severe eczema or an allergy to egg proteins, talk to your doctor first. There is no evidence that waiting to introduce baby-safe (soft), allergy-causing foods, such as eggs, dairy, soy, peanuts, or fish, beyond four to six months of age prevents food allergy, which is why most allergists and pediatricians recommend early introduction of allergy-causing foods to a baby's diet. It may be that when he shows interest in eating he can try tastes of the foods you are eating, while his main source of nutrition remains breastfeeding. Mothers who breastfeed do not need to avoid certain foods, and breast milk helps the baby's body become tolerant of common allergens rather than sensitive to them. Babies are born with a tongue thrust reflex, and a young infant will push his tongue against anything inserted into his mouth, including food. Most babies lose this reflex at about four to five months, so when this reflex disappears, that's a good time to begin "practicing" with solid food. Talk with your pediatrician at the four-month checkup about the timing of the introduction of solid foods, particularly if there is a strong history of food allergies in the family or your baby has severe eczema.

Once you begin, start solid food at whichever time of day feedings works best for you and your baby. However, as he gets older, he will want to eat with other family members, as family mealtimes provide significant benefits to the entire family, including improved nutrition habits, stronger family relationships—and, particularly helpful for a developing infant, exposure to lots of language, which stimulates brain development. To minimize the chances of choking, your baby should sit upright when you introduce solids. If he cries or turns away when you try, don't force the issue. It's more important you both enjoy mealtimes than for him to start foods by a specific date. Go back to nursing or bottle-feeding for a week or two, then try again. Just as you did with nursing or formula-feeding, follow your baby's cues to know when he is hungry and full rather than focusing on the specific amount he eats at each meal.

Options for experimenting with solid foods include using a spoon or a parent's fingers, or allowing your baby to explore the soft, pureed food with his hands. Putting solid foods in a bottle or infant feeder with a nipple is not recommended, as this can drastically increase food intake at each feeding, may be a risk for choking, and could lead to excessive weight gain. Besides, it's important for your baby to get used to the process of eating—sitting up tasting new foods, resting between bites, and stopping when full. This early experience will lay the foundation for good eating habits throughout his life.

Standard spoons may be too wide, but small spoons often work well; a rubber-coated baby spoon is also a good choice and can help avoid injury. Start with small amounts or tiny tastes, and talk your baby through the process ("Mmm, see how good this is?"). He probably won't know what to do the first time or two. He may look confused, wrinkle his nose, roll the food around his mouth, or reject it entirely. This is an understandable reaction, considering how different his feedings have been.

One way to ease the transition is to give your infant small tastes of food, then finish off with his usual breast milk or formula. This will prevent him from being overly frustrated when he's very hungry, and it will link the satisfaction of nursing with this new experience of spoon-feeding. No matter what you do, the first few solid-food feedings are sure to wind up on his face and bib, so increase the size of his feedings very gradually, starting with just a teaspoonful or two, until he gets the idea of swallowing solids.

What foods? Traditionally, single-grain cereals were introduced first. However, there is no medical evidence that introducing solid foods in any particular order has an advantage for your infant. Though many pediatricians recommend starting vegetables before fruits, there is no research indicating your infant will develop a dislike for or allergy to vegetables if they follow fruit. When you are breastfeeding, be sure to eat a variety of foods, including vegetables, as babies who are exposed to these tastes while nursing are less likely to reject them when they start eating solid foods.

Many babies enjoy cereals. You may use premixed baby cereals or dry varieties mixed with breast milk or formula. Pediatricians now advise parents to choose whole-grain cereals rather than highly processed ones. There is no evidence that one whole grain cereal is better than another, though some rice cereals have been found to have higher levels of arsenic compared to other grains, so it is important to use a variety of grains rather than sticking with one. Whichever you choose, make sure it is very soft or completely pureed until your baby is ready and able to safely manage and tolerate more texture.

In the past pediatricians recommended starting one new food every few days, so that you can see if a reaction occurs to that particular food. New research has shown that it is safe to start multiple foods at once. Within two or three months, your baby's daily diet should include breast milk, iron-fortified whole grain cereals, vegetables, meats (including fish), eggs, fruits, and nut butters (but never whole nuts) distributed among three meals. Remember that babies do not need the added sugars and salts that adults have grown used to. Also know that if your baby rejects a given food the first ten times, he may come to love it on the eleventh try. This repeated exposure can be especially important when introducing vegetables like broccoli and asparagus.

Once your baby sits independently, you can begin giving him finger foods to help him learn to feed himself. Parents are often skipping pureed foods altogether in favor of very soft foods that babies can self-feed, a trend called baby-led weaning. Most infants can begin learning to self-feed without assistance around eight months. Make sure anything you give is soft, easy to swallow, and breaks down into small pieces he can't choke on. Well-cooked cut-up sweet potatoes, green beans, peas, diced chicken or meat, small pieces of bread, or whole-grain crackers are good examples. Don't give any food that truly requires chewing, even if he already has teeth. After you are finished with the meal, it is a good idea to gently wipe the infant's mouth with a wet cloth for proper oral care.

When feeding your baby solid foods, use a small dish instead of the container, jar, or pouch the food came in. This will prevent the food from becoming contaminated with bacteria from the baby's mouth. Discard the portion left in the dish rather than trying to save it.

While there is a huge variety of prepared baby foods available at the store, you don't have to rely on jars or packets to feed your baby. Everything you make should be soft and well-cooked. Cooked fresh vegetables and stewed fruits are easy to prepare. Although you can feed your baby mashed raw bananas, most other fruits should be cooked until soft. Immediately refrigerate any food not used, and then inspect carefully for signs of spoilage before giving it again. Never offer foods your baby might choke on, such as whole nuts, uncut grapes or cherry tomatoes, or raw carrots or celery.

Hold off on liquids other than breast milk (or formula if you are not breastfeeding) or small amounts of water in a sippy cup. The American Academy of Pediatrics recommends fruit juice not be given to infants, since it offers no nutritional benefit to babies in this age group, and cow's milk is not recommended until after a year of age. Juice should generally be avoided in this age group and should definitely not be given as a treatment for dehydration or management of diarrhea. Giving fruit juice to infants and young children may get them used to sweet beverages, which can lead to excessive weight gain and tooth decay.

If your infant seems thirsty between feedings, breastfeed him or give him formula, or, after six months, offer small sips of extra water. Getting a child used to plain water is a healthy habit for life. During hot months when your child is losing fluid through sweat, offer water two or more times a day. If your water is fluoridated, this also will help prevent tooth decay. You can test your water with home kits to see if your water source is fluoridated. Most city water is fluoridated, and some well water naturally contains fluoride. Your pediatrician or dentist can guide you if additional fluoride is necessary. If you are using well water, it is important to have the well water tested on a regular basis for contaminants such as bacteria and toxins. The CDC recommends testing wells used for drinking a minimum of every spring, or more often if there are certain contaminants; another option is the addition of a well filtration system.

By the time your baby is six or seven months old, he'll probably sit well enough to use a high chair during mealtime. To ensure his comfort and safety, safety straps should be used, and the chair seat should be cleaned regularly. Also, look for a high chair with a detachable tray with raised rims. (See page 488 for safety recommendations.) The rims help keep dishes and food in place during more rambunctious feeding sessions. The detachable tray can be cleaned easily, a feature you're bound to appreciate in the months to come. (There still may be days when the only solution is to put the entire chair in the shower for a complete wipe-down!) As your child's diet expands and he's feeding himself more regularly, discuss his personal nutritional needs with your pediatrician. Poor eating habits established in infancy can lead to health problems later on.

Your pediatrician will help determine whether your baby is overfed, not eating enough, or eating too much of the wrong kinds of foods. By familiarizing yourself with the caloric and nutritional contents of what he eats, you can ensure he's eating a proper diet. Be aware of other food habits in your family. As your baby eats more and more table foods, he'll imitate the way you eat—the whole family should try to model a healthy, nutrient-rich diet to set a good example, and mealtimes should be a time for interaction and enjoyment, not struggles.

What if you're concerned your baby *already* has overweight? Even when infants are young, some parents are already worried their babies are gaining too much weight. There is a rise in childhood obesity and its potential complications (such as diabetes), thus it's wise to be sensitive to the problem, no matter what your child's age. Some evidence indicates that bottle-fed infants gain weight more rapidly than breastfed babies, perhaps because some parents encourage their infant to finish a bottle. Always remember to let your baby's hunger cues drive how much he eats, rather than urging him to finish a set amount of food.

And it is important to get your pediatrician's advice before making any dietary adjustments. During these months of rapid growth, your infant needs the proper balance of fat, carbohydrates, and protein.

As soon as solid foods are started, his stools will become more solid and variable in color. They'll also have a much stronger odor. Peas and other green vegetables may turn the stool deep green; beets may turn it red. (Beets sometimes make urine red as well.) His stools may contain undigested particles, especially hulls of peas or corn, and the skin of tomatoes or other vegetables. This is normal. If the stools are extremely loose, watery, or full of mucus, however, it may indicate an irritated digestive tract. In this case, consult your pediatrician to determine if there is a digestive problem.

Dietary Supplements

The American Academy of Pediatrics (AAP) currently recommends that infants should be fed breast milk exclusively for the first six months after birth. Exclusive breastfeeding means that the infant does not receive any additional foods (except vitamin D) or fluids unless medically recommended.

Our bodies need sunlight to produce vitamin D. Most of the population in the United States has lower-than-recommended levels of vitamin D, probably due to spending more time inside and the widespread use of sunscreens to prevent skin cancer. Vitamin D deficiency can produce diseases such as rickets (a severe form of vitamin D deficiency characterized by bone softening). While some amount of exposure to sunlight is good in moderation, all children should wear sunscreen, hats, and protective clothing when outdoors for extended periods of time to prevent sunburn and reduce the risk of skin cancer later in life. For this reason, the American Academy of Pediatrics recommends that all infants receive a vitamin D supplement (unless they are consuming more than 27 ounces per day of commercial formula that has the vitamin D supplement added). Vitamin D supplements of 400 IU (10 mcg) per day are recommended for babies up until age one year, with 600 IU (15 mcg) per day for children over one year.

What about iron? For the first four months, your breastfed baby needs no additional iron. The iron in his body at birth was enough for his initial growth. But now the reserves will be low and as his growth increases so will his need for iron. At four months of age infants who are partially or completely breastfeeding should be supplemented with 1 mg/kg per day of oral iron until appropriate iron-containing complementary foods (including iron-fortified cereals) are introduced in their diet. If there were pregnancy or birth complications such as diabetes, low birth weight, or prematurity, or if your baby was small for gestational age and is taking breast milk, iron supplementation may start in the first month after birth. Fortunately, once you start your baby on solid foods, he'll also receive iron from meats, iron-fortified cereals, and green vegetables. (See also *Supplementation for Breastfed and Bottle-Fed Infants*, page 131.)

Sleeping

Most babies this age still need at least two naps a day, midmorning and midday. Some babies may nap a third time later in the afternoon. In general, it's best to let your baby sleep as long as he wants, unless he has trouble falling asleep at his normal nightly bedtime. If this becomes a problem, wake him earlier from his afternoon nap.

Because your child is more alert and active now, he may have trouble winding down at the end of the day. A consistent bedtime routine will help. Experiment to see what works best, taking into consideration household activities and your baby's temperament. A warm bath, massage, rocking, story or lullaby, and a breast- or bottle-feeding will all help relax him and put him in a bedtime mood. *Remember to begin these activities before your baby becomes overtired.* Eventually he'll associate these activities with going to sleep, and that will help relax and soothe him.

Now that your baby is a little older, all the same rules of safe sleep apply (see Chapter 3), except that he is probably rolling over from back to front now on his own. Settle your baby in his crib while he's drowsy but still awake so he learns to fall asleep on his own. Gently place him on his back, whisper your good-night, and leave the room. If he cries, check on him and offer a few comforting words, then leave the room again. As the days pass, gradually give him less attention at night. If parents are consistent, most babies will cry less each night and will be more likely to learn self-soothing. (See Chapter 35 for more information on sleep.)

Teething and Dental Care

Teething usually starts during these months. The two front teeth (central incisors), either upper or lower, usually appear first, followed by the opposite front teeth. The first molars are next, followed by the canines or eyeteeth.

There is great variability in the timing and pattern of teething. If your child doesn't show any teeth until later than this age period, or if they come in out of order, don't worry. The timing may be determined by heredity, and doesn't mean anything is wrong.

Teething *occasionally* may cause mild irritability, crying, a low-grade temperature (but not over 101 degrees Fahrenheit [38.3 degrees Celsius]), excessive drooling, and a desire to chew on something hard. More often, the gums around the new teeth will swell and be tender. To ease your baby's discomfort, try gently rubbing or massaging the gums with one of your fingers. Teething rings are helpful and should be made of firm rubber. (The teethers you freeze tend to get too hard and can cause more harm than good.) Never use teething gels to numb the gums; in rare cases they can poison babies' blood cells and keep them from carrying oxygen. Homeopathic teething tablets also provide no benefit, and in some cases they have been made with potentially harmful toxins. Amber teething necklaces do not do anything at all to relieve pain, and they have caused cases of choking and strangulation; remember never to leave anything around your baby's neck. If your child seems particularly miserable or has a fever higher than 101 degrees Fahrenheit (38.3 degrees Celsius), it's probably not from teething, and you should consult your pediatrician.

Your baby should see a dentist within six months after his first tooth erupts, but no later than twelve months of age, whichever comes first. Pediatric dentists are specially trained to see infants, and you can find a pediatric dentist for your baby at the American Academy of Pediatric Dentistry's website, aapd.org. But going to your family dentist for routine pediatric care is entirely adequate and may be covered by existing health insurance.

Brushing your baby's teeth at home is very important as well. For cleaning when you first start seeing teeth, simply brush with a soft child's toothbrush and a smear of fluoridated toothpaste the size of a grain of rice. To prevent cavities, never let your baby fall asleep with a bottle or on the breast, either at nap time or at night. Doing this will keep milk from pooling around the teeth and creating a breeding ground for decay.

Swings and Play Yards

Many parents find that mechanical swings, especially with cradle attachments, can calm a crying baby when nothing else seems to work. If you use a device like this, check the weight limit and age recommendations on the device. Use only swings that stand firmly on the floor, not those that hang from door frames. Also, don't use a swing for more than half an hour, twice a day; it may quiet your baby, but it is no substitute for attention. Secure your baby properly with the safety harness at all times.

Once your baby starts to move about, you may need to use a play yard. But even before he crawls or walks, a play yard offers a protected place where he can lie or sit outdoors as well as in rooms where you have no crib or bassinet. (See *Play Yards*, page 490, for specific recommendations.) Be sure the play yard has not been recalled. Check the Consumer Product Safety Commission website (cpsc.gov) for recalled products.

Stimulating Infant Brain Growth: Age Four Months Through Seven Months

Many connections are being made in your baby's brain during this time in his young life. They are reflected in his behaviors, such as the strong attachments he has to you and others who take care of him, or his crying when you leave the room, when he is approached by a stranger, or when he wants a particular toy. He is becoming more interested in the world and is better able to communicate his emotions and desires—all the while developing new skills such as grasping, rolling over, and sitting.

Without overstimulating your baby, try these activities to help strengthen the connections in his developing brain:

- Provide a stimulating, safe environment where your baby can begin to explore and roam freely.

- Give consistent, warm, physical contact—hugging, skin-to-skin, body-to-body contact—to establish your infant's sense of security and well-being.

- Be attentive to your baby's rhythms and moods. Respond to him when he is upset as well as when he is happy.

- Talk and sing during dressing, bathing, feeding, playing, walking, and driving. He may not yet understand the language, but as he hears it, his language skills will develop. Check with your pediatrician if your baby doesn't seem to hear sounds or imitate your words.

- Engage your child in face-to-face talk. Mimic his sounds to show interest.

- Read books to your baby every day. He'll love the sound of your voice, and before long he'll enjoy looking at the pictures and "reading" on his own.

- If you speak a foreign language, use it at home.

- Engage in rhythmic movement with your child, such as dancing together to music.

- Avoid subjecting your baby to stressful or traumatic experiences, physical or psychological.

- Introduce your child to other children and parents; this is a very special period for infants. Be sensitive to cues indicating that he is ready to meet new people.

- Encourage your child to reach for toys. Give him baby blocks and soft toys that can stimulate his hand-eye coordination and his fine motor skills.

- Make sure other people who provide care and supervision for your baby understand the importance of forming a loving and comforting relationship with your child.

- Encourage your child to begin to sleep for extended periods at night; if you need advice about this important step in your infant's development, ask your pediatrician.

- Spend time on the floor playing with your child every day.

- If your child will be cared for by others, choose quality childcare that is affectionate, responsive, educational, and safe. Visit your childcare provider frequently and share your ideas about positive caregiving.

Behavior
Discipline

As your baby becomes more mobile and inquisitive, he'll naturally become more assertive as well. This is wonderful for his self-esteem and should be encouraged as much as possible. However, when he wants to do something dangerous or disruptive to the family, you'll need to take charge.

For the first six months or so, the best way to deal with conflicts is to distract him with an alternative activity or toy. Standard discipline techniques won't work until his memory span increases, around the end of his seventh month. Only then can you use a variety of techniques to discourage undesired behavior.

When you begin disciplining, it should never be harsh. Discipline means to teach or instruct, not necessarily to punish. Often the most successful approach is to reward desired behavior and withhold rewards for undesired behavior. If he cries for no apparent reason, first make sure there's nothing wrong physically; when he stops, reward him with extra attention, kind words, and hugs. If he starts again, wait longer before turning your attention to him, and use a firm tone as you talk. This time, don't reward him with extra attention or hugs.

The main goal of discipline is to teach limits. Negative disciplinary strategies, including hitting, yelling at, or shaming children, should never be used

A Word for Grandparents

As a grandparent, you love watching your grandchild develop. Between four and seven months, he's discovering the world around him and has more physical and cognitive abilities to engage his environment.

As laughter abounds and sights and sounds take on more meaning for your grandchild, these are great months for both of you. Smiles, interactive play, and recognition of objects, sounds, people, and names will become part of these discovery months. His vision is better, his hand transfer more efficient, and his curiosity unstoppable. Be sure to reinforce these early learning milestones occurring along the way.

Your grandchild is also beginning to move. Although this is a wondrous period of life, you need to be particularly vigilant as he begins to sit. He will be upright more frequently, and likely to tip over.

You have an important role in stimulating his development. You can make the most of this and enjoying your time with him by taking these steps:

- Follow your own child's lead with respect to activities for your grandchild, adding special things of your own when appropriate. Special names ("Nana," "Grandpa Stan"), places, and books or music you share can be unique to his experiences with you. Also consider inviting other grandparents and their grandchildren to join from time to time, which can be a special treat for your grandchild.

- When buying gifts for your grandchild, choose age-appropriate books, as well as toys that encourage creative play.

- Make yourself available to babysit as often as possible when requested. These times spent alone with your grandchild will be special moments you'll always treasure. Take him on field trips (to the park or zoo), and as the years pass, help him develop hobbies you can do together.

- You will get a better idea of your grandchild's temperament as he grows. Inevitably, you will make comparisons to family members he resembles. Some of his likes and dislikes will emerge, and it is best to respect them. If your grandchild is boisterous and active, you may need extra patience to fully enjoy his company. Give him space, let him be who he is—but rein him in if he gets too far out of bounds. The same with a shy child; don't expect him to be unbashful the moment you appear. Enjoy him for who he is.

■ Diaper changing is often a control exercise, and you may need all your strength to keep a baby who's a "wiggly worm" from rolling onto the floor. Switching from the changing table to the bed or floor is often a good idea; remember to keep all of the diapering supplies close by and within reach.

■ Discuss discipline with the baby's parents, and make sure your own approach is consistent with their wishes.

■ Consider investing in an appropriate crib and other furniture for your home. A high chair will come in handy if he eats meals at your home. A stroller and car safety seat may be useful as well. And keep some everyday medications at your home (for a fever, diaper rash, etc.), along with a few toys he can enjoy.

■ Your grandchild's eating has become more regular, and by the end of this period he will be on solid foods (e.g., infant cereal and pureed vegetables, fruits, and meats). When you're caring for your grandchild, follow the guidance of his parents on what and when to feed him. If they're on his menu, let him explore your versions of "junior foods," such as fruit, soft vegetables, and meats. Stay away from adult canned foods. Avoid giving him large food chunks that could cause choking. If your grandchild is still being breastfed, keep some frozen breast milk in your freezer.

■ Your grandchild should be sleeping through the night, so "overnighters" will be more enjoyable and less disruptive of your schedule.

■ Make your home a safe environment. Follow the guidelines in Chapter 15 to babyproof your home, including placing all medications and matches out of sight and reach.

■ There are times when having your grandchild and his siblings stay at your home will be too much to handle. Try caring for one child at a time, especially at first. Doing this will allow for tailoring the activities, while still providing needed relief to your own child, who can then focus on the remaining child(ren). Your continued, valued role in assisting your child to become the most effective parent possible remains the core purpose for all you do.

■ You can promote your grandchild's development now and in the future by taking family pictures and videos, creating photo albums, and writing down family stories (accompanied by old and new photos).

and are not effective in either the short term or the long term. Try to help him understand what exactly he's doing wrong when he breaks a rule. If you notice him doing something not allowed, such as pulling your hair, let him know it's wrong by calmly saying "no," stopping him by gently pulling his fingers from your hair, and redirecting his attention to something else.

If your child is touching or trying to put something in his mouth he shouldn't, gently pull his hand away as you tell him what is off-limits. But since you want to encourage touching *other* things, avoid saying "Don't touch." More precise phrases, such as "Don't eat the flowers" or "No eating leaves," will convey the message without confusing him.

Never rely only on discipline to keep your child safe. All household chemicals (e.g., soaps, detergents) should be stored out of children's reach, either high up or in locked cabinets. Household water temperature should be checked at the tap and be no higher than 120 degrees Fahrenheit (48.9 degrees Celsius) to prevent scalding. In many cases, you can adjust your water heater to prevent exceeding this temperature. Special care should be taken while cooking, ironing clothes, or using any other heat sources.

Because it's still relatively easy to modify his behavior at this age, this is a good time to establish consistency and your authority. However, be careful not to overreact. He's still too young to misbehave intentionally and won't understand if you punish him or raise your voice. He may become confused or startled when told he shouldn't be doing something. Remain calm, firm, consistent, and loving in your approach. If he learns now you have the final word, it may make life more comfortable for both of you later on, when he naturally becomes more headstrong. It may take many repetitions for an infant to learn what is expected!

Siblings

If your baby has a big brother or sister, you may start to see signs of rivalry at this time, particularly if there are less than two years between the children. Earlier, the baby was more dependent, slept a lot, and didn't require your constant attention. But now that he's becoming more demanding, you'll need to ration your time and energy so you have enough for the children individually and together.

Your older child may still be jealous at having to share your attention. Set aside special "big brother" or "big sister" chores that don't involve the baby. Doing this allows for some extra attention and gets housework done. Be sure to show the child how much you appreciate this help.

You also can help sibling relations by including the older child in activities with the baby. If the two of you sing a song or read a story, the baby will enjoy listening. The older child can also help care for the baby to some extent, assisting at bath or changing time. But unless the child is at least twelve, don't leave him alone with the baby, even if he's trying to be helpful. Younger children can easily drop or injure an infant without realizing what they've done.

(For more information, see the section entitled *Siblings* in Chapter 7. Many issues and guidelines described there also apply to children ages four through seven months.)

Health Watch

Don't be surprised if your baby catches his first cold or ear infection soon after his four-month birthday. Now that he can actively reach for objects, he'll come into physical contact with many more things and people. Also, babies lose the immunity they get from their mothers through the placenta around six months of age, so if you feel like they're getting many more viral infections, you're probably right! This is a normal phenomenon that we all went through at this age.

The first line of defense is to keep your child away from anyone known to be sick. Be especially careful of highly contagious diseases such as influenza (the flu), RSV, chickenpox, or measles (see *Chickenpox*, page 822; *Measles*, page 857). If someone in your play group has one of these diseases, keep your child away from the group until you're sure no one else is infected. However, children and adults are contagious a day or so before they have symptoms, so it is impossible to prevent some exposures.

Your Child and Antibiotics

Antibiotics are among the most powerful and important medicines known. When used properly, they can save lives. When used improperly, antibiotics can harm your child. It is often difficult for parents to leave the doctor's office without a prescription for antibiotics when their child has a fever or bad cold. Understanding the rationale behind limiting antibiotic use is important.

Two main types of germs—viruses and bacteria—cause most infections. Viruses cause all colds and most coughs. There are no medicines effective against the common cold. Antibiotics never cure common viral infections. Your child recovers from these common viral infections when the illness has run its course. *Antibiotics should not be used to treat viral infections.*

(continues on next page)

Antibiotics are used to treat bacterial infections, but some have become resistant to certain antibiotics. If your child is infected with resistant bacteria, he might need a different antibiotic or even hospitalization, where more powerful medicines can be given intravenously. A few new strains of bacteria are already untreatable. To protect your child from antibiotic-resistant bacteria, use antibiotics only when your pediatrician has determined they might be effective, since repeated or improper use of antibiotics contributes to resistant bacteria and viruses.

When are antibiotics needed? When are they not needed?

These complicated questions are best answered by your pediatrician, and it depends on the specific diagnosis. If you think your child might need treatment, contact your pediatrician.

- *Documented ear infection.* Sometimes requires antibiotics.

- *Sinus infections.* These are very uncommon at this age, in large part because the sinuses are so small. Just because your child's mucus is yellow or green does not mean he has a bacterial infection. It is normal for mucus to get thick and change color during a viral cold.

- *Bronchitis.* Children rarely need antibiotics for bronchitis, since these infections are almost always caused by viruses.

- *Colds.* Colds are caused by viruses and sometimes can last for two weeks or more. Antibiotics have no effect on colds. Your pediatrician may have suggestions for comfort measures while the cold runs its course.

- *Influenza.* Once your child reaches six months, he will be old enough for a seasonal flu shot. Until then, other family members—parents and older siblings—should receive theirs to protect the baby. There are antiviral medications for this infection, but not all are appropriate for newborns and very young children, and they may not be as effective as prevention via immunization.

Viral infections sometimes may lead to bacterial infections. Keep your pediatrician informed if the illness gets worse or lasts a long time, so proper treatment can be given as needed.

If an antibiotic is prescribed, your child should take the antibiotic exactly as directed. Never save antibiotics for later use or let other family members use a prescription not intended for them.

No matter how you try to protect your baby, there will be times he gets sick. This is an inevitable part of growing up and will happen more frequently with more direct contact with other children. It's not always easy to tell when a baby is ill, but there are some signs. Does he look pale or have dark circles under his eyes? Is he acting less energetic or more irritable than usual? If he has an infectious disease, he'll probably have a fever (see Chapter 27, *Fever*), and he may lose weight due to loss of appetite, diarrhea, or vomiting. Some difficult-to-detect kidney or lung infections also can prevent weight gain in babies. At this age, weight loss could mean that the baby has a digestive problem, such as an allergy to wheat or milk protein (see *Celiac Disease*, page 533), or lacks the digestive enzymes needed to digest certain solid foods. If you suspect your child may be ill but you can't identify the exact problem, or if you have any concerns about what is happening, call your pediatrician and describe the symptoms.

The following illnesses are the most common ones to occur at this age. (All are described in Part 2 of this book.)

Bronchiolitis	Diarrhea	Sore throat
(see page 603)	(see page 537)	(see page 681)
Colds (URIs)	Earache/ear infection	Vomiting
(see page 667)	(see page 670)	(see page 555)
Conjunctivitis (pinkeye)	Fever	
(see page 739)	(see page 775)	
Croup	Pneumonia	
(see page 608)	(see page 612)	

Immunization Update

At four months, your baby should receive:

- Second DTaP vaccine

- Second polio vaccine

- Second Hib (*Haemophilus influenzae* type b) vaccine

- Second pneumococcal vaccine

- Second hepatitis B vaccine (may be given between one and four months)

■ Second rotavirus vaccine (may be given as early as four weeks after the first dose)

And at six months:

■ First dose of influenza vaccine as soon as it's available in the fall; second dose given one month later

■ Third DTaP vaccine

■ Third polio vaccine (which can be given between six and eighteen months)

■ Third pneumococcal vaccine

■ Third Hib vaccine (depending on vaccine type given for doses one and two)

■ Third hepatitis B vaccine (may be given between six and eighteen months)

■ Third rotavirus vaccine (depending on vaccine type; one requires two doses and the other three)

Safety Check

Car Safety Seats

■ Buckle your baby into an approved, properly installed infant car safety seat before you start the car. It should be equipped with a five-point harness. When your child reaches the top weight or length allowed by his rear-facing-only car safety seat (check the labels or instructions to find these limits), he will need to use a convertible car safety seat. You may choose to use a convertible car safety seat rear-facing from birth; this is safe as long as the seat fits your baby properly. If your car is manufactured after 2002 be sure to take advantage of the LATCH system to secure all car seats.

■ The backseat is the safest place for all children to ride. Never place a rear-facing car safety seat in the front seat of a car with a passenger-side airbag.

Drowning

■ Never leave a baby alone even for a moment in a bath or near a pool of water, no matter how shallow. Infants can drown in just a few inches of water. Baby bath seats or supporting rings are not a substitute for adult supervision. Practice touch supervision by staying within arm's reach anytime your baby is in or near water.

Falls

■ Never leave the baby unattended on any place above floor level, such as tabletops, changing tables, or near stairs. If he does fall and seems to be acting abnormally in any way, call the pediatrician immediately.

Burns

■ Never smoke or eat, drink, or carry anything hot while holding a baby.

■ Keep all hot liquids, like coffee and tea, out of baby's reach.

■ Prevent scalding by making sure the water coming out of the faucet is no more than 120 degrees Fahrenheit (48.9 degrees Celsius).

Choking

■ Never give a baby any food or small object that could cause choking. All foods should be mashed, ground, or soft enough to swallow without chewing.

■ Make sure he cannot get tangled up in cords such as electrical cords or those on window shades.

~ 9 ~

Age Eight Months
Through Twelve Months

DURING THESE MONTHS, YOUR baby is increasingly mobile, a development that will both thrill and challenge you. Being able to move gives your child a new sense of power and control—her first real taste of physical independence. And while this is exhilarating for her, the separation from you it causes is also frightening. So as she eagerly moves out on her own to explore the farthest reaches of her domain, she may also wail if she wanders out of your sight. Mobility does bring dangers that must be constantly monitored, which means there cannot be any unsupervised time.

For you, your baby's mobility may be a source of considerable concern as well as pride. Crawling and walking are signals she's developing on target, but these achievements also mean you'll have your hands full keeping her safe. If you haven't already fully childproofed your home, do it now. (See Chapter 15, on safety.) At her age, your baby has no concept of danger and a limited memory for warnings. The only way to protect her from the hundreds of hazards in your home is to secure cabinets and drawers, place dangerous and precious objects out of reach, and make perilous rooms such as bathrooms inaccessible unless she's supervised.

By childproofing your home, you'll also give your baby a greater sense of freedom. After all, fewer areas will be off-limits, and thus you can let her make discoveries on her own. These personal accomplishments will promote her self-esteem; you might even think of ways of facilitating them. For example:

1. Fill a low kitchen cabinet or drawer with safe objects and let your baby discover it herself.

2. Pad edges of a coffee table or sofa—or consider removing hard tables briefly and replacing them with soft-edged ottomans—and allow her to learn to pull up and cruise.

3. Equip your home with cushions of assorted shapes and sizes and let her experiment with the different ways she can move over and around them.

Knowing when to guide a child and when to let her act alone is part of the art of parenting. At this age, your child is extremely expressive and will give you cues on when to intervene. When she's acting frustrated rather than challenged, don't let her struggle. If she's crying because her ball is wedged under the sofa, or if she's pulled up to a standing position and can't get down, she needs your help. At other times, however, it's important for her to solve problems. Don't let your impatience make you intervene more than necessary. You may be tempted to feed your nine-month-old because it's faster and less messy. However, that deprives her of a chance to learn how to feed herself. The more opportunities you can give to discover, test, and strengthen her new capabilities, the more confident and adventurous she'll be.

Growth and Development
Physical Appearance and Growth

Your baby will continue to grow rapidly during these months. The typical eight-month-old boy weighs between 17.5 and 22 pounds (8–10 kg), with girls about a half pound less. By the first birthday, the average child has usually tripled her birth weight and is 28 to 32 inches (71–81 cm) tall. Do not be alarmed if your child does not follow the typical growth curve in the middle, but follows her own curve. If she was born small, she may stay under the bottom line of the growth curve for the first few years. As long as she is following an upward curve, this is acceptable. Head growth between eight and twelve months slows down from the first six months, a typical circumference at eight months being 17½ inches (44.5 cm) and at one year 18 inches (46 cm). Each baby grows at her own rate, however, so you should check your child's growth curves on the charts in the Appendix to make sure she's following the pattern already established.

When your child first stands, you may be surprised by her posture. Her belly will protrude, her rear will stick out, and her back will sway forward. It may look unusual, but this stance is perfectly normal until she develops a confident sense of balance sometime in the second year.

Your child's feet may also look a little odd. When she lies on her back, her toes may turn inward, appearing pigeon-toed. This common condition usually disappears by twenty-four months. If it persists, your pediatrician may show you foot or leg exercises. If it's severe, your pediatrician may refer you to a pediatric orthopedist. (See *Pigeon Toes*, page 844.)

At this age, your child's feet will seem flat, the arch hidden by a pad of fat. In two to three years, this fat will disappear and her arches will emerge.

When your child takes her first teetering steps, you may notice a different appearance—her feet turning outward. The ligaments of her hips are still loose and her legs naturally rotate outward. During the first half of her second year, the ligaments will tighten and her feet should point straight.

Movement

At eight months, your baby probably will be sitting without support. Although she may topple from time to time, she'll usually catch herself with her arms. As the muscles in her trunk strengthen, she'll also start leaning over to reach objects. Eventually she'll figure out how to roll onto her stomach and get back up to a sitting position. If she is not sitting by herself by nine months, let your pediatrician know.

When lying on a flat surface, your baby is now in constant motion. When on her stomach, she'll arch her neck to look around, and when on her back, she'll grab her feet (or anything else nearby) and pull them to her mouth. She won't be content to stay on her back. She can turn over at will now and flip without a moment's notice. This can be dangerous during diaper changes, so you may want to retire her changing table, using instead the floor or bed, from which she's less likely to fall. Never leave her alone for an instant at any time.

All this activity strengthens muscles for crawling, a skill usually mastered between seven and ten months. For a while she may rock on her hands and knees. Since her arm muscles are stronger than her legs, she may even push herself backward. But with time and practice she'll discover she can propel herself forward across the room toward the target of her choice.

A few children never crawl. Instead, they use alternative methods, such as scooting on their bottoms or slithering on their stomachs. As long as your baby is coordinating each side of her body and using each arm and leg equally, there's no cause for concern. The important thing is that she's able to explore her surroundings and is strengthening her body in preparation for walking. If you feel your child is not moving normally, discuss your concern with the pediatrician.

How can you encourage your child to crawl? Try presenting her with intriguing objects just beyond her reach. As she becomes more agile, create miniature obstacle courses using pillows, boxes, and sofa cushions. Join in the game by hiding behind one of the obstacles and surprising her with a "peekaboo!" Don't ever leave your baby unsupervised, though. If she falls between pillows or under a box, she might not be able to get out. This is bound to frighten her, and she could even smother. Remember not to leave small objects on the floor, under the couch, or in any location where she can find them and put them into her mouth. Things like balloon fragments, small button batteries, and coins are especially dangerous.

Stairs are another ready-made—but potentially dangerous—obstacle course. Although your baby needs to learn how to go up and down stairs, you should not allow her to play on them alone during this time. If you have a staircase, she'll probably head straight for it every chance she gets. Place sturdy gates at the top and bottom of your staircase. (To see a safe, horizontal-type gate, see page 485.) When you're playing with her on stairs, encourage her to work her way down them backward, a skill she's likely to pick up quickly. Even when she does, however, keep the stairs gated at all times.

Although crawling changes dramatically how your baby sees and interacts with the world, don't expect her to be content for long. She'll see everyone else walking, and that's what she'll want to do. In preparation, she'll pull herself to a standing position every chance she gets—although when she first starts, she may not know how to get down. If she cries for help, physically show her how to bend her knees to lower herself without falling. This may help and may save you many trips to her room when she's standing in her crib and crying because she doesn't know how to sit down. Once your baby feels secure standing, she'll

Soon your baby will manage to keep himself up and moving until you catch him several steps later.

try tentative steps while holding on for support. When your hands aren't available, she'll cruise alongside furniture. Just make sure whatever she uses for support has no sharp edges and is properly weighted or attached to the floor.

As her balance improves, she may let go occasionally before seeking support again when she feels herself totter. Her first steps will be shaky. She may take only one before dropping, either in surprise or in relief. Soon, however, she'll manage to keep herself up and moving until you catch her several steps later. As miraculous as it may seem, most children advance from these first steps to confident walking within days.

Although you both will feel excited over this dramatic development, you'll also be unnerved at times, especially when she stumbles and falls. Even if you took pains to provide a safe environment, it's almost impossible to avoid bumps and bruises. Just be matter-of-fact about these mishaps. Offer a quick hug or a reassuring word and send her on her way again. She won't be unduly upset by these falls if you're not. Also, don't be alarmed if she chooses to crawl at times after she has started walking; babies use whatever is easiest and fastest!

At this stage, or even earlier, some parents use a baby walker. Contrary to what the name suggests, these devices do not help children learn to walk. They actually eliminate the desire to walk. To make matters worse, they present a serious tipping hazard when the child bumps into an obstacle, like a small toy or a throw rug. Children in walkers are also more likely to fall down stairs and get into dangerous places otherwise beyond their reach. For these reasons, **the American Academy of Pediatrics strongly urges parents not to use baby walkers.**

A stationary exercise saucer or activity center, with a rotating and bouncy seat but no wheels, is a better choice. You may also consider a sturdy wagon or kiddie push car. Be sure it has a bar to push and is weighted so it won't tip when she pulls herself up on it.

As your child begins to walk outside, she'll need shoes. They should be closed-toe, comfortable, and flexible, with nonskid soles, and they should provide room to grow; sneakers are a great choice. Your child does not need wedges, inserts, high backs, reinforced heels, special arches, or other features designed to shape and support feet. These have no proven benefit for the average child and may actually make it harder to walk. Her feet will grow rapidly during these months, and her shoes will have to keep pace. Her first pair of shoes will probably last two to three months, but you should check the fit monthly during this formative period.

Movement Milestones for Your Eight- to Twelve-Month-Old

- Gets to sitting position without assistance and can stay there without support

- Crawls forward on belly by pulling with arms and pushing with legs

- Assumes hands-and-knees position

- Creeps on hands and knees

- Gets from sitting to crawling or prone (lying on stomach) position

- Pulls self up to stand

- Walks holding on to furniture

- Stands momentarily without support

- May walk two or three steps without support

Many babies' first steps are taken around their first birthday, although it's normal for children to start walking earlier or later. At first, your child will walk with feet wide apart to improve her shaky balance. During those initial days and weeks, she may get going too fast and fall when she tries to stop. As she becomes more confident, she'll learn how to stop and change directions. Before long, she'll be able to squat, pick something up, and stand again. When she reaches this level, she'll get enormous pleasure from push-pull toys—the noisier the better.

Hand and Finger Skills

Your baby's mastery of crawling, standing, and walking are bound to be her most dramatic accomplishments during these months, but don't overlook all the wonderful things she's learning to do with her hands. Her clumsy way of raking things toward her will lead to accurate grasping with her thumb and first or second finger. You'll find her practicing this pincer movement on any small object, from dust balls to cereal, and she may even try to snap her fingers if you show her how.

As your baby learns to open her fingers at will, she'll delight in dropping and throwing things. She'll fling small toys left on her high chair tray or in her play yard and then call loudly for someone to retrieve them, so she can do it again. If she throws hard objects like blocks, she might do some damage and increase the noise level in your household. Your life will be calmer if you redirect her toward softer objects, such as balls of various sizes, colors, and tex-

Milestones in Hand and Finger Skills for Your Eight- to Twelve-Month-Old

- Uses pincer grasp
- Bangs two cubes together
- Puts objects into container
- Takes objects out of container
- Lets objects go voluntarily
- Pokes with index finger
- Tries to imitate scribbling

tures. (Include some with beads inside that make noise as they roll.) One fun activity that allows you to observe your child's developing skills is rolling a large ball toward her. At first she'll slap it randomly, but eventually she'll learn to swat it so that it rolls back to you.

With improved coordination, your baby can now thoroughly investigate the objects she encounters. She'll pick them up, shake them, bang them, and pass them from hand to hand. She'll be particularly intrigued by toys with moving parts—those with wheels, levers, and hinges. Holes are fascinating to poke her fingers in and, when she's a little more skilled, drop things through.

Blocks are another favorite toy at this age. In fact, nothing motivates crawling better than a tower waiting to be toppled. Toward the end of this period, your child may even start building towers of her own.

Language Development

Toward the end of the first year, your baby will begin communicating what she wants by pointing, crawling, or gesturing toward her target. She'll also imitate many gestures she sees adults make as they talk. Nonverbal communication is a temporary measure while she learns how to phrase her messages in words. Remember that hearing problems can manifest as delayed language, so it is important to listen to others' concerns, especially if this is your first baby.

Have you noticed how the coos, gurgles, and screeches of earlier months have given way to recognizable syllables, "ba," "da," "ga," and "ma"? Your child may stumble into words such as "mama" and "bye-bye" accidentally, and when you get excited she'll realize she's said something meaningful. Before long she'll use "mama" to attract your attention. At this age, she may also say "mama" just to practice. Ultimately, however, she'll use words when she wants to communicate their meanings.

Even though you've been talking to your baby from birth, she now understands more language. Your conversations will take on new significance. Many babies can comprehend more words than you suspect, even before they can say them. Watch how she responds when you mention a favorite toy across the room. If she looks toward it, she understands. To increase her understanding, keep talking to her as much as possible. Tell her what's happening around her, particularly as you bathe, change, and feed her. Make your language simple and specific: "I'm drying you with the big blue towel. It's so soft!" Label familiar toys and objects for her, and try to be consistent—that is, if you call the family pet a cat today, don't call it a kitty tomorrow.

Picture books can reinforce her budding understanding that everything has a name. Choose books with large board, cloth, or vinyl pages she can turn herself. Also look for simple but colorful illustrations of things your child will recognize. Look at the pictures, point to things, and say the words for the objects in the book. The more words a child hears, the more she will learn. When you repeat the words as you look at the objects over and over, she will begin to understand that they are connected. At first, you can ask and answer questions like "What do you see? Do you see the ball?" Pause, and then say, "There is a ball. It is a blue ball."

Bilingual Babies

If you speak a second language in your home, don't be concerned your child is going to become confused hearing two languages. More and more American families speak English and another language daily. Research and parental experience show that when children are exposed to two (or even more) languages at a very young age, particularly when they hear both consistently, they are able to learn both simultaneously. Yes, during the child's normal language development, she may be more proficient in one or the other, and at times she may mix words from both languages together. But with time, the two languages will become distinct and separate, and she should be able to communicate in both. (Some studies suggest that while she may be able to understand both languages, she will speak one of them better than the other for a time.)

Certainly you should encourage your child to become bilingual. It's an asset, a skill that will benefit her the rest of her life. In general, the earlier both languages are introduced, the more proficient she'll be; by contrast, she may have a little more difficulty learning the second language if it is introduced during the preschool years after she's learned and spoken the first language exclusively.

Whether you're reading or talking to her, give her plenty of opportunities to join in. Ask questions and wait for a response. Let her take the lead. If she says "Gaagaagaa," repeat it back and see what she does. These exchanges may seem meaningless, but they tell your baby communication is two-way and she's a welcome participant. Paying attention to what she says also will help identify the words she understands and make it more likely you'll recognize her first spoken words.

These first words, incidentally, often aren't proper English. For your child, a "word" is any sound that consistently refers to the same person, object, or event. If she says "mog" every time she wants milk, you should treat "mog" as a legitimate word by giving her milk when she says "mog." However, when you speak back to her, use "milk." Eventually she'll make the correction herself.

Ages vary tremendously for when children begin to say recognizable words. Some can say two to three words by their first birthday. More likely, your baby's speech at twelve months will consist of gibberish with the tones and variations of speech. As long as she's experimenting with sounds that vary in intensity, pitch, and quality, she's getting ready to talk. The more you respond to her as if she were speaking, the more you'll stimulate her urge to communicate. Continuing to read to her daily will help tremendously. She will also enjoy simple songs. Make sure you turn off the television; having the television on in the background keeps parents from talking to their children and harms babies' language development. Limit your own screen time, as your baby needs your attention to learn.

Language Milestones for Your Eight- to Twelve-Month-Old

- Pays increasing attention to speech
- Responds to simple verbal requests
- Responds to "no"
- Uses simple gestures, such as shaking head for "no"
- Babbles with inflection
- Says "dada" and "mama"
- Uses exclamations, such as "oh-oh!"
- Tries to imitate words

Cognitive Development

An eight-month-old is curious about everything, but also has a short attention span and will move rapidly from one activity to the next. Two to three minutes is the most she'll spend with a single toy, and then she'll turn to something new. By twelve months, she may sit as long as fifteen minutes with a plaything, but she'll mostly be a body in motion. You shouldn't expect anything different.

Although toy stores are brimming with expensive playthings, the toys that fascinate children most at this age are ordinary household objects such as wooden spoons, egg cartons, and plastic containers of all shapes and sizes. Your baby will be especially interested in things that differ slightly from what she already knows. If she's bored with the oatmeal box she's been playing with, renew her interest by putting a ball inside or tying a string to it and turning it into a pull toy. These small changes will help her learn to detect small differences between the familiar and unfamiliar. Also, when choosing playthings, remember that objects too much like what she's seen before will be quickly dismissed, while things too foreign may be confusing or frightening. Instead look for objects and toys that gradually expand her horizons. Pots and pans can be noisy but an inexpensive way of entertaining your child.

Often your baby won't need help discovering objects. As soon as she can crawl, she'll be off in search of new things to conquer. She'll rummage through drawers, empty wastebaskets, ransack cabinets, and conduct elaborate experiments on everything she finds. (Make sure that any drawers or cabinets with potential hazards are secured with child safety locks.) She'll never tire of dropping, rolling, throwing, submerging, or waving objects to see how they behave. This may look like random play, but it's your child's way of learning how the world works. Like any good scientist, she's observing an object's properties, and from her observations, she'll develop ideas about shapes (some things roll, others don't), textures (things can be scratchy, soft, or smooth), and sizes (some things fit inside others). She'll even begin to understand some things are edible and others aren't, although she'll still put everything into her mouth just to be sure. (Again, make sure there's nothing dangerous around that she can put in her mouth.)

Her observations during these months also help her understand that objects exist even when out of sight, a concept called object permanence. At eight months, when you hide a toy under a scarf, she'll pick up the scarf in search of the toy—a response that wouldn't have occurred three months earlier. Additionally, if you hide the toy under the scarf and then remove it when she's not looking, she'll be puzzled. By ten months, she'll be so certain the toy still exists she'll continue looking for it. To help your baby learn object permanence, play peekaboo with her. By switching between variations of this game, you'll maintain her interest almost indefinitely.

As she approaches her first birthday, your child becomes increasingly conscious that things have names and also particular functions. You'll see her new awareness weave into her play as a very early form of fantasy. Instead of treating a toy telephone as an object to be chewed, poked, and banged, she'll put it

Variations of Peekaboo

The possible variations of peekaboo are almost endless. As your child becomes more mobile and alert, create games that let her take the lead. Here are some suggestions.

1. Drape a soft cloth over her head and ask, "Where's the baby?" Once she understands the game, she'll pull the cloth away and pop up grinning.

2. With baby on her back facing toward you, lift both her legs together— "Up, up, up"—until they conceal your face from her. Then open them wide: "Peekaboo!" As she gets the idea, she'll move her legs herself. (This is a great game at diaper-changing time.)

3. Hide behind a door or a piece of furniture, leaving a foot or arm in her view as a clue. She'll be delighted to come find you.

4. Take turns with your baby "hiding" your head under a large towel and letting her pull the towel off, then putting it over her head and pulling it off.

to her ear just as she's seen you do. You can encourage important developmental activities like this by offering suggestive props—a hairbrush, toothbrush, cup, or spoon—and by being enthusiastic about her performances.

Brain Development

As you've read in this book, your child's early months are crucial to brain development. The environment she's exposed to and the experiences she has will have a powerful influence on her brain growth.

You have opportunities every day to nurture your child's brain. Just talking with and encouraging her to say words she's learning will provide intellectual stimulation. You can give her a comfortable and safe environment to explore her world. You can provide her with simple toys to challenge her brain to develop. You can play games with her, sing songs, and continue reading to her every day to encourage her memory to stretch.

Following are day-to-day suggestions to use for your baby ages eight to twelve months. They really can make a difference in your child's life, not only immediately but also as a foundation for brain growth for years to come.

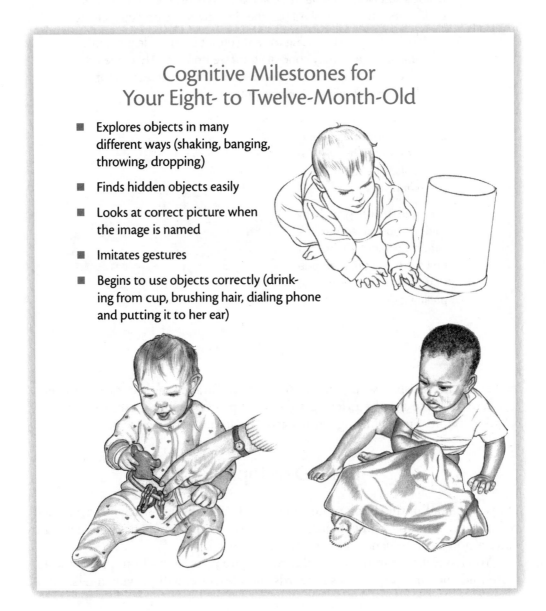

Cognitive Milestones for Your Eight- to Twelve-Month-Old

- Explores objects in many different ways (shaking, banging, throwing, dropping)

- Finds hidden objects easily

- Looks at correct picture when the image is named

- Imitates gestures

- Begins to use objects correctly (drinking from cup, brushing hair, dialing phone and putting it to her ear)

Stimulating Infant Brain Growth: Age Eight Months Through Twelve Months

- Talk to your baby during dressing, bathing, feeding, playing, walking, and driving, using adult talk rather than baby talk. Check with your pediatrician if your baby does not seem to respond to sound or if syllables and words are not developing.

- Be attentive to your baby's rhythms and moods. Respond to her when she is upset as well as when she is happy.

- Your baby will be very tuned in to you and to others she encounters. Her ability to respond to your emotions is an important part of this developmental period. By eight to nine months of age, she can read your face for emotions, which underscores the need for you to temper strong negative expressions.

- Encourage your baby to play with blocks and soft toys. This helps her develop hand-eye coordination, fine motor skills, and a sense of competence.

- Provide a stimulating, safe environment where your baby can begin to explore and roam.

- Give consistent warm, physical contact—hugging, skin-to-skin, body-to-body contact—to establish your child's sense of security and well-being.

- Read to your baby every day.

- If you speak more than one language, use them both at home with your child.

- Try to be sure your baby is not exposed to events that could upset her or overwhelm her, or anything with content intended for older children or adults. This often means keeping the news or other TV shows off when your baby is in the room. You may forget they are on in the background, but she will notice scary sounds and pictures.

- Play games like peekaboo and pattycake to stimulate your baby's memory skills.

- Introduce your child to other children and parents.

(continues on next page)

- Provide toys that are age- and developmentally appropriate, safe, and inexpensive. Toys need not be costly—ordinary household objects are fine. It's much more important to give your child attention by talking, reading, and playing with her than to provide more toys.

- Sing songs that incorporate hand and body movements, repetitive words, etc.

- Teach your baby to wave bye-bye and to nod or shake her head for yes and no.

- Make sure other people who provide care and supervision for your baby understand the importance of forming a loving and comforting relationship with her.

- Understand that it's normal for your baby to be uncomfortable at times around people who are not her primary caregivers.

- Spend time on the floor playing with your child every day.

- Choose quality childcare that is affectionate, responsive, educational, and safe. Visit your childcare provider frequently and share your ideas about positive caregiving.

Emotional Development

At times during these months, your child may seem like two separate babies. There's the one who's open, affectionate, and outgoing with you. Then there's another who's anxious, clingy, and easily frightened around unfamiliar people or objects. Some people may tell you your child is fearful or shy because you're "spoiling" her, but don't believe it. Her diverse behavior patterns aren't caused by you or your parenting; they occur because she is, for the first time, able to tell the difference between familiar and unfamiliar situations. If anything, the predictable anxieties of this period are evidence of her healthy relationship with you.

Stranger anxiety is usually one of the first emotional milestones your baby will reach. You may think something is wrong when the same child who at three months interacted calmly with strangers is now beginning to tense up when they come too close. This is normal, and you need not worry. Even relatives and frequent babysitters once comfortable to her may prompt hiding or crying now, especially if they approach hastily.

The predictable anxieties of this period are evidence of your child's healthy relationship with you.

Social/Emotional Milestones for Your Eight- to Twelve-Month-Old

- Shy or anxious with strangers

- Cries when mother or father leaves

- Enjoys imitating people in play

- Shows specific preferences for certain people and toys

- Tests parental responses to her actions during feedings (what do you do when she refuses a food?)

- Tests parental responses to her behavior (what do you do if she cries after you leave the room?)

- May be fearful in some situations

- Prefers mother and/or regular caregiver over all others

- Repeats sounds or gestures for attention

- Finger-feeds herself

- Extends arm or leg to help when being dressed

At about the same time, she'll become much more clingy about leaving you. This is the start of separation anxiety. Just as she's learning of each object's uniqueness and permanence, she'll also discover there's only one of you. When you're out of sight, she'll know you're somewhere not with her, and this may cause great distress. She'll have little sense of time and she won't know when—or if—you'll come back. Once she's older, her memories of you will comfort her when you're gone, and she can anticipate a reunion. For now, she's only aware of the present, so every time you leave her sight—even when you just go into the next room—she'll fuss and cry. When you leave her with someone else, she may scream as though her heart will break, although this crying will often resolve quickly once you're gone. At bedtime, she may refuse to leave you, and then wake up searching for you in the middle of the night.

Separation anxiety usually peaks between ten and eighteen months and then fades during the last half of the second year. In some ways, this phase will be especially tender for both of you; in other ways it can be stressful. After all, her desire to be with you is a sign of her attachment to you—her first and greatest love. The intensity of her feeling as she hurtles into your arms is irresistible, especially when you realize that no one—including your future child—will ever again think you as perfect as she does at this age. On the other hand, you may feel suffocated by the constant clinging, but also guilty whenever you leave her crying. Fortunately, this emotional roller coaster will eventually subside, along with her separation anxiety. In the meantime, try to downplay your leavetaking as much as possible. Here are some suggestions.

■ Your baby is more susceptible to separation anxiety when she's tired, hungry, or sick. If you know you're going to go out, schedule your departure to occur after she's napped or eaten. And try to stay with her as much as possible when she's sick.

■ Don't make a fuss over your leaving. Instead, have the person caring for her create a distraction (a new toy, a visit to the mirror, a bath). Then say goodbye and leave quickly.

■ Her tears will subside within minutes of your departure. Her outbursts are for your benefit, to persuade you to stay. With you out of sight, she'll soon turn her attention to the person she is with.

■ Help her learn to cope with separation through short sessions at home. Separation will be easier when she initiates it. When she crawls to another room (one that's babyproofed), don't follow her right away; wait a couple of minutes in a place where you can see what she's doing. If she fusses, call to her instead of running to her. Gradually she'll learn that

Acquainting Your Baby with a Sitter

Is your baby about to have a new babysitter for a few hours? Whenever possible, let your child interact with this new person while you're there. Ideally, have the sitter spend time with her on successive days before being left alone. If this isn't possible, allow an extra hour or two for this get-acquainted period before you leave. The same rules apply to daycare and anytime there will be a new caregiver.

During their first meeting, the sitter and your baby should get to know each other very gradually, using the following steps.

1. Hold the baby on your lap while you and the sitter talk. Watch for clues that your child is at ease before you have the sitter make eye contact with her. Wait until the baby is looking at her or playing contentedly by herself.

2. Have the sitter talk to the baby while she stays on your lap. She should not reach toward the child or try to touch her yet.

3. Once the baby seems comfortable with the conversation, put her on the floor with a favorite toy, across from the sitter. Invite the sitter to slowly come closer and play with the toy. As the baby warms up to her, you can move back gradually.

4. See what happens when you leave the room. If your baby doesn't notice you're missing, the introduction has gone well. Don't be discouraged, however, if she cries. That is normal and will improve with time.

You can use leisurely introduction with anyone who hasn't seen the child recently, including relatives and friends. Adults often overwhelm babies this age by coming close and making funny noises or, worse yet, trying to take them from their mothers. Intervene when this occurs. Explain to these well-meaning people that your baby needs to warm up to strangers and that she's more likely to respond well if they go slowly.

nothing terrible happens when you're gone and, just as important, that you always come back when you say you will.

■ If you take your child to a sitter's home or a childcare center, don't just drop her off and leave. Spend a few extra minutes playing with her. When you do leave, reassure her you'll be back later.

If your child has a strong, healthy attachment to you, her separation anxiety will probably occur earlier than in other babies, and she'll pass through it more quickly. Instead of resenting her possessiveness during these months, maintain as much warmth and good humor as you can. Through your actions, you're showing how to express and return love. This is the emotional base she'll rely on in years to come.

From the beginning, you've considered your baby a unique person with specific traits and preferences. She, however, has had only a dim notion of herself as a person separate from you. Now her sense of identity is coming into bloom. As she develops a growing sense of individuality, she'll also become increasingly conscious of you as a separate person.

One of the clearest signs of self-awareness is the way your baby watches herself in the mirror. Up to about eight months, she treated mirrors as fascinating objects. Perhaps she thought the reflection was another baby, or maybe a magical surface of lights and shadows. Now her responses will change, indicating she understands one of the images is hers. Looking at a mirror, she may touch her nose or pull on a stray lock of hair. You can reinforce her sense of identity with mirror games. When you're looking in the mirror together, touch different body parts: "There is Olivia's nose. There is Mommy's nose." Move in and out of the mirror, playing peekaboo with the reflections. Make faces and verbally label the emotions conveyed.

As your child's self-concept becomes more secure, she'll have less trouble meeting strangers and separating from you. She'll also become more assertive. Before, you could count on her to be relatively compliant if she was comfortable. But now, more often than not, she'll want things a particular way. Don't be surprised if she rejects certain foods or objects placed in front of her. And now that she's more mobile, you'll find yourself frequently saying "no" about things she shouldn't touch. However, even after she understands the word, she may still touch anyway. Just wait—this is only a forerunner of challenges to come.

Toys Appropriate for
Your Eight- to Twelve-Month-Old

- Stacking toys in different sizes, shapes, colors

- Cups, pails, and other unbreakable containers

- Unbreakable mirrors of various sizes

- Bath toys that float, squirt, or hold water

- Large building blocks

- "Busy boxes" that push, open, squeak, and move

- Squeeze toys

- Large dolls and puppets

- Cars, trucks, and other vehicle toys made of flexible plastic, with no sharp edges or removable parts

- Balls of all sizes (but not small enough to fit in the mouth)

- Cardboard books with large pictures

- Music boxes, musical toys, and child-safe digital music players

- Push-pull toys

- Toy telephones

- Paper tubes, empty boxes, old magazines, egg cartons, empty plastic water bottles (without a lid or small cap, as that could be a potential choking hazard)

- Remember that pets are not toys and supervision should be the rule at all times

Developmental Health Watch

Each baby develops individually, so it's impossible to predict when your child will perfect a given skill. The developmental milestones listed in this book give you a general idea of expected changes, but don't be alarmed if her development takes a slightly different course. Alert your pediatrician if your baby displays any of the following signs of *possible* developmental delay in the eight- to twelve-month age range.

- Does not crawl or does not sit independently by nine months of age

- Drags one side of body while crawling, or consistently uses one side of the body more than the other

- Cannot stand when supported by twelve months of age

- Does not search for objects that are hidden while she watches

- Says no single words ("mama" or "dada")

- Does not learn to use gestures, such as waving or shaking head

- Does not point to objects or pictures

- Does not respond to name

- Does not make eye contact

Your baby may also become afraid of objects or situations she used to take in stride. Fears of the dark, thunder, and loud household appliances are common. Later you can subdue these fears by talking about them, but for now, the only solution is to eliminate the source as much as possible: use a nightlight, vacuum when she's not around. When you can't shield her from something frightening, try to anticipate her reaction and be close so she can turn to you. Stay calm as you comfort her, so she understands you are not afraid. If you reassure her when she hears thunder or the roar of a jet overhead, her fear will gradually subside until all she has to do is look at you to feel safe.

Basic Care
Feeding

At this age, your baby needs between 750 and 900 calories each day, of which about 400 to 500 should come from breast milk or formula (if you are not breastfeeding)—approximately 24 ounces (720 ml) a day. Breast milk and formula contain vitamins, minerals, and other important components for brain growth. But don't be surprised if her appetite is less robust now. Her rate of growth is slowing, and she has many new and interesting activities to distract her.

At about eight months, you may want to introduce foods that are slightly coarser than strained pureed foods. They require more chewing than baby foods. You can expand your baby's diet to include soft foods such as yogurt, oatmeal, mashed banana, mashed potatoes, or even thicker or lumpy pureed vegetables. Eggs (including scrambled) are an excellent source of protein, as are cottage cheese, Greek yogurt, and avocado.

As your baby's hand use improves, give her a spoon and let her play with it at mealtimes. Once she's figured out how to hold it, dip it in her food and let her try to feed herself. Don't expect much in the beginning. More food is bound to find the floor and high chair than her mouth. A plastic cloth under her chair will help minimize cleanup.

Be patient and resist the temptation to take the spoon away. She needs the practice as well as the knowledge you have confidence in her abilities. For a while you may want to alternate bites from her spoon and one that you hold. Once she can consistently find her mouth with a spoon (which might not be until after her first birthday), you may want to fill her spoon yourself to decrease the mess and waste but leave the actual feeding to her.

In the early weeks of self-feeding, things may go more smoothly when she's really hungry and more interested in eating than playing. Although your baby now eats three meals like the rest of the family, you may not want to impose her disorderly eating on everyone else's dinnertime. Many families compromise by feeding the baby most of her meal in advance and then letting her occupy herself with healthy finger foods at the table with you while the others eat.

Transitional Objects

You may still remember your favorite childhood blanket, doll, or teddy bear. Security objects such as these are part of the emotional support system every child needs in her early years.

Your child may not choose a blanket, of course. She may prefer a soft toy instead. Chances are she'll make her choice between months eight and twelve, and she'll keep it for years to come. When she's tired, it will help her sleep. When she's separated from you, it will reassure her. When she's upset, it will comfort her. When she's in a strange place, it will help her feel at home.

These special comforts are called transitional objects. They help children make the emotional transition from dependence to independence. They work, in part, because they feel good: they're soft, cuddly, and nice to touch. They're also effective because of familiarity. This "lovey" has your child's scent on it, and it reminds her of the comfort and security of her room. It makes her feel everything is going to be OK.

Despite myths to the contrary, transitional objects are not a sign of weakness or insecurity, and there's no reason to keep your child from using one. In fact, a transitional object can be so helpful you may want to help her choose one and build it into her nighttime ritual.

You can also make things easier by having two identical security objects. Doing this allows you to wash one while the other is being used, thus sparing your baby (and yourself) a potential emotional crisis and a bedraggled lovey. If your baby chooses a large blanket for her security object, you can easily cut it into two. She has little sense of size and won't notice. If she's chosen a toy instead, try to find a duplicate as soon as possible. If you don't start rotating them early, your child may refuse the second one because it feels too new and foreign.

Parents often worry that transitional objects promote thumb sucking, and in fact they sometimes do (but not always). But it's important to remember that thumb or finger sucking is a normal, natural way for a young child to comfort herself. She'll gradually give up both the transitional object and the sucking as she matures and finds other ways to cope with stress.

Sample One-Day Menu for Your Eight- to Twelve-Month-Old

1 cup = 8 ounces = 240 ml
¾ cup = 6 ounces = 180 ml
½ cup = 4 ounces = 120 ml
¼ cup = 2 ounces = 60 ml

BREAKFAST
2 to 4 ounces cereal, or 1 mashed or scrambled egg
2 to 4 ounces mashed or diced fruit
Breast milk or 4 to 6 ounces formula

SNACK
Breast milk or 4 to 6 ounces formula
2 to 4 ounces diced cheese or cooked pureed or diced vegetables

LUNCH
2 to 4 ounces yogurt or cottage cheese, or pureed or diced beans or meat
2 to 4 ounces cooked pureed or diced yellow or orange vegetables
Breast milk or 4 to 6 ounces formula

SNACK
1 whole-grain cracker or teething biscuit
2 to 4 ounces yogurt or fork-mashed or diced soft fruit
2 to 4 ounces water

DINNER
2 to 4 ounces diced poultry, meat, or tofu
2 to 4 ounces cooked green vegetables
2 to 4 ounces cooked soft whole-grain
     pasta, rice, or potato
2 to 4 ounces diced or mashed fruit
Breast milk or 4 to 6 ounces formula

BEFORE BEDTIME
Breast milk or 6 to 8 ounces formula, or water (if breast milk or formula,
     follow with water and brush teeth afterward)

In the early weeks of self-feeding, things may go more smoothly when she's really hungry and is more interested in eating than playing.

Finger foods can include small pieces of steamed veggies, soft fruit such as bananas, well-cooked whole-grain pasta, small pieces of whole-wheat bread, chicken, scrambled eggs, or whole-grain cereals. Try offering a selection of flavors, shapes, colors, and textures, but always watch her for choking. (See *Choking*, page 700.) Also, because she's likely to swallow without chewing, never offer a young child chunks of peanut butter, large pieces of raw vegetables, whole nuts, whole grapes, popcorn, uncooked peas, celery, gum, hard candies, or other hard or round foods that could pose a risk for choking. Always observe your child eating. Choking can happen with hot dogs, grapes, chunks of cheese, or meat sticks (baby-food "hot dogs"), so these always should be cut lengthwise and then into smaller pieces before being fed to a child of this age. It is a good idea to have all family members take a basic life support course, which can be lifesaving during a choking episode.

Introducing a Cup

A straw or sippy cup can be introduced anytime after six months. Breastfed babies may transition to a cup more easily than to a bottle. To get started, use a trainer cup with two handles and a snap-on lid with a soft spout, or a straw cup. Either option will minimize spillage as she experiments with different ways to hold (and most likely throw) the cup.

To start, fill the cup with a little water and offer it at one meal a day. Show her how to maneuver and tip it to her mouth so she can drink. Don't become dismayed, however, if she treats it as a plaything for several weeks; most babies do. Just be patient until she's able to get most of the liquid down her throat or out of the straw without it dribbling down her chin or the cup flying around the room. Once she gets the hang of the cup, put breast milk or formula in the cup to get her used to drinking milk from something other than a bottle.

There are advantages to drinking from a cup: namely, improved hand-to-mouth coordination, and preparation for the weaning process. Remember, the American Academy of Pediatrics believes breastfeeding is the best source of nutrition for babies through at least their first birthday.

Even under the best circumstances, the transition to using a cup may not take place overnight. Six months may pass before your baby takes all her liquid from a cup. Even so, you can start the process and proceed gradually, letting her interest and willingness guide you. You'll probably find it easiest to start with the midday feeding first. Once she's adjusted to this, try doing the same in the morning. The bedtime feeding probably will be the last, and for good reason: your baby has become accustomed to this nighttime comfort, and it will take her time to give it up. If she's sleeping through the night and not waking up hungry, she doesn't physically need the extra nourishment from bedtime breast- or bottle-feeding. In this case, you might break the habit in stages, first by substituting water instead of milk for the bedtime bottle and then switching to a drink of water from a cup. Alternatively, just move the bedtime bottle earlier so that it's not associated with bedtime but instead is an evening snack.

During this process, you may be tempted to put milk in her bottle to help her fall asleep, but it's not a good idea for several reasons. If she falls asleep while feeding, the milk will pool around her incoming teeth, and cause them to decay—a condition known as early childhood caries (formerly called baby bottle tooth decay). To make matters worse, drinking while lying flat on her back can contribute to her risk for middle ear infections.

Another disadvantage to prolonged bottle-feeding is that the bottle can become a security object, particularly if your baby keeps it beyond about age one. To avoid this, don't let her carry or drink from a bottle while playing. Restrict the use to feedings when she's sitting down or being held. At all other times, give her a cup. If you never allow the bottle to go with her, she won't realize bringing it is even an option. Don't give in once this decision is made; be consistent or she may get confused and demand a bottle long after she has "officially" been weaned.

Sleeping

At eight months, your baby probably still takes two naps, midmorning and midafternoon. She's also likely to sleep as much as ten to twelve hours at night without needing night feeding. However, as her separation anxiety intensifies in the next few months, she may start to resist going to bed, and she may wake up more often looking for you.

During this difficult period, you may need to experiment to find strategies that help your baby sleep. Some children go to sleep more easily with the door open (so they can hear you); others develop consoling habits, such as sucking their thumbs or rocking. White noise can also be especially helpful, as long as the volume is quiet so as not to damage your baby's sensitive hearing.

To help this stage pass more quickly, don't do anything that will reward your baby for calling you in the middle of the night. Go to make sure she's all right and tell her you're nearby if she really needs you; but don't turn on the light, rock her, or walk with her. You might offer her a drink of water, but don't feed her, and certainly don't take her to your bed. If she's suffering from separation anxiety, doing that will only make it harder for her to return to her crib.

When you do check on her, make her as comfortable as possible and confirm she isn't sick. Some problems, such as ear infections or croup, can come on suddenly at night. Once you're sure there's no sign of illness, check her diaper, changing it only if she's had a bowel movement or if her diaper is uncomfortably wet. Do the change as quickly as possible in dim light and then settle her back in her crib—and on her back. Before leaving, whisper a few comforting words about how it's nighttime and time to sleep. If she still cries, wait a few minutes, then go back in and comfort her a short time. This period can be extremely difficult for parents. After all, it's emotionally and physically exhausting to hear your child cry, and you'll probably respond with a combination of emotions. But remember, her behavior is not deliberate. Instead, she's reacting to natural anxieties and stresses. If you stay calm and follow a consistent pattern each night, she'll soon be putting herself to sleep. Many parents will purchase a wireless baby monitor to watch and hear their baby from their own room. There are many different products available, so research them all before purchasing one. Doing so may make life much easier for both of you. (See Chapter 35 for more information on sleep.)

Teeth

By this age your baby probably has at least one or two teeth, if not more. Don't worry if she doesn't; it's normal for babies as old as twelve months to still have no teeth. As soon as she does, however, it's time to start brushing with a soft toothbrush and a tiny bit of fluoride toothpaste, roughly the size of a grain of rice. She may or may not enjoy this experience. If she resists brushing, have her lie face-up on another person's lap while you make a game of gently cleaning each tooth. Brush her teeth at least once a day, front and back, ideally close to bedtime, since once you're done she should not eat or drink anything other than water. Sugar at night will undo all your hard work! You can also make her first dental appointment. Your child's first dentist visit should occur six months after the first tooth emerges or at one year of age, whichever comes first. The dentist may even apply fluoride varnish. Your child's pediatrician may check the teeth and apply fluoride at well-child exams, but this does not substitute for a dental appointment.

Behavior

Discipline

Your baby's desire to explore is almost impossible to satisfy. As a result, she'll want to touch, taste, and manipulate everything she can get into. She's bound to find her way into places and situations that are off-limits or dangerous. Although her curiosity is vital to her overall development and shouldn't be discouraged unnecessarily, she can't be allowed to jeopardize her own safety or damage valuable objects. Whether she's investigating the burners on your stove or pulling up your flowers, you need to help her stop these activities.

Keep in mind that the way you handle these early incidents will lay the foundation for future discipline. Learning not to do something she very much wants to do is a major first step toward self-control. The better she learns this lesson now, the less you'll have to intervene in years to come.

As we suggested earlier, distraction can usually deal effectively with undesirable behavior. Your baby's memory is still short, and you can shift her focus with minimal resistance. If she's headed for something she shouldn't do, you don't necessarily have to say "no." Overusing that word will blunt its effect. Instead, pick her up and direct her toward something she can play with. Look for a compromise that will keep her interested and active without squelching her curiosity. Never scream or yell at, shake, or hit your baby.

You should reserve your serious discipline for situations where your child's activities can expose her to real danger, like playing with electric cords. This is the time to say "no" firmly and remove her from the situation. Don't expect her to learn from one or two incidents. Because of her short memory, you'll have to repeat the scene over and over before she recognizes and responds to your directions. Never depend on her to keep herself away from danger, no matter how often you've corrected her. Find a spot where she can play safely—a zone where everything is safe and you don't have to say "no."

To improve your discipline's effectiveness, consistency is critical. Make sure everyone taking care of your baby understands what the child is and isn't allowed to do. Keep rules to a minimum, preferably limited to potentially dangerous situations. Then make sure she hears "no" every time she strays into forbidden territory.

Immediacy is also important for good discipline. React as soon as you see your baby heading into trouble, not five minutes later. If you delay, she won't understand the reason you're reprimanding and the lesson will be lost. Likewise, don't be too quick to comfort after scolding. Yes, she may cry, sometimes as much in surprise as distress; but wait a minute or two before reassuring her. Otherwise, she won't know whether she really did something wrong.

In Chapter 10, we'll describe in detail the importance of not spanking or striking your child in any way when disciplining. No matter the age or behavior, physical punishment is always an inappropriate response. Spanking only teaches a child to act aggressively when upset. Yes, it may relieve your own frustration temporarily, and for the moment you actually might believe it did some good. It may stop a particular behavior in the short term, but it is *not* an effective way of disciplining your child in the long term, and it certainly doesn't teach alternative ways to act. It may lead to physical injury, it undermines effective communication between you and her, and it weakens her own sense of security.

What's the alternative? The American Academy of Pediatrics recommends using time-outs when your child is older, instead of spankings—putting a misbehaving child in a quiet place for a few minutes, away from other people, TV, electronics, or books. When the time-out is over, explain exactly why her behavior was unacceptable. Parents of children with special healthcare needs may need to find additional discipline strategies. They should begin by understanding their child's physical, emotional, and cognitive abilities. In some cases, consultation with a developmental-behavioral pediatrician may be helpful. (For more information about spanking and more appropriate ways to discipline, see page 249.)

As you refine your own disciplinary skills, don't overlook the importance of responding positively to your baby's *good* behavior. This reaction is more important for her learning self-control. If she hesitates before reaching for the stove, notice her restraint and tell her how pleased you are. Give her a hug when she does something nice for others. As she grows, her good behavior will depend, in large part, on her desire to please you. If you make her aware now how much you appreciate the good things she does, she'll be less likely to misbehave to get your attention.

Some parents worry about spoiling a child this age by giving her too much attention, but you needn't be concerned. At eight to twelve months, your baby still has a limited ability to be manipulative. You should assume that when she cries, it's not for effect but because she has real needs not being met.

These needs gradually become more complex, and as they do, you'll notice more variation in her cries—and in how you react to them. You'll come running to the shattering wail of something seriously wrong. By contrast, you may finish what you're doing before you answer the shrill come-here-I-want-you cry. You'll probably also recognize a whiny, muffled cry meaning roughly "I could fall asleep now if everyone would leave me alone." By responding appropriately to the hidden message behind your baby's cries, you'll let her know her needs are important, but response comes only to deserving calls.

Incidentally, there probably will be times when you won't be able to figure out why your baby is crying. In these cases, she may not know herself. The best response is comfort from you, combined with making sure she is safe and allowing whatever consoling techniques she chooses. Try holding her while she cuddles her favorite stuffed animal or special blanket, or play a game or read a story with her. Both of you will feel better when she's cheered up. Remember, her need for attention and affection is just as real as her need for food and clean diapers.

Siblings

As your baby becomes more mobile, she'll be better able to play with siblings, and those brothers and sisters will usually be glad to cooperate. Older children, particularly six- to ten-year-olds, often love to build towers for an eight-month-old to destroy. Or they'll lend a finger to an eleven-month-old learning to walk. A baby this age can be a wonderful playmate to her siblings.

However, while mobility can turn your baby into a more active playmate for her brothers and sisters, it also will make her more likely to invade their private territory. This may violate their budding sense of ownership and privacy, and can present serious safety hazards for the baby, since older children's toys often contain small, easily swallowed pieces. You can ensure everyone is protected by giving older siblings a place where they can keep and play with their belongings without fear of a "baby invasion."

Also, now that the baby can reach and grab almost everything in sight, sharing is another issue. Children under three aren't capable of sharing without adult prodding and, in most cases, direct intervention. An adult should always be watching when children are playing together. As much as possible, try to sidestep the issue and encourage tandem play, each child with her own toys. When they do play together, suggest looking at books or listening to music, rolling a ball back and forth, playing hide-and-seek games, or other activities

A baby this age can be a wonderful playmate to his siblings.

requiring limited cooperation. Remember that siblings can become jealous, and they need attention, too.

Grandparents

Eight to twelve months is a wonderful time to enjoy your grandchild. She is much more physically active and has more language expressions and emotional enthusiasm. However, she also may experience stranger anxiety and could show reluctance toward Grandma and Grandpa. Don't take this personally; it's normal. Simply hang on and continue to provide the love and attention you always have. Try not to overcompensate in the midst of these pulling-back episodes. Be patient, and the apparent standoffishness will resolve over time.

You can take advantage of your grandchild's developmental progress in the following areas.

CRAWLING. Get down on the floor with your grandchild as much as you physically can. This floor time is fun and reassuring for the baby. She'll show delight if you are her crawling target or object of exploration. Remember, though, to check the floor for possible hazards, since babies will pick up every object within reach and put it in their mouths.

FINE MOTOR SKILLS. Develop your own set of fine motor games with your grandchild—opening and closing items, operating latches, and dumping out and putting back games and toys. Expect plenty of repetition, since babies seem never to tire of doing the same activity over and over.

LANGUAGE. Read books and listen to music with your grandchild, keeping the language interactive. If you speak a language different from the one your grandchild is learning, don't be afraid to speak your language to her. (For more information on bilingual babies, see page 268.)

BASIC CARE. When it comes to feeding and sleeping, consistency is important. Keep "junior foods" in your home if you live apart from your grandchild. You also can establish "grandparents' special menus" that your grandchild can come to expect. When the baby is staying at your home, nap times and nighttime sleep schedules should be maintained as closely as possible to those at her home. Changes of routine sometimes create confusion for babies.

SAFETY. Follow the safety check items described at the end of this chapter in your own home to ensure your grandchild's well-being. Keep gates at the top and bottom of stairways. Place soft, protective coverings around sharp or round edges. Don't use walkers. Also, since babies of this age can have a strong nature and are wiggly, changing diapers should be a two-person operation if possible; change diapers on the floor or sofa to minimize the risk of falling. While changing the baby, try distracting her with a toy she can hold. Make sure you have all emergency phone numbers quickly available to you.

Immunization Update

At one year of age (or the months immediately after), she should receive the measles, mumps, rubella (MMR) vaccine. This vaccine protects your baby from three serious diseases that can cause fever, rash, and other symptoms, and potentially lead to serious complications (pneumonia or encephalitis [swelling of the brain] in children with measles, and hearing impairment and sterility in children with mumps). The current recommendation is to have your child receive the first MMR vaccine between twelve and fifteen months of age, but children traveling outside the country can receive an extra dose between six and twelve months of age for added protection.

The first dose of varicella (chickenpox) vaccine should be given between twelve and fifteen months. It can be given in combination with MMR (MMRV) or separately. While the MMRV vaccine seems to cause more fevers (and therefore slightly more febrile seizures) than the separate MMR and varicella vaccines, both are safe and effective.

The third hepatitis B vaccine will also be given between six and eighteen months of age, and the first hepatitis A vaccine will be given at or after one year of age.

The fourth pneumococcal vaccine, which protects your child against pneumonia, meningitis, blood infection, and some ear infections, is also given at twelve to eighteen months of age. If you're concerned about giving all the recommended vaccines to your child, consider this: every day your child's immune system fights off more antigens (the foreign substances that challenge the immune system) than are contained in the entire vaccine series. Your child's immune system can easily handle this. Vaccinating her completely and on time is the safest and best way to protect your baby from disease.

Safety Check
Car Safety Seats

- Children should remain in rear-facing car seats until at least the age of two years, and even after that, so long as they are the right size for the seat (this information should be printed on the side of the car safety seat). Car safety seat advice is often available at the fire station in your town, where safety days are held usually in the spring and fall.

- Never leave your baby alone in the car when you're not in it, not even for a short time. Some cars have alarms that remind parents of this. You can also leave an item like a teddy bear in the front seat to remind you of the baby in the back.

- Buckle the baby into an approved, properly installed car safety seat before you start the car. It's important that properly installed seats are in *all* cars your baby will ride in, including those belonging to childcare providers, sitters, and grandparents. (There are other elements of car safety seats you need to be aware of, so for further information, see page 495 in Chapter 15.)

Falls

- Use gates at the top and bottom of stairways, and in doorways to rooms not babyproofed.

- Do not allow an infant to climb on a kitchen chair, as the chair may tip over, resulting in head injury and possible leg or arm fractures.

- Do not use a baby walker. A stationary activity center is a much safer choice.

Burns

- Never smoke or carry hot liquids or foods near your baby or while holding her. When you must handle hot liquids or foods, put your baby in a safe place such as a crib, play yard, or high chair.

- Never leave containers of hot liquids or foods near the edges of tables or counters or on low surfaces, such as coffee tables.

- Do not allow your baby to crawl around hot stoves, floor heaters, or furnace vents.

Drowning

- Never leave your baby alone in a bath or around containers of water, including buckets, wading pools, swimming pools, sinks, or open toilets. Remove all water from containers immediately after use. If you have a swimming pool, install a four-sided fence at least 4 feet high that completely separates the house from the pool.

Poisoning and Choking

- Never leave small objects on or near the floor where your crawling baby could find them. You should look at the floor from their level and crawl around to visualize what they see. Sometimes medications or other small items are dropped unknowingly.

- Have the Poison Help number nearby in case of an emergency (1-800-222-1222).

- Assess your windows and doors for peeling paint so your child doesn't eat the paint chips and get lead poisoning.

- Do not give your baby hard pieces of food, or any soft foods that could become lodged in her airway, such as chunks of hot dogs or uncut grapes.

- Store all medicines and household cleaning products high and out of her reach.

- Use safety latches on drawers and cabinets that contain potentially dangerous objects. It is best to store these items in high, out-of-reach, locked cabinets if possible.

- Make sure that your baby can't become entangled in electrical cords or window shade cords.

- Make sure that all places your child visits, such as their grandparents' house, follow these same guidelines.

~ 10 ~

Your One-Year-Old

YOUR BABY HAS TURNED one and has become a toddler, crawling vigorously, starting or trying to walk, even talking a little; that is a milestone in itself. As he becomes more and more independent, the days of his unquestioning adoration and dependency on you are numbered. You should have a good idea of his personality by now and know his likes and dislikes as you enter this exciting time of his rapidly increasing abilities. Mobility changes his world and yours in an instant.

This might make you feel both sad and excited—not to mention a little nervous, as you think about the coming clash of wills. You may even be getting glimpses of these struggles already. If you take something away from him, he may scream in protest. If you pull him away from a swinging door, he may ignore your warnings and quickly return. And if you make one of his favorite meals, he may reject it unexpectedly. These are early experiments with control—testing your limits and discovering his own.

Exploring the boundaries of established rules and his own physical and developmental limits will occupy much of the next few years. Fortunately, this testing begins slowly, giving both of you time to adjust to his emerging independence. As a toddler just learning to walk, he'll be most interested in finding what the world looks like from an upright position. This curiosity, however, is bound to lead into off-limits situations. He's not consciously trying to be mischievous. He still counts on you to show him what's OK, and he'll look to you frequently for reassurance and security.

His confidence on his feet will lead to more assertiveness. By eighteen months, "no" will probably be his favorite word, and as he nears age two, he may throw a tantrum when asked to do something against his will.

Your toddler may also show more signs of possessiveness with belongings and people close to him. Seeing you pick up another baby might elicit tears. If another child grabs a toy, a strenuous tug-of-war might ensue. In a few months, as his vocabulary grows, "mine" will become another favorite word.

For now, his vocabulary is limited, although expanding rapidly. He understands much of what you say, provided you speak clearly and simply, and you probably can decipher some of what he says. Hard as it is to believe, in a year you'll have running conversations. This is also a time to detect speech problems, which can signal hearing loss or other issues.

Growth and Development
Physical Appearance and Growth

By the end of his first year, your baby's growth rate slows. From now until his next growth spurt (later in adolescence), his height and weight should increase steadily, but not as rapidly as before. As an infant, he may have gained 4 pounds (1.8 kg) in four months or less, but during the entire second year, he'll probably add 3 to 5 pounds (1.4–2.3 kg). Continue to plot his measurements every few months on the growth charts (see Appendix) to ensure he's following the normal growth curve. As you'll see, there's now a broader range of normal than at earlier ages.

At fifteen months, the average girl weighs about 23 pounds (10.5 kg) and is almost 30.5 inches (77 cm) tall; the average boy weighs about 24.5 pounds (11 kg) and is 31 inches (78 cm). Over the next three months, they'll each gain approximately 1½ pounds (0.7 kg) and grow about an inch (2.5 cm). By two, she'll weigh 27 pounds (12.2 kg) and be about 34 inches (about 86 cm) tall; he'll be almost 28 pounds (12.6 kg) and reach 34½ inches (87.5 cm).

Your baby's head growth also will slow dramatically. He'll probably gain only about 1 inch (2.5 cm) in head circumference this entire year, but by age two he'll have about 90 percent of his adult head size.

Your toddler's looks, however, will probably change more than his size. At twelve months, he still looked like a baby. His head and abdomen were still his largest body parts. His belly stuck out when he was upright, and his buttocks, by comparison, seemed small—at least with a diaper off. His arms and legs were relatively short and soft, rather than muscular, and his face had softly rounded contours.

All this will change as he becomes more active, as muscles develop and baby fat is trimmed away. His arms and legs will lengthen, and his feet will start to point forward as he walks, instead of to the sides. His face will become more angular and his jawline better defined. By his second birthday, it will be hard to remember how he looked as an infant.

Movement

If your baby hasn't started walking yet, he should within the next six months. In fact, perfecting this skill will be the major physical accomplishment of this year. If he's already walking, it may take another month or two before he can stand and move smoothly without support. And don't expect him to get up how you would. He'll likely spread his hands on the floor, straighten his arms, and lift his bottom up as he pulls his legs under him, and then straighten his legs and waist and be off. A child who does not walk by age eighteen months should be evaluated by his pediatrician.

In the beginning, he really is toddling. Instead of striding, he'll plant his legs wide apart, toes pointing outward, and lurch from side to side as he moves forward. As slow and painstaking as it may seem at the beginning, he'll quickly pick up speed. Don't be surprised if you're soon running to keep up with him.

An inevitable part of toddling, of course, is falling. Uneven surfaces will be a challenge for some time. He'll trip on even small irregularities—a wrinkle in the carpet or an incline to another room. It will be months before he can handle stairs or turn corners without falling.

He won't use his hands much during walking. While arms are used for balance (held at shoulder level in the "high guard" position), using hands to carry, play, or pick up a toy will be out of the question for a time. After walking for two to three months, however, he'll have the entire process under control. Not only will he be stooping to pick up and carry a toy across the room, he'll also be able to push or pull things, step sideways or backward, and even throw while walking.

About six months after his first steps, your baby's walking style will become more mature. His feet will be close together as he moves, making his gait smoother. With your help he may even walk up and down stairs, though if alone, he'll crawl up and back down. He'll soon take his first short, stiff runs straight ahead, saving running until probably the following year. By his second birthday, your child will be moving with great efficiency. To think—just a year ago he could barely walk!

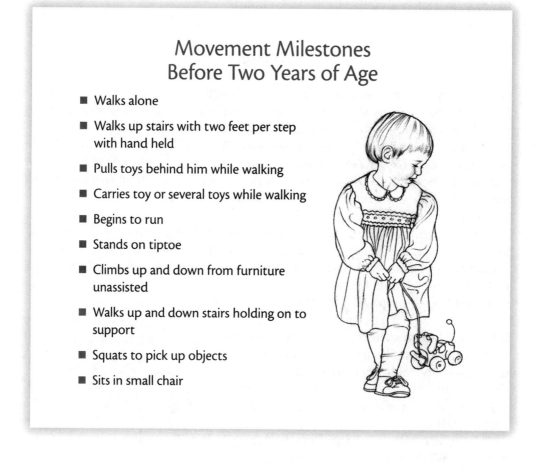

Movement Milestones Before Two Years of Age

- Walks alone
- Walks up stairs with two feet per step with hand held
- Pulls toys behind him while walking
- Carries toy or several toys while walking
- Begins to run
- Stands on tiptoe
- Climbs up and down from furniture unassisted
- Walks up and down stairs holding on to support
- Squats to pick up objects
- Sits in small chair

Hand and Finger Skills

Given all the large motor skills your one-year-old is mastering, it's easy to overlook the subtle changes with his hand skills, using them singly or together, and his hand-eye coordination. These developments allow him more control and precision as he examines objects and tries new movements. They also will greatly expand his exploration of the world around him.

At twelve months, it's a challenge to pick up very small objects between his thumb and forefinger, but by eighteen months, this task is simple. Watch how he manipulates small objects at will, exploring all their attributes. Some of his favorite games might include:

- Building towers of up to four blocks, then knocking them down

- Covering and uncovering boxes or other containers

- Picking up balls or other objects in motion

- Turning knobs and pages

- Putting round pegs into holes

- Scribbling and painting

These activities not only develop hand skills but also teach him spatial concepts, such as "in," "on," "under," and "around." As he nears two years of age and his physical coordination improves, he'll try more complex games, such as:

- Folding paper (if you show him how)

- Putting large square pegs into matching holes (which is more difficult than it is with round pegs, because it involves matching angles)

- Stacking up to five or six blocks

- Taking toys apart and putting them back together

- Making shapes from clay

Milestones in Hand and Finger Skills Before Two Years of Age

- Scribbles spontaneously

- Turns over container to pour out contents; takes objects in and out of container

- Builds tower of four blocks or more

- Might use one hand more frequently than the other

- Makes mark with crayon

- Throws small ball a few feet while standing

By twenty-four months, your toddler may demonstrate a clear tendency toward right- or left-handedness. However, many children don't show this preference for several years. Other children are ambidextrous, using both hands equally well, and may never establish a clear preference. There's no reason to pressure use of one hand over the other or to rush the natural process that leads to a preference.

Language Development

Early during this period, your toddler will suddenly seem to understand everything you say. You'll announce lunchtime and he'll be waiting by his high chair. You'll tell him you've lost your shoe and he'll find it. At first, his rapid response may seem unusual. Did he really understand, or was it just a coincidence? Rest assured, it's not your imagination. He's developing his language and comprehension skills on schedule.

This giant developmental leap will probably alter the way you talk to him and converse with others when he's around. You may edit conversations within his earshot ("Should we stop for i-c-e c-r-e-a-m?"). At the same time, you'll probably feel more enthusiastic about talking to him, because he is so responsive.

The best thing you can do to support your child's language development is to talk and read with him. The more words your child hears, the more he will come to understand. Talk with your child throughout the day. Describe what is happening and what you are doing together. Answer your child's questions and ask your own so he can "answer" you. Have conversations and follow your child's interests. Remember to turn off background television and put away phones or tablets, which tend to get in the way of these important conversations.

You no longer need high-pitched singsong monologues to get his attention. Instead, try speaking slowly and clearly, using simple words and short sentences. Teach him the correct names for objects and body parts and stop using cute substitutes such as "piggies" when you really mean "toes." By providing a good language model, you'll help him learn to talk with minimum confusion. Reading books together is a wonderful way to talk, take turns, and expose your child to new words. Children's books have words that we don't use in everyday conversation and provide a great way to expose your child to more language. Encourage your child to hold the book, turn the pages, and lead you in what he wants to look at and talk about. By talking about the pictures and asking your child questions, you will have rich dialogue that helps your child learn.

Language Milestones Before Two Years of Age

- Points to object or picture when it's named for him ("Where's the . . . ?")
- Uses the names of familiar people, objects, and body parts ("What's that?" "Who's that?")
- Uses six to ten words other than names (by fifteen to eighteen months)
- Uses two- to four-word sentences
- Follows a verbal command without a gesture
- Repeats words overheard in conversation
- Speaks in jargon
- Identifies at least two body parts

Most toddlers master at least fifty spoken words by twenty-four months and can put two words together to form a short sentence, although these milestones vary among children. Even among those with normal hearing and intelligence, some don't talk much during the second year. Boys generally develop language skills more slowly than girls. Whenever your child begins to speak, his first few words will probably include names of familiar people, his favorite possessions, and body parts. You may be the only person who understands these early words, since he'll omit or change certain sounds. He might get the first consonant and vowel right but drop the end of the word. Or he may substitute sounds he can pronounce, such as *d* or *b*, for more difficult ones.

With time and the help of his gestures, you'll learn to understand him. Don't make fun of his language mistakes or rush him. Give him the time he needs to finish what he wants to say, and then answer with correct pronunciation ("That's right, it's a ball!"). If you're patient and responsive, his pronunciation will improve.

By midyear, he'll use a few active verbs, such as "go" and "jump," and words of direction, such as "up," "down," "in," and "out." By twenty-four months, he'll have mastered the words "me" and "you" and use them all the time.

At first, he'll make versions of whole sentences by combining single words with gestures or grunts. He might point and say "ball"—his way of telling you he wants the ball rolled to him. Or he might shape a question, saying "Out?" or "Up?" and raising his voice at the end. Soon he'll combine verbs or prepositions with nouns to make statements, like "Ball up" or "Drink milk," and questions, like "What's that?" By the time he reaches twenty-four months, he'll begin to use two-word sentences. You can help by extending the words and phrases he says to demonstrate what he means. For example, after he says "Ball?" and gestures for it, you can say, "You want the ball? OK, I'm rolling the ball to you. Here is the ball."

Cognitive Development

As you watch your toddler play, have you noticed his hard concentration? Each game or task is a learning proposition, and he'll gather all sorts of information about how things work. He'll also be able to draw on facts already learned to make decisions and find solutions to challenges. However, he'll be interested in solving only problems appropriate for his developmental and learning level. Hand him a toy that fascinated him at eleven months and he may walk away bored, or he may object to a game that's too advanced. Your child will be especially attracted to mechanical devices with switches, buttons, and knobs, or wind-up toys. It may be difficult for you to judge exactly what he can handle, but it's not hard for him. Provide a range of activities, and he'll select the ones challenging but not beyond his abilities.

Imitation is a big part of his learning process at this age. Instead of simply manipulating objects, as he did before, he'll actually use the brush on his hair, babble into the phone, turn the steering wheel of his toy car, and push the wagon back and forth. At first, he'll be alone in these activities, but gradually he'll include other players. He might brush his doll's hair, "read" to you, offer a playmate a pretend drink, or hold his toy phone to your ear. Because imitation is an important part of his behavior and learning now, perhaps more than ever, be aware of the behaviors you model. He may say things he hears you say or do what he sees you do (either to your great pleasure or your dismay). This copying behavior also happens between toddlers and their older siblings. It is an ideal time to take advantage of these natural developmental cues.

Cognitive Milestones Before Two Years of Age

- Finds objects even when hidden under two or three covers

- Begins to sort by shapes and colors

- Begins make-believe play

Well before his second birthday, your toddler will excel at hiding games, remembering hidden objects long after they leave his sight. If you pocket his ball while he's playing, you may forget all about it, but he won't! As he masters hide-and-seek, he'll also understand more about separations from you. Just as he knows a hidden object is somewhere, he'll now recognize that you always come back, even when away for a whole day. If you actually show where you go when you leave him, he'll form a mental image of you there. This may make separation even easier for him. At this age, your toddler lets you know what role you should play in his activities. Sometimes he'll bring you a toy to make it work; other times he'll pull it away and try it by himself. Often, when he knows he's done something special, he'll pause and wait for applause. By responding to these cues, you'll provide support and encouragement to keep him learning.

You also must supply the judgment he still lacks. Yes, he now understands how certain things behave, but—because he can't see the chain of effects—he doesn't yet grasp the full notion of consequences. Even though he understands his toy wagon will roll downhill, he can't predict the effects it will have on the busy street below. Although he knows a door swings open and shut, he doesn't know to keep his hand clear. Even if he found out the hard way once, don't assume he's learned his lesson. Chances are he doesn't associate his pain with the chain of events that led to it, and he almost certainly won't remember this sequence the next time. Until he develops common sense, he'll need your vigilance to keep him safe.

Social Development

Your toddler will develop a very specific image of his social world, friends, and acquaintances. He is at its center, and while you may be close, he is most concerned about things in relation to himself. He knows other people exist, and they vaguely interest him, but he has no idea how they think or feel. As far as he's concerned, everyone thinks like him.

This view of the world (some experts call it egocentric or self-centered) often makes it difficult to truly play with other children socially. He'll play alongside and compete for toys, but he doesn't play cooperative games easily. He'll enjoy watching and being around other children, especially if slightly older. He may imitate them or treat them like dolls (trying to brush their hair), but he's usually surprised and resists when they try the same to him. He may offer toys or things to eat but may get upset if they take what's offered.

The concept of "sharing" is meaningless to a child this age. Every toddler believes he alone deserves the spotlight. Unfortunately, most are also as assertive as they are self-centered, and competition for toys or attention frequently erupts into hitting and tears. How can you minimize the combat when your child's friends are over? Try providing plenty of toys for everyone and be prepared to referee.

As mentioned, your child also may start being possessive over toys he knows are his. If another child even touches the plaything, he may rush over and snatch it away. Try reassuring him the other child is "only looking at it" and "it's OK for him to have a turn with it." But also acknowledge that "yes, it's your toy, and he's not going to take it away from you." It may help to select the particularly prized items and make them off-limits to others. Sometimes this helps toddlers feel they have some control and makes them less possessive about other belongings.

Social Milestones Before Two Years of Age

- Imitates behavior of others, especially adults and older children
- Increasingly aware of himself as separate from others
- Increasingly enthusiastic about company of other children
- Drinks from cup with little spilling
- Points to ask for something or to get help
- Engages with others for play
- Helps dress and undress self
- Points to pictures in book
- Points to object of interest to draw attention to it

Gender Identification

If you took a group of one-year-olds, dressed them alike, and let them loose on a playground, could you tell the boys from the girls? Probably not. Except for minor variations in size, there are very few differences between the sexes at this age. Boys and girls develop skills at about the same rate (although girls tend to talk earlier) and enjoy the same activities. Some studies have found boys more active than girls, but the differences during these first years are negligible.

Although parents generally treat boys and girls this age similarly, they often encourage different toys and games for each sex. Tradition aside, there's no basis for pushing girls toward dolls and boys toward trucks. Left to their own devices, both sexes are equally attracted to all toys, and should be allowed to play with a variety of toys they might be interested in.

Incidentally, young children learn to identify as boys or girls by associating with other members of their own sex. But this process takes years. Dressing your girl exclusively in frills or taking your boy to baseball games won't make much of a difference at this age. What does matter is the love and respect you give your child as a person, regardless of sex. This will lay the foundation for high self-esteem.

Because children this age have little awareness of others' feelings, they can be very physical in their responses to the children around them. Even when just exploring or showing affection, they may poke each other's eyes or pat too hard. (The same is true of their interactions with animals.) When upset, they can hit or slap without realizing they are hurting the other child. For this reason, be alert whenever your toddler is among playmates, and pull him back as soon as this physical aggressiveness occurs. Tell him, "Don't hit," and redirect the children to friendlier play.

Fortunately, your toddler shows his self-awareness in less aggressive ways as well. By eighteen months, he'll be able to say his name. At about the same time, he'll identify his reflection in a mirror and show a greater interest in caring for himself. As he approaches age two, he may be able to brush his teeth and wash his hands if shown how. He'll also help dress and, especially, undress himself. Throughout the day you may find him busily removing shoes and socks, even in the middle of a store.

Because your toddler is a great imitator, he learns important social skills from the way conflicts between the two of you are handled. Model for him

Masturbation

As toddlers explore their bodies, they naturally discover their genitals. Since touching them produces pleasant sensations, they do it often when their diapers are off. Although this may be accompanied by penile erections in boys, it's neither a sexual nor an emotional experience for toddlers. It just feels good. There's no reason to discourage it, worry, or call attention to it. If you show a strong negative reaction when they touch their genitals, you're suggesting there is something wrong or bad about these parts. They may even interpret this to mean there's something wrong or bad about what they're doing. Wait until they're older to teach them about privacy and modesty. For now, accept this behavior as normal curiosity.

how words and listening can, at least on occasion, be used to resolve conflicts ("I know you want to get down and walk, but you must hold my hand so I know you're safe"). As an imitator, he also will eagerly participate in anything you're doing. Whether sweeping the floors, mowing the lawn, or making dinner, he'll want to "help." Even though it may take longer, try turning it into a game. If you're doing something he can't help with, look for another chore he *can* do. Don't discourage these wonderful impulses to be helpful. Helping, like sharing, is a vital social skill, and the sooner he develops it, the more pleasant life will be for everyone.

Emotional Development

Your one-year-old will swing back and forth between independence and clinginess. He can now walk and do things himself. He has the power to move away from you and test his new skills. At the same time, he's not entirely comfortable with the idea he's an individual, separate from you and everyone else. Especially when he's tired, sick, or scared, he'll want you to comfort him and fend off loneliness.

It's impossible to predict when he'll turn his back and when he'll come running. He may seem to change one moment to the next, or he may seem mature and independent for several days before suddenly regressing. You may feel mixed reactions to this as well. While there are moments it feels wonderful to have your baby back, there are bound to be others when his fussing and whin-

The Shy Child

Some children are naturally fearful about new people and situations. They hold back, watching and waiting before joining a group activity. If pushed to try something different, they resist, and when faced with someone new, they cling. For a parent trying to encourage boldness and independence, this behavior can be frustrating. But challenging or ridiculing it will only make a shy child more insecure.

The best solution is to allow your child to move at her own pace. Give her the time needed to adapt, and let her hold your hand when she needs extra assurance. Praise her when she shows bravery. If you take her behavior in stride, outsiders will be less likely to ridicule it, and she'll develop self-confidence quickly. If she continues this kind of behavior, discuss it with your pediatrician. He will be able to give you individual advice and can, if necessary, refer you to a pediatric psychologist or child psychiatrist.

ing is the last thing you need. Some call this period the first adolescence. It reflects your child's mixed feelings about growing up and leaving you, and it's absolutely normal. The best way to help him regain composure is to give him attention and reassurance when he needs it. Snapping at him to "act like a big boy" will only make him feel more insecure and needy.

Brief separations from you may help your toddler become more independent. He'll still suffer some separation anxiety and perhaps fuss when you leave—even for just a few minutes—but the protest will be brief. You may be more upset by these separations than he is, but try to not let him know. If he believes his fussing might cause you to stay, he'll do so with similar occasions in the future. Also, as tempting as it might be to sneak away, if you do that he might actually become more clingy, since he'll never know when you'll disappear next. Instead, leave with a kiss and a promise to return. And when you come back, greet him enthusiastically and devote your full attention to him before moving on to other chores or business. When your child understands you always return and continue to love him, he'll feel more secure.

The Aggressive Child

Before they are two years of age, some children often deal with their frustration through aggressive behavior. They want to take charge and control everything going on. When they don't get what they want, they may turn toward violent behavior, such as kicking, biting, or hitting.

If your toddler does these things, you'll need to watch him closely and set firm, consistent limits. Give him plenty of positive outlets for his energy through physical play and exercise. When he's with other children, supervise him carefully to prevent serious trouble, and praise him when there's a play session without a problem.

In some families, a toddler's aggressive outbursts are considered an omen of future delinquency. Believing they have to come down hard on this behavior as soon as it appears, the parents spank or hit the child as punishment. However, children of this age copy their parents. A child treated like this can begin to believe this is the correct way to handle people whose behavior you don't like—the opposite of what the parent intended. This reaction may just reinforce his aggressiveness. The best way to teach your child how to hold back his aggressive impulses is to remind him how to behave in advance, offer praise for playing well with others, and be firm and consistent when he misbehaves. Also, his siblings and you should offer good examples of how to behave. (See also *Anger, Aggression, and Biting,* page 581.) Sometimes more than words is needed to correct a toddler's misbehavior. Consider using a time-out and/or a time-in (see page 364).

Basic Care
Feeding and Nutrition

You'll probably notice a sharp drop in your toddler's appetite after his first birthday. He's suddenly a picky eater, turns his head after a few bites, or resists coming to the table. It may seem he should be eating more, being so active, but his growth rate has slowed, and he doesn't require as much food.

Your toddler needs about 1,000 calories a day to meet his needs for growth, energy, and good nutrition. A 1,000-calorie diet is not a lot of food for an adult, but your child will do just fine, dividing it among three meals and two snacks a day. Don't count on him keeping this eating schedule, however. The eating habits of toddlers are erratic and unpredictable. He may eat everything in sight at breakfast but almost nothing else for the rest of the day. Or he may eat only his favorite food for three days in a row, and then reject it entirely. He may eat 1,000 calories one day, then noticeably more or less on subsequent days. Your child's needs will vary depending on his activity level, growth rate, and metabolism.

Mealtimes should not turn into sparring matches with your child. He's not rejecting you when he turns down food, so don't take it personally. Besides, the harder you push, the less likely he is to eat. Instead, offer him a selection of nutritious foods at each sitting, and let him choose. Vary the tastes and consistencies as much as you can.

Stimulating Child Brain Growth: Your One-Year-Old

- Your child learns through social interactions and play. Learning happens in the course of safe, stable, and nourishing relationships. If a child is fearful all the time, very little new learning will occur.

- Be consistent and predictable; establish routines for mealtimes, naps, and bedtime.

- Help your child learn more words by naming everyday objects and activities. "We're having breakfast now. This is a bowl. I'm going to pour cereal in the bowl for you to eat."

- Choose toys that encourage creativity. By selecting simple toys, you'll encourage your child to develop his own imagination.

- Encourage playing with blocks and soft toys, which helps your child develop hand-eye coordination, fine motor skills, and a sense of competence.

- Give consistent, warm, physical contact—hugging, skin-to-skin, body-to-body contact—to establish a sense of security and well-being. Avoid using food as a reward; instead verbally praise and hug your child for good behavior.

- Be attentive to your child's rhythms and moods. Respond to him when he is upset as well as happy. Be encouraging and supportive, with firm discipline as appropriate, but without yelling or hitting; provide consistent guidelines.

- Talk (using adult talk) or sing to your child during dressing, bathing, feeding, playing, walking, and driving. Speak slowly and give time for your child to respond. Listen to what your child says and expand on your child's phrases to make more complete sentences. For example, when your child points and says, "Milk?" you might say, "That's right, that is milk. Do you want some milk? We can put it in a blue cup."

- Read to your child every day. Choose books that encourage touching and pointing to objects, and read rhymes, jingles, and nursery stories. Follow your child's lead, letting him turn the pages. Ask questions about the pictures and talk together about what you see.

- If you speak more than one language, use both at home. Speak with your child in whatever language(s) you feel comfortable in.

- Play fun, calm, and melodic music for your child.

- Listen to and answer your child's questions. Ask questions to stimulate language development, thinking, and decision-making processes.

- Begin to explain safety in simple terms; for example, feeling the heat from the stove without touching it teaches the meaning and danger of hot objects.

- Make sure other people who provide care and supervision for your child understand the importance of forming a loving and comforting relationship with him.

- Encourage your child to look at books with you. Draw together.

- Help your child use words to describe emotions and to express feelings such as happiness, joy, anger, and fear. Describe your own emotions with words, and help your child describe his feelings ("glad," "mad," and "sad").

- Spend time on the floor playing with your child every day.

- Choose quality childcare that is affectionate, responsive, educational, and safe. Visit your childcare provider frequently and share your ideas about positive caregiving.

- If at all possible, avoid adverse childhood experiences and other causes of chronic stress that adversely affect brain development. When stressful things happen, take extra time to cuddle with and reassure your child, and consider discussing them with your pediatrician as well.

If he rejects everything, you might try saving the plate for when he's hungry. However, don't allow him to fill up on cookies or sweets after refusing his meal, thereby fueling his interest in empty-calorie foods (foods high in calories, low in nutrients). Hard as it is to believe, your child's diet will balance out over several days if you make a range of wholesome foods available and don't pressure him to eat a particular one at any given time. When parents try to control how much a toddler eats by forcing him to clean his plate, the child may not learn to self-regulate his hunger. This can lead to continued eating while ignoring signs of being full and can lead to obesity. It can also lead to toddlers refusing to eat, and sometimes that results in poor weight gain.

Your toddler needs foods from the same four basic nutrition groups that you do:

1. Meat, fish, poultry, eggs, beans

2. A source of calcium (dairy products, beans, dark green vegetables, seeds, tofu)

3. Fruits and vegetables

4. Whole-grain cereal, bread, and pasta; potatoes; rice

Developmental Health Watch

Because each child develops at his own pace, it's impossible to tell exactly when yours will perfect a given skill. The developmental milestones listed in this book give you a general idea of what you can expect as your child grows, but don't be alarmed if he takes a slightly different course. Alert your pediatrician, however, if he displays any of the following signs of possible developmental delay for this age range.

■ Cannot walk by eighteen months

■ Fails to develop a mature heel-toe walking pattern after several months of walking, or walks exclusively on his toes

■ Does not speak at least fifteen words by eighteen months

■ Does not use two-word sentences by two years

■ Does not seem to know the function of common household objects (brush, telephone, bell, fork, spoon) by fifteen months

- Does not imitate actions or words by two years

- Does not follow simple instructions by two years

- Cannot push a wheeled toy by two years

When planning your child's menu for this age, cholesterol and other fats should not be restricted. They are very important for normal growth and development. Babies and young toddlers should get about half of their calories from fat. You can gradually decrease fat consumption once your child has reached age two (and to about one-third of daily calories by ages four to five). While you should not forget that childhood obesity is a growing problem, children during this period need dietary fat. However, all fats are not created equal. Some are healthy fats, others unhealthy. Healthy fats like those found in avocado, olive oil, fish, nut butters, and dairy are good for your child (and you). Unhealthy fats such as those found in fried foods, fast foods, and many packaged foods are not healthy at any age. If you keep your child's daily caloric intake at about 1,000 calories, you needn't worry about overfeeding and risk of weight gain.

Adult eating preferences are developed now.

Social/Emotional Milestones Before Two Years of Age

- Demonstrates increasing independence

- Begins to show defiant behavior—particularly with adults with whom your child feels comfortable

- Increasing episodes of separation anxiety toward midyear, which then fade

By his first birthday, your child should be able to handle most foods served to the rest of the family—but with a few precautions. First, be sure the food is cool enough to not burn his mouth. Test the temperature yourself, since he'll dig in without consideration. Also, don't give heavily spiced, salted, buttered, or sweetened foods. These additions mask the natural taste of foods and may be harmful to his long-term health. Young children seem to be more sensitive than adults to these flavorings and may reject heavily spiced or seasoned foods.

Your little one can still choke on chunks of food that are large enough to plug his airway. Children don't learn to chew with a grinding motion until they're about four years old. Make sure anything you give is mashed or cut into small, easily chewable pieces. Never offer whole nuts, whole grapes (cut in half or quarters are OK), cherry tomatoes (unless cut in quarters), raw carrots, popcorn, seeds (e.g., processed pumpkin or sunflower seeds), whole or large sections of hot dogs or meat sticks, hard or gummy candies (e.g., jelly beans or gummy bears), or chunks of peanut butter (thinly spread peanut butter on a cracker or bread is OK). Hot dogs and carrots in particular should be quartered lengthwise and sliced into small pieces. Also make sure your toddler eats only while seated and supervised by an adult. Although he may want to do everything at once, eating "on the run" or while talking increases the risk of choking. Teach him as early as possible to finish a mouthful before speaking.

Around his first birthday, your toddler should drink liquids from a cup. He'll need less milk now, since he'll get most of his calories from solid foods.

Breastfeeding Past One Year

The AAP recommends babies be breastfed in combination with the introduction of complementary foods until at least twelve months of age, and continuation of breastfeeding for as long as mutually desired by mother and baby. Many babies continue to breastfeed well into toddlerhood. There is no need to wean your baby from breastfeeding at one year. Your toddler may continue to want to nurse several times during the day and this is normal. As children become more engaged in their surroundings, they will naturally nurse less and less. Feedings around sleep times are usually the last to go (remember to brush the teeth after these feedings). Babies will still be reaping the benefits of breastfeeding past their first birthday. Breast milk continues to be a good source of nutrition and does not lose its disease-fighting properties.

Toys Appropriate Before Two Years of Age

- Board books with large pictures, simple stories
- Books and magazines with photographs of babies
- Blocks
- Nesting toys
- Simple shape sorters and pegboards
- Beginner's jigsaw puzzles
- Toys that encourage make-believe play (child lawnmower, kitchen sets, brooms)
- Digging toys (bucket, shovel, rake)
- Dolls of all sizes
- Cars, trucks, trains
- Unbreakable containers of all shapes and sizes
- Bath toys (boats, containers, floating squeak toys)
- Balls of all shapes and sizes (except balls that could possibly fit in the mouth)
- Push and pull toys
- Outdoor toys (slides, swings, sandbox)
- Beginner's tricycle
- Connecting toys (links, large stringing beads, S-shapes)
- Stuffed animals
- Children's musical instruments
- Large crayons
- Toy telephone
- Unbreakable mirrors of all sizes
- Dress-up clothes
- Wooden spoons, old magazines, baskets, cardboard boxes, other similar safe, unbreakable items he finds around the house (e.g., pots and pans)

DIETARY SUPPLEMENTS. The American Academy of Pediatrics recommends that toddlers consume at least 600 IU (15 mcg) of vitamin D a day. Since most children's diets don't supply this much vitamin D, many pediatricians recommend a daily vitamin supplement. Otherwise, if you provide selections from each of the four basic food groups and let your child experiment with a wide variety of tastes, colors, and textures, he should get a balanced diet with plenty of vitamins. High doses of some vitamins, like the fat-soluble vitamins (A and D), may even pose risks; they're stored in the tissues when consumed in excess, and at very high levels could make your child sick. Large doses of minerals, such as zinc and iron, taken over time can have negative effects as well. Always discuss vitamins and supplements with your pediatrician to ensure your toddler is getting what he needs.

For some children, however, supplementation may be important. Your child may need some vitamin and/or mineral supplementation if your family's dietary practices limit the food groups available. For example, if your household is strictly vegetarian, or one with no eggs or dairy products, he may need supplements of vitamins B_{12} and D as well as riboflavin and calcium. Inadequate vitamin D intake can be associated with rickets, a disease in which the bones soften. Consult your pediatrician about which supplements are needed and their amounts. (See information on vitamin D supplements on page 131.)

Iron deficiency occurs among some young children and can lead to anemia (a limitation of the blood to carry oxygen). In some cases, the problem is dietary. Toddlers need at least 15 mg of daily iron in their food, but many fall short. (See table of sources of iron, page 320.) Drinking large quantities of milk and not eating enough iron-rich foods may lead to iron-deficiency anemia (one of the consequences of which is that the child feels full and is less interested in other foods, some being potential sources of iron). Combining iron-rich foods with fruits high in vitamin C can help children absorb more iron. Cooking in a cast-iron skillet can also add iron to the diet. Other causes of anemia include lead poisoning, which can occur with iron deficiency. It is important to have your child's lead level checked at the one- and two-year check-ups.

If your child is drinking 16 ounces (480 ml) of milk or less each day, there's little cause for concern as long as he is also eating a healthy diet full of iron-rich foods. If he drinks much more than that and you can't get him to eat more iron-rich foods, consult your pediatrician about adding an iron supplement. In the meantime, continue to give him vitamin D drops (600 IU [15 mcg] per day after age one), and keep offering him a wide variety of iron-rich foods so that, eventually, supplementation won't be necessary. (For more information on vitamin D, see page 131 in Chapter 4.)

Discontinuing the Bottle

Infants who sleep with a bottle containing anything other than water are at high risk of tooth decay. It is recommended the bottle be given up entirely at around age one and almost certainly by eighteen months. The sooner you start removing the bottle, the easier the task is. If you are breastfeeding, bottles may be avoided altogether. Cup feeding (sippy or straw cup) can be introduced as early as six months and by one year should be mastered. As long as your baby is drinking from a cup, he doesn't need to take liquids from a bottle. If you must give a bottle, limit the contents to plain water. Unfortunately, weaning from the bottle may not be as easy as it sounds. Eliminate the midday bottle first, then the evening and morning ones; save the bedtime bottle for last, but remember to limit the contents to plain water. If your baby will not initially take a bottle with plain water, gradually dilute the formula or other contents with water over a short time. After a week or two the bottle should contain *only* water.

It's easy to get into the habit of using a bottle to comfort or help a child sleep. But at this age, he no longer needs anything to eat or drink at night. If you are still feeding him at night, you should stop. Even if he demands a bottle and drinks thirstily, nighttime feedings are a comfort rather than a nutritional necessity. The bottle soon turns into a crutch and prevents his learning to fall back to sleep on his own. If he cries for only a short time, try letting him cry back to sleep. After a few nights he'll probably forget all about the bottle. If this doesn't happen, consult your pediatrician and read the other sections on sleep in this book. (See, for example, pages 217 and 246.)

Incidentally, giving your toddler a drink or other healthy snack *before bedtime* is acceptable—provided his teeth are brushed afterward. A short breastfeeding, a drink of cow's milk or other liquid, or even some fruit or another nutritious food will do. If the snack is in a bottle, gradually phase in use of a cup.

Whatever the snack, have your child finish it then clean his teeth, using a small amount (the size of a grain of rice) of fluoridated toothpaste on a soft cloth, gauze, or toothbrush. Not removing the food or liquid from your baby's teeth after he eats allows it to remain on the teeth all night and can result in tooth decay. If he needs comfort to fall asleep, let him use a cuddly toy, blanket, or his thumb—but never a bottle or cup containing anything but plain water.

SELF-FEEDING. At twelve months, your baby was getting used to drinking from a cup and feeding himself with a spoon and his fingers. By fifteen months, he'll have much more control, getting food into his mouth with relative ease and flinging it about the room when that seems like more fun. He'll be able to fill his spoon and get it to his mouth consistently, although occasionally it will tip the wrong way at the last second. Unbreakable dishes, cups, and glasses are essential, since they, too, may go flying when he's bored with their contents. Such behavior should be discouraged by a firm reprimand and replacement of the utensils in the proper location. If these behaviors persist, consider stopping the meal and waiting until the next.

Make sure your toddler eats only while seated and supervised by an adult.

By eighteen months, your toddler can use a spoon, fork, and unbreakable glass or cup, though he may not always want to. There will be times he'd rather finger-paint with his pudding or turn his plate into a Frisbee. Some children get over this chaotic eating behavior by their second birthday, at which time they may actually become upset when they spill or get a smudge of food on their hands. Others, however, will remain messy eaters well past two years of age.

Cutting Down on Sweets

Almost everyone enjoys sweets, and your toddler is no different. Like other human beings, he may have been born with a taste for sugar, and is already sensitive to different concentrations of sweetness. Offer a sweet potato and a baked potato, and he may take the sweet potato every time. Give him a choice between the sweet potato and a cookie, and the cookie may win more often. So it's not your fault if he makes a beeline for candy and ice cream when you'd rather he take a bite of broccoli. But it is your responsibility to limit his access to sweets and provide a diet composed primarily of nutritious foods that promote growth, not tooth decay.

Fortunately, when sweets are out of sight, they won't be on your toddler's mind, so either don't bring them into the house or keep them hidden. Also avoid adding sugar to his food, and don't make dessert an everyday event. As for snacks, instead of sweets or fatty foods, let him have small portions of healthy foods such as fruit, whole-grain bread and crackers, and cheese. In other words, encourage good eating habits that can last a lifetime.

Sample One-Day Menu for a One-Year-Old

This menu is for a one-year-old child who weighs approximately 21 pounds (9.5 kg).

1 cup = 8 ounces = 240 ml
1 ounce = 2 tablespoons = 30 ml
½ ounce = 1 tablespoon = 15 ml = 3 teaspoons
1 teaspoon = ⅓ tablespoon = 5 ml

BREAKFAST
½ cup iron-fortified breakfast cereal or 1 cooked egg
½ cup whole or 2 percent milk
½ banana, sliced
2–3 large sliced strawberries

SNACK
1 slice toast or whole-wheat muffin with 1–2 tablespoons
    cream cheese or peanut butter, or ½ cup yogurt with cut-up fruit
Water or ½ cup whole or 2 percent milk

LUNCH
½ sandwich: sliced turkey or chicken, tuna, egg salad, or peanut butter
½ cup cooked green vegetables
½ cup whole or 2 percent milk

SNACK
1–2 ounces cubed or string cheese, or
2–3 tablespoons fruit or berries
Water or ½ cup whole or 2 percent milk

DINNER
2–3 ounces cooked meat, ground or diced
½ cup cooked yellow or orange vegetables
½ cup whole-grain pasta, rice, or potato
½ cup whole or 2 percent milk

SOURCES OF IRON

Excellent

Red meats   Blackstrap molasses
Iron-fortified whole-grain cereal

Good

Hamburger	Eggs, egg yolks	Kidney beans	Strawberries
Lean beef	Spinach, mustard	Soybeans	Tomato juice
Chicken	greens	Split peas	
Tuna	Asparagus	Dried apricots	
Ham	Potato, baked in	Raisins	
Shrimp	skin	Prunes, prune	
Frankfurter	Navy beans	juice	

WHERE WE STAND

CHILDHOOD OVERWEIGHT AND OBESITY is now a national health emergency. Obesity leads to shorter life spans, lower quality of life, and many chronic medical problems, many of which begin in childhood. We now fear the current generation of children might live shorter lives than their parents due to the long-term effects of obesity. However, a lot can be done to address and prevent obesity, and the earlier we start the better. Small adjustments (regarding approach to food, feeding, physical activity, etc.) in a young child could prevent many future health challenges. That is not to say it will be easy, as currently the healthy choice is not always the easiest, but it is well worth it! It was previously common to think kids might outgrow overweight or grow into their weight, but now, more often than not, this is not happening. In fact, over the past two decades obesity rates have *doubled* in children and *tripled* among adolescents in the United States. Obesity affects all body systems and can lead to potentially serious health problems, including diabetes, high blood pressure, sleep apnea, liver failure, and more. It can also cause psychological stresses associated with children feeling different from their peers, leading to depression, anxiety, and low self-esteem.

The American Academy of Pediatrics believes making small changes early on can prevent a lifetime of complications, and both parents and pediatricians can take steps to help children maintain and achieve a healthy weight. Your pediatrician should monitor your child's weight and rate of weight gain from infancy onward. Your pediatrician will compare your toddler's weight to his length to ensure your child is at a healthy weight for his or her age, sex, and length. Weight-to-length ratio at or above the 85th percentile (higher than 85 percent of children the same age and sex) falls into the overweight category; a weight-to-length ratio at or above the 95th percentile defines the obese category. (See the growth charts in the Appendix.) These categories predict risk for current and future medical problems: the higher the weight-to-length ratio (above the 85th percentile), the greater the risk. The AAP has endorsed the World Health Organization's infant growth charts, meaning that your pediatrician can assess healthy weight from birth onward. Infants aren't put on diets, but these growth charts can provide more confidence that your infant or toddler is growing well, and so may not need extra formula or supplementation. This can be helpful reassurance if you are concerned your child is fussy due to not eating enough.

Some children are prone to extra weight gain because of family history (which includes genetics, metabolism, and family customs), but in almost all cases, making healthy food changes and increasing physical activity can help improve your child's weight. Encourage an active lifestyle at home, in childcare settings, and at school to start your children on the path to lifelong health. Talk to your pediatrician about developing healthy eating habits that begin in infancy, such as minimizing or eliminating juice and offering a variety of healthy foods, especially vegetables and fruits, and continuing these habits throughout childhood. Early on, allow your child to decide when he is full. Taste preferences can change over time, and it can take your child ten times of trying a new food before he enjoys it. Choose nutritious snacks, including vegetables, fruits, low-fat dairy foods, and whole grains. Turn off the TV and have him sit at the table during meals. Enjoy meals together as a family whenever possible, without distractions from phones or the television. Studies show that children who watch too much TV are more likely to have overweight. Meals can be great times for family conversations. (See Chapter 32, *Media*.)

Getting Ready for Toilet Training

As your child approaches age two, you'll begin to think about toilet training. Perhaps you are considering a childcare or preschool program that requires toilet training. Before you launch your campaign, however, be forewarned: toilet training generally becomes easier and is accomplished faster when your child is older. Yes, early training is possible—but not necessarily preferred. It may place unnecessary pressure on your young toddler. He may not have the necessary bowel or bladder control, or the motor skills needed to remove his clothes quickly and reliably before using the toilet.

Many children are ready to be toilet trained after their second birthday (boys often slightly later than girls), but your toddler might be ready earlier. If your toddler appears ready, turn to page 357 for details. Even if he's not ready, you still can familiarize him with the process by keeping his potty chair or toilet seat insert handy and explaining in simple terms how it works. You might also consider choosing the words you'll use at home, such as "pee-pee" and "poop," to familiarize him with what's taking place. Soon he'll be able to tell you after he has gone. While it is not a sign he's completely ready to be toilet trained, it is a first step. You might also consider showing him where stool from his diapers goes, and allow him to flush the toilet. The more familiar he is with the process, the less scary and confusing it will seem when you begin training.

Sleeping

Sometimes it's tempting to give up and let your child fall asleep in his tracks when he's overcome by exhaustion. But doing so will only make it more challenging to implement a routine sleep schedule, important for both daytime and nighttime sleeping. Instead, make note of the time when he shows signs of sleepiness, and make that his regular bedtime. Establish a bedtime ritual and discuss it with your toddler. Whether you include a bath, story, or song, the routine should end with him quiet but awake in his crib, ready for your goodnight kiss before you leave the room. If he cries continuously, consult the methods described in Chapters 9 and 35 for teaching him to fall asleep on his own. Using a transitional object (lovey) may be helpful at this age.

Unfortunately, bedtime resistance isn't the only sleep struggle you may have. Remember the first time he slept through the night and you thought sleep problems were over? As the parent of a toddler, you now know the truth: he may go a few days, weeks, or even months sleeping through the night, then begin waking up almost as frequently as a newborn.

Change in routine is a common cause of nighttime awakening. Switching rooms or beds, losing a favorite cuddly toy or blanket, taking a trip, or having an illness may all disrupt his sleep. Though valid reasons for waking, these are not excuses for you to pick him up or take him to your room. He needs to put himself back to sleep, even if it means crying a bit first. The strategies outlined in Chapter 35 still apply.

If your toddler is used to getting lots of nighttime attention, you'll need to retrain him gradually. If you've been giving milk when he wakes up, it's time to change to water and soon afterward stop the practice entirely. If you've been picking him up, restrict yourself to verbally calming him from a distance. Above all, don't get angry if he continues to protest. Show him kindness, even as you remain firm. It's not easy, but in the long run it will improve your sleep as well as his. (See Chapter 35 for more information on sleep.)

Behavior

Discipline

Having a toddler is a humbling experience and presents new challenges, adventures, and opportunities for fulfillment. Before your child was born, or even when he was a baby, it was easy to watch someone else's toddler throw a temper tantrum and say, "My child will never do that." Now you realize any child will act up unexpectedly. You can guide and teach your child what's right, and that will work most of the time. But you can't force him to act exactly as you want. So face the facts: there are bound to be times when the unruly child everyone stares at is yours!

At this age, your toddler has a limited idea of "good" and "bad," and he does not fully understand the concept of rules or warnings. You may say, "If you pull the cat's tail, he'll bite you," but it may make no sense to him at all. Even "Be nice to the cat" may not be clear. Whether he's running into the street or turning his face away from Grandma's kiss, he's not deliberately behaving badly, nor do his actions mean you've failed as a parent. He's simply acting on impulses. It will take years of firm but gentle guidance before he fully understands what you expect from him and has the self-control to meet those expectations.

Many people think of discipline as punishment. In fact, discipline means to teach or instruct, and while punishment may be part of it, a much more important aspect is love. Affection and caring form the core of your relationship with your child and play a powerful role in shaping his behavior. Your love and respect will teach him to care about others as well as himself. Your daily example of honesty, dedication, and trust will teach him the same. The control you show helping him to learn right from wrong will serve as a model for the self-discipline he will develop. In short, if you want him to behave well, you need to act that way toward him.

If a running tally was kept, your displays of affection should greatly outnumber punishments and criticisms. Even a quick hug or a bit of good-natured roughhousing will reassure your child you love him. And on a day when your toddler is getting into everything and you find yourself being especially snappy with him, make sure you go out of your way when he does behave well to give him a hug and tell him he's doing a good job. Catch him being good as often as you can. Especially during this year, pleasing you is very important to your toddler, so praise and attention are powerful motivational rewards to obey the reasonable rules you set.

Children need healthy forms of discipline, such as positive reinforcement of appropriate behaviors, limit setting, redirecting, and setting future expectations. It's important to have realistic expectations for behavior. They should reflect his temperament and personality, not your fantasies. He may be more active and inquisitive than you would like, but insisting he spend long stretches in the play yard or confined in his high chair will only make him more resistant and frustrated.

Even if your toddler is a "model" child, he still has to learn what you expect. Telling him once won't get the message across. He'll have to learn by trial and error (often several times) before he understands the rule.

If you're a single parent, you may encounter unique challenges trying to manage a child's behavior issues on your own. Remember that while you might feel alone, there are many resources available to help, including family members, friends, faith communities, and parent support groups. Your pediatrician's office can help connect you if you're not sure where to start. (Also see *Single-Parent Families* on page 766.) An important reminder: If you load too many rules on your child at this early age, he'll be hurt and bewildered, and you'll be frustrated. Make things easier for everyone by establishing priorities and build your list of rules gradually. The most important rules should keep him safe. As your child learns to walk, discipline around safety should be paramount, giving him the freedom to explore in safe ways, while ensuring childproof locks are in place where they're needed. Also, be certain he understands that hitting, biting, and kicking are not OK. Once he masters these rules, you can address nuisance behavior, such as screaming in public, throwing food, writing on the wall, and unexpectedly removing his clothes. Save the finer points of social behavior for the next few years. It's too much to ask an eighteen-month-old to return Grandma's kisses when he'd rather be playing.

Despite all your prevention efforts, your toddler will violate some or all of your rules. When that happens, alert him to your displeasure with your facial expression and tone of voice. Then move him to a different place. Sometimes this will be enough, but just as often, other measures may be required. It's best to prepare these responses now, while you are calm and your toddler is young. Otherwise, in the heat of the moment, you may be prone to lose your temper and do something you'll regret. In the next few years, he'll naturally become more mischievous.

Make this important pact with yourself: *never* resort to punishments that physically or emotionally hurt your child. While you need to let him know he's done something wrong, this doesn't require inflicting pain. Spanking, slapping, beating, shaking, and screaming at children of any age does far more harm than good. Here are some of the main reasons this is true.

- Even if it stops the child from misbehaving at the moment, it also teaches him it's OK to hit and yell when he's upset or angry. Think of the mother busily whacking her child as she yells at him: "I told you not to hit!" It's absurd, isn't it? But it's also tragically common, and has an equally tragic result: children who are hit often become hitters themselves, having learned that violence is an acceptable way to express anger and to resolve conflicts. Toddlers will imitate everything that you do.

- Physical punishment can harm your child. If a little spank doesn't work, many parents will slap even harder as they become angrier and more frustrated.

- Physical punishment makes the child angry at and resentful of the parent. So instead of developing self-discipline, the youngster is much more likely to try to get back at the parent by continuing to misbehave, but without getting caught.

- Physical punishment gives a child a very extreme form of attention. Although it's unpleasant, even painful, it tells the child that he's gotten through to his parent. If the mother or father is usually too busy or preoccupied to pay much attention to him, the child may decide the bad behavior and punishment that follows is worth it to get parental attention.

- Yelling and other harsh verbal discipline cause aggression, conduct problems, and depressive symptoms in later years.

Physical punishment is harmful emotionally to both parent and child. It is the least effective way to discipline. So what approach should you take? As difficult as it may be, the best way to deal with your misbehaving toddler is to isolate him briefly. No attention. No toys. No fun. This strategy, known as time-out, works like this:

1. You've told your toddler not to open the oven door, but he persists.

2. Without raising your voice, again say firmly, "No. Don't open the oven door," and pick him up with his back toward you.

3. Begin this "time-out training" in your lap with your child facing away from you. Hold him until he is quiet and still.

The key to this form of discipline—and any other, for that matter—is consistency and calmness. Though it is difficult, try to respond immediately every time your child breaks an important rule, but don't let your irritation get the better of you. If you're like most parents, you won't succeed 100 percent of the time, but an occasional slip-up won't make much difference. Just try to be as consistent as possible.

When you do feel yourself losing your temper, take a few deep breaths, count to ten, and, if possible, leave the room, getting someone else to step in if available. Remind yourself you are older and should be wiser than your toddler. You know at his age he's not deliberately trying to annoy or embarrass you, so keep your own ego in check. In the end, the more self-discipline you exercise, the more effective you'll be at disciplining your child. Remember, he's watching and imitating you!

Coping with Temper Tantrums

While you're busily planning the rules for your toddler, he's attempting to master his own destiny. It's inevitable you'll clash from time to time. Your first taste will come when your one-year-old shakes his head and emphatically says "No!" after you've asked him to do something. By year's end, his protests may have escalated to screaming fits or full-blown tantrums, throwing himself to the floor, clenching his teeth, kicking and screaming, pounding his fists on the floor, and even holding his breath. As difficult as these performances are to tolerate, they are a normal (even healthy) way for your toddler to deal with conflict.

Look at the situation from his point of view. Like all young toddlers, he believes the world revolves around him. He's trying hard to be independent, and most of the time you're encouraging him to be strong and assertive. Yet every now and then, when he's trying to do something he very much wants to do, you pull him away or ask him to do something else. He can't understand why you're getting in his way, nor can he verbally tell you how upset he is. The only way he can express his frustration is by acting it out.

Preventing Temper Tantrums

(See also *Temper Tantrums*, page 596.)

When it comes to discipline, you have several distinct advantages over your child. First, because you know there will be inevitable conflicts (you can probably even predict which issues are likely to spark them), you can plan your prevention strategy in advance.

Use the following guidelines to help you minimize your child's temper tantrums, both in number and in intensity. Make sure everyone who takes care of him understands and follows these policies consistently.

- When you ask your toddler to do something, use a friendly tone and phrase your request like an invitation instead of a command. It also helps to say "please" and "thank you."

- Don't overreact when he says "no." For some time, he may automatically say "no" to *any* request or instruction. He'll even say "no" to ice cream and cake at this stage! What he really means is something like "I'd like to be in control here, so I'll say 'no' until I think it through or until I see if you're serious." Instead of jumping on him, answer his hidden challenge by repeating your request calmly and clearly. Don't punish him for saying "no."

- Choose your battles carefully. He won't throw a temper tantrum unless you push him first, so don't push unless there's something worth pushing. Keeping him safely buckled into his car safety seat is a priority item. Making sure he eats peas before applesauce is not. So while he says "no" to everything, you should say "no" only when it's absolutely necessary.

- Do offer limited choices whenever possible. Let him decide which pajamas to wear, which story to read, which toys to play with. If you encourage his independence in these areas, he'll be much more likely to comply when it counts.

- Don't offer choices where none exists, and don't make deals. Issues like bathing, bedtime, and staying out of the street are nonnegotiable. He doesn't deserve an extra cookie or trip to the park for cooperating with these rules. Bribery will only teach him to break the rule whenever you forget to give him the agreed-on reward.

(continues on next page)

- Anticipate situations that are likely to trigger a tantrum and avoid them whenever possible. If he always makes a scene in the grocery store, arrange for the child to stay with your spouse or partner, or get a sitter, the next few times you go shopping. If one of his playmates always seems to get him keyed up and irritable, separate the children for a few days or weeks and see if the dynamics improve later.

- Reward his good behavior with plenty of praise and attention. Even if you just sit with him while he looks at his books, your companionship shows him you approve of this quiet activity.

- Keep your sense of humor. While it's not a good idea to laugh at your toddler as he kicks and screams (that just plays to his performance), it can be therapeutic to laugh and talk about it with friends or family members when he's out of earshot.

Outbursts, then, are all but inevitable, and your child's general temperament will set the tone for most. If he's adaptable, easygoing, generally positive, and easily distracted, he may never kick and scream. Instead, he might pout and say "no," or head in the opposite direction when you try to guide him. The opposition is there, but it's low-key. On the other hand, if your child is active, intense, and persistent, he'll probably channel the same intensity into his tantrums. You'll need to remind yourself over and over this is neither good nor bad, and it has nothing to do with your parenting skills. Your child is not consciously trying to thwart you, but rather is simply going through a normal stage of development that soon will pass (though perhaps not soon enough to suit you).

Here are some important points to keep in mind about living with temper tantrums.

- You may have an easier time coping with your toddler's outbursts if you think of them as performances. This will remind you of what you have to do to stop them: eliminate the audience. Since you are the only audience that matters to your child, leave the room. If he follows, call time-out and put him in his play yard. Also, if he kicks or bites at any time during the tantrum, call time-out immediately. While it's normal to try out this kind of super-aggressive behavior, you shouldn't let him get away with it.

WHERE WE STAND

THE AMERICAN ACADEMY OF PEDIATRICS strongly opposes striking a child for any reason. Spanking is never recommended; infants and children may be physically harmed by a parent who strikes them. If a spanking is spontaneous, parents should later explain calmly why they did it, the specific behavior that provoked it, and how angry they felt. They also might apologize to their child for their loss of control. This usually helps the youngster to understand and accept the spanking, and it models for the child how to remediate a wrong.

Whenever a parent strikes a child, it may undermine the trust the child needs to thrive. However, infants often frustrate their parents. Here are a few alternatives. First, put your baby in the crib or another safe place while you get control of yourself. Call a friend, relative, or partner to get some support or advice. If these don't help, reach out to your child's pediatrician for advice.

■ When a tantrum takes place away from home, it's much more difficult to remain calm. Especially when out in public, you can't just leave him and go to another room. And because you're trapped and embarrassed, you're much more likely to spank, yell, or snap at him. But that won't work any better here than it does at home, and it has the added disadvantage of making you look worse than your child. Rather than lashing out or letting him have his way—either of which only encourages his tantrums—calmly carry him to a restroom or to the car, so he can finish his performance away from onlookers. Also, sometimes in public a big, immobilizing hug and calming voice will soothe and quiet such a child.

■ When the tantrum or the time-out is over, don't dwell on it. Instead, if a request from you was what triggered his outburst initially, calmly repeat it. Remain composed and determined, and he'll soon realize that acting out is a waste of his and your time.

■ He may hold his breath during a severe temper tantrum. Sometimes this might last long enough to cause him to faint for a very short period of time. This can be frightening, but he will awaken in thirty to sixty seconds. Just keep him safe and protected during this brief episode and try not to overreact, since this tends to reinforce tantrum breath-holding behavior. If not reinforced, this type of activity will usually disappear shortly.

Family Relationships

Because your toddler is self-centered, his older brothers and sisters might find him taxing. Not only does he still consume the bulk of your time and attention, but with increasing frequency he will deliberately invade his siblings' territory and possessions. When they throw him out, he may respond with a tantrum. Even if the older siblings were tolerant and affectionate toward him as an infant, they are bound to occasionally display antagonistic feelings toward him now.

It will help keep the peace if you enforce rules that guard older children's privacy, and set aside time to spend just with them. No matter how old, all your children want your affection and attention. Whether they're preparing for the preschool picnic, planning a second-grade science project, trying out for the middle-school soccer team, or fretting over the junior prom, they need you as much as your toddler does.

If your toddler is the older sibling, the rivalry may be more intense. (See *Sibling Rivalry*, page 764.) The normal feelings of jealousy are heightened by his self-centeredness, and he doesn't have the reasoning abilities to cope. Often his feelings of jealousy don't manifest as outright anger toward an infant, but as anger and belligerence toward you for not providing as much attention as he believes he deserves. And if he isn't getting enough attention for doing the "right" things (playing quietly by himself), he'll have no qualms about pushing your buttons by acting out. To a toddler, there is no such thing as negative attention—all attention is good. At times they'd rather have you angry than feel ignored (which, by the way, is the reason time-out can be so effective). (For more information on preparing a sibling for the new baby, see page 38 in Chapter 1.)

Immunization Update

Between twelve and fifteen months, your toddler will need booster doses of the Hib and pneumococcal conjugate vaccines. These vaccines help prevent meningitis, pneumonia, and joint infection caused by *Haemophilus influenzae* type b and several strains of *Streptococcus pneumoniae* bacteria. Your toddler also should receive his first measles, mumps, rubella (MMR) vaccine, chickenpox vaccine, and hepatitis A vaccine. At twelve to eighteen months, your toddler also will require:

- The fourth dose of the DTaP vaccine (which can be administered as early as twelve months, but is recommended at fifteen to eighteen months of age)

- The third dose of the polio vaccine (if not already given)

- The fourth dose of pneumococcal vaccine

- The fourth dose of Hib vaccine

- The second dose of hepatitis A vaccine, given at least six months after the first dose

Blood Tests

At the twelve-month well-child exam, your child should have a hemoglobin and lead level drawn to assess for anemia and lead poisoning, respectively. Iron-deficiency anemia can be common in infants and toddlers, and iron supplementation may be needed. Also, because of a child's high hand-to-mouth activity, a toddler may chew on objects that may contain lead. These include paint chips, toys painted with lead paint, jewelry, and other objects. Homes that are being renovated may have lead dust that may be ingested. Soil, especially near roadways, may have lead from car exhaust from the days when gasoline contained lead.

Safety Check
Sleep Safety

- Keep the crib mattress at the lowest setting.

- Keep the crib free of any objects that your toddler could stack and climb on to get out.

- If your toddler can climb out of his crib, move him to a low bed.

- Keep the crib away from all windows, drapery, and electrical and other cords.

- Be sure all crib gyms, mobiles, and other hanging toys have been removed.

Toy Safety

■ Do not give your toddler any toy that requires an electrical outlet. If the toy is battery operated, make sure the battery case is secured.

A Message for Grandparents

You have an ongoing role to play in your grandchild's nurturing and development. Though you must carefully re-childproof your house (see Chapter 15), there are many wonderful things grandchildren can do with grandparents. Here are some activities for you and your grandchild to participate in together, and things to keep in mind as you do.

MOTOR SKILLS

Help your grandchild practice skills that involve your own likes. For example:

■ Involve him in physical activities (such as sweeping, preparing food, or arranging items) around the house in which you can lend a helping hand to ensure his success and safety.

■ Devise and initiate outdoor games and exercises that you and he can enjoy together.

COGNITIVE MILESTONES

To help your grandchild develop cognitively:

■ Read special books with him.

■ Play music and sing songs with him.

■ Assist him as he begins to learn his numbers.

■ Play hiding games like hide-and-seek and peekaboo.

■ Mix fantasy play with real play.

SOCIAL DEVELOPMENT

■ Encourage your grandchild to interact with his peers, but keep in mind egocentric behavior is normal for this age.

■ Don't overreact to selfishness or disregard of the feelings of others. Just reinforce that he should be sensitive to other children's feelings.

■ Keep in mind that this period of self-centeredness will taper off by the age of three.

■ Nurture his self-esteem at every opportunity, but not at the expense of others.

EMOTIONAL DEVELOPMENT

■ Repeatedly tell your grandchild how special he is to you. Tell him of the importance of your time together.

■ Don't overreact to his mood swings—clinging one moment, independent the next, then defiant.

■ Don't reinforce his aggressiveness if it becomes abusive. Set limits, but do not physically restrain or punish him. Read the section on brain growth in children this age (page 310). Follow your own inclinations about the activities or areas that promote his development.

■ Do not give him a motorized riding toy.

■ Do not give him a toy with any small parts or sharp edges. Stick with toys intended for toddlers, not for older children. Check the recommended age label to be sure.

Water Safety

■ Never leave your toddler, *even for a few seconds*, in or near any body of water without supervision. This includes a bathtub, toilet, wading pool, swimming pool, fishpond, whirlpool, hot tub, lake, or ocean.

Auto Safety

■ All children this age should ride rear-facing in their car safety seat, appropriately installed in the backseat, with a five-point harness.

■ Never let your toddler climb out of his car safety seat while the car is moving.

■ Never leave him alone in the car, even if it is locked and in your driveway.

■ See the section on car safety seats, pages 495–503, in Chapter 15.

■ Consider engaging the rear door child safety lock.

Home Safety

■ Avoid choking hazard foods (see page 314 of this chapter), and do not let children walk around while eating or with objects in their mouths.

■ Protect any open windows with window guards or barriers your toddler cannot possibly push out or open. Screens do not prevent falls from windows.

■ If possible, block electrical outlets with furniture or use outlet covers that are not a choking hazard. Also make sure all cabinets containing cleaning fluids or other dangerous items have safety locks.

■ Install ground-fault circuit interrupters (GFCIs) where appropriate—usually in the kitchen and bathrooms—to prevent electrocution.

■ Keep electrical cords out of reach.

■ The safest home for a child is one without a gun. If you do have a gun, it is essential to store it unloaded in a locked case, with the ammunition locked in a separate location. In many states, parents are held liable for accidental firearm injuries involving children.

■ Keep all medications (including those you might carry in your purse) out of reach. Do not depend on child safety caps to protect your child from getting into medicine bottles.

■ Always supervise toddlers around animals, especially dogs. Even the friendliest dog has the potential to bite.

■ Ensure that your home has working smoke detectors and carbon monoxide alarms.

Outdoor Safety

- Install door locks, barriers, and alarms to prevent your child from accessing pools, driveways, and streets without your knowledge. Drowning is the number one cause of death in children ages one to four years. It is especially critical that pools be made entirely inaccessible by a four-sided fence completely separating the pool from the house and the rest of the yard.

- Hold on to your toddler whenever you're near streets, parking lots, and driveways, even in quiet neighborhoods.

- Set up fences or other barriers to make sure he stays within his outside play area and away from the street, pools, and other hazards.

- Make sure there is sand, wood chips, or another soft surface under outdoor play equipment.

- Pay special attention anytime you or someone else is backing out of the garage or down the driveway. Make sure you know where your child is and that he cannot run into the path of the vehicle.

- Keep your vehicle locked when not in use so your child cannot get in. Even without starting the engine, he could set the car in neutral, allowing it to roll, or he could suffer heatstroke.

~ 11 ~

Your Two-Year-Old

YOUR CHILD IS NOW advancing toward the preschool years. During this time, her physical growth and motor development will slow, but you can expect to see some tremendous intellectual, social, and emotional changes. Her vocabulary will grow. She'll try to increase her independence from other family members, and—upon discovering that society has certain rules she is expected to observe—she'll begin to develop some real self-control.

From a neurological perspective, your two-year-old's brain is responding to her environment with frequent little "storms" of neurological activity, which is a lot for your little one to process and handle. With your support she can handle this overload of activity in her brain and find the pathways most useful for functioning. Over the next year, you will slowly see that she is becoming more emotionally regulated, showing new connections in her play, demonstrating her rapidly emerging communication skills, and displaying her ability to handle the full spectrum of human emotions. You are key to her success in navigating this exciting and sometimes emotionally challenging chapter in her development.

These changes will present an emotional challenge for you and your child. After all, these are the "terrible twos," when her every other word seems to be "no." This period will seem like a constant tug-of-war between her continuing reliance on you and her need to assert her independence. She may flip-flop between these extremes, clinging to you when you try to leave and running in the opposite direction when you want her to obey. You may find yourself longing for the cuddly infant she was, even as you're also pushing her to behave like a "big kid." It's no wonder you occasionally lose patience with each other.

On the other hand, this is also a time of joy and new independence for your two-year-old. Her language grows, and her ability to be a "real person" blossoms. She plays more games, can entertain herself for longer periods, and can expand her imagination by telling stories and engaging with others.

By acknowledging and accepting these changes over the next hectic years, both the positives and the negatives, you'll make it easier for both of you. She'll learn to feel comfortable, capable, and special, largely through your responses—the encouragement and respect you show her, your appreciation for her accomplishments, and the warmth and security you offer.

These feelings will help later as she goes to school and meets new people. Most importantly, they'll make her proud of herself.

Growth and Development

Physical Appearance and Growth

Although your preschooler's growth rate will slow in her second year, she will continue her remarkable physical transformation from baby to child. The most dramatic change will occur in her bodily proportions. As an infant, she had a relatively large head and short legs and arms; now her head growth will slow, from ¾ inch (2 cm) in her second year alone to ¾ to 1¼ inches (2–3 cm) over the next ten. Her height will increase quickly, primarily in her legs and, to some degree, the rest of her body. With these changes in growth rate, her body and legs will look much more in proportion.

The baby fat that made your infant so cuddly in the first months after birth will gradually disappear during these preschool years. Notice how her arms and thighs become more slender and her face less round. Even the pads of fat under the foot arches, which had been giving the appearance of flat feet, will disappear.

Her posture will change as well during this time. The pudgy, babyish look of a toddler was partly due to her posture, particularly her protruding abdomen and inwardly curving lower back. But as muscle tone improves and her posture becomes more erect, she'll develop a longer, leaner, stronger appearance.

Your child will continue to grow slowly but steadily. Preschoolers grow an average of 2½ inches (6 cm) annually and gain about 4 pounds (2 kg) each year. Plot and track your child's height and weight on the growth charts in the Appendix. If you notice a pronounced lapse in growth, discuss it with your pediatrician. She will probably tell you there is no need to be overly concerned, as some healthy children do not grow as quickly during their second and third years as others.

Less commonly, a dramatic pause in growth during the preschool years may signal something else—perhaps a recurrent infection, or a chronic health problem such as kidney or liver disease. In rare cases, slow growth may be due to a hormone disorder or gastrointestinal complications of some chronic illnesses. Your pediatrician will take all these things into consideration when she examines your child.

Don't be surprised if your two-year-old eats less than you think she should. Children need fewer calories at this time because they're growing more slowly. Even though she's eating less, she can still remain well nourished as long as a variety of healthy foods is available. Encourage healthy snacks and begin establishing sound and healthy eating habits. If she seems overly preoccupied with food and appears to be accumulating excess weight, talk to your pediatrician about ways to manage her weight. Children at this age naturally have wide fluctuations in how much they eat; these coincide with their growth spurts. Don't worry if your child shows less interest in food at any particular meal. If you consistently present a nutritious variety of foods and ensure that mealtime is a quiet, engaging time together, your child will be more attuned to her biological needs and eat accordingly. Early eating behaviors can influence the risk of obesity throughout life, so managing weight in childhood is as important as it will be later.

Movement

At this age, your child will seem continually on the go—running, kicking, climbing, jumping. Her attention span, which was never particularly long, may seem even shorter. Try starting a game with her, and she'll immediately change to a different one. Head in one direction, and she'll quickly detour. This year-long energy spurt between ages two and three will certainly keep you busy. But take heart—this activity level will strengthen her body and develop her coordination.

This is a critical time when childproofing your house really begins to pay off. Consider your child's increased abilities to move, run, and climb. Survey your house. Are there potentially harmful things that were previously inaccessible that are now within her reach? Creating a safe place allows your child to feel safe and free to respond to her innate drive to explore and learn. She will still need supervision. Watch over her without intruding and delight in her new discovery of independence. She will pick up on your positivity, feel good about herself, and further develop her self-esteem and confidence.

In the months ahead, your child's running will become smoother and more coordinated. She'll also learn to kick and aim a ball, walk up and down steps by herself while holding on, and seat herself confidently in a child-size chair. With help, she'll even be able to stand on one leg.

Watch your two-year-old walk. The stiff, spread-legged gait of a young preschooler has been replaced with a more adult, heel-to-toe motion. She has also become much more adept at maneuvering her body, capable of walking backward and turning corners that are not too sharp. She also can do other things while she moves, such as use her hands, talk, and look around.

Don't worry about finding activities to help your child develop her motor skills. She'll probably be able to do that herself. When you are able to join in, bear in mind that children this age love piggyback rides, rolling on mats, going down small slides, and climbing (with help) on a floor-level balance beam. The more running and climbing your games involve, the better.

If you can, set aside specific times when she can go outside to run, play, and explore. This will help minimize wear and tear on your house as well as your nerves. It's also safer for her to run around in the open than bump into walls and furniture. While outdoors, let her use the yard, playground, or park—whichever is available and safe for her. But be aware: since her self-control and judgment lag considerably behind her motor skills, you must remain vigilant and keep safety and injury prevention a priority.

Hand and Finger Skills

At age two, your child can manipulate small objects with ease. She'll turn book pages, build a tower six blocks high, pull off her shoes, and unzip a zipper. She'll also be able to turn a doorknob, unscrew a jar lid, use a cup with one hand, and unwrap candy wrappers.

Movement Milestones for Your Two-Year-Old

- Climbs well

- Kicks ball (wearing closed-toed shoes, which are safer than flip-flops)

- Runs easily and with coordination

- Pedals tricycle (be sure she wears a safety helmet on the tricycle)

- Runs and bends over easily without falling

- Jumps off ground with two feet

- Begins to walk up steps alternating feet

Milestones in Hand and Finger Skills for Your Two-Year-Old

- Makes vertical, horizontal, and circular strokes with pencil or crayon

- Catches large balls

- Turns book pages one at a time

- Stacks objects

- Builds a tower of six blocks

- Holds a pencil in writing position

- Grasps crayon with thumb and fingers instead of fist

- Screws and unscrews jar lids, nuts, and bolts

- Turns rotating handles

One of her major accomplishments this year will be learning to "draw." Hand her a crayon and watch what happens: she'll place her thumb on one side of it and fingers on the other, then awkwardly try to extend her index or middle finger toward the point. Clumsy as this grip may seem, it will give her enough control to create her first artistic masterpieces, using sweeping vertical and circular strokes.

Fortunately, your child's quiet play will be much more focused than it was at eighteen months, when she was into everything. Her attention span is longer, and now that she can turn pages, she'll be an active participant as you look at books together. She'll also be interested in activities like drawing, building, and manipulating objects. Blocks and interlocking construction sets may keep her entertained for long periods. And if you let her loose with a box of crayons or finger paints, her creative impulses will flourish.

Language Development

Your two-year-old not only understands most of what's said, but has a rapidly growing vocabulary of fifty or more words. Over the course of this year, she'll graduate from two- or three-word sentences ("Drink juice," "Mommy want cookie") to those with four, five, or even six words ("Where's the ball, Daddy?" "Dolly sit in my lap"). She's also beginning to use pronouns ("I," "you," "me," "we," "they") and understands the concept of "mine" ("I want my cup," "I see my mommy"). Pay attention to how she uses language to describe ideas and information and to express her physical or emotional needs.

This is a good time to reinforce the labeling of emotions. Your child is experiencing big emotions. Providing the names of those feelings honors her life experience across the wide range of human emotions and helps her understand and appreciate what is happening inside her body and how she can manage her feelings. Helping her label her emotions lets her know that you understand. We all feel better when we know we are understood. This is an especially valuable experience you can provide for your little one.

It's human nature to measure your preschooler's verbal abilities against other children her age, but try to avoid this. There's more variation in language development than in any other area. While some preschoolers steadily develop language skills, others seem more uneven. Some children are also naturally more talkative. This doesn't mean that children who are more verbal are necessarily smarter or more advanced, nor does it mean they have richer vocabularies. The quiet child may know just as many words but is choosier about speaking. Generally, boys start talking later than girls, but this variation—like most others mentioned previously—tends to even out as children reach school age.

Without any formal instruction, just by listening and practicing, your child will master many of the basic rules of grammar when she enters school. You can enrich her vocabulary and language skills by continuing to make a routine out of reading every day. At this age, she can follow a story line and understand and remember ideas and information presented in books. Even so, the books you read should be short, especially if she has a hard time sitting still. To keep her attention, choose activity-oriented books that encourage her to touch, point, and name objects or repeat certain phrases. Toward the end of this year, she'll also have fun with poems, puns, or jokes that play with language by repeating funny sounds or using nonsense phrases.

For some children, however, language development is not smooth. About one in every ten to fifteen children has trouble with language comprehension and/or speech. For some, the problem can be caused by hearing difficulty, a developmental disorder such as autism or a learning disability, lack of verbal stimulation at home, or a family history of speech delays. In most cases, though, the cause is unknown. If your pediatrician suspects difficulty with language, she'll conduct a thorough physical exam and hearing test and, if necessary, refer you to a speech/language or early childhood specialist. Early detection and identification of language delay or hearing impairment is critically impor-

Language Milestones for Your Two-Year-Old

- Follows a two- or three-part command, such as "Go to your room and bring back the teddy bear and the dog"

- Recognizes and identifies almost all common objects and pictures

- Understands most sentences

- Understands physical relationships ("on," "in," "under")

- Uses fifty words

- Uses four- and five-word sentences

- Can say name, age, and gender

- Uses pronouns correctly ("I," "you," "me," "we," "they")

- Uses some plurals ("cars," "dogs," "cats")

- Uses words that are 50 percent understandable by strangers

tant so that treatment can begin before the problem interferes with learning in other areas. Unless you and your pediatrician identify the difficulty and act, your child may have trouble with classroom learning later.

Cognitive Development

Think back to your child's infancy and toddler months, a time when she learned about the world by touching, looking, manipulating, and listening. As a two-year-old, the learning process has become more thoughtful. Her grasp of language is increasing, and she's beginning to form mental images for things, actions, and concepts. She also can solve problems in her head, performing mental trial-and-error instead of manipulating objects physically. And as her memory and intellectual abilities develop, she'll begin to understand time concepts, such as "You can play *after* you finish eating."

Your child is starting to understand relationships between objects. She'll be able to match similar shapes when given shape-sorting toys, and she can complete simple jigsaw puzzles. She'll also begin to recognize the purpose of numbers in counting objects—especially the number two. And as her understanding

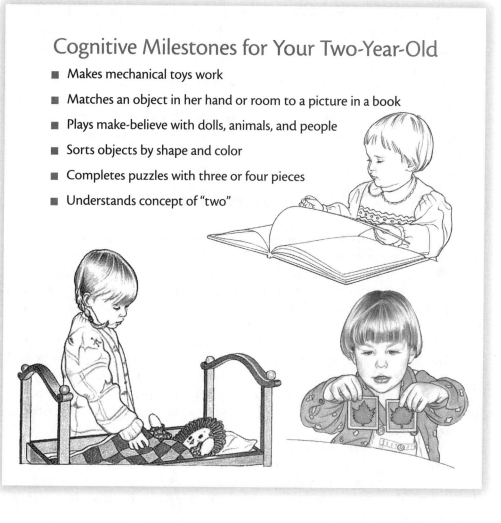

Cognitive Milestones for Your Two-Year-Old

- Makes mechanical toys work
- Matches an object in her hand or room to a picture in a book
- Plays make-believe with dolls, animals, and people
- Sorts objects by shape and color
- Completes puzzles with three or four pieces
- Understands concept of "two"

of cause and effect develops, she'll become much more interested in wind-up toys and turning lights and appliances on and off.

You'll also notice your preschooler's play growing more complex. She'll start stringing together different activities to create logical sequences. Instead of drifting randomly from one toy to another, she may first put a doll to bed, then cover it up. Or she may pretend to feed several dolls, one after the other. Over the next few years, she'll put together longer and more elaborate sequences of make-believe, acting out much of her own routine, from getting up to taking a bath and going to bed.

If there is one major intellectual limitation at this age, it would be your child's feeling that everything that happens is the result of something she did.

With this belief, it becomes very difficult to understand concepts such as death, divorce, or illness without feeling she has played some role. If parents separate or a family member gets sick, children often feel responsible. (See discussion in Chapter 26, *Family Issues*.)

Reasoning with your two-year-old is often difficult. After all, she views everything in extremely simple terms. Unless she's actively playing make-believe, she often confuses fantasy with reality. Choose your words carefully: comments you think are funny or playful—such as "If you eat more cereal, you'll explode"—may actually panic her, as she won't know you're joking.

Social Development

Children this age can often seem concerned about their own needs and act self-ishly. They may refuse to share things that interest them, and they do not inter-act well with other children when playing side by side—that is, unless they want a toy or object from a playmate. At times, your child's behavior may make you upset. But if you look closer, you'll notice all preschoolers are probably acting the same way.

At the same time, two-year-olds are developing the ability to express true empathy. You can help that process by talking about how other people feel: "Emma is crying. She is sad because you took her car. Can you please give it back?" Don't expect your two-year-old to always be able to control her behavior; she is still working on that skill. But with your help she can practice and keep getting better.

With such self-directed behavior, you may find yourself worrying that your two-year-old is spoiled or out of control. Likely, your fears are unfounded, and she'll pass through this phase. Highly active, aggressive children who push and shove usually are just as normal as quiet, shy ones who never seem to act out their thoughts and feelings.

Ironically, despite your child's apparent self-interest, she'll spend much of her playtime imitating other people's mannerisms and activities. "Pretend" is a favorite game at this age. When your two-year-old puts her teddy to bed, you may hear her use the same words and tone you use when telling her to go to sleep. No matter how she otherwise resists your instructions, when she moves into the parent role, she imitates you exactly. These play activities help her learn what it's like to be in someone else's shoes, serve as valuable rehearsals for future social encounters, and help you appreciate the importance of role mod-eling, since children often do as we do, not as we say.

Your two-year-old will best learn how to behave around other people by being given plenty of trial runs. Don't let her relatively antisocial behavior dis-

Social Milestones for Your Two-Year-Old

- Imitates adults and playmates

- Engages in pretend or imitative play

- Plays alongside other children (parallel)

- Urinates in a potty or toilet

- Can remove some of his or her own clothing

- Spontaneously shows affection for familiar playmates

- Can take turns in games

- Understands concepts of "mine" and "his/hers"

courage you from getting play groups together. It may be wise at first to limit groups to two or three children. And although you'll need to monitor the group so that no one gets hurt or overly upset, you should also let the children guide themselves as much as possible. They need to learn how to play with one another, not with one another's parents.

Holding the Line on Tantrums

Frustration, anger, and an occasional tantrum are inevitable for all two-year-olds. You should allow your preschooler to express her emotions but also try to help her channel her anger away from violent or overly aggressive behavior. Here are some suggestions.

■ When you see your child starting to get worked up, try to turn her energy and attention to a new, more appropriate activity.

■ When distraction doesn't work (and it often won't), first acknowledge how your child is feeling and why: "You're mad. We have to leave now, and you don't want to leave." Don't try to reason with her, and don't yell, scold, or punish. Also, don't reward the tantrum by giving her what she wants. Instead, make sure she is safe, and give her some space and time to work through this emotional storm. Then let her know that you're going to give her some time to calm down. In time, she will.

■ If you're in public when her behavior is embarrassing you, simply remove her without discussion or fuss. Wait until she's calmed down before you return or continue with your activities.

■ Do not use physical punishment or hitting to discipline your child. If you do, she will learn that aggression is an acceptable way to respond when she doesn't get her way.

■ If the tantrum involves her hitting, biting, or some other potentially harmful behavior, you can't ignore it. Model an empathic response by giving caring attention to the victim that your child can see and learn from. But overreacting won't help your child. Instead, tell her immediately and clearly she is not to behave this way, and move her off by herself for a few minutes. She can't understand complicated explanations, so don't try to reason with her. Just make sure she understands what she was doing is wrong and give your consequence then and there. If you wait an hour, she won't connect the punishment with the "crime." (See *Temper Tantrums*, page 596.)

■ Limit and monitor her screen time. (See Chapter 32, *Media*.) Preschool children may behave more aggressively if they watch violent programs on TV.

Hyperactivity

By adult standards, many two-year-olds seem "hyperactive." But it's perfectly normal at this age to prefer running, jumping, and climbing to walking slowly or sitting still. She also may speak so fast it's hard to understand, and you may worry about her short attention span, but be patient. This excess energy usually subsides by school age.

Given most two-year-olds' high energy level, it makes more sense for parents to adjust than to force the child to slow down. If your preschooler is a "mover," adjust your expectations accordingly. Don't expect her to stay seated through a long community meeting or restaurant meal. If you take her shopping, be prepared to move at her pace, not yours. In general, avoid putting her in situations you know will be frustrating, and give her plenty of opportunities to release excess energy through games involving running, jumping, climbing, and throwing or kicking a ball.

Without strong guidance, an active child's energy can easily turn aggressive or destructive. To avoid this, establish clear and logical rules and enforce them consistently. You also can encourage low-key behavior with praise whenever she plays quietly or looks at a book for more than a couple of minutes. It helps, too, to keep bedtime, mealtime, bath, and nap routines as regular as possible so that she has a sense of structure to her day.

Some preschool children have very severe problems with hyperactivity and short attention spans that persist beyond the preschool years. Only if these problems significantly interfere with preschool activities, preschool performance, or social behaviors do they warrant special treatment. (See *Hyperactivity and the Easily Distractible Child*, page 590.) If you suspect your child may be having difficulties in these areas, ask your pediatrician to evaluate her.

High-quality early education offers structured opportunities to interact with other children in a safe environment. As she approaches three, your child may develop real friendships. Inviting these new friends to play provides a great opportunity for her to develop her social skills.

Autism Spectrum Disorder

Awareness of autism spectrum disorder (ASD) has increased in recent years, and there has been a notable increase in the number of diagnosed cases of young children with the condition. When a child is diagnosed as having ASD, she will likely have difficulties with communication and social skills.

Pediatricians recognize that the sooner ASD is identified, the sooner an intervention program directed at the child's symptoms of autism can start. For that reason, you need to be aware of the early warning signs of ASD, and talk to your pediatrician if you suspect that any of them are present. These symptoms may include:

- Difficulty making or keeping eye contact

- A lack of, delay in, or loss of language

- A lack of response to a parent's smile or other facial expressions

- Repetitive body movements (such as hand-flapping or rocking)

- A lack of pretend play, or using toys in unusual, repetitive ways

- Difficulty understanding other people's feelings or talking about their own feelings

The American Academy of Pediatrics recommends screening for ASD at eighteen and twenty-four months, and at any age if you or your pediatrician is concerned that problems with development may be present. Children develop at their own pace, but there are general developmental milestones to be aware of during the two- to three-year age range when children are speaking more and developing play skills with other children.

(For more information about ASD, see pages 643–48.)

Emotional Development

It's difficult to follow the ups and downs of a two-year-old. One moment she's beaming and friendly, the next sullen and weepy—often for no apparent reason. These mood swings, however, are part of growing up. They are signs of emotional changes taking place as your child struggles to control actions, impulses, feelings, and her body.

At this age, your child wants to explore and seek adventure. She'll spend most of her time testing limits—her own, yours, and her environment's. Unfortunately, she still lacks many skills required for the safe accomplishment of everything she needs to do, and she often will need your protection.

Developmental Health Watch

The developmental milestones listed in this book give you a general idea of the changes to expect as your child grows, but don't be alarmed if her development takes a slightly different course. Consult your pediatrician, however, if your child displays any of the following signs of possible developmental delay for this age range.

- Frequent falling and difficulty with stairs
- Persistent drooling or very unclear speech
- Inability to build a tower of more than four blocks
- Difficulty manipulating small objects
- Inability to communicate in short phrases
- No involvement in "pretend" play
- Failure to understand simple instructions
- Little interest in other children
- Extreme difficulty separating from a parent
- Poor eye contact
- Limited interest in toys

When she oversteps a limit and is pulled back, she often reacts with anger and frustration, a temper tantrum, or sullen rage. She may even hit, bite, or kick. At this age, she doesn't have much control over her emotional impulses. Her anger and frustration tend to erupt suddenly in the form of crying, hitting, or screaming. It's her only way of dealing with the difficult realities of life. She may even act out in ways that unintentionally harm herself or others. It's all part of being two.

Have sitters or relatives told you your child never behaves badly when they're caring for her? It's not uncommon for preschoolers to be angels when you're not around. They don't trust these other people enough to test their limits. But with you, your preschooler is willing to try things that may be dangerous or difficult. She knows you'll rescue her if needed.

Emotional Milestones for Your Two-Year-Old

- Expresses affection openly
- Expresses a wide range of emotions
- Objects to major changes in routine

Whatever protest pattern developed around the end of her first year will probably persist for some time. When you're about to leave her with a sitter, she may become angry and throw a tantrum in anticipation of the separation; she may whimper, whine, and cling to you; or she may become subdued and silent. Whatever her behavior, try not to overreact by scolding or punishing. The best tactic is to reassure her you will be back, and when you return, praise her for being so patient while you were gone. Take solace in the fact that separations should be much easier when she's three.

The more confident and secure your two-year-old feels, the more independent and well behaved she's likely to be. You can help her develop these positive feelings by encouraging her to behave more maturely. Consistently set reasonable limits that allow her to explore and exercise her curiosity, but draw the line at dangerous or antisocial behavior. She'll soon begin to sense what's acceptable and what's not. The key is consistency. Praise her every time she plays well with another child, whenever she feeds, dresses, or undresses herself without help, and when she completes an activity by herself. When you do this, she'll feel good about these accomplishments and herself. With her self-esteem rising, she'll develop an image of herself as someone who behaves the way you have encouraged, and negative behavior will fade.

Since two-year-olds normally express a range of emotions, be prepared for everything from delight to rage. However, you should consult your pediatrician if your child seems very passive or withdrawn, perpetually sad, or highly demanding and unsatisfied most of the time. These could be signs of depression, caused by either hidden stress or biological problems. If your doctor suspects depression, she'll probably refer your child to a mental health professional for a consultation.

Basic Care
Feeding and Nutrition

By age two, your child should be eating three healthy meals each day, plus one or two snacks. She can eat the same food as the rest of the family. With her improved language and social skills, she'll become an active participant at mealtimes if given the chance to eat with everyone else. Do not fixate on amounts or make mealtimes a battle. Do, however, adopt healthy eating habits and make healthy food choices as a family. Sitting as a family at mealtime is the beginning of a good habit, too!

Fortunately, your child's feeding skills have become relatively "civilized" by now. At age two, she can use a spoon, drink from a cup with one hand, and feed herself a wide variety of finger foods. But while she can eat properly, she's still learning to chew and swallow efficiently, and may gulp her food when in a hurry to get on with playing. For that reason, the risk of choking is high, so avoid the following foods, which could block the windpipe.

Hot dogs (unless sliced lengthwise, then across)
Whole nuts (especially peanuts)
Round, hard candies or gum
Popcorn
Whole grapes
Chunks of apple or other raw fruits or vegetables (unless cut into small slices)
Spoonfuls of peanut butter
Whole raw carrots
Raw cherries with pits
Raw celery
Marshmallows

Ideally, make sure your child eats from each of the four basic food groups each day:

1. Fruits (like apples and grapes)

2. Vegetables (such as spinach, broccoli, and carrots)

3. Grains (ideally whole grains rather than processed)

4. Proteins (such as eggs, tofu, fish, chicken, red meat, and beans)

Sample One-Day Menu for a Two-Year-Old

This menu is for a two-year-old weighing approximately 27 pounds (12.5 kg).

1 teaspoon = 5 ml
3 teaspoons = 1 tablespoon = ½ ounce = 15 ml
⅛ cup = 1 ounce = 30 ml
½ cup = 4 ounces = 120 ml
1 cup = 8 ounces = 240 ml

BREAKFAST

½ cup nonfat or low-fat milk
½ cup iron-fortified cereal or 1 slice whole-wheat toast
⅓ cup fruit (for example, banana, cut-up
     cantaloupe, or strawberries)
1 egg

SNACK

4 crackers with cheese or hummus or ½ cup cut-up fruit or berries
½ cup water

LUNCH

½ cup low-fat or nonfat milk
½ sandwich: 1 slice whole-wheat bread, 1 ounce meat, slice of cheese, veggie
     (avocado, lettuce, or tomato)
2–3 carrot sticks (cut up or cooked) or 2 tablespoons other yellow or green
     vegetable
½ cup berries or 1 small (½ ounce) low-fat oatmeal cookie

SNACK

½ cup nonfat or low-fat milk
½ apple (thinly sliced), 3 prunes, ⅓ cup grapes
     (cut up), or ½ orange

DINNER

½ cup nonfat or low-fat milk
2 ounces meat
⅓ cup whole-grain pasta, rice, or potato
⅓ cup vegetables

Don't be alarmed, however, if she doesn't always meet this ideal. Many preschoolers resist eating certain foods, or insist on eating only one or two foods for long periods. The more you struggle with your child over her eating preferences, the more determined she'll be to defy you. As suggested, if you offer a variety of foods and give her choices, she'll eventually consume a balanced diet on her own. She may be more interested in healthy foods if she can feed them to herself. So, whenever possible, offer finger foods (e.g., fresh fruits or raw or cooked vegetables cut into small pieces) instead of soft food requiring utensils to eat.

DIETARY SUPPLEMENTS. Vitamin supplements (except vitamin D or iron) are rarely necessary for preschoolers eating a varied diet. However, supplemental iron may be needed if your child eats very little meat, iron-fortified cereal, or vegetables rich in iron. Large quantities of milk (more than 16 ounces [480 ml] per day) also may interfere with proper iron absorption, thus increasing the risk of iron deficiency. Two cups of low-fat or nonfat milk each day will provide most of the calcium needed for bone growth and not interfere with her appetite for other foods, particularly those that provide iron.

A vitamin D supplement of 600 IU (15 mcg) per day is important for all children. This amount of vitamin D can prevent rickets.

Teething and Dental Hygiene

By age two and a half, your child should have all twenty of her primary (or baby) teeth, including the second molars, which usually erupt between twenty and thirty months. Her secondary (or permanent) teeth probably won't appear until she's six or seven, although it's quite normal for them to arrive earlier or later than this. While parents have blamed teething for a variety of symptoms, including runny nose, diarrhea, fever, and fussiness, teething doesn't cause any of these. As a rule, take your child to the doctor for any symptom that would normally concern you if not teething. Also, remember that gels that promise to numb the gums contain benzocaine, which is dangerous to children and should not be used.

The number-one dental problem among preschoolers is tooth decay. Approximately 10 percent of two-year-olds already have one or more cavities; by age three, 28 percent of children do; by age five, nearly 50 percent. Many parents assume cavities in baby teeth don't matter because they'll be lost anyway. But that's not true. Dental decay in baby teeth can negatively affect permanent teeth and lead to future dental problems.

The best way to protect your child's teeth is to teach good dental habits. With proper coaching she'll quickly adopt good oral hygiene as a daily routine.

However, while she may be enthusiastic, she won't yet have the control or concentration to brush her teeth by herself. You'll need to supervise for quite some time to come, to help ensure that she brushes well enough to remove plaque—the soft, sticky, bacteria-containing deposits that accumulate on teeth, causing tooth decay. Also, keep an eye out for areas of brown or white spots, which might be signs of early decay.

You should be helping your child brush her teeth twice a day with a child-size toothbrush with soft bristles. There are brushes designed for children of all ages. Select a toothbrush that is appropriate for your child. Start by using a tiny amount (the size of a grain of rice) of fluoride toothpaste, which helps prevent cavities. If your child doesn't like the taste, try another flavor or use plain water. Also teach your child to not swallow it, although she may be still too young to rinse and spit. Swallowing too much fluoride toothpaste can cause white or brown spots on your child's adult teeth.

You'll hear competing advice on the best brushing method: up and down, back and forth, or around in circles. The truth is the direction doesn't matter. What's important is to clean each tooth thoroughly, top and bottom, front and back. This is where you'll encounter resistance. Your child will probably concentrate only on the front teeth she can see. It may help to turn it into a game of "find the hidden teeth." A child cannot brush her teeth without help until older—about six to eight years old. Be sure to supervise or do the actual brushing if necessary.

Besides regular tooth brushing, diet will play a key role in your child's dental health. Of course, sugar is the villain. The longer and more frequently her teeth are exposed to sugar, the greater the risk of cavities. Residue from

sticky, sugary foods such as caramel, toffee, gum, and dried fruit can stay in her mouth and bathe her teeth in sugar for hours, doing serious damage. Make sure to always brush your child's teeth after sugary foods. In addition, do not allow your child any sugary liquid in a sippy cup. During regular well-child visits, the pediatrician will check your child's teeth and gums. If she notices problems, she may refer your child to a pediatric dentist (pedodontist) or a general dentist familiar with the dental needs of children. Both the American Academy of Pediatrics and the American Academy of Pediatric

Dentistry recommend all children see a pediatric dentist and establish a "dental home" by age one, so hopefully your child will be seeing a pediatric dentist by now. A dental home is an ongoing relationship between a dentist and a child to help institute a lifetime of good oral health.

As part of her exam the dentist will make sure all teeth are developing normally, check to see that there are no dental problems, and give you further advice on proper hygiene. Pediatricians and dentists both routinely apply fluoride varnish to the teeth at this age to prevent cavities. If you live in an area where the water is not fluoridated, your child's dentist or pediatrician may prescribe fluoride drops or chewable tablets. (For more guidance on fluoride supplements, talk to your pediatrician, and see page 133.)

Toilet Training

By the time your child is two, you probably can't wait for toilet training. The pressure may be particularly intense if you are considering a preschool or child-care program that requires children to be toilet trained. Be forewarned, though: pushing her too early will likely prolong the process and be disruptive to your relationship with your child. If the pressure to toilet train is coming from an outside source, such as a preschool, try to find a preschool that takes a developmental approach to their expectations of the child, so that your child can develop at her own pace without unrealistic pressure to advance more quickly than she is able to. This approach will preserve her self-esteem and confidence. Rest assured, she will eventually be toilet trained. And when she sees that some of her peers are toilet trained, she may be more encouraged to learn it herself.

If you've started training prior to eighteen months of age, keep your expectations for success realistic and don't punish your child if she has difficulty following instructions or has accidents. Nonetheless, most experts think toilet training is most effective if delayed until the child herself can control much of the process. Studies indicate that many children who begin training before eighteen months are not completely trained until after age four. By contrast, most who start around age two are completely trained before their third birthday. The average age of complete training is a little over two and a half years.

In order for a preschooler to be successfully potty trained, she needs to be able to sense the urge to go, understand what the feeling means, and verbalize that she needs your help to make it to the toilet. Waiting until your child is truly ready will make the experience much faster and more pleasant for everyone involved.

In addition, toilet training probably won't be successful until your child is past the extreme resistance phase of early toddlerhood. She must want to take this major step. She'll be ready when she seems eager to please and imitate you, and also seems to want to become more independent. Since she needs independence, it's important to avoid power struggles, which usually delay training. Most children reach this stage between eighteen and twenty-four months, but a little later is also normal. Often when your child is ready to be toilet trained, she will give you some verbal cues such as "need a clean diaper" or "need to go pee-pee" even if her diaper is already dirty or wet. This awareness indicates your child is ready to be toilet trained.

Once your child is ready to begin this process, things should proceed smoothly as long as you maintain a relaxed, unpressured attitude. Never criticize the child's efforts, even if they fall short. Instead, maintain a positive attitude regarding all aspects of the toilet training process. Setbacks may occur, so provide encouragement, praise her for her successes, and reframe her mistakes as opportunities to do better next time. Punishing her or making her feel bad for an "accident" will only add an unnecessary element of stress.

How should you introduce the concept of using the toilet? The best way is to let her watch other family members of her sex if possible. Also talk to her frequently about the process.

The first goal is bowel training. Urination usually occurs with the bowel movement, so at first it is difficult for the child to separate the two. Once bowel training is established, most children (especially girls) will quickly relate the two. Boys usually learn to urinate in the sitting position but gradually transfer to standing, particularly after watching older boys or their father.

The first step in training is obtaining a potty chair and placing it in your child's room or nearest bathroom. Then do the following:

1. For the first few weeks, let her sit on the potty fully clothed while you tell her about the toilet, what it's for, and when to use it. If your child is initially afraid of the chair, avoid pressuring her to use it. Later, try to reintroduce the concept when she is relaxed and playing.

2. Once she sits on it willingly, let her try it with her diaper off. Show her how to keep her feet solidly on the floor, since this will be important for bowel movements. Make the potty part of her routine, gradually increasing the frequency from once to several times each day.

3. Encourage her to drop the contents of dirty diapers into the pot under her to show that this is the chair's purpose.

4. Once your child grasps how it works, she'll probably be more interested in using the potty properly. To encourage this, let her play near the chair without a diaper and remind her to use the potty when she needs to. Remember that children often have short attention spans; therefore, keeping them focused can be challenging. She's bound to forget or miss at first,

For the first few weeks, let your child sit on the potty fully clothed while you tell your child about the toilet, what it's for, and when to use it.

but don't display disappointment or frustration. Instead, wait until she succeeds, and reward her with excitement and praise. Right after meals is a great time to try, since that's when she is most likely to poop. For children who seem reluctant to have a bowel movement in the potty, it may be useful to check the stools to ensure they are not too hard, which can cause pain on defecation.

5. After she is using the potty chair regularly, gradually switch over from diapers to training pants during the day. Loose-fitting clothing or disposable training pants can be helpful. At this point, most boys quickly learn to urinate into an adult toilet by imitating their fathers or older boys. Both girls and boys may be able to use adult toilets outfitted with training seats.

Like most children, your preschooler will probably take a little longer to complete nap and nighttime toilet training. Even so, encourage these steps along with daytime training, and stress them even more after she's routinely using the potty. The best approach is to encourage use of the potty immediately prior to bed and as soon as she wakes. Be aware that some children will not achieve nighttime dryness until five or six years of age. You can use regular or disposable training pants at night, rather than diapers. There will be accidents, but a plastic sheet on the mattress will minimize cleanup. Reassure your preschooler that all children have accidents, and praise her whenever she makes it through the nap or night without wetting. Also, tell her that if she wakes up in the middle of the night and needs to use the toilet, she can either go by herself or call for you to help.

Your goal is to make this entire process as positive, natural, and nonthreatening as possible so that she's not afraid to make the effort on her own. If naptime or nighttime wetting is still a consistent problem one year after daytime training is complete, discuss the situation with your pediatrician, but keep in mind that nighttime wetting is considered normal until at least age six.

Sleeping

When your child is two, she may sleep between eleven and fourteen hours a day including naps. Most children this age still need to nap, and a two-hour daytime nap is common.

At bedtime, your child is likely familiar with her going-to-sleep ritual. She now knows that at a certain time each day she changes into her nightclothes, brushes her teeth, listens to a story, and takes her favorite blanket, toy, or stuffed animal to bed. If you change this routine, she may complain or even have trouble falling asleep. It is important to keep this routine predictable for your child.

However, even with a predictable bedtime routine, some children resist sleep. If still in a crib, she may cry when alone or even climb out to look for Mom and Dad. If she's graduated to a bed, she may get up again and again, insisting she's not tired (even when clearly exhausted) and asking to join in whatever is going on in the household.

At bedtime, put your child in a good frame of mind for sleep by playing quietly or reading a pleasant story.

Transitioning to a Bed

Begin using a bed instead of the crib by the time your child is 35 inches tall. Transitioning to a regular or "big kid" bed can be difficult for two reasons. First, she is used to the sides of her crib keeping her on her mattress. Initially transitioning to a small mattress (like the one from her crib or a twin mattress) on the floor makes sense, since she's likely to roll out of her new bed anyway; better that it's already on the floor. Over time the crib mattress can be replaced with a larger mattress (placed on the floor), then later raised up onto a frame if desired. The bed can be a child-size bed or, if she feels comfortable with it, a regular-size bed. The second difficulty with transitioning to a big bed involves getting her to stay on the bed. A guardrail can help keep her safe and secure while in bed. At the very least, her room needs to be childproofed; a gate might be needed at the door to keep her from wandering around the house at night. (See Chapter 15 for more information on safety.)

To give a child like this a feeling of control, let her make as many choices as possible at bedtime—which pajamas to wear, what story she wants. Also, use a nightlight and let her sleep with her security objects (see *Transitional Objects*, page 282) to take the edge off her separation anxiety. If she still cries after you leave, give her several minutes (ten, for example) to stop on her own before you go in to settle her down; then leave for several minutes more, and repeat the process as needed. Don't scold, but also don't reinforce her behavior by staying with or feeding her.

When a nightmare awakens your child, the best response is to comfort her. Let her tell you about the dream if possible, and stay until she's calm enough to fall asleep. Your child will have nightmares more frequently when anxious or under stress. If she has bad dreams often, try to determine what's worrying her. For example, if nightmares happen during the toilet training period, relax the pressure to use the potty. Also try talking with her (to the extent she can) about possible issues bothering her. Some of her anxieties may involve separation from you, time spent in childcare, or changes at home. Talking can sometimes help prevent stressful feelings from building up. If your child is watching television, carefully select programs as a precaution against nightmares. Even programs you consider innocent may contain images frightening to her. (See Chapter 32, *Media*.)

Some Golden Rules of Preschooler Discipline

Whether you're a strict disciplinarian or more easygoing, the following guidelines should help shape a strategy of discipline ultimately benefiting both you and your child. Remember, your two-year-old is busy learning the rules—she doesn't want to be bad!

■ Always encourage and reward good behavior and discourage the bad, without ever resorting to spanking or other physical punishments. Whenever you have a choice, take the positive route. If your two-year-old is moving toward the stove, try to distract her with a safe activity instead of waiting for her to get into trouble. When you notice she has independently chosen acceptable behavior instead of misbehaving, congratulate her on making the right decision. By showing you're proud of her, you'll make her feel good about herself and encourage her to behave similarly in the future.

■ Establish rules that help your child learn to control her impulsiveness and behave well socially without impairing her drive for independence. If your rules are overly restrictive, she may be afraid to explore on her own or try out new skills.

■ Always keep your child's developmental level in mind when setting limits. Don't expect more than she's capable of achieving. A two- or three-year-old can't control the impulse to touch attractive things. It's unrealistic to expect her not to touch displays at grocery or toy stores, for example.

■ Set the consequences to your child's developmental level. If you decide to send your preschooler to her room for misbehaving, don't keep her there more than about five minutes; any longer, and she'll forget why she's there. If you prefer to reason with her, first wait until she's no longer upset. Then keep the discussion simple and practical. Never use hypothetical statements such as "How would you like it if I did that to you?" No preschooler can understand this kind of reasoning. Instead, just focus on the rule: "We don't hit. Hitting hurts people."

■ Don't change the rules or the punishments at random. That will only confuse your child. As she grows older, you will naturally expect more mature behavior, and when you change the rules at that time, tell her why. You may tolerate her pulling on your clothes to get your attention when she's two, but by four, you may want her to find a more grown-up way of approaching you. Once you change a rule, explain it to her before you start enforcing it.

- Make sure all adults in the house and other caregivers agree to and understand the limits and punishments used to discipline your child. If one parent says something is OK and the other forbids it, the child is bound to be confused. Eventually she'll figure out she can play one adult against the other, which will make your lives miserable now and in the future. You can prevent this game-playing by presenting a united front.

- Remember that you are a key role model for your child and that your child will do as you do. The more evenhanded and controlled your behavior, the more likely your child will be to pattern herself after you. If, on the other hand, you hit or spank her every time she breaks a rule, you're teaching her it's OK to solve problems through violence.

At bedtime, put your preschooler in a sleeping frame of mind by playing quietly with her or by reading her a pleasant story. Soothing music also may calm her as she falls asleep, and a nightlight will reassure her if she wakes. (See Chapter 35 for more information on sleep.)

Discipline

The greatest challenge facing you as a parent during this and the next few years is, without a doubt, discipline. Your child develops the ability to control her impulses very gradually. At age two (and even through age three), she'll still be very physical, using temper tantrums, pushing, shoving, and quarreling to get her way. Most of these reactions are impulsive; she doesn't plan to behave this way, yet she cannot control herself. Whether she consciously understands it or not, the point of her misbehavior is to find her limits and yours.

Your child is communicating her needs as best as she can. We all react less maturely under emotional distress. This means that your two-year-old will act more like an eighteen- or even twelve-month-old under distress. The learning process for how to stay regulated under physical, emotional, or social stress goes on throughout our lives. Your two-year-old is learning how to develop that skill and establishing patterns of behavior that she will carry forward.

How you choose to establish and enforce these limits is a personal issue.

Time-Out/Time-In

Although you can't ignore dangerous or destructive behavior, you can call a time-out. Beginning relatively early—eighteen to twenty-four months—create a foundation for time-out by teaching your child that it means being quiet and still. You can then build longer quiet-and-still time as your child grows.

As a skill needing to be learned, time-outs are most successful with three-year-olds (as well as four-year-olds), who generally know they've done something wrong and understand that their behavior is why they're being disciplined. It should be coupled with a firm "no" and used only in special circumstances—so pick your battles.

Here's how time-out works:

1. Have your child sit in a chair or go to a boring place with no distractions. By doing this you're separating her from her misbehavior and giving her time to cool off.

2. Briefly explain what you're doing and why. Tell her you love her but her behavior was unacceptable. No long lecture. When children are young, time-out is over as soon as they are calm.

3. End time-out once they are quiet and still. This reinforces that time-out means quiet and still.

4. Once they have learned to calm themselves, a good rule of thumb is one minute of time-out for each year in the child's age.

5. Parenting experts are increasingly recommending starting with the time-in instead of the time-out. Your child may still need some time to cool off, but afterward you spend a moment sitting with her and helping her calm down by attending to her emotions while still putting a stop to the unacceptable behavior. This approach prevents children from feeling isolated while helping them build the skill of controlling their own behavior and emotions.

Some parents are strict, punishing their children whenever they violate a household rule; others are more lenient, preferring reason to punishment. Whatever approach you choose, if it's going to work, it must suit your child's temperament, and you also must feel comfortable enough with it to use it consistently. You'll find other helpful suggestions in *Some Golden Rules of Preschooler Discipline* on pages 362–63.

Extinction

Extinction is a disciplinary technique most effective with two- and three-year-olds, although it can be useful into the school years. The idea is to ignore the child systematically whenever she breaks certain rules. This method should be used for misbehavior that's annoying or undesirable, like whining, but not dangerous or destructive; the latter needs the direct, immediate approach already discussed.

Here's how extinction works.

1. Define exactly what your child is doing wrong. Does she scream for attention in public? Does she cling to you when you're trying to do something else? Be very specific about the behavior and the circumstances in which it occurs.

2. Keep track of how often your child does this, and what you do in response. Do you try to pacify her? Do you stop what you're doing to pay attention to her? If so, you're unwittingly encouraging her to keep misbehaving.

3. Keep recording the frequency of her misbehavior as you begin to ignore it. The key is consistency. Even if every person in the grocery store glares at you, do not show your child you hear her screaming. Just keep doing what you're doing. At first, she'll probably act out more intensely and more frequently to test your will, but eventually she'll realize she's not getting the desired response. Be strong and—most important—ignore the misbehavior. If you give in to the outburst, you may reinforce the behavior you're trying to eliminate.

4. When your child acts properly in a situation where she usually misbehaves, be sure to compliment her. If, instead of screaming over a toy you won't buy, she talks to you in a normal voice, praise her for acting so grown-up.

5. If you manage to extinguish the misbehavior and it reappears, start the process over again. It probably won't take as long the second time.

Family Relationships
A New Baby

During this year, if another baby is due, you can expect your preschooler to greet this news with considerable jealousy. After all, she doesn't yet understand the concept of sharing time, possessions, or your affection. Nor is she eager to have someone else become the center of the family's attention.

The best way to minimize her jealousy is to start preparing her several months in advance. If she understands, you can let her help shop for baby items

Stimulating Child Brain Growth: Your Two-Year-Old

Age two is an important time in your child's life and brain development. As previously described, your child's physical growth may slow during this time, but her brain and intellectual growth are moving ahead full speed. Just as you've stimulated her brain growth from birth, you should continue doing so during this crucial year. Here are some suggestions:

- Encourage creative play, building, and drawing. Provide the time and tools for playful learning.

- Be attentive to your child's rhythms and moods. Respond when she is upset as well as happy. Be encouraging and supportive, with firm discipline as appropriate, but without yelling, hitting, or shaking. Provide consistent guidelines and rules.

- Give consistent warm, physical contact—hugging, skin-to-skin, body-to-body contact—to establish a sense of security and well-being.

- Talk to or sing to your child during dressing, bathing, feeding, playing, walking, and driving, using adult talk. Speak slowly and give your child time to respond. Avoid replying with "uh-huh," because your child will recognize you're not listening; instead, expand on your child's phrases.

- Read to your child every day. Choose books that encourage touching and pointing to objects, and read rhymes, jingles, and nursery stories.

- If you speak a foreign language, use it at home.

- Introduce your child to musical instruments (toy pianos, drums, etc.). Musical skills can influence math and problem-solving skills.

- Play calm and melodic music for your child.

- Listen to and answer your child's questions.

- Spend one-on-one personal time with your child each day.

- Offer your child simple choices in appropriate situations throughout the day ("Do you want peanut butter or cheese?" "Do you want to wear the red T-shirt or the yellow one?").

- Help your child use words to describe emotions and to express feelings such as happiness, joy, anger, and fear.

- Limit your child's television viewing and video time; avoid violent programming and games. Monitor what your child watches and discuss programs with her. Don't use the TV as a babysitter.

- Keep the television off and phones put aside. Even if your toddler doesn't seem to be paying attention, adults tend to talk or engage much less when they are distracted, and every word is important for your toddler's language development.

- Promote out-of-home social experiences such as preschool programs and play groups in which your child can play and interact with other children.

- Acknowledge desirable behavior frequently (e.g., "I like it when the two of you play together").

- Make sure other people providing care and supervision for your child understand the importance of forming a loving and comforting relationship with her.

- Spend time on the floor playing with your child every day.

- Choose quality childcare that is affectionate, responsive, educational, and safe (you may want to consider programs that are accredited by the National Association for the Education of Young Children [NAEYC]); visit your childcare provider frequently and share your ideas about positive caregiving.

or help get the house or room ready. If your hospital offers a sibling preparation class, take her during the last month of pregnancy so she can see where the baby will be born and where she can visit. Discuss what it will be like having a new member of the family, how fun and important it is to be a big sibling, and how she can help her little brother or sister. (See *Preparing Your Other Children for the Baby's Arrival*, page 38.)

Once the baby is home, encourage your preschooler to help and play with the newborn (after washing her hands, of course), but don't force her. If she shows interest, give her tasks to make her feel like a big sister, such as bringing you diapers or blankets for the baby and picking out the baby's clothes or bath toys. And when you're playing with the baby, invite her to join and show her how to hold and move the baby. Make sure she understands, however, that she's not to do these things unless you or another adult is present. Remember to reserve special time alone to spend with older siblings.

Hero Worship

Does your preschooler have older siblings? If so, you'll probably start seeing signs of hero worship around age two. In the young child's eyes, older brothers or sisters can do no wrong. They are perfect role models—people who are strong and independent, but still play like kids.

This relationship has both benefits and drawbacks. Your preschooler will probably follow her older sibling around like a puppy. This gives you some freedom, and it's usually fun for both children for a while. But before long, your older child will want his freedom back, which is bound to cause disappointment— and perhaps tears or misbehavior—from your little one. Nevertheless, it's up to you to make sure she doesn't overstay her welcome with her big brother or sister. If you don't step in, their relationship is likely to become strained.

If the older child is eight or more, he probably already has a fairly independent life, with friends and activities outside the home. Given the chance, your preschooler will tag along with him everywhere he goes. You shouldn't allow this unless the older child desires it or you are going along and can keep the

In your young child's eyes, his older brother or sister can do no wrong.

little one from becoming a pest. If the older child is of babysitting age, compensating him for taking care of your preschooler when you're out will help prevent resentment.

A Message for Grandparents

Age two is often challenging for parents, and therefore grandparents as well. A child at this age is showing increased physical activity, greater mood swings, frequent tantrums or demanding behavior, and testing the limits of adults.

You may have forgotten what two-year-olds are like; it's been many years since your own children were this age. Here are some guidelines for when you spend time with your two-year-old grandchild (some of these steps are easier said than done).

- Make an effort to keep your cool. Don't overreact to outbursts. Try to take them in stride, and realize that much of this behavior is designed to get you to react. Maintain a flexible but firm and loving response.

- Be consistent in your approach to discipline, and make sure it's consistent with the disciplinary style of the child's parents. Never use physical punishment.

(continues on next page)

- Reinforce good behaviors with praise and compliments. Become a role model for the way you would like your grandchild to act.

- Try to encourage self-control.

- Always be affectionate.

- Recognize that children of this age are very egocentric (i.e., they think mostly of "me," less of the others), so don't take their lack of interest in you personally. This is normal for a two-year-old, and it won't last forever.

Toilet training will be one of your grandchild's most important accomplishments at this age. Talk to her parents about the stage of training she's in, and how you can reinforce what she has already achieved, particularly when you're caring for her—say, babysitting on a Saturday afternoon or for the weekend. If she spends time in your home, purchase some extra training pants and have a potty chair identical to the one at home.

Safety remains important, so make sure your home is childproofed. See Chapter 15 for the specifics. Be especially careful of medications. Never leave them out for her curious eyes or fingers; put them out of sight and reach in a safe place you will remember. Try to leave the medication there even after they leave, so that your home stays safe if they stop by for a quick, unexpected visit. This is even more important if you have chosen to put your pills in containers without child-resistant caps. Such containers can be easily opened by curious two-year-olds, so be especially vigilant. Finally, always remember to place your grandchild in a car safety seat in the backseat for every trip in the car.

Pressures and rivalries are inevitable between siblings, but with a healthy balance between comradeship and independence, the bond between your children should grow and contribute to both children's self-esteem. Through her older sibling, your preschooler will get a sense of family values and a preview of being a "big kid." The older child, meanwhile, will discover what it means to be a hero in his own home.

Being a role model for a younger brother or sister is a big responsibility, and if you point this out to your older child, it may prompt improved behavior. If you feel he's a bad influence on his younger sibling, however, and doesn't improve, you have no choice but to separate them whenever he's misbehaving. Otherwise, your preschooler will mimic him and soon pick up bad habits. Don't embarrass the older child by punishing him in front of the preschooler, but make sure the younger one understands the difference between "good" and "bad" behavior.

Visit to the Pediatrician

Beginning at twenty-four months, your child should see the pediatrician for routine examinations twice a year. In addition to screening tests performed during earlier examinations, she may undergo the following laboratory tests.

- A blood test to check for lead exposure and hemoglobin (oxygen-carrying protein in red blood cells)

- A skin or blood test for tuberculosis (depending on the risk of possible exposure)

Immunization Update

By age two, your child should have received most of her childhood immunizations. These include:

- The hepatitis B series

- The Hib vaccine series against *Haemophilus influenzae* type b

- The vaccine series against pneumococcus

- The first three doses of the polio vaccine

- The first four doses of DTaP (diphtheria, tetanus, and pertussis [aka whooping cough])

- The first dose of the MMR vaccine (measles, mumps, rubella)

- Two doses of the hepatitis A vaccine

- Two or three doses of the rotavirus vaccine (depending on the vaccine type given for doses one and two)

- The chickenpox (varicella) vaccine

Once a year, beginning at six months, your child should also receive the influenza vaccine. Also remember to have your child get booster shots for DTaP, polio, MMR, and varicella at elementary school entry or four to six years of age. For more information on immunizations, please see Chapter 31.

Safety Check

Your preschooler is now able to run, jump, and learn to ride a tricycle. With her natural curiosity she'll explore many new things, including some dangerous places. Unfortunately, her self-control and ability to rescue herself are not yet fully developed, so she still needs careful supervision. (See Chapter 15 for additional information on safety.)

Falls

■ Lock doors to any dangerous areas and hide the keys, and secure all doors to the outside so that children cannot wander out.

■ Install stairway gates and window guards.

Burns

■ Keep her away from kitchen appliances, irons, and wall or floor heaters (check for safety features on both newer heaters and those in old houses).

■ Block outlets with furniture or use outlet covers that are not a choking hazard.

■ Keep electrical cords out of reach.

■ Install and maintain working smoke and carbon monoxide detectors.

■ Do not have lit candles in areas that are easily reachable by a child.

Poisoning

■ Keep all medicines in child-resistant containers, locked up high, and out of sight and reach. Make sure you engage the child-resistant closure every time.

■ Store household cleaning products and medicines in their original containers in a locked cabinet.

■ It is safest to use liquid or powder laundry detergent instead of concentrated liquid laundry packets until your child is at least six years old.

■ Post the Poison Help phone number (1-800-222-1222) next to every telephone and in your cellphone contacts list. This number can be used everywhere in the United States.

■ Ensure that dangerous items, especially laundry detergent pods, small lithium button batteries, and powerful rare earth magnets, are safely locked away.

Car Safety

■ Supervise your child closely whenever playing outside. Do not allow your child to play near the garage or driveway, where cars may be coming or going. Many children are killed when someone, often a family member, unintentionally runs them over with a car. Most vehicles have large blind spots where a child cannot be seen as a car is backing up or moving. Keep cars locked when not in use so your child cannot get in without permission.

■ Use approved and properly installed car safety seats for every ride, and keep them rear-facing as long as possible. Once your child outgrows the height or weight limit for rear-facing in their convertible seats, she should ride forward-facing in a car seat equipped with a five-point harness as long as possible, or until she reaches the highest weight or height allowed by the seat's manufacturer. Most convertible car safety seats have limits that permit nearly all children to ride rear-facing well past their second birthday. Remember, never put your child in the front seat, even for a short ride. Airbags are not child-friendly, and if a crash sets off the airbag, your small child could get seriously injured. Always put the car safety seat in the rear seat, and if your car was manufactured after 2002, use the included LATCH system to secure the seat. Never let her unbuckle or climb out of her car safety seat while the car is in motion.

■ Never leave your child alone in the car. The internal temperature of a car can rise rapidly, leading to heat stroke and potentially to death.

~ 12 ~

Your Three-Year-Old

WITH YOUR CHILD'S THIRD birthday, the "terrible twos" may be officially over and the "magic years" can begin. This is approximately a two-year period (ages three and four) when your child's world will be dominated by fantasy and vivid imagination. No longer a toddler, he is more independent and, at the same time, more responsive to other children. This is a perfect age to introduce him to school or an organized play group, where he can stretch his skills while learning to socialize.

During this time, your child will mature in toilet training and learning how to take proper care of his body. Since he can control and direct his movements, he'll be able to play more organized games and sports. He also has mastered the basic rules of language and built an impressive vocabulary that increases daily as he experiments with words. Language will play an important role in his behavior, as he learns to express his desires and feelings verbally instead of through physical actions such as grabbing, hitting, or crying. He will learn to share for the first time. Guiding his self-discipline as he puts all his new skills together to feel confident and capable is one of the most important ways you help during this period.

The relationship with your child will change dramatically during this time. Emotionally, he is able to view you as a separate person, with feelings and needs he's beginning to understand. When you're sad, he may render sympathy or offer to solve your problems. If you become angry at another person, he may announce he, too, "hates" that individual. He wants very much to please you and knows he must do certain things and behave in certain ways to do so. However, he wants to please himself as well, so he'll often try to bargain with you: "If I do this for you, will you do that for me?" His bargaining may be irritating when you simply want him to behave as you desire. But it's a healthy sign of independence, and shows he has a clear sense of justice.

Growth and Development

Physical Appearance and Growth

Your child's body should continue to lose baby fat and gain muscle during this time, giving him a stronger and more mature appearance. His arms and legs become more slender and his upper body more narrow and tapered. In some, height gains are not matched in weight and muscle gains, and children may begin to look skinny and fragile as a result. This doesn't mean they are unhealthy or anything is wrong; such children fill out gradually as their muscles develop.

In general, a preschooler's growth gradually begins to slow this year and subsequently—decreasing from about a 5-pound (2.3 kg) gain and about a 3½-inch (8.9 cm) gain during the third year to about 4½ pounds (2 kg) and 2½ inches (6.4 cm) during the fifth. However, after age two, children of the same age can vary noticeably in size and weight, so try not to spend too much time comparing your child's measurements with others. As long as he's maintaining his own individual growth rate, there's no reason to worry.

Measure and record your child's measurements twice a year on his growth charts in the Appendix. If his weight seems to be rising faster than his height, he may have overweight. If his height does not increase at all in six months, he may have a growth problem. In either case, discuss this with your pediatrician.

Your child's face will also mature during these years, the length of his skull increasing slightly and his lower jaw becoming more pronounced. At the same time, the upper jaw widens to make room for permanent teeth. As a result, his face becomes larger and his features more distinct.

Movement

At age three, your preschooler no longer has to concentrate on the mechanics of standing, running, jumping, or walking. His movements are agile, whether he's going forward, backward, or up and down stairs. He walks erect, shoulders pulled back and belly held in by firm abdominal muscles. He uses regular heel-toe motions, taking steps of the same length, width, and speed. He can also ride a tricycle with ease.

However, not everything comes easily. Your child still may need to make a conscious effort while standing on tiptoes or one foot, getting up from a squat, or catching a ball. But if he keeps his arms extended in front of him he can catch large balls, and he can smoothly throw smaller ones overhand.

Your three-year-old may still be as active as he was at two, but he'll probably be more interested in structured games. Instead of running aimlessly or flitting from one activity to another, he'll probably ride his tricycle or play in the sandbox for long periods. He may also enjoy active games such as tag, catch, or playing ball but will still appreciate unstructured play.

Your preschooler may seem in constant motion much of the time. He uses his body to convey thoughts and emotions he still can't describe through language. Moving his body also helps him better understand many new words and concepts. If you start talking about an airplane, he may spread his wings and "fly" around the room. This level of activity may be annoying and distracting for you, but it's a necessary part of his learning process and his fun.

Because your child's self-control, judgment, and coordination are still developing, adult supervision remains essential to prevent injuries. However, it's a mistake to fuss too much over him. Bumps and bruises are inevitable and even necessary to help discover his limits in physical activity. As a general rule, you can leave him alone when he is playing by himself in a nearby room. He'll play at his own pace, attempting only those tasks within his abilities. Your concern and attention should be reserved for situations when he's around other children, hazardous equipment or machinery, and especially traffic. Other children may tease or tempt him to do dangerous things, while he lacks the ability to predict what machines, equipment, and traffic may do. He still cannot anticipate the consequences of his actions such as chasing a ball into traffic or sticking his hand through the spokes of his tricycle, so you'll have to protect him in these situations.

Movement Milestones for Your Three-Year-Old

- Hops and stands on one foot for up to five seconds

- Goes upstairs and downstairs without support

- Kicks ball forward

- Throws ball overhand

- Catches bounced ball most of the time

- Moves forward and backward with agility; jumps forward

- Pedals tricycle

- Climbs on and off couch or chair

Hand and Finger Skills

At age three, your child is developing both the muscular control and the concentration he needs to master many precision finger and hand movements. You'll notice he now can move each finger independently or together, which means that instead of grasping his crayon in his fist he can hold it like an adult, with thumb on one side and fingers on the other. He can now trace a square, copy a circle, or scribble freely.

Because his spatial awareness is better developed, he's more sensitive to the relationships among objects. He'll position his toys with care during play and control the way he holds utensils and tools to perform specific tasks. This increased sensitivity and control allows him to build a tower of nine or more blocks, pour water from a pitcher into a cup (using two hands), unbutton clothes, possibly put large buttons into buttonholes, and use a fork and feed himself independently, spilling only occasionally.

He's also extremely interested in tools such as scissors and in materials such as clay, paint, paper, and crayons. He has the skill to manipulate these objects and experiment with them to make other things. At first he'll play randomly with craft materials, perhaps identifying the end product only after completion. Looking at his scribbles, he might decide they look like a dog. But soon this will change, and he'll decide what he wants to make before starting. This change in approach will motivate him to develop even more precision with his hands.

Quiet-time activities that can help improve your child's hand abilities include:

■ Building with blocks

■ Solving simple jigsaw puzzles (four or five large pieces)

- Playing with pegboards

- Stringing large wooden beads

- Coloring with crayons or chalk

- Building sand castles

- Pouring water into containers of various sizes

- Dressing and undressing dolls in clothing with large zippers, snaps, and laces

Milestones in Hand and Finger Skills for Your Three-Year-Old

- Copies square shapes
- Draws a person with head and one other body part
- Uses child-safe scissors
- Draws circles and squares
- Begins to copy some capital letters

You can encourage your child to use his hands by teaching him to use certain adult tools. He'll be thrilled to use a real screwdriver, a lightweight hammer, an eggbeater, or gardening tools. You'll need to supervise closely, of course, but if you let him help as you work, you may be surprised by how much he can do himself.

Language Development

At age three, your child should have an active vocabulary of three hundred or more words. He can talk in sentences of three to four words and imitate most adult speech sounds. At times he'll seem to chatter constantly—a phenomenon that sometimes may disturb you but is essential to learning new words and gaining experience thinking with and using them. Language allows him to express thoughts, and the more advanced he is in speaking and understanding words, the more tools he'll have to think, create, and tell you about it.

You should be able to see how your child uses language to help him understand and participate in the things around him. He can name most familiar objects, and he'll freely ask "What's this?" when he doesn't know something by name. You can help expand his vocabulary by providing additional words he might not even request. If he points to a car and says, "Big car," you might answer, "Yes, that's a big gray car. Look how shiny the surface is." If he's helping pick flowers, describe each one he collects: "That's a beautiful white-and-yellow daisy, and that's a pink geranium."

You can also help him use words to describe things and ideas he can't see. When he's describing the "monster" in his dream, ask if the monster is angry or friendly. Ask him about the monster's color, where he lives, and whether he has friends. Not only will this help your child use words to express thoughts, but it also may help overcome his fears.

Stuttering

Many parents worry over their child's stuttering, even though such concern is usually unnecessary. It's quite common for children to repeat syllables, sounds, or words occasionally, or to hesitate between words at around age two or three. Most children never realize their mistake, and they grow out of it without any help. It's only considered true stuttering when this pattern persists over a long period (greater than two to three months) and interferes with communication.

About one in twenty preschool children stutters at some point, most often between the ages of two and six, when language is being developed, with a threefold greater incidence in boys than in girls. The cause is unknown. Some children may have trouble learning the normal timing and rhythm of speech, but most have no medical or developmental problems. Stuttering may in-

(continues on next page)

crease when a child is anxious, tired, ill, or excited and tries to talk too rapidly. Some children stutter when learning too many new words at once. At other times, the child's thoughts are running ahead of his speech and he loses track of what he was saying midsentence. Repeating a sound or word allows him to catch up. In some children who stutter, the pitch of their voices may rise as they repeat syllables or sounds; or they may open their mouths to speak but nothing comes out for a few moments.

The more frustrated a child becomes about stuttering, the more trouble he will have with it. The best approach is to simply ignore the stuttering. Listen when he speaks, but don't correct him. Don't interrupt or finish sentences for him, and make it clear through body language you're interested in listening. At the same time, you can set a good example by talking calmly and correctly, and using simple language when addressing him. It may also help if you slow the entire pace of your household, including the speed at which you (and other family members) speak; your slower rate of speech will be more helpful than telling your child he needs to talk slower. It is important to tell him that you have all the time in the world to listen to him.

You should also set aside relaxed time each day to play and talk quietly with your child. Give him your full attention, free from distractions, and let him decide the activities you'll do together. You can build his self-esteem and confidence by praising him for all the activities he's doing correctly, while not drawing attention to his speech difficulties. Don't show any signs you're annoyed, frustrated, or embarrassed by his stuttering (avoid statements like "Talk slower!" or "Say it again more clearly this time!" or "Relax!"), and demonstrate that you accept him. Reinforce the things he does well. In an environment of acceptance, stuttering-associated anxiety will be reduced, which will help him conquer the problem. With support, a child can usually overcome his stuttering difficulty before entering school.

With severe stuttering, speech therapy may be necessary to avoid long-term problems. If your child frequently repeats sounds or parts of words, is very self-conscious, and shows obvious signs of tension (e.g., facial twitches or grimaces), let your pediatrician know. Also inform your doctor of any family history of serious stuttering. Your pediatrician will probably refer you to a speech and language specialist.

Language Milestones for Your Three-Year-Old

- Understands the concepts of "same" and "different"
- Understands simple prepositions such as "on" and "under"
- Uses three-word sentences
- Uses words that are 75 percent understandable by strangers
- Tells stories

Your three-year-old is still learning pronoun use ("I," "me," and "you"). As simple as these words seem, they're difficult ideas to grasp. They indicate where his body, possessions, and authority end and someone else's begins. To further complicate matters, the terms change depending on who's talking. Often, he may use his name instead of "I" or "me." Or when addressing you, he may say what he calls you ("Mommy," "Daddy," or "Grandma," for example) instead of "you." If you try to correct him (e.g., by suggesting, "Say 'I would like a cookie' "), you'll confuse him more, because he'll think you're talking about yourself. Instead, use pronouns correctly in your own speech. Say "I would like you to come" instead of using the word that he calls you ("Daddy would like you to come," for example). Not only will this help him learn correct use, but it will also help him establish a sense of you as an individual apart from your role as his parent.

At this age, your child's speech should be clear enough even strangers can understand most of what he says. Even so, he may still mispronounce as many as half the speech sounds he uses. He may use *w* for *r* ("wabbit," "wice," "wose"), *d* for *th* ("dis," "dat," "den"), or *t* for any sounds he has trouble with ("tee" for "three," "tik" for "six"). The sounds *b*, *p*, *m*, *w*, and *h* will only emerge midway through this year, and it may take months for him to perfect his use.

If your child's language abilities are delayed or poorly developed, he should be evaluated by a developmental or speech specialist. If he also has shown behaviors such as social withdrawal, limited interests, or repetitive movements, he should be evaluated by a specialist skilled in diagnosing autism spectrum disorder (ASD). The earlier ASD is detected and treated, the greater likelihood your child will function to his full potential. (For more information about ASD, see descriptions of this disorder and its management on pages 350 and 643.)

If the question is "Why can't the dog talk to me?" you can invite your child to look into the question further by finding a book about dogs.

Cognitive Development

Your three-year-old will spend most of his time questioning everything happening around him. He loves to ask "Why do I have to . . . ?" and he'll pay close attention to your answers as long as they're simple and to the point. Don't feel you have to explain your rules fully; he can't yet understand such reasoning and isn't interested anyway. If you try to have a "serious" conversation, he'll stare into space or turn his attention to more entertaining matters. Instead, telling him to do something "because it's good for you" or "so you don't get hurt" will make more sense than a detailed explanation.

The abstract "why" questions may be more difficult, partly because there may be hundreds each day and also because some have no answers—or none you know. If the question is "Why does the sun shine?" or "Why can't the dog talk to me?" you can answer that you don't know, or invite him to find out by reading a book about the topic. Take these questions seriously. You will be helping to broaden your child's knowledge, feed his curiosity, and teach him to think more clearly.

When your three-year-old is faced with specific learning challenges, you'll find his reasoning still one-sided. He can't yet see an issue from two angles, nor solve problems requiring him to look at more than one factor. If you take two equal cups of water and pour one into a short, fat container and the other into a tall, skinny one, he'll probably say the tall container holds more water. Even if he sees the two equal cups and watches you pour, he'll come up with the same answer. By his logic, the taller container is "bigger" and therefore holds more. At around age seven, children finally understand they have to consider multiple aspects of a problem before finding an answer.

Cognitive Milestones for Your Three-Year-Old

- Correctly names some colors
- Understands the concept of counting and may know a few numbers
- Approaches problems from a single point of view
- Begins to have a clearer sense of time
- Follows three-part commands
- Recalls parts of a story
- Engages in imaginative play

At about three years of age, your child's sense of time will become much clearer. He'll know his daily routine and will try hard to figure out the routines of others. He may eagerly watch for the daily visit by the mail carrier but be perplexed that trash is only picked up weekly. He'll understand that certain special events, such as holidays and birthdays, occur every once in a while, but even if he knows how old he is, he'll have no real sense of the length of a year.

Social Development

At age three, your child will be much less selfish than before. He'll be less dependent on you, a sign his own sense of identity is stronger and more secure. Now he'll actually play with other children, interacting instead of just playing side by side. In the process, he'll recognize that not everyone thinks exactly as he does and that each of his playmates has many unique qualities, some attractive and others not. You'll find him drifting toward certain children and developing friendships. As he creates these friendships, he'll discover that he, too, has special qualities that make him likable—a revelation giving a vital boost to his self-esteem.

There's more good news about your child's development at this age: As he becomes more aware of and sensitive to the feelings and actions of others, he'll gradually stop competing and learn to cooperate when playing with friends.

He'll take turns and share toys in small groups, though sometimes he still won't. But instead of grabbing, whining, or screaming for something, he'll actually ask politely much of the time. You can look forward to less aggressive behavior and calmer play sessions. Three-year-olds are often able to work out solutions to disputes by taking turns or trading toys.

However, particularly in the beginning, you'll need to encourage this cooperation. You might suggest he "use his words" to deal with problems instead of acting out. Also, remind him that when two children are sharing a toy, each gets an equal turn. Suggest ways to reach a simple solution when he and another child want the same toy, perhaps drawing for the first turn or finding another toy or activity. This doesn't work all the time, but it's worth a try. Also, help him find appropriate words to describe his feelings and desires so that he doesn't feel frustrated. Above all, show him by example how to cope peacefully with conflicts. If you have an explosive temper, try to tone it down in his presence. Otherwise, he'll mimic your behavior whenever he's under stress.

No matter what you do, however, there will probably be times your child's anger or frustration becomes physical. When that happens, restrain him from hurting others, and if he doesn't calm down quickly, move him away from the other children. Talk to him about his feelings and try to determine why he's upset. Let him know you understand and accept his feelings, but make it clear that physically attacking another child is not how to express these emotions.

Help him see the situation from the other child's point of view by reminding him of a time when someone screamed at him, and then suggest more peaceful ways to resolve conflicts. Finally, once he understands what he did wrong—but not before—ask him to apologize to the other child. However, simply saying "I'm sorry" may not help your child correct his behavior; he needs to know why he's apologizing. He may not understand right away, but give it time; by age four these explanations will begin to mean something.

Fortunately, the normal interests of three-year-olds keep fights at a minimum. They spend much of playtime in fantasy activity, which tends to be more cooperative than play focused on toys or games. As you've probably seen, preschoolers enjoy assigning different roles in an elaborate game of make-believe using imaginary or household objects. This type of play helps develop important social skills, such as taking turns, paying attention, communicating (through actions, expressions, and words), and responding to one another's actions. And there's still another benefit: because pretend play allows children to try any role they wish—including superheroes or the fairy godmother—it helps them explore complex social ideas. Plus it helps improve executive functioning such as problem-solving.

By watching the role-playing in your child's make-believe games, you may see that he's beginning to identify his own gender and gender identity. While playing house, boys may naturally adopt the father's role and girls the mother's, reflecting whatever they've noticed in the world around them. At this age, your son may also be fascinated by fathers, older brothers, or other boys in the neighborhood, while your daughter may be drawn to girls and women.

Research shows that few of the developmental and behavioral differences that typically distinguish boys from girls are biologically determined. The average preschool boy tends to be more aggressive, while girls are more verbal, although there is much overlap. However, most gender-related characteristics at this age are more likely shaped by culture and family. Regardless of the makeup of your family and the roles people play, your child will still find role models who are both men and women in television, magazines, books, billboards, and the families of friends and neighbors, and some of these representations may reinforce certain gender stereotypes. Your daughter, for example, may be encouraged to play with dolls by advertisements, gifts from well-meaning relatives, and approving comments from adults and other children. Boys, meanwhile, may be guided away from dolls in favor of rough-and-tumble games and sports. Children sense the approval and disapproval in these labels and adjust their behavior accordingly. By the time they enter kindergarten, children's gender identities are often well established.

As children start to think in categories, they often understand the boundaries of these labels without understanding that boundaries can be flexible, and children this age will often take this identification process to an extreme. Girls may insist on wearing dresses, nail polish, and makeup to school or playground. Boys may swagger, be overly assertive, and carry their favorite ball, bat, or truck everywhere.

On the other hand, some girls and boys reject these stereotypical expressions of gender identity, preferring to choose toys, playmates, interests, mannerisms, and hairstyles that are more often associated with the opposite sex. These children are sometimes called gender expansive, gender variant, gender nonconforming, gender creative, or gender atypical—all synonymous terms. Among these gender expansive children are some who may come to feel that their deep inner sense of being female or male—their gender identity—is the opposite of their biologic sex, somewhere in between male and female, or another gender; these children are sometimes called transgender. As children are better able to express themselves through language, they are more able to communicate their preferences for how they express gender (through choice of clothes, toys, playmates, hairstyle) and how they understand their own gender identity. Given that many three-year-old children are doubling down on gender stereotypes, this can be an age in which a gender-expansive child stands out from the crowd. These children are normal and healthy, but it can be difficult for parents to navigate their child's expression and identity if it is different from their expectations or the expectations of those around them.

As your child develops his own identity in these early years, he's bound to

Social Milestones for Your Three-Year-Old

- Interested in new experiences
- Cooperates with other children and shares
- Plays "mom" or "dad"
- Increasingly inventive in fantasy play
- Dresses and undresses self (coat, jacket, shirt)
- Negotiates solutions to conflicts
- Eats independently
- Enters bathroom and urinates by self

experiment with attitudes and behaviors of both sexes. There's rarely reason to discourage such impulses, except when the child is resisting or rejecting strongly established cultural standards. If your son wants to wear dresses every day or your daughter only wants to wear sport shorts like her big brother, allow the phase to run its course unless the behavior is inappropriate for a specific event. If the child persists, however, or if he seems unusually upset about his gender, discuss the issue with your pediatrician.

Your child may also imitate certain behaviors adults consider sexual, such as flirting. If he's very dramatic and expressive, you may be concerned by "suggestive" looks and movements, but often this perception is an adult way of looking at the situation. The child is just playing and not aware of his actions. At this age, he has no mature sexual intentions, and his mannerisms are mere mimicry, so don't worry. If, however, his imitation of sexual behavior is explicit or otherwise indicates he may have been personally exposed to sexual acts, you should discuss this with your pediatrician, as it could be a sign of sexual abuse or the influence of inappropriate media or videogames.

(For more information about how the media could affect your child, see Chapter 32.)

Emotional Development

Your three-year-old's vivid fantasy life will help him explore and come to terms with a wide range of emotions, from love and dependency to anger, protest, and fear. He'll not only take on various identities himself, but also assign human qualities and emotions to inanimate objects, such as a tree, clock, truck, or the moon. Ask him why the moon comes out at night, and he might reply, "To say hello to me."

From time to time, expect your preschooler to introduce you to one of his imaginary friends. Some children have a single make-believe companion for as long as six months, others change pretend playmates daily or prefer imaginary animals, while still others never have one at all. Whatever the form, don't think these phantom friends signal loneliness or emotional upset; they're actually a creative way for your child to sample different activities, lines of conversation, behavior, and emotions.

You may also notice your preschooler moving back and forth between fantasy and reality throughout the day. At times he may become so involved in his make-believe world that he can't tell where it ends and reality begins. His play experience may even spill into real life. One night he'll come to the dinner table convinced he's Spider-Man; another day he may be sobbing after hearing a ghost story he believes is true.

While it's important to reassure your child when he is frightened or upset by an imaginary incident, be careful not to belittle or make fun of him. This stage in emotional development is normal and necessary and should not be discouraged. Above all, never joke with him about "locking him up if he doesn't eat his dinner" or "leaving him behind if he doesn't hurry up." At this age he believes everything you say is true, and he's liable to feel terrified the rest of the day or remember it later. Likewise, never suggest that the doctor is going to give him a shot if he misbehaves; he will believe that vaccines and other procedures are punishments and may fear his check-ups.

From time to time, join in his fantasy play. This can help him find new ways to express his emotions and even work through problems. You might suggest that he "send his teddy bear to school" to see how he feels about preschool. Don't insist on participating in these fantasies, however. Part of the joy of fantasy for him is controlling these imaginary dramas. If you plant an idea for make-believe, stand back and let him make it what he will. If he asks you to play a part, keep your performance low-key. Let the world of pretend be the place where *he* runs the show.

Back in real life, let your preschooler know you're proud of his new independence and creativity. Talk with him, listen to him, and show him that his opinions matter. Give choices whenever possible—in the foods he eats, the clothes he wears, the games you play together. This will give him a sense of importance and help him learn to make decisions. Keep his options simple. When you go to a restaurant, narrow his choices down to two or three items. Otherwise he may be overwhelmed and unable to decide. (A trip to an ice cream store that sells many flavors can be agonizing if you don't limit his choices.)

What's the best approach? One of the best ways to nurture his independence is to maintain fairly firm control over all parts of his life, while at the same time giving him some freedom. Let him know you're still in charge and you don't expect him to make big decisions. When he is older and his friend is daring him to climb a tree, and he's afraid, it will be comforting to have you say no, so that he doesn't have to admit his fears. As he conquers many of his early anxieties and becomes more responsible in making his own decisions, you'll naturally give him more control. In the meantime, it's important he feels safe and secure.

Emotional Milestones for Your Three-Year-Old

- Imagines that many unfamiliar images may be "monsters"

- Views self as a whole person involving body, mind, and feelings

- Often cannot distinguish between fantasy and reality

Developmental Health Watch

Because each child develops in his own manner, it's impossible to tell exactly when or how he'll perfect a given skill. The developmental milestones listed will give you a general idea of changes you can expect as your child grows, but don't be alarmed if his development takes a slightly different course. Alert your pediatrician, however, if your child displays any of the following signs of possible developmental delay for this age range.

- Cannot throw a ball overhand
- Cannot jump in place
- Cannot ride a tricycle
- Cannot grasp a crayon between thumb and fingers
- Has difficulty scribbling
- Cannot stack four blocks
- Still clings or cries whenever his parents leave him
- Shows no interest in interactive games
- Ignores other children
- Doesn't respond to people outside the family
- Doesn't engage in fantasy play
- Resists dressing, sleeping, using the toilet
- Lashes out without any self-control when angry or upset
- Cannot copy a circle
- Doesn't use sentences of more than three words
- Doesn't use "me" and "you" appropriately

Basic Care
Feeding and Nutrition

As a preschooler, your child should have a healthy attitude toward eating. Ideally, he no longer uses eating—or not eating—to show defiance, nor confuses food with love or affection. Generally (but not always), he'll view eating as a natural response to hunger and meals as a pleasant social experience.

Despite your preschooler's enthusiasm for eating, he still may have specific food preferences, some even varying from day to day. Your child may gobble down a particular food one day, then push away the same plate the next day. He may want certain foods several days in a row, then insist he doesn't like them anymore. As irritating as you may find it for him to reject a dish he devoured the day before, it's normal behavior for a preschooler. It's best to not make an issue of it. Let him eat the other foods on his plate or select something else. As long as he chooses foods that aren't overly sugary, fatty, or salty, don't object. However, encourage trying new healthy foods by offering small amounts to taste, not by insisting he eat a full portion of something unfamiliar.

Your job is to make sure your preschooler has nutritious food choices at every meal. If healthy options are on the table, let him make the decision of what (and how much) to eat. If he's picky—resisting eating vegetables, for example—don't get discouraged or frustrated. Keep giving them even if he repeatedly turns up his nose at the sight of them. Before long, he may change his mind, developing a taste for foods once ignored. Kids may need as many as fifteen exposures to a given food before they accept it. This is the time healthy snacking and other habits get reinforced or established.

Meals need not be elaborate to be nutritious. If you have only a few minutes to prepare a meal, try a turkey sandwich, a serving of green beans, an apple, and a glass of nonfat or low-fat milk. A simple lunch like this takes less time to prepare than driving through a fast-food restaurant, and it's much healthier. Try to avoid frequent snacking during the day. When snacks are offered, make them healthy options. Limit snacking to the table so that when he leaves the table snack-time is over.

Television advertising, incidentally, can be a serious obstacle to your preschooler's good nutrition. Studies show children who watch more than fourteen hours of TV weekly (more than two hours daily) have a greater tendency to become obese. Children this age are extremely receptive to ads for sugary cereals and sweets, especially after visiting homes where these foods are served. Obesity is a growing problem among children in America. You need to be aware of your child's eating habits, at home and away, to ensure he's eating in as healthy a way as possible.

Beyond Toilet Training

By about age three, many children are already fully toilet trained. As a toddler, your child may have gotten used to a potty chair instead of a toilet. But now is a good time to transition to toilets. If your child will be in preschool, ask about their policies on potty training.

If the small potty chair isn't already in the bathroom, move it next to the regular toilet. If your child isn't yet used to going into the bathroom, this will help establish that routine. When he has fully adjusted to the potty seat, get a child-size seat for the toilet, and provide a sturdy box or stool to climb up and down. This will also give him a surface for his feet while using the toilet. Once he has completely and voluntarily made the transition from potty to toilet, remove the potty from the bathroom.

Little boys generally sit down to urinate during early toilet training, but as preschoolers, they'll begin to copy their fathers, friends, or older brothers and stand up. As your son is learning, make sure he lifts the toilet seat beforehand. Be prepared for some extra cleaning around the toilet bowl for a while. He probably won't have perfect aim for some time. (Note: Check your toilet lid hinges to make sure the lid doesn't fall easily once it's been raised; falling seats have caused injuries.)

Away from home, teach your child to recognize restroom signs, and encourage use of public bathrooms whenever necessary. You'll need to accompany and assist him in the beginning (although by five he should be comfortable enough to manage by himself). Whenever possible, however, an adult or older child should accompany him or at least wait outside the stall door.

He'll also need to learn to use facilities when they're available, whether or not he has a strong need to go. Doing this will make outings and especially car trips much more pleasant. Sometimes, however, a bathroom will not be available when it's really needed, so you may need a portable potty chair.

During the entire process, you'll

need to help your child in the bathroom—whether at home or away. Plan not only on wiping, but also on helping dress and undress. However, before he goes to school teach him to manage entirely on his own, especially if he is in a school that expects children to be fully trained. A boy must learn to pull down his pants (if elastic-waist) or use the fly front. To make this as simple as possible, dress your child in clothes easily undone without help. Overalls, for example, may be practical in some ways, but they're very difficult for a child to get in and out of without help. Elastic-waist pants or shorts are generally the most practical clothing at this age. A dress with elastic-waist underpants will work equally well.

Sometimes when a child is excited to play with other children, he may try to hold off going to the bathroom and end up having an accident. This is common, and experiences like this are part of growing up. Never punish a child in circumstances like this. He'll outgrow it. If you notice that holding urine is becoming a pattern, it is important to start your child on a timed voiding regimen every few hours so that the bladder does not get too full and become irritated and prone to infection.

Bed-Wetting

All young children occasionally wet their beds when going through nighttime toilet training. Even after your preschooler is able to stay dry at night for a number of days or weeks he may start wetting again, perhaps in response to stress or changes around him. When this happens, don't make an issue of it. Simply put him back in training pants at night for a while, but not as punishment, only as a means to keep the sheets dry. As the stress decreases, he should stop wetting.

Most children with an ongoing bed-wetting pattern have never been consistently dry at night. Some may have functionally small bladders, and at age three (even four or five) they can't last a whole night without urinating. For some, successful bladder control can take longer to develop. Preschoolers may not have learned to wake up and urinate at night when their bladders are full.

If your preschooler persistently wets his bed, the problem will probably disappear gradually as he matures. Medication is not advisable during the preschool years, nor should he be punished or ridiculed. He is not wetting the bed on purpose; usually it simply indicates that he is a deep sleeper. Limiting fluid intake in the hour before bed and waking him up to urinate may help some, but don't be disappointed if these steps don't stop the wetting. Reassuring him these mishaps are "no big deal" may help him feel less ashamed. Also, make sure he understands that bed-wetting is not his fault and that it will likely stop as he gets older. If there's a family history of bed-wetting, let him know that, too. It will further take the burden off his shoulders. If it persists, however, check with your pediatrician, particularly if your child snores severely at night, as the return to bed-wetting may be a sign of obstructive sleep apnea. Should the bed-wetting continue after age five, your pediatrician may recommend one of several treatment programs. (See *Wetting Problems or Enuresis*, page 792.)

If a child has been dry at night for six months or longer and suddenly begins wetting his bed again, there may be an underlying physical or emotional cause. Constipation frequently causes bed-wetting, so talk to your pediatrician if your child has large, painful, or infrequent bowel movements. Stressful situations can also contribute to bed-wetting. Maybe he's reacting to a new baby in the family, a move to a new neighborhood, or a divorce. If he has frequent accidents during the day, dribbles urine constantly, or complains of burning or pain while urinating, he may have a urinary tract infection or other medical problem. In any of these cases, see your pediatrician as soon as possible.

Sleeping

For many parents, their child's bedtime is the most challenging part of the day. This is more likely to be difficult if he has older brothers or sisters who stay up later. The younger one is bound to feel left out and afraid of missing something. These feelings are understandable, and there's no harm in granting some flexibility in bedtimes. However, most children this age need at least ten to thirteen hours of sleep each night. At age three, about 90 percent of children still take a nap each day, typically lasting one to two hours.

The best way to prepare your preschooler for sleep is by establishing a consistent and predictable bedtime routine. Brush his teeth (every night and every morning). Read him a story. But once the story is over and good-nights are said, don't let him stall or talk you into staying until he falls asleep. He needs to get used to doing this on his own. Also, don't let him roughhouse or get involved in a lengthy play project right before bedtime. The calmer and more comforting the activity preceding bed, the better and more easily he'll go to sleep. Screens—televisions, mobile phones, tablets, and videogames—should be turned off at least one hour prior to bedtime.

Although most preschoolers sleep through the night, some rouse several times to check their surroundings before falling asleep again. There may be nights when your child's very active dreams awaken him. They may reflect some impulse, aggressive feeling, or inner fear coming to the surface by way of frightening images or dreams. When a little older (five or even older), he'll be better able to understand these images are only dreams. But as a preschooler, he still may need to be reassured they're not real. When he wakes in the middle of the night and is afraid and crying, try holding him while talking about the dream, and stay until he's calm. For your own peace of mind, don't forget these are only nightmares and not a serious problem.

Night terrors can seem like nightmares, but they occur in the deepest part of sleep, usually earlier in the evening. During a night terror your toddler may sit upright in bed screaming, but not wake up immediately, and he won't acknowledge your presence. Once the night terror has passed, he should fall back asleep easily. In the morning, *you* will likely remember the event vividly, but your *child* is unlikely to remember it at all.

To further help overcome his nighttime fears, you might read your child stories about dreams and sleep. He'll better understand that everyone has dreams and he needn't be frightened of them. But always make sure the books themselves aren't frightening to him. (For more information about nightmares and night terrors, see pages 425–27.)

In some cases, your child may call out for you at night simply because he has awakened. In those instances, simply reassure him everything is all right, put him back to sleep, and then leave. Don't reward him for waking up by giving him food or by taking him to your room. (See Chapter 35 for more information on sleep.)

Discipline

As a parent, your challenge is to teach your child which behaviors are acceptable and which are not. This learning process won't happen overnight, but you've already been doing it since your child was very young. All along, you should have been—and should continue to be—consistent about your expectations regarding behavior. Set rules clearly, and stick to them. Caregivers' discipline techniques are often influenced by the way that they themselves were disciplined. If they feel that they were raised too strictly, they may be overly lenient. The reverse is true as well.

At this age, your child's misconduct tends to be more deliberate than before. As a toddler, he acted out of curiosity, finding and testing his limits; now that he's a preschooler, his misbehavior may be less innocent. A three-year-old who is reacting to something stressful may do something he knows is forbidden. He may not understand the emotions driving him to break the rules, but he certainly realizes he's breaking them.

To discourage such behavior, help your child express his emotions through words instead of violent or disruptive actions. The parent whose son hits his brother might say, "Stop it! You are very angry. Please tell me why." If he doesn't stop, a time-out may be necessary (see page 364 for a discussion on time-outs and time-ins).

Sometimes your child won't be able to explain his anger, and it will be up to you to help him. This can be a real test of skill and patience, but it's well worth it. Usually the problem is fairly obvious if the situation is seen from his viewpoint. The parent can suggest, "You're very angry. Let's think of some ways you can feel better." This approach works best if you encourage your child to talk about problems and feelings on an ongoing basis.

When setting limits, you'll need to be patient. Describe the undesirable behavior your child has shown, and then tell him he needs to stop. Keep things simple: "Don't hit your brother. That's not allowed."

Children test rules, particularly when those rules are new. But if you stay consistent and repeat the new rule at appropriate times for a few days, he'll get the message and accept it. Remember that hitting a child is *never* OK and is likely to make the situation worse over time. When you're especially angry or frustrated, you may need to give *yourself* a "time-out" to calm down.

(For more information about discipline, see pages 323 and 364, as well as the description of extinction on page 365.)

Preparing for School

Kindergarten is usually considered the official start of school. But many children get a taste much earlier, through preschool or group childcare programs that accept children as young as two or three. These programs are generally not designed for academic or book-learning education, but they will get him used to leaving home each day and introduce him to learning in a group.

A good preschool is designed to prepare your child for kindergarten. If the preschool's programming is aligned with your child's developmental level and is emotionally supportive, your child will make a smoother transition to kindergarten. He'll also be more likely to enjoy greater school success in the years ahead. Preschool gives a chance to improve social skills by meeting and playing with other children and adults, and it introduces rules that may be more formal than the ones you have at home. A preschool program may be especially beneficial if your child doesn't have many opportunities to meet other children or adults, or if he has unusual talents or developmental problems that might benefit from special attention.

Aside from these advantages, a preschool or childcare program may help you meet your own needs. Perhaps you're going back to work, or have a new baby. Maybe you just want a few hours to yourself each day. At this stage of your child's development the separation can be good for both of you.

If you haven't spent much time apart from your child, you may feel sad or guilty about this new separation. You also may feel jealous if he becomes attached to his preschool teacher, especially if—in a moment of anger—he insists he likes his teacher better than you. But face it: you know his teacher can't replace you, any more than preschool can replace home. These new relationships help him learn there's a world of caring people in addition to his family, an important lesson as he gets ready for the much larger world of elementary school.

When you're hit by pangs of sadness, guilt, or jealousy, remind yourself these structured separations help your child become more independent, experienced, and mature and also give you valuable time to pursue your interests and needs. In the end, this time apart will actually strengthen the bond between the two of you.

Ideally, every preschool program should offer children a safe and stimulating environment supervised by attentive, supportive adults. At the same time, the community at large should be sensitive to and supportive of the need for high-quality early childhood education. But unfortunately, not all preschool programs meet even the most basic requirements for an excellent environment for young children.

How can you tell if a preschool is appropriate? Here are some things to look for:

■ The school should have stated goals with which you agree. A good preschool tries to help children gain self-confidence, become more independent, and develop interpersonal skills. Be wary of programs claiming to teach academic skills or "speed up" children's intellectual development. From a developmental standpoint, most preschoolers are not ready to begin formal education, and pushing them may take away the fun of learning and decrease their drive to learn. If you suspect your child is

A preschool program may be especially beneficial if your child doesn't have many opportunities to meet other youngsters or adults.

ready to take on more educational challenges, ask your pediatrician to refer him to a child development specialist. If testing supports your suspicions, look for a program that will nurture his natural curiosity and talents without pressuring him to perform.

■ For a child with special needs—such as language, hearing, behavioral, or developmental problems—contact the director of special education in your local school system for a referral to appropriate programs in your area. Many neighborhood programs are not equipped to provide special therapy or counseling and may make your child feel "behind" or out of place among other children.

■ Look for programs with a relatively small class size. One- to three-year-olds do best in classes of eight to ten children, with close adult supervision. By the time your child is four, he will need slightly less direct supervision and may enjoy groups of up to sixteen. Here are the American Academy of Pediatrics' standards for child-to-staff ratios:

Age	Maximum Child-to-Staff Ratio	Maximum Group Size
≤12 months	3:1	6
13–35 months	4:1	8
3-year-olds	7:1	14
4- and 5-year-olds	8:1	16

■ Teachers and aides should be trained in early childhood development or education. Be suspicious of schools with an extremely high turnover rate among staff. This may reflect poorly on the school's appeal to good teachers, and it also makes it difficult to find people who know anything about the teachers currently there.

■ Make sure you agree with the disciplinary methods used. Limit-setting should be firm and consistent without discouraging each child's need to explore. Rules should reflect the developmental level of the children in the program, and teachers should be supportive and helpful without stifling creativity and independent learning.

■ You should be welcome to observe your child at any time. While it may disrupt the daily routine to have parents coming and going, this openness reassures you the program is consistent and the school has nothing to hide. Some schools even offer webcam access so parents can check on their child's classroom throughout the day without being a distraction.

- The school and grounds should be thoroughly childproofed. (See Chapter 15 on keeping your child safe.) Make sure there's an adult present at all times who knows basic first aid, including CPR and how to care for a choking child.

- There should be a clear policy about illness among children. In general, children with fever should be excluded whenever the fever is accompanied by behavioral changes or symptoms that may need a doctor's attention. At the same time, the presence of a fever alone should not keep a child from participating in childcare, since the fever itself isn't particularly relevant to whether the disease will spread. Many childcare centers have fever rules that are stricter than these, often to comply with state or local regulations.

- Hygiene is important to minimize the spread of infectious illness. Make sure there are child-height sinks and that children are encouraged to wash their hands when appropriate, especially after using the toilet and before eating. If the school accepts children who are not yet toilet trained, a diaper-changing area isolated from activity and eating areas is critical to controlling the spread of infectious disease.

- Be certain you agree with the program's overall philosophy. Find out ahead of time how the school's philosophy affects the curriculum, and decide whether this is right for your family. Many preschools are connected with churches, synagogues, or other religious organizations. Children do not generally have to belong to the congregation in order to attend, but they may be exposed to certain rituals of faith.

(For more information about childcare and preschool programs, see Chapter 14.)

Traveling with Your Preschooler

As your child gets older and more active, traveling may become more challenging. Your three-year-old will be restless when confined to a seat and, with his increasing willfulness, may protest loudly when you insist he stay put. For safety, you will need to be firm, but if you provide enough distractions he may forget his restlessness. The specific tricks of traveling will vary with your mode of transportation.

TRAVELING BY CAR. Even on short trips, your child must stay in his car safety seat. (See *Car Safety Seats*, page 495, for guidelines on selection and installation of car safety seats.) Most automobile crashes occur within five miles of home and at speeds under twenty-five mph, so there can be no exceptions to the rule. If your child protests, refuse to start the car until he's buckled. If you are driving and he escapes from his car safety seat, pull over until he is secured again.

TRAVELING BY PLANE. When flying with a young child, choose a direct flight whenever possible to keep travel time to a minimum, and consider flying during your child's nap time or on a red-eye (overnight) flight. Don't forget to pack healthy food and snacks: even if a meal is served, it may not appeal to your toddler. Do not request seating in an emergency exit row, since you will be moved.

Due to airport security policies, the Federal Aviation Administration (FAA) recommends that you give yourself more time than usual to negotiate security when traveling with small children. All child-related equipment—including strollers, car safety seats, infant carriers, and toys—must be visually inspected, as well as pass through an X-ray machine. You'll probably be asked to fold child-related equipment when you reach the X-ray belt so it can pass through faster.

Your three-year-old is safest flying in his own car safety seat installed with the aircraft seatbelt. Alternatively, the FAA has approved a harness-type restraint for children 22 pounds to 44 pounds that is only certified for use on airplanes. Remember that you will need to have a car safety seat available to use at your destination.

For safety, dress your child in bright colors when traveling, to easily spot him in a crowd. Tuck a card into his pocket with his name (and yours), your phone number, your address, and your travel itinerary. Have an up-to-date photograph of your child in your possession. (If possible, take a picture of him with your phone on the day of your flight, wearing the clothes he's traveling in.) It's also a good idea to carry a change of clothes in case your child needs to be changed on board.

While it makes sense to pre-board when traveling with a baby, pre-boarding with a toddler or preschooler may not be wise if you think your child will become more restless with the added wait. An advantage of air travel is you and your child can take brief walks when the "Fasten Seatbelt" sign is off. This is the best antidote to restlessness, especially if you should meet another preschooler in the aisles. To amuse your child in his seat, take along an assortment of books, games, and toys similar to those you would pack for a car trip.

Visit to the Pediatrician

Starting at the age of three years, your preschooler should be examined by the pediatrician once a year. Now that he is better able to follow instructions and communicate, some screening procedures such as more accurate hearing and vision testing can be done. Your pediatrician will check your child's teeth and gums during routine visits, although your child should keep seeing a children's dentist for routine dental examinations (by age three, 28 percent of children have at least one cavity, and by age five, nearly 50 percent do; good dental care is important).

Especially for Grandparents

A three-year-old child is becoming more of a real person. As that happens, your grandparent-grandchild relationship may become more meaningful and unique and will present many opportunities for additional growth for both of you.

Ages three through five are often known as "the magic years." Children are becoming more sociable, engage in more make-believe and fantasy play, and may even have an "imaginary friend." Your role as a grandparent is to be part of his activities, play along, enjoy his creative mind at work, and develop favorite play scenarios that you can return to whenever you're with him. Make time for adventures at or near your house that allow you to interact with him. For example:

- Take him to the zoo or the aquarium, which your grandchild will find very enjoyable at this age.

- Visit and explore a museum.

- Go with him to a safe playground with equipment that allows him to exercise many of his muscle groups, while you hold, hug, and catch him.

- Attend young people's concerts and plays, which are short (about one hour long) and a good way to introduce him to music and the theater.

- Become a volunteer, reading to your grandchild's class at preschool.

Be sure to follow all of the travel rules and advice that appear in this chapter.

Immunization Update

During your child's preschool years, you and your pediatrician should work together to ensure your child's immunizations are up-to-date. Refer to the chart on page 893 for an overview of vaccines he should have received in the first three years. Your doctor may recommend giving any missed vaccinations according to a "catch-up" schedule approved by the American Academy of Pediatrics and other medical organizations. And remember the annual influenza vaccine, given in the fall.

Safety Check
Falls

Be sure to guard against falls from the following:

- *Play equipment.* Watch your child on slides, swings, and monkey bars. Do not allow him to use playground equipment without an impact-absorbing surface underneath, such as wood chips, shredded rubber, sand, or rubber mats. Even with soft mats or chips, broken arms are extremely common in kids who fall off playground equipment, especially the monkey bars, so watch carefully and keep your child at a reasonable height for getting off and landing. Do not go down slides with your child in your lap, as this is a common cause of broken bones.

- *Tricycles.* Avoid unstable tricycles, and use the kind with a low-to-the-ground profile. Use a properly fitted bicycle helmet. It should bear a label indicating certification by the Consumer Product Safety Commission. Do not allow your child to ride in the street.

- *Stairs.* Continue to use gates at the top and bottom of staircases.

- *Windows.* Continue to use window guards on all windows.

Burns

- Keep matches, cigarette lighters, candles, and hot objects out of your child's reach. Install and maintain working smoke and carbon monoxide detectors in your home. If the microwave is within your child's reach, stay close and do not permit your child to remove hot food or liquids.

Car Safety

■ If your child reaches the top weight and height limits for his car safety seat (see the manufacturer's recommendation), he may need a car safety seat that can be used to a higher weight and height. The majority of convertible, three-in-one, and combination car safety seats have forward-facing weight limits of 65 pounds or more, which should accommodate nearly all children this age. A five-point harness is much safer than a booster seat as long as your child fits within the weight and height limits. Continue to use the LATCH system if your car was manufactured after 2002.

■ Your young child is not safe around cars. Keep him away from places where there are cars. Driveways and quiet streets can be dangerous, with injuries sometimes occurring when cars back into a child playing on the sidewalk or driveway. Always hold your child's hand in parking lots, as drivers backing out of parking spots often cannot see a small child behind them. Keep cars locked when not in use so your child cannot get in without permission. Do not leave your child alone in the car even for a second. Leaving a child in a vehicle can lead to illness or even death in a matter of minutes.

■ Do not allow children to ride tricycles in the street or near traffic; do not allow them to ride down driveways into the street.

Drowning

■ Never leave your preschooler unattended near water, even if he has taken swimming lessons and has swimming skills. (See Chapter 15, pages 514–17, for guidelines on when to give your child swimming lessons.) This includes the bathtub. Also make sure there are no large buckets filled with water inside or outside of the home.

■ Swimming lessons do not provide "drownproofing" for any child. Continue practicing touch supervision (an adult is within arm's reach at all times) anytime your child is in or near water.

■ If you have a pool at home, make sure it is surrounded by a four-sided fence that is separate from the house. The fence should have a self-closing and self-latching gate.

Poisoning and Choking

■ Make sure that lithium button batteries and powerful rare earth magnets are out of reach, as swallowing these items can cause life-threatening injuries of the digestive tract.

■ Do not allow your child to walk around with food or other items in his mouth.

■ Keep medications and poisons, including laundry detergent packets, locked away and out of reach.

■ Always supervise your child around pets, especially dogs.

~ 13 ~

Your Four- and Five-Year-Old

TIME PASSES QUICKLY. BEFORE you know it, your child has turned four and then five years old. You may find your calm child of three is now a dynamo of energy, drive, bossiness, belligerence, and general out-of-bounds behavior. You may be reminded of the trials and tribulations of her terrible twos, but by age four, she is now taking different directions. Although she may seem to be going in all directions at the same time, she is learning from all these experiences. Eventually this will subside (just when you couldn't take it for another day), and gradually a more confident child will emerge around her fifth birthday.

Meanwhile, this is a difficult age to handle. Each day brings new challenges. The emotional highs and lows have her appearing secure and bragging one minute and insecure and whining the next. In addition, four-year-olds become set in some routines, not wanting to change for fear they will not know what to do. This fixation reveals the insecurity they feel during these months.

Their out-of-bounds behavior also extends to their language. They enjoy using inappropriate words, and love to watch your expression when they say them. They use these words more to get a response than for any other reason, so don't overreact.

Your child's mind is now a font of imaginative ideas. The "monsters" they talk with at school or the "dragon" who helps them across the street are normal tall tales for four- to five-year-olds. They reflect your child's push to distinguish fact from fantasy, and their fantasies sometimes get a bit out of control. All this behavior and thinking will help your child build a secure foundation as she approaches kindergarten.

In fact, around her fifth birthday, your baby will be ready to tackle "real" school—the major occupation of childhood. This enormous step demonstrates she's able to behave within the limits expected by school and society and has the skills to take on complex learning challenges. It also means she's able to separate comfortably from you and move out on her own. Not only can she now share with and show concern for others, but she has also learned to value friends—both children and adults—outside her family.

Development

Movement

Your preschooler now has coordination and balance nearer to that of an adult. Watch her walk and run with long, swinging, confident strides, use stairs without holding the handrail, stand on tiptoes, whirl in a circle, and pump herself on a swing. She also has the muscular strength to perform challenging activities such as somersaults and standing broad jumps. It will be a toss-up as to who is excited more by her progress—you or her. You should talk to your pediatrician if you are concerned that your child can't keep up with other kids or is more clumsy.

In your child's eagerness to prove her independent capabilities, she'll often run ahead when out on a walk. However, her motor skills are still way ahead of her judgment, so you'll need to remind her frequently to wait and hold your hand when crossing the street. The need for vigilance is just as important near water. Even if she can swim, she probably can't swim well or consistently. Should she go under, she may become frightened and forget how to keep afloat. To prevent drowning, never leave her alone in or near a pool, hot tub, lake, ocean, or any body of water, even for a moment (including the bathtub). Be sure to practice "touch supervision"—being no farther away than arm's length while she is in the water—and avoid distractions like mobile phones.

Hand and Finger Skills

Your four-year-old's coordination and ability with her hands is almost fully developed. She's becoming able to take care of herself. She can brush her teeth (still with your help) and get dressed with little assistance, and may even be able to tie her shoes.

Notice how she uses her hands with far more care and attention when drawing. She'll decide in advance what she wants to create then create it. Her figures may or may not have a body, and the legs may be sticking out of the head, but they'll have eyes, a nose, and a mouth. And most important for your child, the drawing is a person to her.

Movement Milestones for Your Four- and Five-Year-Old

- Stands on one foot for ten seconds or longer

- Climbs stairs alternating feet without support

- Hops, somersaults

- Swings, climbs

- May be able to hop on one foot

Milestones in Hand and Finger Skills for Your Four- and Five-Year-Old

- Copies triangle and other geometric patterns
- Draws person with at least three body parts
- Grasps pencil with thumb and fingers instead of fist
- Prints some letters
- Dresses and undresses without assistance
- Unbuttons and buttons medium-sized buttons
- Uses fork and spoon
- Usually cares for own toilet needs

Because of this growing hand control, arts and crafts in general are becoming more exciting. Her favorite activities may include:

- Writing and drawing, holding the paper with one hand and the pencil or crayon with the other

- Tracing and copying geometric patterns, such as stars or diamonds

- Card and board games

- Painting with a brush and finger painting

- Clay modeling

- Cutting (using safety scissors) and pasting

- Building complex structures with many blocks

These kinds of activities will permit her to use and improve many of her emerging skills, and she'll also discover the fun of creating. In addition, because of her successes with these activities her self-esteem will grow. You may even notice emerging talents, but at this age it's not advisable to push your child in any one direction. Provide a broad range of opportunities to exercise all her abilities. She'll take the direction she enjoys most.

Language Development

At about age four your child's language skills will blossom. She'll now pronounce most sounds in the English language, with the following exceptions: *f*, *v*, *s*, and *z*. These sounds may remain difficult until midway through age five, and she may not fully master *sh*, *l*, *th*, and *r* until six or later.

Language Milestones for Your Four- and Five-Year-Old

- Recalls part of a story
- Uses four-word sentences
- Uses words that are 100 percent understandable by strangers
- Uses future tense
- Tells longer stories
- Says name and address

Your preschooler's vocabulary has expanded to around fifteen hundred words and will grow by another thousand or so over the course of this year. She can now tell elaborate stories using relatively complex sentences of up to eight words. And she will tell you not only about things happening to her and things she wants, but also about her dreams and fantasies.

Don't be surprised, however, if some words are not those you want to hear. She's learned how powerful words can be, and she'll enthusiastically explore this power, for better or worse. If your four-year-old is like most, she'll be very bossy at times, perhaps commanding you to "stop talking" or her playmates to "come here now." To counter this, teach her "please" and "thank you." Also, review how you and other adults in the family address her and each other. She will repeat many of the commands she hears most often.

Your child may pick up swear words at this age. From her point of view,

Learning to Read

Is your child interested in learning the names of letters? Does she look through books and magazines on her own? Does she like to "write" with a pencil or pen? Does she listen attentively during story time? If the answer is yes, she may be ready to learn the basics of reading. If not, she's like most preschoolers and will take another year or two to develop the language skills, visual perception, and memory needed to begin formal reading.

Although a few four-year-olds sincerely want to learn to read and will begin to recognize familiar words, there's no need to push your child. Even if you succeed in giving her this head start, she may not maintain it once school begins. Some early readers lose their advantage during the second or third grade, when the other students acquire the same basic skills.

The most crucial fact determining a student's success in school is a child's enthusiasm, not how aggressively she was pushed early on. Parents should make learning to read fun, without forcing their child. Encouraging your child's enthusiasm in learning is more important than the age at which a child actually learns to read.

What's the most successful approach to early learning? Let your child set her own pace and have fun. Don't drill her on letters, numbers, colors, shapes, or words. Instead, encourage her curiosity and tendencies to explore on her own. Read her books she enjoys, but don't push her to learn the words. Provide her with educational experiences, but make sure they're also entertaining.

When your child is ready for letters and reading, there are plenty of valuable tools to help—books, puzzles, games, songs, educational television programs, and even some of the latest age-appropriate video/computer games and DVDs. But don't expect them to do the job alone. You need to be involved, too. If she's watching an educational TV show, sit with her and talk about the concepts shown. If she's playing a computer game, do it with her to ensure it's appropriate for her abilities. If the game is too frustrating, it may diminish her enthusiasm and defeat the purpose. Active learning in a warm, supportive environment is the key to success.

these are the most powerful words of all. She hears adults say them when they are most angry or emotional, and whenever she uses them, she gets quite a reaction. What's the best way to stop this behavior? Be a good role model and make a conscious effort to avoid these words, even when stressed. In addition, try to minimize your child's use of them without drawing too much attention to them. She probably has no idea what these words really mean; she just enjoys their energy.

When your child's upset, she may use words as insults. This is certainly preferable to physical violence, although it can be disturbing to you. Keep in mind that when your child uses these words, she's disturbed, too. If she says "I hate you!" what she really means is "I am very angry, and I want you to help me sort out my feelings." Getting angry and shouting back will only hurt and confuse her more. Instead, remain calm and tell her you know she doesn't really hate you. Then let her know it's OK to feel angry, and talk about the events leading up to her outburst. Try giving her the words that show how she feels.

If the insults she chooses are mild, the best response may be a joke. If she calls you a "wicked witch," you might laugh and respond: "And I just boiled up a pot of bats' wings and frogs' eyes. Want some?" This kind of humor can take the edge off her anger as well as your own.

From time to time your preschooler may be extremely talkative. Try redirecting her verbal energy. Instead of allowing her to chant mindless sound rhymes, teach her some limericks or songs, or take time out to read some poems. This will help her pay more attention to the words she speaks and will boost her appreciation for written language as well.

Cognitive Development

By age four, your child is exploring many basic concepts to be taught in greater detail in school. She now understands the day is divided into morning, afternoon, and night, and that there are different seasons. By the time she's five, she may know some days of the week and that each day is measured in hours and minutes. She also may comprehend counting, the alphabet, size relationships (big versus small), and the names of geometric shapes.

There are many children's books illustrating these concepts, but don't feel compelled to rush. There's no advantage to her learning early, and if she feels pressured to perform now, she actually may resist learning when she gets to school.

The best approach is to offer a wide range of learning opportunities. This is the perfect age to introduce zoos and museums, if you haven't done so already. Many museums have special children's sections, where she can actively experience the learning process.

At the same time, you should respect her special interests and talents. If your child seems very artistic, take her to art museums and galleries, or try a preschool art class. If you know an artist, take her for a visit so she can see a studio. If she's most interested in dinosaurs, take her to the natural history museum. Whatever her interests, books can help answer her questions and open her horizons even further. At this age, your child should be discovering the joy of learning so that she can be self-motivated when formal education begins.

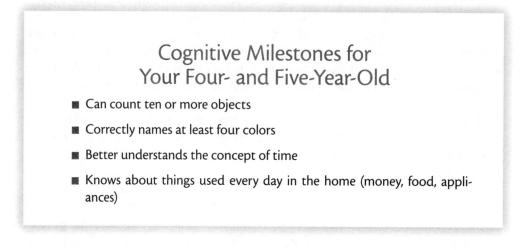

Cognitive Milestones for Your Four- and Five-Year-Old

- Can count ten or more objects

- Correctly names at least four colors

- Better understands the concept of time

- Knows about things used every day in the home (money, food, appliances)

You'll also find, in addition to exploring practical ideas, your four-year-old will probably ask universal questions about subjects such as the origin of the world, death and dying, and the composition of the sun and sky. Now is when you'll hear the classic question "Why is the sky blue?" Like many parents, you may struggle to answer these questions, particularly in language your child understands. Don't make up answers; rely instead on children's books. These questions provide the perfect opportunity to visit libraries or bookstores with your child. If you choose to look this information up online, refer to reliable scientific websites and take time to look at pictures and videos together.

Social Development

By age four, your child should have an active social life filled with friends, maybe even a "best friend." Ideally, she'll have neighborhood or preschool friends she sees routinely.

What if your child is not enrolled in preschool and doesn't live near other children the same age? In these cases, you might arrange play sessions with other preschoolers. Parks, playgrounds, and preschool activity programs all provide excellent opportunities to meet other children.

Once your preschooler has found playmates she seems to enjoy, you need to take initiative to help build their relationships. Encourage her to invite these friends to your home. It's important for her to show off her home, family, and possessions to other children. This will establish a sense of self-pride. Incidentally, to generate this pride, her home needn't be luxurious or filled with expensive toys; it need only be warm and welcoming.

Social Milestones for Your Four- and Five-Year-Old

- Wants to please friends
- Wants to be like her friends
- More likely to agree to rules
- Dresses and undresses without much help
- Engages in well-developed imaginative play
- Enters bathroom and has bowel movement by self
- Brushes teeth
- Shows more independence and may even visit a next-door neighbor by self

It's also important to recognize that her friends are not just playmates. They actively influence her thinking and behavior. She'll desperately want to be like them, even during times when they break rules and standards you've taught her from birth. She now realizes there are other values and opinions besides yours, and she may test this new discovery by demanding things you've never allowed—certain toys, foods, clothing, or watching certain TV programs.

Don't despair if your relationship changes dramatically in light of these new friendships. She may be rude to you for the first time in her life. Hard as it may be to accept, this sassiness is actually a positive sign she's learning to challenge authority and test her independence. Once again, deal with it by expressing disapproval, and possibly discussing with her what she really means or feels. If you react emotionally, you'll encourage her to continue misbehaving. If the subdued approach doesn't work and she persists in talking back, a time-out (or time-in) is the most effective form of punishment (see page 364).

Bear in mind that even though your child is exploring the concepts of good and bad, she still has an extremely simplified sense of morality. When she obeys rules rigidly, it's not necessarily because she understands them, but more likely because she wants to avoid punishment. In her mind, consequences count, but not intentions. When she breaks something of value, she probably assumes she's bad, even if she didn't break it on purpose. She needs to be taught the difference between accidents and misbehaving.

To help her learn this difference, you need to separate her from her behavior. When she does or says something that calls for punishment, make sure she understands she's being punished for the act, not because she's "bad." Describe specifically what she did wrong, clearly separating the person from the behavior. If she is picking on a younger sibling, explain why it's wrong, rather than saying "You're bad." When she does something wrong without meaning to, comfort her and tell her you understand it was unintentional. Try not to get upset, or she'll think it's her you're angry with rather than what she did.

It's also important to give your preschooler tasks you know she can perform and then praise her when she does them well. She's ready for simple responsibilities, such as setting the table or cleaning her room. On family outings, explain that you expect her to behave well, and congratulate her when she does. Along with responsibilities, give her ample opportunities to play with other children, and tell her how proud you are when she shares with or is helpful to another child.

Finally, it's important to recognize that the relationship with older siblings can be particularly challenging, especially if the sibling is three to four years older. Often your four-year-old is eager to do everything her older sibling does; just as often, your older child resents the intrusion. She may resent the intrusion on her space, her friends, her more daring and busy pace, and especially her room and things. You often become the mediator of these squabbles. It's important to seek middle ground. Allow your older child her own time, independence, and private activities and space, but also foster cooperative play when appropriate. Family vacations are great opportunities to enhance the positives of their relationship while giving each child his or her own activity and special time.

Emotional Development

Just as it was when she was three, your four-year-old's fantasy life remains very active. However, she's now learning to distinguish between reality and make-believe, and she'll be able to move back and forth between the two without confusing them.

Developmental Health Watch

Because each child develops in her own manner, it's impossible to predict exactly when or how your own preschooler will perfect a given skill. The developmental milestones listed will give you a general idea of the expected changes as your child grows, but don't be alarmed if her development takes a slightly different course. Alert your pediatrician, however, if your child displays any of the following signs of possible developmental delay for this age range.

- Exhibits extremely fearful or timid behavior

- Exhibits extremely aggressive behavior

- Is unable to separate from parents without major protest

- Is easily distracted and unable to concentrate on any single activity for more than five minutes

- Shows little interest in playing with other children

- Refuses to respond to people in general, or responds only superficially

- Rarely uses fantasy or imitation in play

- Seems unhappy or sad much of the time

- Doesn't engage in a variety of activities

- Avoids or seems aloof with other children and adults

- Doesn't express a wide range of emotions

- Has trouble eating, sleeping, or using the toilet

- Can't differentiate between fantasy and reality

- Seems unusually passive

- Cannot understand two-part commands using preposition ("Put the cup on the table"; "Get the ball under the couch")

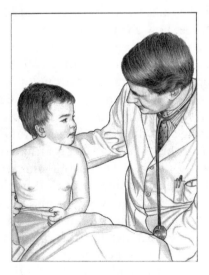

(continues on next page)

- Can't correctly give her first and last name
- Doesn't use plurals or past tense properly when speaking
- Doesn't talk about her daily activities and experiences
- Cannot build a tower of six to eight blocks
- Seems uncomfortable holding a crayon
- Has trouble taking off her clothing
- Cannot wash and dry her hands

As pretend games advance, don't be surprised if your child experiments with make-believe games involving some form of violence. War games, dragon-slaying, and even games like tag all fall into this category. Some parents forbid store-bought toy guns, only to find their child cutting out cardboard guns or pointing a finger and shouting "Bang!" Parents shouldn't panic over these activities. This is no evidence these children are violent. A child has no idea what it is to kill or die. For him, toy guns are an innocent and entertaining way to be competitive and boost self-esteem.

If you want a gauge of your child's developing self-confidence, listen to the way she talks to adults. Instead of hanging back, as she may have done at two or three, now she is probably friendly, talkative, and curious. She is also likely to be especially sensitive to the feelings of others—adults and children—and enjoys making people happy. When she sees they're hurt or sad, she'll show sympathy and concern. This will probably come out as a desire to hug or "kiss the hurt," because this is what she wants most when in pain or unhappy.

At about four and five, your preschooler may begin to show an avid interest in basic sexuality, both her own and that of others. She may ask where babies come from and about the organs involved in reproduction and elimination. She may want to know how boys' and girls' bodies are different. When confronted with these questions, answer in simple but correct terminology. A four-year-old doesn't need to know details about intercourse but should feel free to ask questions, knowing she'll receive direct and accurate answers.

Along with this increased interest in sexuality, she'll probably play with her own genitals and may demonstrate an interest in the genitals of other children. These are not adult sexual activities but signs of normal curiosity and don't warrant scolding or punishment.

Emotional Milestones for Your Four- and Five-Year-Old

- Aware of sexuality
- Able to distinguish fantasy from reality
- Sometimes demanding, sometimes eagerly cooperative

What limits should parents set on such exploration? It's probably best to not overreact, since in moderation the behavior is normal. However, children need to learn what's socially appropriate. You may decide to tell your child:

- Interest in genital organs is healthy and natural.

- Nudity and masturbation in public are not acceptable.

- No other person, including close friends and relatives, may touch her "private parts." The exceptions to this rule are doctors and nurses during physical examinations and her own parents when they are trying to find the cause of pain or discomfort in the genital area.

At about this same time, your child may also become fascinated with a parent or adult figure of the opposite sex. There's no need to feel threatened or jealous.

Basic Care

Healthy Lifestyle

Preschool years are a good time to adopt a healthy lifestyle for the entire family, and to encourage your child's healthy habits. The lifestyle she becomes accustomed to at four and five is likely to influence health-related choices for the rest of her life. That means being conscientious about the food she eats and exercise she gets.

Pediatricians are more aware than ever that a growing number of children have overweight. Your doctor has been keeping track of your child's height and weight since infancy. She'll be able to calculate whether your child weighs more than she should. Fortunately, steps can be taken now to reduce your child's likelihood of becoming obese, and to keep her on track for a healthy life. Give thought to your child's physical activity. Even as she's a bundle of endless energy, much often goes to waste. Many preschoolers spend several hours a day in front of the TV or computer screen, rather than playing outdoors. In fact, today's children are only one-fourth as active as their grandparents were.

Whether or not your four- or five-year-old has overweight, you need to make sure physical activity becomes and remains a priority in her life. These preschool years are when she should be developing her motor skills, improving her coordination, and playing games and sports with greater skill. Make sure she has access to age-appropriate play equipment, such as balls and plastic bats, that will make exercise fun and something she looks forward to doing. Of course, play periods must be supervised; keep her away from dangerous situations like running into the street to chase a ball. You can serve as a playmate and role model by practicing exercise and active play yourself.

Make an effort to have family time be physically active. Rather than going to an afternoon movie, take the entire family on a hike. Or fly a kite, play tag, or throw a ball back and forth.

Television, computers, videogames, tablets, and mobile phones all compete with more active pursuits for your child's attention and time. Some gaming consoles can promote activity ("exergaming"), which may be useful when weather or other circumstances limit outside play. Mobile phone and tablet apps may also encourage activity or exploration. At the same time, most screen-based pursuits can distract your child from more active or imaginative play. In order to determine the role screen time will play in your child's life, first think about your goals for activity, sleep, and family time, then assign some remaining time to age-appropriate, constructive electronic activities. Your participation can help your child get the most from these programs and apps. (See Chapter 32, *Media*.)

Feeding and Nutrition

Good nutrition is an important part of your child's healthy lifestyle. Fast-food restaurants may be tempting because of cost and convenience, but there are now many acceptable alternatives to the higher-calorie, less nutritious items on the menu. During the preschool years, your child should eat the same foods as the rest of the family, with an emphasis on those with nutritional value. This includes fresh vegetables and fruits, nonfat or low-fat dairy products (milk, yogurt, cheeses), lean meats (chicken, turkey, fish, lean hamburger), and whole-grain cereals and bread. At the same time, limit or eliminate junk food from

Sample One-Day Menu for a Preschooler

This menu is planned for a four-year-old child who weighs approximately 36 pounds (16.5 kg).

1 cup = 8 ounces = 240 milliliters
1 ounce = 30 milliliters
1 teaspoon = ⅓ tablespoon = 5 milliliters

BREAKFAST
½ cup nonfat or low-fat milk
½ cup whole-grain cereal
4–6 ounces or ½–¾ cup cantaloupe, strawberries, or banana

SNACK
½ cup nonfat or low-fat milk
½ cup fruit such as melon, banana, or berries
½ cup yogurt

LUNCH
½ cup nonfat or low-fat milk
1 sandwich: 2 slices whole-wheat bread with 1–2 ounces meat and cheese, veggie, and dressing (if needed), or peanut or almond butter (and jelly if needed)
¼ cup yellow or green vegetable

SNACK
1 teaspoon peanut or almond butter with 1 slice whole-wheat bread; 5 whole-grain crackers; string cheese; or cut-up fruit

DINNER
½ cup nonfat or low-fat milk
2 ounces lean meat, fish, or chicken
½ cup whole-grain pasta, rice, or potato
¼ cup vegetable

   If your family would like to include margarine, butter, or salad dressing as a side option to any meal, choose low-fat or healthier versions, if possible, and give only 1 or 2 teaspoons to your child.

your child's diet, and get rid of sweetened beverages as well. Junk food includes foods with low nutritional value, especially food that has too much fat and sugar. Dairy is important for your child's diet. Research demonstrates that regardless of flavoring (such as chocolate), milk does not adversely affect body mass index measurements in children. So, if your child will only drink flavored milks, it still helps meet her recommended daily dairy servings. The AAP's 2014 report on optimizing bone health recommends that children consume low-fat or fat-free flavored milks, cheeses, and yogurts containing modest amounts of added sugars to meet calcium recommendations. Desserts like ice cream and cake are fine occasionally but shouldn't be an everyday indulgence. Particularly if your child has overweight, pay attention to portion sizes, and for four- and five-year-olds, servings should be less than an adult-size portion.

While three-year-olds are frequently picky eaters and four-year-olds may continue to be so, the older child may be more vocal about her preferences. She may become more insistent about refusing to eat certain foods. Her nutritional needs are the same as when she was a year younger, but she may have unpredictable emotional responses to foods. She may talk back if she doesn't like what's being served, but if you put well-balanced meals on her plate, she'll have enough wholesome choices to keep her healthy.

At this age, your child should be good company at meals and ready to learn basic table manners. By four, she'll no longer grip her fork or spoon in her fist, but rather hold them like an adult. With instruction, she also can learn proper use of a table knife. You can teach other table manners as well, such as not talking with her mouth full, using her napkin, and not reaching across another person's plate. While it's necessary to explain these rules, it's more important to model them; she'll behave as she sees the family behaving. She'll also develop

Handwashing is an important part of a healthy lifestyle, too.

How Much Is Enough?

Many parents worry whether their children are getting enough to eat. Here are some guidelines to help you make sure your child gets enough, but not too much.

■ Your child does not need the serving size of an adult. Offer her small portions, typically about half adult size, with seconds only if she asks. For many foods, a child portion is about the size of her palm (not yours). Using child-size plates can help guide portions as well. Here are some acceptable child-size portions.

1 teaspoon = 5 ml
1 ounce = 30 ml

1 tablespoon = 15 ml
1 cup = 8 ounces = 240 ml

4–6 ounces milk or juice
½ cup cottage cheese or yogurt
2 ounces hamburger
1 slice toast
4 tablespoons vegetables

½ cup cereal
2 ounces chicken
1 teaspoon margarine, butter,
   or dressing

■ In general, limit snacks to two a day; more may spoil her appetite for main meals. Choose healthy items instead of unhealthy foods such as soft drinks, candy, pastries, or salty or greasy items. To minimize the risk of cavities and excess calories, rely on nutritious snack foods like those listed below. If needed, consider cutting them into small pieces for easier chewing and to avoid any choking hazards. It often takes about twelve to fifteen times for a child to develop a taste for an unfamiliar food.

Fruit
Carrot, celery, or cucumber
   sticks (can dip into low-fat
   ranch dressing or hummus)
Yogurt

Whole-grain toast or crackers
   (with healthy nut butter)
Low-fat bran muffins
String cheese

■ On special occasions, your child can have dessert items or a sweet treat, but don't make dessert dependent on what she eats for a meal. Instead pick a couple of days a week as "dessert days." Also, pay attention to portion sizes of desserts: one scoop of ice cream provides pretty much exactly the same pleasure as two.

(continues on next page)

- Don't use food as a reward for good behavior.

- Make sure your child actually is hungry or thirsty when she asks for food or drink. If what she really wants is attention, talk or play with her. Don't use food as a pacifier.

- Don't allow her to eat while playing, listening to stories, or watching television. Allowing her to do so will lead to mindless eating well past the point of fullness.

- Don't worry if your child's food intake is inconsistent. One day she may seem to eat anything she gets her hands on, and the next she'll grimace at the sight of everything. When she refuses to eat, she may not be hungry because she's been less active that day. Also consider the possibility she's using food as a means of control. Especially when she's being negative about nearly everything, she's bound to resist your efforts to feed her. When that happens, don't force her. She will not starve herself, and she'll seldom, if ever, lose weight. If, however, a markedly decreased appetite persists for more than one week, or there are other signs of illness, such as fever, nausea, diarrhea, or weight loss, consult your pediatrician.

- Your child needs to drink approximately 2 cups (16 ounces [480 ml]) of nonfat or low-fat milk daily to meet her calcium requirement. Milk is an important food, mainly because of its calcium and vitamin D content. Too much milk, however, may reduce her appetite for other important foods, and some children don't like dairy. Children should take a daily vitamin D supplement anyway, and other high-calcium foods include seeds, cheese, oily fish such as salmon, beans, almonds, and leafy green vegetables.

better table manners if your family is accustomed to eating together. Try to make at least one meal a day a special and pleasant family meal, and have your child set the table or help in the meal preparation.

Monitor your child's television viewing and exposure to advertisements. Television advertising, even after the best of explanations, presents a serious obstacle to your preschooler's good nutrition. Research shows a strong relationship between time spent watching television and obesity; cutting back on television time improves weight in kids with overweight. Four- and five-year-olds are extremely receptive to ads for sugary cereals and sweets, especially after they've visited other homes where these foods are served. Be aware of your child's eating habits, at home and away, and monitor them to ensure she's eating as healthyfully as possible.

To combat unhealthy influences, keep your own home as healthy as possible. Stock up on nutrient-rich foods without added fats or sugars. Eventually she'll become accustomed to healthy whole foods, which may make her less susceptible to the temptation of the sugary, salty, or greasy ones.

Sleeping

If your child is having difficulty with nighttime sleep, it often helps to establish routines before bedtime. A four-year-old may respond positively to having a schedule of a bath, brushing her teeth, and a bedtime story before the lights are turned off. You might also try setting bedtime earlier rather than later; the nighttime struggles over sleep might subside when your child is less tired and cranky. Your child's need for naps may also gradually subside during this period.

Night terrors can be an issue for this age group. Occasionally your preschooler will be in bed and appear to be awake and upset, perhaps even screaming and thrashing, eyes wide open and terrified, but won't respond to you. In this case, she's neither awake nor having a nightmare. Rather, you're witnessing a night terror (or sleep terror)—a mysterious and, to parents, distressing form of sleep behavior common during the preschool and early school years. Typically, the child falls asleep without difficulty but wakes up a few hours later, wide-eyed and terrified. She may point to imaginary objects, kick, scream, call out ("No, no!" or "I can't!"), and be generally inconsolable. Parents find these experiences particularly disturbing because the child looks and acts so differently from usual. (These events are much more unsettling for parents than for the child.) The only thing you can do is hold your child to protect her from hurting herself. Reassure her: "You're fine. Mommy and Daddy are here." Keep the lights dim and speak softly. After ten to thirty minutes, she'll settle down and go back to sleep. Prolonged interactions with your child may extend these episodes. The next morning, she'll remember nothing about the occurrence.

Some children may have just one ep-

How to Tell a Nightmare from a Night Terror

Sometimes it's difficult to tell the difference between a nightmare and a night terror. This chart should help.

	Nightmare	Night Terror
Appearance and behavior	Frightening dream; child may awaken afraid and crying	Screaming, crying, thrashing during sleep; may appear partially aroused, anxious, and agitated
At what age does it start?	Frequently first occurs in toddlers and older	May begin at age four or five (or occasionally later)
Timing of episodes	Often in the second part of the night during intense dreaming	Mostly during non-dreaming sleep; episodes start within two hours of going to sleep and last five to fifteen minutes; occur most often when child has a fever or sleep schedules are disrupted
Return to sleep	May have trouble going back to sleep due to anxiety	Goes back to sleep quickly
Memory of experience	May remember the dream and talk about it	No memory of the episode
Underlying issues	Not associated with emotional problems, but may reflect inner fears surfacing in dreams	Not associated with emotional problems
Management	Awaken and comfort your child; talk to her to ease any stress that may be bothering her; avoid watching TV before bedtime	Treatment with medications not effective; try putting child to bed a little earlier to avoid over-tiredness
Long-term	Talk to pediatrician if child complains of nightly nightmares	Most children outgrow having night terrors

Source: Adapted with permission from *Healthy Sleep Habits, Happy Child,* by Marc Weissbluth (Ballantine Books, 2015).

isode of night terrors, while others experience several. It's not typical, however, for them to recur frequently or for a prolonged period. In cases of very frequent night terrors, sleep medications prescribed by your pediatrician may help, but the best strategy seems to be to wait them out. Since some children have night terrors when they're overtired, try putting your child to bed thirty minutes earlier than usual and see if the episodes diminish in frequency. In any case, they'll disappear naturally as the child grows older. (For more information on night terrors, see the box opposite.)

Discipline

By age four, your preschooler may be controlling some of her unpredictable emotional responses, but she still can't manage her feelings of defiance. At this age, she may openly disobey rules and, as mentioned earlier, even talk back or swear. Often she'll behave badly just to test you and to see your response. As irritating and embarrassing as this behavior may be, it's rarely a sign of emotional illness and usually disappears by school age if a relaxed approach is taken.

Children want guidance and to be shown expected behaviors in a consistent way. They need to feel safe and protected even if their behavior gets out of hand. Time-outs and time-ins continue to be effective. If you use a time-out, follow it with a brief time-in to review with your child the reason for it. Another technique is the loss of privileges. However, do not use empty threats, and never resort to physical punishment. You must teach what is and isn't acceptable behavior. The only way she'll learn to set her own limits later is by having you set reasonable limits now and having you guide her in learning emotional control. If you are loving, firm, and consistent, she will become more secure. It's also important to create opportunities for autonomy. If you're heading out the door together on a cool day, ask if she wants a sweater or jacket and ask her to help find it. At the grocery store, ask her to help point out a product you're looking for.

Fibbing

Not telling the truth is common at this age. Preschoolers fib for a variety of reasons. Sometimes they're afraid of punishment, other times because they've gotten carried away with fantasies, or perhaps they're imitating behavior seen in adults. Before you punish your child for fibbing, make sure you understand her motives.

When she's trying to avoid punishment, she may have broken a household rule. She may have damaged something she shouldn't have been handling. Or maybe she was too rough and hurt one of her playmates. In any case, she's concluded it is best not to admit to what she has done. You will want to explain why it is important for her to understand what she has done and to be able to talk about it with you. Say something like "This is broken. I wonder how it happened." If she confesses, remain calm and even-tempered, and if there will be a punishment, make it reasonable and meaningful. This way she may be less afraid to admit to her behaviors the next time.

Telling tall tales is entirely different from lying. Tall tales are usually just an expression of your child's imagination and do no harm. It becomes a problem only if you—or your child—can no longer distinguish truth from fantasy. Although a tall tale doesn't require punishment, it does call for a lesson. Tell her the story of "The Boy Who Cried Wolf" and explain how it could be dangerous for her to keep making up falsehoods. (What if she was hurt and you didn't know whether to believe her or not?). Make it clear it's in her best interests to tell the truth.

When your child's lying is just a copy of your behavior, you can best stop it by eliminating the model. When your child hears you telling "white lies," she may not understand you're doing it to be tactful or in an effort not to hurt someone's feelings. All she knows is that you're not telling the truth, so she feels free to lie as well. You can try teaching her the difference between outright and white lies, but she probably won't understand most of it. You're more likely to succeed by changing your behavior.

In deciding limits, keep in mind that many strategies used when she was younger are also suitable now. Rewarding and praising desired behaviors and ignoring unwanted behaviors work better than punishing. Avoid physical punishments. It's still essential to deal with misbehavior promptly and fairly, not waiting so long your child forgets why she's being disciplined. Now more than ever, you need to model appropriate behavior by controlling your emotions, selecting your words carefully (label the behavior, not the child), and using words (not violence) to address emotions and settle disputes. Be sure to share your discipline strategies with your child's caregivers so your child receives consistent messages and appropriate forms of discipline. (For more information, see *Discipline* on page 396, which is also largely applicable to four- and five-year-olds.)

Preparing for Kindergarten

Many four-year-olds will attend preschool. Many school districts offer free or lower-cost preschool options which are actually part of the school system. Kindergarten, however, is a major turning point. Even if your child attended preschool, she'll be expected to be more mature as she enters elementary school, and she'll be given more responsibilities and independence. "Regular" school is also a larger and more confusing social setting than any she's known before. Even though her class may be the same size as preschool, she may spend part of each day mixing with children from older classes. She must be emotionally prepared for the tasks of kindergarten and the challenge of being among the youngest in a big school.

As your child nears school age, you can start preparing by talking to her about going to kindergarten. Explain how her routine will change, and involve her in choosing her back-to-school clothes. It will also help to drive or walk her by the school occasionally and even go in and show her the classroom so she'll know firsthand what to expect. Many schools open their classrooms before school begins so you can take your child in and meet the teacher. This prepa-

Kindergarten is a major turning point for your child.

ration will help build her enthusiasm and lessen her anxiety about the next big step.

Prior to beginning school, your child should also have a thorough physical examination. (Many states require it.) Your doctor will evaluate your child's vision, hearing, and overall physical development, and make sure she has the necessary immunizations or give any boosters needed. (See Chapter 31, *Immunizations*, and the immunization schedule in the Appendix.) Depending on state law and likelihood of exposure, she also may administer a test for tuberculosis and do routine labs in the office or send you to a laboratory for other tests.

Most school systems accept children for kindergarten based on age, often with a rigid cutoff date. While this approach works well for most children, it's not perfect for everyone. Developmental rates vary so widely that one child may be prepared for school at age four while another isn't ready until six.

If you are in doubt about your child's readiness to start kindergarten, or if you are debating whether to start or give an extra year of preschool before kindergarten, there are experts who may be able to help you determine what's best. If your child is attending preschool, her teacher may be able to help, as she has seen her in action with other children and should be able to tell you if she's ready for a more structured classroom experience. Your pediatrician can also help evaluate your child or make arrangements for developmental testing to help determine whether she has the necessary skills to do well in kindergarten. These same experts and tests can also help if you feel your child is advanced for her age and you wish her to start school early.

Talking About Bullying

Bullying can be a fact of life for many preschoolers. Bullying occurs when one child picks on another, and it can happen at preschool, in the neighborhood, at playgrounds, or in parks. The targeted child is often smaller or weaker, shy, and feels helpless when confronted by bullying that can be physical (punching, pushing, kicking, choking), verbal (teasing, taunting, threatening, hate speech), or social (excluding from activities).

When children are bullied, they are often afraid to go to school. They may have difficulty paying attention at school, and may complain of headaches or stomach pains. Make sure your child understands bullying is not her fault. Talk to her about ways to stay safe when she's being subjected to this aggressive behavior. Here are some often effective strategies your child can use:

- Look the bully directly in the eye.

- Stand tall and stay calm.

- Walk away.

- Say (in a firm voice) things such as "I don't like what you're doing" or "Please don't talk to me like that."

Have your child practice these approaches at home so they will happen more naturally when they're needed. Also, let her know that when bullying takes place, she should ask an adult for help. At the same time, you need to let preschool teachers and playground monitors know bullying is going on, and ask them to help stop it if they see it occurring. When you are not around, an adult should be nearby who can keep watch and protect your child's safety.

Now, what if your child is the one doing the bullying? What if she is bullying other children in her preschool or neighborhood? Take steps to put a stop to this behavior as soon as possible. Bullying needs to be taken seriously. This is the time to change undesirable behavior, before things get worse. Here are some guidelines:

- Set consistent limits on your child's aggressive behavior. Make sure your child understands bullying is never acceptable.

- Be a positive role model. Show your child she can get what she needs without threatening or teasing other children.

(continues on next page)

- When you need to discipline your child for her behavior, use nonphysical approaches—such as time-outs, time-ins, and the loss of privileges. Make sure your child understands why this behavior is unacceptable.

- If you're having trouble putting a stop to your child's bullying, seek help from a teacher, a counselor, or your pediatrician.

Many school districts conduct screening assessments for all kindergarten-age children to assess school readiness and, in some instances, to identify children who will need an Individualized Education Program (IEP) and special education services. Testing of developmental skills is generally held at the school during the spring or summer before the child is scheduled to enter kindergarten. At the same time, school nursing personnel may collect information about the child's health, making sure she's been fully immunized, and perhaps examining her hearing and vision if there is no documentation your pediatrician has already done so.

Unless there's evidence your child may need modifications or accommodations to succeed, the best test may be a trial run when school opens. If there is a serious question about progress during the school year, your child may need a psychoeducational evaluation to decide whether an IEP is necessary. This decision will be based largely on her ability to learn, follow directions and routines, and relate to other children as well as the teacher.

Visit to the Pediatrician

Continue to visit your pediatrician once a year. She will confirm your child is up to date on immunizations and give booster doses of vaccines against polio, diphtheria, tetanus, pertussis, measles, mumps, rubella, and chickenpox for ages four to six years. Many states require these before kindergarten. (For a schedule of recommended immunizations, see the Appendix.)

HEARING. Around age four, your child can talk well enough to describe different sounds. Your pediatrician may suggest a thorough hearing check, using tones at different frequencies. This test should be repeated every year or two, or more often if hearing problems are found.

VISION. At ages four and five, your child can understand directions and cooperate well enough to have a formal vision test, although photo vision screening devices used at younger ages are also acceptable for screening at this age. Using either device, her visual acuity should be 20/30 or better. More important than the absolute vision in each eye is any difference in visual acuity between the two. If you suspect a problem or anything is picked up on a vision screening or exam, she should be evaluated by a pediatric optometrist or ophthalmologist.

Safety Check

Throughout this book, there are recommendations for keeping your child safe at and away from home. In particular, Chapter 15 is devoted to safety in a number of areas, including playgrounds, on bicycles and tricycles, and in your own backyard.

Here are some guidelines applicable specifically to four- and five-year-old children:

- As your child learns to ride a bicycle, she should *always* wear a helmet. When you purchase a bike, buy a helmet at the same time, and make sure it fits correctly. Set a good example by wearing your own helmet every time you ride a bicycle.

- Never let your child ride a bike in the street. She is too young to ride safely in the street.

- If your child darts into a street, she's in danger of being struck by a car. Accompany your child to the park or playground. Instruct her on the importance of stopping at the curb and of never crossing the street without an adult. Keep in mind, though, your child may not remember this safety rule and must be supervised closely when near a street.

- While your child can learn to swim at this age, *never* let her swim alone, even if she seems capable, as drowning is the second-leading cause of death in this age group. Your child should never play around a body of water (a lake, stream, pool, or ocean) or bathtub unless an adult is nearby supervising and watching at all times. Preferably at this age, "touch supervision"—staying no farther away than an arm's distance—should be used so an adult can quickly take hold of the child if she unintentionally goes under the water.

■ Whenever you're on a boat with your child, she should wear a life jacket. Teach her never to dive or jump into the water unless an adult has checked the water depth.

■ Teach your child never to play with matches, lighters, sparklers, or fireworks, and make sure these items are never left around the house where she can have access to them.

■ If there are firearms in your home or any other home she spends time at, always keep them locked, with ammunition locked in a separate location.

(For additional information about safety, see Chapter 15.)

Traveling with Your Child

Car crashes are the greatest danger to your child's life and well-being. A collision or sudden stop, even when traveling at slow speed, can cause devastating injuries. Your child should still be in a car safety seat with a five-point harness. The backseat is still the safest place for your child to ride.

Particularly for lengthy car trips with your four- or five-year-old, your child is less likely to resist the confinement of a car safety seat if you make the trip fun. Here are some suggestions to help pass the time.

■ Talk about the passing sights. Ask your child what she sees out her window. Point out interesting sights. When she begins to learn colors, letters, and numbers, ask her to identify them in signs and billboards. Remember to keep your eyes on the road, however.

■ Keep a variety of picture books and small, lightweight toys in the car within reach of her car safety seat.

■ Keep children's songs or stories in the car. Encourage your child to sing along with her favorite tunes.

■ For longer trips, bring a small box filled with age-appropriate activities, such as coloring or activity books, crayons, paper, stickers, or paper dolls. (Do not allow scissors in the car; they could be hazardous in the event of a sudden stop.) Your child may travel with a tablet or mobile phone, but take time beforehand to consider what games, stories, and shows or movies will be best, and be sure to build in some screen-free time to talk, sing, or play travel bingo. Avoid violent and age-inappropriate content, and remember that what she sees on her screen is likely to set her mood for the trip. Monitor children's use of screens in order to avoid overuse or nausea.

- Stop at least every two hours to break up the trip. This will allow your child a chance to stretch, perhaps eat a snack, and use the toilet.

- If your child is prone to motion sickness, it may help to give her an appropriate dose of non-drowsy motion-sickness medication one-half hour before getting in the car. (See *Motion Sickness*, page 800.)

The trip will be more pleasant and comfortable for everyone if you follow these additional rules consistently, wherever you are:

- Never leave a child alone in a car, even for a minute.

- Don't allow yelling, hitting, biting, or loud noisemaking.

- Don't allow children to touch door handles. It may be helpful to use the child safety lock if your car has one.

- Remind children to be considerate of other people in the car.

Especially for Grandparents

As you spend time with your grandchild, you'll probably notice changes in her personality as she moves from a four-year-old to the more independent five-year-old. She may test your authority, show aggressiveness, be bossy, and at times even use foul language. Fear not and stay calm. This stage is only a stepping-stone to gaining greater mastery over her surroundings. Discipline her firmly but not harshly (and never physically), and don't overreact to language you may find surprising or offensive.

During this period in your grandchild's young life, she also will be developing larger social networks and some "best friends." You can expand this net-

(continues on next page)

work even further if you can locate some other children nearby when she visits you, particularly if she's staying a few days or more. Take her to places where she can interact with other children her own age.

What if you live many miles from your grandchild and frequent visits are not possible? There are many long-distance strategies for grandparents, taking advantage of the fact that children of this age are now quite verbal. Here are some suggestions.

- The telephone is an obvious option. Establish a regular time when your grandchild can expect you to call. During these phone calls, talk about her activities. Ask questions about what she's doing and who her friends are. Preschool activities and events are often first on her mind. Keep notes so you can refer to her friends or special places by name in later conversations.

- Use video conferencing to communicate. Simply viewing each other is worth a thousand words. Remember, though, that four-year-olds may not understand that you are not in the room. An adult will likely have to explain how they can see Grandpa or Grandma even though he or she is far away.

- Children love to get regular mail or email (using a parent's account). Sending cards and playful mementos of trips you have been on can keep the connection real.

- Exchanging family pictures and movies can mean a lot.

- Call to sing "Happy Birthday" and send a card to arrive on special occasions and holidays when you can't be there. It is important to make some contact for special celebrations.

- Despite the distance, visits should become a priority. As important as the above suggestions are, nothing replaces actually being there with your grandchild. Even if it's only a weekend, repeated contact and familiarity are keys to a meaningful relationship.

~ 14 ~

Early Education and Childcare

WHO WILL CARE FOR your child during the hours when you are away? Sooner or later you're bound to face this question. Whether you need someone to care for your child a few hours a week or nine hours a day, you'll want to feel confident about the person. But finding the right caregiver or team of caregivers for your child can be a big challenge. When selecting childcare, your top priority should be the well-being of your child, overriding all other considerations. This chapter provides suggestions to make your search easier, and also contains guidelines for preventing, recognizing, and resolving problems once your choice is made.

To find good childcare it is important to judge both the quality of the childcare program and the character and abilities of the caregivers involved with your child. Approximately six of every ten families with children between three years and six years of age use center-based care. Parents may also choose to share care between themselves or have relatives or nonrelatives provide care. Some children participate in different types of childcare at different times of the day or week. If your child's caregiver is not a family member, chances are you will meet this person only a few times before entrusting your child to her or him. Even so, you will want to feel as confident about your choice as if she were a family member. While it is impossible to be absolutely sure under these circumstances, you can tell a great deal by observing caregivers at work for a day or two and by carefully checking references. Entrust your child to someone only after you have watched her with your child and other children and you feel confident in her abilities and dedication.

What to Look for in a Care Provider: Guidelines for the Toddler and Preschool Child

(For infants, see Chapter 6, *Your Baby's First Sitter*," page 182.)

Children thrive when cared for in a safe, healthy environment by warm, affectionate, and supportive adults who help them learn, interact, and work out solutions while protecting them from making harmful choices. The following list describes several things to look for when observing someone who might take care of your child. More specific suggestions appear throughout this chapter, but remember they are general guidelines. They apply to all out-of-home and in-home care, including babysitters, nannies, and teachers during preschool and the early primary school years. Also, keep all this in mind as you play with your child or supervise groups of children.

A good caregiver will:

■ Listen carefully to children and observe their behavior

■ Set reasonable limits for children and maintain them consistently

■ Promote children's intellectual and physical growth and development through exposure to reading, singing, hands-on activities, and physical activity

■ Tell children why certain things are not allowed and offer acceptable alternatives

Never entrust your child to anyone until you have taken time to watch him or her with your child and other children.

- Deal with difficult situations as they arise, before they get out of control

- Anticipate trouble and intervene early to prevent it

- Live up to promises made to the children

- Join children at play without disrupting their activity

- Ease stressful transitions for children

- Encourage children to think of their own ideas before offering suggestions

- Reward children's efforts and relieve their "hurts" with an affectionate physical gesture, such as a hug or a pat

- Talk naturally and conversationally with the children about what they are doing

- Help children encourage each other by asking them to share their accomplishments

- Encourage children to complete projects, even if they take longer than originally planned

■ Limit adult conversations in the children's presence

■ Show respect for the children's ideas and decisions

■ Avoid offering children choices when there are none

■ Allow children to make mistakes and learn from them (as long as there is no danger involved in doing so)

Choices in Care

In addition to these general suggestions, you will want to identify your specific needs and desires. Before you meet and interview potential caregivers, questions you need answered should include:

■ *Where* do I want my child to be during the day? At home? In someone else's home? In a childcare center? If out-of-home care, how far away? What other family members or friends will my child be near?

■ *What days and hours* do I need or want childcare each week?

■ *How will I transport* my child to and from the program? If the caregiver needs transportation during the day or evening, how will it be handled?

■ *What backup arrangements* can I make? How will I handle days when my child is sick or when my child's caregiver is unavailable because of illness or personal business? What are the arrangements for holidays, summertime, and vacations?

■ *How much* can I realistically afford?

■ *What size program* do I want for my child? How much group interaction do I want for my child?

■ *How much structure and stimulation* do I want for my child?

■ *What qualifications* do I want the caregiver(s) to have?

■ *What type of discipline* do I want used for my child?

■ *What other basic conditions* would make me feel comfortable about leaving my child with someone else?

While a majority of young children in the United States are in some form of childcare, over a quarter of this care is provided by relatives, mostly grandmothers. Not only are many grandparents caring for children for part of the day, but more and more are involved in taking children to and from other childcare arrangements.

If you have family members or friends whom you would like to care for your child and who live nearby, ask yourself if you are comfortable with their care and whether they would be willing to provide it (perhaps for a few hours a day or two to three days a week), either on a regular basis or as a backup if other arrangements fail. When possible, consider offering payment for these services to make the arrangement fairer and to create an additional incentive for the person to help you.

Other options include bringing someone into your home or taking your child to another person's home or a childcare center. Your financial resources, the age and needs of your child, and your own preferences about child rearing will help you decide.

Remember that your child will grow and develop quickly and that the correct choice today may not be the best choice tomorrow. Keep reevaluating your child's needs and the fit of your current childcare arrangement over time.

Here are suggestions to keep in mind when deciding among in-home care, family childcare, or a childcare center.

In-home Care/Nanny

If you are returning to work while your child is an infant, one choice for childcare (often a more expensive one) is to have someone come into your home on a live-in or live-out basis. A person you hire to work in your home is not required to be licensed, so there are important considerations that should be part of your evaluation and the hiring process.

- Check references.

- Perform a background check, if possible.

- Ask for documented work experience (preferably for the previous five years).

- Ask about the person's approach to discipline, scheduling, feeding, comforting, and providing appropriate activities. Determine if that approach matches your style of child rearing and is right for your child. Make sure the person you select shares your philosophy about how to react to excessive crying, how to respond when your child has an accident, or what to do when he doesn't want to take a nap or go to bed. (Sharing this kind of information is applicable no matter the type of care setting.)

■ How will the caregiver report back about the child's day?

How Do I Find an In-home Caregiver?

■ Ask friends, work colleagues, and neighbors for recommendations.

■ Scan or place ads online or in the paper (especially local publications for parents).

■ Go through a service.

■ Contact a childcare resource and referral agency in your community or an au pair service.

After Choosing an In-home Caregiver

■ Arrange a trial period of at least a week when you can be home to watch the caregiver work under your supervision.

■ In the days and weeks ahead, carefully monitor the caregiver's performance.

Advantages of In-home Care

1. Your child will stay in familiar surroundings and receive individualized care and attention.

2. He will not be exposed to the illnesses and negative behaviors of other children.

3. When your child is sick, you won't have to stay home from work or make additional arrangements to care for him.

4. Some caregivers do light housework and prepare family meals. If you want your caregiver to do household work in addition to childcare, make it clear from the start.

Disadvantages of In-home Care

1. You may have difficulty finding someone willing to accept the wages, benefits, and confinement of working in your home; or you may find the costs of qualified in-home care prohibitive.

2. Since you will be considered an employer, you must meet minimum-wage, Social Security, and tax-reporting requirements.

3. The presence of a caregiver may infringe on your family's privacy, especially if she lives in your home.

4. Because your caregiver will be alone with your child most of the time, you have no way of knowing exactly how she will perform her job.

5. Your caregiver may not always have backup help available for when she is sick, has a family crisis, or wants time off. You will be responsible for securing a replacement.

6. Your caregiver will likely have less initial or ongoing training in child development and health and safety issues such as CPR, first aid, and medication administration. CPR and first aid are skills she *has* to learn. Consider signing her up for a class in these lifesaving skills, and offer to pay for it.

7. You may need to provide a car for your caregiver if you expect your child to be taken on outings.

Family Childcare

Many people provide informal care in their homes for small groups of children, often looking after their own children or grandchildren at the same time. Some even offer evening care or sick care. Family childcare is generally less expensive and more flexible than care offered by childcare centers. A small family childcare home typically has fewer than six children and one caregiver. Large family childcare homes may have up to twelve children and one caregiver and an assistant, though the exact numbers are dependent on the ages of the children and state and local regulations. See the suggested staff-to-child ratios on page 399 in Chapter 12.

Family childcare may be licensed, registered, or unregulated. It is always best to seek out a licensed setting. (Licensing regulations vary from state to state and can be found at places like the website of the National Center on Early Childhood Quality Assurance, childcareta.acf.hhs.gov.)

A Message for Grandparents

As a grandparent, you may become a part-time care provider for your grandchild, perhaps on scheduled days during the week or for a few hours here and there. Many of the guidelines in this chapter will apply to you. The recommendations about the best environment, safety issues, special needs, and the size of the group (if you care for more than one child) should be considered.

As a grandparent, you have a unique and important role. You are not just "another babysitter," as you have a fundamental connection to your grandchild and provide the continuity between generations that your grandchild will come to understand and respect. Take advantage of this irreplaceable role! Your involvement with your grandchild and introducing him to your world is especially valuable. Treasure the experience and make the most of special days when you babysit. Offer to do it regularly if you can, sharing stories and reading to him often.

At times you may not be the actual caregiver but you may be asked to help out by taking him to and from childcare. You can make sure he is transported safely in an appropriate car safety seat, and provide another evaluation of the quality of the center or sitter, which helps his parents feel secure in their choice of childcare. Introduce yourself to the responsible persons at the childcare place and leave your telephone number as a contact person.

As you know, times have changed, although caring love is still the universal ingredient helping children to thrive. Educate yourself on new medical discoveries since you raised your children by asking your grandchild's parents to share information. In your home, make sure you secure any of your medications up and away from sight and out of reach so your grandchild can't get them. The medical profession has learned a lot about having infants sleep safely on their backs and about safer over-the-counter medications, as well as many other things. Learning new things keeps us young.

In Choosing a Family Childcare Home

■ Observe the caregiver's work.

■ Look for signs of good-quality care, such as hygienic diaper changing and safety measures.

In family childcare, your child can be involved in many of the same household activities he'd find at home.

- Ask for references.

- Check certification and licensing compliance.

- Look over the home to ensure its safety.

- Find out how many children the provider has enrolled and during what hours. It also helps to know the ages of the other children and whether they have any special needs or behavioral challenges.

- Inquire about substitute arrangements when the caregiver is sick or cannot provide care.

- Request information on the caregiver's emergency situation plans.

- Ask the provider what training he or she has.

- Ask if the provider's program is accredited by the National Association for Family Child Care.

- Ask how the caregiver will report back about your child's day.

- Ask for the provider's approach to discipline, scheduling, feeding, comforting, and providing appropriate activities. Determine if that approach matches your style of child rearing and is right for your child. Make sure the family care home you select shares your philosophy about how to react to excessive crying and squabbles between children, how to respond when your child has an accident, or what to do when he doesn't want to take a nap or go to bed.

How Do I Find a Family Childcare Provider?

- Ask friends for recommendations.

- Scan or place ads online and in local parenting-oriented publications.

- Contact a local resource and referral agency: Child Care Aware at 1-800-424-2246 or childcareaware.org or naccrra.org. Or the National Association for Family Child Care: nafcc.org.

After Choosing a Family Childcare Provider

- Monitor your child's adjustment and carefully observe interactions between the caregiver and your child, and between your child and the other children.

- Keep the lines of communication open and address issues that arise.

Advantages of Family Childcare

1. In good family childcare settings, there is a favorable child-to-adult ratio. In general, the total number of children to adults should be no more than about three children for one adult, especially if some children are under twenty-four months. (See page 399 for additional information on optimal child-to-staff ratios.)

2. Your child will have the comforts of being in a home and can be involved in many of the same household activities he'd find at home.

3. Your child will have social stimulation coming from having playmates when other children are present.

4. Family childcare has the potential to be relatively flexible. Special arrangements can often be made to meet your child's individual interests and needs.

5. Your child may have more individualized attention and quiet time.

6. Your child may be exposed to fewer infectious diseases or less negative behavior from other children.

Disadvantages of Family Childcare

1. You cannot observe what happens to your child in your absence. While many providers carefully organize activities appropriate for children, there are instances where they may use the TV as a babysitter and even let children watch shows inappropriate for them.

2. Many family childcare providers work without supervision or advice from other adults.

3. The caregiver might share the care of your child with relatives, boyfriends, or other people who might not give high-quality care.

4. Family childcare centers may have fewer protocols or trained staff for assisting with children and youth who have special healthcare needs. On the other hand, they may be able to provide more personalized care. During your selection process, if your child has special needs or if other children in the center have special needs, be sure to understand whether there are enough caregivers to address each child's needs.

Childcare Centers

Childcare centers may also be called daycare, child development centers, nursery schools, preschools, or other similar names. These facilities typically provide care for children in a nonresidential building with classrooms for children of different age groups. Most centers are licensed, caring for children from birth to six years. Of the approximately four million children in childcare in the United States, about 2.7 million children are in licensed facilities, meaning that about 25 percent are cared for in unlicensed and unregulated settings. Centers demonstrate a higher commitment to quality by participating in the accreditation process.

There are several types of childcare centers, most notably the following:

- *Chain centers* offer a wide variety of programs and appealing activities for children. Because they are chains and run under central management, some do not offer variation and room for individual creativity in their operations.

- *Independent for-profit centers* depend on enrollment fees to pay their overhead, typically earning a narrow profit for their owners. Because many of these programs are built around one or two dedicated people, they can be excellent—as long as those individuals remain actively involved in the daily operations.

- *Nonprofit centers* are sometimes linked to religious institutions, community centers, universities, social service agencies, or independently incorporated facilities. Some have access to additional public funding, permitting discounted fees for lower-income families. Any income earned above expenses goes back into the program, directly benefiting the children.

■ *Head Start* is a national child development program for children from birth to age five providing services to promote academic, social, and emotional development, as well as social, health, and nutrition services for income-eligible families.

■ *State-funded pre-kindergarten or transitional-kindergarten programs* are for children not quite at the cutoff age to enter kindergarten or those who aren't quite ready to start. They are fully or partially funded by state education agencies and are operated in schools or under the direction of state and local education agencies.

■ *Centers for children and youth with special healthcare needs* may be for-profit or nonprofit chains or may have some public support. These centers are specially designed and staffed to meet the needs of children with developmental disabilities, chronic illnesses, or behavioral concerns.

How Do I Find a Childcare Center?

■ *The Internet or the phone book* often list childcare centers.

■ *Ask your pediatrician or other parents* with children in childcare to recommend a center.

■ *Contact your community's health or welfare agency,* or a local or national resource and referral organization, such as Child Care Aware at childcareaware.org or 1-800-424-2246.

Advantages of Childcare Centers

1. More information is generally available about them, since the majority of centers are regulated by licensing agencies.

2. Many centers have structured programs designed to meet children's developmental needs, functional abilities, and medical care needs.

3. Most centers have several caregivers, so you are not dependent on the availability of just one person.

4. Workers in these centers have higher educational requirements and tend to be better supervised than caregivers in other settings.

5. Some centers may allow you to arrange shorter hours or fewer days if you work part-time.

6. Many centers encourage parental involvement, so you can help make the center better. Co-op daycare centers rely on parents' involvement, and the daycare contract lists the days a parent must volunteer.

Disadvantages of Childcare Centers

1. Regulations for childcare centers vary widely based on the type of center.

2. Good programs in high demand may have waiting lists for admissions.

3. Due to the number of children cared for in this type of program, your child may receive less personalized attention than in a smaller program.

4. Many childcare centers suffer from low pay and high staff turnover. Keeping staff skilled in the care of children with special needs can be challenging in these settings.

Selecting a Childcare Center

When considering childcare centers, you need to know the rules and practices that would affect your child. If the program is formal enough to have a printed or electronic handbook, this may answer many of your questions. Otherwise, ask the program director the following (some of which apply to in-home or family childcare as well).

1. What are the hiring requirements for staff members? (Regulations vary state to state.) In many good programs, caregivers must have at least two years of college, pass minimum health requirements, and receive basic immunizations. Ideally, they will have some background in early child development and perhaps have children themselves. Directors generally have a college degree or many years of experience, qualifying them as experts in both child development and administration. Staff members should also have training in CPR and first aid.

2. What is the ratio of staff to children? Although some children need highly personalized attention and others do well with less, the general rule to follow is: the younger the child, the more adults are needed per group. Each child should have one primary caregiver responsible for that child's

The younger the child, the more adults there should be in each group.

care, providing most of the child's feeding, diapering, and putting the child to sleep.

3. How many children are in each group? Generally, smaller groups offer children a better chance to interact with and learn from one another. While fewer children per adult is usually better, there is a desirable maximum ratio and group size for each age category. The designated ratios vary from state to state, and some good facilities do not reach the ideal child-staff ratios (see page 399).

4. Are there frequent staff changes? If so, this may suggest there are problems with the facility's operations. Ideally, most caregivers should have been with the program for several years, since consistency is desirable. Unfortunately, staff turnover in this profession is an issue for a variety of reasons, including low wages.

5. Are caregivers prohibited from smoking, even outside? This is important for your child's health.

6. Are caregivers required to have updated immunizations, including whooping cough and influenza vaccines?

7. What are the goals of the program? Some are organized and try to teach children new skills, or attempt to change or mold their behavior and beliefs. Others are relaxed, with an emphasis on helping children develop at their own pace. Still others fall somewhere in between. Decide what you want for your child, and make sure the program you choose meets your desires. Avoid programs offering no personalized attention or support for your child.

8. What are the admission procedures? Quality childcare programs require relevant background information on each child. Be prepared for specific questions about your child's individual needs, developmental level, and health status. You may also be asked about your child-rearing desires and about your other children.

9. Does the childcare provider have a valid license and recent health certificate, and does the provider enforce health and immunization requirements in the program? Standard immunizations and regular checkups should be required for all children and staff members.

10. How are illnesses handled? Parents should be notified if a staff member or child contracts a significant communicable disease (not just a cold, but illnesses such as chickenpox or hepatitis). The program should also have a clear policy regarding sick children. You should know when to keep your child home and how the center will respond if he becomes ill during the day.

11. What are the costs? How much is it to start, and when are the payments due? What do the payments cover specifically? Will you need to pay when your child is absent for illness or vacations with the family?

12. What happens on a typical day? Ideally, there should be a mix of physical activity and quiet times. Some activities should be group-oriented, others individualized. Times for meals and snacks should be set. While a certain amount of structure is desirable, there also should be room for free play and special events.

13. How much parental involvement is expected? Some programs rely on parent participation, while others request very little. At the least, quality programs should welcome your opinions and allow you to visit during the day. If the school maintains a closed-door policy for part or all of the day—typically for educational reasons—be sure you are comfortable with this practice.

14. What are the general procedures? A well-organized program should have clearly defined rules and regulations regarding:

■ Hours of operation

■ Transportation of children

■ Field trips

■ Meals and snacks, whether they are provided by parents or are prepared on-site

- Administration of medication and first aid

- Emergency evacuations

- Notification of child's absence

- Weather cancellations

- Withdrawal of children from the program

- Supplies or equipment parents must provide

- Sleep arrangements, especially for infants

- Special celebrations

- How parents are to contact staff during the day or night

- Exclusion of children while they are sick with certain illnesses

- Security to ensure that everyone who enters the facility, including outdoor play areas, is screened by childcare personnel. Strangers should not be able to enter any childcare area, indoors or out, nor should familiar adults who act oddly be allowed to stay.

- How discipline or behavior challenges are addressed

- Ask for their approach to discipline, scheduling, feeding, comforting, and providing appropriate activities. Determine if their approach matches your style of child rearing and is right for your child. Make sure the center you select shares your philosophy about how to react to excessive crying, how to respond when your child has an accident, or what to do when he doesn't want to take a nap or go to bed.

Once you've received this basic information, take a tour of the building and grounds during operating hours to see how the caregivers interact with the children. First impressions are especially important, since they'll influence all your future dealings with the program. If you sense warmth and a loving approach to the children, you'll probably feel comfortable placing your child there. If you see a worker spank or restrain a child too forcefully, you should reconsider sending your child, even if that's the only sign of abusive behavior you notice.

Try to observe daily routines, paying attention to how the day is organized and what activities are planned. Watch how food is prepared, and find out how often children are fed. Check how frequently children are taken to the toilet or diapered. While touring the childcare home or center, also check if the following basic health and safety standards are being met:

■ The premises are clean and reasonably neat (without discouraging play).

■ There is plenty of play equipment, and it is in good repair.

■ The equipment is appropriate for the developmental skills of the children in the program.

■ Children are closely supervised when climbing on playthings, roughhousing, or playing with blocks (which are sometimes thrown) and other potentially dangerous toys.

■ Food is stored appropriately. If the childcare site is preparing the food, it is nutritious.

Napping in Childcare Settings

Many parents know the importance of placing a baby to sleep on his back to minimize the risk of sudden unexpected infant death (SIDS). Obviously, this same precaution should be followed in childcare settings, where 20 percent of all SIDS cases occur—a disproportionately high amount. Although the American Academy of Pediatrics stresses the importance of using the back-sleeping position to lower the incidence of SIDS during childcare, not all states in the United States have licensing regulations to mandate that childcare facilities place infants on their backs to sleep.

If your baby will be napping at his childcare site, you must discuss this issue with the caregivers before making a final selection about a facility. Make sure the childcare setting you choose routinely follows this simple procedure. (For more information about SIDS, see page 193.) For older children, make sure that bedding is clean and hypoallergenic. (Additional information about crib safety is available on pages 477–79.)

While touring the childcare home or center, also check to see if basic health and safety standards are being met.

- Areas where food is handled are separate from toilets and diaper-changing areas.

- Diaper-changing areas are cleaned and sanitized before and after being used for each child.

- Handwashing sinks are available where needed and are used by the children and also staff members during the following:
  —Upon arrival
  —When moving from one childcare group to another
  —Before and after eating or touching food or food preparation surfaces
  —Before and after giving medication
  —Before and after playing in water used by more than one person
  —After diapering
  —After using the toilet or helping children use the toilet
  —After handling any body fluid, such as nasal discharge, blood, vomit, drool, or sores
  —After playing in sandboxes
  —After handling garbage

- Potty chairs are avoided to decrease risk of spreading diarrheal illnesses.

- Children are supervised by sight and sound at all times, even when napping.

Once you are satisfied a particular program will provide your child with a safe, loving, healthy environment, let him test it out while you're present. Watch how the caregivers and your child interact, and make sure all of you are comfortable with the situation.

Building a Relationship with Your Child's Care Providers

For your child's sake, develop a good relationship with the people who care for him in your absence. The better you get along with his caregiver, the more comfortable your child will feel as he interacts with both of you. The better you communicate with the caregiver, the more continuity there will be in your child's care throughout the day.

Talk with the caregiver—even briefly—each time you drop your child off or return for your child. If something exciting or upsetting happened during the early morning, it might affect your child's behavior the rest of the day, so the caregiver should know about it. Share family stresses, both good and bad, like an expected birth or a family illness.

When you arrive for pickup, you should be told about any important events from the day, from a change in bowel movements or eating patterns to a new way of playing or his first steps. Also, if he's developed symptoms of illness, you and the caregiver should discuss the situation and agree on what to do if symptoms get worse.

A rivalry may develop between you and the caregiver for your child's affection and control of his behavior. You may hear "Funny, he never does that for me" when he misbehaves. Don't take this seriously, as children usually save their worst behavior for those they trust most.

If you treat caregivers as partners, they will feel you respect them and will probably be more enthusiastic about looking after your child. Here are some ways to build this sense of partnership on a daily basis.

- *Show the caregiver* something your child made at home or talk about particularly funny or interesting things he's done. Explain that sharing this kind of information is important to you, and encourage two-way communication.

- *Extend basic courtesy* to your child's caregivers.

- *Provide materials and suggestions* for special projects the caregivers can do with your child and the group, or ask for ways you can help with planned activities.

Tips for Transitioning

Getting the day started can be a challenge. So here are some suggestions to make childcare drop-off a little easier for everyone.

Your Child's Developmental Stage	Your Response

0 to 7 months

In early infancy your baby primarily needs love, comforting, and good basic care to satisfy his physical needs.

Although this period may be a difficult time of separation for you, young infants generally will transition to a consistent childcare worker in almost any setting. Be patient during this initial settling-in period.

7 to 12 months

Stranger anxiety normally occurs at this time. Suddenly your baby may be reluctant to stay with anyone outside his family. The unfamiliar setting of a childcare center also may upset him.

If starting childcare during this period, ease into it and know it may take a little longer to adjust. If your child is already in a program, take extra time each day before you say goodbye. Create a short goodbye ritual, perhaps letting him hold a favorite stuffed animal. Say goodbye and then quietly leave. Above all, be consistent from day to day.

12 to 24 months

This is when separation anxiety peaks and your child has the most difficulty with your leaving. He may not believe you will return, and may weep and cling to you as you try to leave.

Be understanding but firm and persistent. Reassure him you will return when you're done with work or have finished your errands, and then make a quick departure. Once you have left, do not reappear unless you are prepared to stay or take your child home.

■ *Your child should always know you are leaving.* Keep a positive tone, and be sure to say goodbye before you disappear, but leave without prolonging your departure. Don't just slip away.

■ *Help plan and carry out* special activities with the caregiver.

Periodically, you and the caregiver should also have longer discussions to review your child's progress, discuss any problems, and plan for future changes. Schedule these extended conversations at a time when you won't be rushed, your child's caregiver isn't busy, and you are both in a place with no distractions. If possible, arrange for someone else to care for your child during the conversation. Allow enough time to discuss all of your child's achievements and concerns from both perspectives, and agree on specific objectives and plans.

Most parents find this discussion goes more smoothly if a topic list is made beforehand. You should start on a positive note by talking about some of the good things the caregiver is doing, and then move on to any concerns. After presenting your own thoughts, ask for her opinions and listen carefully, remembering that there is little that's strictly right or wrong when it comes to child rearing. Most situations have several "right" approaches. Be open-minded and flexible in your discussion. Close the conversation with a specific plan for action and follow-up communication. Everyone will be more comfortable if something concrete comes from the meeting, even if it's only a decision to stay on the same course for another month or two.

Resolving Conflicts

Most parents are pleased with the childcare they've chosen. Nevertheless, whenever two or more people share responsibility for a child, conflicts sometimes arise. In many cases, you can resolve a disagreement about childcare simply by talking through the problem. You may find the conflict is nothing more than a misunderstanding of the situation. Other times, especially when several people are involved in the care of your child, you may need a more organized approach. The following step-by-step strategy can help.

1. Define the problem clearly. Understand who is involved, but avoid blaming anyone. If your child has been involved in a biting or hitting incident with another child, find out which caregivers were on hand at the time. Ask what they observed and focus your attention on realistic measures that can be taken to prevent the likelihood of further incidents. Maybe you can suggest an alternative way in which caregivers can respond if the incident recurs.

The better you get along with her caregiver, the more comfortable your child will feel as she interacts with both of you.

2. Listen to everyone's ideas to find other possible solutions.

3. Agree on a specific plan of action with clearly defined time limits and assignments to each of the caregivers—including you.

4. Consider everything that could go wrong with the plan and decide how these problems might be avoided or how they will be handled if they occur.

5. Put the plan into action.

6. Meet again at a specified time to decide whether the plan is working. If it's not, go through the process again to decide what changes need to be made.

What to Do When Your Child Is Sick

If your child is like most, he will get his share of illnesses, whether he is in a childcare program or not. Most illnesses are colds or other respiratory infections, which tend to occur more often between early fall and late spring. At times your child may get infections one right after another and be sick for weeks. If both parents work full-time, this can be a problem and cause a great deal of stress, since often one will need to stay home with the ill child.

Even children who seem only mildly ill may be sent home from childcare programs; if the program's policies are based on sound principles, this may be for good reason. A sick child may be contagious and risks giving his illness to other children. Also, a sick child may need more individual care and attention than a provider can offer without interfering with the care of others.

States often have regulations requiring childcare programs to send sick children home. This makes sense, particularly when a child has a fever or symptoms like rashes that are weeping, vomiting two or more times in a twenty-four-hour period, or frequent diarrhea that is not contained in the diaper and/or more than two stools above normal, since those circumstances enable contagious diseases to spread. The ultimate goal is to provide your child with care and to limit the spread of contagious illnesses.

Ideally, you would stay home when your child is sick. However, there may be times when this option is particularly difficult or simply not possible. Be sure to talk to your employer ahead of time to see what arrangements might be available. You might suggest telecommuting, taking work home, or identifying coworkers who can fill in for you when this situation arises. Spouses, other family members, and trusted friends may be able to help as well.

If your job and your spouse's employer require full-time attendance, you will have to make other arrangements for a sick child. These are days when you might arrange alternative care, preferably where both the caregiver and setting are familiar. If you rely on a relative or hire a sitter, make sure the caregiver understands the nature of the illness and how to manage it.

If your child requires medication, confirm your childcare provider's policies regarding giving medication to children, and always obtain written instructions from your pediatrician to give to your caregiver. Do not expect your caregiver to follow your instructions without a pediatrician's authorization. Also, both prescription and over-the-counter medications should have a pharmacy or drugstore label on them with the child's name, medication dosage, and expiration date. Giving medication to children is a significant responsibility and can be a challenge for caregivers. It should be requested only when necessary. Often medication dosages can be adjusted so that they are given in the morning, before childcare, and in the evening, after childcare. Address any questions to your pediatrician.

Your child's caregiver will need to know the reason for giving the medication, how it should be stored and administered (what doses, intervals, and for how long), and what side effects to look for and what to do if they occur. Again, this should all be put in writing. Do not disguise medicine as food or describe it as candy; instead, your child should know that it's medicine and why it's needed. Ask the caregiver to record the time each dose is given.

If your child is in a childcare center, be prepared to sign a consent form authorizing staff to administer medication. Also, expect your child's medications to come home each evening (regulations typically do not allow medicine to be kept at childcare facilities overnight).

A few communities have services specializing in care for mildly ill children. These include the following:

Home-based Programs

■ Family childcare homes equipped to care for both sick and well children. If a child becomes ill in such a program, he can continue attending in a segregated area, if necessary. Not all infections are contagious.

■ Family childcare homes that care only for sick children. Some of these are associated with well-childcare centers.

■ Agencies or childcare centers that provide caregivers to work in your home.

Center-based Programs

■ Regular childcare centers that have trained staff members to care for sick children in the usual childcare setting, but apart from the main group.

■ Centers offering a separate "get-well room" for sick children, staffed by a caregiver.

■ Sick-childcare centers set up specifically to care for ill children.

In sick-child programs, caregivers adjust the activity level to the child's ability to participate, and the children receive a lot of cuddling and personal attention. These programs should pay extra attention to hygiene for both caregivers and children. The premises and equipment, especially toys, should be cleaned thoroughly and often. Disposable toys may be necessary, depending on the nature of the illnesses. A pediatrician and public health consultant should be on call for every sick-childcare facility.

Controlling Infectious Diseases

Whenever children gather, their risk of getting sick increases. Infants and toddlers are particularly affected, since they place their hands and toys in their mouths, making the spread of infections even easier.

While it's impossible for adults to keep toys and other objects in perfect sanitary condition, many precautions and practices can help control the spread of infection. Childcare programs should be extremely careful about maintaining good hygiene. Children and teachers should have easy access to sinks with soap. They should be reminded, and children assisted, to wash hands with soap and water after using the bathroom. Staff members also should wash at the times listed earlier in this chapter (page 454), and especially after changing diapers. Both the caregiver's and child's hands should be wiped after removing the soiled diaper, and then washed at the end of the diaper change routine. Handwashing or the use of alcohol-based hand sanitizers after blowing or wiping noses and before handling food or food surfaces can also significantly reduce infections.

If a center cares for infants, toddlers, and toilet-trained children, each group should have separate areas with accessible sinks for handwashing. The facility and all equipment should be cleaned at least daily. Changing tables should be cleaned after each diaper change, and toilets should be washed and disinfected regularly.

If an injury involving blood occurs, the caregiver should put on gloves and wash the wound, administer first aid, and apply a bandage. All blood-contaminated surfaces or clothing should be washed and disinfected. Diluted bleach kills the virus. Also, since breast milk can transmit HIV and other viruses, be sure the childcare facility has procedures to prevent feeding one mother's breast milk to another mother's child. If such an incident occurs, the situation should be handled following the national standards described in *Caring for Our Children,* published by the National Resource Center for Health and Safety in Child Care and Early Education (nrckids.org/CFOC). (Also see descriptions of HIV on pages 634–37.)

As a parent, you can help control the spread of disease by keeping your child at home when he has a contagious illness with fever or one requiring medical attention. Also notify his caregiver as soon as anyone in your family is diagnosed as having a particular illness, and request that all parents be alerted if a child in the program has a serious or highly contagious illness. Many childcare centers exclude children with fever for twenty-four hours, although this measure has never been shown to reduce the spread of illness.

Immunizations can greatly reduce outbreaks of serious infectious diseases. Centers should require children to be immunized (at appropriate ages) against hepatitis B, rotavirus, diphtheria, tetanus, pertussis, polio, influenza, *Haemophilus influenzae* type b, pneumococcus, measles, mumps, rubella, hepatitis A, and chickenpox (also, the meningococcal vaccine is available for certain high-risk children). The immunity of your child's caregivers should be checked as well, and if there is any doubt, they should receive appropriate immunizations.

Teach your child proper hygiene and handwashing habits so he is less likely to spread illnesses. Finally, educate yourself about common illnesses in childcare settings, so you know what to expect and how to respond if they occur. These include the following.

Colds

Children in childcare typically have about seven to nine colds each year and are more likely to get these infections than infants cared for at home. Fortunately, the chances of contracting some of the most severe illnesses or complications associated with colds can be decreased by immunizing children. In childcare centers, toys, tables, doorknobs, and other surfaces touched by hands should be sanitized frequently.

Colds are spread by direct or close contact with the mouth or nose secretions of an infected individual, or by touching contaminated objects. In childcare settings, children can be taught to wash their hands frequently, and to sneeze into their upper arm rather than their hands. They should also be taught proper disposal of tissues and not to share cups or eating utensils. (For more information about colds and influenza, see pages 667–70 and pages 609–12, respectively.)

Cytomegalovirus (CMV) and Parvovirus Infection

Cytomegalovirus and parvovirus usually don't cause any (or only mild) illness in children and adults. However, these viruses can be dangerous to pregnant women who are not immune to them and can sometimes also cause a serious infection in the unborn child. The infection is transmitted through direct contact with body fluids (tears, urine, saliva). Fortunately, most adult women are already immune to CMV and parvovirus, but if a woman is pregnant, has a child in daycare, or works in a childcare home or center, she has an increased risk of exposure and should discuss her risk with her obstetrician. Good hand hygiene is the most effective way to decrease transmission of CMV when caring for sick children. If necessary, her obstetrician can order a blood test to see if she has already had these diseases.

Diarrheal Diseases

The average child has one or two episodes of diarrhea a year. These illnesses can spread easily in childcare homes and centers. If your child has diarrhea, do not take him to childcare unless his stools have become manageable by normal diaper changes or by using the toilet. This will help avoid the chance of the infection being transmitted to others. If diarrhea is persistent with dehydration, or stools have blood or mucus, the child should undergo medical evaluation, and further lab tests may be required to identify the responsible bacteria, virus, or parasite for treatment and management before returning to childcare. (See *Diarrhea*, page 537.)

Eye and Skin Infections

Conjunctivitis (pinkeye), impetigo, scabies, and cold sores are common problems in young children. These infections of the skin and mucous membranes can spread by contact. Childcare staff should notify you if any child in the program contracts one of these illnesses. If so, watch for symptoms in your child and if symptoms appear, contact your pediatrician for early diagnosis and possible treatment. (See *Eye Infections*, page 739; *Impetigo*, page 857; *Ringworm*, page 865; *Scabies*, page 868; *Herpes Simplex* [cold sores], page 678.)

Head Lice

Head lice are small, tan-colored insects less than one-eighth inch long that live on blood they draw from the scalp. Although families and caregivers often become very upset about lice, the insects do not carry disease, though they do cause annoying symptoms such as itching. Lice are spread by direct contact with infested hair. By using medications that kill lice and nits, the infestation can be controlled. Children should not be excluded by childcare due to head lice. (Also see *Head Lice*, page 855.)

Hepatitis A Virus

Because of the success of the hepatitis A vaccine, this infection in childcare settings is now rare, but it remains contagious. In infants and preschool children, most infections are asymptomatic or cause mild, nonspecific symptoms. Older infected children may have only mild fever, nausea, vomiting, diarrhea, or jaundice (a yellowish skin color). However, adults who get this illness usually experience these symptoms to a much greater degree. (See *Hepatitis*, page 549.)

Hepatitis B Virus

Infants receive the hepatitis B vaccine series starting at birth. The virus can be acquired during birth from an infected mother or after birth by exposure to infected blood such as during a needle stick, but children also can contract the virus through frequent casual contact with household members. Transmission rarely occurs in a childcare setting, so there is no need to exclude a child with hepatitis B infection from group childcare. (Also see descriptions of hepatitis B and the vaccine on pages 549–51.)

Human Immunodeficiency Virus (HIV)/AIDS

HIV (the virus that causes AIDS) can produce a serious chronic infection. Some children acquire HIV from their infected mothers before or during birth. HIV can also be transmitted from one child to another by exposure to blood; however, there have been no reports of HIV transmission in childcare. There is no need to exclude an HIV-infected child from childcare in the belief that this would protect others, since the risk of HIV transmission in this setting is extremely low when standard appropriate blood and body fluid precautions are used. If an injury involving blood occurs, see pages 701–3 for standard clean-up procedures.

Ringworm

Ringworm (or tinea) is not a worm but a mildly contagious fungal infection, causing red, circular patches with raised edges. On the scalp, ringworm can lead to patchy areas of dandruff-like scaling. Ringworm is spread by direct contact with contaminated combs, brushes, towels, clothing, or bedding. To control infection, children should be treated early with medication. Ringworm is a common condition and should not exclude a child from childcare settings. (See also *Ringworm*, page 865.)

Preventing Injuries and Promoting Car Safety

Many injuries occurring at home or in childcare settings are predictable and preventable (see pages 449–55 for sections on assessing and selecting childcare). Safety for children (and adults) in and around cars is a special concern. The center should have well-marked pickup and drop-off areas where children and adults are protected from street traffic, with "Children at Play" or similar signs placed in the pickup/drop-off areas as well as along nearby streets. The center should never allow a child in these areas, or in any area where cars come and go, unless he is being picked up or dropped off and is accompanied by an adult. Children should also never go behind vehicles that could back over them. Keep in mind that adults may need assistance dealing with more than one child in the car. Cars should not be left running, and should always be driven slowly near childcare centers.

If your child shares a ride to and from childcare, be sure the drivers have good driving records and are using appropriate car safety seats for all children. The driver must check to ensure that everyone is properly buckled in a car safety seat before pulling away, and that everyone has left the vehicle before locking up and leaving the car. School buses and vans also need to follow measures ensuring child safety while in transit (see page 434).

Car-Pool Safety

If you use a car pool, you are responsible for every child in the car in addition to your own. This means making sure each child is properly restrained in a car safety seat appropriate for his or her size, installing each car safety seat correctly, not overloading the car, disciplining children who disobey safety rules, and checking that your insurance covers everyone on board. In addition, make sure you and other drivers observe the following precautions.

- Pick up and drop off children only in an area where they are protected from other cars. They should be dropped off on the same side of the street as the school to avoid having them cross the street in traffic areas. There are too many vehicle-pedestrian collisions involving children crossing a street with no specific crosswalk or crossing guard.

- If possible, have each child's own parents or another responsible adult buckle him into the car safety seat and take him out when returning home.

- Turn all children over to the direct supervision of a parent or childcare staff.

- Close and lock all car doors, but only after checking that fingers and feet are inside.

- Open passenger windows only a few inches, and lock all power window and door controls from the driver's seat if possible.

- Remind children about safety rules and proper behavior before starting out.

- Plan your routes to minimize travel time and avoid hazardous conditions.

- Pull over if a child gets out of control or misbehaves. If any child consistently presents a problem, discuss the difficulty with his parents and exclude him from the car pool until his conduct improves.

- Have available emergency contact information (ideally in your phone) for each child.

- Ideally, equip each vehicle with a fire extinguisher and first-aid kit.

- Be sure no child is ever left in the car without a supervising adult.

If your childcare program includes swimming, appropriate safety precautions must be followed. Any pool, lake, creek, or pond used by children should first be checked by public health authorities. If the pool is at or near the childcare center, it should be entirely surrounded by at least a 4-foot-high (1.2 m), four-sided childproof fence with a self-closing, self-latching gate that completely separates the center from the pool. For hygienic and safety reasons, portable wading pools should not be used.

Care for Children with Special Needs

If your child has a developmental disability or chronic health condition, don't let that keep him from preschool or childcare. Quality childcare may be good for him. He is likely to benefit from the social contact, physical exercise, and variety of experiences of a group program.

The time your child spends in a childcare program will be good for you, too. Tending a child with special needs often places great demands on your time, energy, and emotions. The challenge is to find a program that encourages normal childhood activities and meets his special needs; fortunately, these are more available than in the past.

WHERE WE STAND

TO ENSURE THE SAFETY of children while being transported to school, the American Academy of Pediatrics strongly recommends all children travel in age-appropriate and properly secured child restraint systems in all motor vehicles.

The AAP has had a long-standing position that new school buses should have safety restraints. Parents should work with school districts to encourage that new buses be equipped with lap/shoulder seatbelt restraints that can also accommodate car safety seats, booster seats, and harness systems. School districts should provide height- and weight-appropriate car safety seats and restraint systems for all children of preschool age; these systems include booster seats with a three-point belt.

When districts have policies on seatbelt use, children tend to be better behaved and less likely to distract the driver.

School Transportation Safety

Whether you rely on a bus or on alternative vehicles (such as vans) to take your child to school, preschool, or childcare, specific safety measures must be taken to protect him on that daily commute. The box on page 466, *Where We Stand*, describes the American Academy of Pediatrics' strong recommendation for the use of lap/shoulder seatbelts on school buses. Also, make sure your child understands that on the school bus, he should:

- Stay seated on the bus, never moving around once he's found and taken a seat

- Always remain within view of the bus driver

- Follow the instructions of the driver

- Talk softly with classmates, so the driver can concentrate

- Never stick his hands, books, or other objects out the window

Because most school-bus-related injuries happen while the child is getting on or off the bus, safe habits are also important *before* he boards and *after* he is dropped off at school or home. For example, he should:

- Walk to the bus stop with you or another responsible adult

- Arrive at the bus stop five minutes before the bus arrives, to avoid rushing

- Wait for the bus to stop before approaching it to board

- Tell the driver if he drops something near the bus; your child shouldn't try to pick it up himself until he tells the driver that the item is there

- Take his time while boarding and leaving the bus

- Look both ways for traffic before crossing the street—looking to the left, then right, then left again

(For other guidelines on car safety, see page 373.)

Federal law (the Individuals with Disabilities Education Act [IDEA]) requires all states to develop special education programs for preschool-age (three- to five-year-old) children with developmental disabilities. This act also gives states the option to develop special education programs for infants and toddlers with developmental disabilities or delays, and ensures that childcare centers provide children with special needs with an equal opportunity to participate in all programs and services. Centers are expected to evaluate the child's needs on an individual basis, and make reasonable accommodations and inclusions for the child. When selecting a childcare program, be sure to discuss your child's strengths and abilities. Parents should also check with their pediatrician or their state education or health department regarding the availability of these early intervention programs.

Safety Walk Checklist

Next time you walk through your child's childcare setting, use the following checklist to ensure the facility is safe, clean, and in good repair. If there is a problem with any item on the list, bring it to the attention of the director or caregiver and follow up later to ensure it was corrected.

Indoors in All Programs

- Floors are smooth, clean, and have a nonskid surface.

- Medicines, cleaning agents, and tools are locked up and out of children's sight and reach.

- First-aid kit is fully supplied and out of children's reach.

- Windowsills, walls, and ceilings are clean and in good repair, with no peeling paint or damaged plaster. (Windowsills are the highest-risk areas for lead poisoning.)

- Children are never left unattended.

- Bookcases, dressers, and other tall furniture are secured to the wall so they cannot tip over if a child climbs on them. Televisions are mounted or strapped to the wall or secured to low, sturdy furniture that is designed to hold them.

- Electrical outlets are covered with childproof caps that are not a choking hazard.

- Electric lights are in good repair, with no frayed or dangling cords.

- Be especially careful about batteries being left around, particularly button batteries, which can be very damaging to the GI tract if swallowed.

- Heating pipes and radiators are out of reach or covered so children cannot touch them.

- Ask if the hot water is set at or below 120 degrees Fahrenheit (48.9 degrees Celsius) to lessen the risk of a scald burn.

- There are no poisonous plants or disease-bearing animals (e.g., turtles or iguanas).

- Trash containers are covered.

- Exits are clearly marked and easy to reach.

- Smoking is not allowed in the childcare facility.

- Windows at or above the second story have guards to prevent falls, and all drapery or window blind cords are secured out of children's reach. If possible, it is best to use cordless window products.

- Leaks are fixed promptly and any mold is properly treated.

Outdoors in All Programs

- Grounds are free of litter, sharp objects, and animal droppings.

- Play equipment is smooth, well anchored, and free of rust, splinters, and sharp corners. All screws and bolts are capped or concealed.

- Outdoor playground equipment is mounted over impact-absorbent surfaces for a distance of at least 6 feet (1.8 m) on all sides of the equipment. Playground surfaces should be made of at least 12 inches (30 cm) of wood chips, mulch, sand, pea gravel, or other impact-absorbing material under and around areas where falls are more likely to occur (under monkey bars, slides).

- Swing seats are lightweight and flexible, and there are no open or S-shaped hooks.

- Slides have wide, flat, stable steps with good treads, rounded rims along the sides to prevent falls, and a flat area at the end of the slide to help children slow down.

(continues on next page)

- Metal slides are shaded from the sun.

- Sandboxes are covered when not in use.

- Childproof barriers keep children out of hazardous areas.

Infant and Toddler Programs

- Toys do not contain lead or have any signs of chipping paint, rust, or small pieces that could break off. (A clue that suggests a toy might contain lead is that the toy feels unusually heavy or soft for its appearance.)

- High chairs have wide bases and safety straps.

- Toddlers are not allowed to walk around with bottles or take bottles to bed.

- Infant walkers are not used.

- Cribs, portable play yards, and beds meet safety standards and are free of pillows, blankets, bumpers, toys, and loose bedding.

- No recalled products or old products with broken or missing parts are used. Recalled products can be determined by checking the website of the Consumer Product Safety Commission: cpsc.gov. Caregivers can subscribe to email alerts from the CPSC alerting them when any toy or other children's product is recalled.

Start your search with your pediatrician by asking about the best type of group programs for your child. Ask for referrals to suitable centers. Your pediatrician can draft an individualized care plan to address your child's special healthcare needs and help your childcare providers understand what is needed. Although only one appropriate site may be available in smaller communities, in many communities you will have several to choose from. The one you select should meet the same basic requirements outlined earlier, plus the following.

1. The program should include children with and without chronic health conditions and special needs, to the extent possible. Having relationships with typically developing playmates helps a child with a disability feel more relaxed and confident socially, and helps build self-esteem. The arrangement also benefits the typically developing child and those with no special

health needs by teaching them to look past surface differences and helping them develop sensitivity and respect.

2. The staff should be trained in the specific care your child requires. Some of the training needs can be specified in your child's care plan.

3. The program should have at least one physician consultant who is active in the development of policies and procedures affecting the type of special needs present. Your own pediatrician should also play an active role. Give permission for your childcare providers to discuss questions and issues with your pediatrician.

4. All children should be encouraged to be as independent as their abilities allow, within the bounds of safety. They should be restricted only in activities that might be dangerous or that have been prohibited by doctor's orders.

5. The program should be flexible enough to adapt to slight variations in the children's abilities. This may include altering equipment or facilities for physically challenged or visually or hearing-impaired children.

6. The program should offer special equipment and activities to meet the special needs of children, such as breathing treatments for children with asthma. The equipment should be in good repair, and the staff should be trained to operate it correctly.

7. The staff should be familiar with each child's medical and developmental status. The staff should recognize symptoms and determine when the child needs medical attention.

If your child has a developmental disability or chronic health condition, don't let that keep him out of child care.

8. If the program includes off-site field trips or activities, the staff should be trained in safe transportation of children with special needs.

9. The staff should know how to reach each child's physician in an emergency and be qualified to administer any necessary emergency medications. Emergency planning should be specified in the child's care plan.

These are general recommendations. Because special needs vary widely, it's impossible to advise more precisely how to determine the best program. If you're having trouble deciding among the programs your pediatrician suggested, go back and discuss your concerns with her. She will work with you to make the right choice.

Whatever your child's special needs, how he will be cared for in your absence is an important decision. The information here should help. However, you know your child better than anyone. Rely most heavily on your impressions when choosing a childcare arrangement.

~ 15 ~

Keeping Your Child Safe

EVERYDAY LIFE IS FULL of well-disguised dangers for children: sharp objects, shaky furniture, reachable hot water faucets, pots on hot stoves, hot tubs, swimming pools, and busy streets. Adults navigate this minefield so well we no longer think of things like scissors and stoves as hazards. To protect your child from the dangers she'll encounter in and out of your home, you have to see the world as she does, and you must recognize she cannot yet distinguish hot from cold or sharp from dull.

Keeping your child physically safe is your most basic responsibility—a never-ending one. Unintentional injuries are the number-one cause of death and disability in children over age one, with drowning and car crashes accounting for a large number of injuries or death. Each year, children experience more than six million emergency department visits for unintentional injury, and more than four thousand children and adolescents under the age of fifteen die from injuries.

Many children are injured or killed by equipment designed specifically for them. In one recent twelve-month period, high-chair-related injuries sent almost 13,000 children to the hospital. In 2017, toys caused more than 183,000 injuries serious enough to require an emergency department visit in children under fifteen.

These are worrisome numbers, but many injuries can be prevented. In the past, injuries were called "accidents" because they seemed unpredictable and unavoidable. Today we know injuries are not random but are often predictable and preventable. By understanding how a child grows and develops, and the risk of injury at each developmental stage, parents can take precautions to prevent most, if not all, of these injuries.

Why Children Get Injured

Every childhood injury involves three elements: factors related to the child, the object that causes the injury, and the environment in which it occurs. To keep your child safe, you must be aware of all three.

Your child's age greatly affects the kind of protection he needs. The three-month-old cooing in an infant seat requires different supervision from the walking ten-month-old or the toddler who's learned to climb. At each stage of your child's life, you must revisit the present hazards and consider how to eliminate them. As your child grows, you must repeatedly ask: How far and how quickly can he move? How high can he reach? What objects attract his attention? What can he do today that he couldn't yesterday? What about tomorrow versus today?

During the first six months, you can secure your child's safety by never leaving him alone, even for a moment, in dangerous situations—for example, on a bed or a changing table where he might fall off. As he grows, he'll create dangers of his own—perhaps by creeping into places he shouldn't, or actively seeking out dangerous things to touch and taste.

For the child on the move, you'll certainly tell him "no" whenever he approaches something potentially hazardous, but he won't understand the significance of your message. Many parents find the ages between six months and eighteen months extremely frustrating, because the child doesn't seem to learn from reprimands. Even if you tell him twenty times a day to stay away from the toilet, he's still in the bathroom every time you turn your back. Your child is not being willfully disobedient; his memory isn't developed enough to recall your warnings when he's attracted by the forbidden object or activity. What looks like naughtiness is actually the testing and retesting of reality—the normal way a child this age learns.

The second year is also risky because a child's physical abilities exceed his understanding of the consequences of his actions. Although judgment has improved, his sense of danger won't be intense enough and his self-control developed enough to make him stop once he's spotted something interesting. At this point, even things he can't see will interest him, so curiosity may take him to the bottom shelf of the refrigerator, the medicine cabinet, or under the sink—to touch things and perhaps to taste.

Young children are extraordinary mimics and may try to take medicine as they've seen Mom do or play with a razor just as Dad does. Yes, your child may realize after the fact that the tugging of the cord is what pulled the curtain rod down on his head, but his ability to anticipate this is still months away.

Gradually, between the ages of two and four years, your child develops a more mature sense of himself as an agent of change—when he flips a switch, the light goes on. Although this thinking eventually helps children avoid danger, at this age they are so self-involved they're likely to see only their part in the action. A child who sees his ball roll into the street will think only about retrieving it, not about the danger of being hit by a car.

The risks of thinking like this are obvious, and they're compounded by something called magical thinking, where a child behaves as if his wishes and expectations actually control what happens. A four-year-old may light a match to recreate the beautiful bonfire he saw on television. It won't occur to him the fire could get out of control; but even if it did, he might discount the possibility because it isn't his idea of what *should* happen.

This type of self-centered, magical thinking is entirely normal. Nonetheless, you must be twice as careful about your child's safety until he outgrows this stage. You can't expect your two- to four-year-old to understand that his actions can have harmful consequences for himself or others. He may throw sand at a playmate because it amuses him and is fun. He will find it difficult to understand that his friend might not enjoy the game.

For all these reasons, you must establish and consistently enforce rules related to safety during the early preschool years. Explain the reasons behind the rules: "You can't throw stones, because you'll hurt your friend"; "Never run into the street, because you could be hit by a car." But don't expect these reasons to be persuasive—or for the rules to be consistently remembered. Repeat the rule every time your child is on the verge of breaking it until he understands that unsafe actions are always unacceptable. For most children, it takes dozens of repetitions before even the most fundamental safety rules are remembered. Be patient. Also, even if he seems to understand, don't assume he will always follow the rules. You still must watch him very closely.

Your child's temperament also may be a factor. Studies suggest that extremely active and unusually curious children have more injuries. At certain stages of development, your child is likely to be stubborn, easily frustrated, aggressive, or unable to concentrate—all characteristics associated with injuries. When you notice your child having a bad day or going through a difficult phase, be especially alert: that's when he's most likely to test safety rules, even those he ordinarily follows.

Since you can't change your child's age, and you have little influence over his basic temperament, most of your efforts to prevent injury should focus on objects and surroundings. By designing an environment where obvious hazards are removed, you can ensure the freedom your child needs to explore.

Some parents feel that childproofing their home is unnecessary because they intend to supervise their children closely. It's true that with constant vigilance, most injuries *can* be avoided. But even the most conscientious parents can't watch a child every moment. Most injuries occur not when parents are alert and at their best but when they're under stress. The following situations are often associated with injuries:

- Hunger and fatigue (e.g., the hour or so before dinner)

- Mother's pregnancy

- Illness or death in the family

- Changes in the child's regular caregiver

- Tension between parents

- Sudden changes in the environment, such as moving to a new home or going on vacation

All families experience some of these stresses. Childproofing eliminates or reduces opportunities for injury, so even with momentary distraction—the telephone or doorbell—your child is less likely to encounter harm-causing situations or objects.

The pages that follow include advice about how to minimize dangers in and out of the home. The intention is to alert you to hazards—particularly those that might seem harmless—so you can take the sensible precautions to keep your child safe and still allow him the freedom to grow up happy and healthy.

Safety Inside Your Home

Room to Room

Your lifestyle and your home's layout will determine which rooms should be childproofed. Examine every room where your child spends time (for most families, that means the entire house). It's tempting to exclude a formal dining or living room behind closed doors, but remember that the forbidden rooms are the ones your child will want most to explore. Any areas not childproofed require extra vigilance on your part, even if entrances are normally locked or blocked. At the very least, your child's room should be a place where everything is as safe as it can be.

Nursery

CRIBS. Your baby is usually unattended in his crib, which should be a totally safe environment. Newborns are at risk for suffocation-related deaths and injuries, especially when there are soft materials in the crib or basinet such as blankets, crib bumpers, pillows, or stuffed animals. In older infants and toddlers, falls are the most common injury associated with cribs, even though they are easiest to prevent. Children are most likely to fall when the mattress is raised too high for their height or not lowered properly as they grow.

It is strongly recommended to use a crib manufactured after June 2011, when a stronger mandatory safety standard was implemented. If your crib has a side that lowers and raises, it is probably too old and should be replaced. Older cribs pose too high a risk of injury to infants.

No matter the age of your crib, inspect it carefully for the following features.

- Slats should be no more than 2⅜ inches (6 cm) apart so a child's head cannot become trapped between them. Widely spaced slats can allow an infant's legs and body to fall through but will trap the infant's head, which can result in death.

- There should be no decorative cut-outs in the headboard or footboard, as your child's head or limbs could become trapped in them.

- If the crib has corner posts, they should be flush with the tops of the end panels, or else be very, very tall (such as posts on a canopy bed). For posts that stick up past the end panels, clothing and ribbons can catch on them and strangle an infant.

- All screws, bolts, nuts, plastic parts, and other hardware should be present and original equipment. Never substitute something from a hardware store for the original parts; obtain replacement parts from the manufacturer. They must be tightly fastened to prevent the crib from coming apart, as otherwise a child's activity could cause the crib to collapse, trapping and suffocating her.

- Before each assembly and weekly thereafter, inspect the crib for damage to hardware, loose joints, missing parts, or sharp edges. Do not use a crib if any parts are missing or broken.

Prevent other crib hazards with the following guidelines.

1. The mattress should be the same size as the crib, with no gaps to trap arms, body, or legs. If more than two fingers can be inserted between the mattress and sides or ends of the crib, the crib/mattress combination should not be used.

2. For a new mattress, remove and destroy all plastic wrapping that comes with it. It can suffocate a child.

3. Before your baby can sit up by himself, lower the mattress to the level where he cannot fall out by leaning against the side or by pulling himself over it. Set the mattress at its lowest position before your child learns to stand. Most falls occur when a baby tries to climb out. Move your child to another bed when he is 35 inches (89 cm) tall, or when the height of the side rail is less than three-quarters his height (approximately nipple level).

4. Periodically check the crib to ensure that no rough edges, sharp metal points, and no splinters or cracks in the wood have developed. If you notice tooth marks on the railing, cover the wood with a plastic strip (available at most children's furniture stores).

5. Do not use bumper pads in cribs. There is no evidence they prevent injuries, and there is risk of suffocation, strangulation, or entrapment. Infant deaths in cribs have been associated with bumper pads. In addition, toddlers can use a bumper guard to climb and fall out.

6. Pillows, quilts, comforters, sheepskins, stuffed animals, and other soft products should not be placed in a crib. Babies can suffocate on such items in the crib.

7. If you hang a mobile, be sure it is securely attached to the side rails. Hang it high and out of reach of the baby, and remove it when he's able to

get up on his hands and knees, or reaches five months, whichever comes first.

8. Crib gyms are not recommended, as infants and toddlers may injure themselves falling forward onto the gym or pulling it down on top of themselves.

9. To prevent the most serious of falls and to keep children from getting caught in window or drapery cords and strangling, don't place a crib—or any other child's bed—near a window. The Consumer Product Safety Commission recommends using cordless window coverings if possible.

10. Keep baby monitor cords at least 3 feet away from the crib and do not place any item with a cord near the crib or under the crib mattress.

CHANGING TABLES. Changing tables make dressing and diapering easier, but falls from such a height can be serious. Don't trust vigilance alone to prevent falls; you should also consider the following recommendations.

1. Choose a sturdy, stable changing table with a 2-inch (5 cm) guardrail on four sides.

2. The top of the changing table pad should be concave, with the middle slightly lower than the sides.

3. Buckle the safety strap, but don't depend on it alone to keep your child secure. Always keep a hand on your baby. Never leave a child unattended on a dressing table, even for a moment, even if he is strapped.

4. Keep diapering supplies within reach—but not your child's reach—so you don't have to leave your baby's side. Baby powder can get in your child's lungs and cause damage, so instead of powder use a diaper cream.

5. If you use disposable diapers, store them out of your child's reach and cover them with clothing when he wears them. Children can suffocate on swallowed, torn-off pieces of the plastic liner.

BUNK BEDS. Although some children love them, bunk beds pose several serious dangers. The child on the top bunk can fall out, and the child on the lower bunk can be injured if the top collapses. The bunk beds might be improperly constructed or assembled, resulting in dangerous structural flaws. Or a mattress that doesn't properly fit could entrap your child. If, despite these warnings, you choose to use bunk beds, take the following precautions.

1. Don't allow a child under six to sleep in the top bunk. She won't have the coordination needed to climb safely or to keep from falling out.

2. Place the beds in a corner of the room so there are walls on two sides. This provides extra support and blocks two sides from possible falls.

3. Don't place beds beside a window. This will help prevent children from falling out of the window or being strangled by window or drapery cords. The Consumer Product Safety Comission (CPSC) recommends using cordless window coverings if possible.

4. The top mattress should fit snugly and not possibly slip over the edge of the frame. If there's a gap, your child might get trapped and suffocate.

5. Attach a ladder to the top bunk bed. Use a nightlight so your child can see the ladder.

6. Install a guardrail on the top bunk. The gap between the side rail and guardrail should be no more than 3½ inches (8¾ cm). Be sure your child can't roll under the guardrail when the mattress on the top bunk is compressed by the weight of her body. If her head gets stuck under the guardrail, she may suffocate or be strangled. You may need a thicker mattress to prevent this.

7. Check the supports under the upper mattress. Wires or slats should run directly under the mattress and be fastened in place at both ends. A mattress supported only by the frame of the bed or unsecured slats could come crashing down.

8. If you separate bunks into two individual beds, remove all dowels or connectors.

9. To prevent falls and collapse of the bed, don't allow children to jump or roughhouse on either bunk.

10. Choose bunk beds with a label stating they comply with ASTM Standard F1427 to ensure they are designed and constructed to be as safe as possible.

Kitchen

The kitchen can be a very dangerous environment for young children. While your child is with you in the kitchen, use a high chair or play yard. He should be securely strapped in (if in a high chair) and within your sight. Keep a toy box or drawer with safe play items in the kitchen to amuse him. Eliminate the most serious dangers by taking the following precautions.

1. Store strong cleaners, lye, furniture polish, dishwasher soap (especially detergent packets), and other dangerous products in a high cabinet, locked and out of sight. Detergent packets pose a special risk for young children, who mistake them for candy; buy powdered or liquid detergent if at all possible. Lye is similarly dangerous and few households use it these days; it's better simply not to have it in the home. If you must store items under the sink, an automatically fastening child safety lock should be used (most hardware, baby supply, and department stores have them). Never transfer dangerous substances into containers that look as if they might hold food, as this may tempt a child to taste them.

2. In the kitchen, keep knives, forks, scissors, and other sharp instruments in a latched drawer separate from "safe" kitchen utensils. Store sharp cutting appliances such as food processors out of reach and/or in a locked cupboard.

3. Unplug appliances when not in use. Don't allow electrical cords to dangle where your child can reach and tug on them, possibly pulling a heavy appliance down on himself.

4. Always turn pot handles toward the back of the stove so your child can't reach up and grab them. Whenever you have to walk with hot liquid—coffee, soup—know where your child is so you don't trip over him. Do not try to carry your child at the same time!

5. When shopping for an oven, choose one that's well insulated to protect your child from the heat if he touches the oven door. Never leave the oven door open.

6. If you have a gas stove, turn the dials firmly to the off position. If they're easy to remove, do so when you aren't cooking so that your child can't turn the stove on. If they cannot be removed easily, use child-resistant knob covers and block access to the stove as much as possible.

7. Keep matches out of reach and out of sight.

8. Don't warm baby bottles in a microwave oven. The liquid heats unevenly, and there may be pockets of milk hot enough to scald your baby. Also, overheated baby bottles have exploded when removed from the microwave.

9. If the microwave is within your child's reach, stay nearby when it is on and never permit your child to open the microwave or remove food or liquids that have finished heating.

10. Keep a fire extinguisher in your kitchen, and on every floor of your home, in a place you'll remember.

11. Do not use small refrigerator magnets your baby could choke on or swallow.

Laundry Room

Children love to help with laundry, but because this room contains several potential hazards, they should never be allowed into the laundry room without adult supervision.

1. Keep detergent, fabric softener, and other products in their original containers. Keep the containers closed tightly and store them in a high, locked cabinet.

2. Single-use detergent packets are highly concentrated and toxic. The packets can burst open if bitten or squeezed by a child, and the contents can shoot down the child's throat or into his eyes and cause breathing or stomach problems, coma, and even death. Detergent packets are often brightly colored and resemble candy or gummy treats. It is best to use traditional liquid or powder detergent products instead of concentrated packets until your child is at least six years old. If you do use detergent packets, the container must be sealed after each use and stored out of sight and reach in a locked cabinet.

3. Clean the dryer lint trap after each use to prevent fires.

Bathroom

The simplest way to avoid bathroom injuries is to make this room inaccessible unless your child is with an adult. This may mean installing a latch on the door at adult height or a top lock. Also, be sure any lock can be unlocked from the outside, in case your child locks himself inside.

Prevent bathroom injuries with the following suggestions.

1. Children can drown in only a few inches of water. **Never leave a young child alone in the bath, even for a moment.** Practice touch supervision by staying within arm's reach of your child anytime he is in or near water, such as a bathtub or swimming pool. If you can't ignore the doorbell or phone, wrap your child in a towel and take him with you to answer it. Bath seats and rings are strongly *not* recommended and will not prevent drowning if the infant is left unattended. Babies can slip out of the seat and be trapped underwater. Do not rely on a bath seat or ring to keep your baby safe, even for a moment. Never leave water in the bathtub when not in use.

2. Install no-slip strips on the bottom of the bathtub. Put a cushioned cover over the water faucet to prevent hurtful bumps on the head.

3. Get in the habit of closing the toilet lid, and use a toilet lid lock. A curious toddler playing in the water can lose his balance, fall in, and drown. A toddler's head is disproportionately heavy, and he may not be able to lift it out of the water.

4. To prevent scalding, the hottest temperature at the faucet should be no more than 120 degrees Fahrenheit (48.9 degrees Celsius). In many cases, you can adjust your water heater. If you're unsure how to set your water heater's temperature, check with the manufacturer. When your child is old enough to turn the faucets, teach him to start the cold water before the hot.

5. All medicine containers should have safety caps. However, remember these caps are child-*resistant,* not childproof. Store all medicines and cosmetics high and out of sight and reach in a locked cabinet. Don't keep toothpaste, soaps, shampoos, and other frequently used items in the same cabinet as medicines. Instead, store all medications in a hard-to-reach cabinet equipped with a safety latch or lock. Get rid of old or unused medications. Refer to the package insert or label for direction on safe ways to dispose of medications. If the label does not provide instructions on safe disposal, look for take-back programs in your community, often sponsored by your local hospital, law enforcement, or waste management facility.

6. If you use electrical appliances in the bathroom, particularly hair dryers and razors, unplug and store them in a cabinet with a safety lock when not in use. All bathroom wall sockets should be GFCI outlets, which automatically shut off when in contact with water, to lessen the likelihood of electrical injury if an appliance falls into the sink or bathwater. It's even better to use them in another room where there is no water. Ask an electrician to check your bathroom electrical outlets and install GFCI safety outlets if needed.

Garage and Basement

Garages and basements are places where potentially lethal tools and chemicals are stored. Keep doors locked, with self-closing doors, and make both areas strictly off-limits. To minimize the risk when children do gain access to the garage and basement:

1. Keep paints, varnishes, thinners, pesticides, and fertilizers in a locked cabinet or locker. Always keep these substances in their original, labeled containers.

2. Store tools in a safe locked area out of reach. This includes sharp items like saw blades. Be sure power tools are unplugged and locked in a cabinet when not in use.

3. Do not allow your child to play near the garage or driveway where cars may be coming and going. Many children are killed when playing in the driveway when someone, often a family member, unintentionally backs over them. Most vehicles have large blind spots where a child cannot be seen even if the driver is watching the mirrors carefully. Even backup cameras are no match for small, fast-moving children.

4. If you have an automatic garage door opener, be sure your child is nowhere near the door before it's opened or closed. Keep the opener out of reach and sight. Make sure the automatic reversing mechanism is properly adjusted to avoid crushing a child as the door is closing.

5. Never leave a car running in the garage, as dangerous carbon monoxide gas can collect quickly in a partly enclosed space.

6. If, for some reason, you must store an unused refrigerator or freezer, remove the door so a child cannot become trapped if he crawls inside.

7. Do not allow your child to ride on a riding lawnmower, as children can fall off and be injured by the blades. Do not mow while a child is playing on the lawn, since lawnmowers can send rocks and other dangerous projectiles flying at high speeds.

All Rooms

Certain safety rules and preventive actions apply to every room. The following safeguards against commonplace household dangers will protect not only your small child, but your entire family.

1. To prevent injuries from fire and carbon monoxide, install smoke and carbon monoxide detectors throughout your home, at least one on every level and inside and outside bedrooms. Check them monthly to be sure they are working. It is best to use smoke detectors with long-life batteries, but if these are not available, change the batteries annually on a date you will remember. If possible, install networked smoke detectors so that when one alarms they all alarm. Develop a fire escape plan and practice it so that you'll be prepared if an emergency does occur.

2. To prevent electrocution injuries, put non-choking-hazard safety plugs or covers in all unused electrical outlets so your child can't stick her finger or a toy into the holes. If your child won't stay away from outlets, block access to them with furniture. Keep electrical cords out of reach and sight.

3. To prevent slipping, carpet your stairs where possible. Be sure the carpet is firmly tacked down at the edges. When your child is just learning to crawl and walk, install safety gates at both the top and bottom of stairs. Avoid accordion-style gates, which can trap an arm or neck, and instead use gates firmly mounted to the home's studs.

4. Certain houseplants may be harmful. The Poison Help line (1-800-222-1222) or the National Capital Poison Center (poison.org/articles/plant) has a list or description of plants to avoid. You may want to forgo house plants for a while, or, at the very least, keep house plants out of reach.

Safe, horizontal-type gate with slats 2⅜ inches (6 cm) apart

5. To prevent a choking injury, check floors constantly for small objects a child might swallow, such as coins, buttons, beads, pins, and screws. The best way to check is to get down at your child's level and see what's there. This is particularly important if someone in the household has a hobby involving small items, or if there are older children who have small items.

6. Small button batteries can cause life-threatening risks when inhaled or swallowed. These batteries are found in many common household and personal products, such as small remote controls, cameras, garage door openers, flameless candles, watches, toys, and hearing aids. If ingested, they can cause serious damage to the esophagus or intestines and may result in death. They also can burn holes inside the nose if lodged in there. Know what products in the house use these batteries and keep them out of reach of children. Swallowing a button battery is a medical emergency, and children suspected of having swallowed a button battery or inserted one into their nose should be immediately taken to the emergency department.

7. Children can suffer head injuries and cuts or injuries to their teeth when they fall while running. If you have hardwood floors, don't let your child run around in socks, which make slippery floors even more dangerous.

8. The Consumer Product Safety Commission recommends using cordless window coverings in all homes with children to prevent children from becoming strangled by cords. If your window products are not cordless, attach cords for window blinds and drapes to floor mounts that hold them taut, or wrap cords around wall brackets to keep them out of reach. Use safety stop devices on the cords. Cords with loops should be cut and equipped with safety tassels.

9. Pay attention to doors between rooms. Glass doors are particularly dangerous, because a child may run into them. Fasten them open if possible. Swinging doors can knock a small child down, and folding doors can pinch little fingers. If you have either, consider removing them until your child is old enough to understand how they work.

10. Sharp edges of furniture can injure a running or falling child. Check your home for furniture with hard edges and sharp corners that could injure your child (coffee tables are a particular hazard). If possible, remove dangerous furniture from traffic areas, particularly when your child is learning to walk. You also can buy cushioned corner and edge protectors that can be applied to furniture.

11. To prevent crush injuries from furniture, test the stability of large pieces of furniture, such as floor lamps, bookshelves, and television stands.

Put floor lamps behind other furniture and anchor bookcases, dressers, and TV stands to the wall. Deaths and injuries occur when children climb onto, fall against, or pull themselves up on large pieces of furniture. Secure televisions to the wall or to a low, stable stand designed to hold them; children have died from being crushed by a falling television.

12. Keep computers out of reach so that your child cannot pull them over onto themselves. Cords should be out of sight and reach.

13. To prevent fall injuries from windows, open windows from the top if possible. If you must open them from the bottom, install operable window guards only an adult or older child can open. A screen is not strong enough to prevent a fall. Never put chairs, sofas, low tables, or anything else a child might climb on in front of a window. Doing so gives her access to the window and creates an opportunity for a serious fall.

14. To prevent suffocation injuries, never leave plastic bags lying around the house, and don't store children's clothes or toys in them, as children can suffocate inside them. Dry-cleaning bags are particularly dangerous. Knot them before you throw them away so that it's impossible for your child to crawl into them or pull them over her head. Even a small torn-off piece can become a potential choking hazard.

15. Think about the potential hazard of anything you put into the trash. Any trash container used for potentially dangerous items—spoiled food, discarded razor blades, batteries—should have a child-resistant cover or be kept out of reach.

WHERE WE STAND

THE MOST EFFECTIVE WAY to prevent firearm-related injury to children is to keep guns out of homes and communities. The American Academy of Pediatrics strongly supports gun-safety legislation. We believe that assault weapons and high-capacity ammunition magazines should be banned.

Furthermore, the AAP recommends that handguns and handgun ammunition be regulated, that restrictions be placed on handgun ownership, and that the number of privately owned handguns be reduced. Firearms should be removed from environments where children live and play, but if they are not, they *must* be stored locked and unloaded. Safe storage practices can reduce the risk of death or injury, but loaded firearms, unloaded firearms, and ammunition represent a serious danger to children.

16. To prevent burns, check your heat sources. Fireplaces, woodstoves, and kerosene heaters should be screened so your child can't get near them. Gas fireplaces with glass doors get extremely hot and can cause severe burns when touched. Check electric baseboard heaters, radiators, and even vents from hot-air furnaces to see how hot they get when the heat is on. They, too, may need to be screened.

17. A firearm should not be kept in the home or environment of a child. If you must keep a firearm in the house, keep it unloaded and locked away. Lock ammunition in a separate location. If your child plays in other homes, ask if guns are present there, and if so, how they are stored. (Also see *Where We Stand* on page 487.)

18. Alcohol can be very toxic to a young child. Keep all alcoholic beverages in a locked cabinet and empty any unfinished drinks immediately.

Baby Equipment

During the past thirty years, the Consumer Product Safety Commission has taken an active role in setting safety standards to assure the safety of equipment manufactured for children and infants. Because many of these rules went into effect in the early 1970s, you must pay special attention to the safety of furniture made before then. The following guidelines will help you select the safest possible baby equipment, whether used or new, and utilize it properly.

High Chairs

Falls are the most serious danger associated with high chairs. To minimize the risk of your child falling:

1. Select a chair with a wide base, so it can't tip over.

2. If the chair folds, make sure the locking device is secure each time you set it up.

3. Strap your child in with the shoulder, waist, and crotch safety straps whenever he sits in the chair. Never allow him to stand in the high chair.

4. Don't place the high chair near a counter or table or within reach of a hot or dangerous object. Your child may be able to push hard enough against these surfaces to tip the chair over.

5. Never leave a young child unattended in a high chair, and don't allow older children to climb or play on it, as this could cause it to tip over.

6. A high chair that hooks onto a table is *not* a substitute for a more solid one. But if you plan to use such a model when you eat out or travel, look for one that locks onto the table. Be sure the table is heavy enough to support your child's weight without tipping. Also, check to see whether his feet can touch a table support. If he can push against it, he may be able to dislodge the seat from the table.

7. Check that all caps or plugs on chair tubing are firmly attached and cannot be pulled off; these could be choking hazards.

Infant Seats and Bouncers

Infant seats and bouncers should be labeled to meet CPSC safety standard F2167. Use care in selecting an infant seat. Check the weight guidelines provided by the manufacturer, and don't use the seat after your baby has outgrown it. Here are some other safety guidelines to follow.

1. Do not put the seat above floor level. The most serious injuries associated with infant seats occur when a baby falls from a high surface, such as tables, countertops, and chairs. Even small infants can jiggle a seat or carrier off a surface and fall, suffering head trauma and other injuries. To keep an active, squirming baby from tipping the seat over, place it on a carpeted area near you and away from sharp-edged furniture. Infant seats also may tip over when placed on soft surfaces, such as beds or upholstered furniture; these are not safe places for infant seats.

2. Never leave a baby unattended in an infant seat.

3. Never use an infant seat as a substitute for a car safety seat. Infant seats are designed only for propping a baby up so that she can see, play, or be fed more easily.

4. Always buckle the safety strap and harness.

5. Choose a seat with an outside frame that allows the infant to sit deep inside. Be sure the base is wide, to prevent tipping over.

6. Look at the bottom of the infant seat to ensure that it's covered with a nonskid material.

7. Parents should remove the infant from the seat when moving the location of the seat to avoid falling or other injuries to the baby.

8. Never place a baby in an infant seat or a car safety seat on the roof or back of a car, even for a moment.

9. Infants should never sleep in a sitting device without direct line-of-sight supervision and should be moved to an approved crib when feasible.

Play Yards

Most parents depend on play yards (sometimes called playpens) as a safe place to put a baby when Mom or Dad isn't available to watch him every moment. Yet play yards, too, can be dangerous under certain circumstances. To prevent mishaps:

1. Choose a play yard with a label stating it meets ASTM F406, a safety standard that will ensure it is designed and built to prevent injuries. This standard is mandatory for all new play yards.

2. Do not add a supplemental mattress to the play yard. These are a suffocation hazard. Your baby will be comfortable using just the mattress that came with the play yard. If your baby sleeps in the play yard, follow safe sleep practices: remove pillows, blankets, and stuffed toys and put your baby on his back.

3. Never leave the side of a mesh play yard lowered. An infant who rolls into the pocket created by the slack mesh can become trapped and suffocate.

4. Do not tie toys to the sides or across the top of a play yard, as a baby or toddler can become entangled.

5. If your play yard has a raised changing table, always remove the changing table when your child is in the play yard so he cannot become entrapped or strangled in the space between the changing table and the side rail.

6. When your child can pull himself to a standing position, remove any boxes or large toys in the play yard he could use to climb out.

7. Teething children may gnaw on the top rails. Check them periodically for tears and holes in the fabric. If the tears are small, repair them with heavy-duty cloth tape; if more extensive, contact the manufacturer to find out how to repair.

8. Be sure a play yard's mesh is free of tears, holes, or loose threads and the openings are less than ¼ inch (0.6 cm) across, so your child cannot get caught in it. The mesh should be securely attached to the top rail and floor plate. If staples are used, they should not be missing, loose, or exposed. Slats on wooden play yards should be no more than 2⅜ inches (6 cm) apart, so your child's head cannot become trapped between them.

9. Circular enclosures made from accordion-style fences are extremely dangerous. Children can get their heads caught in the diamond-shaped openings and the V-shaped border at the top of the gate. Never use such an enclosure, either indoors or out.

Walkers

The American Academy of Pediatrics does not recommend the use of mobile infant walkers. Children can fall down stairs, leading to head injuries. If the walker runs into an object like a table or bookshelf, objects may fall off them and injure the child. Walkers do not help a child learn to walk, and they can delay normal motor development. A stationary walker or activity center is a better choice. These do not have wheels, but seats that rotate and bounce. You may also consider a sturdy wagon or a kiddie push car. The toy should have a bar she can push and be weighted so it won't tip over when she pulls herself up on it.

Pacifiers

Pacifiers will not harm your baby. In fact, there is evidence that pacifiers may help reduce the risk of sudden infant death syndrome (SIDS) when your infant is being put to sleep. However, for maximum safety use the following tips when using a pacifier:

1. Do not use the top and nipple from a baby bottle as a pacifier, even if you tape them together. If the baby sucks hard, the nipple may pop out of the ring and choke her.

2. Purchase pacifiers that cannot possibly come apart. If you are in doubt, ask your pediatrician for a recommendation.

3. The shield between the nipple and the ring should be at least 1½ inches (3.8 cm) across, so the infant cannot take the entire pacifier into her mouth. Also, the shield should be made of firm plastic or silicone with ventilation holes.

4. Never tie a pacifier to your child's crib or around your child's neck or hand. This is very dangerous and could cause serious injury or even death.

5. Pacifiers deteriorate over time. Inspect them periodically to see whether the rubber is discolored or torn. If so, replace them.

6. Follow the recommended age range on the pacifier, as older children can sometimes fit smaller newborn-size pacifiers in their mouths and choke.

Toy Boxes and Toy Chests

A toy box can be dangerous for two reasons: a child could become trapped inside, or a hinged lid could fall on your child's head or body while he is searching for a toy. If possible, store toys on open shelves your child can get to easily. If you must use a toy box:

1. Look for one with no top, a lightweight removable lid, or sliding doors or panels. However, little fingers can easily be injured under lids and between sliding doors and panels.

2. If you use a toy box with a hinged lid, be sure it has a lid support that holds the lid open at any angle. If your toy box didn't come with such a support, install one yourself—or remove the lid.

3. Look for a toy box with rounded or padded edges and corners, or add the padding yourself.

4. Children occasionally get trapped inside toy boxes. Your box should have ventilation holes or a gap between the lid and the box. Don't block the holes by pushing the box tight against a wall. The lid should not latch.

Toys

Most toy manufacturers want to produce safe toys, but they cannot always anticipate the way a child might use—or abuse—their products. In 2017, there were an estimated 251,000 toy-related injuries treated in US emergency rooms. Of these, 35 percent (89,483) involved children under age five. If your child is injured by an unsafe product or you would like to report a product-related injury, visit saferproducts.gov. The Consumer Product Safety Commission keeps a record of complaints and initiates recalls of dangerous toys, clothing, jewelry, and other household products. Your phone call may protect not only your child, but others as well.

When selecting or using toys, always observe the following safety guidelines:

1. Match toys to your child's age and abilities. Follow the manufacturers' guidelines on the packaging.

2. Rattles—probably your child's first toy—should be at least 1⅝ inches (4 cm) across. An infant's mouth and throat are very flexible, and a smaller rattle could cause choking. Rattles should have no detachable parts.

3. Toys should be constructed of sturdy materials that won't break or shatter when a child throws or bangs them.

4. Check squeeze toys to ensure the squeaker can't become detached.

5. Before giving your child a stuffed animal or a doll, the eyes and other parts should be firmly attached; check them periodically. Remove all ribbons. If a doll comes packaged with accessories, don't allow your child to suck on a doll pacifier or any other accessory small enough to be swallowed.

6. Swallowing or inhaling small toy parts is a serious danger to young children. Inspect toys carefully for small parts that could fit in your child's mouth and throat. Look for toys labeled for children three and under, because they must meet federal guidelines requiring they have no small parts likely to be swallowed or inhaled.

7. Toys with small magnets are especially dangerous. If more than one magnet is swallowed, the magnets can attract each other in the child's body and cause intestinal blockages, perforations, and even death. Keep toys with small magnets away from children.

8. Toys with small parts purchased for older children should be stored out of reach of younger ones. Impress on your older child the importance of picking up all the pieces from such toys when she's finished playing. You should check that there are no items dangerous for your baby left out. Consider restricting the use of these toys to a small area or places inaccessible to the baby.

9. Don't let a child play with balloons; she may inhale a balloon if she tries to blow it up. If a balloon pops, pick up and discard all the pieces. Mylar balloons are a safer choice than latex.

10. To prevent both burns and electrical shocks, don't give young children (under age ten) a toy that must be plugged into an electrical outlet. Instead, buy battery-operated toys. Be sure that the battery cover is securely fastened in an enclosure that requires a screwdriver or other tool to open to prevent a loose battery from becoming a choking hazard. All newer battery-powered toys meet this guideline, but check older toys, and do not use them if the batteries can be accessed without a screwdriver.

11. Ensure that teething children do not have access to electrical cords, which they might bite through, risking electrical burns.

12. Carefully inspect toys with mechanical parts for springs, gears, or hinges that could trap a child's fingers, hair, or clothing.

13. Register any applicable toys with the manufacturer in order to be informed of any recalls.

14. To prevent cuts, check toys to ensure they don't have sharp edges or pointed pieces. Avoid toys with parts made of glass or rigid plastic that could crack or shatter.

15. Don't allow your child to play with very noisy toys, including squeeze toys with unexpectedly loud squeakers. Noise levels at or above 100 decibels can damage hearing.

How to Report Unsafe Products

If you become aware of an unsafe product used by children—or if your child suffers an injury related to a particular product—report it to the Consumer Product Safety Commission (CPSC) at saferproducts.gov. Your report is important for helping the CPSC identify hazardous products requiring further investigation or a potential recall.

16. Projectile toys such as dart guns or slingshots are not suitable for children. They can easily cause eye injuries. Never give your child a toy that fires anything except water.

Safety Outside the Home

Even if you create the perfect environment inside your home, your child will spend a lot of time outside, where surroundings are less controllable. Obviously, your personal supervision will remain the most valuable protection, but even a well-supervised child is exposed to many hazards. The following information will show how to eliminate many of these hazards and reduce the risk your child will be injured.

Car Safety Seats (Child Safety Seats)

Each year more children between the ages of one and nineteen are killed in car crashes than any other way. Many deaths can be prevented if the children are properly restrained in a car safety seat when riding in a motor vehicle. Contrary to what some believe, a parent's lap is the most dangerous place for a child to ride. In a car crash or even a sudden stop or swerve, you wouldn't be able to hold on to your child, and your body would crush hers as you were thrown against the dashboard and windshield. Not even the strongest adult can hold a child while experiencing the massive forces of a crash. The single most important thing to keep your child safe in the car is to buy, install, and use an approved car safety seat, appropriate for the age and size of your child, every time she rides in the car. Children should ride in the rear seat until they turn thirteen years old in order to prevent brain or spine injuries from front seat airbags.

Car safety seats are required by law in all fifty states, the District of Columbia, and US territories. Unfortunately, studies consistently show that many parents do not use them properly. The most common mistakes include facing car safety seats in the wrong direction (facing forward too soon), not keeping your child in a car safety seat long enough, placing rear-facing seats in front of an airbag, failing to strap or fasten the child into the car safety seat,

Rear-facing-only car safety seat

failing to securely fasten the child's car safety seat to the vehicle seat, not adequately tightening the straps, not using a booster seat for older children, and letting a child ride in the front seat. Also, some parents don't use the car safety seat on short trips. They are not aware that most fatal crashes occur within 5 miles (8 km) of home and at speeds of less than 25 miles (40 km) per hour. For all these reasons, children continue to be at risk. It's not enough to have a car safety seat—you must use it correctly, every time, in the backseat.

Choosing a Car Safety Seat

Here are guidelines to select a car safety seat.

1. The American Academy of Pediatrics annually publishes a list of car safety seats available, "Car Safety Seats: Product Listing," which can be found online at healthychildren.org/carseatlist.

2. No one seat is "safest" or "best." The "best" car safety seat is one that fits your child's size and weight, and can be installed correctly in your car and used correctly on every trip.

3. Price does not always make a difference. Higher prices can mean added features that may or may not make the seat easier to use.

4. When you find a seat you like, try it out. Put your child in the seat and adjust the harnesses and buckles. Make sure it fits in your car and that the harnesses are easy to adjust when the seat is in your car. Many big-box stores will allow you to take a loaner seat out to your car to see how it fits.

5. If your baby is born preterm or at low birth weight, she should be observed in her car safety seat by hospital staff before leaving the hospital to ensure that the semi-reclined position does not cause low heart rate, low oxygen, or other breathing problems. If the pediatrician advises you that your baby needs to lie flat during travel, use a crash-tested car bed. If possible, an adult should ride in the backseat next to your baby to watch her closely.

6. Children with special health problems may need other restraint systems. Discuss this with your pediatrician. (More information about safe transportation of children with special health needs is available from the Automotive Safety Program by phone at 1-800-543-6227 or on their website at preventinjury.org.)

7. If your car was manufactured after 2002, always install your car safety seat using the LATCH system, which provides reinforced steel rings between and behind the seats. Just clip, tighten, and go. If you're not sure where to find the rings, check your car's owner's manual.

Belt-positioning booster seat

8. Do not use a car safety seat that is too old. The label has the date of manufacture. Many manufacturers recommend seats be used for only six years. Check the instruction manual for the expiration date; this may also be found on a label on the seat or stamped into the plastic shell. Over time, and with exposure to heat and cold, the car safety seat parts can become weakened. It is important *not* to use a car safety seat past the manufacturer's expiration date.

Forward-facing car safety seat

9. If a car safety seat was in a moderate or severe crash, it may have been weakened and should *not* be used, even if it looks fine. Seats that were in minor crashes may still be safe to use. A crash is considered minor if the vehicle can be driven away from the crash, the door closest to the car safety seat was not damaged, no one in the vehicle was injured, the airbags did not go off, and you can't see any damage to the car safety seat. Some manufacturers still recommend replacing a seat after even a minor crash. Call the car safety seat manufacturer if you have questions about your seat. Only use a seat if you know its full history.

10. It is best to use a new car safety seat. If you choose a used car safety seat, be absolutely sure it has never been in any crash, all the labels and instructions are present, and it has not been recalled.

11. Do not use a car safety seat missing a label with the date of manufacture and seat name or model number. Without these, you cannot check on recalls.

12. Do not use a car safety seat with missing instructions. You need them to know how to use the car safety seat. Do not rely on the former owner's directions. Get a copy of the instruction manual from the manufacturer or download a copy from the manufacturer's website before you use the seat.

13. Do not use a car safety seat with cracks in the frame of the seat or missing parts.

14. Register your car safety seat with the manufacturer so you can be notified promptly in the event of a recall. If you do not have the original registration card, you can register the seat on the manufacturer's website or by calling its customer service department.

15. You can find out if your car safety seat has been recalled by calling the manufacturer or the US Department of Transportation's Vehicle Safety Hotline at 1-888-327-4236 from 8 A.M. to 8 P.M. ET, Monday through Friday. This information is also available on the National Highway Traffic Safety Administration website: odi.nhtsa.dot.gov/recalls/childseat.cfm. If the seat has been recalled, follow instructions to fix it or get the necessary parts.

Types of Car Safety Seats

Infants/Toddlers

All infants and toddlers should ride in a rear-facing car safety seat as long as possible, or until they reach the highest weight or height allowed by the car safety seat manufacturer. They should be positioned in the rear seat. This is the safest way to ride. Nearly all convertible car safety seats have rear-facing weight and height limits that allow most children to ride rear-facing well past the second birthday.

Toddlers/Preschoolers

Children who have outgrown the rear-facing weight or height limit for their car safety seat should use a forward-facing car safety seat with a five-point harness positioned in the rear seat of the vehicle. Children should use a car safety seat for as long as possible, up to the highest weight or height allowed by their car safety seat's manufacturer.

School-Age Children

All children whose weight or height is above the forward-facing limit for their car safety seat should use a belt-positioning booster seat until the vehicle seatbelt fits properly, typically when they have reached about 4 feet 9 inches in height and are between eight and twelve years old. They should always ride in the backseat to avoid injury from front seat airbags.

Older Children

When children are old enough and large enough to use the vehicle seatbelt alone, they should always use lap and shoulder seatbelts for optimal protection. All children younger than thirteen years should be restrained in the rear seats for optimal protection. **Children seven years and younger are not old enough or large enough to ride safely without a car safety seat or booster seat.**

Travel Vests

A travel vest may be an option while traveling, if your car or taxicab has only lap belts. Travel vests are designed for children between 20 and 168 pounds and are an alternative to traditional forward-facing seats. They are useful in a vehicle with lap-only seatbelts in the rear or for children whose weight exceeds that allowed by traditional car safety seats. These vests may require use of a top tether.

Installing a Car Safety Seat

1. Read your vehicle owner's manual for important information on how to install the car safety seat correctly in your vehicle.

2. To prevent head and spine injuries from the deployment of an airbag in the event of a crash, the safest place for all children to ride is in the backseat. Avoid driving more children than can be buckled safely in the backseat.

3. Never place a child in a rear-facing car safety seat in the front seat of a vehicle with a passenger airbag. All new cars have airbags. When used with seatbelts, airbags work very well to protect older children and adults. However, airbags are very dangerous when used with rear-facing car safety seats. If your car has a passenger airbag, children in rear-facing seats *must* ride in the backseat. Even in a low-speed crash, the airbag can inflate, strike the car safety seat, and cause serious brain injury and death. Toddlers who ride in forward-facing car safety seats are also at risk from airbag injuries. Remember, *all* children younger than thirteen are safest in the backseat.

If you have a pickup truck without a backseat or with a backseat that is too small for a properly installed car safety seat, it may be possible in some cases to install a car safety seat in the front seat. Keep in mind, though, that a rear-facing car safety seat can **never** be installed in a seating position with an active front airbag. Do not rely on the vehicle sensor to disable the airbag; only use that seating position if the airbag can be deactivated with a key. Installing a car safety seat in a pickup truck, even in the backseat if there is one, can be more complicated than installing in a typical vehicle, so read the owner's manuals for both the pickup truck and the car safety seat and follow the instructions carefully.

4. Car safety seats can be installed using either the vehicle seatbelts or LATCH (Lower Anchors and Tethers for Children). LATCH is a system of lower anchors located in the seat bight (where the vehicle cushions meet) and tether anchors located on the shelf behind the seat (in most sedans) or on the floor, ceiling, or back of the seat (in most minivans, SUVs, and hatchbacks). The systems are equally safe, but in some cases, it may be easier to install a seat tightly using LATCH.

5. Place the seat facing the correct direction for the size and age of your child. Route the seatbelt or LATCH strap through the correct path on the car safety seat (check your instructions to make sure) and pull it tight. Before each trip, check to make sure the car safety seat is installed tightly enough by pulling on the car safety seat where the seatbelt or LATCH strap passes through. It should not move more than an inch side to side or toward the front of the car.

6. If your infant's head flops forward, the seat may not be reclined enough. Recline the seat to the correct angle according to the manufacturer's instructions; there may be different recline settings for very young infants and for older babies. Your seat may have a recline indicator to help determine whether the angle is correct and a built-in adjuster for this purpose. If not, you may wedge firm padding, such as a rolled towel, under the seat's front base.

7. If the seatbelt buckle lies just at the point where the belt bends around the car safety seat, it may be impossible to make the belt tight enough. If you cannot get the belt tight, try another position in the car or consider using LATCH if it is available.

8. If you install a car safety seat using the vehicle seatbelt instead of LATCH, the seatbelt must be locked tightly in place. In many vehicles, you can lock the seatbelt by pulling the shoulder belt all the way out, then feeding it back into the retractor. In many cases, it may be easier or the car safety seat manufacturer may advise using a built-in lock-off or locking clip that comes with the car safety seat to lock the seatbelt. Read your car owner's manual and car safety seat instructions to determine the best way to lock the seatbelt.

9. In rare situations, a lap-only belt may need a special, heavy-duty locking clip, available from the vehicle manufacturer. Check your car owner's manual for more information.

10. Before using LATCH, check the car safety seat and vehicle instructions for information, including the weight limits for the lower anchors and attachments and which seating positions can be used for LATCH installation. Check the vehicle instruction manual to ensure you don't attach the tether to a cargo tie-down or other attachment point not designed as a tether anchor.

11. Tethers should always be used with forward-facing car safety seats. Most anchors are located on the rear window ledge, the back of the vehicle seat, or the floor or ceiling of the vehicle. Tethers give extra protection by keeping the car safety seat from being thrown forward in a crash. All new cars, minivans, and light trucks are required to have tether anchors for securing the tops of car safety seats. If your vehicle was manufactured before September 2000, it may be possible to have a tether anchor installed by a dealer, often at no cost.

12. For specific information about installing your car safety seat, consult a certified child passenger safety (CPS) technician. A list of certified CPS technicians is available by state or ZIP code at cert.safekids.org. A list of inspection stations staffed by certified CPS technicians is also available online at nhtsa.gov/equipment/car-seats-and-booster-seats. In addition, the information can be accessed by telephone on the Department of Transportation's Vehicle Safety Hotline at 1-888-327-4236, from 8 A.M. to 8 P.M. ET, Monday through Friday.

Using the Car Safety Seat

1. A car safety seat protects your child only if she is buckled securely *every* time she rides—no exceptions, beginning with your baby's first ride home from the hospital. Help your child form a lifelong habit of buckling up by *always* using your seatbelt. If you have two cars, buy two seats or transfer the seat to the car in which your child will be traveling. Remember never to place a rear-facing car safety seat in the front seat if there is an airbag. The safest place for all children to ride is in the back.

2. Read and follow the car safety seat manufacturer's instructions, and always keep them with the car safety seat. If you lose the instructions, call or write the manufacturer for a replacement. In many cases, you can download the instructions from the manufacturer's website.

3. Most children go through a stage when they protest whenever you put them in the car safety seat. Explain firmly you cannot drive until everyone is buckled. Then back up your words with action.

4. Use the correct harness slots for the child. When riding rear-facing, the harness straps should be at or below your child's shoulder level. When riding forward-facing, they should be at or above the shoulders. Some seats do not have slots, but instead use a sliding mechanism to move the harness straps up and down. Read the instructions to see how and where to adjust the harness strap height.

5. The harness straps should be snug against your child's body. Dress your baby in clothes that allow the straps to go between her legs. Keep the straps snug so they hold your child securely; if you can pinch a fold of webbing between your fingers, it is too loose. Be certain the straps lie flat and are not twisted.

6. If needed to keep your newborn from slouching, pad the sides of the seat and behind the crotch strap with rolled-up diapers or receiving blankets. Do not use add-on products behind the baby or between the baby and the harness straps; these can cause the straps to not restrain the baby properly in a crash. Never use any add-on products unless they came with your car safety seat or are specifically allowed by the manufacturer's instructions.

7. In cold weather, dress your baby in thinner layers rather than thickly padded clothes, and tuck blankets around your baby *after* adjusting the harness straps snugly. Do not use bunting products that have a layer that goes underneath your baby.

8. In hot weather, drape a towel over the seat when the car is in the sun. Before putting your child in the seat, test the fabrics and metal buckle with your hand to ensure they aren't hot.

9. No matter how short your errand is, **never leave an infant or child alone in a car.** She can get overheated or too cold very quickly, even if the temperature outside seems mild, or she may become frightened and panicky when she realizes she's alone. Children left alone in cars in hot weather can die from hyperthermia (overheating) in less than ten minutes. Any child alone in a car is also a target for abduction, and older children may be tempted to play with things like cigarette lighters, power windows, or the gear shift, which could cause serious injury or death. Any parent, no matter how loving and attentive, is capable of forgetting a child in the car. Take steps to prevent this by incorporating visual reminders or check-ins into your routine:

■ Put something you need at your destination, like your purse or briefcase or a shoe, in the backseat, where you have to open the back door to retrieve it.

- Put a large stuffed toy in the car safety seat when your child is not in the car, and when your child rides with you, move the toy into the front seat where you will see it.

- Ask your childcare provider to call if your child does not arrive when expected.

- Be especially vigilant when the usual routine is changed; the risk of forgetting a child is higher during such disruptions.

- Lock your car and set the parking brake when not in use so children cannot get inside. Overheating deaths have occurred when children got into cars to play. If a child is missing, check the pool or other body of water first, and then check the car, including the trunk.

10. Always use your seatbelt. In addition to setting a good example, you'll reduce your own risk of injury or death in a crash by 60 percent.

11. Children will outgrow their booster seats when they are older, often eight to twelve years of age. They can use the seatbelt alone when it fits properly over strong bones, meaning that the lap belt fits low and snug across the thighs, the shoulder belt lies across the middle of the chest, and they can sit all the way back on the vehicle seat with knees bent over the edge without slouching and can stay in that position for the whole ride.

12. Never let your infant sleep in a car safety seat outside of the car.

13. Never place your infant in a car safety seat with partially buckled straps, as there is a risk of strangulation.

Airbag Safety

An airbag can save your life. However, airbags and young children do not mix. The following information will help keep you and your children safe. (This information is worth repeating.)

- The safest place to ride for all infants and children under thirteen years is in the backseat. When front seat airbags deploy, they can injure children's brains or spines.

- Never put a rear-facing car safety seat in the front seat of a car with an airbag. Your child can suffer a serious injury or death from the impact of the airbag against the back of the car safety seat. (See pages 499–500 of this chapter for information on pickup trucks and car safety seats.)

■ Infants and toddlers should ride in a rear-facing car safety seat until they reach the height or weight limit set by the manufacturer. Nearly all convertible car safety seats have weight and height limits that will allow most children to ride rear-facing well past the second birthday. Rear-facing is the safest way to ride. It is best to ride that way as long as possible.

■ All children should be properly secured in car safety seats or booster seats correct for their age and size.

■ Side airbags improve safety for adults in side impact crashes. When children ride next to side airbags, it is essential they be restrained in the proper position. Read your car safety seat manual for guidance on placing the seat next to a side airbag, and refer to your vehicle owner's manual for recommendations that apply to your vehicle.

Keeping Your Child Happy and Safe on the Road

As hard as you may try to enforce car safety seat and seatbelt use, your child may resist these constraints as he gets older. Here are some tips to keep him occupied and content—and also safe—while the car is in motion.

BIRTH TO NINE MONTHS

■ Ensure your newborn's comfort by padding the sides of his car safety seat with receiving blankets if necessary to prevent slouching. Padding should only be added outside the harness straps, **never** under your baby or between your baby and the harness straps.

■ If needed, place a small rolled-up cloth diaper or receiving blanket between the crotch strap and your baby to prevent his lower body from sliding too far forward.

■ If your infant's head flops forward, double-check whether the seat has been reclined enough. Follow the manufacturer's instructions on how to achieve the proper recline angle.

NINE MONTHS TO TWENTY-FOUR MONTHS

■ Children this age love to climb and may want desperately to get out of the car safety seat. If this describes your child, remind yourself this is only a phase. As mentioned, in a calm but stern voice, insist he stay in his seat whenever the car is on the road. Let him know the car cannot move unless everyone is buckled in, then follow through if he tries to escape his seat. Keep the harness straps snug and the harness clip at chest level to make it more difficult for him to escape.

■ Entertain your toddler by talking or singing with him as you drive. However, never do this to the point where it distracts you from paying attention to driving.

TWENTY-FOUR MONTHS TO THIRTY-SIX MONTHS

■ Make driving a learning experience by talking about what your child sees out the window, as long as this doesn't distract from driving.

■ Encourage your child to buckle his toy animals or dolls into a seatbelt and talk about how safe the toy is being buckled in.

PRESCHOOLERS

■ Talk about safety as "grown-up" behavior, and praise your child whenever he voluntarily buckles in.

■ Encourage your child to accept the car safety seat or booster seat by suggesting make-believe roles, such as astronaut, pilot, or race-car driver.

■ Explain why the car safety seat is important: "If we have to stop suddenly, the straps keep you from bumping your head."

■ Show him books and pictures with safety messages.

■ Always wear your seatbelt, and make sure everyone else in the car does, too.

■ Seatbelts must be worn correctly at all times by all passengers to provide the best protection.

Kids Around Cars

From a young age, teach children not to walk or play in the street or driveway. Young children are not safe around streets and should not play near them. While they have the skills to get to roads and streets, they do not have the ability to recognize streets and cars are dangerous. Children move quickly and impulsively. They are curious. Yet they have difficulty seeing cars in their peripheral vision, localizing sounds, and understanding traffic and the meaning of signs and signals. They cannot judge speed and vehicle distance. Add in drivers who may be multitasking and not looking out for young children playing near the street, and a disaster could be in the making. If children are near streets, hands-on supervision is necessary for quick intervention if your child darts into the street to get a ball or to run after an older child.

To avoid injuries from vehicle backovers, driveways, alleyways, and any adjacent unfenced front yards should not be used as play areas. Parents should remember the large blind spots behind cars (especially in bigger, elevated vehi-

WHERE WE STAND

ALL FIFTY STATES require children to ride in car safety seats. The American Academy of Pediatrics urges that all newborns discharged from hospitals be brought home in rear-facing car safety seats. The AAP has established car safety seat guidelines for low-birth-weight infants, which include riding in a rear-facing seat and supporting the infant with ample padding around the sides, outside the harness system. A convertible car safety seat is recommended as a child gets older.

Infants and young children must always ride in car safety seats—preferably in the backseat. Never use a rear-facing car safety seat in the front seat of a vehicle equipped with a passenger-side airbag. An infant or child should never ride in an adult's arms. Children age twelve and younger should ride in the rear seat.

Older children should use booster seats until the vehicle safety belt fits well, meaning the shoulder belt crosses the middle of the child's chest, the lap belt is low and snug across the thighs, the child can sit all the way back on the vehicle seat with knees bent at the edge, and the child is able to sit this way the entire ride. This position helps avoid injuries to the neck and internal organs from the seatbelt in case of an accident.

cles) and the need to walk completely around the car before getting in and starting the engine. Never assume that having a backup camera is adequate to prevent backing over a fast-moving small child. Adults should make a point of knowing where the children are before putting a vehicle in reverse.

Baby Carriers: Backpacks, Front Packs, and Slings

Back and front carriers for infants are very popular. For your baby's—and your own—comfort and safety, follow these guidelines when purchasing and using baby carriers.

1. Infants born prematurely or with respiratory problems should not be placed in backpacks or other upright positioning devices, as the positioning in these devices may make it harder for them to breathe.

2. Some sling carriers may curl your baby's body into a C-shape, which greatly increases the risk of breathing problems. If you use a sling, your baby's neck should be straight and his chin not pressed into his chest, and make sure you can always see his face.

3. In any type of carrier, check frequently to ensure that your baby's mouth and nose are not blocked by fabric or your body and that airflow is not restricted. The CPSC warns about the suffocation hazard to infants, particularly those younger than four months, carried in infant sling carriers. When infant slings are used for carrying, it is important to ensure that the infant's head is up and above the fabric, the face is visible, and the nose and mouth are clear of obstructions.

4. Take your baby with you when you shop for the carrier so you can match it to his size. Make sure the carrier supports his back and the leg holes are small enough that he can't possibly slip through. Look for sturdy material.

5. If you buy a backpack, the aluminum frame should be padded, so your baby won't be hurt if he bumps against it. A sunshade is also a good idea to shield your baby from the sun.

6. Check the pack periodically for rips and tears in the seams and fasteners.

7. When using a baby carrier, bend at the knees, not the waist, if you need to pick something up. Otherwise, the baby may tip out of the carrier, and you may hurt your back.

8. Babies over five months old may become restless in the carrier, so continue to use the restraining straps. Some children will brace their feet against the frame or against your body, changing their weight distribution. You should be certain your child is seated properly before you walk.

Strollers

Look for safety features and take the following precautions.

1. If you string toys across your stroller, fasten them securely so they can't fall on the baby. Remove such toys as soon as the baby can sit or rise on all fours.

2. Strollers should have easy-to-operate brakes. Use the brake whenever stopped, and ensure your child can't reach the release lever. A brake that locks two wheels rather than just one provides an extra measure of safety.

3. Select a stroller with a wide base, to avoid tipping.

4. Children's fingers can become caught in the folding hinges of the stroller. Keep your child at a safe distance when opening and closing. Securely lock open the stroller before putting your child in. Check that your baby's fingers cannot reach the stroller wheels.

5. Don't hang bags or other items from the handles of your stroller—they can make it tip backward. If the stroller has a basket for carrying things, be sure it is low and near the rear wheels.

6. The stroller should have a five-point harness (with straps over both shoulders, hips, and between the legs) that should be used whenever your child goes for a ride. For infants, use rolled-up baby blankets on either side of the seat if necessary to prevent slouching.

7. Never leave your child unattended in a stroller. If he falls asleep in his stroller, make sure you can see him at all times.

8. If you purchase a side-by-side twin stroller, the footrest should extend all the way across both sitting areas. A child's foot can become trapped between separate footrests.

9. There are also strollers that allow an older child to sit or stand in the rear. Be mindful of weight guidelines and especially careful that the child in the back doesn't become overly active and tip the stroller.

Shopping Cart Safety

More than twenty thousand children are treated in emergency departments for shopping cart–related injuries each year. The most frequent kinds of injuries are contusions, abrasions, and lacerations, and most injuries are to the head or neck. Shopping cart–related injuries can be serious enough to require hospitalization, often because of head injuries and serious fractures. Some deaths have even occurred.

Shopping carts are often unstable; it may take as little as 16 pounds (7.26 kg) of force on the handle to tip a cart. The design of shopping carts makes them tip over easily when a child is in the cart or the seat designed to fit on the cart. The seats attached to the top of shopping carts or built into them won't prevent a child from falling out if she isn't properly restrained; these seats also won't prevent the cart from tipping over even if the child is restrained.

If possible, seek an alternative to placing your child in a shopping cart; consider using a stroller or baby carrier instead. If you must use a shopping cart, make sure she is restrained at all times. Never allow her to stand in the cart, be transported in the basket, or ride on the outside. Do not snap an infant car safety seat onto the built-in cart seat, as this can make the cart even more unstable. If one is available, use a shopping cart designed to carry children in a seat lower to the ground. Never leave a child alone in a shopping cart, even for a moment.

Bicycles and Tricycles

If you like to ride a bicycle, you'll probably consider getting a child carrier that attaches to the back of the bike. You should be aware that even with the best carrier and safety helmet, your child is at risk for serious injury. This can occur when you lose control of the bike, or if you should happen to strike or be struck by another vehicle. It is wiser to wait and enjoy bicycling together when your child is old enough to ride on his own. (Further information about child carriers can be found later in this section.)

As your child outgrows babyhood, he will want a tricycle of his own, and when he gets one, he'll be exposed to a number of hazards. A child on a tricycle is low to the ground and can't be seen by motorists who are backing up. Nevertheless, riding trikes and bikes is almost an essential part of growing up. Here are some safety suggestions to help reduce the risk to your child.

1. Don't buy a tricycle until your child is physically able. Most children are ready around age three.

2. Buy a tricycle built low to the ground with big wheels. This type is safer because it is less likely to tip over.

3. Obtain a properly fitting bicycle helmet, and teach your child to use it every time he rides. The chin strap should fit snugly under his chin, and the helmet should not have excessive movement over his forehead when strapped properly. Your child should always wear closed-toe shoes to protect his toes and feet when on a tricycle or bike.

4. Tricycles should be used only in protected places. Don't allow your child to ride near automobiles, driveways, or swimming pools.

5. Do not push your child to ride a two-wheel bicycle before he is ready. Choose a bicycle that is small enough for him to put both feet on the ground comfortably and start with training wheels if needed. Consider a bike with no pedals to help your child develop balance and muscle coordination. To protect your child from injury, he should wear an approved and appropriately fitting bicycle helmet (meeting Consumer Product Safety Commission standards, certified on the label).

6. If you're considering having your child ride as a passenger in a rear-mounted seat on an adult's bike, keep in mind that not only will he make the bike unstable, but he will also increase braking time and raise the risk of serious injury to both of you. If you must carry your child on a bike, never put him in a seat on the back of your bicycle until he's at least one year old. A much better choice is for your child to ride in a bicycle-towed child trailer, although trailers should not be used on roadways, as they are low and may not be seen by motorists. Children old enough (twelve months to four years) to sit well unsupported and whose necks are strong enough to support a lightweight helmet may be carried in a rear-mounted seat, although it is not the preferred choice. *Never* carry infants in backpacks or front packs on a bike.

7. A rear-mounted seat must:

    a. Be securely attached over the rear wheel

    b. Have spoke guards to prevent feet and hands from being caught in the wheels

    c. Have a high back and a sturdy shoulder harness and lap belt to support a sleeping child

8. A young passenger should always wear a lightweight infant bike helmet certified for young children, to prevent or minimize head injury.

9. The child must be strapped into the bike seat with a sturdy harness.

10. Never ride with a child on the front handlebars or place a seat there.

Playgrounds

Whether it's a backyard swing set or a more elaborate apparatus in a park, there are many positive things about playground equipment. This equipment encourages children to test and expand their physical abilities. However, there are inevitable dangers. The risks are minimized when equipment is well designed and children are taught basic playground manners. Use the following guidelines in selecting playground equipment and sites.

1. Children under five should play on equipment separate from older children.

2. To prevent or mitigate injuries from falls from playground equipment, make sure there is well-maintained sand, wood chips, or rubberized matting of proper depth under swings, seesaws, and jungle gyms. On concrete or asphalt, a fall can cause serious injury to the head—even from just a few inches high.

3. Wooden structures should be made from all-weather wood, which is less likely to splinter. Examine the surfaces periodically to be sure they are smooth. Metal structures can get extremely hot in warmer months, so take a moment to check the temperature of metal equipment yourself before allowing your children on it.

4. Conduct a periodic inspection of equipment, looking especially for loose joints, open chains that could come loose, and rusted cotter pins. Be sure there are no open S-shaped hooks or protruding pieces that could hook a child's clothing. On metal equipment, check for rusted or exposed bolts as well as sharp edges and points. At home, cover them with protective rubber. In a public playground, report the hazard to the appropriate authorities.

5. Be sure swings are made of soft and flexible material. Insist your child sit in the middle of the seat, holding with both hands. Don't allow two children to share the same swing. Teach your child never to walk in front of or behind a swing while used by another child. Avoid equipment in which the swings hang from overhead climbing bars.

6. Your child should wear closed-toe shoes at all times, as surfaces can become hot enough to cause serious burns to bare feet.

7. Be sure children on slides use the ladder instead of climbing up the sliding surface. Don't permit pushing and shoving on the ladder, and have children go up one at a time. Teach your child to leave the bottom of the slide as soon as he reaches it. If a slide has been sitting in the sun, check the sliding surface to see if it's too hot to use.

8. Don't allow children under four to use climbing equipment taller than they are (e.g., jungle gyms) without close supervision.

9. Between the ages of three and five, your child should use a seesaw only with other children of comparable age and weight. Children under three don't have the arm and leg coordination to use the equipment.

10. Although trampolines often are considered fun for children, about a hundred thousand people per year are injured on them, including backyard models. Childhood injuries have included broken bones, head injuries, neck and spinal cord injuries, sprains, and bruises. Parental supervision and protective netting aren't adequate to prevent these injuries. Between 2013 and 2017 there were approximately 96,500 trampoline-related injuries each year, resulting in about 1,120 hospitalizations annually. Children five years and younger have a greater risk of injury, compared with older children. The American Academy of Pediatrics strongly discourages the use of trampolines for recreational use, whether at home, a friend's house, playground, or a routine gym class. Older children should use trampolines only in training programs for competitive sports such as gymnastics or diving, and only when supervised by a professional trained in trampoline safety.

If, despite these warnings, you choose to have a home trampoline, take the following precautions:

■ Place the trampoline on a level surface free from surrounding hazards.

■ Inspect the protective padding and the net enclosure often. Replace any damaged parts. (About 20 percent of trampoline injuries are related to direct contact with the springs and frame.)

■ Allow only one person on the trampoline at a time. (Most trampoline injuries occur when there are multiple jumpers, particularly younger ones.)

■ Do not permit users to do somersaults or flips.

■ An adult should supervise any child while she's on the trampoline and enforce the rules.

■ Check your homeowners insurance policy to make certain you are covered for trampoline-related claims. If not, a rider to the policy may be needed.

Your Backyard

Your backyard can be a safe play area for your child if you eliminate potential hazards.

1. If you don't have a fenced yard, teach your child the boundaries where he should play. He may not always follow your guidelines, so watch him very closely. Always have a responsible person supervise outdoor play, as young children may wander off or get injured. (See a description of trampoline safety on pages 512–13.)

2. Check your yard for dangerous plants, and teach your child never to pick and eat anything from a plant, no matter how good it looks, without your permission. Among preschoolers, plants are a leading cause of poisoning. If you are unsure about the plants in your yard, call the Poison Help line (1-800-222-1222) and request a list of poisonous plants common to your area. If you have poisonous plants, either replace them or securely fence and lock that area of the yard.

3. If you use pesticides or herbicides on your lawn or garden, use only organic-approved products, and read and follow the instructions carefully. Don't allow children to play on a treated lawn for at least forty-eight hours.

4. Don't use a power mower to cut the lawn when young children are around. Mowers may throw sticks or stones with enough force to injure children. Never have your child on a riding mower even when you are driving. It is safest to keep young children indoors while the lawn is being mowed.

5. When you cook food outdoors, screen the grill so your child cannot touch it, and explain that it is hot like the stove in the kitchen. Store propane grills so your child cannot reach the knobs. Be sure charcoal is cold before dumping it.

6. Never allow your child to play unattended near traffic or in the street, and do not allow her to cross the street by herself, even to a waiting school bus.

Water Safety

Water is one of the most dangerous hazards your child will encounter. Young children can drown in only a few inches of water, even if they've had swimming instruction. All children should learn to swim starting at age four, but parents should know swimming instruction and skills do not provide "drownproofing" for children of any age. The American Academy of Pediatrics now believes children ages one to four may be less likely to drown if they have had formal

WHERE WE STAND

THE AMERICAN ACADEMY OF PEDIATRICS feels strongly that parents should never—even for a moment—leave children alone near open bodies of water (lakes, swimming pools), nor near water in homes (bathtubs, spas). For backyard pools, rigid, motorized pool covers are not a substitute for four-sided fencing, since pool covers are unlikely to be used appropriately and consistently. Parents should learn CPR and keep a telephone and emergency equipment (e.g., life preservers) at poolside. Parents should stay within arm's length of young children whenever they are swimming and avoid distractions such as mobile phones.

swimming instruction with a focus on water survival. Even so, because the studies are small, and because they don't define what type of lessons work best, the American Academy of Pediatrics is not recommending *mandatory* swim lessons for all children ages one to four at this time. Instead, a parent's decision to enroll young children in swim lessons should be based on the child's frequency of exposure to water, his emotional development, his physical abilities, and certain health concerns related to pool water infections and pool chemicals. The following can be helpful when considering swimming lessons.

1. You may be lulled into being less cautious because you think your child can swim, and children themselves may be emboldened to enter water without supervision.

2. Young children repeatedly immersed in water may swallow so much they develop water intoxication. This can result in convulsions, shock, and even death.

3. Children aged four and older can learn swimming skills more quickly than at a younger age, particularly as their motor development reaches the five-year-old level. All children should be taught to swim once they are developmentally ready.

4. Safety training does not result in a significant increase in poolside safety skills of young children.

Children under age one may participate in swimming programs with a parent as a fun, recreational activity, but because there is no evidence programs intended to prevent drowning in infants less than one year are effective or safe, they should *not* be given this type of swim lessons.

When selecting a swimming program, choose a class that adheres to guidelines established by the national YMCA. Remember, even a child who knows how to swim needs to be watched constantly. Whenever your child is near water (e.g., swimming pools, ponds, beach, etc.), follow these safety rules.

1. Be aware of small bodies of water your child might encounter, such as fishponds, ditches, fountains, rain barrels, watering cans—even a five-gallon bucket used for car washing. Empty water containers when done using them. Children are drawn to water and need constant supervision to ensure they don't fall in. Remember that bacterial and chemical contamination can render any body of water unsafe, so check advisories before allowing your child to swim anywhere.

2. Children who are swimming—even in a shallow toddler's pool—always should be watched by an adult, preferably one who knows CPR. (See *Cardiopulmonary Resuscitation [CPR] and Mouth-to-Mouth Resus-*

citation, page 699.) The adult should be within arm's length, providing "touch supervision," whenever young children and those without swimming skills are in or around water. Empty and put away inflatable pools after each play session.

3. Enforce safety rules: no running near the pool and no pushing others underwater.

4. Don't allow your child to use inflatable toys or mattresses to keep him afloat. These toys may deflate suddenly, or your child may slip off them into water that is too deep.

5. Be sure the deep and shallow ends of any pool are clearly marked. Never allow your child to dive into the shallow end.

6. If you have a home swimming pool, it should be completely surrounded with at least a 4-foot-high (1.2 m) four-sided fence that is not attached to the house. It should have a self-closing, self-latching gate that opens away from the pool. Check the gate frequently to ensure that it is in good working order. Keep the gate closed and locked at all times. Be sure your child cannot manipulate the lock or climb the fence. No opening under the fence or between uprights should be more than 4 inches (10 cm) wide. Keep toys out of the pool area when not in use so children are not tempted to get through the fence.

7. If your pool has a cover, remove it completely before swimming. Also, never allow your child to walk on the pool cover; water may have accumulated on it, making it as dangerous as the pool itself. Your child also could fall through and become trapped underneath. Do not use a pool cover in place of a four-sided fence because it is unlikely to be used appropriately and consistently.

8. Keep a safety ring with a rope beside the pool at all times. If possible, have a phone in the pool area with emergency numbers clearly marked.

9. Spas and hot tubs are dangerous for young children, who can easily drown or become overheated. Don't allow young children to use these facilities unless the temperature is turned down to 98 degrees Fahrenheit (approximately 36.6 degrees Celsius) and you are within arm's reach at all times. Even then, limit soaks to no more than fifteen minutes.

10. Your child should always wear a life jacket or "boat coat" when swimming or riding in boats. A life jacket fits properly if you can't lift it off over your child's head after being fastened in. For the child under age five, particularly the non-swimmer, it also should have a flotation collar to keep the head upright and the face out of the water.

11. Adults should not drink alcohol or use sedating medications when swimming or boating. It presents a danger for them as well as children they might be supervising. Adult supervisors should know CPR and how to swim.

12. Eliminate distractions while children are in the water. Talking on the phone, working on the computer, and other tasks need to wait until children are out of and away from water.

Safety Around Animals

Children are more likely than adults to be bitten by domesticated animals, including your family pet. This is particularly true when a new baby is brought home. At such times, the pet's response should be observed carefully, and it should not be left alone with the infant. After a two- or three-week get-acquainted period, the animal may become used to the baby. However, it is always wise to be cautious when the animal is around, regardless of how much your pet seems to enjoy the relationship.

If you are getting a companion pet for your child, wait until he is mature enough to handle and care for the animal—usually around age five or six. Younger children have difficulty distinguishing an animal from a toy, so they may inadvertently provoke a bite through teasing or mistreatment. Remember you have ultimate responsibility for your child's safety around any animal, so take the following precautions.

1. Look for a pet with a gentle disposition. An older animal is often a good choice, because a puppy or kitten may bite out of sheer friskiness. Avoid older pets raised in homes without children, however.

2. Treat your pet humanely so it will enjoy human company. Don't tie a dog on a short rope or chain. Extreme confinement may make it anxious and aggressive.

3. Never leave a young child alone with an animal. Many bites occur during periods of playful roughhousing, because the child doesn't realize the animal is overexcited.

4. Teach your child not to put his face close to an animal.

5. Don't allow your child to tease your pet by pulling its tail or taking away a toy or a bone. Make sure he doesn't disturb the animal when it's sleeping or eating.

6. Have all pets—both dogs and cats—immunized against rabies.

7. Obey local ordinances about licensing and leashing your pet. Be sure your pet is under your control at all times.

8. Find out which neighbors have dogs, so your child can meet animals he's likely to come into contact with. Teach your child how to greet a dog: After asking the owner for permission, the child should stand still while the dog sniffs him; then he can slowly extend his hand to pet the animal.

9. Warn your child to stay away from yards with seemingly high-strung or unfriendly dogs. Teach older children the signs of an unsafe dog: rigid body, stiff tail at "half mast," hysterical barking, crouched position, staring expression.

10. Instruct your child to stand still if approached or chased by a strange dog. Tell him not to run, ride his bicycle, kick, or make threatening gestures. Your child should face the dog and back away slowly until out of reach, while avoiding eye contact, which dogs find challenging.

11. Wild animals can carry serious diseases that may be transmitted to humans. You (and family pets) need to avoid contact with rodents and other wild animals (raccoons, skunks, foxes) that can carry diseases ranging from hantavirus to plague, toxoplasmosis to rabies. To avoid wild animal bites, notify the health department or animal control whenever you see an animal that seems sick or injured, or one acting strangely. Don't try to catch the animal or pick it up. Teach your child to avoid all undomesticated animals. Fortunately, most wild animals are nocturnal and tend to shy away from humans. A wild animal found in your yard or neighborhood during the daytime might have an infectious disease like rabies, and you should contact local authorities.

In the Community and Neighborhood

Many parents worry about keeping their child safe in and around the neighborhood. Fortunately, child abductions are rare, although they understandably get plenty of media attention when they occur. Most abductions occur when children are taken by noncustodial parents, although a smaller number of abductions by strangers do take place each year.

Here are some suggestions to help keep your child safe.

- When shopping with your child, keep an eye on him at all times. He is able to move quickly in and out of sight in an instant. You might encourage your child to hold on to your hand whenever you're out.

- When choosing a preschool, ask about safety issues. Make sure a policy exists where your child is picked up only by a parent or another designated person.

- Although your child should be supervised by a trusted adult at all times, it is still important to teach him to never get into a car or go along with someone unfamiliar. If a stranger tells him something like "There's a lost puppy in my car; come into the car for a minute and see if you know him," he should emphatically say "no." In fact, he should run away as fast as possible from dangers like this and yell very loudly and find a trusted adult in any situation where he feels threatened.

- When hiring babysitters, always check references and/or ask for recommendations from friends and family members.

- For more information, contact the National Center for Missing & Exploited Children (1-800-843-5678; missingkids.com).

When planning ways to keep your child safe, remember he is constantly changing. Strategies that protect him from danger when he's one year old may no longer be adequate as he grows and becomes stronger, more curious, and more confident. Review your family's home and habits often to ensure your safeguards remain appropriate for your child's age and balance supervision with opportunities to learn and play independently.

A Message for Grandparents

Your grandchild's well-being and safety are extremely important. Particularly when he is under your care—at your home, in his, in the car, or elsewhere—make sure you've taken every step possible to ensure he is safe and secure.

Take the time to read this chapter from beginning to end. It will provide you with guidelines to protect your grandchild in the situations he's most likely to encounter. Before you have your grandchild visit or stay at your home, make certain you've reviewed and adopted the recommendations you'll find here. In this special section, you'll find the most important safety points for grandparents to follow.

(continues on next page)

SAFETY INSIDE THE HOME

There are plenty of safety measures you should implement to protect your grandchild.

- Smoke detectors and carbon monoxide detectors should be placed in the proper locations throughout the house.

- Pets and pet food should be kept out of a child's reach.

- Escape plans should be thought about in advance, and fire extinguishers should be readily available.

- Gates should be positioned at the top and bottom of stairs.

- Medications should always be out of sight and out of reach of children and stored in child-resistant containers. Store your purse or any bags away from grandchildren if any medications are kept in there.

- Soft covers or bumpers should be positioned around sharp or solid furniture.

In addition to these general rules, be sure to keep important phone numbers by the telephone and programmed into your mobile phone. In an emergency, you'll want to call not only 911 when appropriate, but also certain specific family members.

Another safety consideration is that walking aids could be unstable and present a risk; if possible, move them into the closet or a room your grandchild won't be able to enter when he visits. Read on to review safety measures for specific areas of your home.

NURSERY/SLEEPING AREA

- If you stored your own child's crib in your attic or garage, perhaps awaiting the arrival of a grandchild someday, replace it with a new one. Guidelines for children's furniture and equipment have changed dramatically, and a crib made before June 2011 will not meet today's safety standards. This is likely true for other saved and aging furniture that could pose risks to children, such as old play yards.

- Buy a changing table (see page 479), use your own bed, or even place a towel on the floor to change the baby's diapers. As he gets older and more likely to squirm, you may need a second person to help change his diaper.

■ Don't allow your grandchild to sleep in your bed.

KITCHEN

■ Put "kiddie locks" on lower cabinets; to be extra safe, move unsafe cleansers and chemicals so they're completely out of reach.

■ Remove any dangling cords, such as those from the coffeepot or toaster.

■ Take extra precautions before giving your grandchild food prepared in microwave ovens. Microwaves can heat liquids and solids unevenly, and food may be mildly warm on the outside but *very hot* on the inside.

BATHROOMS

■ Store pills, inhalers, and other prescription or nonprescription medications, as well as medical equipment, locked and out of the reach of your grandchild. Be especially vigilant that medications of any kind are kept up and away from a child's reach and sight. Dispose of old or unused medications by following the instructions on the medicine label or package insert. If the label doesn't give instructions, look for a drug take-back program in your community.

■ Put nonslip material in the bathtub to avoid dangerous falls.

■ If there are handles and bars in the bathtub for your use, cover them with soft material if bathing the baby there.

■ Never leave a child unattended in a tub or sink filled with water.

BABY EQUIPMENT

■ Never leave your grandchild alone in a high chair or in an infant seat located in high places, such as a table or countertop.

■ Do not use mobile baby walkers.

TOYS

■ Buy new toys for your grandchild with a variety of sounds, sights, and colors. Simple toys can be just as good as more complex ones. Remem-

(continues on next page)

ber, no matter how fancy the toy, your own interaction with your grand-child is much more important.

■ Toys, books, programs, and other electronic content should be age-appropriate and challenge children at their developmental level.

■ Avoid toys with small parts babies could put into their mouths and swallow. Follow the package recommendations to find toys suitable for your grandchild's age.

■ Keep small button batteries, used in hearing aids and some remote controls, out of reach of children. When children swallow or inhale these batteries or put them in their noses, they can cause life-threatening chemical burns.

■ Because toy boxes can be dangerous, keep them out of your home, or look for one without a top or lid.

GARAGE/BASEMENT

■ Make sure the automatic reversing mechanism on the garage door is operating.

■ Never leave a car running in the garage, as deadly carbon monoxide gas can collect quickly.

■ Keep all garden chemicals and pesticides as well as tools in a locked cabinet and out of reach.

SAFETY OUTSIDE THE HOME

Buy a car safety seat to keep inside your car. Make sure it's installed properly (or have a trained professional install it) and that you can strap your grandchild into it easily. Experiment with the buckles and clasps before you buy the car safety seat, since their ease of use varies. Make sure you know your grandchild is out of harm's way before backing your car out of the garage or down the driveway.

■ Purchase a stroller to use in your neighborhood.

■ On shopping trips, whenever possible choose stores offering child-friendly shopping carts with seats low to the ground. Don't place your car safety seat into a shopping cart, and avoid putting your grandchild in the seat at the top of the cart if possible.

- If you have a tricycle or bicycle at your home for your grandchild, make sure you also have a helmet for him, and make sure he wears closed-toe shoes to protect his feet and toes. You can let him choose a helmet in a special design or color so he wants to wear it.

- Although playgrounds can be fun, they also can be dangerous. Select one that has been designed to keep children as safe as possible; those at schools or at community-sponsored parks are often good choices.

- Inspect your own backyard for anything hazardous or poisonous.

- Keep your grandchild out of the yard when a lawnmower or other power yard tool is being used. Never let your child ride on your lap while mowing.

- If you have a backyard swimming pool, or if you take your grandchild to another home or park with a pool, **carefully read the water safety guidelines in this chapter (see pages 514–17). There should be at least a 4-foot-high (1.2 m) four-sided fence with a self-closing, self-latching gate surrounding the pool.** Make sure neighbors' pools are enclosed by fences as well. Even if your grandchild seems to be a good swimmer, practice touch supervision anytime your grandchild is in or near water. You should also know CPR and how to swim.

~ PART 2 ~

~ 16 ~

Abdominal/Gastrointestinal Tract

Abdominal Pain

Children of all ages experience abdominal pain occasionally, but the causes of such pain in infants tend to be quite different from what they are in older children. So, too, is the way children of different age groups react to the pain. An older child may rub her abdomen and tell you she's having a "bellyache" or "tummyache," while a very young infant will show her distress by crying and pulling up her legs or by passing gas. Vomiting or excessive burping also may accompany crying in babies with abdominal pain.

Fortunately, most stomachaches disappear on their own and are not serious. However, if your child's complaints continue or worsen over a period of three to five hours, or if she has a fever, severe sore throat, or extreme and sustained change in appetite or energy level, you should notify your pediatrician immediately. These symptoms may indicate a more serious disorder.

In this section, you'll find descriptions of problems that lead to abdominal pain in children, from colic to intestinal infections. Also, because some causes of abdominal pain occur predominantly in older children rather than infants, a separate portion is devoted to those particular disorders (like constipation). You'll be referred to other sections of this chapter and other chapters in the book as well, for more detailed descriptions of some of these disorders.

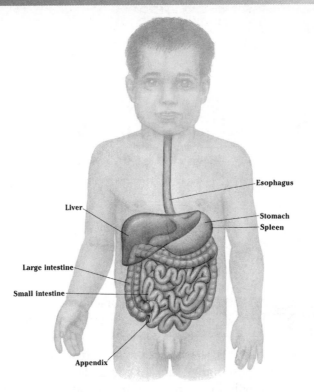

Abdomen/Gastrointestinal Tract

Abdominal Pain in Infants

Colic usually occurs in infants between the ages of ten days and three months of age and typically improves after three months, resolving by one year of age at the latest. While no one knows exactly what causes it, colic certainly looks like abdominal discomfort. The discomfort often is more severe in the late afternoon and early evening, and may be accompanied by inconsolable crying, pulling up of the legs, frequent passage of gas, and general irritability. You can try a variety of approaches to colic, which might include rocking your baby, walking with her in a baby carrier, swaddling her in a blanket, or giving her a pacifier. Some probiotic supplements have shown promise in easing colic symptoms. (For more information about colic, see page 167 in Chapter 6, *The First Month*.)

Intussusception is a rare condition that may cause abdominal pain in young infants. Intussusception is the most common abdominal emergency in children under age two. This problem occurs when one part of the intestine slides inside another and becomes trapped, creating a blockage that causes severe pain. The child will intermittently and abruptly cry and pull her legs toward her stomach. This will be followed by periods without stomach pain and often without any distress. These children also may vomit and have dark, mucus-filled, bloody stools that often look like blackberry jelly. The pain is frequently severe, with periods of screaming followed by periods of quiet or even periods of lethargy.

It is important to recognize this cause of abdominal pain and to talk to your pediatrician immediately. She will want to see your child and perhaps order an ultrasound or an X-ray called an air contrast or barium enema. Sometimes doing this test not only enables the diagnosis but also unblocks the intestine. If the enema does not unblock the intestine, an emergency operation may be necessary to correct the problem.

Viral or bacterial infections of the intestine (gastroenteritis) are usually associated with diarrhea and/or vomiting. On-and-off abdominal pain is often also present. Most cases are viral, require no treatment, and will resolve on their own within several days to a week; the pain itself generally lasts one or two days and then disappears. One exception is an infection caused by the *Giardia lamblia* parasite. This infestation may produce periodic recurrent pain not localized to any one part of the abdomen. The pain may persist for weeks or months and can lead to a marked loss of appetite and weight. Treatment with appropriate medication can cure this parasitic infection and the abdominal pain that accompanies it. (For more

information, see *Diarrhea*, page 537, and *Vomiting*, page 555.)

Abdominal Pain in Older Children

Appendicitis is very rare in children under age three and uncommon under the age of five. When it does occur, the first sign is often a complaint of constant stomachache in the center of the abdomen, and later the pain moves down and over to the right side. (See *Appendicitis*, page 531, for more detailed information.) Children with appendicitis typically stop eating and won't want to eat their favorite food if offered.

Constipation often is blamed for abdominal pain, and while it's rarely a problem in younger infants, it's a common cause of pain in older children, especially when pain is in the lower part of the abdomen. When a child's diet lacks plenty of fluids, fresh fruits and vegetables, and whole grains rich in fiber, bowel problems are more likely to occur. (For more information, talk to your pediatrician, and see *Constipation* on page 534.)

Emotional upset in school-age children sometimes causes recurrent abdominal pain that has no other obvious cause. Although this pain rarely occurs before age five, it can happen to a younger child who is under unusual stress. The first clue is pain that tends to come and go over a period of more than a week, often associated with activity that is stressful or unpleasant. In addition, there are no other associated findings or complaints (fever, vomiting, diarrhea, coughing, lethargy or weakness, urinary tract symptoms, sore throat, or flu-like symptoms). There also may be a family history of this type of illness. Finally, your child probably will act either quieter or noisier than usual and have trouble expressing her thoughts or feelings. If this type of behavior occurs with your child, find out if there's something troubling her at home or school or with siblings, relatives, or friends. Has she recently lost a close friend or a pet? Has there been a death of a family member, or the divorce or separation of her parents?

Your pediatrician can suggest ways to help your child talk about her troubles. For example, he may advise you to use toys or games to help the child act out her problems. If you need additional assistance, the pediatrician may refer you to a child therapist, psychologist, or psychiatrist.

Lead poisoning most often occurs in toddlers living in an older house (built before the 1960s) where lead-based paint has been used. Children in this age group may eat small chips of paint off the walls and woodwork. The lead is then stored in their bodies and can create many serious health problems. Parents also should be aware of toys, dishes, or other products with unacceptable lead content. (Recalls are posted on the US Consumer Product Safety Commission website at cpsc .gov.) Symptoms of lead poisoning include not only abdominal pain, but

also constipation, irritability (the child is fussy, crying, difficult to satisfy), lethargy (she is sleepy, doesn't want to play, has a poor appetite), and convulsions. If your child is exposed to lead paint, has eaten paint chips, has been exposed to toys with cracking, peeling, or chipping paint, and has any of the above symptoms, call your pediatrician. She can order a blood test for lead and advise you as to what else needs to be done. For all children, it is a good idea to be tested for lead as early as nine to twelve months of age, as often there are no symptoms, especially in young infants. (See *Lead Poisoning*, page 727.)

Milk allergy is a reaction to the protein in milk, usually in younger infants, and can produce cramping abdominal pain, often accompanied by vomiting, diarrhea, blood in the stool, and skin rash.

Strep throat is a throat infection caused by bacteria called streptococci, or strep. It occurs frequently in children over two years of age. The symptoms and signs include a sore throat, fever, and ironically, abdominal pain. This is because swallowed bacteria can cause irritation of the bowels. Children can also get perianal strep, which is a strep infection around their anus. This can cause pain, constipation (because they don't want to stool), and abdominal pain as well. Your pediatrician can examine your child for either type of infection and may swab her throat or anus to check for the bacteria. If the results are positive for strep, your child will need to be treated with an antibiotic. (See *Sore Throat*, page 681.)

Urinary tract infections (UTIs) are much more common in one- to five-year-old girls than in younger children. UTIs may produce pain in the lower abdomen (the bladder area) but are also usually associated with pain and burning when urinating. Children with UTIs typically urinate small volumes and more frequently, have blood in their urine or have urinary accidents, and may or may not have a fever. If your child complains of these symptoms, take her to the pediatrician, who will examine her and check her urine. Both a urinalysis and urine culture should be obtained to confirm a UTI. If an infection is present, an antibiotic will be prescribed, which will eliminate both the infection and the abdominal pain. (See *Urinary Tract Infections*, page 790.)

Appendicitis

The appendix is a narrow, finger-shaped, hollow structure attached to the large intestine. While it serves no known purpose in humans, it can cause serious problems when it becomes inflamed. Because of its location, this can happen quite easily; for instance, a piece of food or stool can get trapped inside, causing the appendix to swell and become inflamed and infected. This is called appendicitis. It is most common in children over the age of six but can occur in younger

children. Once infected, the child must be hospitalized. Treatment commonly includes antibiotics, IV fluids, and often surgery. If surgery is needed, the appendix will be removed. Otherwise it may burst, allowing the infection to spread within the abdomen. Since this problem is potentially life-threatening if left untreated, it's important to know the symptoms of appendicitis so you can tell your pediatrician at the first sign of trouble. In order of appearance, the symptoms are:

1. Abdominal pain. This usually is the first complaint the child will have. With infants it may present as crying and the inability to get comfortable in any position. Almost always, the pain is felt first around the belly button (periumbilical), and then may intensify in the lower right side. Sometimes, if the appendix is not located in the usual position, the discomfort may occur elsewhere in the abdomen or in the back, or there may be urinary symptoms, such as increased frequency or burning. Even when the appendix lies in its normal position and the pain is in the right lower abdomen, it may irritate one of the muscles that leads toward the leg, causing the child to limp or walk bent over.

2. Vomiting. After several hours of pain, vomiting may occur. It is important to remember that a stomachache usually comes before the vomiting with appendicitis, not after vomiting. Abdominal pain that follows vomiting is very commonly seen in viral stomach infections such as gastro-enteritis.

3. Loss of appetite. The absence of hunger occurs shortly after the onset of the pain.

4. Fever. Fever can vary, but is often around 101 or 102 degrees Fahrenheit (approx. 38 or 39 degrees Celsius). If the appendix ruptures (breaks open), fever can be higher.

Unfortunately, the symptoms associated with appendicitis sometimes may be hidden by a viral or bacterial infection that preceded it. Diarrhea, nausea, vomiting, and fever may appear before the typical pain of appendicitis, making the diagnosis much more difficult.

Also, your child's discomfort may suddenly vanish, thus persuading you that all is well. Unfortunately, this disappearance of pain also could mean that the appendix has just burst or ruptured. Although the pain may leave for several hours, this is exactly when appendicitis becomes dangerous. The infection will spread to the rest of the abdomen, causing your child to become much more ill, develop a higher fever, and require hospitalization for surgery and intravenous antibiotics. Recovery may take much longer, and there may be more complications than when appendicitis is diagnosed and treated earlier.

Treatment

Detecting the signs of appendicitis is not always easy, particularly with children under the age of three, who cannot tell you where it hurts or that the pain is moving to the right side. This is why it's better to act sooner rather than later if you have any suspicion that your child's pain or discomfort seems different, more severe than usual, or out of the ordinary. While most children with abdominal pain don't have appendicitis, only a physician should diagnose this serious problem. If the abdominal pain persists for more than an hour or two, and if your child also has nausea, vomiting, loss of appetite, and fever, notify your pediatrician immediately.

If the doctor is not certain that the problem is appendicitis, she may decide to observe your child closely for several hours, either in or out of the hospital. During this time, she will perform additional tests or examinations to see if more conclusive signs develop. If there is a strong probability of appendicitis, the child will be hospitalized, further studies will be done, and any necessary treatment will be administered, which may include IV fluids, antibiotics, or surgery.

Celiac Disease

Celiac disease is a problem that causes malabsorption—that is, a failure of the bowels to absorb nutrients. It's caused by an abnormal immune reaction to gluten (the protein found in wheat, rye, and barley—and sometimes oats, which can be contaminated with gluten) that takes place in the intestine and stimulates the body's immune system to attack and damage the lining of the intestine, preventing nutrients from being absorbed into the system. As a result, food simply passes through the intestines, only partially digested. The result may be crampy abdominal pain, foul-smelling stools, diarrhea, weight loss, irritability, and a continuous feeling of being sick. In many cases, however, there may be no symptoms at all with celiac disease.

Treatment

Once your pediatrician suspects celiac disease, he'll order certain blood tests that can be used to screen for celiac disease. However, to make a definitive diagnosis, your pediatrician will refer your child to a pediatric gastroenterologist. This specialist will do a small-bowel biopsy, which entails the removal of a very tiny piece of the intestine for laboratory examination. This procedure usually is done by passing a small scope through the mouth and into the small intestine, where the biopsy is obtained.

If the intestinal lining turns out to be damaged in a way that is suggestive of celiac disease, you will be recommended to feed your child a gluten-free diet. This means staying away from wheat, rye, barley, and contaminated oat products. Your pediatrician or gastroenterologist will give you a complete list of foods to avoid, but you also need to carefully check the labels of any foods you purchase, since wheat flour is a hidden ingredient in many items. Because rice and rice products do not contain gluten, they'll probably become a major part of your child's diet. The number of gluten-free products in the grocery stores continues to increase, and some restaurants even have gluten-free menus. Consultation with a dietitian is recommended, as the diet is very strict and must be followed exactly.

Some parents ask if they can just try a gluten-free diet without doing diagnostic testing. This is not recommended for several reasons. First, as stated before, the gluten-free diet in celiac disease is very strict. Few families can adhere rigidly enough to the diet without confidence that the diagnosis is correct. Second, it may take months for symptoms to completely resolve in a patient with celiac disease on a gluten-free diet. Finally, the gluten-free diet will cause both the serum and tissue markers of celiac disease to disappear, making it impossible to diagnose the disease accurately without putting your child back on a gluten-containing diet for several months.

Incidentally, your child may not be able to tolerate the sugar in milk for as long as several months after the initial diagnosis is made. In this case, you may be advised to eliminate milk temporarily, as well as gluten products, from her diet. During this time she might be given milk treated with enzymes, so that it will be predigested before reaching the intestine. Extra vitamins and minerals also might be necessary.

If your child does have celiac disease, she must remain on a gluten-free diet for her entire life, completely avoiding wheat, rye, barley, and contaminated oat products. Luckily, this is easier to do now than it was years ago due to the many gluten-free products and recipes available.

(See also *Diarrhea*, page 537; *Malabsorption*, page 554; *Anemia*, page 627.)

Constipation

Bowel patterns vary in children just as they do in adults. Because of this, it is sometimes difficult to tell if your child is truly constipated. One child may go two or three days without a bowel movement and still not be constipated, while another might have relatively frequent bowel movements but have difficulty passing the stool. Or a child's constipation may go unnoticed if he passes a small stool each day, while a buildup of stool develops in his colon. In general, it is best to watch for the following signals if you suspect constipation:

■ In a newborn, firm stools less than once a day, though this can be normal in some exclusively breastfed infants (some breastfed babies will stool only once a week)

■ In an older child, stools that are hard and compact, with three or four days between bowel movements

■ At any age, stools that are large, hard, and dry ("rabbit pellets") and associated with painful bowel movements (see *Is My Child Constipated?* opposite)

■ Episodes of abdominal pain relieved after having a large bowel movement

■ Blood in or on the outside of the stools

■ Soiling between bowel movements

Constipation generally occurs when the muscles at the end of the large intestine tighten, preventing the stool from passing normally. The longer the stool remains there, the firmer and drier it becomes, making it even more difficult to pass without discomfort. Then, because the bowel movement is painful, your child may actively try to hold it in, making the problem still worse.

The tendency toward constipation seems to run in families. It may start in infancy and remain as a lifetime pattern, becoming worse if the child does not establish regular bowel habits or withholds stool. Stool retention occurs most commonly between the ages of two and five, at a time when the child is coming to terms with independence, control, and toilet training. Older children may resist having bowel movements away from home because they don't want to use an unfamiliar toilet. This, too, can cause constipation or make it worse.

If your child does withhold, he may produce such large stools that his rectum stretches. Then he may no longer feel the urge to defecate until the stool is too big to be passed without the help of an enema, laxative, or other treatment. In some of these cases, soiling occurs when liquid waste leaks around the solid stool. This looks like diarrhea or soiling on the child's underpants or diaper. In these severe cases, the rectum must be emptied under a physician's supervision, and the child must be retrained to establish normal bowel patterns. Consulting a pediatric gastroenterologist may be necessary.

Is My Child Constipated?

The following descriptions of stool consistency can help you gauge whether your child is constipated:

Type 1: Painful, very thick, dense, heavy rocks/pebbles/pellets, hard to push out
Type 2: Hard to push out initially, clumped-together pebbles
Type 3: Soft and easy to push out in log shapes
Type 4: Super-soft, semi-solid, comes out easily and/or explosively
Type 5: Liquid, runs out, hard to control

Source: Used with permission from Tanya Altmann, *Baby & Toddler Basics* (Itasca, IL: American Academy of Pediatrics, 2018).

Treatment

Mild or occasional episodes of constipation may be helped by the following suggestions.

Constipation due to breast milk is unusual, unless your supply has decreased or your baby is also eating solid food, but if your breastfed infant is constipated, it is probably due to a reason other than diet. Consult your doctor before substituting formula for breast milk. (Keep in mind that the American Academy of Pediatrics recommends breastfeeding and avoiding cow's milk for the first twelve months after birth.)

For infants, ask your pediatrician about giving small amounts of water or prune juice. In addition, for infants older than six months, fruits (especially prunes and pears) can often help resolve constipation.

For a toddler or older child who is eating solid foods and has problems with constipation, you may need to add high-fiber foods to his daily diet. These include prunes, apricots, plums, raisins, high-fiber vegetables (peas, beans, broccoli), and whole-grain cereals and bread products. At the same time, cut back on junk food and on cereals or breads that are not high in fiber. Increasing the daily water intake also may help.

In more severe cases, your pediatrician—alone or in consultation with a pediatric gastroenterologist—may prescribe a stool softener, stimulant laxative, or enema. Follow such prescriptions exactly. Although some newer softeners are sold over the counter and are simpler to use than these products used to be, never give your child a stool-loosening medication without first consulting with your doctor.

For all children, having their feet flat on the floor or on a stepstool or other flat surface is ideal to promote ease of pushing stool out. This way, they are able to use their abdominal muscles to push, rather than to help them balance on the toilet. If your child is constipated and relearning to go to the bathroom normally, it may be helpful to have him sit on the toilet ten minutes after a meal, without distraction, for five minutes or so, to reacquaint him with the feeling of needing to push poop out.

Prevention

Parents should become familiar with their children's normal bowel patterns and the typical size and consistency of their stools. Doing this is helpful in determining when constipation occurs and how severe the problem is. If the child does not have regular bowel movements each day or two, or is uncomfortable when they are passed, he may need help in developing proper bowel habits. This may be done by providing a proper diet and establishing a regular bowel routine.

In a child who is not yet toilet trained, the best way to guard against constipation is to provide a high-fiber diet. Increase the fiber as he gets older. A child should eat at a minimum his age plus five in grams of fiber. For example, a three-year-old should eat at least 8 grams of fiber per day. To help reach that target, buy grains (cereals, crackers, breads, tortillas, pastas) that have at least 3 grams of fiber per serving. Make sure your child is getting five servings of fruits and vegetables each day. Read product labels for fiber content before choosing which items to serve your family.

Once the child is mature enough to be toilet trained, urge him to sit on the toilet every day, preferably after a meal. A book, puzzle, or toy can occupy him during this time so that he feels relaxed. Encourage him to stay on the toilet until he has a bowel movement, or for about fifteen minutes. Praise him if he is successful; if he is not, encourage him with positive statements. Eventually he should be able to use the toilet himself without parental guidance.

If the combination of a high-fiber diet, increases in fluid in the diet, and a daily toilet routine does not result in regular bowel movements, the child may consciously be withholding stool. In this case, you should consult your pediatrician, who may suggest an individualized approach to resolve the problem (every child's condition is unique). Your doctor can supervise the use of stool softeners, laxatives, or suppositories should they be necessary. Occasionally stool withholding becomes so severe that both the child and the family become upset by the symptoms, and much of each day's interactions focus on bowel movements. Programs have been devised to deal effectively with this problem.

Usually the withholding begins around the time of toilet training. The child is reluctant to move his bowels on the potty or toilet and withholds. The next bowel movement is painful. The child associates pain with bowel movements and now withholds stool because of this. The situation can progress to an all-consuming fear. When such severe symptoms develop, the rectum must be cleansed with enemas, or medications including laxatives and stool softeners need to be given orally. In some cases, rectal suppositories are also used. Following this, a stool softener is given on a regular basis in amounts large enough to prevent the child from voluntarily withholding stool. Because the bowel movements are now no longer painful, the child will start to go on the potty without fear. This treatment may go on for several months while the laxative is slowly withdrawn. A diet high in fiber, fluids, and regular toileting are also part of the routine.

Diarrhea

Normally your child's bowel movements will vary in number and consistency, depending on her age and diet. Breastfed newborns may have up to twelve small bowel movements a day, but by the second or third month, they may have some days without passing any stool. By age two, most children will have only one or two large bowel movements a day, but your child can have several smaller ones and still be normal, especially if his diet includes juices or fiber-containing foods, such as prunes or bran.

An occasional loose stool is not cause for alarm. If, however, your child's bowel pattern suddenly changes to loose, watery stools that occur more frequently than usual, he has diarrhea.

Diarrhea often occurs when the inner lining of the intestine is injured. The stools become loose because the intestine does not properly digest or absorb the nutrients from the foods that your child eats and drinks. Also, the injured lining tends to leak fluid. Minerals and salt are lost along with the fluid. This loss can be made even worse if your child is fed food or beverages that contain large amounts of sugar, such as fruit juice and sweetened beverages, since unabsorbed sugar draws even more water into the intestine, increasing the diarrhea.

When a child has diarrhea, the body may lose too much salt and water, leading to dehydration. This can be prevented by replenishing losses due to the diarrhea with adequate amounts of fluid and salt, as described under *Treatment* (opposite).

The medical term for intestinal inflammation is "enteritis." When the problem is accompanied by or preceded by vomiting, as it often is, there is usually some stomach and small-intestine inflammation as well, and the condition is called "gastroenteritis."

Causes of Diarrhea

In young children, the intestinal damage that produces diarrhea is caused most often by viruses such as norovirus and rotavirus. Such viruses are easily transmitted from person to person, so it is very important that your family practices excellent handwashing if a member of the house has a diarrheal illness. Diarrhea caused by bacteria and parasitic infections has decreased in frequency as a result of improvements in public health such as clean drinking water and proper disposal of sewage. Other causes of diarrhea are:

- Food poisoning (from things such as mushrooms, shellfish, or contaminated food)

- Side effects of antibiotics and other oral medications

- Food or milk allergy

- Drinking excessive amounts of fruit juice

- Overflow constipation (when loose stool leaks around an area of constipation)

The causes of diarrhea are described in the box *Causes of Diarrhea* and include viral or bacterial infections of the intestine. Children with viral diarrheal illnesses often have symptoms such as vomiting, fever, and irritability. (See *Vomiting*, page 555; Chapter 27, *Fever*.) Their stools tend to be more greenish yellow in color and have a significant amount of water with them. (If they occur very frequently, they may not have any solid stool at all.) If the stools appear red or blackish, they might contain blood; this bleeding may arise from the injured lining of the intestine or, more likely, simply may be due to irritation of the rectum by frequent, loose bowel movements. In any event, if you notice this or any other unusual stool color, you should notify your pediatrician.

A rotavirus vaccine is now given routinely to infants starting at two months of age. This is a liquid vaccine that is given by mouth in your pediatrician's office. Infants are given the vaccine in a two- or three-dose regimen (depending on the formulation) at two months, four months, and (if the three-dose regimen is used) six months of age. It is very good at preventing diarrhea and vomiting caused by rotavirus. Almost all babies who get rotavirus vaccine will be protected from severe rotavirus diarrhea. However, this vaccine will not prevent diarrhea or vomiting caused by other infections.

Treatment

There are no effective medications for treating viral intestinal infections, which cause most cases of diarrhea in infants. The most important treatment of a young child with vomiting or diarrhea is to keep him adequately hydrated with breast milk, formula, electrolyte solution, or other fluids recommended by your pediatrician. Prescription medications should be used only to treat certain types of bacterial or parasitic intestinal infections, which are much less common. When the latter conditions are suspected, your pediatrician will ask for stool specimens to be tested in the laboratory; other tests also may be done.

Some studies indicate that probiotics may be beneficial for certain causes of infectious diarrhea and may shorten the duration if started early and given daily. These dietary supplements are believed to help with the digestive process, as well as allergies, vaginal infections, and preventing some illnesses. (See *Probiotics and Prebiotics*, page 543.)

Over-the-counter antidiarrheal medications are not recommended for children under age two and should be used with caution in older children. They often worsen the intestinal injury and cause the fluid and salt to remain within the intestine instead of being absorbed. With these medications, your child can become dehydrated without your being aware of it, because the diarrhea appears to stop. Always consult your pediatrician before giving your child any medication for diarrhea.

MILD DIARRHEA

If your child has a small amount of diarrhea but is not dehydrated (see the box on page 547 for signs of dehydration), does not have a high fever, and is active and hungry, you may not need to change her diet.

If your child has mild diarrhea and is vomiting, substitute a commercially available electrolyte solution for her normal diet. Your pediatrician will recommend these solutions to be given in small amounts frequently, to maintain normal body water and salt levels, until the vomiting has stopped. In most cases, they're needed for only one to two days. Once the vomiting has subsided, gradually restart the normal diet.

SIGNIFICANT DIARRHEA

If your child has a watery bowel movement every one to two hours, or more frequently, and/or has signs of dehydration (see the box on page 547), consult his pediatrician. She may advise you to withhold all solid foods for at least twenty-four hours and to avoid liquids that are high in sugar (Jell-O, soft drinks, full-strength fruit juices, or artificially sweetened beverages), high in salt (packaged broth), or very low in salt (water and tea). If you are breastfeeding, she will probably have you continue, but in other cases she may recommend only prepared electrolyte solutions, which contain the ideal balance of salt and minerals. (See the table *Estimated Amount of*

Fluid Children Should Drink Daily (Depending on Body Weight) on page 542.)

Remember, if your child has diarrhea, keeping him hydrated is very important. If he shows any signs of dehydration (such as decreased wet diapers, no tears, sunken eyes, or sunken fontanelle [soft spot]), call your pediatrician right away and withhold all foods and milk beverages until she gives you further instructions. Also contact your doctor if your child looks sick and the symptoms aren't improving with time. *Take your child to the pediatrician or nearest emergency department immediately if you think he is moderately to severely dehydrated.* In the meantime, give your child a commercially prepared electrolyte solution.

For severe dehydration, hospitalization is sometimes necessary so that your child can be rehydrated intravenously. In milder cases, all that may be necessary is to give your child an electrolyte replacement solution according to your pediatrician's directions. The table on page 542 indicates the approximate amount of this solution to be used.

Exclusively breastfed babies are less likely to develop severe diarrhea. If a breastfed infant does develop diarrhea, generally you can continue breastfeeding, giving additional electrolyte solution if your doctor feels this is necessary. Many breastfed babies can continue to stay hydrated with frequent breastfeeding alone.

Once diarrhea is decreasing and your child wants to eat, you can gradually expand the diet with a goal of returning to his usual diet as he tolerates. Sometimes milk ingestion worsens diarrhea, so in children over age one your pediatrician may recommend holding off on milk or may advise giving lactose-free formula or milk for a period of time.

It is not necessary to withhold food for longer than twenty-four hours, as your child will need some normal nutrition to start to regain lost strength. After you have started giving him food again, his stools may remain loose, but that does not necessarily mean that things are not going well. Look for increased activity, better appetite, more frequent urination, and the disappearance of any of the signs of dehydration. When you see these, you will know your child is getting better.

Diarrhea that lasts longer than two weeks (chronic diarrhea) may signify a more serious type of intestinal problem. When diarrhea persists this long, your pediatrician may want to do further tests to determine the cause and to make sure your child is not becoming malnourished. If malnutrition is becoming a problem, the pediatrician may recommend a special diet or special type of formula.

If your child drinks too much fluid, especially too much juice or sweetened beverages, a condition commonly referred to as toddler's diarrhea could develop. This causes ongoing loose stools but shouldn't affect appetite or growth or cause dehydration. Although toddler's diarrhea is not a dangerous condition, the pediatrician may suggest that you limit the amounts of juice and sweetened fluids your child drinks. Ideally, toddlers and children would drink mainly milk and water.

When diarrhea occurs in combination with other symptoms, it could mean that there is a more serious medical problem. Notify your pediatrician immediately if the diarrhea is accompanied by any of the following:

- Fever that lasts longer than twenty-four to forty-eight hours

- Bloody stools

- Vomiting that lasts more than twelve to twenty-four hours

- Vomited material that is green-colored, blood-tinged, or like coffee grounds in appearance

- A distended (swollen-appearing) abdomen

- Refusal to eat or drink

- Severe abdominal pain

- Rash or jaundice (yellow color of skin and eyes)

- Signs of dehydration such as no urination for six to twelve hours

If your child has another medical condition or is taking medication routinely, it is best to tell your pediatrician about any diarrheal illness that lasts more than twenty-four hours without improvement, or anything else that really worries you.

Estimated Amount of Fluid Children Should Drink Daily (Depending on Body Weight)

1 pound = 0.45 kilograms   1 ounce = 30 milliliters

Body Weight (in pounds)	Minimum Daily Fluid Requirements (in ounces)*	Electrolyte Solution* Requirements for Mild Diarrhea (in ounces for 24 hours)
6–7	10	16
11	15	23
22	25	40
26	28	44
33	32	51
40	38	61

* Note: This is the smallest amount of fluid that a normal child requires. Most children drink more than this.

Prevention

The following guidelines will help lessen the chances that your child will get diarrhea.

1. Most forms of infectious diarrhea are transmitted by direct hand-to-mouth contact following exposure to contaminated fecal (stool) material. This happens most often in children who are not toilet trained. Promote handwashing after using the toilet or changing diapers and before handling food, as well as other sanitary measures, in your household and in your child's daycare center or preschool.

2. Do not give your child raw (unpasteurized) milk or foods that may be contaminated. (See *Food Poisoning*, page 544.)

3. Avoid unnecessary medications, especially antibiotics.

4. If your child needs to take antibiotics, consider the use of probiotics, to potentially prevent antibiotic-associated diarrhea.

5. If possible, breastfeed your child through early infancy.

6. Limit the amount of juice and sweetened beverages your child drinks.

7. Make sure your child has received the rotavirus vaccine, as it protects against the most common cause of diarrhea and vomiting in infants and young children.

Probiotics and Prebiotics

Probiotics are types of "good" bacteria. These living organisms inhabit the intestines and may have beneficial health effects, although the evidence is not yet conclusive. Some studies have shown that foods or infant formula containing probiotics can prevent or even treat diarrhea in children, whether this condition is chronic, acute, or associated with the use of antibiotics. Other studies have found a correlation in children between taking daily probiotics and experiencing fewer illnesses and therefore fewer missed days of school. Newer research has shown that giving specific probiotics to newborns can help colonize the gut with beneficial bacteria and actually decrease harmful bacteria later in life. Many studies are currently underway and ongoing research will provide more guidance on the role of probiotics in newborns and children, but if your child has diarrhea or other gastrointestinal issues, talk to your doctor about the use of these organisms.

Probiotics are available in many forms. Many infant formulas are now supplemented with probiotics. Some dairy products such as yogurt and kefir contain them, too. So do some miso, tempeh, and soy beverages. Probiotic supplements (powders, capsules, and liquids) are sold in health food stores. Pediatricians are still debating the most appropriate use of these commercial probiotics—for example, what are the best organisms and dosages, how frequently should they be taken, and should they be used at all for preventing or managing certain health conditions?

Foods containing probiotics appear to be safe for most children, although they can cause mild bloating or gas in some cases. If probiotic supplements have been exposed to heat or moisture, the living "good" bacteria may be killed, and thus the products will become useless. For now, if you're interested in trying probiotics, talk to your pediatrician first. (For more information about probiotics, see page 123.)

Some doctors recommend that rather than giving your child *probiotics*, you should consider using *prebiotics* instead. While probiotics are living bacteria, prebiotics are nondigestible food components—special carbohydrates naturally found in breast milk and other complex sugars and fiber—that promote the growth of beneficial bacteria that are already present in the intestines, thus increasing the number of these good bacteria while also suppressing the growth of unhealthy strains. Breast milk is a good source of prebiotics, as are foods like bran, legumes, barley, certain vegetables such as asparagus, spinach, and onions, and fruits such as berries and bananas.

(See also *Abdominal Pain*, page 527; *Celiac Disease*, page 533; *Malabsorption*, page 554; *Rotavirus*, page 825; and *Vomiting*, page 555.)

Food Poisoning and Food Contamination

Food poisoning occurs after eating food contaminated by bacteria. The symptoms of food poisoning are basically the same as those of a stomach virus: abdominal cramps, nausea, vomiting, diarrhea, and sometimes fever. But if your child and other people who have eaten the same food all have the same symptoms, the problem is more likely to be food poisoning than a stomach virus. The bacteria that cause food poisoning cannot be seen, smelled, or tasted, so your child won't know when she is eating them. Some sources of food poisoning include poisonous mushrooms, contaminated fish products, and foods with special seasonings. Young children do not care for most of these foods and so will eat very little of them. However, it still is very important to be aware of the risk. If your child has unusual gastrointestinal symptoms, and there is any chance she might have eaten contaminated or poisonous foods, call your pediatrician.

BOTULISM

This is the deadly food poisoning caused by *Clostridium botulinum*. Although these bacteria normally can be found in soil and water, illness from them is extremely rare because they need very special conditions in order to multiply and produce poison. *Clostridium botulinum* grows best without oxygen and in certain chemical conditions, which explains why improperly canned food is most often contaminated and low-acid vegetables such as green beans, corn, beets, and peas are most often involved. Honey also can be contaminated and frequently causes severe illness, particularly in children under one year of age. This is the reason **honey should never be given to an infant under the age of one year.**

Botulism attacks the nervous system and causes double vision, droopy eyelids, decreased muscle tone, and difficulty in swallowing and breathing. It also can cause vomiting, diarrhea, and abdominal pain. The symptoms develop within eighteen to thirty-six hours and can last weeks to months. Without treatment, botulism can cause death. Even with treatment, it can cause nerve damage.

CAMPYLOBACTER

One form of infectious food poisoning is caused by the bacteria *Campylobacter*, which a child may ingest when he eats raw or undercooked chicken, or drinks unpasteurized milk or contaminated water. This infection typically leads to symptoms such as watery (and sometimes bloody) diarrhea, cramps, and fever about two to five days after the germs are consumed in food.

To diagnose a *Campylobacter* infection, your doctor will have a stool specimen analyzed in the laboratory. Fortunately, most cases of this infection run their course without any formal treatment, other than making sure that your child drinks plenty of fluids in order to replace the fluids lost from diarrhea. When symptoms are severe, however, your pediatrician may prescribe antibiotics. In most cases, your child will be back to normal in about two to five days.

CLOSTRIDIUM PERFRINGENS

Clostridium perfringens (C. perfringens) is a bacterium frequently found in soil, sewage, and the intestines of humans and animals. It usually is transferred by the food handler to the food itself, where it multiplies and produces its toxin. *C. perfringens* often is found in school cafeterias because it thrives in food that is served in quantity and left out for long periods at room temperature or on a steam table. The foods most often involved are cooked beef, poultry, gravy, fish, casseroles, stews, and bean burritos. The symptoms of this type of poisoning, such as vomiting and diarrhea, start eight to twenty-four hours after eating, and can last from one to several days.

CRYPTOSPORIDIOSIS

Cryptosporidiosis is a parasitic infection, usually caught from swimming or drinking water, that causes watery diarrhea, low-grade fever, and abdominal pain. This infection can occur in anyone, but it is of special concern in children who do not have a normal immune system.

E. COLI

Escherichia coli (or *E. coli*) is a group of bacteria that normally live in the intestines of children and adults. A few strains of these bacteria can cause food-related illnesses. Undercooked ground beef is a common source of *E. coli*, although raw produce and contaminated water have caused some outbreaks.

Symptoms of an infection typically include diarrhea (which can range from mild to severe and can be bloody) to abdominal pain, and in some cases nausea and vomiting. Some *E. coli* outbreaks have been quite severe and have even caused deaths in rare instances. The optimal treatment for an *E. coli*–related illness is rest and fluids (to counteract dehydration). But if symptoms are more severe, you should have a discussion with your pediatrician.

SALMONELLA

Salmonella bacteria (there are many types) are another major cause of food poisoning in the United States. The most commonly contaminated foods are raw meat (including chicken), raw or undercooked eggs, unpasteurized milk, and vegetables. Fortunately, salmonella are killed when the food is cooked thoroughly. For vegetables, make sure they are washed thoroughly. Symptoms caused by salmonella poisoning start six to forty-eight hours after eating, may last two to seven days, and may include vomiting and diarrhea, though rarely bloody diarrhea. Although a salmonella infection is usually self-limiting, it can be severe, so if your child appears sick and has a high fever, call your doctor. Children with sickle cell disease, or other problems with their spleens, will need antibiotics if they have this infection.

SHIGELLOSIS

Shigella infections, or shigellosis, are intestinal infections caused by one of many types of shigella bacteria. These bacteria can be transmitted through contaminated food and drinking water, as well as via poor hygiene (in childcare centers, for example). The organisms invade the lining of the intestine and can lead to symptoms such as bloody diarrhea, fever, and cramps.

Shigellosis and its symptoms usually subside after about five to seven days. In the meantime, your child should consume extra fluids and (if your pediatrician recommends it) a rehydrating solution. In severe cases, your doctor may prescribe antibiotics, which can shorten the duration and intensity of the infection. Shigella is one of the few bacterial causes of gastroenteritis that is usually treated with antibiotics. Also, infants and toddlers should not be at daycare until treated or until the infection is completely resolved.

STAPHYLOCOCCUS AUREUS (STAPH)

Staph contamination is the leading cause of food poisoning. These bacteria ordinarily cause skin infections, such as pimples or boils, and are transferred when foods are handled by an infected person. When food is left at a specific temperature (100 de-grees Fahrenheit [37.8 Celsius])—generally one that is lower than the temperature needed to keep food hot—the staph bacteria multiply and produce a poison (toxin) that ordinary cooking will not destroy. The symptoms begin one to six hours after eating the contaminated food, and the discomfort usually lasts about one day.

Treatment

In most cases of food-borne illnesses, all that's necessary is to limit your child's eating and drinking for a while. The problem will then usually resolve itself. Infants can tolerate three to four hours without food or liquids; older children, six to eight. If your child is still vomiting or her diarrhea has not decreased significantly during this time, call your pediatrician.

Also notify the doctor if your child:

■ Shows signs of dehydration (see the box *Signs and Symptoms of Dehydration*, opposite)

■ Has bloody diarrhea

■ Has continuous diarrhea with a large volume of water in the stool, or diarrhea alternating with constipation

■ May have been poisoned by mushrooms

■ Suddenly becomes weak, numb, confused, or restless, and feels a tin-

Signs and Symptoms of Dehydration (Loss of Significant Amounts of Body Water)

The most important part of treating diarrhea is to prevent your child from becoming dehydrated. Be alert for the following warning signs of dehydration, and notify the pediatrician immediately if any of them develop.

MILD TO MODERATE DEHYDRATION

- Plays less than usual
- Urinates less frequently (for infants, fewer than six wet diapers per day)
- Parched, dry mouth
- Fewer tears when crying
- Sunken soft spot of the head in an infant or toddler
- Stools will be loose if dehydration is caused by diarrhea; if dehydration is due to other fluid loss (vomiting, lack of fluid intake), there will be decreased bowel movements

SEVERE DEHYDRATION (IN ADDITION TO THE SYMPTOMS AND SIGNALS ALREADY LISTED)

- Very fussy
- Excessively sleepy
- Sunken eyes
- Cool, discolored hands and feet
- Wrinkled skin
- Urinates only one to two times per day

gling sensation, acts drunkenly, or has hallucinations or difficulty breathing

Tell the doctor the symptoms your child is having, what foods she has eaten recently, and where they were obtained. The treatment your pediatrician gives will depend on your child's condition and the type of food poisoning. If she is dehydrated, fluid replacement will be prescribed. Some-times antibiotics are helpful for specific bacteria. Antihistamines help if the illness is due to an allergic reaction to a food, toxin, or seasoning, although if the reaction or symptoms are severe, call your doctor, as other medications, such as epinephrine, may be required. If your child has botulism, she will require hospitalization and treatment in the intensive care unit.

Prevention

Most food-borne illness is preventable if you observe the following guidelines.

CLEANLINESS

■ *Be especially careful when preparing raw meats and poultry.* Wash your hands, and all surfaces that have come in contact with the raw meat and poultry, with hot, sudsy water before continuing your preparation.

■ *Always wash your hands* before preparing meals and after going to the bathroom or changing your child's diaper.

■ *If you have open cuts or sores* on your hands, wear gloves while preparing food.

■ *Do not prepare food when you are sick,* particularly if you have nausea, vomiting, abdominal cramps, or diarrhea.

FOOD SELECTION, PREPARATION, AND SERVING

■ Carefully examine any canned food (especially home-canned goods) for signs of bacterial contamination. Look for milky liquid surrounding vegetables (it should be clear), cracked jars, loose lids, and swollen cans or lids. *Don't use canned or jarred goods showing any of these signs. Do not even taste them. Throw them away so that nobody else will eat them.* (Wrap them first in plastic and then in a heavy paper bag.)

■ Buy all meats and seafood from reputable suppliers.

■ Do not use raw (unpasteurized) milk or cheese made from raw milk.

■ *Do not eat raw or undercooked meat.*

■ *Do not give honey to a baby under one year of age.*

■ If your child turns away from a particular food or drink, smell or taste it yourself; you may find that it is spoiled and that it shouldn't be eaten.

■ Do not let prepared foods (particularly starchy ones), cooked or cured meats, cheese, or anything with mayonnaise stay at room temperature for more than two hours.

■ Do not interrupt the cooking of meat or poultry to finish the cooking later.

■ Do not prepare food one day for the next unless it will be frozen or refrigerated right away. (Always put hot food right into the refrigerator. Do not wait for it to cool first.)

■ Make sure all foods are cooked thoroughly. Use a meat thermometer for large items like roasts or turkeys, and cut into other pieces of meat to check if they are done.

■ When reheating meals, cover them and reheat them thoroughly.

■ You also may want to visit usda .gov for more information. The department has a number of helpful pamphlets and newsletters, including topics such as cooking on a grill and preparing holiday turkeys.

Hepatitis

Hepatitis is an inflammation of the liver that, in children, is almost always caused by one of several viruses. In some children it may cause no symptoms, while in others it can provoke fever, jaundice (yellow skin), loss of appetite, nausea, and vomiting. There are multiple forms of viral hepatitis. The most common forms include:

■ *Hepatitis A*. Routine vaccination is recommended for all children at one year of age with a booster dose six to twelve months later.

■ *Hepatitis B*. Routine vaccination is now recommended for all infants at birth, with two booster doses given.

■ *Hepatitis C*. Currently there is no vaccine, but effective treatment is available and curative for infected patients.

Most children in the United States are now vaccinated against hepatitis A, but the infection can be transmitted directly from person to person or through contamination of food or water (such as while swimming or eating in a restaurant or traveling). In a childcare or household setting, the infection can be spread when hands are not washed after having a bowel movement or after changing the diaper of an infected infant. Anyone who drinks water contaminated with infected human feces or who eats raw shellfish taken from polluted areas also may become infected. A child infected with hepatitis A virus may develop no symptoms or will become ill two to six weeks after the virus is transmitted. The illness usually disappears within one month after it begins.

Hepatitis B infection is transmitted during sexual activity and via contact with infected blood, semen, or other body fluids. In young children, however, it can also be contracted through nonsexual, person-to-person contact, such as at daycare or school, which is why the hepatitis B vaccine is recommended for all young children.

Risk is greatest from contaminated needles, shared syringes, or drug paraphernalia, sex partners of infected persons, and in the newborns of women who are infected with the virus. When a pregnant woman has acute or chronic hepatitis B, she may transmit the infection to her newborn at the time of delivery. Therefore, all pregnant women should be tested for hepatitis B infection and all newborn babies should be vaccinated against hepatitis B.

Hepatitis C can be acquired by intravenous (IV) drug abusers who use contaminated needles or, less commonly, through needle injections, sexual contact with an infected person, and birth to an infected mother. In the United States, the use of sterile disposable needles and the screening of all blood and blood products has essentially eliminated the risk of transmission of hepatitis B and C in hospitals and doctors' offices.

Infection with the hepatitis C virus commonly produces no symptoms, or only mild symptoms of fatigue and jaundice. In many cases, however, this form of hepatitis becomes chronic and can result in severe liver disease, liver failure, cancer of the liver, and even death later on in life. There are antiviral medications available that can cure hepatitis C, and anyone at risk should be tested so that effective treatment may be offered.

Signs and Symptoms

A child could have hepatitis without anyone being aware of it, since many affected children have few, if any, symptoms. In some children the only signs of disease may be malaise and fatigue for several days. In others there will be a fever followed by jaundice (the sclera, or whites of the eyes, and the skin develop a noticeable yellowish color). This jaundice is due to an abnormal increase in bilirubin (a yellow pigment) in the blood, caused by liver inflammation.

With hepatitis B, fever is less likely to occur, although the child may suffer loss of appetite, nausea, vomiting, abdominal pain, and malaise, in addition to jaundice. In children, hepatitis C doesn't always have symptoms.

If you suspect that your child has jaundice, notify your pediatrician. She may order blood tests to determine if hepatitis is causing the problem or if it is due to another condition. You should contact your doctor anytime vomiting or abdominal pain persists beyond a few hours, if appetite loss, nausea, or malaise (a vague feeling of low energy or feeling sick) continue for more than a few days, or if your child becomes jaundiced. These may be indicators of hepatitis.

Treatment

In most settings, there is no specific treatment for hepatitis. As with most viral infections, the body's own defense mechanisms usually will overcome the infecting agent. Although you do not need to rigidly restrict the diet or activity of your child, you may need to make adjustments depending on his appetite and energy levels. Your doctor may recommend your child avoid aspirin and ibuprofen (and other nonsteroidal anti-inflammatory drugs), but acetaminophen can be used in children with chronic liver disease as long as aggressive hepatitis is not present. Also, children on certain medications for long-term illnesses should have their dosages carefully reviewed by the pediatrician, to avoid the side effects that might result because the liver is unable to handle the usual medication load.

Medications are available to treat hepatitis B and hepatitis C. If your child's hepatitis becomes a chronic condition, your pediatrician will refer you to a pediatric gastroenterologist or infectious disease specialist to help decide on appropriate management.

Most children with hepatitis do not need to be hospitalized. However, if loss of appetite or vomiting is interfering with your child's fluid intake and posing a risk of dehydration, your pediatrician may recommend that he be hospitalized. You should contact your doctor immediately if your child appears very lethargic, unresponsive, or delirious, as these may indicate that his illness is worsening and hospitalization is indicated.

There is no chronic infection following hepatitis A; in comparison, among unimmunized children, chronic hepatitis B occurs more frequently in infants than in older children and adults. A high percentage of infants who are born to mothers with acute or chronic hepatitis B become chronically infected if they are not properly immunized after birth. Children with chronic hepatitis B will need monitoring and medication management to reduce the lifetime risk of liver damage, cirrhosis, and liver cancer.

Prevention

All newborns should be immunized with the hepatitis B vaccine at birth; a second dose should be given at age one to two months. Two doses of hepatitis A vaccine are recommended for all children between their first and second birthdays (twelve to twenty-three months of age), as well as older children and adolescents who have not yet been vaccinated. In addition, most international travelers, adults employed in certain high-risk occupations, and people with chronic liver disease, among other conditions, should ask their physician about receiving the hepatitis A vaccine. (See immunization schedules on page 892.)

Handwashing before eating and food preparation, and after using the toilet, is the most important preventive measure against hepatitis. Children should be taught as young as possible to wash their hands at these times. If your child is in childcare, check to be sure that members of the staff wash their hands after handling diapers and before feeding the children.

If you find out that your child has been exposed to a person with active hepatitis, immediately contact your pediatrician, who will determine if the exposure has placed your child at risk. If there's a risk that the infection might have been passed to your child, the doctor may recommend post-exposure measures such as an injection of gamma globulin or a hepatitis vaccine, depending on which hepatitis virus was involved.

Prior to foreign travel with your child, consult your physician to determine the risk of exposure to hepatitis in the countries you plan to visit and consider vaccination against hepatitis A and B if your family has not yet received it.

Inguinal Hernia

If you notice a small lump or bulge in your child's groin area or an enlargement of the scrotum, you may have discovered an inguinal hernia. This condition, which is present in up to five of every hundred children (most commonly in boys), occurs when an opening in the lower abdominal wall allows the child's intestine to squeeze through. This inguinal hernia may be confused with a more benign condition, a communicating hydrocele (see below).

The testicles of the developing male fetus grow inside his abdominal cavity, moving down through a tube (the inguinal canal) into the scrotum as birth nears. When this movement takes place, the lining of the abdominal wall (peritoneum) is pulled along with the testes to form a sac connecting the testicle with the abdominal cavity. Normally this connection closes before or shortly after birth. Hernia is due to a failure of this normal protrusion from the abdominal cavity to close properly, leaving a space for a small portion of the bowel to later push through into the groin or scrotum.

Most hernias do not cause any discomfort, and you or the pediatrician will discover them only by seeing the bulge either in the groin or in the scrotum. Although this kind of hernia must be treated, it is not an emergency condition. You should, however, notify your doctor, who may instruct you to have the child lie down and elevate his legs. Sometimes this will cause the bulge to disappear. However, your doctor will still want to examine the area as soon as possible.

Rarely, a piece of the intestine gets trapped in the hernia, causing swelling and pain. (If you touch the area, it will be tender.) Your child may have nausea and vomiting as well. This condition is called an incarcerated (trapped) hernia and *does* require immediate medical attention. Call your pediatrician immediately if you suspect an incarcerated hernia.

Treatment

Even if the hernia is not incarcerated, it still should be surgically repaired. The surgeon also may check the other side of the abdomen to see if the defect is present there, too, which is very common.

If the hernia is causing pain, it may indicate that a piece of intestine has become trapped or incarcerated. In that case, consult with your pediatrician immediately. He may try to move the trapped piece of intestine out of the sac. Even if this can be done, the hernia still needs to be surgically repaired soon thereafter. If the intestine remains trapped despite your doctor's efforts, emergency surgery must be performed to prevent permanent damage to the intestine.

Communicating Hydrocele

If the opening between the abdominal cavity and the scrotum has not closed properly and completely, abdominal fluid can pass into and out of the sac around the testis, causing a changing fluid collection called a communicating hydrocele. Many newborn boys have this problem; however, it usually disappears within one year without any treatment. Although most common in newborns, hydroceles also can develop later in childhood, sometimes with a hernia.

If your son has a hydrocele, he probably will not complain or be bothered by it, but you or he will notice that one side of his scrotum is swollen. In an infant or young boy, this swelling increases with activity or crying but it will decrease when he is resting or lying down. Sometimes you will not be able to notice any change in size. Your pediatrician may make the final diagnosis by shining a bright

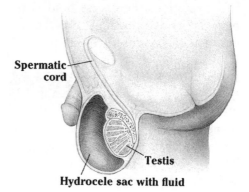

light through the scrotum, to show the fluid surrounding the testicle. Your doctor also may order an ultrasound examination of the scrotum if it is very swollen or hard.

If your baby is born with a hydrocele, your pediatrician will examine it at each regular checkup until around one year of age. During this time your child should not feel any discomfort in the scrotum or the surrounding area. But if it seems to be tender in this area or he has unexplained discomfort in his scrotum with associated nausea or vomiting, call the doctor at once—these are signs that a piece of intestine may have entered the scrotal area along with abdominal fluid. (See *Inguinal Hernia*, opposite.) If this occurs and the intestine gets trapped in the scrotum, your child may require immediate surgery to release the trapped intestine and close the opening between the abdominal wall and the scrotum.

If the hydrocele persists beyond one year without causing pain, a simple surgical procedure may be recommended to correct the hydrocele. In

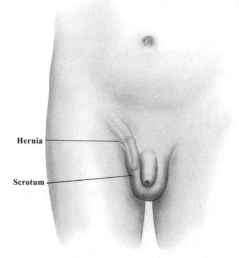

In boys, an internal opening leading to the scrotum allows abdominal contents to slide downward. In girls, the hernia may simply appear as a bulge in the groin area.

this operation, the excess fluid is removed and the opening into the abdominal cavity closed.

Malabsorption

Sometimes children who eat a balanced diet suffer from malnutrition. The reason for this may be malabsorption, the body's inability to absorb nutrients from the digestive system into the bloodstream.

Normally the digestive process converts nutrients from the diet into small units that pass through the wall of the intestine and into the bloodstream, where they are carried to other cells in the body. If the intestinal wall is damaged by an infection (from a virus, bacterium, or parasite) or an immune disorder (such as celiac or inflammatory bowel disease), its surface may change so that digested substances cannot pass through. When this happens, the nutrients will be eliminated through the stool.

Malabsorption commonly occurs in a normal child for a day or two during severe cases of stomach or intestinal virus. It rarely lasts much longer since the surface of the intestine heals quickly without significant damage. In these cases, malabsorption is no cause for concern. However, chronic malabsorption may develop, and if two or more of the following signs or symptoms persist, notify your pediatrician.

Signs and Symptoms

Possible signs and symptoms of chronic malabsorption can include the following:

■ Persistent abdominal pain and vomiting

■ Frequent, loose, bulky, foul-smelling stools

■ Increased susceptibility to infection

■ Weight loss with the loss of fat and muscle

■ Increase in bruises

■ Bone fractures

■ Dry, scaly skin rashes

■ Personality changes

■ Slowing of growth and weight gain (may not be noticeable for several months)

Treatment

When a child suffers from malnutrition, malabsorption is just one of the possible causes. She might be undernourished because she's not getting enough of the right types of food, or she has digestive problems that prevent her body from digesting them. She also might have a combination of these problems. Before prescribing a treatment, the pediatrician must determine the cause. This can be done in one or more of the following ways.

■ You may be asked to list the amount and type of food your child eats.

■ The pediatrician may collect and analyze stool samples. In healthy people, only a small amount of the fat or protein consumed each day is lost through the stool. If too much is found in the stool, it is an indication of malabsorption.

■ Collection of sweat from the skin, called a sweat test, may be performed to see if cystic fibrosis (see page 630) is present. In this disease, the body produces insufficient amounts of certain enzymes.

■ In some cases the pediatrician might request that a pediatric gastroenterologist obtain a biopsy from the wall of the small intestine, and have it examined under the microscope for signs of infection, inflammation, or other injury.

Ordinarily, these tests are performed before any treatment is begun, although a seriously sick child might be hospitalized in order to receive special feedings while her problem is being evaluated.

Once the physician is sure the problem is malabsorption, she will try to identify a specific reason for its presence. When the reason is infection, the treatment usually will include antibiotics. If malabsorption occurs because the intestine is too ac-

tive, certain medications may be used to counteract this, so that there's time for the nutrients to be absorbed.

Sometimes there's no clear cause for the problem. In this case, the diet may be changed to include foods or special nutritional formulas that are more easily tolerated and absorbed.

Reye Syndrome

Reye syndrome (often referred to as Reye's syndrome) is a rare but very serious illness that usually occurs in children younger than fifteen years of age. It can affect all organs of the body, but most often injures the brain and the liver. It is strongly associated with the use of aspirin or aspirin-containing medication during a viral illness.

Since the medical community issued a public warning against the use of aspirin during viral illnesses, the number of cases of Reye syndrome has decreased greatly. Do not use aspirin or aspirin-containing products in your child without consulting a pediatrician.

Vomiting

Because many common childhood illnesses can cause vomiting, you should expect your child to have this problem several times during these early years. Usually it ends quickly without treatment, but this doesn't make it any easier for you to watch. That feeling of helplessness combined with the fear that something serious might be wrong and the desire to do something to make it better may make you feel tense and anxious. To help put your mind at ease, learn as much as you can about the causes of vomiting and what you can do to treat your child when it occurs.

First of all, there's a difference between real vomiting and just spitting up. Vomiting is the forceful throwing up of stomach contents through the mouth. Spitting up (most commonly seen in infants under one year of age) is the easy flow of stomach contents out of the mouth, frequently with a burp.

Vomiting occurs when the abdominal muscles and diaphragm contract vigorously while the stomach is relaxed. This reflex action is triggered by the "vomiting center" in the brain after it has been stimulated by:

■ Nerves from the stomach and intestine when the gastrointestinal tract is either irritated or swollen by an infection or blockage

■ Chemicals in the blood (e.g., drugs)

■ Psychological stimuli from disturbing sights or smells

■ Stimuli from the middle ear (as in vomiting caused by motion sickness)

The common causes of spitting up or vomiting vary according to age. During the first few months, for instance, most infants will spit up small amounts of formula or breast milk, usually within the first hour after being fed. It may occur less often if a child is burped frequently and if active play is limited right after meals. This spitting up tends to decrease as the baby becomes older, but it may persist in a mild form until ten to twelve months of age. Spitting up is not serious and doesn't interfere with normal weight gain. (See *Spitting Up*, page 134.)

Occasional vomiting may occur during the first month. If it appears repeatedly or is unusually forceful, call your pediatrician. It may be just a mild feeding difficulty, but it also could be a sign of something more serious.

Around two weeks to four months of age, persistent forceful vomiting may be caused by a thickening of the muscle at the stomach exit. Known as hypertrophic pyloric stenosis, this thickening prevents food from passing into the intestines. It requires *immediate* medical attention. Surgery usually is required to open the narrowed area. The important sign of this condition is forceful vomiting occurring approximately fifteen to thirty minutes or less after every feeding. Anytime you notice this, call your pediatrician as soon as possible.

GER (gastroesophageal reflux). Occasionally the spitting up in the first few weeks to months after birth gets worse instead of better—that is, even though it's not forceful, it occurs all the time. This happens when the muscles at the lower end of the esophagus become overly relaxed and allow the stomach contents to back up. This condition is known as gastroesophageal reflux, or GER. It is important to note that when an infant is growing typically and spitting up, this is most likely normal physiologic spitting up, and it does not require therapy or management. This is certainly not convenient or pleasant for a parent, but it's not bad for the baby. Common ways to treat GER include:

1. Avoid overfeeding or give smaller feeds more frequently.

2. Burp the baby frequently.

3. Leave the infant in a safe, quiet, upright position for at least thirty minutes following feeding.

4. Thicken the breast milk or formula with small amounts of baby cereal as directed by your pediatrician. Some newer formulas, labeled "anti-reflux," are designed with this thickening included.

If these steps are not successful, if your baby isn't gaining weight or growing typically, or if your child is upset by the spitting up or vomiting, your pediatrician may consider starting medication and/or refer you to a pediatric gastrointestinal (GI) specialist.

Infectious Causes. After the first few months after birth, the most common cause of vomiting is a stomach or intestinal infection. Viruses are by far the most frequent infecting agents, but occasionally bacteria and even parasites may be the cause. The infection also may produce fever, diarrhea, and sometimes nausea and abdominal pain. The infection is usually contagious; if your child has it, chances are good that some of her playmates also will be affected.

Viruses are a leading cause of vomiting in infants and young children, with symptoms often progressing to diarrhea and fever. Rotavirus is one of the viral causes of gastroenteritis, but other types of viruses—such as noroviruses and adenoviruses—

Normal pylorus

Stomach

First part of the duodenum of small intestine

Hypertrophied (enlarged) pylorus muscle with narrowed stomach outlet can cause it as well. Rotavirus has become much less frequent due to the availability of a vaccine that can prevent severe disease. (For more information about gastroenteritis, see page 529.)

Occasionally infections outside the gastrointestinal tract will cause vomiting. These include infections of the respiratory system (also see discussions of middle ear infections, page 670; pneumonia, page 612), infections of the urinary tract (see page 790), meningitis (see page 797), and appendicitis (see page 531). Some of these conditions require immediate medical treatment, so be alert for the following trouble signs, whatever your child's age, and call your pediatrician if they occur.

■ Blood or bile (a green-colored material) in the vomit, or the vomit appears to consist of coffee-ground-like material

■ Severe abdominal pain

■ Strenuous, repeated vomiting

■ Swollen or enlarged abdomen

■ Lethargy or severe irritability

■ Convulsions

■ Jaundice

■ Signs or symptoms of dehydration (see *Signs and Symptoms of Dehydration* on page 547.)

■ Inability to drink adequate amounts of fluid

■ Vomiting continuing beyond twenty-four hours

Treatment

In most cases, vomiting will stop without specific medical treatment. The majority of cases are caused by a virus and will get better on their own. You should never use over-the-counter or prescription remedies unless they've been specifically prescribed by your pediatrician for your child and for this particular illness.

When there is continued vomiting, you need to make certain that dehydration doesn't occur. *Dehydration* is a term used when the body loses so much water that it can no longer function efficiently (see *Signs and Symptoms of Dehydration,* page 547). If allowed to reach a severe degree, it can be serious and life-threatening. To prevent this from happening, make sure your child consumes enough extra fluids to restore what has been lost through throwing up. If she vomits these fluids, notify your pediatrician.

For the first twenty-four hours or so of any illness that causes vomiting, keep your child off solid foods, and encourage her to suck or drink small amounts of fluids such as electrolyte solution instead of eating. Liquids not only help to prevent dehydration, but also are less likely than solid foods to stimulate further vomiting.

Be sure to follow your pediatrician's guidelines for giving your child fluids. Your doctor will adhere to requirements like those described in the box on page 542 (*Estimated Amount of Fluid Children Should Drink Daily [Depending on Body Weight]*).

In most cases, your child will just need to stay at home and receive a liquid diet for twelve to twenty-four hours. Your pediatrician usually won't prescribe a drug to treat the vomiting, but some doctors will prescribe anti-nausea medications to children.

If your child also has diarrhea (see page 537), ask your pediatrician for instructions on giving liquids and restoring solids to her diet.

If she can't retain any clear liquids or if the symptoms become more severe, notify your pediatrician. He will examine your child and may order blood and urine tests or imaging tests such as X-rays to make a diagnosis. Occasionally hospital care may be necessary.

Until your child feels better, remember to keep her hydrated, and call your pediatrician right away if she shows signs of dehydration. If your child looks sick, if the symptoms aren't improving with time, or if your pediatrician suspects a bacterial infection, he may perform a culture of the stool, and treat appropriately.

~ 17 ~

Asthma and Allergies

Asthma

Asthma is a chronic disease of the breathing tubes that carry air to the lungs. In the last twenty years, there has been a major increase in the number of people with asthma, especially young children and those living in urban areas. In fact, asthma is now one of the most common chronic diseases of childhood, affecting about five million children. We don't know what caused this increase, but some reasons or triggers for asthma or wheezing episodes include air pollution (including tobacco smoke early in life), exposure to allergens or not enough exposure to allergens, obesity, and respiratory illnesses.

Asthma symptoms can be different for each person, but wheezing is a hallmark sign. Wheezing is the high-pitched sound on breathing out that occurs when the breathing tubes in the lungs are narrowed, typically due to inflammation. In asthma, wheezing occurs most often at night or in the early morning. Still, not everyone who wheezes has asthma. Although no specific test can determine asthma, the diagnosis is often made after a child has had three or more wheezing attacks. Many times, in between attacks children do well, but since they often get colds (a common trigger for wheezing in children), the attacks can be as frequent as every month, particularly in toddlers or children less than three years of age who get sick often. If a child has no other allergies—meaning that she does not have eczema or food allergy—and neither parent has asthma, wheezing will likely decrease between three and six years of age once they outgrow catching frequent colds that often trigger the wheezing. If these children begin wheezing in the first years after birth and continue to have repeated wheezing attacks, they are diagnosed with asthma.

Every child is unique, and thus it is important to discuss your child's health with your primary physician or specialist. Asthma is such a variable disease that some infants and children may wheeze without much distress while others have such severe wheezing and breathing difficulty that it may create an emergency situation. In general, most exacerbations are manageable at home if symptoms are recognized early and treatment initiated as directed by your doctor.

If there is a history of asthma or allergy, a child who frequently wheezes is likely to continue wheezing for a number of years. However, asthma can also occur in children who are not allergic. It is not possible to cure asthma, but it *is* possible to control asthma symptoms. Proper treatment reduces wheezing and prevents future attacks. How you breathe starts with what you breathe. Irritants and allergens can cause asthma problems. Irritants are a problem for everyone. Allergens are a problem only if you are allergic to the allergen.

Tobacco smoke is one of the most important asthma triggers. Tobacco smoke exposure increases risk of wheezing from viral infections and decreases response to some of the most important medications used to control asthma. One of the most important things that a family can do to protect a child is to eliminate his or her exposure to tobacco smoke. Keeping the home and car smoke free is an important start, but it is difficult to eliminate a child's exposure as long as close family members are smokers. The best thing a family member can do to protect the child would be to stop smoking. Free help with stopping is available from the National Smokers' Helpline at 1-800-QUIT-NOW.

Electronic cigarettes (also called vapes, Juul, e-hookah, and others) are very dangerous, especially to children with asthma. They are not safe to use around children. Their emissions can and do expose children to nicotine as well as a number of irritating, inflammation-producing, and carcinogenic chemicals. Use of fire-

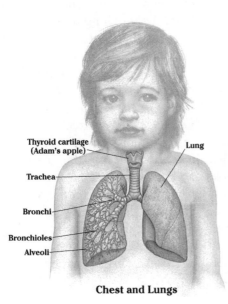

Thyroid cartilage
(Adam's apple)

Lung

Trachea

Bronchi

Bronchioles

Alveoli

Chest and Lungs

places and burning of incense also can trigger asthma. Other common irritant asthma triggers include strong-smelling household cleaners, insecticides (bug spray), other strong chemicals, paint, air fresheners, and perfumes.

Viral infections—even the common cold—can trigger asthma attacks, especially in young children. It is difficult to keep a child from catching a cold, but you can practice healthy habits by ensuring they get the flu shot (influenza vaccine) every fall and encouraging them to wash their hands.

Allergens—irritants that your child is allergic to—also can trigger asthma. Since asthma is a breathing problem, the common allergens that trigger asthma are the ones that are breathed in. Food allergy would not cause asthma alone, as the food proteins that are absorbed travel to all parts of the body. Allergy testing can help determine what your child is allergic to.

Common allergic triggers of asthma include:

■ House dust mites (microscopic insects that live in house dust and feed on shed skin; bedding can also have high concentrations of house dust mites)

■ Cockroaches

■ Pet (animal) dander (the shed skin from animals with fur or feathers)

■ Pollens (from trees, grasses, or weeds)

■ Molds and mold spores (from either water damage in the home or decomposing plant material outside)

Other asthma triggers include:

■ Stress and emotional upset—especially if the underlying asthma is not well controlled

■ Sinus infections

■ Outdoor air pollution

■ Cold air

■ Certain medications (sensitivity to NSAIDs such as ibuprofen, aspirin, etc.)

Signs and Symptoms

When your child has an asthma flare-up (or "attack"), the major symptom will be a cough or wheeze that gets worse at night, with physical activity, or after contact with an irritant (e.g., cigarette smoke) or an allergen (e.g., animal dander, mold, dust mites, or cockroaches). As the attack progresses, the wheezing actually may decrease, as less air is able to move in and out. She also may experience shortness of breath, breathe fast, and have "retractions," when the chest and neck pull in while she works harder to take in air.

Many children with asthma have chronic symptoms, such as daily (or nightly) cough, cough whenever they exercise, or cough after exposure to pets, dust, or pollen. Asthma is considered persistent if there is a need for rescue medication (see *Treatment* section) more than twice a week or if there are more than two awakenings at night for asthma symptoms per month.

In some children, the physician may hear wheezing (especially when the child blows out hard) even without more obvious signs. Abnormalities may be detected by pulmonary function testing (PFT) or functional exhaled nitric oxide (FE_{NO}) in children old enough to cooperate with this breathing test.

When to Call the Pediatrician

Children with well-controlled asthma can participate in the same activities as other children, including play outdoors and exercise. Watch your child closely when she's outside or exercising, and if symptoms develop or worsen, talk to your pediatrician.

For a child with asthma, you should know the situations that require *immediate* medical attention. As a rule, call your pediatrician immediately or consider going to the emergency room if:

■ Your child has *severe* trouble breathing and seems to be getting worse, especially if she is breathing rapidly and there is pulling in of the chest wall when she inhales and forceful grunting when she exhales.

■ Your child's mouth or fingertips appear blue.

■ Your child acts agitated, unusually sleepy, or confused.

■ There is any chest pain with breathing.

You also should call your pediatrician without delay if:

■ Your child has a fever and persistent coughing or wheezing that is not responding to treatment.

■ Your child is vomiting repeatedly and cannot take oral medication or drink fluids.

■ Your child has difficulty speaking or sleeping because of wheezing, coughing, or troubled breathing.

Treatment

Asthma always should be treated under your pediatrician's supervision. The goals of treatment are to:

1. Prevent asthma symptoms such as coughing, wheezing, chest tightness, and shortness of breath.

2. Allow your child to run and play as hard as he or she wants to.

3. Prevent serious asthma attacks.

4. Control your child's asthma with the smallest amount of medication possible.

Preventing severe asthma problems starts by preventing mild asthma problems. Work with your child's doctor to develop an asthma action plan. Like a traffic light, an asthma action plan has green, yellow, and red zones and discusses what to do at each step, including which medications to give. The green zone plan is the action you take every day to keep your child well. The yellow zone plan is what actions you take when your child has mild asthma symptoms. The red zone plan is what actions you follow when your child experiences moderate or severe asthma problems. Work with your doctor to create a written asthma action plan for your child.

With these goals in mind, your pediatrician will prescribe medication and may refer you to a specialist who can evaluate your child's asthma—a pediatric pulmonologist (breathing specialist) or allergist (allergy specialist). Your doctor also will help you plan your child's specific home treatment program. **This will include learning how to use the medicines and treatments that are prescribed and developing a plan to avoid the irritants and allergens that may be causing your child to cough or wheeze.**

The medication prescribed for your child will depend on the nature of the asthma. There are two main types of asthma drugs. One type opens up the breathing tubes and relaxes the muscles causing obstruction. These quick-relief or rescue medicines are called bronchodilators. The second type is controller or maintenance medications, which are used to treat the airway inflammation (swelling and mucus production).

■ *Quick-relief or rescue medications are intended for short-term use.* If your child has an asthma attack, with coughing and/or wheezing, a rescue medication should be given. Medicines such as albuterol are a common choice. By relaxing the muscle squeezing down around the breathing tubes, these rescue medicines can relieve the tightness in her chest and ease her wheezing and feelings of breathlessness. They are prescribed on an as-needed basis. After using a rescue inhaler, breathing will usually improve for a few hours. Rescue inhalers provide a few hours of symptom relief but are not meant to fix the underlying problem. The rescue medication can be given by an HFA-propelled inhaler (HFA = hydrofluoroalkanes)—also known as a puffer—or by nebulizer (see page 566).

It is important to note that if there is no improvement or change after giving the rescue medicine, the child may need further evaluation, the asthma problems may be severe and need stronger medicine, or the problem may not be asthma, but something else such as an infection or other lung problem. Should an attack become severe, your doctor may prescribe an additional medication, such as an oral corticosteroid (usually prednisone, prednisolone, or dexamethasone). The oral corticosteroids are powerful medicines to shrink the swelling and inflammation of the breathing tubes.

■ *Controller medications are intended to be used every day.* They are designed to control your child's asthma and reduce the number of days and nights that he has asthma symptoms. In general, controller medicines are appropriate for children who have symptoms two or more times a week, who awaken with symptoms more than twice a month, who require more than two oral steroid courses within a year, or who have been hospitalized due to asthma symptoms.

■ *The most effective controller medication is an inhaled corticosteroid.* Inflammation of the breathing tubes typically leads to an asthma reaction. By controlling the inflammation and making the breathing tubes less sensitive, these medications help to prevent asthma symptoms and asthma attacks. Daily use can help to keep your child's breathing regular. There are several different types, but they all work by preventing inflammation in the airway. By making the airways less sensitive to allergens and irritants, these medicines can reduce the number and severity of asthma episodes. In infants and young children, inhaled corticosteroids may be administered via nebulizer with face mask or via inhaler. An inhaler requires using a

plastic tube called a spacer or volume holding chamber, which is required to allow the particles space to spread out and reach the small areas of the lungs. Without the spacer, most of the medication will travel to the back of the throat and be swallowed instead of inhaled. In infants and small children this is usually done with a mask (small or medium), which needs to be placed on the face with a good seal while the child takes several breaths. Spacers also come with a mouthpiece for older children, which requires the child to slowly inhale and hold her breath for ten seconds. After taking an inhaled steroid, it is important for your child to rinse and spit or brush her teeth, as the medicine is very good for the lungs but not so good for the teeth.

Spacers come in various shapes and sizes.

Another way to deliver the medication is by nebulizer (sometimes called a breathing machine). The compressor connects by tubing to a device that is like a small cup into which the medication is placed. The compressor converts the liquid into a mist that is then breathed in. In small children a mask is used (see illustration on page 566) and needs to be on the face with a good seal. If there is not a good seal, most of the medication escapes into the air and never reaches the lungs.

It is ideal to give the medication when your child is not crying, as crying decreases the amount of medicine that can reach the lungs. This may not always be possible, but over time most children learn to accept the medication. Although both techniques are equally effective, your child may be more cooperative with one over the other. It may appear that the rescue medication (e.g., albuterol) is more effective through a nebulizer, but nebulized doses of albuterol are typically much greater than two puffs delivered through an inhaler.

Leukotriene receptor antagonists block the activity of chemicals (leukotrienes) that are associated with airway inflammation; they are available only in oral preparations (pill form, granule powder, and chewable tablet). They are not as strong as the inhaled corticosteroid medications, but they can be very helpful when used in combination with an inhaled corticosteroid. Anti-inflammatory medications, inhaled corticosteroids, and/or leukotriene receptor antagonists are recommended for all children with asthma who have persistent symptoms. Another way for a child to receive certain medication is through a

dry powder inhaler. These release the medicine without a propellant. Your child must rely on the force of her own inhalation to take in the medicine and get it into her lungs.

As prevention, all of these medications work best when used regularly. Often they fail because they are not taken consistently. Giving your child medicine when he or she feels well can be challenging; however, having a routine, such as giving the medicine before brushing the teeth, can make taking the medicine daily a lot easier.

Be sure to give medications according to your doctor's directions. *Do not stop medicines too soon*, give them less often than recommended, or switch to other drugs or treatments without first discussing the change with the doctor. In some children, several medicines may be prescribed at the same time to get the asthma controlled, and then the number of medications is reduced once asthma symptoms are under control. If you do not understand why a particular treatment has been recommended, or how it should be given, ask for an explanation.

Asthma treatment should alleviate your child's symptoms so they do not interfere with sleep, activity, or sports. If your child is not achieving the goals of treatment, the asthma action plan needs to be reevaluated. Maybe there is an asthma trigger that can be controlled or a problem with how your child takes his or her medicine, or perhaps more or different asthma medication may be needed. Sometimes the reason that asthma medicines don't work is that your child might not have asthma or it could be another medical condition. Your pediatrician will examine your child and check for problems that could be making her asthma worse, and consider if your child needs a referral to an asthma specialist.

Prevention

A common allergic trigger of asthma is house dust mites. While you cannot eliminate dust and other irritants, there are some things that can be done to reduce exposure and lower your child's chances of having asthma symptoms. For example, in your home you can:

■ Cover your child's bed mattress and pillow with special allergen-proof encasings.

■ Use pillows or comforters that can be machine-washed.

■ Wash sheets, blankets, pillows, throw rugs, and stuffed animals every week in hot water to kill dust mites.

■ Limit stuffed animals in your child's room.

■ Keep pets out of your child's room and consider removing pets from your home if the child is allergic.

■ Keep your child out of rooms while you're vacuuming carpets and dusting furniture.

■ Consider investing in a special air filter (called a high-efficiency particulate air filter, or HEPA filter) to keep your child's room clean.

■ Maintain the humidity in your house below 50 percent when possible; dust mites and mold grow best in damp areas.

■ Avoid perfumes, scented cleaning products, and other items with scents that could become irritants.

■ Reduce mold in your house by repairing leaky plumbing.

■ Keep your child away from cigarette, cigar, or pipe smoke, as well as smoke from a fireplace.

■ Don't allow anyone to smoke in your home or car.

Eczema

Although many patients and practitioners use the terms "eczema" and "atopic dermatitis" interchangeably, "eczema" is a general term used to describe a group of skin conditions characterized by a red itchy rash. Atopic dermatitis and contact dermatitis are two of the most common types of eczemas in children. Acute eczema may appear as red skin that is dry and peeling or moist and oozing. When eczema is persistent, the skin tends to thicken, darken, and become scaly.

ATOPIC DERMATITIS

Atopic dermatitis often occurs in infants and children in families with a history of atopic dermatitis, food allergies, asthma, hay fever, and/or environmental allergies. Although the cause of atopic dermatitis is unknown, genetics clearly plays a role. The relationship to allergies is unclear. Additionally, atopic dermatitis is often the first condition to develop in many children who will go on to develop the other conditions listed above.

Atopic Dermatitis usually develops in three different phases. The infantile phase occurs between several weeks and six months of age, with itching, redness, and the appearance of small bumps on the cheeks, forehead, or scalp. The bumps may spread to the trunk and extremities as well. Although atopic dermatitis can be confused with other types of dermatitis, severe itching is typically a prominent feature. In many cases, the rash improves by two or three years of age.

In school-age children (between four and ten years old), atopic dermatitis often affects the skin at the elbows and knees, and sometimes on the backs of the wrists and ankles. One common feature is red, scaly patches. There may be dry, scabby and irritated areas due to excessive scratching. Over time, the skin becomes discolored and thicker. The third phase, characterized by itching and dry, scaly skin, begins at age twelve and may continue into adulthood.

CONTACT DERMATITIS

Contact dermatitis can occur when the skin comes in contact with an irritating substance or allergen. One form of this problem results from repeated contact with irritating substances such as citrus or other acidic foods, bubble baths, harsh soaps, and wool or rough fabrics. One of the most common irritants is a child's own saliva. Constant drooling or licking the lips can cause an eczematous dermatitis of the lips and skin around the mouth.

Another form of contact dermatitis develops after contact with substances the child is allergic to. The most common potential allergens are:

■ Nickel in jewelry or snaps on jeans or pants

■ Flavorings or additives to toothpastes and mouthwashes

■ Glues, dyes, or leather used in the manufacture of shoes

■ Dyes used in clothing

■ Plants, especially poison ivy, poison oak, and poison sumac (this rash usually appears within several hours after contact, or within one to three days with poison ivy)

■ Medications such as antibiotic/antibacterial ointments

Treatment

If your child has a rash that looks like eczema, your pediatrician will need to examine it to make the correct diagnosis and prescribe the proper treatment. In some cases she may arrange for consultation with a pediatric dermatologist. Although there is no cure for eczema, it can be controlled and will often go away after several months or years. The most effective treatment is to prevent the skin from becoming dry and itchy and to avoid triggers that cause the condition to flare. To do this:

■ Use skin moisturizers regularly and frequently to decrease the dryness and itchiness. Ointments often work better than creams, which often work better than lotions.

■ Give your child a short daily bath in lukewarm water. After a bath, rinse twice to remove any residual soap (which might be an irritant). Then apply the moisturizing cream or ointment within three minutes of getting out of the bath to lock in the moisture.

■ Avoid harsh or irritating clothing (wool or synthetic material).

■ If there is extreme itching, use cool compresses on the area, followed by the application of prescribed medications.

There are many types of prescription creams and ointments available, so ask your pediatrician to prescribe one that she prefers to control inflammation and itching. These preparations often contain a form of steroid, which is the first line of treatment. These creams or ointments should be used under the direction of your child's doctor. It's important to continue to apply the medications for as long as your pediatrician recommends their use.

In addition to the skin preparations, your child also may take an antihistamine by mouth to relieve the itching and may need antibiotics if the skin becomes infected. If your child develops frequent infections, your pediatrician may suggest a very dilute bleach bath, usually made by adding ⅛ to ½-cap bleach in a regular-size bathtub of water.

Treatment of allergic contact dermatitis is similar. Although a little detective work will often help identify the trigger, your pediatric dermatologist or allergist may conduct a series of patch tests. These tests are done by placing small patches of allergens against your child's skin for forty-eight hours. If the skin reacts with redness and itching, that substance should be avoided.

Alert your pediatrician if any of the following occurs:

■ Your child's rash is severe and is not responding to home treatment.

■ There is any fever or evidence of infection (i.e., blisters, extensive redness, yellow crusts, pain, or oozing of fluid).

Food Allergy

While many foods can cause allergic reactions, true food allergies are less common than you might think. Food allergies are most likely to happen in infants and children, as well as in children with other allergies or whose family members have allergies. When food allergies do occur, they may be in response to any food, although particular items are more likely to cause reactions (see the list below). While in many cases food allergies may reveal themselves with mild symptoms, they can be potentially life-threatening.

While any food can trigger a food allergy, several cause the vast majority of cases in children. Cow's milk is among them. Other common foods associated with allergies include:

- Eggs

- Peanuts and tree nuts (such as cashews, walnuts, etc.)

- Soy

- Wheat

- Fish (such as tuna, salmon, and cod) and crustacean shellfish (such as shrimp, crab, and lobster)

- Sesame seeds

If your child has a food allergy, her immune system responds in an exaggerated way to otherwise harmless proteins in foods. When this food is consumed, her immune system manufactures antibodies that attempt to fight off the offending food. In the process, substances called histamines and other chemicals are released that cause allergic symptoms.

Another condition, food intolerance or food sensitivity, occurs more often than true food allergies. Although the terms are often confused and sometimes used interchangeably, food intolerance does not involve the immune system. For example, a child with lactose intolerance (a condition of food sensitivity) is deficient in an enzyme required to digest milk sugar, leading to stomachaches, bloating, and diarrhea.

Symptoms

A true food allergy happens when the body reacts against proteins found in foods. The reaction usually happens shortly after a food is eaten. Food allergy reactions can vary from mild to severe and include:

- Skin problems (itchy skin rashes, hives, swelling)

- Stomach problems (nausea, vomiting, diarrhea)

- Breathing problems (sneezing, wheezing, throat tightness)

- Circulation problems (pale skin, light-headedness, loss of consciousness)

The intensity of the allergic reaction can range from mild to severe. If

How Allergies Develop

When an allergy-prone child is exposed to an allergen, his immune system produces an antibody (called IgE) in a process called allergic sensitization. The IgE sticks to mast cells in the skin and the linings of the airways and gut. The next time he comes in contact with allergens, these cells release chemicals (e.g., histamine and leukotrienes) that cause allergic symptoms.

your child is highly allergic, even trace amounts of the food may trigger a potentially dangerous allergic response called anaphylaxis. Anaphylaxis can develop without warning and can progress rapidly; it must be treated immediately with a prescribed emergency injectable medication (called epinephrine autoinjector), which should be on hand at all times. Symptoms of anaphylaxis include:

- Swelling of the throat and tongue

- Difficulty breathing

- Wheezing

- A sudden drop in blood pressure, which would make your child look pale, feel lethargic, or lose consciousness

- Turning blue

- Loss of consciousness

(See the box *Anaphylactic Reactions: What You Should Do* on page 577.)

Diagnosis and Management

Because some food allergies can be serious, talk to your pediatrician if you suspect that your child has one. To help make the diagnosis, your pediatrician will review your concerns and may perform some tests or refer you to an allergist, who may recommend additional testing. Sometimes the presence of a food allergy is obvious, like when a child gets hives and lip swelling after eating a walnut, but sometimes it's less obvious, such as dry skin patches. Tests, including a skin prick test and blood tests, can provide more information and answers.

- With the skin prick test (or scratch test), the doctor will prick the skin with drops of the suspicious food allergens on your child's back or forearm. This can result in redness, swelling, and itching at the site, which the doctor will measure after twenty minutes.

- A blood test can measure antibodies to foods as well; these antibodies are called immunoglobulin E, or IgE. A sample of your child's blood will be drawn and sent to the laboratory for testing.

It is important that your doctor tests your child only for the specific foods that have caused potential reactions. General blood panels are not recommended unless reactions have occurred. A positive skin or blood test alone is not sufficient to diagnose food allergy. Your doctor should discuss with you the specifics of your child's diet, including any of your concerns about reactions to particular foods, to know what tests to consider and how to interpret the results.

There is no treatment for food allergies at this time. Avoidance of what your child is allergic to is the only way to avoid food allergy symptoms including a life-threatening reaction. However, with some foods such as milk, soy, wheat, and eggs, many children will outgrow their food allergy over time. Some children can tolerate certain forms of milk and egg, depending on how it is cooked or processed. Some children can eat baked food with milk and eggs, such as in a muffin, without symptoms of an allergic reaction. In such cases, your pediatrician or allergist may recommend continuing to feed your child a small amount of the food such as egg or milk regularly, as this might help your child outgrow her food allergy. In other cases, your pediatrician or allergist may recommend that you avoid the food your child is allergic to altogether and retest your child in the future to see if she is still allergic. Certain food allergies—like those to

peanuts and fish—are less likely to be outgrown. Only 20 percent of children with peanut allergy outgrow or develop a natural tolerance.

Even once you're successful in keeping allergenic foods out of your refrigerator and off your dining room table, it may be more difficult to keep your child away from those items when she is out of your care. As your child gets older you'll have to educate her, as well as her friends, grandparents, teachers, childcare workers, and other caregivers, about the importance of avoiding specific foods that could trigger allergy symptoms. Every time you shop, read food labels and look for major allergens to which your child is allergic. Also, when your family is eating in restaurants or traveling, ask questions about the ingredients of menu items. While the waiter may be helpful, confirm the information by speaking with the chef.

As you make adjustments in your child's diet, talk to your pediatrician regularly about compensating for the missing foods and keeping her diet balanced. For example, if your child is allergic to milk, you will need to include other calcium-rich foods (like green leafy vegetables and calcium-fortified drinks) in her diet. If your infant is allergic to breast milk or milk formula, refer to page 122 about choosing an elemental formula.

Nasal Allergy/Allergic Rhinitis

If your child's nose starts to run and his eyes become itchy, red, and swollen, but there are no other symptoms of a cold or an infection, he may be having allergic rhinitis. This is a reaction to allergens in the environment. The most common environmental allergens are pollen, dust mites, mold, and animal dander. Like other allergies, this condition tends to run in families. The symptoms may not appear immediately, however. Seasonal respiratory allergies (e.g., to pollen) are quite uncommon in children under age two because infants have to be exposed to a few pollen seasons to develop allergies.

It is sometimes difficult to tell the difference between a common cold and nasal allergy, because many of the symptoms are the same. Here are some of the signs of a possible nasal allergy:

- Sneezing, sniffling, stuffiness; itchy and runny nose (usually clear discharge)

- Tearing; itchy, red, or swollen eyes

- A horizontal crease across the bridge of nose from frequent wiping (nasal salute)

- Nosebleeds (see *Nosebleeds*, page 679)

- Dark rings under the eyes (allergic shiners)

- Mouth breathing because of nasal congestion

- Fatigue (mostly from not sleeping well at night)

- Frequent throat clearing or clucking (rubbing tongue against roof of mouth)

If your child has nasal allergies, potential complications include frequent sinus and ear infections (see *Middle Ear Infections*, page 670, and *Sinusitis*, page 675). If the allergy causes eye irritation and rubbing, she may be more susceptible to eye infections (see page 739). Since chronic allergies also can interfere with sleep, this may also affect school performance.

Treatment

Call your pediatrician if your child's nasal allergies start to interfere with sleep, school, or other activities. To prevent or treat allergy symptoms, the doctor can suggest treatment, including prescription and nonprescription antihistamines, nose sprays of various types (including saline), and other medications. In many cases, she will recommend an oral antihistamine; most are now available over the counter, including loratadine, fexofenadine, and cetirizine. For more severe or persistent allergy symptoms, your physician may recommend a prescription or over-the-counter steroid nasal spray that, when used on a daily basis, will help prevent nasal allergy symptoms. If your child's eyes are swollen, itchy, and red, your pediatrician may also recommend prescription or over-the-counter allergy eye drops.

Common Household Allergens

Source	What to Do
Pets (dogs, cats, guinea pigs, rabbits, and hamsters) The best pets for allergenic families are fish and reptiles because they don't cause allergies.	If your child is allergic to an animal, it's best not to have that animal in the house, but at the very least, keep it out of the child's bedroom. Have your child wash his hands and face after playing with a pet, and shower and wash his hair at night before bed so he doesn't sleep in pet dander. Also, run a HEPA filter in the child's bedroom to remove airborne allergens.
Mold Mold grows outdoors in cool, damp, dark places, such as in soil, grass, and dead leaves. Indoors, it's found in cluttered storage areas, recently flooded areas, basement areas, plumbing spaces, and areas with poor ventilation such as closets and attics, as well as pillows and blankets that haven't been aired out in a long time.	The key to controlling mold is to limit humidity. Avoid using vaporizers, humidifiers, and swamp coolers. A dehumidifier in a damp basement can be helpful. Throughout the house, replace any carpet that's been saturated by a big water spill, or dry it completely. You can destroy mold with several types of disinfectants, but be careful to store them in a safe place, away from curious toddlers.
House Dust Mites Many people are allergic to house dust mites, which are found in bedding (pillows, blankets, sheets, and mattresses), upholstery, furniture, and carpet. These mites, which are too small to be seen by the naked eye, thrive in humid environments (humidity greater than 50 percent).	The most important measures for reducing exposure to house dust mites should be focused on the bedroom. Put dust-mite-proof covers on mattresses and pillows, and wash sheets and blankets in hot water once a week to remove allergens and kill the mites. It's also helpful to keep the humidity in the home at less than 50 percent to control the growth of mites. If you're remodeling the bedroom, consider removing carpets from the room.

The best thing you can do for your allergic child is to remove the sources of allergens from your home, if possible. Refer to the box on page 575 for more information on common household allergens.

Hives

Another allergic type of rash that is characteristically very itchy and comes and goes is called hives. Hives are red, swollen bumps that tend to move around; individual lesions typically resolve within about twenty-four hours. When the rash remains in the same place for more than twenty-four hours, other diagnoses should be considered.

Among the most common causes of hives are:

■ Response to an infection, most commonly a virus

■ Foods (most commonly peanuts, tree nuts, egg whites, milk, shellfish, and sesame)

■ Medications, either over-the-counter or prescription (such as ibuprofen and antibiotics)

■ Bites or stings from bees or other insects

In at least half of cases of acute hives, it is not possible to identify the cause. An episode of acute hives can last up to six weeks before resolving. If hives persist longer than six weeks, they are considered chronic and may need further evaluation by your pediatrician or allergist. Foods, medications, and venom stings are generally not responsible for chronic hives (those lasting more than six weeks).

Treatment

Oral antihistamine medication should relieve or at least help reduce the itching of hives. This can be obtained without a prescription. You may need to use this type of medication around the clock for several days. Some of these medicines may need to be given to your child as often as every four to six hours, while others can be given once or twice a day. Applying cool compresses to the area of itching and swelling may help.

If your child is wheezing or having trouble swallowing, seek emergency treatment. The doctor usually will prescribe self-injectable epinephrine to stop the allergic response. Self-injectable epinephrine should be available at all times for such patients, including at home, in childcare, or at school, in case of such reactions in the future. (For more information about these emergency kits, see the box *Anaphylactic Reactions: What You Should Do*, opposite.)

Prevention

Your doctor will try to determine what is causing the hives. For example, does it usually happen an hour after eating a specific food? Or after taking a specific medication? Does your child have any other illness

Anaphylactic Reactions: What You Should Do

An anaphylactic reaction is the most serious of allergic reactions and is always an emergency. It is potentially fatal and requires immediate medical attention. If symptoms such as swelling of the face or throat and wheezing occur, administer self-injectable epinephrine and then call 911 or go to the emergency room immediately. When used properly and promptly, self-injectable epinephrine can reverse most serious reactions and allow for time to get to an emergency room for further treatment. In most cases, it reduces symptoms rapidly, but if it doesn't, another injection should be given five minutes later.

To use an auto-injector, you'll press the device against your youngster's thigh and hold it there for ten seconds. Make sure to ask your doctor or nurse to give you precise instructions and demonstrate its use with a trainer. At the same time, your childcare center or preschool should have written instructions on how to recognize and react to a severe allergic reaction that may be life-threatening, and epinephrine should be available to care providers, along with a step-by-step guide and demonstration on how to administer it. Keep in mind that unused medication in these auto-injectors should be replaced at regular intervals, so check the expiration date and replace it as recommended by your doctor.

If your child has an anaphylactic reaction, see your pediatrician afterward, and find out exactly why the reaction happened and how to avoid another one. Your child should also wear a medical identification bracelet if she has had an anaphylactic episode in the past. This bracelet should give information about the allergies that your child has.

symptoms? How quickly does it resolve? Does it start within one hour of eating and resolve quickly (food allergy) or last days to weeks (infection)? Consult your doctor for evaluation and management.

Insect Bites and Stings

Your child's reaction to a bite or sting will depend on her sensitivity to the particular insect's venom. While most children have only mild reactions, those who are allergic to certain insect venoms can have severe symptoms that require emergency treatment.

In general, bites are usually not a serious problem, but in some cases, stings may be. While it is true that most stings and bites (from honeybees, yellow jackets, hornets, wasps, and fire ants, for example) may cause pain and localized swelling, severe anaphylactic reactions are also possible. Delayed allergic reactions to fleas, bedbugs, and mosquito bites are common, and although uncomfortable, they are not life-threatening.

Treatment

Although insect bites can be irritating, they usually begin to disappear by the next day and do not require a doctor's treatment. To relieve the itchiness that accompanies bites by mosquitoes, flies, fleas, and bedbugs, apply a cool compress and calamine lotion or a low-potency topical steroid on the affected areas. Use oral antihistamines to control itch.

If your child is stung by a wasp or bee, this can be more serious. If redness, pain, and itching is present at the site of the sting, this is a local reaction. Soak a cloth in cold water and press it over the area of the sting to reduce pain and swelling. Nonsteroidal anti-inflammatory drugs (ibuprofen) may also be helpful. Call your pediatrician if symptoms persist or become difficult to control. Your child may be prescribed an oral steroid if the swelling is significant. If the reaction occurs in another area of the body (or all over the body), this is a systemic reaction and needs immediate medical attention. If there is throat swelling or trouble breathing, administer self-injectable epinephrine and call 911.

If your child disturbs a beehive or wasps' nest, get him away from it as quickly as possible. Any disturbance makes other bees and wasps more likely to sting as well. Keep your child's fingernails short and clean to minimize the risk of infection from scratching. If infection does occur, the bite will become redder, larger, and more swollen. In some cases you may notice red streaks or yellowish fluid near the bite or your child may get a fever. Have your pediatrician examine any infected bite right away because it may need to be treated with antibiotics.

Call for medical help immediately if your child has any of these other symptoms after being bitten or stung:

■ Sudden difficulty in breathing

■ Weakness, collapse, or unconsciousness

■ Hives or itching all over the body

■ Extreme swelling near the eyes, lips, or penis that makes it difficult for the child to see, eat, or urinate

Insect Bites and Stings

Insect/Environment	Characteristics of Bite or Sting	Special Notes
Mosquitoes		
Water (pools, lakes, birdbaths)	Stinging sensation followed by small, red, itchy mound with tiny puncture mark at center	Mosquitoes are attracted by bright colors, sweet scents, and sweat.
Flies		
Food, garbage, animal waste	Painful, itchy bumps; may turn into small blisters	Bites often disappear in a day but may last longer.
Fleas		
Cracks in floor, rugs, pet fur	Multiple small bumps clustered together on exposed areas, particularly arms, legs, face	Fleas are most likely to be a problem in homes with pets.
Bedbugs		
Cracks of walls, floors, crevices of furniture, bedding	Itchy red bumps occasionally topped by a blister; usually 2–3 in a row (same as fleas but may affect covered areas)	Bedbugs are most likely to bite at night and are less active in cold weather.
Fire ants		
Mounds in pastures, meadows, lawns, and parks in southern states	Painful, itchy bumps; may turn into small blisters	Fire ants usually attack intruders.
Bees and wasps		
Flowers, shrubs, picnic areas, beaches	Immediate pain and rapid swelling	A few children have severe reactions, such as difficulty breathing and hives/swelling all over the body.
Ticks		
Wooded areas	May not be noticeable; hidden by hair or on skin	Don't remove ticks with matches, lighted cigarettes, or nail polish remover. Grasp the tick firmly with tweezers near the head; gently pull the tick straight out.

It is impossible to prevent all insect bites, but you can minimize the number your child receives by following these guidelines.

■ Avoid areas where insects nest or congregate, such as garbage cans, stagnant pools of water, uncovered foods and sweets, and orchards and gardens where flowers are in bloom.

■ When you know your child will be exposed to insects, dress her in long pants and a lightweight long-sleeved shirt as well as closed-toe shoes.

■ Avoid dressing your child in clothing with bright colors or flowery prints, because they seem to attract insects.

■ Don't use scented soaps, perfumes, or hair sprays on your child, because they also are inviting to insects.

Insect repellents are generally available without a prescription, but they should be used sparingly on infants and young children. The most common insecticides are DEET (N,N-diethyl m-toluamide) and picar-idin. DEET is a chemical that can be used in children older than two months of age. The AAP recommends that when used on children, repellents should contain *no more than 30 percent DEET.* The concentrations of DEET vary significantly from product to product—from less than 10 percent to over 30 percent—so read the label of any product you purchase. DEET's effectiveness peaks at a concentration of 30 percent, which is also *the maximum concentration currently recommended for children.*

In children who consistently get itchy bumps after insect bites, topical treatment and oral antihistamines are of little help. For these children, wearing protective clothing, treating household pets for fleas, and applying insect repellent are the most effective ways to manage the situation. These repellents are effective in preventing bites by mosquitoes, ticks, fleas, chiggers, and biting flies, but they have virtually no effect on stinging insects such as bees, hornets, and wasps. (The table on page 579 summarizes information about common stinging or biting insects.)

~ 18 ~

Behavior

Anger, Aggression, and Biting

There are many times when your child's behavior warms your heart. But there are other times when it probably drives you a little crazy. From temper tantrums to dancing around your living room, he's expressing his feelings and needs, although not always in ways that you'd prefer.

Your child's behavior is partly innate; in a real sense, he was born to act this way. But there are a lot of other influences on his behavior in addition to his genetic makeup. For example, your own parenting style will affect your child's behavior. So will the role models that he encounters and may imitate. So will the media, from television to movies to the Internet. Family circumstances are important, too, as are the stresses and transitions he'll encounter, including starting a new preschool or dealing with sickness.

Your child's behavior doesn't happen in isolation. But no matter the underlying cause or the message that he's trying to communicate, his behavior will get your attention every day. Consequently, there will be issues you'll have to deal with. We all have feelings of anger and aggression, including your child. These impulses are normal, healthy, and part of your child's expected behavior. As a toddler or preschooler, your child may lack the self-control to express his anger peacefully. Instead, he may naturally lash out, perhaps hitting or biting in frustration. It's a behavior you should anticipate as he moves through this period of his life.

In a toddler (ages fifteen to thirty months), expressive language skills (the speech and language your child produces) and the ability to articulate emotions such as happiness, anger, and sadness are not well developed. From the child's perspective, these are the "terrific twos," because he is so excited about all of the new things he is developmentally able to do. It's as if he is saying, "Look at what I can do!" But one consequence of this is that your toddler can get frustrated at anyone or anything limiting his ability to do what he wishes to do, even if he's not capable of it. This lack of independence leads to immediate and intense frustration and loss of control, which may manifest as a temper tantrum or other behavioral episode. When this happens, he needs you to take control for him and to help him develop judgment, self-discipline, and other tools to express his feelings in more acceptable and age-appropriate ways.

This is very hard for parents, since before the "terrific twos," your child was a cuddly, warm, interactive, and loving infant and toddler. Some parents will even think, "He is like a monster and just out to get me!" But do not take this behavior personally. Your toddler is simply overwhelmed. During this time, your overarching goal is to teach him how to regain control and to set limits on behaviors so he won't cause harm to himself, to others, or to property—but not to punish him.

While many parents think that discipline and punishment are the same thing, they are not. Discipline is a way of teaching and a way of enhancing a good parent-child relationship. When you discipline, you should provide your child with praise along with instruction in a firm tone, with the intent of improving his behavior. By contrast, punishment is a negative, in which you're dispensing an unpleasant consequence when your child does or doesn't do something. Punishment is a part of discipline, but only a small part. Until age three and sometimes later, children simply don't understand the concept of punishment. Setting limits is a much better approach than punishment; most children will respond to clear, calm, and decisive limit-setting. Effective disciplinary strategies, appropriate to the child's age and development, teach the child to regulate his own behavior, keep him from harm, enhance his cognitive, socio-emotional, and executive functioning skills, and reinforce the behavioral patterns taught by the child's parents and caregivers.

A child's behavior or temper can change frequently and quickly and is easily affected by many things such as sleep, nutrition, and what is going on around them. Keep in mind that while some temper tantrums (see page 596) and outbursts are completely normal in young children, anything that causes injury to the child or others should be discussed with your pediatrician.

Your child might go through a brief period of different or unusual behavior, particularly if he's worried, tired, or overstressed, but if it continues for more than a few weeks or is especially aggressive, consult your pediatrician. Parents of children with special healthcare needs may need additional assistance regarding discipline strategies. These strategies begin with an understanding of the child's physical, emotional, and cognitive capacities. In some cases, consultation with a developmental-behavioral pediatrician may be helpful.

What You Can Do

The best way to prevent behavior problems is to give your child a stable, secure home life with firm, loving discipline and full-time supervision during the toddler and preschool years. Choose people to care for your child who can be good role models and who agree to follow the rules you've outlined—both in terms of your expectations for your child and in terms of responding to misbehavior.

Children don't know the rules of the house until they're taught them, so that is one of your important parenting responsibilities. Toddlers are normally interested in touching and exploring, so if there are valuables you don't want them to handle, hide or remove them. Consider setting up a separate portion of your home where your child can play with age-appropriate, safe books and toys.

For discipline to be most effective, it should take place on an ongoing basis, not just when your child misbehaves. In fact, it begins with parents smiling at their smiling baby, and it continues with praise and genuine affection for all positive and appropriate behaviors. Over time, if your child feels encouraged and respected, rather than demeaned and embarrassed, he is more likely to listen, learn, and change when necessary. It is always more effective to positively reinforce desired behaviors and to teach children alternative behaviors rather than just say "Stop it or else." Briefly ignore minor misbehavior, then tell him what to do instead. Provide praise when your child behaves in a way that you like. Let him know exactly what it was about his behavior that you liked, such as "Thank you for talking in your quiet voice in the library," so he knows what to do more of.

Distracting your child can also be helpful when he is starting to get upset. This can help take his mind off something that's upsetting and get him involved in another activity to help him calm down. Try to avoid bribing him to behave differently and instead set clear expectations for how you'd like to see him behave.

Remember, young children have little natural self-control. Your child needs you to teach him not to kick, hit, or bite when he is angry, but instead to express his feelings through words. It's important for him to learn the difference between real and imagined insults and between appropriately standing up for his rights and attacking out of anger. The best way to teach these lessons is to supervise your child carefully when he's involved in disputes with his playmates.

As long as a disagreement is minor, you can keep your distance and let the children solve it on their own. However, you must intervene when children get into a physical fight that continues even after they're told to stop, or when one child seems to be in an uncontrollable rage and is assaulting or biting another. Pull the children apart and keep them separate until they have calmed down. If the fight is extremely violent, you may have to end the play session. Make it clear that it doesn't matter who "started it." There is no excuse for trying to hurt each other.

To avoid or minimize high-risk situations, teach your child ways to deal with his anger without resorting to aggressive behavior. Teach him to say "no" in a firm tone of voice, to turn his back, or to find compromises instead of fighting with his body. Through example, teach him that settling differences with words is more effective—and more civilized—than using physical violence. Praise him for his appropriate behavior and tell him how "grown-up" he is acting whenever he uses these tactics instead of hitting, kicking, or biting. And always reinforce and praise his behavior when he is demonstrating kindness and gentleness.

There's nothing wrong with using a time-out when his behavior is inappropriate, and it can be used in children as young as one year old. These time-outs should be a last resort, however. Have him sit in a chair or go to a boring place where there are no distractions; in essence, you're separating him from his misbehavior, and giving him time to cool off. Briefly explain to your child what you're doing and why—but no long lectures. Initially, when children are young, time-out is over as soon as they have calmed down and are quiet and still. Once they have learned to calm themselves (to be quiet and still), a good rule of thumb is one minute of time-out for each year of your child's age—thus, a three-year-old should have a three-minute time-out. When the time-out is over, there needs to be a time-in, while giving him plenty of positive attention when doing the right thing. (See Time-Out/Time-In on page 364.)

Always watch your own behavior around your child. One of the best ways to teach him appropriate behavior is to control your own temper. If you express your anger in quiet, peaceful ways, he probably will follow your example. That said, there may be times when you must discipline him. In such cases, do not feel guilty about it and certainly don't apologize. If he senses your mixed feelings, he may convince himself that he was in the right all along and you are the "bad" one. Although disciplining your child is never pleasant, it is sometimes a necessary part of parenthood. Your child needs to understand when he is in the wrong so that he will take responsibility for his actions and be willing to accept the consequences.

When to Call the Pediatrician

If your child seems to be unusually aggressive for longer than a few weeks and you cannot cope with his behavior on your own, consult your pediatrician. Other warning signs include:

- Physical injury to himself or others (teeth marks, bruises, head injuries)

- Attacks on you or other adults

- Being sent home or barred from play by neighbors or school

- Your own fear for the safety of those around him

The most important warning sign is the frequency of outbursts. Sometimes children with behavior disorders will go for several days or even a week or two without incident, and may even act quite charming during this time, but few can go an entire month without getting into trouble at least once. Keep in close contact with your child's teacher, school, and other caregivers in order to monitor his behavior.

Your pediatrician can suggest ways to discipline your child and will help you determine whether your expectations of his behavior are appropriate for his age, whether his behavior is within the normal range for children his age, or whether he may have a true behavior disorder. When a child has a true behavior disorder, a mental health intervention with a child psychologist, child therapist, and/or behavioral therapist can help. Ask your pediatrician for a referral.

The pediatrician or other mental health specialist will interview both you and your child and may observe your child in different situations (home, preschool, with adults, with other children). A behavior management program will be outlined. Not all methods work on all children, so there will be a certain amount of trial and reassessment.

Once several effective ways are found to reward good behavior and discourage bad behavior, they can be used in establishing an approach that works both at home and away from home. The progress may be slow, but such programs usually are successful if started when the disorder is just beginning to develop.

Behaviors Raising Concerns About Abuse or Neglect

Sexual behaviors in children are more normal than many parents realize. Up to half of children will display some sort of sexual behavior before age thirteen. That said, many parents find these behaviors concerning and wonder whether they indicate that a child has been a victim of sexual abuse or molestation. While both sexual abuse and neglect can lead to increased sexual behaviors, it's hard even for experts in child abuse to tell if any particular behavior is a result of molestation. Complicating matters further, sexually explicit images and videos are increasingly available to children, and seeing these materials can also prompt behaviors that parents might not expect at such young ages.

One behavior that is common, especially in the preschool years, is simple curiosity about bodies and their differences. At this age children are becoming aware that not everyone is the same, and they may engage in curious touching and comparison of body parts, usually in the context of comparing other features like height, weight, and hair. You may see more of these behaviors after a child welcomes a new sibling, sees a parent without clothes, or observes his mother breastfeeding. Usually these behaviors go away once you've calmly explained to your child that they are inappropriate. If you're concerned about a particular behavior or pattern of behavior, however, talk to your child's pediatrician.

Coping with Disasters and Violence

Disastrous events—earthquakes, hurricanes, tornadoes, floods, and fires—can be frightening and traumatic for both children and adults. Events like these have always demanded that parents be available to talk with and reassure their children and be particularly sensitive to their children's needs. The AAP has compiled information for parents on talking with children about tragedies and other events at Healthy Children.org and AAP.org.

Parents are understandably concerned about the effects of terrorism on their children, including the effects of the media's coverage of those events. In general, it is best to share only the basic information with children, not graphic details or unnecessary details about tragic circumstances. Therefore, it's best to turn off the TV and any other screens that a child may see. It's especially important to keep young children away from repetitive graphic images and sounds that may appear on television, radio, social media, and the Web. If you have older children as well as younger ones, you may make different, age-specific decisions about allowing their exposure to disturbing news. If you decide to let the older children watch the news or a segment online, review it first, and protect your younger children appropriately.

Children will generally follow good advice, but you have to give them some latitude to make decisions about what they're ready for. You can block them from seeing the newspaper that comes to the door, for example, but not the one on the newsstand or at the grocery store. Today, most older children will have access to the news and graphic images through social media and other applications right from their cellphone. You need to be aware of what's out there, take steps in advance to talk to children about what they might hear or see, and ask them if they have any questions or concerns.

What to Expect

Even if terrorism, natural disasters, or other traumatic events occur hundreds or thousands of miles from you and your child, television, online, and print news coverage can make the aftermath traumatizing. If the disaster actually has occurred in your own community, it can be especially frightening for your child.

In the aftermath of a crisis, children may react in different ways. Some may experience a type of post-traumatic stress reaction, with symptoms that may vary from child to child, depending in part on his age. A child up to age five:

■ May have difficulty sleeping

■ May exhibit a decreased appetite

■ May cry and become cranky

■ May show defiance, have tantrums, and exhibit hostility toward siblings

■ May cling to you, shadowing you as you move from one room of the house to another, and show anxiety on leaving your side

■ May have nightmares and refuse to sleep in his own bed

■ May have bed-wetting episodes, even if he has previously been toilet trained

■ May develop physical symptoms, such as stomachaches and headaches

■ Might refuse to go to the preschool that he had attended enthusiastically for months or years

What You Can Do

Remember that children tend to personalize events. They may think that a terrorist attack or disaster is going to strike them or their family members. One of your primary goals as a parent is to talk with your child and make him feel secure and safe. Your words and actions can be very powerful in comforting him; talking with him about the events won't increase his fear and anxiety. As you interact with him, speak to him at a level he can understand. Here are some guidelines to keep in mind.

■ Listen to what your child says to you. Help him use age-appropriate words to describe his feelings—perhaps "sad," "mad," or "scared." Don't make assumptions, and don't downplay what he's saying. Accept what he's feeling.

■ If your child has difficulty expressing himself, encourage him to get his feelings out in other ways—perhaps by drawing pictures or playing with toys.

■ At his age, your child may not need a lot of information about the events that have happened. Don't be surprised if he asks the same questions over and over. While you should be honest about what you tell him, don't overload him with information.

■ If a terrorist attack has happened nearby, explain that there are some bad people in the world, and bad people do bad things. But make sure he understands that most people are not bad and that most people of all ethnic and religious groups are good. Use this event to teach inclusion to your child.

■ For an event like a terrorist attack that occurred elsewhere, let him know that the violence was isolated to particular areas far away, and not in your community.

■ Although you always should monitor what your child watches on television, this advice is *particularly* important when terrorism or other disasters are filling the screen. No matter what your child's age, he can be traumatized by what he sees on television or online, so restrict his viewing of any screens. When he does watch TV, make sure you are there with him, and talk about what you've seen.

■ If you appear particularly anxious over what has happened, he'll feel it and find coping more difficult. Try to stay as calm as possible in his presence, and maintain as many of the routines of the family's life as you can. If your child has been going to preschool, for example, the structure of continuing to do so can be comforting to him.

■ Teach your child the importance of helping out those who have been directly affected by the tragedy or disaster. Let him help you send a letter or care package, or explain to him that you are sending money or supplies to help the victims.

■ If your child has been particularly traumatized by the events that have happened, talk with your pediatrician. She may suggest seeking the help of a mental health professional who specializes in treating children in tough emotional times.

■ It is easier for adults and children when there is a plan in place in advance of an emergency or disaster situation. Parents should develop a written disaster plan and discuss this plan with their children. Talking to children in advance of an emergency or disaster helps them to get better prepared and to develop strategies for coping with emergency situations. It is important to engage them in conversation and help them develop strategies to cope and adjust. (For more information on helping children cope and adjust after a disaster, visit the Advocacy and Policy section at AAP .org.)

Death of a Loved One

The death of an important person in a child's life is among the most stressful events that a child can experience. When the death involves a parent or sibling, the potential for an adverse response by the child is compounded. A number of behavioral changes may be seen, and parents should be on the lookout for problems needing professional help. When dealing with bereavement, here are some key things to consider.

■ The child should be told about a death honestly and in language that is developmentally appropriate.

■ The family can be reassured that showing their feelings, such as shock, disbelief, guilt, sadness, and anger, is normal and helpful. A bereaved parent or other close family member who shares these feelings and memories (e.g., with pictures and stories) with a child reduces the child's sense of isolation.

■ Children need reassurance that they will be cared for and loved by a consistent adult who attends sensitively to their needs. In addition, they must be assured that they did not cause the death, could not have prevented it, and cannot bring back the deceased. Parents should be encouraged to continue family routines and discipline.

■ The funeral services can provide even a young child with an important way to grieve a loved one if such involvement is supportive, appropriately explained, and compatible with the family's values and approach. The child's opinion about attending the service should be considered. Children need to be prepared if they are to participate in the funeral process. The participation should be tailored according to the developmental level of the child.

A trusted person should be with the child to explain what is happening and to offer support. Encouraging a child to commemorate loss through some form of participation, such as drawing pictures, planting a tree, or giving a favorite object, will promote inclusion in the process and provide a meaningful ritual.

■ For a child, grief is a process that unfolds over time. The initial shock and denial of death may evolve into sadness and anger that can last for weeks to months and eventually end, in the best circumstances, with acceptance and readjustment.

Teeth Grinding (Bruxism)

Teeth grinding, also known as bruxism, can occur when your child is awake but more often happens when she is asleep. About a third of children will exhibit some form of teeth grinding. There may be several reasons a child develops this habit, including emotional stress, parasomnias (sleep disturbances), traumatic brain injury, and neurologic disabilities. When chronic, teeth grinding can cause enamel wear, headaches, temporomandibular joint problems, and soreness of the chewing muscles. Preliminary evidence suggests that in most cases grinding in young children is self-limiting and does not continue into adulthood, though occasionally it may. Options for managing bruxism depend on how severe it is and may include the use of a dental night guard, psychological techniques, or medications. Your pediatrician may refer your child to a pediatric dentist to help manage and treat.

Hyperactivity and the Easily Distractible Child

Almost every young child has days when she seems inattentive and hyperactive. Effective behavior management on the part of parents and teachers will likely help any child to stay more focused and attentive. Marked inattention (persistent trouble focusing and concentrating) and hyperactivity could be a condition called attention-deficit/hyperactivity disorder (ADHD), which affects almost 10 percent of school-age children in the United States. Children who have ADHD are inattentive, impulsive, move about a great deal, and/or have difficulty sitting still when it is required. They also can be easily distracted, often act on impulse, and/or have difficulty paying attention when listening to or watching events around them, compared with other children of their age. They also may have trouble sleeping.

A diagnosis of ADHD is made only if a child has persistent symptoms and in more than one setting, for example, home and school. Symptoms that are present in only one context may represent an adjustment to that setting or relationship. Parental expectations that are out of sync with a child's developmental capacity may cause a child to be frustrated and appear inattentive and hyperactive. Also, symptoms in children exposed to traumatic events can mimic ADHD.

Particularly when your child is a toddler, you may worry that she shows signs of hyperactivity, but if you compare her with others her age, you probably will discover that her behavior is typical of her childhood peers. Around ages two and three, children naturally are very active and impulsive and have a short attention span. All children occasionally seem overactive or easily distractible—for example, when they're very tired, excited about doing something special, or anxious about being in a strange place or among strangers. Children with ADHD, however, are noticeably more active, more easily distracted, and more excitable than their peers. Most important of all, these children never seem to be calm from one day to the next, and their behaviors continue into their school years, which is when their behaviors become more problematic because children with ADHD often struggle in school and other group settings, especially those that require focused attention.

Although most children with ADHD have normal intelligence, they frequently do not perform well in school settings, because they can't pay attention or follow instructions through to completion. They also are slower to develop control over their impulses and emotions and slower in developing the age-appropriate ability to concentrate and pay attention. They tend to be more talkative, emotional, demanding, disobedient, and noncompliant than others their age. Their behavior often remains immature throughout childhood and adolescence, and may lead to problems doing things that they need to do at home, in school, or among friends. Without support and treatment, children with ADHD have difficulty developing the self-esteem they need to lead healthy, productive lives.

Most children with ADHD have other family members with the same condition, which suggests that it may be mostly inherited. Sometimes the condition can be traced to illnesses affecting the brain or nervous system, such as meningitis, encephalitis, fetal alcohol syndrome, or severe prematurity. Most children with ADHD have never had such an illness, however, and most children who do suffer these ailments do not develop a disorder. Boys are diagnosed with ADHD at a ratio of approximately 2 to 1 or 3 to 1. Research has demonstrated that some children with ADHD experience worse symptoms, such as increased hyperactivity, when they are exposed to food additives and environmental exposures (such as tobacco smoke or lead). More research is needed, but many experts will recommend that these children eat a healthy diet of whole, real foods and avoid food preservatives and artificial colors whenever possible.

Often children with ADHD elicit negative, punitive, and controlling responses from adults or parents who may not understand the true nature of their disorder. Being subjected to much criticism only makes these children feel more negative about themselves, which is why it is important to fully evaluate the behavioral issue, find the cause, and come up with a treatment plan.

Whatever the cause of ADHD, the way the problem is perceived, understood, and treated, and the way parents and teachers respond, can influence the outcome for the child. The children who see the best results have parents who are emotionally healthy and who understand how to help children manage their behavior.

When to Call the Pediatrician

Observing your child alongside others her age over a period of days or weeks is the best way to determine if she is unusually inattentive or hyperactive. For this reason, those who care for her at preschool or in a childcare setting may be your best source of information. They can tell you how she behaves in a group and whether she is acting in a typical manner compared with other children her age. Specific signs of ADHD include:

■ Difficulty paying attention to activities that interest other children her age

■ Difficulty following even simple instructions due to not paying attention

■ Being impulsive, such as repeatedly running into the street without looking, interrupting other children's play, or racing through off-limits areas without considering consequences

■ Unnecessarily hurried activity, such as running and jumping without periods of rest

■ Sudden emotional outbursts, such as crying, angry yelling, hitting, or frustration, that seem inappropriate

■ Persistent misbehavior because of not listening despite being told "no" many times

If you and others observe several of these warning signs on a continuing basis, consult your pediatrician. The doctor will go through the criteria for ADHD and examine your child to rule out any medical cause for the behavior, and then either conduct a further evaluation or refer you to a developmental behavioral pediatrician, psychologist, or child psychiatrist for a more formal evaluation. If this specialist determines that your preschooler has ADHD, the doctor or therapist probably will recommend some specific behavior strategies for managing her behavior and may suggest that you learn a system for fine-tuning your own behavior management skills, using so-called behavioral therapy or behavioral parent training (see also the section *How to Respond* on page 594). Ensuring that your child gets adequate sleep, proper nutrition, plenty of exercise and time outdoors every day, and limits on screen time may help with some symptoms. In addition, specific vitamins and supplements may be recommended or prescribed, such as omega-3 fatty acids, iron, zinc, methylated folate, vitamin B_{12}, and vitamin D.

Medications also may be recommended, depending on the effectiveness of behavioral measures with your child. Toddlers and preschoolers change so rapidly and so dramatically that what might seem like a behavioral problem at one point could disappear a few months later. Therefore it is important to determine if the behaviors have persisted for more than six months.

Keep in mind that medications are used in more severe cases of ADHD in younger children only after trying to control the behaviors with good parenting techniques and healthy lifestyle choices. The American Academy of Pediatrics recommends that children with ADHD have a thorough patient history, family history, and physical exam before being diagnosed and starting any treatment, especially with medications (specifically with stimulant drugs). In some cases, if the history or physical exam raises concerns, your doctor may advise that your child undergo an electrocardiogram (a test measuring the heart's activity) before she prescribes these medications.

As a parent of a child with ADHD, you may hear about complementary treatments, some of which are still unproven or have not been shown to be effective. Talk with your pediatrician before involving your child in any complementary therapies to ensure that you won't waste your time and money or do anything that might harm your child.

Effective Discipline

Child's Behavior*	Your Responses	
	Effective	*Constructive*
Temper tantrums	Give a time-out and walk away.	When child is calm, discuss the incident in an age-appropriate manner.
Overexcitement	Distract with another activity.	Talk about his behavior in an age-appropriate manner when he's calm.
Hitting or biting	Immediately remove him from the situation or in anticipation of this behavior.	Discuss consequences of his actions (pain, damage, bad feelings) to him and others in an age-appropriate manner. Try a one-minute time-out after a brief response.
Not paying attention	Establish eye contact to hold his attention.	Make sure your expectations are age-appropriate for your child's developmental level (ask him to listen to a story for three minutes instead of ten; don't insist he sit through a full church service).
Refuses to pick up toys	Don't let him play until he does his job.	Show him how to do the task and help him with it; praise him when he finishes.

* Note: In all these situations, try to determine what influences might cause or prolong the behavior: Is the child in need of attention, tired, worried, or fearful? What is your own mood or behavior? Remember, you always should praise your child for good or improved effort.

How to Respond

If your child shows signs of ADHD, it may mean that she cannot control her behavior on her own. In her hurry and excitement, she may be accident-prone and may destroy property. To discipline a hyperactive child, you need to respond both effectively and constructively. If your actions are effective, your child's behavior will improve as a result. If they are constructive, they also will help develop her self-esteem and make her more personable. The box on page 593 (*Effective Discipline*) provides some examples of effective and constructive responses to common problems among hyperactive children.

It is important to respond immediately whenever your child misbehaves and to make sure that everyone caring for her responds to these incidents in the same way. Discipline means teaching self-control. If done effectively, you will rarely need to use punishment. Do not spank or slap your child, since it does not encourage her to control herself and may contribute to a continued negative self-image and resentment toward you; at the same time, this approach tells her that it's OK to strike other people. Instead, acknowledge and point out those times when she displays appropriate behaviors (that is, catch her being good), and learn to actively ignore inappropriate behaviors that are not dangerous; this approach is far more effective in the long run. Children with ADHD can be very challenging to manage, and parents may find they need help or coaching in how to effectively manage their child's behaviors.

Pacifier, Thumb, and Finger Sucking

Nonnutritive sucking habits (pacifier, thumb, or other finger) are common in infants and young children—half or more of all children engage in this activity at some time early in life. It is largely the result of the normal rooting and sucking reflexes present in all infants at birth. There is evidence that some infants suck their thumbs and fingers even before delivery, and some, particularly finger suckers, will show that behavior immediately after birth. Very young babies suck their thumb or fingers to calm themselves, satisfy their urge for contact, and help themselves feel more secure.

Because sucking is a normal reflex, pacifier, thumb, and finger sucking can be considered a normal habit in the youngest of children. Beyond the soothing effects of sucking, pacifier use has been associated with a decrease in the risk of sudden infant death syndrome (SIDS), and most pacifier users do not develop a thumb or finger sucking habit. It is recommended that use of the pacifier be discontinued once your child turns one, as SIDS is no longer a risk at that point and she is unlikely to develop an interest in thumb or finger sucking afterward.

Over half of thumb or finger suckers stop by age six or seven months.

Sometimes young children, especially when they are feeling most vulnerable, still will suck their thumb occasionally, even until the age of eight years or so. Don't worry about it until your child is four to five years old. But because thumb sucking beyond the fifth birthday may cause changes in the roof of the mouth (palate) or in the way the teeth are lining up, you and your child's dentist might become concerned at that time. This also is a time when your child might begin to be affected by social pressure, such as negative comments by his playmates, siblings, and relatives. If these factors become worrisome, consult your pediatrician about treatment.

Treatment

Parents can help their children overcome habits like thumb sucking, but it takes time. Severe emotional or stress-related problems that might prolong this habit should be ruled out before any treatment program is begun. Also, your child should have the ability to understand why thumb sucking can be a problem, and must want to stop the habit. Friends or relatives might suggest that you introduce a pacifier, but there is no evidence that this is effective at this stage—it only substitutes one sucking habit for another.

Since habits are often unconscious, the first step is to help the child build an awareness of the habit. Generally, the process begins with gentle reminders when you see her sucking her thumb, particularly during the daytime hours. You can also have her purposely suck her thumb while looking in the mirror, so that she becomes more aware of what she's doing. Then you and your child need to work together to find a substitute for the habit, such as squeezing a stress ball or a small plush animal or even just taking deep breaths. Then, whenever you see your child start to suck her thumb, you bring her attention to it and suggest the substitute habit instead. Praise her when you see her catching herself. Over time she should be able to shift to the new habit.

Other pediatricians recommend motivating the child to unlearn the habit of thumb sucking by setting a series of attainable goals (e.g., no thumb sucking for an hour before bed, then after dinner, then all day), with praise or rewards for accomplishing those goals. But only once the child begins to catch herself doing it will the behavior stop.

In those cases where there is notable jaw growth alteration or severe tooth misalignment and the techniques described have all failed, a pediatric dentist can install a device in the mouth that goes across the palate and serves as a reminder to the child, breaking the pattern and reducing the soothing effects of the habit. Other, often less effective ways of achieving this result include using a sock, a bandage, or adhesive tape on the thumb to serve as a reminder to your child to stop sucking. It is important to realize that whatever approach you use, it will work only if your child agrees that she wants to participate in stopping the thumb sucking.

It also is important to remember that your child may be one of the very few who for one reason or another cannot seem to stop sucking her thumb or finger. If this is the case, putting excessive pressure on your child to stop this type of behavior can cause more harm than good. Be assured that most of these children stop daytime sucking habits before they progress very far along in school due to peer pressure.

Temper Tantrums

As an adult, you have learned to control your strong emotions when it's not appropriate to fully express them—but your preschooler probably hasn't yet. His temper tantrums certainly are not fun for you or for him, but they are a normal part of life with most preschoolers. The first time your child screams and kicks because he can't have his way, you may feel angry, frustrated, humiliated, or frightened. You may wonder where you've gone wrong as a parent to produce such a miserable child. Rest assured, you are not responsible for this behavior, and tantrums are not ordinarily a sign of severe emotional or personality disorders. Almost all children have these episodes occasionally, especially around ages two and three. If handled successfully, they usually diminish in intensity and frequency by age four or five.

The section *Anger, Aggression, and Biting* (see page 581 in this chapter) explains the development of emotions in young children, and much of it applies to temper tantrums. Tantrums are often an expression of frustration. Preschoolers are very eager to take control. They want to be more independent than their skills and safety allow, and they don't appreciate their limits. They want to make decisions, but they don't know how to compromise, and they don't deal well with disappointment or restraint. They also can't express their feelings well in words, so instead they act out their anger and frustration by crying or withdrawing, and sometimes by having temper tantrums. Although these emotional displays are unpleasant, they rarely are dangerous.

You often can tell when a temper tantrum is coming. For some time before it begins, the child may seem more sullen or irritable than usual, and neither gentle affection nor playing with her will change her mood. She may be tired, hungry, or lonely. Then she tries, or is expected, to do something beyond her capabilities, or asks for something she can't have. She begins to whimper or whine and becomes more demanding. Nothing will distract or comfort her, and finally she starts to cry. As the crying increases, she begins to flail her arms and kick her legs. She may fall to the ground or hold her breath—some children actually hold their breath until they turn blue or faint. As frightening as it is to watch these breath-holding spells, the child's normal breathing resumes as soon as she faints, and she will recover quickly and completely. Children may also bang their head on the ground, sometimes hard enough to produce a bruise.

Don't be surprised if your child has tantrums only when you are around—most children act up only around their parents or other family members, seldom when with outsiders. She is testing your rules and limits, whereas she wouldn't dare do this with someone she knows less well. When her challenge goes too far and you restrain her, she may respond with a tantrum. Don't take tantrums personally. Try to remain calm and understand the behavior. Ironically, her occasional outbursts are actually a sign that she trusts you.

This emotional explosion serves as a kind of energy release, which often exhausts the child so that she falls asleep soon afterward. When she awakens she usually is calm and her behavior is quiet and pleasant. If she is ill or there is a great deal of tension among the people around her, however, the frustration may start building all over again. Children who are anxious, ill, or temperamental, who get too little rest, or who live in very stressful households tend to have tantrums more frequently.

Prevention

You can't prevent every tantrum, but you may be able to decrease the number, duration, or intensity by making sure your child does not get overtired, overly anxious, or unnecessarily frustrated. Your child's temper may become very short if she doesn't have enough quiet time, particularly when she is sick or anxious, or has been unusually active. Even if she doesn't sleep, lying down for fifteen or twenty minutes can help restore her energy and reduce the likelihood of tantrums from exhaustion. Children who do not nap may be particularly prone to tantrums and often need such a quiet period on a daily, scheduled basis. If your child resists, you might lie down with her or read her a story, but do not allow her to play or talk excessively.

Children whose parents fail to set appropriate limits, are overly strict, or forget to reinforce good behaviors tend to have more frequent and severe tantrums than children whose parents take a moderate approach. As a rule, it's best to set very few limits but to be firm about those that are set. You can allow her to have her way when the issue is minor—for example, if she wants to wander around slowly instead of walking quickly to the park, or if she refuses to get dressed before breakfast. But when she starts to run into the street, you must stop her and insist that she obey you, even if you have to hold her back physically. Be loving but firm, and respond the same way every time she violates the rule. She won't learn these important lessons immediately, so expect to repeat these interventions many times before her behavior changes. Also, make sure that every adult who cares for her observes the same rules and disciplines her in the same way.

One of the best strategies for preventing temper tantrums is to give your child appropriate choices. You might say, "Do you want me to read to you, or would you rather get dressed and go to the park?" Clearly each choice must be possible and reasonable—there may be days when the park is out of the question—and you will need to show some flexibility at times. Or what happens if you want to take your child outside in the winter so she can play in the snow—but she refuses to wear her snow clothes? In this instance, you might say, "Either you wear your snow clothes, or you have to carry them with you, or I will carry them. Which choice do you want?" Once outside, she'll quickly realize that she is cold and she'll want to put on her snow clothes.

How to Respond

When your child has a temper tantrum, it's important that you try to remain calm yourself. If you have loud, angry outbursts, your child naturally will imitate your behavior. If you shout at her to calm down, you probably will make the situation worse. Maintaining a peaceful atmosphere will reduce the general stress level and make both you and your child feel better and more in control. In fact, sometimes gentle restraint, holding, or distracting comments such as "Did you see what the kitty is doing?" or "I think I heard the doorbell" will interrupt behavior such as breath holding before it reaches the point of fainting.

Sometimes, if you feel yourself losing control, humor will save the day. Turn a dispute over taking a bath into a fun race to the bathroom or create a new bath toy out of a plastic cup or bowl. Soften your command to "pick up your toys" by making a funny face or singing a silly song. Unless your child is extremely irritable or overtired, she is more likely to be distracted into obedience if you temper discipline with a bit of fun or whimsy. Doing this might also make you feel better.

Some parents feel guilty every time they say "no" to their children. They try too hard to explain their rules, or apologize for them. Even at age two or three, children can detect uncertainty in a tone of voice, and they will try to take advantage of it. If the parent sometimes gives in, the child becomes even more outraged on those occasions when she doesn't get her way. There is no reason to be apologetic about enforcing your rules. It only makes it more difficult for your child to understand which of them are firm and which can be questioned. This does not mean that you should be unfriendly or abusive when you say no, but state your position clearly. As your child gets older, you can offer brief, simple reasons for your rules, but do not go into long, confusing explanations.

These important rules should be based on your child not hurting herself or destroying property. Also, everyone providing care for your child needs to agree to the same rules. It's wise to pick your battles as well. Toddlers can stay in a conflict situation for some time, which runs counter to the goal of limiting or avoiding the clash altogether. When you ask your child to do something against her will, follow through on the order with her. If you've asked her to put away her toys, offer to help her. If you've told her not to throw her ball against the window, show her where she *can* throw it. If you've reminded her not to touch the hot oven door, either remove her from the kitchen or stay there with her to make sure that she minds you. (Never issue a safety order to a two- or three-year-old and then leave the room.)

Finally, use the cooling-off or time-out strategy described on page 364. Give your child some time alone to calm down and regain control. Put her in a separate place, removed from the activity in the house, and tell her clearly that her behavior was unacceptable (but that you still love her). The time-out plus your words will help her understand the reasons why.

When to Call the Pediatrician

Although occasional temper tantrums during the preschool years should be expected, they should become less frequent and less intense by the middle of the fourth year. Between tantrums, the child should behave like other kids her age and seem healthy. At no time should the behavior cause the child to harm herself or others or destroy property. When the outbursts are very severe, frequent, or prolonged, they may be an early sign of emotional disturbance.

Consult your pediatrician if your child shows any of the following warning signs.

■ Tantrums persist or intensify after age four.

■ Your child injures herself or others, or destroys property during tantrums.

■ Your child has frequent nightmares, extreme disobedience, reversal of toilet training, headaches or stomachaches, refusal to eat or go to bed, extreme anxiety, constant grumpiness, or clinging to you.

■ Your child holds her breath and faints during tantrums.

In cases where your child holds her breath and faints, the doctor may want to check for other causes of fainting, such as seizures (see page 803) or iron deficiency (which is associated with breath-holding spells). The pediatrician also can offer suggestions for disciplining your child and suggest parent education groups that might provide additional support and guidance. If your doctor feels the tantrums indicate a severe emotional disturbance, she will refer you to a child psychiatrist, psychologist, or mental health clinic.

Tics and Stereotypies

Tics and stereotypies are repetitive movements that generally look or sound about the same each time they are performed, such as eye blinking.

Although they can look disturbing or uncomfortable, they often cause more distress for the parent than they do for the young child. In some cases, other developmental or psychiatric problems may be present or may emerge later on.

Stereotypies generally begin before three years of age and often involve arms, hands, or the entire body. Examples include rhythmic arm flapping, body rocking, and finger wiggling. Sometimes there may also be body clenching, mouth gaping, or a vocalization of a sound along with the movement. They tend to appear many times per day, can occur in short bursts or randomly, and seem to stick around for months to years. They may occur in certain situations, such as when a child is focusing on something, excited, or stressed, making it easy for parents to video them. The child is not doing this because he feels as if he has to or wants to do it, it just happens. A child may seem to stare off or not be responsive briefly during these episodes but, unlike seizures, you can interrupt and stop them. Although some children outgrow them, other times they may persist many years, sometimes into adulthood.

Tics generally begin between three years and eight years of age and initially involve muscles of the face or of vocalizations/sounds. Examples include blinking, mouth gaping, eye widening or deviation, head jerking, throat clearing, sniffing, coughing, or grunting. They generally begin gradually, although to caregivers they may appear to start suddenly when they get worse. They can be exacerbated by illness, or family or social stress. They can worsen when a child is anxious, tense, sleep deprived, or when a child is at home and not otherwise occupied. They can become less frequent during focused motor activities like sports or musical performance. Tics can emerge, resolve, and change in appearance over time. Children generally report an initial sensation or urge and experience at least some of their tics as voluntary responses and as, at least briefly, suppressible. They may persist many years, sometimes into adulthood.

When a tick occurs sporadically for less than a year, it is called a provisional tic disorder. Chronic tic disorders are diagnosed when tics last longer than twelve months and tend to start later, such as in early elementary school years, compared with preschool years. The primary chronic tic disorder is called *Tourette's syndrome,* in which children have both motor tics and vocal tics. Vocal tics may include involuntary uttering of words or phrases (sometimes including obscene words). Chronic tic disorders are often associated with other disorders, including ADHD (attention-deficit/hyperactivity disorder), OCD (obsessive compulsive disorder), and anxiety.

A sudden onset of tics can be highly concerning for parents and caregivers. This is most often a more dramatic onset of typical tic disorders. An explosive onset can raise concerns about a condition termed PANDAS, or Pediatric Autoimmune Neuropsychiatric Disorder Associated with Streptococcal Infection. PANDAS may be diagnosed when sudden and dramatic episodes of obsessive-compulsive behaviors and tics occur close in time to an infection such as streptococcal infection (Group A Strep). The role of auto-immunity and connection between this condition and streptococcal infections remains controversial. All PANDAS cases are unique and treatment varies based on the cause and symptoms. Most cases wax and wane as a child grows. Talk to your pediatrician about what treatment options are available and the best way to evaluate and treat your child.

Management

In general, stereotypies and tics do not need to be treated unless they interfere with daycare, preschool, or the child's other activities, cause physical pain, or produce significant social distress for the child. Sometimes parents find their child's tics annoying and are tempted to say, "Stop doing that." But this is unlikely to be helpful.

If your pediatrician believes that there is a psychological or medical component that is making your child's stereotypies and tics worse, these underlying conditions should be treated. Make an effort to reduce the stress, worries, or conflicts in your child's life, which may help relieve the severity of his tics.

For chronic tic disorders, your doctor may prescribe medications or refer you to a specialist. Cognitive behavioral therapy with a psychologist is also an effective method of reducing the severity of tics.

~ 19 ~

Chest and Lungs

Bronchiolitis

Bronchiolitis is an infection of the small breathing tubes (bronchioles) of the lungs. It is one of the most common diseases of early childhood. (Note: The term "bronchiolitis" sometimes is confused with "bronchitis," which refers to an infection of the larger, more central airways.) Bronchiolitis is caused most commonly by respiratory syncytial virus (RSV),

which is especially common between October or November through March, though other viruses can be responsible.

Signs and Symptoms

Almost all children get an RSV infection by the time they are three years old. The majority of them develop only an upper respiratory infection (a cold) with a runny nose, mild cough, and sometimes fever. Unfortunately, in a small number of infants, especially those under the age of one year, the RSV infection leads to inflammation and swelling of the bronchioles. When this happens, after a day or two the cough becomes more pronounced, and the child begins to breathe more rapidly and with more difficulty.

If your baby shows any of the following signs of breathing difficulty, or if his fever lasts more than three days (or if fever is present at all in an infant under three months), call your pediatrician immediately.

■ He makes a high-pitched whistling sound, called a wheeze, each time he breathes in (inhales) or out (exhales).

■ Drawing in of the skin between and around the ribs and breastbone.

■ He is unable to drink fluids well because he is working so hard to breathe that he has difficulty sucking and swallowing.

■ He develops a bluish color around his lips or fingertips. This means the airways are so blocked that not enough oxygen is getting into his lungs and into the blood.

Also call the pediatrician if your child develops any of the following signs or symptoms of dehydration (not enough fluid in the body), which also can appear with bronchiolitis:

■ Dry mouth

■ Drinking less than his normal amount of fluids

■ Not making tears when he cries

■ Urinating less often than usual

■ Lethargic or not acting as usual (not playing, smiling, or interacting)

If your child has any of the following conditions, notify your pediatrician:

■ As soon as you suspect that he has bronchiolitis

■ A persistent cough and runny nose (symptoms not improving after a week)

■ Any difficulty breathing

■ An underlying medical condition such as:
   —Cystic fibrosis
   —Congenital heart disease
   —Bronchopulmonary dysplasia, seen in some infants who were born prematurely or were on a respirator (breathing machine) as newborns

■ Low immunity

■ Organ transplant

■ Cancer for which he is receiving chemotherapy

Treatment

There are no medications to treat bronchiolitis. All you can do during the early phase of the illness is ease your child's cold symptoms. You can relieve some of the nasal stuffiness with a humidifier and salt water (saline) nose drops, with or without gentle nasal suction (aspiration). Coughing is one way for the body to clear the lungs, and normally a cough should not need to be treated with cough suppressant medicine.

If your child has a fever and is over three months old, you can give children's acetaminophen (Tylenol) as instructed on the box, or children's ibuprofen (Motrin, Advil) if your child is six months of age or older. Also, to avoid dehydration, make sure your child drinks lots of fluid during this time. He may prefer clear liquids rather than milk or formula. Because of his breathing difficulty, he also may feed more slowly or eat smaller amounts more frequently. He also may not eat solid foods very well due to decreased appetite. It's usually fine if he eats less solid food while sick as long as he is drinking enough fluids to avoid dehydration.

In contrast to asthma treatment, no breathing treatments have been shown to help children with bronchiolitis. Your pediatrician may try treatments that open up the lungs (bronchodilators) and steroids (medication inhaled or taken by mouth to decrease inflammation) to see if there is any improvement, but such medications do not prevent hospitalization or change the course of illness in otherwise healthy children with bronchiolitis. If your child is having difficulty breathing, is having trouble feeding, or shows signs of dehydration, your pediatrician will likely tell you to take your child to the hospital's emergency department, where they can provide additional supportive treatment.

Prevention

The best way to protect your child from bronchiolitis is to keep him away from the viruses that cause it. Whenever possible, and especially when your child is an infant, avoid close contact with children or adults who are in the early (contagious) stages of respiratory infections. What produces just a mild cold in an older child or adult can cause breathing problems for an infant. If he is in a childcare center where other children might have the virus, make sure that those who care for him wash their hands thoroughly and frequently. Infants should not be exposed to secondhand smoke, as this can increase the risk of infection.

If your child under twenty-four months is at high risk because of premature birth (less than twenty-nine weeks of gestation) or a medical condition, an injectable drug is available to protect against severe RSV disease; it is given on a monthly basis for three to five months prior to and during the RSV season. Your pediatrician will be able to tell you whether your child might benefit from this.

Cough

Coughing is almost always an indication of an irritation in your child's air passages. When the nerve endings in the throat, windpipe, or lungs sense the irritation, a reflex causes air to be ejected forcefully through the passageways.

Coughs frequently accompany colds (see page 667). When a child has a cold, the cough may be either productive (bringing up mucus) or dry and irritating. The cough may last longer than the accompanying runny nose, up to two to three weeks.

Other respiratory illnesses can produce a cough as well, including bronchiolitis (see page 603), croup (see page 608), flu (see page 609), or pneumonia (see page 612). Your pediatrician can often tell by the sound of the cough what may be causing it. For example, an irritation in the larynx (voice box), caused by an illness such as croup, causes a cough that sounds like the bark of a dog or seal, while irritation of the larger airways (bronchi) or the trachea (windpipe) produces a deeper, raspy cough.

In a very young infant, anything more than an occasional cough has to be taken seriously, and merits a visit to the pediatrician. If your child has a cough plus a fever and difficulty breathing (the breathing is too fast, too slow, or noisy, or you see a drawing in of the skin between and around the ribs and breastbone when he inhales), he may have a serious infection in the lungs, such as pneumonia. If he has these symptoms, see your doctor immediately.

Allergies and sinus infections can cause a chronic cough because mucus drips down the back of the throat (a condition known as postnasal drip), producing a dry, hard-to-stop cough, particularly at night upon lying down. A child who coughs only while asleep may have asthma (see page 561) or gastroesophageal reflux (a condition where the contents of the stomach rise up into the esophagus, causing irritation and cough).

Here are some other cough-related issues that can affect children:

■ Anything more than an occasional cough in an infant has to be taken seriously. The most common causes are colds and bronchiolitis, which usually get better in a few days. It is important to watch for signs of breathing difficulties and seek medical help if needed. These signs include not only rapid breathing, especially while asleep, but also drawing in of the skin between and around the ribs and breastbone (sternum).

■ Sometimes children cough so hard that they throw up. Usually they vomit liquid and food from the stomach, but there also may be a lot of mucus, especially during a cold or an asthma attack.

■ Wheezing is a high-pitched sound during breathing that occurs when there is an obstruction of the airway inside the chest. It is one of the symptoms of asthma, but also can occur if your child has bronchiolitis, pneumonia, or certain other disorders.

■ Children with asthma often cough and wheeze together. This may happen when they are active or playing, or at night. Sometimes their cough can be heard, but the wheezing may be evident only to your doctor when she listens with a stethoscope. The cough and the wheeze usually get better after using asthma medications.

■ A cough is commonly worse at night. When your child coughs at night, it may be caused by irritation in the throat or a sinus infection with postnasal drip. Asthma is another major reason for a nighttime cough.

A sudden cough in children can mean that some food or liquid or an object (such as a coin or toy) has "gone down the wrong way" and ended up in the lungs. The coughing is an attempt to clear the airways. However, if coughing continues for more than a few minutes, or if your child is having difficulty breathing, seek medical help right away. Don't put your fingers in your child's mouth to clear the throat because you may push the food or other cause of the obstruction down farther. (See *Choking,* page 700.)

When to Call the Pediatrician

An infant under two months of age who develops a cough should be seen by the doctor. For older infants and children, consult your physician immediately if the coughing:

■ Makes it difficult for your child to breathe

■ Is painful, persistent, and accompanied by whooping, vomiting, or turning blue

■ Interferes with eating and sleeping

■ Appears suddenly and is associated with a fever

■ Begins after your child chokes on food or any other object (see *Choking,* page 700)—though in about 50 percent of cases when a foreign body (food or toy) is inhaled into lungs, the cough may not develop until a few hours or days later

Your pediatrician will try to determine the cause of your child's cough; most commonly it's due to an upper respiratory virus. When the cough is from a medical problem other than a cold or the flu, such as a bacterial infection or asthma, it will be necessary to treat that condition before the cough will clear. Occasionally when the cause of a chronic cough (lasting longer than four weeks) is not apparent, further tests such as chest X-rays or even testing for tuberculosis may be necessary.

Treatment

Treating a cough depends on its cause. Adding moisture to the air with a cool-mist humidifier or vaporizer may make your child more comfortable, especially at night. However, be sure to clean the device thoroughly each morning as recommended in the manufacturer's manual, so it doesn't become a breeding ground for harmful bacteria or fungi.

Nighttime coughs associated with allergies or asthma can be especially problematic, because they prevent the child (and often the rest of the family)

from getting a good night's sleep. If the night cough is due to asthma, use a bronchodilator or other asthma medication as directed by your pediatrician.

Although cough medicines can be purchased without a prescription, the American Academy of Pediatrics' position is that these cough medicines are not effective for children younger than six years old, and may even pose a health risk from serious side effects.

Croup

Croup is an inflammation of the voice box (larynx) and windpipe (trachea). It causes a barking cough and a high-pitched sound when breathing in. Croup is usually caused by a virus, most commonly the parainfluenza virus. Other less common viral causes of croup include the flu, RSV, adenovirus, and enteroviruses. The illness most often is caught from someone who is infected, sometimes from air droplets or from your child's own hand, which he uses to transfer the virus into his nose or mouth.

Croup tends to occur in the fall and winter in children between three months and three years old. Initially your child may develop nasal stuffiness (resembling a cold) and fever. After a day or two, the sound of the cough will turn into something resembling a barking or seal-like cough. The cough tends to become worse at night.

The greatest danger with croup is

that your child's airway will continue to swell, further narrowing his windpipe and making it difficult to breathe. As your child tires from the effort of breathing, he may stop eating and drinking. He also may become too fatigued to cough. Some children are particularly prone to getting a croup-like cough whenever they have a respiratory illness.

Treatment

If your child has mild croup symptoms, steam up the bathroom by turning on the hot water in the shower. Take your child into the steamy bathroom, close the door, and sit in the bathroom with your child. Inhaling the warm, humidified air should ease her breathing within fifteen to twenty minutes. Or, weather permitting, you can take her outside to breathe in the cool, wet night air. While she is sleeping, use a cool-mist humidifier in her room.

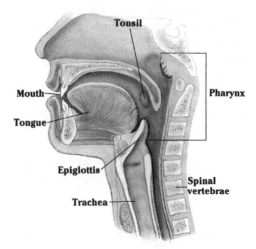

Do *not* try to open your child's airway with your finger. Her breathing is being obstructed by swollen tissue beyond your reach, so you can't clear it away. She may throw up because of the coughing, but don't try to make her vomit. Pay close attention to your child's breathing. Take her to the nearest emergency room *immediately* if:

■ She seems to be struggling to get a breath.

■ She can't speak because of a lack of breath.

■ She gets excessively sleepy.

■ She turns blue when she coughs.

Your pediatrician may prescribe various medications, usually steroids, to help decrease the swelling in the upper airway and throat and make it easier for her to breathe. Steroids will also decrease the amount of time your child has symptoms of croup. Antibiotics are not helpful for croup because the infection is usually caused by a virus. Cough syrups do not help, either. In fact, as stated earlier, over-the-counter cough medicines may pose a health risk.

In the most serious cases, which are quite rare, if your child has a lot of difficulty breathing, your pediatrician may recommend you go to the emergency department for a special breathing medication (racemic epi) or admit her to the hospital until the swelling in the airway gets better.

Influenza (Flu)

Influenza (flu) is an illness caused by the influenza virus. The infection can spread rapidly through communities as the virus is passed from person to person. When someone with the flu coughs or sneezes, the influenza virus gets into the air, and people nearby, including children, can inhale it. The virus also can be spread when a contagious person touches a hard surface, such as a door handle, and then someone else touches the same surface and then his nose, mouth, or eyes. The virus is most likely to be transmitted to other people during the first several days of illness. Flu is most common from fall through spring.

Flu symptoms include:

■ A sudden fever, usually above 101 degrees Fahrenheit (38.3 degrees Celsius)

■ Chills and body shakes

■ Headache, body aches, and being a lot more tired than usual

■ Sore throat

■ Dry, hacking cough

■ Stuffy, runny nose

While influenza may cause some abdominal pain, vomiting, and diarrhea, it does most of its damage in the respiratory system; it should not be confused with viruses that cause what is commonly known as the "stomach flu."

You may wonder whether your child has a cold or the flu. A child with a common cold (see *Colds/Upper Respiratory Infection*, page 667) usually has a lower fever, a runny nose, and only a small amount of coughing. Children with the flu usually feel much sicker, more achy, and more miserable.

Most children get over the flu in about a week or two without any lingering problems. However, you might suspect a complication if your child says that his ear hurts or that he feels pressure in his face and head, or if his cough and fever persist beyond two weeks.

Children who appear to have the greatest risk of complications from influenza are those with an underlying chronic medical condition, such as heart, lung, or kidney disease, an immune system problem, diabetes, some blood diseases, or a malignancy. Such children should be kept away from anyone showing symptoms suggestive of influenza, such as fever, cough, and runny nose, and your pediatrician may suggest additional precautions.

Treatment

For all children with the flu who don't feel well, lots of tender loving care is in order. Children can benefit from extra bed rest, extra fluids, and light meals. A cool mist humidifier or vaporizer in the room may add additional moisture to the air and make breathing a little easier.

If your child is uncomfortable because of a fever, acetaminophen or ibuprofen in doses recommended by your pediatrician for his age and weight will help him feel better. (See Chapter 27, *Fever*.) Ibuprofen is approved for use in children six months of age and older; however, it should never be given to children who are dehydrated or who are vomiting continuously. **It is extremely important never to give aspirin to a child who has or may have the flu. Giving a child aspirin during a viral illness is associated with an increased risk of developing Reye syndrome.** (For more information about Reye syndrome, see page 555.)

Prevention

Every child six months or older (including infants who were born preterm) should get the flu vaccine each year—the vaccine is safe, and it's the best way to prevent the illness. The best time to get the flu vaccine is the late summer or early fall, or as soon as it is available in your community.

Currently there are two types of the vaccine to protect against the flu—an inactivated (killed) vaccine, also called the flu shot, which is given by injection; and a live, attenuated (weakened) influenza vaccine that is sprayed into the nostrils, often called the flu mist. Ask your pediatrician which is preferred for your child. If your child is receiving the flu vaccine for the first time, he will need two doses given at least one month apart.

All healthcare personnel and adults who live in the same household as someone who has a high risk for flu complications or who care for children under the age of five years should receive the flu vaccine yearly. All women who are pregnant, are considering pregnancy, have recently delivered, or are breastfeeding during the flu season should also receive a flu vaccine.

The flu vaccine has few side effects, the most common being redness, soreness, or swelling at the injection site, and fever. Although flu vaccines are produced using eggs, the vaccine itself has been shown to contain minimal egg protein, so virtually all children with presumed egg allergy may still safely receive the flu vaccine. For those having a history of severe egg allergy (anaphylaxis or respiratory and/or cardiovascular symptoms after egg ingestion), speak with your child's allergist about receiving the flu vaccine in their office.

In addition to being vaccinated, here are some tips that will help protect your family from getting sick.

1. Wash hands often. Use soap and warm water, and lather up for at least twenty seconds—about as long as it takes to sing the "Happy Birthday" song two times. An alcohol-based hand sanitizer works well, too. Put enough on your hands to make them all wet, and then rub them together until dry.

2. Teach your child to cover his mouth and nose when coughing or sneezing. Show your child how to cough into the elbow or upper sleeve (not a hand) or use a tissue.

3. Throw all tissues used for runny noses and sneezes in the trash right away.

4. Wash dishes and utensils in hot, soapy water or the dishwasher.

5. Don't let children share pacifiers, cups, spoons, forks, washcloths, or towels without washing. *Never* share toothbrushes.

6. Teach your child to try not to touch her eyes, nose, or mouth.

7. Clean doorknobs, toilet handles, countertops, and even toys. Use a disinfectant wipe or a cloth with soap and hot water.

If your child does become ill, antiviral medications to treat some kinds of influenza infection are now available by prescription. Antiviral medications work best if started within the first one to two days of showing signs of the flu, so call your pediatrician right away, especially if your child is at high risk of complications. Call your pediatrician within twenty-four hours to ask about antiviral medications if your child is at high risk of influenza complications or if your child:

■ Has any serious health problem like asthma, diabetes, sickle cell disease, or cerebral palsy.

■ Is younger than two years, but especially if younger than six months, as young children are at an increased risk of influenza infection, hospitalization, and serious complications including death.

Pneumonia

The word "pneumonia" refers to an infection of the lung. While such infections were extremely dangerous in past generations, today most children recover from pneumonia if they receive proper medical attention.

Most cases of pneumonia follow a viral upper respiratory tract infection. Pneumonia also can be caused by bacteria. Also, if a viral infection has irritated the airway enough or weakened a child's immune system, bacteria may begin to grow in the lung, adding a second infection to the original one.

Children whose immune defenses or lungs are weakened by other illnesses, such as cystic fibrosis, asthma, or cancer, are more likely to develop pneumonia. Children whose airways or lungs are abnormal in any other way also have a higher risk.

Because most forms of pneumonia are linked to viral or bacterial infections that spread from person to person, they're most common during the fall, winter, and early spring, when children spend more time indoors in close contact with others. The chance that a child will develop pneumonia is not affected by how warmly she is dressed or by air temperature on cold days.

Signs and Symptoms

Like many infections, pneumonia usually produces a fever, which in turn may cause sweating, chills, flushed skin, and general discomfort. The child also may lose her appetite and seem less energetic than normal. Babies and toddlers may seem pale and limp, and cry more than usual.

Because pneumonia can cause breathing difficulties, you may notice these other, more specific symptoms, too:

■ Cough (see page 605)

■ Fast, labored breathing

■ Drawing in of the skin between and around the ribs and breastbone

■ Flaring (widening) of the nostrils

■ Pain in the chest, particularly with coughing or deep breathing

■ Wheezing

■ Bluish color to the lips or nails, caused by decreased oxygen in the bloodstream

Although the diagnosis of pneumonia usually can be made by a pediatrician on the basis of the signs, symptoms, and examination, a chest X-ray sometimes is necessary to make certain and to determine the extent of lung involvement.

Treatment

When pneumonia is caused by a virus, usually there is no specific treatment other than rest and the usual measures for fever control (see Chapter 27). Cough suppressants containing codeine or dextromethorphan should not be used, because coughing is helpful in clearing the excessive secretions caused by the infection. Viral pneumonia usually improves after a few days, although the cough may linger for several weeks.

Because it is often difficult to tell whether the pneumonia is caused by a virus or by bacteria, your pediatrician may prescribe an antibiotic. All antibiotics should be taken for the full prescribed course and at the specific dosage recommended. Your child will feel better after just a few days, and you may be tempted to discontinue them early, but you should not do so—some bacteria may remain, and the infection might return unless the entire course is completed. Check back with the doctor if your child shows any of the following signs that the infection may be worsening or spreading:

■ Fever lasting more than a few days despite using antibiotics

■ Fever that goes away and then returns after a few days

■ Breathing difficulties

■ Increased lethargy and sleepiness

■ Evidence of an infection elsewhere in the body: red, swollen joints, bone pain, neck stiffness, vomiting, or other new symptoms or signs

Prevention

Your child should be vaccinated against pneumococcal infections, a bacterial cause of pneumonia. The American Academy of Pediatrics recommends that all children younger than two years old receive this immunization (called pneumococcal conjugate or PCV13). A series of doses needs to be given at two, four, six, and twelve to fifteen months of age, at the same time that children receive other childhood vaccines.

If your child did not receive the initial doses at the recommended times, talk to your pediatrician about a catch-up schedule. One dose of PCV13 should be given to all healthy children aged two through five years who have not previously received their recommended doses before the age of two years and to children aged two years through eighteen years with certain underlying medical conditions who have not previously received a dose of PCV13.

Another pneumococcal vaccine (pneumococcal polysaccharide or PPV23) also is recommended for older children (two through five years of age) who have a high risk of developing a pneumococcal infection. These include children with sickle cell anemia, heart disease, lung disease, kidney failure, damaged or no spleen, organ transplant, and HIV (human immunodeficiency virus) infection. It's also recommended for children taking certain medications or who have diseases that weaken their immune system. Some children with certain underlying medical conditions may require a second dose of pneumococcal vaccine given at least eight weeks later.

See also *Asthma*, page 561; *Colds/Upper Respiratory Infection*, page 667; Chapter 27, *Fever*.

Tuberculosis

Tuberculosis (TB) is an airborne infection that primarily affects the lungs. While TB is less common than it once was, some groups of children have a higher risk of developing tuberculosis, including:

■ Children living in a household with an adult who has active tuberculosis or has a high risk of contracting TB

■ Children infected with HIV or another condition that weakens the immune system

■ Children born in a country that has a high prevalence of TB

■ Children visiting a country where TB is regularly found (endemic) and who have extended contact with people who live there

■ Children from communities that generally receive inadequate medical care

■ Children living in a shelter or living with someone who has been in jail

Tuberculosis usually is spread when an infected adult coughs the bacteria into the air. These germs are inhaled by the child, who then becomes infected. Children younger than about ten years old with TB of the lungs rarely transmit infection to other people, because they tend to have very few bacteria in their mucous secretions and also have a relatively ineffective cough.

Fortunately, most children exposed to tuberculosis do not become ill. When the bacteria reach their lungs, the body's immune system attacks the bacteria and prevents further spread. However, the child still must be treated to prevent the disease from becoming active. Occasionally, in a small number of children without proper treatment, the infection does progress to disease, causing fever, fatigue, irritability, a persistent cough, weakness, heavy and fast breathing, night sweats, swollen glands, weight loss, and poor growth.

In a very small number of children (mostly those less than four years old), the tuberculosis infection can spread through the bloodstream, affecting virtually any organ in the body. This illness requires much more complicated treatment, and the earlier treatment is started, the better the outcome. These children have a much greater risk of developing tuberculosis meningitis, a dangerous form of the disease that affects the brain and central nervous system.

If your child has any of the risk factors mentioned earlier, your pediatrician may recommend a test to see whether he has ever been exposed to the illness. The tuberculin skin test, sometimes called a PPD (purified protein derivative of tuberculin), is the only way to check for tuberculosis in children less than two years old, and it can be used to screen children older than two years as well. Your child may need a skin test if you answer yes to at least one of the following questions:

■ Has a family member or contact had tuberculosis disease?

■ Has a family member had a positive tuberculin skin test?

■ Was your child born in a high-risk country (countries other than the US, Canada, Australia, New Zealand, or Western European countries)?

■ Has your child traveled (had contact with resident populations) to a high-risk country for more than one week?

The test is performed in the pediatrician's office by injecting a purified, inactive piece of TB germ into the skin of the forearm. If there has been an infection, your child's skin will gradually swell and redden at the injection site. Your pediatrician must check the skin forty-eight to seventy-two hours

after the injection and measure the diameter of the reaction. The test will be able to tell if the bacteria have ever entered the child's body, even if the child has had no symptoms.

Doctors may instead choose to use a blood test to check for tuberculosis, the interferon gamma release assay (IGRA). This type of test is especially useful for people who received a tuberculosis vaccine in another country or who cannot return to the clinic in two to three days to have their skin test read. Like the PPD, the IGRA only tells doctors if the tuberculosis germ has ever entered a person's body, not if there is still an active infection.

If your child's skin or blood test for TB comes back positive, a chest X-ray will be ordered to determine if there is evidence of an active or past infection in the lungs. If the X-ray does indicate the possibility of an active infection, the pediatrician also will search for the TB bacteria in your child's cough secretions or in his stomach. This is done in order to determine the type of treatment needed.

Treatment

If your child's skin or blood test is positive but he does not have symptoms or signs of active tuberculosis infection, he still has the tuberculosis bacteria hiding out in his body and will need to be treated in order to prevent the bacteria from becoming active and causing symptoms. The medication used for treatment, isoniazid, must be taken by mouth once a day every day for a minimum of nine months (antibiotics for shorter lengths of time may be possible).

For an *active* tuberculosis infection, your pediatrician will prescribe three or four medications. You will have to give these to your child every day for six to twelve months. Your child may have to be hospitalized initially for the treatment to be started, although most of it can be carried out at home.

Prevention

If your child has been infected with TB, regardless of whether he develops symptoms, it is *very* important to attempt to identify the person from whom he caught the disease. Usually this is done by looking for symptoms of TB in everyone who came in close contact with him, including family members and childcare providers, and having TB skin tests or IGRA tests done. The most common symptom in adults is a persistent cough, especially one that is associated with coughing up blood. Anyone who has a positive skin test or IGRA test should receive a physical examination, a chest X-ray, and treatment.

When active tuberculosis infection is found in an adult, he should be isolated as much as possible—especially from young children—until treatment is underway. Certain family members who have been in contact with that person, including all children under five years old and those with conditions like HIV, usually are also initially treated with isoniazid, regardless of the results of their own skin tests. Anyone

who becomes ill or develops an abnormality on a chest X-ray should be treated as an active case of tuberculosis.

Whooping Cough (Pertussis)

Pertussis, or whooping cough, is caused by bacteria that attack the lining of the breathing passages (bronchi and bronchioles), producing inflammation and narrowing of the airways. Severe coughing is a prominent symptom. Because the child is short of breath, she inhales deeply and quickly between coughs. These breaths frequently make a "whooping" sound—which is how this illness got its common name. The intense coughing scatters the pertussis bacteria into the air, spreading the disease to other susceptible persons.

Many years ago, there were several hundred thousand cases of whooping cough each year in the United States. After the development of a vaccine for pertussis, that figure decreased. But in recent years there has been a rise in the number of cases seen in the United States. As a result, giving the pertussis vaccine to children and their caregivers is even more important than ever. Infants under one year of age are at greatest risk of developing severe breathing problems and life-threatening illness from whooping cough.

Pertussis often acts like a common cold for a week or two. Then the cough gets worse (rather than better, as usually happens with a cold), and older children may start to have the characteristic "whoop." During this phase (which can last two weeks or more), the child often is short of breath and can look bluish around the mouth. He also may tear, drool, and vomit. Young infants with pertussis may have episodes where they appear to stop breathing or have vomiting after a long bout of cough. Infants with pertussis become exhausted and develop complications such as susceptibility to other infections, pneumonia, and seizures. Pertussis can be fatal in some infants, but the usual course is for recovery to begin after two to four more weeks. The cough of pertussis, which has also been called the "100-day cough," may not disappear for months, and may return with subsequent respiratory infections.

When to Call the Pediatrician

Pertussis infection starts out acting like a cold. You should consider whooping cough if the following conditions are present.

■ The child is a very young infant who has not been fully immunized and/or has been exposed to someone with a chronic cough or the disease.

■ The child's cough becomes more severe and frequent, or his lips and fingertips become dark or blue.

■ He becomes exhausted after coughing episodes, eats poorly, vomits after coughing, and/or looks "sick."

Treatment

The majority of infants less than six months old with whooping cough need to be initially treated in the hospital. In addition, slightly less than half of older babies with the disease are initially treated in the hospital. This more intensive care can decrease the chances of complications. These complications can include pneumonia, which occurs in slightly less than one-fourth of children under one year old who have whooping cough. (If your child is older, he is more likely to be treated only at home.)

While in the hospital, your child may need to have the thick respiratory secretions suctioned. His breathing will be monitored, and he may need to have oxygen administered. Your child will be isolated from other patients to keep the infection from spreading to them.

Whooping cough is treated with an antibiotic that is most effective when given in the first stage of the illness, before coughing spells begin. Although antibiotics can stop the spread of the infection, they cannot prevent or treat the cough itself. Because cough medicines do not relieve the coughing spells, your pediatrician probably will recommend other forms of home treatment to help manage the cough. Let your child rest in bed and use a cool-mist vaporizer to help soothe his irritated lungs and breathing passages. A vaporizer also will help loosen secretions in the respiratory tract. Ask your pediatrician for instructions on the best position for your child to help drain those secretions and improve breathing. Also ask your doctor whether antibiotics or vaccine boosters need to be given to others in your household to prevent them from developing the disease. Children who have been diagnosed with pertussis should be kept home from school or daycare until finishing five days of antibiotics.

Prevention

The best way to protect your child against pertussis is with the DTaP vaccine (immunizations at two months, four months, and six months of age, and booster shots at twelve to eighteen months and at four or five years of age or prior to starting school). Parents or family members who will be in close contact with infants younger than one year old should also receive the Tdap booster to decrease the risk of passing the infection to the infant. In addition, all women who are pregnant should receive the Tdap vaccine during each pregnancy. This allows mothers to pass on protection against pertussis to their newborns.

~ 20 ~

Chronic Health Conditions and Diseases

Coping with Chronic (Long-Term) Health Problems

We tend to think of childhood as a carefree and healthy time of life, but some children face chronic health problems during these early years. What distinguishes a *chronic* health problem from an *acute* health problem is that the acute problem is expected to resolve in a relatively short time frame and the child will return to normal. An acute health problem could mean an injury or a fracture that will heal, or an infection such as pneumonia, from which your child will recover completely. There are also a number of conditions that the child will outgrow without any treatment or intervention. For example, a child with bed-wetting or intoeing will usually outgrow such health issues by school age.

In contrast, a chronic health problem is usually expected to last a year or more and requires ongoing medical attention for management. For example, a child with asthma may require inhalers every day to prevent an asthma attack. Parents should take steps to reduce exposure to irritants and allergens in the child's environment, and will need to learn about asthma, the treatment plan, and what to do if the child has an asthma attack. The child will need to visit his primary care doctor, specialist, or both several times throughout the year. Parents also need to learn how to navigate the health-care system so their child gets the treatment he needs. Finally, parents need to help their child cope with the chronic condition emotionally and physically, and to be able to help themselves and other family members cope as well. You could substitute diabetes, autism, leukemia, or any other number of diagnoses for asthma, and the challenges would be very similar.

The information that follows is aimed at helping parents and caregivers deal with the emotional and practical challenges of living with any child who has a long-term health condition, special healthcare need, or disability. (The specific medical treatment of many chronic conditions is discussed elsewhere, under the names of those conditions; see the Index.)

Some long-term health conditions in children are relatively mild, and some children with chronic health conditions will not have any physical or psychological disability due to the success of ongoing medical treatment. Regardless, any type of long-lasting condition, special healthcare need, or disability is stressful for both the child and his family. It is important to be able to manage all of these aspects and take care of yourself in the process.

Learning about a child's chronic condition is a slow process, and it can be very frustrating at times; occasionally you may feel alone with these challenges. Rest assured that you are *not* alone. Your reactions, grief, and frustrations are normal, and your journey will be filled with many highs and lows; you will meet other parents on the same journey; and you will have many victories. Also remember that your child is still *your child*—he is not, and should not be, defined by the medical condition.

Receiving the Diagnosis of a Chronic Condition in Your Child

All parents, from the time they find out they are expecting a child, start out assuming the child will be healthy. You may have found out about your child's condition during pregnancy, in the newborn nursery, or afterward when you noticed that something was not quite right about your child's health. Regardless of when your child was diagnosed, being given the diagnosis of a chronic condition can cause a parent to feel sadness, fear, guilt, or grief at losing the expectation of a healthy child. This is a normal reaction and an adjustment that all parents of a child with a chronic condition endure.

You may feel that your hopes and expectations for your child have been replaced by fear of the unknown. You may think: "What will happen to my child in two years? Five? Ten? Will the condition get better or worse? How am I going to manage all of these medications? Will I have to take time off from work? How much pain will my child have? Will my insurance cover all the costs?" You never forget the day that you were given the diagnosis for your child. It's a lot of information to absorb, and it takes time to process it all.

This may be a brand-new world for you, with a lot to learn in a relatively short period of time—because your child's health depends on it. There may be highs and lows, flares and periods of quiet, denial and fear of the unknown. There may be days when you think you are the only parent with a child who has special needs, and you may wonder if anyone else knows how you feel. All of this can take a toll on your own well-being and health, which in turn can affect how you can take care of your child. Recognizing these emotions will help you learn how to care for your child, your family, and yourself.

If your child is born with a serious medical problem or develops a chronic medical condition during his first years, you may face some of the following stressors and decisions.

■ The realization that your child is not perfectly healthy often leads to feelings of disappointment and guilt, and fear for the child's future. In trying to deal with these feelings, you may find yourself struggling with unexplained emotional swings ranging from hopefulness to depression and anxiety.

■ You will need to select and work with a team of medical and community partners who can help your child and work with you in shared decision-making.

■ You may be faced with learning about a new diagnosis and understanding your child's prognosis.

■ You may face decisions about treatment or surgery.

■ You may have to be responsible for giving your child certain medications, guide him in usage of special equipment, or perform special therapies.

■ You will be called on to provide the time, energy, money, and emotional commitment necessary for your child to receive the best possible treatment and coordinated care.

■ You will need to learn how to access appropriate services and information.

■ In adapting your life to meet your child's needs without neglecting other family members, you will face many difficult choices, some of which may require compromise solutions.

Navigating the Healthcare System

Parents of children with chronic conditions routinely describe navigating the healthcare system as one of their biggest challenges. Depending on your child's condition, you may be dealing with a few extra doctor visits per year, or you could be working with multiple specialists, pharmacies, therapists, insurance companies, and home healthcare agencies and personnel as well as hospitalizations. All of this may sometimes seem overwhelming and take up a great deal of time. Empowering yourself with information about your child's condition is a necessary start to learning how to navigate the healthcare system as effectively as possible.

You know your child and his needs better than anyone else. Read about your child's condition, ask questions of your child's doctors and nurses, and talk with other parents. The information you learn—and particularly the answers to questions that you don't know to ask in the early stages—will help you engage with your child's doctors in making decisions. Healthcare and developmental outcomes are improved when the parents are part of the decision-making process and knowledgeable about the child's condition. Keep a notebook with questions and make sure they are answered. If you see something at home that concerns you, call the doctor or use the patient portal of your health system's electronic health record; do not assume that you have to wait until the next scheduled appointment. Doctors depend on and respect the information parents and caregivers provide them to make the right medical decision for your child.

It's best to make sure your child has a *medical home*. The American Academy of Pediatrics defines a medical home as care that is accessible, continuous, comprehensive, family-centered, coordinated, compassionate, and culturally effective. The medical home model of care means that the medical care team, child, and family work in partnership together to meet all of the child's special needs. At a minimum, ensure that your child has regularly scheduled visits with his doctors to actively manage the child's condition; this will help keep your child as healthy as possible. It is essential that you and your family have a strong relationship with your child's primary care physician, who will help oversee all aspects of care. It is also helpful to select one medical person as the overall coordinator of your child's medical care. This person may be someone in your pediatrician's office or another health professional who is closely involved with your child's treatment. It should be someone who knows your family well, fosters shared decision-making, values you as an equal team member, makes you feel comfortable, and is willing to spend time answering questions, partnering with you, and working with other doctors and therapists involved in your child's care. In some health systems, this may be a care manager, often a nurse or social worker, who is knowledgeable about your child's condition, your child's care team, and the community services, equipment, medications, and other resources he requires.

Keep track and manage what goes on at home to ensure that you can carry out the medical care recommendations, and that your child gets good nutrition and all of his medications as recommended. Make sure that your child's medical care needs are met *proactively*—that is, everyone works to keep your child healthy and make sure he does not get sicker due to a complication of the chronic health problem. Many children with chronic healthcare conditions have relatively long periods in which those conditions are well controlled; at other times, the condition may flare up. Your goal is to keep the condition under control and learn the signs and symptoms of a flare so you can intervene early and prevent complications, whether those are emergency department visits, hospital admissions, or even long-term consequences to your child.

Parent support groups will have meetings, either online or in person, and provide literature and emotional support. Learn about the options for treatment, including those that your doctor may not know about or is not familiar with. Regardless of whether those options are what you decide to choose, information enables you to take control of the treatment plan and have the knowledge to make the right decision for your child and family.

WHERE WE STAND

WHEN CHILDREN HAVE a chronic, serious illness or disability, their parents may turn to "natural" therapies, wanting to try everything and anything to help their child. Words that describe these therapies include "alternative," "complementary," and "folk remedy." These treatments often are used in addition to the care their child is receiving from her pediatrician or other mainstream practitioner. In most cases, parents use these therapies even though they are happy with traditional medical care, however, in some cases, parents may turn to them when they become frustrated with all that mainstream medicine can offer their child.

If you've made the decision to seek natural therapies for your child's care, involve your pediatrician in the process. In most cases, such therapies work best when used in combination with traditional medical care. Your doctor may be able to help you better understand these therapies, whether they have scientific merit, whether claims about them are accurate or exaggerated, and whether they pose any risks to your child's well-being. Keep in mind that a "natural" treatment does not always mean a safe one. Your pediatrician can help you determine whether there is a risk of interactions with your child's other medications.

The American Academy of Pediatrics has encouraged pediatricians to evaluate the scientific merits of natural therapies, determine whether they might cause any direct or indirect harm, and advise parents on the full range of treatment options. If you decide to use a natural therapy, your pediatrician also may be able to assist in evaluating your child's response to that treatment.

Getting Help for Your Child

There are many ways that you can help with a chronic condition. You can start by making sure that your child gets to all of his doctor appointments. If you have to miss a doctor's appointment, call the doctor's office right away and get it rescheduled—preferably *before* you miss the appointment. That way, your child's doctors can help you manage the medical condition before there is a disease flare. If you find that you are unable to give your child his medications because of scheduling conflicts, financial barriers to filling the prescription, or your child is refusing, call the doctor. Doctors will give you advice on how to help your child accept the regimen, or they may be able to propose an alternative treatment plan. It is important that you let your child's doctors know what is going on at home and if something needs to be changed.

It is very important to provide your child with as much of a typical childhood experience as possible. No one wants to feel different from his friends, and to the extent that it is medically safe to do so, your child should be given the same opportunities as any other child to run and play. No child should be defined by his medical condition—your child is not an "asthmatic" or a "diabetic." Rather, yours is a child "who has asthma" or "who has diabetes."

Good nutrition and growth are at the root of helping a child with special healthcare needs. Some children with a chronic health condition have diffi-culty eating and swallowing. It is especially important for your child to be offered a good, healthy diet. If necessary, a parent or caregiver can work with the doctors or nutritionists to make sure your child is not gaining too little weight or too much. Some children with difficulty swallowing will cough or retch with feeds. If that is the case, you may also need to speak with a speech therapist, who can focus on helping your child learn to swallow with less difficulty to avoid inhaling food particles into the lungs.

Not all of your child's special needs will be medical, of course. He may require community supports such as special schooling, counseling, or other therapy. Many children with chronic conditions will attend daycare or school. Some children may be in private daycare; others may be in a center-based learning center specifically for children with disabilities. It is important that you speak with your child's teachers and caregivers about the medical needs. Specifically, you should let your child's teachers and caregivers know what the medical condition is, medications or therapies that are needed during the day, and warning signs about which you need to be called. School nurses may be available to help you and your child manage any medical condition.

Your family may need outside financial or governmental assistance. The team that coordinates your child's medical care also should provide some guidance in obtaining this extra help, but the best way to make sure you and your child get the services and support needed is to learn about the resources and regulations that apply to special services for children with special healthcare needs. You also should find out what you can do if the services received do not meet your child's needs.

Focus on emotional state and well-being. Help your child adapt to his chronic condition. You should offer your child every opportunity to enjoy typical activities and participate to the extent that it is medically safe to do so. That means going to the park to run and play if he is able, making friends, and attending school. As your child gets older, he will become increasingly aware of the medical treatments and the sense of being "different," regardless of whether there is any actual physical disability or appearances. Many children may not talk about their feelings but will act out in different ways, including tantrums, having a short fuse, or being sad. Meeting other children with a chronic condition can help. It is also important to acknowledge your child's feelings and help caregivers and teachers understand how your child is coping so they can help.

Balancing the Needs of Family and Child

For a while, the child with special needs may take all your attention, leaving little for other family members and outside relationships. Although this is normal, everyone in the family can be affected, so try to find some way to restore a sense of balance and routine to your activities. No one will benefit—not the sick child, not other children, not your spouse or partner—if the health problem becomes the central and overwhelming issue in your family's life. Eventually your child's medical care must become a part of the daily routine rather than its focus.

If your child must be hospitalized, returning to normal family and community life is vital, not only for the family but also for the child's health and well-being. The longer one is treated like a patient instead of a growing child, the more problems she may have socially and emotionally later on. Although it's natural to want to protect a sick child, overprotection may make it more difficult for her to develop the confidence, security, and self-discipline needed to mature properly. Also, if there are other children in the household, you can't expect them to observe rules that you allow the child who is sick or disabled to ignore. Make sure these siblings receive adequate attention as well.

Your child needs encouragement far more than protection. Rather than concentrating on what she cannot do, try to focus instead on what she *can* do. Build on the child's strengths. If given a chance to participate in normal activities with similar-aged children, she probably will do things that surprise everyone. Establishing this sense of normalcy is difficult if your child's condition is uncertain. You may withdraw from your friends due to worrying about your child, and you may hesitate to plan social activities if you're not sure she will be well enough to attend. If you give in to these feelings all the time, resentment is bound to build up, so try not to let this happen. Even if there is a chance that the medical condition may worsen unexpectedly, take the risk and plan special outings, invite friends to your home, and get a babysitter from time to time so you can go out for an evening. Both you and your child will be better off in the long run if you take this approach.

The following suggestions may help you cope more effectively with your child's condition.

■ Whenever possible, both parents and all caregivers should be included in discussions and decisions about medical treatment, even if the parents are separated or divorced. Too often, one parent may go alone to the medical appointment and then must explain what was said to the other parent. This may prevent one parent from getting some of his or her questions answered or learning enough about the choices.

■ Keep an open line of communication with your pediatrician. Express concerns and ask questions. Ask for a care plan to be developed with your input and regularly updated with relevant medical information and summaries.

■ Do not be offended if your child's doctors ask personal questions about your family life. The more they know about the family, the better they can help manage your child's care. For example, if your child has diabetes, a special schedule of meals may be necessary, so the pediatrician may want to suggest ways to work this diet into your family's normal meal plan. Or if a wheelchair is necessary, the doctor may ask about your home in order to suggest the best places for wheelchair ramps. If caring for your child is causing notable stress, your child's pediatrician may ask to explore that with you and offer guidance. If there are any concerns about the doctor's suggestions, discuss them so you can reach an acceptable plan of action together.

■ Remember that although everyone involved in the care plan wants to be optimistic about your child's condition, you must be honest about it. If things are not going well or you have concerns about your child's future, you should discuss these worries. Your child depends on you to speak up at these times and to work with the doctor to adjust the treatment or find a solution that will make the situation as manageable as possible. Asking for additional help, including child life counseling, psychological counseling or therapy, and social services, makes long-term coping easier.

■ Discuss your child's condition frankly, not only with the child but also with the other members of your family. If you do not tell your child the truth, there will be a sense that you are lying; this can lead to feelings of isolation and rejection. Furthermore, she will imagine all the things that could be wrong—most of which may be worse than the real problem. So talk openly, and listen to her responses to make sure all is understood. Answer questions in clear, simple language.

■ Call on friends and family members for support. You cannot expect to handle the strain created by your child's chronic condition all by yourself. Asking close friends to help meet your own emotional needs will in turn help you to meet your child's.

■ If you have other children, be sure to give them your attention and try to balance their needs and fears as well. There are resources available for siblings of children and youth with special healthcare needs.

■ Connecting with other parents or caregivers who have children with the same or similar conditions as your child is helpful to many families. Each state has a Family-to-Family Health Information Center that can help link you to other parents. In addition, for families whose children have certain diagnoses (such as cystic fibrosis, sickle cell disease, or diabetes), there are specific family support networks that your healthcare providers or community partners can link you to.

■ Remember that your child needs to be loved and valued as an individual. If you let the medical problems overshadow your feelings for her as a person, they may interfere with the bond of trust and affection between parent and child. Be sure to reach out to your child's medical care team if you are feeling overwhelmed, lost, or don't know how to give proper medical or emotional care. Don't become so worried that you cannot relax and enjoy your child.

You are not alone. It is important to reach out to other parents who have a child with a chronic condition to see how they have coped with the journey. Family support groups are often an important part of the journey. Knowing other families will help reassure you, your child, and other family members.

The topics that follow address some of the more commonly seen chronic conditions. It is important for you to be proactive in learning about your child's condition as much as possible and what you can do to help. Read about the condition, talk with other families, and get to know your doctors well—they will be a tremendous resource and help you understand how to take care of your child's medical needs.

Anemia

Blood contains several different types of cells. The most numerous are the red blood cells, which absorb oxygen in the lungs and distribute it throughout the body. These cells contain hemoglobin, a red pigment that carries oxygen to the tissues and carries away carbon dioxide (the waste material). Anemia can be either an acute or chronic condition in which a decreased amount of hemoglobin is available in the red blood cells, or there is a reduced number of red blood cells in the blood itself, making the blood less able to carry the amount of oxygen necessary for all the cells in the body to function and grow.

Anemia may occur for any of the following reasons:

1. The production of red blood cells is too slow.

2. Too many red blood cells are destroyed.

3. There is not enough hemoglobin within the red blood cells.

4. Blood cells are lost from the body.

Many cases of anemia are treatable. Young children most commonly become anemic when they fail to get enough iron in their diet. Iron is necessary for the production of hemoglobin. This iron deficiency causes a decrease in the amount of hemoglobin in the red blood cells.

An infant may get iron-deficiency anemia if he starts drinking cow's milk too early, particularly if he is not given an iron supplement or healthy food that contains enough iron. Cow's milk contains very little iron, and the iron it does have is not easily absorbed. Furthermore, cow's milk can interfere with the absorption of iron from other foods. Cow's milk given to an infant under twelve months of age can irritate the bowel and cause small amounts of blood loss. This results in a decrease in the number of red blood cells, which can cause anemia. Finally,

drinking too much milk may limit a child's interest in other foods that are rich in iron, placing them at risk for iron-deficiency anemia. Other nutritional deficiencies, such as a lack of folic acid, can cause anemia as well, but such causes are rare.

Anemia can also be a result of a chronic condition that will need ongoing treatment and follow-up by your child's doctor. For example, blood loss may occur because a child is slowly losing blood in his stool in amounts tiny enough that it can't be seen. Another group of conditions is called hemolytic anemia. In this condition, red blood cells are prone to being easily destroyed because of changes in the shape of the cells, disturbances on their surface, or other abnormalities. Certain enzyme deficiencies can alter the function of red blood cells and increase the chances they will die or be destroyed early, causing anemia. A severe condition called sickle cell anemia involves an abnormal structure of hemoglobin, which is seen most often in children of African heritage but can affect children of all ethnicities. This disorder can be very severe and is associated with frequent episodes of pain and worsening anemia, often requiring repeated hospitalizations. Fortunately, it is now tested for in the newborn screen in all states (see page 637).

Disorders called thalassemias are inherited blood conditions that tend to occur most frequently in children of Asian, African, Middle Eastern, Greek, and Italian heritage. Children with these disorders have an abnormally low number of red blood cells, or not enough hemoglobin. They can develop anemia, sometimes severe cases.

Signs and Symptoms

In some cases, the anemia develops so slowly over time that symptoms aren't noticed. More typically, though, anemia causes the skin to be mildly pale, usually most apparent as a decreased pinkness of the lips, the lining of the eyelids (conjunctiva), and the nail beds (pink part of the nails). Anemic children also may be irritable, mildly weak, or easily tired. Those with severe anemia may have shortness of breath, rapid heart rate, and swelling of the hands and feet. If the anemia continues, it may interfere with normal growth. Children with hemolytic anemia may become jaundiced (turn yellow), although many newborns are mildly jaundiced for reasons that don't involve anemia.

If your child shows any of these symptoms or signs, or if you suspect he is not getting enough iron in his diet, consult your pediatrician. A simple blood count can diagnose anemia in most cases.

Although some cases of thalassemia have no symptoms, more moderate to severe cases can cause lethargy, jaundice, a poor appetite, slow growth, and an enlarged spleen.

Some children are not anemic but still are deficient in iron. They may have a decreased appetite and be irritable, fussy, and inattentive, which may result in developmental delays or poor school performance. These problems may improve when the children are given iron. Other signs of iron deficiency that may be unrelated to anemia include a tendency to eat unusual things, such as ice, dirt, clay, and cornstarch. This behavior, called pica, is not harmful unless the material eaten is toxic (e.g., lead). Usually the behavior improves after the iron deficiency is treated and as the child becomes older, although it may persist longer in children who are developmentally delayed.

Treatment

Since there are so many different types of anemia, it is very important to identify the cause before any treatment is begun. Do not attempt to treat your child with vitamins, iron, or other nutrients or over-the-counter medications unless it is at your physician's direction. This is important, because such treatment may mask the real reason for the problem and thus delay the diagnosis. The treatment for anemia may include medications, dietary supplements, or dietary restrictions.

If the anemia is due to a lack of iron, your child will be given an iron-containing medication. This comes in a drop form for infants and a liquid or tablet form for older children. To avoid giving your child too much iron, or continuing it once it is no longer needed, your pediatrician will check your child's blood hemoglobin and/or iron levels at regular intervals. Do not stop giving the medication until the physician tells you it is no longer needed.

The following are a few tips concerning iron medication.

■ It is best not to give iron with milk because milk blocks iron absorption.

■ Vitamin C increases iron absorption, so you might want to follow the dose of iron with a glass of orange juice or a serving of fresh fruit.

■ Since liquid iron tends to turn the teeth a grayish black color temporarily, have your child swallow it rapidly and then rinse his mouth with water. You also may want to brush your child's teeth after every dose of iron. Tooth-staining from iron is not permanent.

■ Iron medications cause the stools to become a dark or black color. Don't be worried by this change.

Safety precautions: Iron medications can be poisonous if taken in excessive amounts. (Iron is one of the most common causes of poisoning in children under five years of age.) For that reason, *keep this and all medication out of reach of small children.*

Severe cases of thalassemias are typically treated with folate supplements, transfusions of red blood cells, and, when possible, hematopoetic stem cell (bone marrow) transplantation.

Cystic Fibrosis

Cystic fibrosis (CF) is the second most common inherited, life-shortening disease of childhood in the United States (second only to sickle cell anemia). The overall prevalence is approximately 1 out of every 3,500 live births. Considerable progress has been made in treating cystic fibrosis and its symptoms, although there is still no cure. CF is a disease that changes the secretions of certain glands in the body. It is inherited from parents who carry the gene that causes this disease. For a child to get cystic fibrosis, both parents must be carriers of a genetic abnormality that can cause the disease. Although the sweat glands and the glandular cells of the lungs and pancreas are affected most often, the sinuses, liver, intestines, and reproductive organs also can be involved. In 1989 researchers discovered the most common gene defect that causes CF. Couples planning to have children can undergo genetic testing and counseling to find out if they carry one of the identified abnormal CF genes. They can also receive prenatal testing to detect the gene in the fetus. If both parents are carriers, there are other options available, such as IVF (in vitro fertilization). Talk to your doctor about these alternatives.

Signs and Symptoms

The majority of CF cases are diagnosed within the first two years after birth; in all US states, newborn screenings now include mandatory testing for CF, though not all states test as extensively as others. Therefore, even if the newborn screen was reported as "not suggestive of cystic fibrosis," additional testing is routinely done if there are symptoms of CF present. More than half of CF cases are diagnosed because of repeated lung infections. These infections tend to recur because mucus in the airways is thicker than normal and more difficult to cough out, leading to a persistent cough and potentially pneumonia or bronchitis. Over time, these infections cause damage to the lungs, and are the major cause of death in CF patients in later life. Most children with CF are also deficient in digestive enzymes, making it difficult for them to digest fats and proteins as well as they should. As a result, these children can have large, bulky, foul-smelling stools, accompanied by poor weight gain, if the enzymes are not supplemented (see *Treatment* for more information on enzymes).

To confirm the diagnosis, your pediatrician will order a sweat test to measure the amount of salt your child loses as he perspires. Children with cystic fibrosis have much more salt in their sweat than children who do not have CF. Two or more of these tests may be required to ensure an accurate diagnosis, since the results are not always clearly positive or negative. Often, genetic testing is performed as well, as different abnormal CF genes can indicate the most likely course of the illness in the child. If your child is diagnosed as having the disease, your pediatrician will help you get the additional specialized medical help that is necessary. At a medical center that specializes in treating children with CF you can find multidisciplinary experts to help your child and family.

Treatment

CF treatment is lifelong and typically requires many visits to a CF center, where your child will be treated by a healthcare team specializing in CF care. Treating the lung infections that develop in children with CF is the most important aspect of your child's care. The goal is to help clear the thick secretions from your child's lungs, which may involve various techniques and medications that help him cough out the sputum more easily. The lung infections themselves are treated with antibiotics. Your child may also be prescribed capsules containing digestive enzymes to be taken with every meal and snack. The amount of enzymes is based on the composition of the diet and the weight of your child. Once the correct amount of enzymes is taken, your child's stool pattern should become more normal and he'll begin gaining more weight. Close observation by your child's primary care physician, the CF center physicians, and the center care team is designed to detect failure to respond to treatment and allow additional therapy.

The majority of children with CF can expect to grow up and lead productive adult lives with continuous treatment according to care guidelines. It is important to raise your child as you would if he did not have this disease. With very few exceptions, there is no reason to limit educational or career goals. Your child needs both love and discipline, and should be encouraged to develop and test limits. Balancing the physical and emotional demands created by this disease is hard on both the CF patient and his family, so it is very important that you get as much support as possible. Ask your pediatrician to put you in touch not only with the nearest CF center but also with CF support groups. The Cystic Fibrosis Foundation also can be of help (cff.org; 1-800-344-4823). Connecting with other parents is essential to support you, your child, and your family.

Diabetes Mellitus

Type 1 diabetes occurs when specialized cells of the pancreas (a gland located behind the stomach) do not produce adequate amounts of the hormone insulin. Insulin enables the body to process the nutrients (proteins, fat, and carbohydrates) to make body tissues, promote growth, produce energy, and store energy. These nutrients are broken down into glucose, a type of sugar used by the cells of the body as a source of energy. Glucose is fuel for the body to use. Insulin is needed to transport glucose from the bloodstream into the cells, providing cells with the energy they depend on; insulin maintains blood sugar levels within a tight range.

People with type 1 diabetes have a reduced supply of insulin or none at all. Therefore, when a person with type 1 diabetes eats, her blood glucose levels rise (hyperglycemia) and her body does not produce normal amounts of insulin to combat the rise in glucose. Without insulin, the nutrients in the food cannot be used by the cells but remain in the bloodstream. When cells don't receive the energy source they need, they act as if they are starving, and the liver in turn is prompted to make sugar from the body stores of protein and fat, which also cannot be used without insulin. This leads to weight loss and weakness, because muscle and fat are being broken down and the body is not getting the energy it needs.

Normally the kidneys remove glucose from waste water (urine) before it is excreted from the body. In patients with diabetes, however, the kidneys become overwhelmed, and excess glucose leaks into the urine, bringing more water with it. This is why people who have diabetes urinate more frequently and can become very thirsty as they try to replace the fluid loss. Without insulin, the body tries to get energy from stored fat. The fat is broken down to certain kinds of acids that are converted to ketones, which are also excreted in the urine.

Currently, there is no way to prevent type 1 diabetes. There is a genetic predisposition to developing type 1 diabetes, but only about 30 percent of children with type 1 diabetes have any close relatives with the disease. The destruction of the cells that make insulin results from a process in which the body's immune system views these cells as foreign invaders and mounts an immune response against them. This autoimmune process starts months to years before the first symptoms of diabetes show up. The trigger for this process is unknown, although in rare cases certain viruses or other environmental factors have been implicated. Although clinical research trials are exploring these links, currently there is no known way to prevent the autoimmune response.

In *type 2 diabetes*, the body does not use insulin properly (known as insulin resistance) nor produce enough insulin to make up for the extra insulin it needs. Type 2 diabetes was once considered a disease that only adults had to worry about (indeed, the condition was once called "adult-onset diabetes"). Today, type 2 diabetes in young children and adolescents is closely associated with obesity, and is increasing in children as rates of obesity grow. Among children diagnosed with type 2 diabetes, eighty-five out of one hundred are obese, and in the United States virtually all have at least overweight. Children who have overweight, are inactive, overeat or eat unhealthy diets, and have a family history of diabetes have the greatest risk of developing type 2 diabetes. Children in minority groups also have a higher incidence of type 2 diabetes. According to the American Diabetes Association, an estimated two million children have pre-diabetes, which is a collection of risk factors that often leads to type 2 diabetes.

Type 1 diabetes can appear at any age, although it most commonly appears in school-age children. Unfortunately, the diagnosis often is delayed in infants and toddlers until the child is very sick, because the symptoms may be attributed to other illnesses. Type 2 diabetes more commonly appears in older children and teens. It is important to notify your pediatrician immediately if your child displays any of the following warning signs and symptoms of diabetes:

- Increased or frequent urination. A toilet-trained child may start bedwetting, or a baby in diapers will need more frequent changes.

- Increased thirst (due to the increased or frequent urination).

- Weight loss with either increased appetite and food intake or marked persistent loss of appetite (more common in younger children)

- Dehydration (see page 547 for signs)

- Unexplained tiredness or fatigue

- Persistent vomiting, particularly if it is accompanied by weakness or drowsiness

- Blurred vision

If your child goes to the doctor with any suspicious symptoms, be sure that a urine or blood test is done to determine whether her glucose levels are too high. This simple test will provide a clue to diabetes and prevent your child from becoming more ill.

Treatment

When blood tests confirm diabetes, treatment begins immediately. Insulin injections are required for type 1 diabetes, whereas an oral medication is sometimes effective for type 2 diabetes. When the child does not require intravenous fluids to correct dehydration and vomiting, many specialists do not recommend hospitalization, but provide outpatient family diabetes education and care with frequent office visits.

A healthcare team that specializes in diabetes will teach the entire family how to manage diabetes. Members of the healthcare team include a physician (usually with advanced training in the care of youth with diabetes), a nurse educator, a dietitian, and a social worker, who all work together to educate the family. With type 1 diabetes you'll learn how to test blood glucose levels from a drop of blood from a finger stick and how to give insulin injections. You will learn about food, planning meals and snacks, and activity and exercise. Your team will help determine how many insulin injections your child may need to control her blood sugars and successfully manage her diabetes. Eventually, your child will likely transition to receiving insulin by means of a portable pump; this is more flexible than the standard injections but still requires regular blood glucose checks. Newer pumps that also measure blood glucose are under development. Parents should learn as much as possible about the care and management of their child's diabetes.

Having children participate as much as possible in their diabetes management gives them some measure of control. For example, a child under age three might choose which finger to stick for blood sugar tests or choose which place to use for the insulin injection, then gradually learn how to do her own blood glucose testing and insulin shots (or insulin pump care) as she gets older.

Childcare and school personnel need to know about your child's diabetes, her insulin and testing schedule, and her snack needs. They need to be able to recognize and treat hypoglycemia (low blood sugar). They also need to know how to test blood sugar levels and have guidelines for giving insulin and testing for urine ketones. They should always have the parent's emergency phone number on hand. Most diabetes education teams have a school packet and will help you communicate with school or daycare personnel. To learn more about type 1 diabetes, contact the Juvenile Diabetes Research Foundation (jdrf.org; 1-800-533-2873) and the American Diabetes Association (diabetes.org; 1-800-342-2383).

HIV Infection and AIDS

HIV (human immunodeficiency virus) is a virus that can lead to AIDS (acquired immunodeficiency syndrome). Infants acquire HIV infection primarily from their mothers living with HIV, either in utero (the virus passes across the placenta), during delivery (when the newborn is exposed to the mother's blood and body fluids), or by ingesting infected breast milk; rarely, transmission occurs when the infant is given food pre-chewed by an infected person.

Perinatal HIV transmissions have decreased 90 percent since the 1990s; infants born to mothers living with HIV have a less than 1 percent chance of being infected when their mothers are on medications that control the virus. Currently, a combination of anti-HIV therapy is recommended for all infected pregnant women living with HIV, followed by prophylaxis for the infant at birth and shortly afterward. In 2016 there were fewer than 100 children diagnosed with perinatally acquired HIV in the United States, and many of those were born overseas; the number of foreign-born infected children living with HIV has exceeded the number of US-born infected children since 2011.

Once a person is infected with HIV, the virus will be in his body for life. People with HIV infection may be free of symptoms for months or even years; AIDS occurs only after the progressive weakening of the immune defense system by the virus. Without treatment, children usually develop signs of HIV infection by the age of two, but the average time to develop AIDS is about five years. Infants with the HIV infection initially may appear well, but need to be started on medications as soon as the diagnosis is confirmed because problems gradually develop. For example, untreated infants can fail to grow appropriately within the first six months to one year. They have frequent episodes of diarrhea or frequent respiratory infections. The lymph nodes (glands) anywhere in the body may enlarge, and there is a persistent fungus infec-tion of the mouth (thrush). The liver and spleen may enlarge. Because neurological development may be affected, children may have a delay in walking and other motor skills, a delay in their ability to think and talk, and diminished head growth during infancy.

Eventually, if the untreated HIV infection progresses as the body's immune system further deteriorates, AIDS-related infections and cancers may occur. The most common of these, *Pneumocystis jirovecii* pneumonia, is accompanied by fever and breathing difficulties.

Care of a Child Living with HIV

Children living with HIV can now grow well and lead productive and fulfilling lives with good medical care. Your child with HIV is typically cared for by an infectious disease specialist or pediatric immunologist as well as a primary care pediatrician. Other specialists and therapists may work with you and your family. It is important to keep all of your appointments and for your child to take all medications that are prescribed. Anti-retroviral (ARV) medications suppress virus reproduction and improve the child's growth and development. They also delay the progression of the disease.

It is important that you advocate for your child and ensure that people understand HIV cannot be transmitted by just holding a child living with HIV. Call the doctor if your child living with HIV develops a fever, breathing difficulties, diarrhea, or swallowing problems, or if he's been exposed to a communicable disease. In fact, any change in your child's health status should prompt you to seek medical attention, since the child living with HIV may have few reserves to combat illnesses. With the use of combination anti-HIV therapy, however, infected children living with HIV whose immune systems are not seriously compromised can be expected to respond to common bacterial and viral infections the same way as children not living with HIV.

Whenever seeking any medical attention for your child, be sure to inform the physician of the HIV infection so that she can assess and care for the illness appropriately, as well as give correct immunizations.

WHERE WE STAND

THE AMERICAN ACADEMY OF PEDIATRICS supports legislation and public policy directed toward eliminating any form of discrimination based on whether a child is infected with HIV (the virus that causes AIDS).

- *HIV in the schools.* All infected children living with HIV should have the same right as those without the infection to attend school and childcare. Infected children should receive access to special education and other related services (including home instruction) if their disease progresses and the need arises. The confidentiality of a child's HIV infection status should be respected, with disclosure given only with the consent of the parent(s) or legal guardian(s).

- *HIV legislation.* The Academy supports federal funding for AIDS research and healthcare services for infected individuals living with HIV and their families and for HIV prevention programs.

- *HIV testing.* The Academy recommends that information about HIV infection, prevention of mother-to-child HIV transmission, and HIV testing be routinely provided as part of a comprehensive healthcare program for pregnant women. Documented, routine HIV testing should be performed for all pregnant women in the United States after notifying them that testing will be performed, unless the patient declines HIV testing (called "opt-out" consent or "right of refusal"). The Academy also recommends expedited HIV testing for newborns whose mothers' HIV status (i.e., whether the virus is present in her blood) is not known, using consent procedures consistent with state and local law.

If You're Pregnant

All pregnant women should be tested for HIV infection during every pregnancy. When a pregnant woman is infected with HIV, it is important that she be treated appropriately to reduce the likelihood of transmission of the virus from mother to infant. Once the baby is born, women who are HIV-infected should not breastfeed their infant because of the risk of transmitting the virus via breastfeeding; safe alternative sources of infant nutrition are available, such as infant formulas.

In the Classroom

There is no risk of HIV transmission in routine classroom activities. The virus is not spread through casual contact. It cannot be transmitted through the air, by touching, or via toilet seats. School-age children with HIV infection can attend a regular school. You are not required to disclose the HIV status of your child in order for him to attend school and participate in all school-related activities.

Although HIV transmission has not occurred in schools and childcare centers, these settings are required to adopt routine precautionary procedures for handling blood, stool, and bodily secretions. The standard precaution is to wash exposed skin immediately with soap and water after any contact with blood or body fluids. Soiled surfaces should be cleaned with disinfectants such as bleach (a 1-to-10 dilution of bleach to water). Dispos-

able towels or tissues should be used whenever possible. Gloves are recommended when contact with blood or blood-containing body fluids may occur, and therefore gloves should be available in schools and childcare centers. It is important for staff members to wash their hands thoroughly after changing diapers, whether gloves are used or not.

Schools should ensure that children wash their hands before eating, and the staff should wash their hands before food preparation or feeding children. Though many parents worry about biting, HIV has not been transmitted in school settings. Also, it is critically important that schools incorporate HIV education into their curriculum. All children should learn that HIV is spread through blood or body secretion exposures, and not through casual contact. They should learn how to avoid exposure to blood and body fluids that might contain HIV or other viruses.

Sickle Cell Disease

Sickle cell disease (SCD) is a group of chronic genetic disorders affecting the red blood cells. In children with SCD, the red cells in the blood become sickle-shaped, impacting how well the red blood cells transport oxygen around the body.

There are several types of sickle cell disease. The best-known is sickle cell anemia. Others include sickle–hemoglobin C disease and two types of sickle β-thalassemia. All of these disorders in the SCD complex have similar symptoms, such as anemia (shortage of red blood cells), episodes of severe pain, and infections. (See *Signs and Symptoms*, to the right.)

In the United States, about 2,000 newborns each year are diagnosed with SCD. Although it is commonly thought of as affecting only people of African ancestry, it can occur in children of any race or ethnicity, in particular those whose ancestors come from South and Central America, India, Saudi Arabia, Italy, Greece, or Turkey.

In healthy children, red blood cells are normally round and flexible, and travel easily through blood vessels, transporting oxygen from the lungs to every part of the body. Children with SCD have abnormalities in hemoglobin (a component of every red blood cell) that can distort the shape of these red cells. The irregularly shaped red cells become sticky, clumping together and interfering with the flow of nourishing blood to organs and limbs. These cells also survive only a few days from the time they are released into the circulation, in contrast to several months for normal red blood cells. This causes ongoing anemia.

Some children do not have the disease itself, but they carry the gene responsible for causing it, and they can pass it along when they have children of their own. If a child inherits the sickle cell gene from one parent but not the other, pediatricians categorize the child as having sickle cell trait.

Signs and Symptoms

In most cases, infants with SCD appear healthy at birth. However, after a child is a few months old, symptoms may emerge that can range from mild to severe.

Common signs and symptoms of SCD include:

■ Inflammation and swelling of the hands and/or feet (called dactylitis or hand-foot syndrome); this is commonly the first symptom of SCD

■ Anemia

■ Pain

■ Pallor

■ Jaundice (yellowing of the skin and eyes)

■ Susceptibility to infections

■ Delayed growth

A sickle cell crisis may occur suddenly, with an episode of pain that typically affects the bones, joints, or abdomen. The intensity of pain can vary, and it can last from hours to many weeks. The trigger for these crises is unclear in many cases, although blocked blood flow plays a role, and in some cases so can infections. Serious SCD complications can develop, including pneumonia, stroke, and organ damage (spleen, kidney, liver, or lung).

Treatment

If your child has SCD, she should be diagnosed as early as possible so that appropriate treatment can be planned and started. Fortunately, most cases of SCD can be detected through a simple screening blood test that is universally given to newborns in all states.

Children with SCD need long-term care in order to minimize the risk of complications, to address problems when they occur, to prevent life-threatening infection, and to be able to access new treatments as they are developed. Commonly prescribed treatments include the following:

■ Mild pain can be relieved with over-the-counter analgesic medications, such as acetaminophen or nonsteroidal anti-inflammatory drugs (NSAIDs) such as ibuprofen. Heating pads also can be used for pain relief. In addition, good hydration is important.

■ Antibiotics should be prescribed for all children with sickle cell anemia (HbSS and HbSβ°thalassemia) and other types of SCD, beginning by two months of age and given continuously until at least the age of five years. These medications are a preventive measure to reduce the risk of serious bacterial infection.

■ Children with SCD should receive all childhood immunizations as recommended by the American Academy of Pediatrics (see page 892).

■ Children with sickle cell anemia (HbSS or HbSβ°thalassemia) should begin hydroxyurea treatment at nine months of age. Hydroxyurea is a once-daily medication that decreases the number of pain crises, pneumonias, and blood transfusions.

■ Children with sickle cell anemia should have a transcranial Doppler (TCD) every year beginning at two years of age. TCD is an ultrasound of the brain that helps to identify children who are at highest risk of stroke so that they can begin treatment to reduce that risk.

Your child with SCD can benefit from various lifestyle measures. She should get plenty of rest and sleep. She should drink lots of water (particularly in warm weather) and avoid becoming overly hot or cold. Some doctors recommend folic acid supplements, which can help the body make more red blood cells.

If your child's pain becomes severe, or she develops other serious symptoms or complications, your pediatrician may recommend hospitalization. While hospitalized, your child could receive:

■ Morphine or other drugs given intravenously (through a vein) for pain relief

■ Intravenous antibiotics that can manage an infection if one develops

■ Blood transfusions that can raise the number of red blood cells

■ Supplemental oxygen given through a mask that can add oxygen to the blood

Because relatively mild symptoms (fever, pale skin, abdominal pain) can quickly progress to serious illness, parents should talk with their pediatrician in advance to make sure that the family has around-the-clock access to a medical facility experienced in treating SCD. If your child develops a fever, contact your pediatrician at once because of the risk of a major infection.

~ 21 ~

Developmental Disabilities

IT'S NATURAL TO compare your child with others his age. When the neighbor's baby walks at ten months, for example, you may worry if yours isn't walking by twelve months, although many children do not walk until they are fourteen or fifteen months of age. And if your toddler is using words at an earlier age than his playmates, probably you'll be very proud. Usually, however, such differences are not significant in the long run. Each child has his own unique rate of development, so some learn certain skills faster than others. Sometimes, when a child is slightly delayed, he or she may simply need a little more time to catch up to other peers. However, any significant delay should be identified and intervened upon as early as possible to ensure that the child reaches his full developmental potential.

A true developmental disability, however, is likely to be a more permanent issue and to require more intensive intervention. Yet only when a baby or preschooler fails to reach the developmental milestones outlined in Chapters 6 through 13 of this book, or loses a previously acquired skill, is there reason to suspect a mental or physical problem serious enough to be considered a developmental disability. Developmental disabilities that can be identified during childhood include intellectual disability, language and learning disorders, attention-deficit/hyperactivity disorder, cerebral palsy, autism spectrum disorder, and sensory impairments such as vision and hearing impairments. (Some pediatricians include seizure disorders in this category, but a large percentage of children who have seizures have typical development.)

Within each developmental disability there is a range of mild to severe that may impact daily functioning just a little bit or a lot. Also, some children may have more than one disability, each requiring different types of support. Your pediatrician and medical home will be integral to helping you navigate any developmental disability.

If your child does not seem to be developing at the same pace as other children the same age, you should mention this to your child's pediatrician. Your child should have a complete medical and developmental evaluation, perhaps including a consultation with a developmental-behavioral pediatrician, child neurologist, geneticist, or pediatric rehabilitation medicine physician, all of whom are specialists trained in evaluation, diagnosis, and care planning for children with disabilities. Your pediatrician will refer you to the most appropriate professional for further assessment. Doing this will give your pediatrician the information she needs to determine whether a true disability exists, and, if so, how it should be managed. Your physician may recommend additional evaluation by a physical, speech and language, or occupational therapist. Early intervention services are typically recommended for children under the age of three with developmental delays or medical conditions

that place children at high risk for delay. You don't need a referral from a doctor for an evaluation by an early intervention specialist or the school system, but your pediatrician is often available to help you arrange these consultations. These evaluations may be available through the public early intervention system by your county for children under three years of age or by the school district if your child is over three. If you or your physician has concerns about developmental delays, you should contact your school district to find out if they can do these evaluations.

Today every child over the age of three years with a developmental disability is entitled by federal law to a free and appropriate public education in the least restrictive environment. Most states also offer special early intervention programs for infants and toddlers. For children under three, such intervention may be provided in your home. Between the ages of three and five years, therapy or education for identified delays may take place in a preschool or at home.

The families of children with disabilities also need special support and education. Families often worry about how they can help their child once a developmental disability is identified. To understand how your child can realize his full potential, each member of your family should be educated about the child's developmental condition and counseled about how to help him develop new skills. One of the most important tenets of early intervention, in fact, is to teach parents appropriate therapeutic techniques that can be practiced and utilized even outside therapy sessions.

Autism Spectrum Disorder

Autism spectrum disorder (ASD) affects a child's behavior, social skills, and communication abilities. ASD is a lifelong condition and can impair the way an individual interacts with others. Although there is a range of symptoms with varying levels of severity, from mild differences in social awareness to severe disabilities in relating to and communicating with others, the scientific consensus is now that autism spectrum disorder is a single diagnosis. (Previously, ASD symptoms were classified under four separate disorders: autistic disorder, Asperger disorder, childhood disintegrative disorder, and pervasive developmental disorder not otherwise specified [PDD-NOS].) The diagnosis of ASD can be further modified by indicating whether a child has an additional language disorder and/or intellectual disability, and whether there is a known neurogenetic condition associated with or predisposing to the autism.

The social symptoms associated with ASD are typically seen in the first year after birth (although they may be subtle). Children may have difficulty with nonverbal communication, such as use of gestures, pointing, making eye contact, and imitation. Language problems—unusual or delayed language—are more obvious in the second year. Repetitive behaviors, such as turning a light switch off and on, repetitive speech, a singular interest in one topic, or physical behaviors like rocking from side to side or hand flapping, may appear even later. Some children also have intellectual deficits, although the majority have typical scores on formal intellectual testing done after six years of age.

Many children with ASD do not have language delays and have typical intelligence. They may, however, have trouble taking the point of view of others and thus difficulties in understanding how they should interact with others. They may be preoccupied with their own world, be unaware of their impact on other people, talk about only one or two topics that they focus on repeatedly, and interpret language literally, having trouble with humor, teasing, and figures of speech. They may be described as having "quirky" interests and behavior. Their voice may have little variation in tone and they may exhibit only limited facial expressions or eye contact. Many also have symptoms of ADHD and anxiety.

Children with fewer overall symptoms may still have challenging behaviors that impair function and benefit from intervention. Children who do not display any repetitive or restrictive patterns of behavior but have difficulties with social communication may now be classified as having social communication disorder.

Autism affects children of all races, ethnicities, and socioeconomic groups. It occurs about four times more often in boys than in girls, and is diagnosed in nearly one of every fifty-nine children in the United States. Although autism was once thought of as relatively rare, the number of children identified as having this diagnosis has risen in recent years. This increase in reported cases is likely due in part to a greater awareness of autism's signs and symptoms on the part of parents, teachers, and pediatricians, which means that more children are being diagnosed. In addition, some children who are diagnosed as having autism today might have been classified in the past as having a different diagnosis, like intellectual disability; this would contribute to the increase in numbers.

As noted, autism is a diagnosis that describes a spectrum of symptoms. Likely there are many different underlying reasons for these symptoms, so in most individual cases the exact cause of autism still remains unclear. Studies of families, including those with twins, have shown that genetics plays an important role in autism. Researchers are also studying factors in the environment that may interact with genes to increase a child's risk of developing symptoms of autism. Better awareness leads to diagnosis in children with milder symptoms. This allows for treatment, which has been shown to help, especially when started earlier in life.

Some parents have been concerned about a possible link between autism and certain childhood immunizations. Numerous studies have now exam-ined the claim that childhood vaccines cause autism, and **they have effectively ruled out any link between vaccines and autism.** The changes in the brain that lead to autism start in the womb, long before the baby is born and receives any vaccines. If you have questions about vaccines for your child, talk to your pediatrician, who can provide scientifically confirmed information about the safety of vaccines and the important benefits of vaccinating your child.

Signs and Symptoms

The following characteristics may be seen in children with ASD. Keep in mind that no two children with these disorders are alike, and signs and symptoms can differ from one child to another, and across the lifespan of any one child.

Some children with ASD never develop the ability to speak, or may have delayed or poorly developed language skills. They may use words without attaching the usual meanings to them, or simply repeat what they hear others saying (known as echolalia). They may not be capable of starting or continuing a conversation, using language for social discussions, or following rules for conversations and story-telling (language pragmatics). Fortunately, this is a minority of children now diagnosed with ASD.

Some children may not be able to understand what people say to them, or interpret or respond appropriately to cues such as the facial expressions and the body language of others. They may have delayed use of pointing, unusual qualities of pointing or requesting, or limited use of pointing to indicate what they want or to interact with others. They might not respond when their name is called, but may react when they hear other types of sounds (a dog's bark, the crinkle of a bag of potato chips).

These children may be socially withdrawn and have trouble relating to people and making eye contact. They may appear to be unaware of their surroundings or in their own world. Their behavior and body movements are sometimes repetitive. For instance, they may have repetitive motor movements like rocking, spinning, flapping their hands, or lining things up. They may be fascinated by spinning objects like fans or tops. They also may develop maladaptive behavior patterns that could be harmful to themselves, such as head banging or biting, or may be aggressive toward others. They may become upset and have tantrums or disruptive behavior when changes in everyday routines occur (e.g., mealtimes) or when they have to transition from one activity to another.

They may have a limited (restricted) range of interests and activities. Their play may not be creative or imaginative in the usual sense of "play," and may include repetitive behavior. They may play with toys in ways in which the toys are not designed to be used. They may play with parts of a toy (only the wheels on a toy truck, for example) rather than the entire toy. They may line up toys repeatedly and may have delays in use of make-believe or pretend play.

Instead of forming attachments to a blanket or stuffed animal, they might prefer unusual objects (e.g., string, sticks, figures), and may not want to give up holding them all the time.

They may be very sensitive to smells, lights, sounds, touch, and textures; they may seem to have a high threshold for pain.

Diagnosis

The earlier that therapies are started after diagnosis, the better the response. Therefore, if your child has shown delays in developing language, has difficulties with social communication, or has unusual behaviors, talk to your pediatrician. Other early signs should raise concerns and should be evaluated for a potential diagnosis. Contact your doctor if your child is not doing the following activities by the stated age:

BY TWELVE MONTHS

■ Looks at an object when you point to it and say "Look!"

■ Uses simple gestures like waving bye-bye

■ Says "mama," "dada," and at least one other word

BY EIGHTEEN MONTHS

■ Points to show you interesting objects or events

■ Uses at least ten words correctly

■ Will do pretend play, e.g., feed a doll

BY TWENTY-FOUR MONTHS
■ Points to several body parts, objects, and pictures

■ Imitates behavior of others, especially adults and older children

■ Speaks two-word phrases and has a fifty-word vocabulary

BY THIRTY-SIX MONTHS
■ Enjoys playing with (not just alongside) other children and imitating them

■ Speaks three-word sentences and can use some pronouns

■ Talks for doll or action figure in pretend play

BY FORTY-EIGHT MONTHS
■ Can name friends when asked

■ Answers "wh" questions (what, when, who, where)

■ Speaks clearly in five- to six-word sentences

Further signs and symptoms can be found at the Centers for Disease Control and Prevention website, cdc .gov/actearly.

If you observe signs like these in your child, or are concerned about other aspects of his language and social development, let your pediatrician know—and the earlier, the better. In fact, as soon as the diagnosis of autism is suspected, treatment should begin, even before a diagnosis is conclusively made. Children with other types of delays may have some of these symptoms as well, but these other developmental diagnoses also benefit from intervention, so getting your child evaluated is important even if you are not concerned about autism.

Unfortunately, no laboratory test is available to diagnose autism, nor, as we have seen, does a single set of symptoms always characterize it. But your pediatrician should refer you to a team of healthcare specialists with expertise in ASD (developmental pediatricians, neurologists, child psychiatrists, etc.) who will make the diagnosis based largely on the presence (or absence) of a collection of symptoms. As part of the diagnostic process, your child's play behavior will be observed, as will his interactions with his caregivers. The physician will take a detailed history, conduct a physical examination, and perhaps order laboratory tests to look for medical conditions that can cause symptoms associated with autism. The diagnostic process should also include evaluation of your child's language and cognitive ability using standardized testing. Children with language delays should always be evaluated to make sure they can hear normally.

To help make the diagnosis, you can contact a specialist in ASD, typically found in major medical centers. Ask your pediatrician for a referral. You can also call your state's public early childhood system or school district to request a free evaluation, without a doctor's referral, to find out if your child qualifies for intervention services.

Treatment

There is no known cure for autism spectrum disorder, but there are effective treatments that improve many of the difficulties associated with ASD.

A child diagnosed with ASD will need specialized services aimed at the management of the specific findings associated with his ASD. Early treatment will likely improve the ability of a child with autism to function more independently.

Some commonly used approaches include applied behavior analysis (ABA), developmental interventions (e.g., Floortime), and TEACCH (Treatment and Education of Autistic and Communications-handicapped Children). The most effective techniques are intensive, and help the child develop communication and social skills while teaching appropriate behaviors.

WHERE WE STAND

THE AMERICAN ACADEMY OF PEDIATRICS encourages doctors to be aware of the signs of ASD, and to be on the lookout for these signs during every well-child visit.

At the same time, the Academy urges parents to always let their pediatricians know of any concerns they may have about their child's behavior and development. The AAP recommends autism-specific screening when children are at eighteen and twenty-four months of age; the sooner an intervention program is started, the better. However, children should be evaluated at any age if a parent or professional has concern about the possibility of ASD. If ASD is suspected or diagnosed, parents should seek a referral for early intervention and local specialists (like speech therapy or behavioral intervention to promote social skills). Public early intervention programs are specific for children from birth to three years of age. Above the age of three, a referral should be made to your school district. Parents should make an effort to become as familiar as possible with available treatments and programs in their community, and support their child in learning the skills needed to be successful in the least restrictive educational setting.

Children with ASD require an Individualized Education Program (IEP) that addresses their language and social learning needs in the least restrictive environment. Sometimes children will benefit from smaller learning environments that provide less distraction. For other children, more inclusive environments with typical peer modeling can be beneficial. Generally, younger children benefit from intensive educational programs and other therapies that may include up to twenty-five hours a week of one-on-one work, twelve months a year. As for other children with developmental disabilities, families should evaluate educational options that promote development of social skills. Social skills group therapy approaches can be very helpful for children of all ages. At times, medications also are helpful to manage the behavioral difficulties with autism and related disorders as part of an overall behavioral plan. The use of medication is more common in children and youth of school age.

Children with ASD can vary considerably in their ability for independence in adulthood, as well as in their behavior and language skills. It is impossible to predict in early childhood the adult abilities of a young child with ASD, so it is important to begin interventions for language, social, academic, and behavioral symptoms as early and intensely as possible with involvement of the family in treatment. No two children with ASD have the same needs, and the approach that is appropriate for one child may be different from what is used for another. Be as involved as you possibly can in your child's treatments. Your pediatrician can help you find community agencies that provide services for your child, as well as family support networks, counseling, and advocacy groups. On the Internet, seek out reliable sources of information and education, such as the Centers for Disease Control and Prevention (cdc.gov) or the American Academy of Pediatrics (aap.org/autism). You may get conflicting advice about interventions besides those recommended at the time of your child's evaluation. It is important to confer with your pediatrician or specialist about therapies that you might be considering. Through support groups, you also can meet parents of other children with ASD and share experiences, concerns, and solutions.

As mentioned earlier, there is a genetic factor involved in ASD, so if one of your children is diagnosed as having autism, there is an increased risk that the same disorder will be identified in your other children. Speak to your pediatrician about receiving counseling to discuss this increased risk. (Also see the section on autism in Chapter 11 [*Your Two-Year-Old*] on page 350.)

Cerebral Palsy

Children with cerebral palsy (CP) have abnormal development of or damage to the area of the brain that controls movement, posture, and muscle tone. About two or three children per thousand have CP. About half of children with cerebral palsy have typical intelligence, even though they have difficulty with motor control and movement. The condition causes different types of motor difficulties, which can vary from quite mild and barely noticeable to very profound. Depending on the severity of the problem, a child with cerebral palsy may have clumsy movement patterns, or he may be unable to walk. Some children have weakness and poor motor control of one arm and one leg on the same side of the body (called hemiparesis), some have difficulties with both their legs (diplegia), and some have problems with control of both upper and lower extremities (quadriplegia). In some children the muscle tone generally is increased (called spasticity or hypertonia), while in others it is very low (called hypotonia), and in some it is mixed. While many children with cerebral palsy have no trouble understanding language, they may have difficulty in coordinating the mouth movements needed to produce speech.

Cerebral palsy is caused by malformation or damage to the brain. Often the damage occurs before birth, while the brain is being formed, but occasionally it occurs during delivery or after birth. Premature birth is associated with an increased risk of cerebral palsy due to the fragility of the developing brain. Other causes of cerebral palsy include underlying genetic or metabolic abnormalities, in-utero stroke, congenital infections, and abnormal formation or development of

certain parts of the brain. A baby also can get cerebral palsy from very severe jaundice after birth, or later on in infancy from an injury or illness affecting the brain.

Although parents often look for an explanation as to why this happened, a report by the American Academy of Pediatrics and the American College of Obstetricians and Gynecologists concluded that the majority of cases of cerebral palsy are not the result of events during labor and delivery, such as an insufficient supply of oxygen (hypoxia).

Signs and Symptoms

The signs and symptoms of cerebral palsy vary tremendously because there are many different types and degrees of motor problems. The main clue that your child might have cerebral palsy is a delay in achieving the motor milestones listed in Chapters 5 through 13 of this book. Here are some specific warning signs.

IN A BABY OVER TWO MONTHS

■ His head lags when you pick him up while he's lying on his back and he has poor head control in sitting.

■ He feels stiff.

■ He feels floppy.

■ When held cradled in your arms, he seems to overextend his back and neck—constantly acts as if he is pushing away from you.

- When you pick him up, his legs get stiff and they cross or "scissor."

IN A BABY OVER NINE MONTHS
- He is not yet able to sit without support.

- He uses one side of the body more than the other, such as crawling in a lopsided manner, pushing off with one hand and leg while dragging the opposite hand and leg.

- He hops on his knees, but does not crawl on all fours.

- He does not walk independently by eighteen months of age.

If you have any concerns about your child's development, talk to your pediatrician right away. Because children's rates of development vary widely, it is sometimes difficult to make a definite diagnosis of mild cerebral palsy right away. Often a consultation with a developmental pediatrician, pediatric neurologist, or pediatric rehabilitation medicine physician will assist in the diagnosis. Your pediatrician will refer you to the appropriate professional. Your child will also be referred to a physical and/or occupational therapist for additional assessment of his motor skills. A CT (computed tomography) or MRI (magnetic resonance imagery) of the head or spine (or both) should be done in all children with cerebral palsy to determine whether a brain abnormality exists. When a CT or MRI is normal and there is no birth history suggestive of brain injury, additional genetic or metabolic testing is sometimes needed. Even when a firm diagnosis is made during these early years, it often is difficult to predict how severe the motor problems will be in the future.

Treatment

If your pediatrician suspects that your child has cerebral palsy, you may be referred to an early intervention program. These programs are staffed by early childhood educators; physical, occupational, and speech and language therapists; nurses; social workers; and medical consultants. In such a program, your child will get therapies specifically targeting his needs and you'll learn how to become your child's own teacher and therapist. You will be taught by a physical and/or occupational therapist what exercises to do with your infant, what positions are most comfortable and beneficial to him, and how to help with specific problems such as feeding difficulties. Sometimes medications such as baclofen or botulinum toxin type A are used to minimize the spasticity or decrease muscle tightness in the legs or arms, though medication for spasticity is not typically recommended for younger children. Older children may be treated with implantable baclofen pumps or have surgical procedures to decrease spasticity or treat problems with the hips or spine. You may receive information about adaptive equipment that can help your child participate in everyday activities and position him so he can use his hands better in play. Special equipment may include customized utensils to make eating easier, adapted bath or potty chairs, pencils that can be held more easily, wheelchairs, and walkers. These adaptations allow children to be more independent and participate with peers and within the community. Through support groups, you also can meet parents of other children with similar disabilities and share experiences, concerns, and solutions.

The most important thing you can do for your child is to help him develop skills, become resilient, and gain positive self-esteem. Encourage him to perform the tasks he is capable of and practice more challenging tasks so that he learns to do them with as little assistance as possible. The professionals at early intervention centers can help you evaluate your child's abilities and teach you how to reach appropriate goals. You may be offered advice about other types of therapies besides those provided by the conventional therapy team. Discuss any nonstandard therapies with your pediatrician before trying them.

A number of organizations are available to help parents learn more about how best to take care of their child with cerebral palsy. These include the United Cerebral Palsy Association (ucp.org); the Cerebral Palsy Foundation (yourcpf.org); and the Cerebral Palsy Now Foundation (cpnow foundation.org).

Associated Problems

INTELLECTUAL DISABILITY

It has been estimated that more than half of children with cerebral palsy have global developmental delays that include thinking and problem-solving. Many children with cerebral palsy also are diagnosed with intellectual disabilities such as learning difficulties, while others have average intellectual abilities. (See also *Intellectual Disability*, page 663.)

SEIZURES

One out of every three people with cerebral palsy has or will develop seizures. They may not start until later in childhood. Fortunately, these seizures often can be controlled with anticonvulsant medications. (See also page 803.)

VISION DIFFICULTIES

Because the injury to the brain often affects eye muscle coordination, more than three out of four children with cerebral palsy have vision difficulties. Some of the vision issues include strabismus (eyes not properly aligned; see page 744), amblyopia (one eye turning in or out), or cortical visual impairment (where the brain can't understand what the eyes are seeing). It is extremely important to have your child's eyes checked regularly by your pediatrician and a pediatric ophthalmologist. Many of these vision difficulties can be corrected if identified and treated early, but if left untreated they may worsen and may even cause permanent vision loss.

JOINT CONTRACTURES

In children with spastic forms of cerebral palsy, it is often difficult to prevent contracture, a loss of range of motion of a stiff joint, caused by the unequal pull of one muscle over the other. Possible problems that may result include scoliosis (curvature of the spine) or dislocation of the hips. Some children with asymmetry of their muscle tone may have differences in the size of the affected arm or leg or contractures of joints.

A physical therapist, developmental pediatrician, or pediatric rehabilitation medicine physician can teach you how to stretch the muscles to try to prevent the onset of contracture. Sometimes braces, splints, casting, or medication may be used to improve joint mobility and stability. In some situations, orthopedic surgery is performed as part of contracture management.

DENTAL PROBLEMS

Many children with cerebral palsy have a greater risk of developing oral diseases. This can mean more gingivitis (gum disease) and cavities. One reason may be that it is difficult for them to brush their teeth. However, they also have more enamel defects than other children, which may make their teeth more susceptible to decay. In addition, some medications such as seizure or asthma drugs may contribute to cavity formation. Because of the special skills needed to monitor their dental needs, families often seek out pediatric dentists with training in children with special needs.

HEARING LOSS

Some children with cerebral palsy have a complete or partial hearing loss as part of the injury or illness that caused the damage to the brain. All babies in the United States are screened for hearing loss before leaving the nursery, but if you find that your baby does not blink or startle at loud noises by one month, is not turning his head toward a sound by three to four months, or is not saying words by twelve months, discuss it with your pediatrician. The results of newborn hearing screening should be reviewed and follow-up hearing evaluation should be obtained along with formal speech and language testing. (See also *Hearing Loss,* page 659.)

PROBLEMS WITH SPATIAL AWARENESS

Over half the children with cerebral palsy affecting one side of the body have challenges sensing the position of their arm, leg, or hand on the affected side. (For example, when a child's hands are relaxed, he cannot tell whether his fingers are pointing up or down without looking at them.) If this problem exists, the child may limit use of the involved hand, even if the motor disability is minimal. He might act as if it is not there. Physical or occupational therapy can help him learn to use the affected parts of his body, despite this disability.

Congenital Abnormalities

Congenital abnormalities are caused by problems during the fetus's development before birth. About three of every one hundred babies born in the United States have congenital abnormalities.

There are five categories of these abnormalities, grouped according to the cause.

CHROMOSOME ABNORMALITIES

Chromosomes carry the genetic material inherited from one generation to the next in the egg and sperm. Normally, twenty-three chromosomes come from the father and twenty-three from the mother, and all are found in the center of every cell in the body except the red blood cells. The genes carried on the chromosomes provide the instructions for how the body is made and determine a child's characteristics.

When a child does not have the normal forty-six chromosomes, or when pieces of the chromosomes are missing or duplicated, there may be problems in the development and function of organs including the brain. Down syndrome (trisomy 21) is an example of a condition that can occur when a child is born with an extra chromosome.

SINGLE-GENE ABNORMALITIES

Sometimes the chromosomes are normal in number, but one or more of the genes on them are abnormal. Some of these genetic abnormalities are inherited from a parent who also has that abnormality. This is known as autosomal dominant inheritance. Each child has a one in two chance of inheriting this gene from the parent.

Other genetic problems can be passed to the child only if both parents carry the same gene. Cystic fibrosis, Tay-Sachs disease, and spinal muscular atrophy are all examples of disorders inherited in this fashion. In these cases neither parent has the disorder, but each carries one gene for it, and the disorder results when the child inherits the abnormal gene from both parents. Each child has a one in four chance of inheriting this gene from both parents and being affected. This is known as autosomal recessive inheritance.

A third type of genetic abnormality is called sex-linked, and generally is passed on to boys only, though the abnormality runs on their mother's side of the family. Girls may carry the abnormal gene that causes these disorders on one of their X chromosomes but not show the actual disease because they have an extra X chromosome with a normal gene. Because boys have only one X chromosome, if they inherit an abnormal gene on the X chromosome they will have the disorder. (Examples of this problem include hemophilia, color blindness, and the common forms of muscular dystrophy.) Each boy has a one in two chance of inheriting this gene.

The fourth type of genetic abnormality is of the mitochondria, which are the parts of the cell that make energy. Mitochondrial DNA is inherited from the mother only. Mitochondrial diseases may cause a wide variety of problems, including seizures, developmental delays, hearing and vision abnormalities, or kidney and intestinal problems.

CONDITIONS DURING PREGNANCY THAT AFFECT DEVELOPMENT

Some infections, illnesses, and conditions that affect the mother during pregnancy, particularly during the first nine weeks, can cause serious congenital abnormalities—Zika, German measles, and cytomegalovirus, for example. That is why infections and other disorders such as diabetes are screened for during pregnancy. In many cases, working closely with your physician and following strict management protocols can help decrease complications during pregnancy and later problems for your baby. Other things that can affect your baby during development are alcohol consumption, illegal drugs, particular medications, and certain chemicals that can pollute air, water, and food. Always check with your doctor before using any medication or nutritional supplement while you are pregnant.

COMBINATION OF GENETIC AND ENVIRONMENTAL PROBLEMS

Spina bifida and cleft lip and palate are types of congenital abnormalities that may occur when there is a genetic tendency for the condition combined with exposure to certain environmental influences, toxins, chemicals (alcohol, cigarette smoke, etc.) or vitamin deficiencies (folic acid, etc.) within the womb during critical stages of the pregnancy. Women are prescribed prenatal vitamins containing folic acid even while they are planning to become pregnant to help prevent the fetus from having spina bifida.

UNKNOWN CAUSES

The vast majority of congenital abnormalities have no known cause. If you and your family have had one child with congenital abnormalities or developmental problems without a known cause, ask your pediatrician or obstetrician for a referral to a geneticist or genetic counselor. They can review with you your risk for having another child with similar problems.

When Your Child Has a Congenital Disorder

Despite advances in prenatal diagnostics, such as ultrasound, many families learn their baby has a congenital abnormality after she is born. It is very important to ask the doctors caring for your baby to explain everything so you understand what is happening with her, and so you can enlist the support of friends and family. Siblings need to be informed about the condition of the baby in words that are appropriate to their developmental level. Once a diagnosis is made, many families find it very helpful to be put in contact with family support groups for that disorder.

Congenital Conditions

Congenital abnormalities are so diverse and require such different types of treatment that it would be impossible to discuss them all in this section. Instead, we will look only at the medical management of two conditions: Down syndrome and spina bifida. However, clinical symptoms accompanying congenital conditions might include global developmental delay or intellectual disability, cerebral palsy, sensory impairment, or autism spectrum disorder; in these cases, the evaluations and interventions described for those clinical conditions would apply.

DOWN SYNDROME

Approximately one out of every eight hundred babies is born with Down syndrome. Fortunately, through prenatal testing, Down syndrome can often be detected prenatally. Down syndrome is caused by the presence of an extra chromosome. One result of this extra chromosome is a typical appearance that includes up-slanted eyes with extra folds of skin at the inner corners, flattening of the bridge of the nose, a tongue that looks larger in the setting of a small mouth, and a decrease in the muscle and ligament tone of the body.

Most children with Down syndrome will have mild to moderate intellectual disability and will benefit from early intervention services, which can be started in infancy. However, it is important to remember that children with Down syndrome are more like other children than they are different. Children with Down syndrome form deep and meaningful relationships with others, can learn in special education and inclusive classrooms, and can participate in community activities and sports. Many can be employed competitively or in a workshop setting and can live independently or in a group home setting as adults.

Children with Down syndrome are at higher risk for a number of medical conditions. Congenital heart disease is common in children with Down syndrome, so your doctor will arrange for an ultrasound of the heart (echocardiogram) shortly after birth. Children with Down syndrome may be born with problems with the gastrointestinal tract or with other organ systems; these can usually be found by exam and by monitoring how the baby eats and moves her bowels.

Many children with Down syndrome are shorter and weigh less than average for their age when they are infants. However, older children with Down syndrome may struggle with excess weight gain. More than half have vision and hearing impairments. Many children will develop sleep apnea, so all children should have a sleep study by the time they start school. Some children with Down syndrome will develop hypothyroidism, which can lead to decreased metabolism, weight gain, and slowed behavior. Children with Down syndrome are also at higher risk for loosening of the ligaments that provide neck stability and connect the vertebral column to the base of the skull. If these ligaments are too loose, overextension (bending backward) of the neck can occur, causing serious spinal injury. For this reason, caution should be taken with contact sports that could place a child at increased risk of spinal cord injury, such as football, soccer, and gymnastics.

SPINA BIFIDA

Spina bifida occurs when the tissue surrounding the spinal cord fails to close properly during early fetal development. There are many different subtypes of spina bifida. The most common form, spina bifida occulta, occurs when the spinal bones don't close but there are no problems with the nerves, as they are protected by the spinal column. Most people with spina bifida occulta don't even know they have it. Another form is meningocele, in which a sac of fluid that protects the spinal cord pushes out between the opening in the spinal bones, but no spinal nerve tissue is involved. A third type is myelomeningocele, in which the protruding sac of fluid also contains parts of the spinal nerves and spinal cord. Most of the time when people say spina bifida, they are referring to myelomeningocele, so that is what this section will discuss.

Spina bifida is often caused by an interaction between genes and the environment. A parent who has one child with spina bifida has a greater chance (one out of one hundred) of having another. This increased frequency appears to be due to some combined effect of heredity and environment. One factor we know of is inadequate intake of folic acid during very early pregnancy, so supplements including this vitamin are given to all women of childbearing age, sometimes even before pregnancy, to minimize the risk for spina bifida in the fetus. Ultrasound examination can usually identify spina bifida during pregnancy, and blood tests done on the mother can help to identify an increased risk of having a baby with spina bifida. Knowing that a baby will have spina bifida allows the family to plan for delivery at a medical center that offers specialty care. At some centers with experts in high-risk maternal-fetal medicine and specialist surgeons, pregnant women may choose to be evaluated for fetal surgery (surgery done while the fetus is still in the womb), which is not a cure but may lessen the impact of the condition in some children.

A newborn with spina bifida has a sac protruding from the spine that contains spinal fluid and a portion of the spinal cord. These are the nerves that control the lower part of the body. On the first or second day after birth, surgery must be performed to close the opening in the spine. Unfortunately, little can be done to repair the damaged nerves, but a lot can be done to help children be as functional as possible. Most babies with spina bifida have several other medical complications. These include:

Hydrocephalus. Up to nine out of ten children with spina bifida eventually develop hydrocephalus, or increased fluid in and around the brain. The increase occurs because the path through which the fluid ordinarily flows is blocked. This condition is serious and must be treated surgically. The pediatrician should suspect hydrocephalus if the baby's head is growing more rapidly than expected, if the child has a bulging fontanelle, or has symptoms of irritability, lethargy, or seizures. The condition is confirmed by a CT (computed tomography), magnetic resonance imagery (MRI), or ultrasound scan of the head. If the condition exists, surgery will be required to relieve fluid buildup by placement of a shunt to remove the fluid.

Latex allergies. People with spina bifida are more likely to be allergic to latex, likely because of early surgeries and latex sensitization. Allergic reactions can vary from mild to very severe. All children with spina bifida should take precautions to avoid latex. Children with latex allergies should have an emergency care plan in place should an allergic event occur. You can reduce the chances that your child will acquire this sensitivity by avoiding exposure to latex. But be aware that many infant products contain latex (bottle nipples, pacifiers, teething toys, changing pads, mattress covers, and some diapers).

Muscle weakness or paralysis. Because the congenital abnormality of the spinal cord impacts the development of nerves connecting the brain to the lower limbs, the muscles in the legs may be very weak or not function at all in children with spina bifida. Because they may not be able to move their feet, knees, or hips, they may be born with contractures of these joints (shortening or tightening of the joints or muscles). Surgery can be performed to correct some of these contractures, and the muscle weakness

can be treated with physical therapy and bracing. Depending on the level of the spinal lesion, children with spina bifida may be able to walk independently or with walkers. Many use wheelchairs, however.

Bowel and bladder problems. Often the nerves that control bowel and bladder function do not work properly with spina bifida. As a result, these children are more likely to develop urinary tract infections and can have urine back up from the bladder and damage the kidneys. Your pediatrician will refer your child to a urologist, who will monitor your child's bladder function and determine if he needs to have urine drained through a catheter to protect his kidneys. These children are prone to urinary infections, which might cause fever, or abdominal or back pain.

Bowel control may be a problem because of the lack of nerve control of the rectum. Careful dietary management to keep the stools soft, including stool softeners, suppositories, or enemas, may be recommended to help with bowel management.

Educational and social problems. Seven out of ten children with spina bifida have developmental and learning disabilities requiring some educational supports for learning needs. Issues of health and wellness, including weight control, physical activity, and social inclusion, are particularly important to the long-term physical, emotional, and social well-being of children with spina bifida.

Parents of a child with spina bifida need more than one physician to manage their child's medical care. In addition to the basic care your pediatrician delivers, this condition requires a team approach that involves neurosurgeons, orthopedic surgeons, urologists, rehabilitation experts, physical therapists, psychologists, and social workers. Many medical centers run special spina bifida clinics, which offer the services of all these health professionals in one location. Having all members of the team together makes it easier for everyone to communicate and usually provides better access to information and assistance when parents need it.

Resources

Information and support for parents of children born with congenital conditions are available from various organizations.

March of Dimes
1-888-663-4637
marchofdimes.com

The National Down Syndrome Congress
1-800-232-NDSC (6372)
ndsccenter.org

WHERE WE STAND

IN AN EFFORT to reduce the prevalence of spina bifida, the American Academy of Pediatrics endorses the recommendation of the US Public Health Service that all women capable of becoming pregnant consume 400 mcg per day of folic acid (a B vitamin). Folic acid helps to prevent neural tube defects (NTDs), which include spina bifida. Although some foods are fortified with folic acid, it is not possible for women to meet the 400-microgram goal through a typical diet. Thus, an Academy policy statement recommends a daily multivitamin tablet that contains folic acid in the recommended dose. Studies show that if all women of childbearing age met these dietary requirements, 50 percent or more of NTDs could be prevented.

Women who are at high risk for an NTD-affected pregnancy (for example, because of a previous NTD-affected pregnancy, having diabetes mellitus, or taking antiseizure medications) are advised to discuss their risk with their doctor. This includes possible treatments with very high doses of folic acid (4,000 mcg per day), beginning one month before becoming pregnant and continuing throughout the first trimester. As the doctor will explain, however, women should not attempt to achieve this very high dose of folic acid by taking multivitamin supplements (because then they may receive too much of other vitamins), but rather only under the care of a physician.

The Spina Bifida Association
1-800-621-3141
spinabifidaassociation.org

United Cerebral Palsy
1-800-872-5827
ucp.org

Hearing Loss (Hearing Impairment)

Although hearing impairment can occur at any age, hearing difficulties at birth or that develop during infancy and the toddler years can have serious developmental consequences if unrecognized and untreated. This is because normal hearing is needed to understand spoken language and then, later, to produce clear speech. Consequently, if your child experiences hearing impairment during infancy or early childhood, immediate attention is required. Even a temporary but significant hearing impairment during this time can make it very difficult for the child to learn spoken language or speech patterns.

Most children experience mild hearing loss when fluid accumulates in the middle ear from congestion, colds, or ear infections. This hearing loss is usually only temporary; normal hearing commonly returns once the congestion or infection subsides and the Eustachian tube (which connects the middle ear to the throat) drains the remaining fluid into the back of the throat. In many children, perhaps one in ten, fluid stays in the middle ear following an ear infection (see page 670) because of problems with the Eustachian tube. Children with this problem don't hear as well as they should, and sometimes develop speech delays. Much less common is the permanent kind of hearing impairment that always impacts normal speech and language development. Permanent hearing impairment varies from mild or partial to complete or total deafness.

There are two main kinds of hearing loss or impairment: conductive and sensorineural. When a child has a conductive hearing impairment, there may be an abnormality in the structure of the outer ear canal or middle ear, there may be a large amount of cerumen (wax) lodged in the ear canal, or there may be fluid in the middle ear that interferes with the transfer of sound.

By contrast, a sensorineural hearing impairment is caused by an abnormality of the inner ear or the nerves that carry sound messages from the inner ear to the brain. The impairment can be present at birth or occur anytime thereafter. Even without a family history of deafness, the cause is frequently genetic, with parents and other family members often unaffected because each parent is only a carrier for a hearing loss gene; because future children have an increased risk of being hearing impaired, genetic counseling is recommended. Or if the mother had rubella (German measles), cytomegalovirus (CMV), toxoplasmosis, or another infectious illness that affects the inner ear during pregnancy, the fetus could have been infected and may lose hearing as a result. Some infections cause hearing loss in early childhood. The problem also may be due to a malformation of the inner ear.

Hearing impairment must be diagnosed as soon as possible, so that your child isn't delayed in learning language—a process that begins the day she is born. The American Academy of Pediatrics recommends that before a newborn infant goes home from the hospital, she undergo a formal hearing screening. In fact, every state and territory in the United States now has an Early Hearing Detection and Intervention (EHDI) program, which mandates that all newborns be screened for hearing impairment before they are discharged from the hospital. At any time during your child's life, if you and/or your pediatrician suspect that she has a hearing impairment, insist that a formal hearing evaluation be performed promptly. (See *Hearing Impairment: What to Look For* on page 662.) Some family doctors, pediatricians, and well-baby clinics can test in the office for hearing loss or fluid in the middle ear, a common cause of hearing loss. If a problem is detected, your child may be referred to an audiologist (hearing specialist) and/or ear, nose, and throat doctor (ENT; otolaryngologist).

If your child is under six months of age, is unable to cooperate with or understand a hearing examination, or has significant developmental delays, she may be given one of two available tests, which are similar to the tests performed during newborn hearing screenings. They are painless and can take anywhere from five to sixty minutes.

■ The *auditory brainstem response test (ABR)* measures how the brain responds to sound during deep sleep. Clicks or tones are played into the baby's ears through soft earphones, and electrodes placed on the baby's head measure the brain's response. This allows the doctor to test your child's hearing without having to rely on her cooperation. ABRs are performed during a natural sleep in infants under three or four months old. Older babies and toddlers need to be sedated to undergo an ABR.

■ The *otoacoustic emissions test* measures sound waves produced by the ear. A tiny probe is placed just inside the baby's ear canal, which then measures the response when clicks or tones are played into the baby's ear. Babies and young children usually do not need to be napping or sedated for this, as it is a brief screening exam. This can be done at any age.

Behavioral audiometry, or conditioned response audiometry, can be performed with a cooperative baby as young as six months old. A combination of visual and auditory stimuli is provided, and the test can determine frequency-specific (although not ear-specific) hearing levels in infants and toddlers.

Formal behavioral audiometry can determine hearing levels as well as eardrum function in each ear. This is performed using soft earphones that send sounds and words to the ear, and is typically well tolerated by children in the three- to five-year age range.

Not all of these tests may be available in your immediate area, but the consequences of undiagnosed hearing impairment are so serious that your doctor may advise you to travel to where the tests and potential treatment can be done. Certainly, if these tests indicate that your baby may have a hearing problem, your doctor should recommend a more thorough hearing evaluation as soon as possible to confirm whether your child's hearing is impaired. Even a mild hearing impairment can still affect overall hearing and should be properly diagnosed and treated.

Treatment

Treating a hearing impairment will depend on its cause. If it is a mild conductive hearing loss due to fluid in the middle ear, the doctor may simply recommend that your child be retested in a few months to see whether the fluid has cleared by itself. Medications such as antihistamines, decongestants, or antibiotics are ineffective in clearing up middle ear fluid.

If there is no improvement in hearing over a three-month period, and there is still fluid behind the eardrum, the doctor may recommend a referral to an ENT specialist. If the fluid persists and there is sufficient (even though temporary) conductive hearing impairment from the fluid, the specialist may recommend draining the fluid through ventilating tubes. These are surgically inserted through the eardrum. This is a minor operation and takes about fifteen minutes, but your child must receive a general anesthetic for it to be done properly, so she usually will spend part of the day in a hospital or an outpatient surgery center.

Even with the tubes in place, future infections can occur, but the tubes help reduce the amount of fluid and decrease your child's risk of repeated infection. If the cause for the hearing loss was purely the fluid, the tubes will improve hearing.

If a conductive hearing impairment is due to a malformation of the outer or middle ear, a hearing aid may restore hearing to normal or near-normal levels. However, a hearing aid will work only when it's being worn. You must make sure it is on and functioning at all times, particularly in a very young child. Reconstructive surgery may be considered when the child is older.

Early placement of hearing aids for infants with hearing impairment is important to give them awareness of sound and language. Early exposure to either aural (spoken) or visual (sign) language has a very positive impact on language development. In children with mild to moderate sensorineural hearing impairment, hearing aids can improve hearing so much that most can develop normal speech and spoken language. Should your child have severe or profound hearing impairment in both ears and receive little or no benefit from hearing aids, she could be a candidate for cochlear implants. Cochlear implants have been approved by the Food and Drug Administration for children since 1990. If your family is considering an implant for a child whose hearing loss occurred at birth, outcomes for developing useful speech and hearing are better with early (ideally by one year of age) rather than late (over three years old) implantation. Therefore it is extremely

Hearing Impairment: What to Look For

Here are the signs and symptoms that should make you suspect that your child has a hearing impairment and alert you to call your pediatrician.

- Your child doesn't startle at loud noises by one month or turn to the source of a sound by three to four months of age.

- He doesn't notice you until he sees you.

- He concentrates on gargling and other vibrating noises that he can feel, rather than experimenting with a wide variety of vowel sounds and consonants. (See *Language Development* in Chapters 8 and 9.)

- His speech is delayed or hard to understand, or he doesn't say single words such as "dada" or "mama" by twelve to fifteen months of age.

- He does not say five to ten words by eighteen months of age.

- He does not put two to three words together at two years of age.

- His speech is not understandable 50 percent of the time by two and a half years of age.

- He doesn't always respond when called. (This is usually mistaken for inattention or resistance, but it could be the result of a partial hearing impairment.)

- He seems to hear some sounds but not others. (Some hearing impairments affect only high-pitched sounds; some children have hearing impairment in only one ear.)

- He seems not only to hear poorly but also has trouble holding his head steady, or is slow to sit or walk unsupported. (In some children with sensorineural hearing impairment, the part of the inner ear that provides information about balance and movement of the head is also damaged.)

important to seek out early and efficient evaluation and treatment of hearing impairment. Most children with typical development and early implantation coupled with intensive therapy after the surgery can develop good to excellent hearing and can be supported in a mainstream educational setting; almost all children with cochlear implants gain better awareness of sounds in their environment.

Parents of children with sensorineural hearing impairment usually are most concerned about whether their child will learn to talk. The answer is that although optimally timed cochlear implantation will greatly improve the chances of learning spoken language, not all may learn to speak clearly. However, all children with a hearing loss can be taught to communicate. Some children learn to lipread well, while others never fully master the skill. However, speech is only one form of communication. For children in whom hearing aids or cochlear implants cannot offer enough improvement in hearing to develop spoken language, or for those families who have chosen not to pursue spoken language, sign language is another mode of communication that can be learned. If your child is learning sign language, you and your immediate family also must learn it. This way you will be able to teach, praise, comfort, and laugh with her. You should encourage friends and relatives to learn signing, too. Written language is very important as well, because it is the key to educational and future career success.

Intellectual Disability

The term "intellectual disability" (ID) is used when a child's intelligence and adaptive behavior, which covers many everyday social and practical skills, is significantly below average and affects the way he learns, develops new skills, and participates in the world around him. The more severe the disability, the more delayed a child's skills will be in comparison to his chronological age.

There are several different ways to test a child for intellectual disability. Traditional intelligence tests, such as an IQ test, show a child's ability to learn and solve problems. More important, however, is the child's ability to function in his everyday life. This is known as adaptive behavior, and can also be tested formally.

IQ testing is not thought to be reliable until age six years or older. To determine IQ, the child is given a test to assess his language abilities, memory, problem-solving, visual spatial skills, and nonverbal reasoning. The tests are designed around an average score of 100, and most people test within a range of 30 points above and below that. In some cases, standard IQ tests are not accurate or reliable because cultural differences, language problems, or physical problems interfere with testing. In such cases, tests that measure the child's ability to function and reason should be used.

The diagnosis of intellectual disability no longer relies on an IQ measurement below 70, which used to be the standard definition. Now, specialists who diagnose this condition tend to focus more on assessing adaptive behavior, as this correlates most with functioning and levels of independence. Generally, lower intellectual functioning correlates with more difficulties in different areas of adaptive functioning. This includes conceptual skills (language, literacy, time, number concepts), practical skills (personal care skills, travel and transportation, schedules/routines, safety, use of money), and social skills (interpersonal skills, gullibility, ability to follow rules).

Signs and Symptoms

Generally, the more severe the degree of intellectual disability, the earlier you will notice the signs. It may be difficult to predict in young children who have delays in both language and problem-solving skills what their level of function might be as they develop.

When a baby is late in developing basic motor skills (e.g., holding his head up by himself by three to four months or sitting unsupported by seven to eight months), there also may be some associated intellectual disability. However, this is by no means always the case. Nor does normal motor development guarantee normal intelligence. Some children with mild to moderate degrees of intellectual disability have normal physical development. In such cases, the first sign of intellectual disability may be a delay in language development or in learning simple imitation skills, such as waving bye-bye or playing pattycake.

In many cases of mild disability, the young child may reach developmental milestones at typical times. Later, when he begins preschool or school, he may have difficulty performing academic skills at his grade level. He might have trouble completing puzzles, recognizing colors, or counting when his classmates already have mastered these tasks. Remember, however, children do develop at very different rates, and problems in school are usually not a sign of intellectual disability. In fact, specific learning disabilities—which are not the same as intellectual disability—are often diagnosed only when a child has more difficulty learning than would be expected for the child's overall intelligence level. The key is watching a child's trajectory over time. Children with learning disabilities can close the gap with their peers with the help of targeted interventions. If that is not the case, then an intellectual disability should be considered.

Early developmental delays also can be caused by disorders such as hearing loss, vision problems, learning disabilities, or lack of experience due to environmental challenges. Formal testing can be done closer to kindergarten.

When to Call the Pediatrician

If you are concerned about a delay in your child's development (see the sections on development in Chapters 6 through 13), call your pediatrician, who will review your child's overall development and determine whether it is appropriate for his age. If the pediatrician is concerned, she will probably refer you to a pediatric developmental specialist, a pediatric neurologist, or a multidisciplinary team of professionals for further assessment. Children under three years of age should be referred to the public early intervention program, and children over three years of age should be referred to your school district for formal testing. With older children, formal psychological testing may be helpful.

Treatment

The main treatment for children with intellectual disability is educational. Children with intellectual disability often benefit from life-skills and vocational training through the end of high school and can often qualify for public school education through twenty-one years of age. Many are capable of graduating with diplomas, though some are better suited to graduate with a certificate.

Intellectual disability has a range of impact, with symptoms that can be mild, moderate, or severe in degree. Adults with mild intellectual disability may develop the academic or trade skills for community employment, often read at a fourth- to sixth-grade level, and can frequently live independently with some minor supervision. However, with increasing functional impairment, there is a greater likelihood that the person will need supports for daily needs and employment support. People with severe to profound intellectual disability are often dependent upon others for care and supervision through adulthood and will require thoughtful planning for transition to adulthood.

In the past, people with ID often were forced to live in large residential facilities. The goal is now for adults with ID to live with their families, in their communities, or in small supported living units with meaningful work options. (For more information, visit the American Association on Intellectual and Developmental Disabilities, aaidd.org/home, and the CDC, cdc.gov/ncbddd/actearly/pdf/parents_pdfs/intellectualdisability.pdf.)

Prevention

Preventable causes of intellectual disability include alcohol consumption by the mother during pregnancy and other fetal exposures. Women planning to become pregnant should consult with their obstetricians regarding support they may need to have the healthiest pregnancy. A cause for intellectual disability can be identified in up to 40 percent of cases, though the likelihood of finding an identifiable genetic cause is lower in children with milder levels of disability.

While an increasing number of genetic causes for ID can be identified, early screening can only prevent symptoms due to metabolic disorders such as phenylketonuria (PKU) and hypothyroidism. Currently, there are eighty-one treatable inborn errors of metabolism, which may account for 5 percent of intellectual disability cases.

If these conditions are detected soon after birth through standard screening tests performed in the hospital nursery, they can be treated. Other examples of conditions that can cause intellectual disability if not detected and treated early in life include lead poisoning, hydrocephalus (excess fluid causing increased pressure in the brain; see page 656) and epilepsy (seizures).

Consult your pediatrician, local advocacy organizations, and other reputable professionals to find out what programs (e.g., Special Olympics, Best Buddies, etc.) are available in your community. Professional assistance can be extremely helpful. In the long run, however, you and your family members will be your child's most important advocates. With your child's teachers and therapist, you can set realistic objectives for him and encourage him to reach them. Assist him if necessary, but let him do as much as possible on his own. You and your child will feel most rewarded when he reaches a goal by himself.

~ 22 ~

Ears, Nose, and Throat

Colds/Upper Respiratory Infection

Your child probably will have more colds, or upper respiratory infections, than any other illness. In the first two years alone, most children have around eight to ten colds. And if your child spends time in a childcare setting, or if there are school-age children in your house, she may have even more, since colds spread easily among children who are in close contact with one another. That's the bad news, but there is some good news, too: most colds go away by themselves and do not lead to anything worse.

Colds are caused by viruses, which are extremely small infectious particles (much smaller than bacteria). A sneeze or a cough may directly transfer a virus from one person to another. The virus also may be spread indirectly, when someone infected with the virus transfers some of the virus particles onto her hand by coughing, sneezing, or touching her nose. She then touches a surface such as a toy or doorknob, and a healthy person touches it after, or she may touch the healthy person's hand directly. This healthy person touches her newly contaminated hand to her own nose, introducing the infectious agent to a place where it can multiply and grow—the nose or throat. Symptoms of a cold soon develop. The cycle then repeats itself, with the virus being transferred from this newly infected child or adult to the next susceptible one, and so on.

Once the virus is present and multiplying, your child will develop the familiar symptoms and signs:

■ Runny nose (first, a clear discharge; later, a thicker, often colored one)

■ Sneezing

■ Mild fever (101–102 degrees Fahrenheit [38.3–38.9 degrees Celsius]), particularly in the evening

■ Decreased appetite

■ Sore throat and, perhaps, difficulty swallowing

■ Cough

■ On-and-off irritability

■ Slightly swollen glands in the neck

If your child has a typical cold without complications, the symptoms should disappear gradually in seven to ten days.

Treatment

An older child with a cold usually doesn't need to see a doctor unless the condition becomes more serious. If she is three months old or younger, however, call the pediatrician at the first sign of illness. With a young baby, symptoms can be misleading, and colds can quickly develop into more serious ailments, such as bronchiolitis (see page 603), croup (see page 608), or pneumonia (see page 612). For a child older than three months, call the pediatrician if:

■ The nostrils are widening with each breath, there is drawing in of the skin between and around the ribs and breastbone as the child inhales, your child is breathing rapidly, or there are any other signs of difficulty breathing.

■ The lips or nails turn blue.

■ Nasal mucus persists for longer than ten to fourteen days.

■ A daytime cough lasts more than ten days.

■ She has pain in her ear (see *Middle Ear Infections*, page 670) or persistent fussiness or crying.

■ Her temperature is higher than 102 degrees Fahrenheit (38.9 degrees Celsius).

■ She is excessively sleepy or cranky.

Your pediatrician may want to see your child, or he may ask you to watch her closely and report back if she doesn't improve each day and is not completely recovered within one week from the start of her illness.

Unfortunately, there's no cure for the common cold. Antibiotics may be used to combat *bacterial* infections, but they have no effect on viruses, so the best you can do is to make your child comfortable. Make sure she gets extra rest and drinks a lot of fluids. If she has a fever or is uncomfortable, give her single-ingredient acetaminophen or ibuprofen. Ibuprofen is approved for children six months of age and older; however, it should never be given to children who are dehydrated or who are vomiting repeatedly. (Be sure to follow the recommended dosage for your child's age and the time interval for repeated doses.)

It's important to note that the American Academy of Pediatrics' position is that over-the-counter cough medicines are not effective for children younger than six years old; in fact, they can have potentially serious side effects. In addition, keep in mind that coughing clears mucus from the lower part of the respiratory tract, and ordinarily there's no reason to suppress it.

If your infant is having trouble breathing or drinking because of nasal congestion, clear her nose with saline (salt water) nose drops or spray, which are available without a prescription. This can then be followed by suction with a bulb syringe every few hours, or before each feeding and before bed. For the nose drops, use a dropper that has been cleaned with soap and water and rinsed well with plain water. Place two drops in each nostril fifteen to twenty minutes before feeding, and then immediately suction. *Never use nose drops that contain any medication, since too much of the medication can be absorbed and cause problems in an infant. Only use normal saline nose drops.*

When using the suction bulb, remember to *squeeze the bulb part of the syringe first, gently stick the rubber tip into one nostril, and then slowly release the bulb.* This slight amount of suction will draw the clogged mucus out of the nose and should allow her to breathe and suck at the same time once again. You'll find that this technique works best when your baby is under six months of age. As she gets older, she'll fight the bulb, making it difficult to suction the mucus, but the saline drops will still be effective. Alternatively, there are nasal aspirators on the market powered by battery or by parents' oral suction.

Placing a cool-mist humidifier or vaporizer in your child's room also will help keep nasal secretions more liquid and make her more comfortable. Set it close to her (but safely beyond her reach) so that she gets the full benefit of the additional moisture. Be sure to clean and dry the humidifier thoroughly each day as recommended in the manufacturer's manual to prevent bacterial or mold contamination. *Hot-water vaporizers are not recommended, since they can cause serious scalds or burns.*

Prevention

If your baby is under three months old, the best way to prevent colds is to keep her away from people who have them. This is especially true during the winter, when many of the viruses that cause colds are circulating in larger numbers. A virus that causes a mild illness in an older child or an adult can cause a more serious one in an infant. If your child is in childcare and has a cold, teach her to cough and sneeze away from others, and to use a tissue to cough into and wipe her nose. Doing this may prevent her from spreading the cold to others. Similarly, if your child would be in contact with children who have colds and it is convenient for you to keep her away from them, by all means do so. Also teach her to wash her hands regularly during the day, or use an alcohol-based hand sanitizer when soap and water are not available; this will cut down on the spread of viruses.

Teach your child to sneeze or cough into the crook of her elbow or shoulder. Even using a tissue or a handkerchief is better than having your child cover her mouth with her hand when sneezing and coughing. If the virus lands on her hand, it can be transmitted to whatever she touches—a sibling, a friend, or a toy.

Middle Ear Infections

During your child's first few years, there's a good chance that he'll get a middle ear infection. At least 70 percent of the time, middle ear infections occur after colds that have weakened the body's ability to prevent bacteria from entering the middle ear. Doctors refer to this middle ear infection as acute otitis media.

Middle ear infections are one of the most prevalent treatable childhood illnesses, occurring most often in children between six months and three years of age. Two-thirds of all children have at least one ear infection

by their second birthday. It's a particularly common problem among young children because they are more susceptible to colds and because of the length and shape of their tiny Eustachian tubes, which normally ventilate the middle ear.

Children under one year of age who spend time in childcare programs tend to get more middle ear infections than those cared for at home, primarily because they are exposed to more viruses. Also, infants who self-feed from a bottle when lying on their backs are susceptible to ear infections, as this way of feeding may allow small amounts of formula to enter the Eustachian tube. Two things may explain the fact that by the time your child reaches school age, his likelihood of getting a middle ear infection will decrease: the growth of his middle ear structures reduces the likelihood of fluid blockage, and the body's defenses against infection improve with age.

A number of other factors may place children at a higher risk of middle ear infections:

Secondhand smoke. Children who breathe in secondhand tobacco smoke have a markedly increased risk of ear infections as well as respiratory infections, bronchitis, pneumonia, and asthma.

Gender. Although researchers are not sure why, boys have more middle ear infections than girls.

Heredity. Ear infections can run in families. Children are more likely to

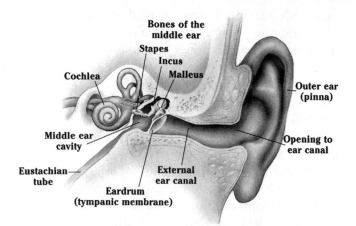

Cross Section of Ear

have repeated middle ear infections if a parent or a sibling also had numerous ear infections.

There are certain things you can do to protect your infant from ear infections, such as breastfeeding, not smoking and not allowing smokers around your child, making sure she is up to date on her vaccines, and practicing good hygiene and proper nutrition to prevent illness.

Signs and Symptoms

Middle ear infections are usually painful, but not always. A child old enough to talk will tell you that his ear hurts; a younger child may pull at his ear and cry. Babies with ear infections may cry even more during feedings, because sucking and swallowing cause painful pressure changes in the middle ear. A baby with an ear infection may have trouble sleeping. Fever is another warning signal: ear infections sometimes (about a third of the time) are accompanied by elevated temperatures ranging from 100.4 to 104 degrees Fahrenheit (38–40 degrees Celsius). In addition, children may appear off balance or clumsier because the fluid or infection in the middle ear may affect their sense of balance (vestibular system).

You might see blood-tinged yellow fluid or pus draining from the infected ear. This kind of discharge means that the eardrum has developed a small hole (called a perforation). This hole usually heals by itself without complications, but you will want to describe the discharge to your pediatrician.

You also may notice that your child does not hear well. This occurs because the fluid behind the eardrum interferes with sound transmission. But the hearing loss is usually temporary; normal hearing will be restored once the middle ear is free of fluid. Occasionally, when ear infections recur, fluid may remain behind the eardrum for many weeks and continue to interfere with hearing. If you feel your child's hearing is not as good as it was before his ear became infected, consult your pediatrician. Good hearing is important for proper speech development, so if your child is having any speech delay, ask your pediatrician if a referral for a hearing test or a consultation with an ear, nose, and throat doctor (ENT; otolaryngologist) or an audiologist (hearing specialist) would be appropriate. Even when there's no speech delay, if your child has had middle ear fluid in both ears for more than three months, or in one ear for more than six months, referral for a hearing test is important.

Middle ear infections are most common during the cold and flu season of winter and early spring. When your child complains of moderate or severe pain in his ear during the summer, especially when you touch or pull on the ear, he could be suffering from an infection of the *outer* ear canal, called swimmer's ear. Swimmer's ear is essentially an infection of the skin lining the inside of the outer ear canal. Although this may temporarily affect hearing, it poses no risk of long-term hearing loss. Swimmer's ear can be extremely painful and should be treated. (See *Swimmer's Ear*, page 685.)

Treatment

Whenever you suspect an ear infection, call your pediatrician. In the meantime, try to make your child more comfortable. If he has a high fever, cool him using the procedures described in Chapter 27. Give acetaminophen or ibuprofen in the dose appropriate for his age to help decrease the pain. (Don't give aspirin to your child; it has been associated with Reye syndrome, a disease that affects the liver and brain. See page 555 for more information about Reye syndrome.)

If there's a fever, the doctor will examine your child to determine whether there are any other problems. To treat middle ear infections, the doctor will recommend steps to ease pain and may prescribe an antibiotic. For swimmer's ear or a middle ear infection with perforation, antibiotic ear drops may be prescribed as well.

An antibiotic is one of the treatment options for ear infections. If one is recommended, your doctor will specify the schedule for giving it to your child; it usually includes dosing once, twice, or three times a day. It's important to follow the medication schedule precisely. If an antibiotic is prescribed by an urgent care or emergency department doctor, it's often a good idea to let your pediatrician know so that he can check the dose and also make a note in your child's chart.

As the infection begins to clear, some children experience a sense of fullness or popping in the ears; these are normal signs of recovery. There should be clear signs of improvement and disappearance of ear pain and fever within two days.

When your child starts feeling better, you may be tempted to discon-

Antibiotic Overuse

Antibiotics are an important treatment in managing bacterial infections such as severe ear infections and strep throat. But infections caused by viruses will not improve with antibiotics. That is why the common cold, certain types of mild ear infections, and the vast majority of sore throats do not require an antibiotic. When an antibiotic is prescribed, the goal is to make sure that the antibiotic is specific for the type of bacteria causing the infection and that it is given for the right length of time.

If antibiotics are used when they are not needed—or if patients do not take the drug consistently—new strains of bacteria may develop. When that happens, antibiotics eventually may stop working and the infections they're designed to treat will no longer be curable by the use of these medications, because the bacteria have become resistant to them. In addition, antibiotics can produce side effects, including allergic reactions and a potentially serious form of antibiotic-associated diarrhea.

Here are three important points to keep in mind if your child has an infection, to make sure your child gets the right kind of antibiotic and only when it's necessary.

■Ask your pediatrician if the infection causing your child's illness is caused by bacteria. Antibiotics work only against bacterial illnesses, not those caused by viruses. So while these medications may be appropriate for treating severe ear infections, you should not ask your pediatrician for a prescription for antibiotics to treat your child's colds and flu (as well as many sore throats and coughs), which are viral infections.

■If an antibiotic is not necessary because your child has a viral infection, ask what other measures are recommended to help with your child's symptoms. For children with mild ear infections, your child's doctor may recommend pain medicine to treat ear pain while the infection clears on its own.

■If your child's doctor prescribes an antibiotic for an ear infection or other bacterial infection, ask how to follow up if your child's condition worsens or has not improved in forty-eight to seventy-two hours. Make sure that your child takes the prescribed antibiotic exactly as your doctor instructs. And don't give your child antibiotics that have been prescribed for another family member or for another illness. If your child develops an itchy rash, hives, or watery diarrhea while taking antibiotics, notify your child's doctor.

tinue the medication—but don't. Some of the bacteria that caused the infection still may be present, and stopping the treatment too soon may allow them to multiply again and permit the infection to return with full force. Your pediatrician may want to see your child after the medication is finished, to check if any fluid is still present behind the eardrum, which can occur even if the infection has been controlled. This condition (fluid in the middle ear), known as otitis media with effusion, is extremely common: five out of every ten children still have some fluid three weeks after an ear infection is treated. In nine out of ten cases, the fluid will disappear within three months without additional treatment. Also, this fluid accumulation may be caused by something other than an ear infection, such as swollen adenoid tissue in the upper throat that interferes with drainage; for that reason, seeing a doctor is especially important to determine the cause of and best care for the problem.

Occasionally an ear infection won't respond to the first antibiotic prescribed. If your child continues to complain of significant ear pain and still has a high fever for more than two days after starting an antibiotic, call your pediatrician. To determine if the antibiotic is working, your doctor will examine your child and take another look at your child's eardrum. Sometimes the antibiotic may need to be changed, or another antibiotic added. In more severe or persistent cases, an antibiotic shot or shots may

be needed to treat the infection. If none of those options works, your pediatrician may refer you to an ENT specialist for another exam. In rare cases the ENT may take a sample of the fluid from the ear by inserting a needle through the eardrum. This will help determine the specific cause of the infection and assist in determining treatment. In very rare instances a child may be hospitalized so that antibiotics can be given intravenously and the ear can be drained surgically.

Should a child with an ear infection be kept home? Not unless he has a fever, is in serious pain, or feels or looks sick. If he's feeling well, and if medication can be given before and after school (or perhaps by a school nurse), he can go to school. If your child's eardrum has ruptured, he'll be able to engage in most activities, although he may not be permitted to swim until the ear is dry and healed. Ordinarily, there's no reason to prevent him from flying in an airplane, although he may have some discomfort from the pressure change. Pain medication and drinking fluids during takeoff and landing can help prevent and ease discomfort.

Prevention

Occasional ear infections cannot be prevented. In some children, ear infections may be related to seasonal allergies, which also can cause congestion and block the natural drainage of fluid from the ear to the throat. If your child seems to get ear infections more frequently when his allergies flare up, mention this to your pediatrician, who may suggest additional testing or recommend nasal saline spray, antihistamines, or a nasal allergy spray.

If your baby is being bottle-fed, hold his head higher than his stomach during feedings. Doing this keeps the Eustachian tubes from becoming blocked. You and others should not smoke around your baby, as children exposed to secondhand tobacco smoke have more ear infections—and more respiratory infections, bronchitis, pneumonia, poor lung function, and asthma—than children who aren't exposed to smoke. In addition, careful handwashing can help protect your baby from illness and subsequent ear infections. Breastfeeding is also associated with fewer ear infections in children. Pacifier use after the age of six months is associated with ear infections as well, so it may be a good idea to stop pacifier use, especially if your child is prone to ear infections.

And what about children who recover from one ear infection only to get another shortly thereafter? If your child continues to have ear infections, and continues to have hearing loss, he will be referred to an ear, nose, and throat doctor (ENT; otolaryngologist), who may recommend that tiny ventilation tubes (sometimes called tympanostomy tubes) be inserted in the eardrum under anesthesia. While the tubes are in place, they usually restore hearing to normal, and also prevent fluid and harmful bacteria from becoming trapped in the middle ear, where they can cause another infection.

Eardrum

One type of ear tube (tympanostomy tube)

Use of tubes has become standard care for the following specific indications: (1) persistent fluid in both middle ears for more than three months with hearing loss; (2) recurrent ear infections with significant symptoms occurring more than three times in six months or more than four to five times in twelve months. If the placement of ventilation tubes is proposed for your child, discuss his specific problem with your child's specialist and pediatrician so you fully understand the advantages and disadvantages.

Keep in mind that although ear infections are bothersome and uncomfortable, they are usually minor and clear up without causing any lasting problems. Most children stop getting ear infections by the time they are four to six years old.

Sinusitis

Sinusitis is an inflammation of one or more of the sinuses (bony cavities) around the nose. It usually occurs as a complication of a cold or allergic inflammation in children over two years of age. These conditions cause swelling of the lining of the nose and sinuses. This swelling blocks the openings that normally allow the sinuses to drain into the back of the nose, so the sinuses fill with fluid. Although nose blowing and sniffing may be natural responses to this blockage, they can make the situation worse by pushing bacteria from the back of the nose into the sinuses. Since the sinuses can't drain properly, the bacteria will multiply there, causing an infection.

Several signs of sinusitis should alert you to call your pediatrician:

■ Persistent cold or upper respiratory infection symptoms, including daytime cough and/or nasal discharge lasting for more than ten days without any improvement. The nasal discharge may be thick and yellow, clear, or whitish, and the cough usually will continue during the day as well as at night. In some cases a child with sinusitis will have swelling around the eyes when he wakes up in the morning. Also, a preschooler with sinusitis

sometimes may have persistent bad breath along with cold symptoms. (However, this also could mean that he has put something into his nose or has a sore throat, or that he isn't brushing his teeth.)

■ Your child's cold is severe and is accompanied by high fever and thick yellow nasal discharge for at least three days. His eyes might be swollen in the early morning, and he might have a severe headache that he describes (if he's old enough) as behind or above the eyes.

In very rare cases, a sinus infection may spread to the eye. If this occurs, you'll see swelling around the eye not just in the morning but all through the day, and you should call your pediatrician immediately. Another very rare but serious possibility is that the infection spreads to the central nervous system (the brain), so if your child has a very severe headache, becomes sensitive to light, or is increasingly irritable or sleepy and difficult to arouse, seek immediate medical attention.

Treatment

If your pediatrician thinks your child has sinusitis, she may prescribe an antibiotic, usually for one to two weeks, typically to continue for one week after your child has shown improvement. Once your child is on the medication, his symptoms should start to go away very quickly. In most cases the nasal discharge will clear and the

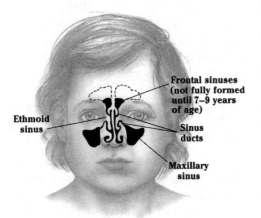

Frontal sinuses (not fully formed until 7–9 years of age)

Ethmoid sinus

Sinus ducts

Maxillary sinus

cough will improve over a week or two. *But even though he may seem better, he must continue to take the antibiotics for the prescribed length of time.* If there's no improvement after two to four days, your pediatrician might want to conduct some further tests, such as a sinus X-ray or referral to an ENT or allergist, after which a different medication may be prescribed or an additional one added for a longer period of time.

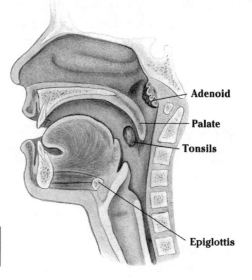

Epiglottitis

The epiglottis is a tongue-like flap of tissue at the back of the throat that may become infected, usually by bacteria called *Haemophilus influenzae* type b. Fortunately, this infection (epiglottitis) is now uncommon thanks to the Hib vaccine, which prevents infections from this bacteria.

Epiglottitis, which can be life-threatening when it occurs, begins with a sore throat and a fever that usually is greater than 101 degrees Fahrenheit (38.3 degrees Celsius) and quickly makes your child feel very sick. Her throat will become extremely sore. With each breath, she may make a harsh or raspy noise, called stridor. She may have such difficulty swallowing that she begins to drool.

If your child has an unusually sore throat and is drooling and/or breathing with difficulty, call your physician immediately or go to the emergency room. Because epiglottitis progresses so rapidly and has such serious conse-

quences, do not attempt to treat it at home. After contacting your pediatrician, try to keep your child calm. Don't try to examine her throat or insist that she lie down. Also, avoid offering food or water, because that might cause vomiting, which often makes breathing even more difficult. It's important to remember that epiglottitis can become life-threatening if it goes untreated. If the doctor determines that your child has epiglottitis, she will be urgently admitted to the hospital for treatment including antibiotics.

Prevention

The Hib vaccine is available to combat the bacteria that most commonly cause epiglottitis. Your child should receive the full series of the Hib vaccine, according to your pediatrician's recommendations. (See *Recommended Immunizations* on page 892.)

However, even if she has had the vaccine, consult your doctor if you know there has been an exposure to another child who has the infection. Your physician might want to take added precautions.

Herpes Simplex

Oral herpes is a common viral disease of childhood. This condition produces sores (cold sores), blisters (fever blisters), and swelling of the inside of the mouth and lips. Oral herpes is highly contagious and is spread by direct contact, frequently by kissing. Most infants are protected by their mothers' antibodies up to about age six months, but they become susceptible after that.

When the virus is transmitted to a child for the first time, she is said to have primary herpes. This may cause pain, swelling, and reddening of the gums, and an increase in saliva, followed a day or two later by blisters inside the mouth. When the blisters break, they leave sore areas that take several days to heal. The child also may develop a fever and headache, act irritably, lose her appetite, and have swollen lymph glands for a week or so. Many children, however, have such mild symptoms that no one realizes they have the virus.

Once a child has had primary herpes, she becomes a carrier of the virus. This means that the virus, usually in an inactive state, remains within her system. However, during episodes of stress (including other infections), injury to the mouth, sunburn, allergies, and fatigue, the virus can become reactivated, producing what's called recurrent herpes. This condition is usually milder than the primary infection, and usually doesn't occur until later in childhood or adulthood. Cold sores and fever blisters are the symptoms of recurrent herpes.

Treatment

If your child complains of symptoms resembling those of herpes, consult your pediatrician. Primary herpes is not a serious illness, but it can make your child uncomfortable. The treatment, which should be aimed at reducing this discomfort, includes:

■ Bed rest and sleep.

■ Plenty of cold fluids, including non-acidic drinks like apple or apricot juice.

■ Acetaminophen, if there's fever or excessive discomfort.

■ Mouth rinse or gargles prescribed by your pediatrician. These medications may contain a painkiller that will numb the areas affected by the mouth sores. Carefully follow the directions for these preparations.

■ A soft, bland, but nutritious diet.

■ Antiviral medication (such as acyclovir or a similar type of drug) that may be prescribed by your pediatrician in some severe cases. If started early in the illness, this will stop the virus from multiplying, but it will not prevent reactivation after the medication is stopped. It is important to keep in mind that antiviral medication will likely decrease symptom duration only by a day or so and may not make your child feel immediately better.

Occasionally a child infected with primary herpes refuses to drink fluids because of the associated mouth pain. Such a child must be hospitalized if she is showing signs of dehydration. Never use any creams or ointments containing steroids (cortisone) on mouth sores if there is the slightest suspicion that the sores are due to herpes, as these preparations can make the viral infection spread.

Prevention

Direct contact is required to spread the herpes virus, so you should not let anyone with herpes blisters or sores kiss your child. People with a history of oral herpes often shed the virus in their saliva even when they have no sores. In general, to prevent spread of germs, discourage individuals from kissing your baby or child directly on the lips. Also, try to discourage your child from sharing eating utensils with other children or touching a water fountain with their mouth. (This is more easily said than done.) If your child has active open primary herpes cold sores, keep her home to prevent other children from getting this infection from her.

Nosebleeds

Your child is almost certain to have at least one nosebleed—and probably many—during these early years. Some preschoolers have several a week. This is neither abnormal nor dangerous, but it can be very frightening. If blood flows down from the back of the nose into the mouth and throat, your child may swallow a great deal of it, which in turn may cause vomiting.

There are many causes of nosebleeds, most of which aren't serious. Beginning with the most common, they include:

■ *Colds and allergies.* A cold or allergy causes swelling and irritation inside the nose and may lead to spontaneous bleeding.

■ *Trauma.* A child can get a nosebleed from picking his nose, putting something into it, or just blowing it too hard. A nosebleed also can occur if he is hit in the nose by a ball or other object or if he falls and hits his nose.

■ *Low humidity or irritating fumes.* If your house is very dry, or if you live in an arid climate, the lining of your child's nose may dry out, making it more likely to bleed. If he is frequently exposed to toxic fumes (fortunately, an unusual occurrence), they may cause nosebleeds, too.

■ *Anatomical problems.* Any abnormal structure inside the nose may lead to crusting and bleeding.

■ *Abnormal growths.* Any abnormal tissue growing in the nose may cause bleeding. Although most of these growths (usually polyps) are benign (not cancerous), they still should be treated promptly.

■ *Abnormal blood clotting.* Anything that interferes with blood clotting can lead to nosebleeds. Medications, even common ones like ibuprofen, can alter the blood-clotting mechanism just enough to cause bleeding. Blood diseases and bleeding disorders, such as hemophilia, also can provoke or worsen nosebleeds.

■ *Chronic illness.* Any child with a long-term illness, or who may require extra oxygen or other medication that can dry out or affect the lining of the nose, is likely to have nosebleeds.

Treatment of Nosebleeds

There are many misconceptions and folktales about how to treat nosebleeds. Here's a list of dos and don'ts.

DO...
1. Remain calm. A nosebleed can be frightening, but is rarely serious.

2. Keep your child still in a sitting or standing position. Tilt his head slightly forward.

3. Pinch the lower half of your child's nose (the soft part) between your thumb and finger and hold it firmly for at least ten minutes. If your child is old enough, he can do this himself. *Don't release the nose during this time to see if it is still bleeding* (no peeking!). Stopping the pressure may interfere with the forming of the clot and allow the bleeding to continue.

Release the pressure after ten minutes and wait, keeping your child quiet and still. If the bleeding hasn't stopped, hold pressure again. If after ten more minutes of pressure the bleeding hasn't stopped, continue to hold pressure, and call your pediatrician or go to the nearest emergency department.

DON'T...
1. Panic. You'll scare your child.

2. Have him lie down or tilt back his head.

3. Stuff tissues, gauze, or any other material into your child's nose to stop the bleeding.

Also, call your pediatrician if:

■ You think your child may have lost too much blood or continues to bleed heavily. (But keep in mind that the blood coming from the nose always looks like a lot.)

■ The bleeding is coming only from your child's mouth, or he's coughing or vomiting blood or brown material that looks like coffee grounds.

■ Your child is unusually pale or sweaty, or is not responsive. *Call your pediatrician immediately in this case, and arrange to get your child to the emergency department.*

■ He has a lot of nosebleeds, along with a chronically stuffy nose. This may mean he has a small, easily broken blood vessel in the nose or on the surface of the lining of the nose, or a growth in the nasal passages.

If a blood vessel is causing the problem, the doctor may touch that point with a chemical substance (silver nitrate) to stop the bleeding.

Prevention

If your child gets a lot of nosebleeds, ask your pediatrician about using salt water (saline) nose drops every day and/or putting a small amount of petroleum jelly in each nostril at night. Doing so may be particularly helpful if you live in a very dry climate, or when the furnace is on. In addition, a humidifier or vaporizer will help maintain your home's humidity at a level high enough to prevent nasal drying. Also tell your child not to pick his nose. If your child still gets nosebleeds despite the moisture to the nostrils, the doctor may need to refer your child to an ear, nose, and throat doctor (ENT; otolaryngologist) and/or do tests to evaluate for a bleeding disorder.

Sore Throat (Strep Throat, Tonsillitis)

The terms "sore throat," "strep throat," and "tonsillitis" often are used interchangeably, but they don't mean the same thing. Tonsillitis refers to tonsils that are inflamed. (See *Tonsils and Adenoid*, page 683.) Strep throat is an infection caused by a specific type of bacteria, *Streptococcus.* When your child has a strep throat, the tonsils are usually very inflamed, and the inflammation may affect the surrounding part of the throat as well. Other causes of sore throats are viruses, which may cause inflammation only of the throat around the tonsils and not of the tonsils themselves.

In infants, toddlers, and preschoolers, the most frequent cause of sore throats is a viral infection. No specific medicine is required when a virus is responsible, and the child should get better over a seven- to ten-day period. Often children who have sore throats due to viruses also have a cold at the same time. They may develop a mild fever, too, but they generally aren't very sick.

One particular virus (called Coxsackie), seen most often during the summer and fall, may cause the child to have a somewhat higher fever, more difficulty swallowing, and a sicker overall feeling. If your child has a Coxsackie infection, she also may have one or more blisters in her throat and on her hands and feet (often called hand, foot, and mouth disease).

Infectious mononucleosis can produce a sore throat, often with marked tonsillitis; however, most young children who are infected with the mononucleosis virus have few or no symptoms.

Strep throat is caused by a bacterium called *Streptococcus pyogenes* or group A streptococcus. Strep throat is most common among school-age children and adolescents, peaking at seven to eight years of age. Children over three years of age with strep may have an extremely painful throat, fever over 102 degrees Fahrenheit (38.9 degrees Celsius), swollen glands in the neck, and pus on the tonsils. Cough, runny nose, hoarseness (changes in your voice that make it sound raspy), and conjunctivitis (also called pinkeye) are not symptoms of strep throat and suggest that a virus is the cause of the illness instead. It's important to be able to distinguish a strep throat from a viral sore throat, because strep infections are treated with antibiotics.

Diagnosis and Treatment

If your child has a sore throat that persists (not one that goes away after her first drink in the morning), whether or not it is accompanied by fever, headache, stomachache, or extreme fatigue, you should call your pediatrician. That call should be made even more urgently if your child seems extremely ill, or if she has difficulty breathing or extreme trouble swallowing (causing her to drool). This may indicate a more serious infection (see *Epiglottitis*, page 677).

If your pediatrician is concerned that your child may have strep throat, he may want to perform a swab of the back of the throat and tonsils to test for bacteria. Most pediatric offices perform rapid strep tests that provide findings within minutes. If the rapid strep test is negative, your doctor may confirm the result with a culture. A negative test means that the infection is presumed to be due to a virus. In that case, antibiotics (which work against bacteria, not viruses) will not help and need not be prescribed.

If the test shows that your child does have strep throat, your pediatrician will prescribe an antibiotic to be taken by mouth or by injection. If your child is given the oral medication, it's very important that she take it for the full course, as prescribed, even if the symptoms get better or go away. If a child's strep throat is not treated with antibiotics, or if she doesn't complete the treatment, the infection may worsen or spread to other parts of her body, leading to conditions such as abscesses of the tonsils or kidney problems. Untreated strep infections also can lead to rheumatic fever, a disease that affects the heart. However, rheumatic fever is rare in the United States and in children under five years old.

Prevention

Most types of throat infections are contagious, being passed primarily through the air on droplets of moisture or on the hands of infected children or adults. For that reason, it makes sense to keep your child away from people who have symptoms of this condition. However, most people are contagious before their first symptoms appear, so often there's really no practical way to prevent your child from contracting the disease. In the past when a child had several incidents of sore throat, her tonsils might have been removed in an attempt to prevent further infections. But this operation, called a tonsillectomy, is recommended today only for the most severely affected children. Even in difficult cases, where there is repeated strep throat, antibiotic treatment is usually the best solution.

(See also *Swollen Glands*, page 687.)

Tonsils and Adenoid

If you look into your child's throat, you may see a pink, oval-shaped mass on each side. These are the tonsils. The tonsils are small in infants and increase in size over the early years of childhood. They produce antibodies during periods when the body is fighting infection. Like the tonsils, the adenoid is part of your child's defense against infections. The adenoid is located in the very upper part of the throat, above the uvula and behind the nose. This area is called the nasopharynx. The adenoid can be seen only with special instruments passed through the nose or mouth, or indirectly by X-ray.

A common illness associated with the tonsils is tonsillitis. This is an inflammation of the tonsils, usually due to an infection. Sometimes tonsils can be enlarged and not be infected; however, most of the time there is an infection that has caused them to be larger than normal. There are several signs of tonsillitis, including:

■ Red and swollen tonsils

■ White or yellow coating over the tonsils

■ A "throaty" voice

■ Sore throat

■ Uncomfortable or painful swallowing

■ Swollen lymph nodes (glands) in the neck

■ Fever

It is not always easy to tell when your child's adenoid is enlarged. Some children are born with a larger adenoid. Others may have temporary enlargement of their adenoid due to

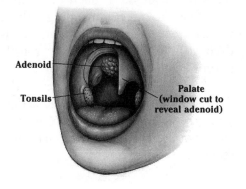

Adenoid

Tonsils

Palate
(window cut to reveal adenoid)

colds or other infections; this is especially common among young children. Also, the symptoms just described are more frequently due to chronic rhinitis (a persistent runny nose), which can be treated with corticosteroid nasal sprays. But the constant swelling or enlargement of the adenoid can cause other health problems, such as ear and sinus infections. Some signs of adenoid enlargement are:

- Breathing through the mouth instead of the nose most of the time

- The nose sounds blocked when the child talks

- Noisy breathing during the day

- Snoring at night

Both the tonsils and the adenoid may be enlarged if your child has the above symptoms along with any of the following:

- Breathing stops for a short period of time at night during snoring or loud breathing; this condition is called sleep apnea

- Choking or gasping during sleep

- Difficulty swallowing, especially solid foods

- A constant "throaty" voice, even when there is no tonsillitis

In severe cases, your child may have such difficulty breathing that it interferes with the normal exchange of oxygen and carbon dioxide in his lungs. This is important to recognize since it may interrupt your child's normal sleep pattern. If your child has breathing difficulties, seems drowsy during waking hours, and lacks energy despite what should have been adequate amounts of sleep, consult your pediatrician; when breathing problems are severe, call 911.

Treatment

If your child shows the signs and symptoms of enlarged tonsils or adenoid and doesn't seem to be getting better over a period of weeks, mention it to your pediatrician.

SURGERY TO REMOVE TONSILS AND/OR ADENOID (TONSILLECTOMY AND ADENOIDECTOMY)

Although these two operations (often combined and called T & A) were done almost routinely in the past and remain one of the most common major operations performed on children, not until recently has their long-term effectiveness been adequately tested. In light of current studies, today's physicians are much more conservative in recommending these procedures, even though some children still need to have their tonsils and/or adenoid taken out.

According to the guidelines of the American Academy of Pediatrics, your pediatrician may recommend surgery in the following circumstances:

■ Tonsil or adenoid swelling makes normal breathing difficult (causing problems such as behavioral issues, bed-wetting, sleep apnea, school performance problems, etc.).

■ Tonsils are so swollen that your child has a problem swallowing.

■ An enlarged adenoid makes breathing uncomfortable, severely alters speech, and possibly affects normal growth of the face. In this case, surgery to remove only the adenoid may be recommended.

■ The child has an excessive number of severe sore throats each year.

If your child needs surgery, make sure he knows what will happen before, during, and after surgery. Don't keep the surgery a secret from your child. An operation can be scary, but it's better to be honest than to leave your child with fears and unanswered questions.

The hospital may have a special program to help you and your child get familiar with the hospital and the surgery. If the hospital allows, try to stay with your child during the entire hospital visit. Let your child know that you'll be nearby during the entire operation. Your pediatrician also can help you and your child understand the operation and make it less frightening.

Swimmer's Ear (External Otitis)

Swimmer's ear is an infection of the skin inside the ear canal (or outer ear) that occurs most often after swimming or other activities that allow water into the ears. Swimmer's ear develops because moisture in the ear canal encourages the growth of certain bacteria and, at the same time, causes the skin that lines the ear canal to soften (like the white, swollen area that forms under a wet bandage). The bacteria then invade the softened skin and multiply there, causing an often painful infection.

For reasons that are not clear, some children are more prone to swimmer's ear than others. Injury to the canal (sometimes from the improper use of cotton swabs) or conditions such as eczema (see page 568) and seborrheic dermatitis (see page 852) can increase the likelihood of getting swimmer's ear.

With the mildest form of swimmer's ear, your child will complain only of itchiness or a plugged feeling in the ear, or—if he's too young to tell you what's bothering him—you might notice him sticking his finger in his ear or rubbing it with his hand. Within hours to days the opening of his ear canal may become swollen and slightly red, causing a dull pain. If you push on the opening or pull up on his ear, it may be painful.

In more severe cases of swimmer's ear, the pain will be constant and in-

Swollen, inflamed external ear canal

tense, and your child may cry and hold his hand over his ear. The slightest motion, even chewing, will hurt a lot. The ear canal opening may be swollen shut, with a few drops of pus or cheesy material oozing out, and there may be a low-grade fever (rarely more than one or two degrees above normal). In the most serious infections, the redness and swelling may spread beyond the ear canal to the entire outer ear. Since swimmer's ear doesn't involve the middle ear or the hearing apparatus, any loss of hearing due to blockage of the canal is temporary.

Treatment

If your child has pain in his ear, or if you suspect swimmer's ear, call your pediatrician. Although the condition usually isn't serious, it still needs to be examined and treated by a doctor. Until you see your pediatrician, you can help relieve your child's pain with acetaminophen or ibuprofen. Keep him out of the water for several days, and see if the pain subsides.

Do *not* insert a cotton swab or anything else into the ear in an attempt to relieve itching or promote drainage; doing so will only cause further skin damage and provide additional sites for bacteria to grow. At the pediatrician's office, the doctor first will examine the affected ear and then, perhaps, carefully clean out pus and debris from the canal. Most doctors also prescribe eardrops for five to seven days. The eardrops combat infection and thereby decrease swelling, which helps to relieve the pain. In order to be effective, however, eardrops have to be used properly. Here's how to administer them:

1. Lay your child on his side with his affected ear up.

2. Put the drops in so that they run along the side of the ear canal, permitting air to escape as the medicine flows in. You can gently move the ear to help the drops along.

3. Keep your child lying on his side for two or three minutes to make sure that the drops reach the deepest part of the ear canal.

4. Use these drops as directed for the length of time prescribed.

If the ear canal is too swollen for drops to enter, your pediatrician may insert a wick—a small piece of cotton or spongy material that soaks up the medicine and holds it in the canal. In this case, you'll need to resaturate the wick with the drops three or four times per day. Rarely, oral antibiotics also are prescribed.

When your child is being treated for swimmer's ear, your doctor may recommend he stay out of the water for a few days. However, he can take brief showers or baths daily and have his hair washed, as long as you dry the ear canal afterward with the corner of a towel or a blow-dryer (on a very low setting, held away from the ear). Once that's done, put in more eardrops.

Prevention

There's no need to try to prevent swimmer's ear unless your child has had this infection frequently or very recently. Under these circumstances, limit his stays in the water, usually to less than an hour. Then, when he comes out, remove the excess water from his ear with the corner of a towel, or have him shake his head.

As a preventive measure, many pediatricians recommend acetic acid eardrops. They are available in various preparations, some of which require a prescription. They usually are used in the morning, at the end of each swim, and at bedtime. A mixture of white vinegar and rubbing alcohol is a practical and effective home remedy. A few drops in each ear can be used after swimming.

Resist the temptation to clean out your child's ear with cotton swabs, your finger, or any other object, as doing so can cause trauma to the ear canal or eardrum.

Swollen Glands

Lymph glands (or lymph nodes) are an important part of the body's defense system against infection and illness. These glands normally contain groups of cells, called lymphocytes, which act as barriers to infection. The lymphocytes produce substances called antibodies that destroy or immobilize infecting cells or poisons. When lymph glands become enlarged or swollen, it usually means that the lymphocytes have increased in number due to an infection or other illness and that they are being called into action to produce extra antibodies. Rarely, swollen glands—particularly if long-lasting and without other signs of inflammation, such as redness or tenderness—may indicate a tumor.

If your child has swollen glands, you'll be able to feel them or actually see the swelling. They also may be tender to the touch. Sometimes, if you look near the gland, you can find the infection or injury that has caused it to swell. For example, a sore throat often will cause glands in the neck to swell, or an infection on the arm will produce swollen glands under the arm. Sometimes the illness may be a generalized one, such as those caused by a virus, in which case many glands might be slightly swollen. In general, because children have more viral infections than adults, lymph nodes, particularly in the neck, are more likely to be enlarged. Swollen glands at the base of the neck and just above the collarbone may be an infection or even a tumor within the chest, and should be examined by a physician as soon as possible.

Treatment

In the vast majority of cases, swollen glands are not serious. Young children almost always have a few small glands (less than 1 cm) in their neck, behind their ears, or at the back of their heads that can be felt, but it is nothing to be concerned about. Lymph node swelling usually disappears after the illness that caused it is gone. The glands

Cervical lymph nodes

gradually return to normal over a period of weeks. You should call the pediatrician if your child shows any of the following:

■ Lymph glands swollen and tender for more than five days

■ Fever higher than 101 degrees Fahrenheit (38.3 degrees Celsius)

■ Glands that appear to be swollen throughout the body

■ Tiredness, lethargy, or loss of appetite

■ Glands that enlarge rapidly, or the skin overlying them turning red or purple

As with any infection, if your child has a fever or is in pain, you can give her acetaminophen or ibuprofen in the appropriate dosage for her weight and age until you can see the pediatrician. When you call, your doctor probably will ask you some questions to try to determine the cause of the swelling, so it will help if you do a little investigating beforehand. For instance, if the swollen glands are in the jaw or neck area, check if your child's teeth are tender or her gums are inflamed, and ask her if there is any soreness in her mouth or throat. Mention to your doctor any exposure your child has had to animals (especially cats) or wooded areas. Also check for any recent animal scratches, tick bites, or insect bites or stings that may have become infected.

The treatment for swollen glands will depend on the cause. If there's a specific bacterial infection in nearby skin or tissue, antibiotics will clear it, allowing the glands gradually to return to their normal size. If the gland itself has an infection, it may require not only antibiotics but also warm compresses to localize the infection, or surgical drainage. If this is done, the material obtained from the wound will be cultured to determine the exact cause of the infection. Doing this will help the doctor choose the most appropriate antibiotic.

If your pediatrician cannot find the cause of the swelling, or if the swollen glands don't improve after antibiotic treatment, further tests will be needed. For example, infectious mononucleosis might be the problem if your child has a fever and a bad sore throat (but not strep), is very weak, and has swollen (but not red, hot, or tender) glands, although mononucleosis occurs more often in older children. Special tests can confirm this diagnosis. In cases where the cause of a swollen gland is unclear, the pediatrician also may want to do a tuberculosis skin test.

If the cause of prolonged swelling of lymph nodes cannot be found in any other way, it may be necessary to perform a biopsy (remove a piece of tissue from the gland) and examine it under a microscope. In rare cases this may reveal a tumor or fungal infection, which would require special treatment.

Prevention

The only swollen glands that are preventable are those that are caused by bacterial infections in the surrounding tissue. In cases of suspected infection, you can avoid involving the lymph nodes by properly cleaning all wounds (see *Cuts and Scrapes*, page 701) and receiving early antibiotic treatment.

~ 23 ~

Emergencies

THE INFORMATION IN this section, such as first-aid procedures for the choking child and cardiopulmonary resuscitation (CPR), is constantly changing. Visit healthy children.org and ask your pediatrician or other qualified health professional for the latest information on these procedures. It is rare for children to become seriously ill with no warning. Based on your child's symptoms, you should usually contact your child's pediatrician for advice. Timely treatment of symptoms can prevent an illness from getting worse or turning into an emergency.

At the same time, take steps *before* an emergency occurs to prepare for such an event if it should happen (see guidelines for emergency phone numbers on page 692). Also read the description of how to assemble a first-

aid kit (page 703). For the CPR guidelines chart, please see pages 902–3.

A true emergency is when you believe a severe injury or illness is threatening your child's life or may cause permanent harm. In these cases, a child needs emergency medical treatment immediately. Discuss with your child's pediatrician in advance what you should do in case of a true life-threatening emergency.

Many true emergencies involve sudden injuries. These injuries are often caused by the following:

■ Motor-vehicle-related injuries (car crashes, pedestrian injuries), or other sudden impacts such as from bicycle-related injuries, falling TVs or furniture, or falls from heights such as a window.

Emergency Phone Numbers

Keep the following phone numbers and addresses handy by programming them into your cellphone and the phone of anyone who cares for your child. You can also post them on your refrigerator or near other phones and insert a copy in your wallet.

- Your cellphone number

- Home phone number and address

- Phone number of a nearby relative, trusted neighbor, or friend

- Your pediatrician's contact information

- Emergency medical services (ambulance) (911 in most areas)

- Police (911 in most areas)

- Fire department (911 in most areas)

- Poison Help (1-800-222-1222)

- Hospital

- Dentist

It is important that everyone who cares for your child, including care providers or sitters, knows where to find emergency phone numbers. If you have 911 service in your area, make sure your older children and your sitter know to dial 911 in case of an emergency. Be certain that they know your home address and phone number, since an emergency operator will ask for or confirm this information. Always leave your cellphone number and the phone number and address where you can be located. You should also make sure your sitter knows about any medications your child takes and any food and medication allergies he may have. Those caring for your child (including you and your spouse and family) also should take a CPR class.

Remember, for a medical emergency, always call 911 first, then your child's pediatrician. If your child is seriously ill or injured, it may be safer for your child to be transported by emergency medical services (an ambulance).

- Poisoning (if the child is not seriously ill, call Poison Help first)

- Burns or smoke inhalation

- Choking

- Drowning (even nonfatal or near drowning) in a swimming pool, bathtub, etc.

- Head or other serious injury after a significant fall or sports-related injury

- Firearms or other weapons

- Electric shock

Other true emergencies can result from either medical illnesses or injuries. Often you can tell that these emergencies are happening if you observe that your child has any of the following symptoms:

- Acting strangely or becoming more withdrawn and less alert

- Increasing difficulty with breathing

- Skin or lips that look blue or purple (or gray for darker-skinned children)

- A cut or burn that is large or deep

- Bleeding that does not stop

- Rhythmical jerking and loss of consciousness (a seizure)

- Unconsciousness

- A head injury followed by any change in level of consciousness, confusion, a bad headache, or vomiting

- Very loose or knocked-out teeth, or other major mouth or facial injuries

- Increasing or severe persistent pain

- Decreasing responsiveness when you talk to your child

Call your child's pediatrician or Poison Help (1-800-222-1222) at once if your child has swallowed or come in contact with a suspected poison or any medication you did not intend him to ingest, even if your child has no signs or symptoms. You should not make your child vomit (do not give him syrup of ipecac, make him gag, or give him salt water) unless specifically instructed to by Poison Help or your pediatrician, as it can cause further injury to your child's body.

Always call for help if you are concerned that your child's life may be in danger or your child is seriously hurt.

IN CASE OF A TRUE EMERGENCY
- Stay calm.

- If your child is unresponsive and is not breathing, and you know how, start CPR (cardiopulmonary resuscitation). (For information on CPR, see page 699.)

- If you need immediate help, call 911. For example, if your child is having trouble breathing, having a seizure, or is unresponsive, dial 911. If you do not have 911 service in your area, call your local emergency ambulance service or county emergency medical service. Otherwise, call your child's pediatrician's office and state clearly that you have an emergency.

■ If there is bleeding, apply continuous pressure to the site with a clean cloth.

■ If your child is having a seizure, place her on a carpeted floor with her head turned to the side, and stay with her until help arrives. Do not put anything in her mouth. She can bite down while unaware of her actions. Turning her head to the side will help the tongue move to the side, which will help open her airway.

After you arrive at the emergency department, make sure you tell the emergency staff the name of your child's pediatrician; he will work closely with the emergency department and can provide them with additional information about your child. Bring any medication your child is taking and her immunization record with you to the hospital. Also bring any suspected poisons or medications your child might have taken. If your child has a medically complicated condition, it's a good idea to keep a notebook/folder on their past medical history, including information such as dates of and types of surgeries.

In the event of a car crash, the driver or other adults in the car may be unconscious or otherwise unable to give first responders information about the child. Medical personnel may be delayed in providing needed care to your child if they cannot find you to give permission. To help ensure that your child can be identified and treated promptly, consider attaching a sticker to his car safety seat with his name, date of birth, parents' names and phone numbers, and any other information you think might be important to emergency personnel (e.g., special healthcare needs or severe allergies). Place the sticker in a spot where first responders will be able to find it but where it is not easily visible from outside the car. Many police and fire departments, hospitals, and health departments keep a stock of pre-printed stickers for this purpose, or you can make your own.

Bites

Animal Bites

Keep your child safe around animals, including family pets. Review *Safety Around Animals* on page 517. Many parents assume that children are most likely to be bitten by strange or wild animals, but in fact most bites are inflicted by animals the child knows, including the family pet. Although the injury often is minor, biting does at times cause serious wounds, facial damage, and emotional problems.

As many as 1 percent of all visits to pediatric emergency centers during the summer months are for human or animal bite wounds. An estimated 4.7 million dog bites, 400,000 cat bites, 45,000 snake bites, and 250,000 human bites occur annually in the United States. About six in ten of those bitten by dogs are children.

Treatment

If your child is bleeding from an animal bite, apply firm continuous pressure to the area for five minutes or until the bleeding stops. Then wash the wound gently with soap and water, and consult your pediatrician. Animal bites to the face, head, and neck (which are common in small children) can be serious, and your child will need to be examined by an emergency health provider.

If the wound is very large, or if you cannot stop the bleeding, continue to apply pressure, and call your pediatrician to find out where to take your child for treatment. If the wound is so large that the edges won't come together, it probably will need to be sutured (stitched). Although this will help reduce scarring, in an animal bite it increases the chance of infection, so your doctor may prescribe antibiotics or choose not to suture the wound.

Contact your pediatrician whenever your child receives an animal bite that breaks the skin, no matter how minor the injury appears. The doctor will need to check whether your child has been adequately immunized against tetanus (see the immunization schedule on page 892) or might require protection against rabies. Both

of these diseases can be spread by animal bites.

Rabies is a viral infection that can be transmitted by an infected animal through bites or scratches. It causes a high fever, difficulty swallowing, convulsions, and ultimately death. Fortunately, rabies in humans is rare today, with an average of two to three deaths each year in the United States; the decline in recent years is due to the availability of animal control and vaccination programs, as well as effective human rabies vaccines and immunoglobulin treatments. Nevertheless, because the disease is so serious and the incidence has been increasing in animals, your pediatrician will carefully evaluate any bite for the risk of contracting this disease. Bites from wild animals—especially bats but also skunks, raccoons, coyotes, and foxes—are much more dangerous than those from tame, immunized (against rabies) dogs and cats. Avoid contact with the animal and call animal control to evaluate any dead animal for rabies and dispose of it.

When your child is evaluated, either by emergency department physicians or your pediatrician, they will determine if the risk of contracting rabies is high; if so, they will refer your child to receive immunoglobulin and a rabies vaccine series to prevent contracting the disease. If the animal that bit your child is a healthy dog or cat, the animal should be observed for ten days, and treatment for your child should be started only if the animal shows signs of rabies.

As noted earlier, an animal bite,

even when it doesn't cause rabies, can become infected. Notify your pediatrician immediately if you see any of the following signs of infection.

■ Pus or drainage coming from the bite

■ The area immediately around the bite becoming swollen and tender (it normally will be red for two or three days, but this in itself is not cause for alarm)

■ Red streaks that appear to spread out from the bite

■ Swollen glands above the bite

(See also *Safety Around Animals*, page 517.)

Your pediatrician may recommend antibiotic therapy for a child who has:

■ Moderate or severe bite wounds

■ Puncture wounds, especially if the bone, tendon, or joint has been penetrated

■ Facial bites

■ Hand and foot bites

■ Genital area bites

Children who have a weakened immune system or have no spleen often receive antibiotic treatment for a bite. Your pediatrician may recommend a follow-up visit to inspect any wound for signs of infection within forty-eight hours. Many children who have been bitten by dogs may also show signs of traumatic stress in the weeks and months after the incident, long after the physical wound has healed. These children may feel fear, including anxiety about being bitten again, especially when they see or hear about another dog. They may withdraw, or cling to their parents. They may resist going outside to play, have trouble sleeping, have nightmares, and wet the bed.

To help the healing process, be attentive to what your child is saying and feeling. Give her extra attention, particularly when you sense that she needs it. Some children with traumatic stress may require treatment by a mental health professional.

Human Bites

Children often experience a human bite from a sibling or a playmate. If your child is bitten by another person, call your pediatrician immediately to describe the severity of the injury. Doing this can be especially important if the biter's teeth pierced your child's skin or if the injury is large enough to require stitches.

Be sure to wash the bite carefully with cool water and soap right away to help prevent infection. For a bite that barely breaks the skin, such as a cut or scrape, a good washing with soap and water, followed by bandaging and close follow-up, is all that is needed. For more serious bites, your pediatrician should evaluate the wound. Your pediatrician will also check your child's tetanus and hepatitis B vaccine status and assess the risk for other infections. (For more information on human biting, aggressive behavior, or biting in situations with HIV, see Chapter 14, page 464; Chapter 20, page 634.)

Burns

Burns are divided into three categories, according to their severity. First-degree burns are the mildest and cause redness and perhaps slight swelling of the skin (like most sunburns). Second-degree burns are painful and cause blistering and considerable swelling. Third-degree burns lack sensation and may appear white or charred and cause serious injury, not just to the surface but also to the deeper skin layers.

There are many different causes of serious burns in children, including sunburn, scalds from hot water or other liquids, and those due to fire, electrical contact, or chemicals. All of these can cause permanent injury and scarring to the skin and important organs such as the eyes, mouth, and genitalia.

Treatment

Your *immediate* treatment of a burn should include the following.

1. As quickly as possible, soak the burn in cool water. Don't hesitate to run cool water over the burn long enough to cool the area and relieve the pain immediately after the injury. *Do not use ice on a burn, as it may delay healing.* Also, do not rub a burn; it can increase blistering.

2. Cool any smoldering clothing immediately by soaking with water, then remove any clothing from the burned area unless it is stuck firmly to the skin. In that case, cut away as much clothing as possible.

3. If the injured area is not oozing, cover the burn with a sterile gauze pad or a clean, dry cloth.

4. If the burn is oozing, cover it lightly with sterile gauze if available and immediately seek medical attention. If sterile gauze is not available, cover burns with a clean sheet or towel.

5. Do not put butter, grease, mustard, or powder on a burn. All of these so-called home remedies actually can make the injury worse.

For anything more serious than a superficial burn, or if redness and pain continue for more than a few hours, consult a physician. *All* electrical burns and burns of the hands, mouth, or genitals should receive immediate medical attention. Chemicals that cause burns also may be absorbed through the skin and cause other symptoms. Call Poison Help (1-800-222-1222) or your pediatrician after washing off all the chemicals. (For treatment of a chemical contact to a child's eye, see *Poison in the Eye*, page 713.)

If your physician thinks the burn

is not too serious, he may show you how to clean and care for it at home using medicated ointments and dressings. Under the following circumstances, however, hospitalization may be necessary:

■ If the burns are third-degree

■ If 10 percent or more of the body is burned

■ If the burn involves the face, hands, feet, or genitals, or involves a moving joint, or is circumferential (goes completely around the part of the body)

■ If the child is very young or fussy, and therefore too difficult to treat at home

When treating a burn at home, watch for any increase in redness or swelling or the development of a bad odor or discharge. These can be signs of infection, which will require medical attention.

Prevention

Chapter 15, *Keeping Your Child Safe,* provides ways to safeguard your child against fire and scalding at home. For added protection, here are a few more suggestions.

■ *Install smoke detectors* (and carbon monoxide detectors) in hallways outside bedrooms, the kitchen, the living room, and near the furnace, with at least one on every floor of the house.

Test them every month to be sure they work. It is best to use alarms that have long-life batteries, but if these are not available, change batteries at least annually on a specific date that you'll remember (such as January 1 of each year). Consider investing in an alarm that allows you to record your own voice calling to your children by name; these new alarms may be more effective in rousing sleeping children than alarms with only loud beeping tones. Smoke alarms are coming on the market with new technologies that make them more sensitive to flaming and smoldering fires and less prone to nuisance alarms caused by cooking heat or steam. This may give you more time to evacuate in case of a fire. Consider investing in new alarms if yours are several years old.

■ *Practice home fire drills.* Make sure every family member and others who care for your children in your home know at least two ways to leave any area of the home safely in case of a fire.

■ *Have several working fire extinguishers readily available* and familiarize yourself with how to use them. Place fire extinguishers around the home where the risk of fire is greatest, such as in the kitchen, in the furnace room, and near the fireplace.

■ *Teach your children to crawl to the exits* if there's smoke in the room. (They will avoid inhaling the smoke by staying below it.)

■ *Purchase a safety ladder* if your home has a second story, and teach your children how to use it. If you live in a high-rise building, teach your children the locations of all exits and make sure they understand never to use the elevator in a fire. (It can become trapped between floors or open on a floor where the fire is burning.)

■ *Agree on a family meeting point* outside the house or apartment so you can make certain everyone has gotten out of the burning area.

■ *Teach your children to stop, drop, and roll* on the ground if their clothing catches fire.

■ *Avoid smoking indoors.*

■ *Do not leave food cooking* on the stove unattended.

■ *Lock up flammable liquids* in the home. It is best to store them outside the home, out of children's reach, and away from heat or ignition sources.

■ *Lower the temperature of your water heater* so the temperature at the faucet is no more than 120 degrees Fahrenheit (48.9 degrees Celsius) to prevent hot-water scalds and burns.

■ *Don't plug appliances or other electrical equipment into extension cords* if they place too much amperage or load on the cord, thus creating a potentially unsafe situation.

■ *Keep matches and lighters away from children*, locked up and out of reach.

■ *Avoid all fireworks,* even those meant for consumer use.

■ *Keep lit candles out of reach* of children

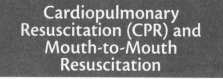

Cardiopulmonary Resuscitation (CPR) and Mouth-to-Mouth Resuscitation

CPR can save your child's life if his heart stops beating or if he has stopped breathing for any reason, such as drowning, poisoning, suffocation, smoke inhalation, or choking. Become familiar with the CPR instructions in the Appendix of this book. However, reading about CPR is not enough to teach you how to perform it. **The American Academy of Pediatrics strongly recommends that all parents and anyone who is responsible for the care of children should complete a course in basic CPR and treatment for choking.**

This training is especially vital if you own a swimming pool or live near water, such as a lake or community swimming pool or spa. Contact your local chapter of the American Heart Association or the American Red Cross to find out where and when certified courses are given in your community. Most of the classes teach basic first aid, CPR, and emergency prevention, along with what to do for a choking infant or child.

Choking

Choking occurs when a person inhales something other than air into the windpipe or when food or other objects block the windpipe. Among children, choking often is caused by liquid that "goes down the wrong way." The child will cough, wheeze, gasp, and gag until the windpipe is cleared, but this type of choking is usually not harmful.

Choking becomes life-threatening when a child swallows or inhales an object—often food—that blocks airflow to the lungs. This is an emergency that calls for immediate first aid. For specific and complete choking/CPR instructions, familiarize yourself with the chart in the Appendix on pages 902–3, and take a course on CPR for children. A child who begins to breathe by herself two or three minutes after a choking incident probably will not suffer any long-term damage. The longer she is deprived of oxygen, however, the greater the risk of permanent injury.

Occasionally a choking episode is followed by persistent coughing, gagging, wheezing, excessive salivation, or difficulty in swallowing or breathing. If this occurs, it may mean that an object is still partially blocking the airway—possibly in the lower breathing tubes. In this case, the object can cause continued breathing difficulty, irritation, and possibly pneumonia.

See your pediatrician or go to the emergency department if any symptoms persist, so that further tests, such as chest X-rays, can be done. If they show that your child has inhaled something, she probably will need to be admitted to the hospital for a procedure to remove the object. Any choking incident that lasts more than a few seconds warrants medical attention.

Prevention

Choking is a significant danger for children, especially until age seven. Objects such as small balls or marbles, balloon fragments, small parts from toys, and coins cause choking, but food is responsible for most incidents. You must be particularly watchful when children around the age of one are sampling new foods. Here are some additional suggestions to prevent choking.

■ *Don't give young children hard, smooth foods* (e.g., peanuts, raw vegetables) that must be chewed with a grinding motion. Children don't master that kind of chewing until around age four, so they may attempt to swallow the food whole. Do not give whole peanuts or other nuts to young children. When your child does start to eat peanuts (and you know she doesn't have an allergy to peanuts), watch her very closely while she is chewing and give only one nut at a time.

■ *Don't give your child round, firm foods* (like hot dogs, grapes, and carrot sticks) unless they are chopped completely. Cut them lengthwise and then into bite-size pieces (no larger than ½ inch [1.27 cm]) and encourage your child to chew thoroughly.

■ *Do not give your child compressible foods* like marshmallows or fruit snacks until at least four years of age.

■ *Supervise mealtime* for your infant or young child. Only permit eating while your child is seated and supervised, never while she is playing or running. Teach her to chew and swallow her food before talking or laughing.

■ *Chewing gum* is a choking hazard for young children.

Foods that pose particular risk include hot dogs; hard, gooey, or sticky candy or vitamins; grapes; and popcorn.

Because young children put everything into their mouths, small nonfood objects are also responsible for many choking incidents. Look for age guidelines in selecting toys and follow the manufacturer's recommended ages, especially for children younger than three years of age. Also be aware that certain objects have been associated with choking, including uninflated or broken balloons, baby powder, items from the trash (e.g., eggshells, poptops from beverage cans), safety pins, coins, marbles, small balls, pen or marker caps, magnets, and small, button-type lithium batteries.

If you're unsure whether an object or food item could be harmful, you can purchase a standard small-parts cylinder at juvenile products stores that you can use to determine whether any object is small enough to choke a child.

Cuts and Scrapes

Your child's natural curiosity and eagerness are likely to produce some scrapes and cuts along the way. His reaction may be far more severe than the actual damage. In most cases, good treatment will require little more than cleansing the injury, protecting it, and providing plenty of reassurance (and perhaps a kiss on the minor bump or bruise).

Cuts, Lacerations, and Bleeding

A cut or laceration is a wound that breaks through the skin and into the tissues beneath. The deeper the cut, the more likely there are to be problems, such as bleeding and the possibility of damage to nerves and tendons. The following simple guidelines will help you prevent serious bleeding and other problems such as scarring when your child gets a cut.

1. *Apply pressure.* Almost all active bleeding can be stopped by applying direct pressure with clean gauze or cloth over the site for five to ten minutes. The most common mistake is interrupting the pressure too early in order to peek at the wound. Doing this may result in more bleeding or the buildup of a clot that can make it harder to control the problem with further pressure. If bleeding starts again after five minutes of continuous pressure, reapply pressure and call your doctor for help. Do not use a tourniquet or tie-off on an arm or leg unless you are trained in its use, since this can cause severe damage if left on too long. However, if the cut is on an extremity, you can elevate the arm or leg to help decrease bleeding.

2. *Stay calm.* The sight of blood can be frightening, but this is an important time to stay in control. You'll make better decisions if you are calm, and your child will be less likely to get upset by the situation. Remember, by using direct pressure you will be able to control bleeding from even the most severe lacerations until help can arrive. Relatively minor cuts to the head and face will bleed more than cuts to other parts of the body because of the greater number of small, superficial blood vessels.

3. *Seek medical advice for serious cuts.* No matter how much (or how little) bleeding occurs, call your doctor if the laceration is deep (all the way through the skin and into the tissue below) or more than ½ inch (1.27 cm) long. Deep cuts can severely damage underlying muscles, nerves, tendons, and joints even if on the surface the wound does not appear serious. Long lacerations and those on the face, chest, and back are more likely to leave disfiguring scars. In these situations, if the wound is properly closed, the scar probably will be much less

apparent. In some circumstances a skin adhesive (a glue-like substance) may be used to close the wound. If in doubt about whether stitches, adhesives, or staples are needed, call your doctor right away for advice, as it's important for repair to occur within eight to twelve hours of the injury.

You should be able to treat short, minor cuts yourself as long as the edges come together by themselves or can be brought together with the aid of a butterfly bandage, and if there is no numbness beyond the wound and no reduction in sensation or movement. (A butterfly bandage is a strip of adhesive with ends that flare. It's used to keep the edges of a cut together during the healing process.) However, have your doctor examine your child if there is any possibility that foreign matter, such as dirt or glass, is trapped in the cut. Any injury that you cannot manage should be seen by your pediatrician or emergency medical services as soon as possible to maximize healing. Your child may not like to let you examine a laceration thoroughly because of the pain involved. The pediatrician, however, can use a local anesthetic if necessary to ensure a thorough exam. He may also use topical skin adhesives.

4. *Clean and dress the wound.* If you feel comfortable handling the problem, wash the wound with plain water and examine it carefully to be sure it is clean. Apply an antibiotic ointment, then cover it with a sterile dressing. It's easy to underestimate

First-Aid Supplies for Your Home and Car

You should prepare a first-aid kit for your home as well as one for each of your cars. The kit should contain:

- Fever- or pain-reducing medication: acetaminophen or a nonsteroidal anti-inflammatory medication such as ibuprofen

- Antihistamine for allergic reaction

- Antibiotic ointment

- Prescription medications that anyone in your family takes

- Sterile adhesive bandages (in various sizes)

- Gauze pads

- Medical tape

- Scissors

- Tweezers

- Soap or another cleansing agent

- Petroleum jelly or another lubricant

- Moistened towelettes

- Thermometer

the extent or severity of a cut, so even if you choose to treat it yourself, don't hesitate to call your pediatrician for advice. If any redness, swelling, or pus appears around the wound, or if bleeding recurs, consult your physician as soon as possible. Antiseptics such as iodine and alcohol are not necessary and increase your child's discomfort, so do not use them on cuts. If your child's immunizations are current, tetanus shots are not necessary after most abrasions and lacerations. However, if your child is not up to date on his tetanus booster or it is time for a booster dose, your pediatrician may recommend that one be given.

(See the box above, *First-Aid Supplies for Your Home and Car,* for information on assembling items needed to treat your family's wounds and injuries.)

Scrapes

Most minor injuries in young children are scrapes, or abrasions, which means that the outer layers of skin literally have been scraped off. If the abrasion covers a large area, it may appear to be very bloody, although the actual amount of blood lost is small. The area should be rinsed first with cool water to flush away debris and then washed gently with warm water and soap. Avoid using iodine and other antiseptic solutions. They have little protective value and can add to the pain and discomfort.

If left alone, most abrasions scab over quickly, and formerly this was thought to be the best natural remedy. But scabs actually slow the healing process and can lead to more scarring. Treat large or oozing scrapes with an antibiotic ointment and then cover them with a sterile (germ-free) dressing. These can be obtained at your local pharmacy, in the form of either an adhesive bandage or a separate gauze pad that is held in place by rolled gauze or adhesive tape. Some dressings are made of materials such as Telfa, which are less likely to adhere to the raw surface of a wound. Antibiotic ointment also helps prevent the dressing from sticking to the healing wound surface. The purpose is to prevent the injury from becoming infected while healing occurs. It is best to keep the bandage in place, except for dressing changes, until the wound heals. Take care that dressings around such areas as fingers or toes are not so tight as to interfere with circulation.

Examine the wound daily during the dressing change, or whenever it becomes dirty or wet. If a bandage sticks when you try to remove it, soak it off with warm water. Most wounds require a dressing for only two or three days, but your child may be reluctant to stop applying bandages that quickly, because small children tend to regard bandages as badges or medals. There is no harm in leaving the area loosely covered as long as the bandage is kept dry and clean and the wound is checked daily.

Call your pediatrician if you can't get a wound clean or if you notice drainage of pus, increasing tenderness or redness around the site, or fever. These are signs that the wound may be infected. If necessary, the doctor can use a local anesthetic to prevent severe pain while cleaning out dirt and debris that you are not able to remove. If the wound is infected, she may prescribe antibiotics in the form of an oral medicine or an ointment or cream.

Prevention

It is almost impossible for a curious and active child to avoid some scrapes and minor cuts, but there are things you can do to decrease the number your child will have and to minimize their severity. Keep potentially dangerous objects like sharp knives, easily breakable glass objects, and scissors out of his reach. When he gets old enough to use knives and scissors himself, teach him how to handle them properly and insist that they be used safely. At regular intervals make a safety check of your house, garage, and yard. If you find objects that are potentially dangerous because your child is older and can get into them, store them securely out of his reach.

Also see Chapter 15, *Keeping Your Child Safe*.

Drowning

Drowning is a leading cause of death among children, including infants and toddlers. Most infant drownings occur in bathtubs and buckets. Toddlers between one and four years most commonly drown in swimming pools. However, many children in this age group drown in ponds, rivers, and lakes. Children older than five years old are more likely to drown in rivers and lakes, but this varies from one area of the country to another. It is important to know that children can drown in even 1 inch of water, such as a bathtub or toilet. When a child is rescued before death, the episode is called a nonfatal drowning.

What You Should Do

Without putting yourself in harm's way, get your child out of the water immediately, then check to see if she is breathing on her own. If she is not, begin CPR immediately (see Appendix). If someone else is present, send him or her to call for emergency medical help (911), but don't spend precious moments looking for someone, and don't waste time trying to drain water from your child's lungs. Concentrate instead on giving her rescue breathing and CPR until she is breathing on her own. While you are doing CPR, it is very likely your child will vomit some of the swallowed water. Only when the child's breathing has resumed should you stop and seek emergency help. Call 911 if you haven't already. Once the paramedics arrive, they will administer oxygen and continue CPR if necessary.

Any child who has come close to drowning should be given a complete medical examination, even if she seems all right. If she stopped breathing, inhaled water, or lost consciousness, she should remain under medical observation for at least twenty-four hours to be sure there is no damage to her respiratory or nervous system. A child's recovery from a nonfatal drowning depends on how long she was deprived of oxygen. If she was underwater only briefly, she is likely to recover completely. Longer periods without oxygen can cause damage to the lungs, heart, or brain. A child who doesn't respond quickly to CPR may have more serious problems, but it's important to keep trying, because sustained CPR has revived children who have appeared lifeless or who have been immersed in very cold water for lengthy periods.

Prevention

For newborn infants and all children under five years of age (and older children who are not strong swimmers), parents and caregivers should never—not even for a moment—leave children alone or in the care of another child while in or near bathtubs, pools, spas, or wading pools, or near irrigation ditches or other open bodies of water. With children of this age, use "touch supervision"; that means that a supervising adult should be within an arm's length of the child, with full attention focused on the child at all times, when she is in or near water. The supervising adult should not be engaged in distracting activities, such as using a telephone, reading, socializing, or tending to household chores. If you are hosting a pool party, hire or designate an adult lifeguard, so that a supervising adult always has eyes on the water in case of emergency.

Home swimming pools should be surrounded by a fence that is not connected to the house to prevent a child from getting to the pool from the house. There is no substitute for a four-sided, nonclimbable fence that is at least 4 feet high, with a self-closing, self-latching gate that opens away from the pool. Parents, caregivers, and pool owners should know CPR and how to swim and should keep a telephone and equipment approved by the US Coast Guard (life preservers, life jackets, shepherd's crook) at poolside.

Toddlers, children with intellectual disabilities, and children with seizure disorders are particularly vulnerable to drowning, but all youngsters are in danger if unsupervised in or near water. Even a child who knows how to swim may drown a few feet from safety. Remember, children should be supervised at all times. Swimming lessons should *not* be considered as a way to "drownproof" your child. (For more information on water safety, see page 514.)

Electric Shock

When the human body comes in direct contact with a source of electricity, the current passes through it, producing what's called an electric shock. Depending on the voltage of the current and the length of contact, this shock can cause anything from minor discomfort to serious injury and even death. Young children, particularly toddlers, experience electric shock most often when they bite into electrical cords or poke metal objects such as forks or knives into unprotected outlets or appliances. These injuries also can take place when electric toys, appliances, or tools are used incorrectly, or when electric current makes contact with water in which a child is sitting or standing. Christmas trees and their lights are a seasonal hazard.

What You Should Do

If your child comes in contact with electricity, *always* try to turn the power off first. In many cases you'll be able to pull the plug or turn off the switch. If this isn't possible, consider an attempt to remove the live wire— but *not with your bare hands*, which would bring you in contact with the current yourself. Instead, try to cut the wire with a wood-handled ax or well-insulated wire cutters, or move the wire off the child using a dry stick, a rolled-up magazine or newspaper, a rope, a coat, or another thick, dry object that won't conduct electricity.

If you can't remove the source of the current, try to pull the child away. Again, *do not touch the child with your bare hands* when he's attached to the source of the current, since his body will transmit the electricity to you. Instead, use a nonconducting material such as rubber or those described previously to shield you while freeing him. (*Caution:* None of these methods can be guaranteed safe unless the power can be shut off.)

As soon as the current is turned off (or the child is removed from it), check the child's breathing, skin color, and ability to respond to you. If his breathing or heartbeat has stopped or seems very rapid or irregular, immediately use cardiopulmonary resuscitation (CPR; see page 699) to restore it, and have someone call for emergency medical help. At the same time, avoid moving the child needlessly, since such a severe electrical shock may have caused a spinal fracture.

If the child is conscious and it seems the shock was minor, check him for burned skin, especially if his mouth was the point of contact with the current. Call 911. Electric shock can cause internal organ damage that may be difficult to detect without a medical examination. For that reason, *all* children who receive a significant electric shock should see a doctor. In the pediatrician's office, any minor burns from the electricity will be cleansed and dressed. The doctor may order laboratory tests to check for signs of damage to internal organs. If the child has severe burns or any sign

of brain or heart damage, he will need to be hospitalized.

Prevention

The best way to prevent electrical injuries is to use outlet covers that are not a choking hazard, make sure all wires are properly insulated, tuck wires away from your child's reach, and provide adult supervision whenever children are in an area with potential electrical hazards. Small appliances are a special hazard around bathtubs, sinks, or pools. (See also Chapter 15, *Keeping Your Child Safe.*)

Fingertip Injuries

Children's fingertips get smashed frequently, usually getting caught in closing doors. Either the child is unable to recognize the potential danger, or she fails to remove her hand quickly enough before the door is shut. Fingers also sometimes get crushed when children play with a hammer or other heavy object, or when they're around a car door. Because fingertips are exquisitely sensitive, your child will let you know immediately that she's been injured. Usually the damaged area will be blue and swollen, and there may be a cut or bleeding around the cuticle. The skin, tissues below the skin, and the nail bed—as well as the underlying bone and growth plate—all may be affected. If bleeding occurs underneath the nail, it will turn black or dark blue, and the pressure from the bleeding may be painful.

Home Treatment

When the fingertip is bleeding, wash it with soap and water, and cover it with a soft, sterile dressing. An ice pack or a soaking in cold water may relieve the pain and minimize swelling. If the swelling is mild and your child is comfortable, your doctor may recommend that you allow the finger to heal on its own. But be alert for any increase in pain, swelling, redness, or drainage from the injured area, or a fever beginning twenty-four to seventy-two hours after the injury. These may be signs of infection, and you should notify your pediatrician. When there's excessive swelling, a deep cut, blood under the fingernail, or if the finger looks as if it may be broken, call your doctor immediately. Do not attempt to straighten a fractured finger on your own.

Professional Treatment

If your doctor suspects a fracture, he may order an X-ray. If the X-ray confirms a fracture—or if there's damage to the nail bed, where nail growth occurs—an orthopedic consultation may be necessary. A fractured finger can be straightened and set under local anesthesia. An injured nail bed also must be repaired surgically to minimize the possibility of a nail deformity developing as the finger grows. If there's considerable blood under the nail, the pediatrician may drain it by making a small hole in the nail, which should relieve the pain.

Although deep cuts may require stitches, often all that's necessary is sterile adhesive strips (thin adhesive strips similar to butterfly bandages). A fracture underneath a cut is considered an open fracture and is susceptible to infection in the bone. In this case, antibiotics will be prescribed. Depending on your child's age and immunization status, the doctor also may order a tetanus booster.

(See also *Fractures/Broken Bones*.)

Fractures/Broken Bones

Although the term "fracture" may sound serious, it is just another name for a broken bone. Fractures are the fourth-most-common injury among children under age six. Falls cause most of the fractures in this age group, but the most serious bone breaks usually result from car crashes.

A broken bone in a child is different from one in an adult, because young bones are more flexible and have a thicker covering, which makes them better able to absorb shock. Because children's bones are still growing, the bones have tremendous potential to repair themselves, so perfect alignment is often not necessary. Children's fractures rarely require surgical repair. They usually just need to be kept free of movement, most often through the use of a molded cast.

Often children's fractures are either greenstick fractures, in which the bone bends like green wood and breaks only on one side, or torus fractures, in which the bone is buckled, twisted, and weakened but not completely broken. A bend fracture is a bone that is bent but not broken, and is relatively common among children as well. Complete fractures, in which the bone breaks all the way through, also occur in young children.

Because your child's bones are still growing, he is vulnerable to an additional type of fracture that does not occur in adults. This involves damage to the growth plates at the ends of the bones, which regulate future growth. If this part of the bone does not heal properly after the fracture, the bone may grow at an angle or more slowly than the other bones in the body. Unfortunately, the impact on the bone's growth may not be visible for a year or more after the injury, so these fractures must be followed carefully by the pediatrician for twelve to eighteen months to make sure no growth damage has occurred. Fractures that involve injury to the growth plate sometimes need surgery to minimize the risk of future growth problems.

Fractures around the elbow often cause the arm to heal abnormally, resulting in a crooked position. Many require surgery to minimize this risk. Children with fractures near the elbow may be referred to a sports medicine or orthopedic specialist.

Signs and Symptoms

It's not always easy to tell when a bone is broken, especially if your child is too young to describe what he's feeling. Ordinarily with a fracture, you will see swelling and your child will clearly be in pain and unable—or unwilling—to move the injured limb. However, just because your child can move the limb doesn't necessarily rule out a fracture. Often with a fracture there is tenderness at one spot where the fracture is when you press along the limb. Anytime you suspect a fracture, notify your pediatrician immediately.

Home Treatment

Until your child can be seen in the pediatrician's office, emergency room, or urgent care center, use an improvised sling or rolled-up newspaper or magazine as a splint to protect the injury from unnecessary movement. If you think your child may have a broken bone, do not give him anything to eat or drink (even pain medication) before going to the doctor in case he needs to be sedated or put to sleep with general anesthesia to fix the fracture. For older children, you can use a cold pack or a cold towel, placed on the injury site, to decrease pain. Extreme cold can cause injury to the delicate skin of babies and toddlers, so do not use ice with children this young.

If your child has broken his leg, do not try to move him yourself. Call 911 for an ambulance; let the paramedics supervise his transportation and make the child as comfortable as possible. If part of the injury is open and bleeding, or if bone is protruding through the skin, place firm pressure on the wound (see *Cuts, Lacerations, and Bleeding*, page 701), then cover it with clean (preferably sterile) gauze. Do not try to put the bone back underneath the skin. After this injury has been treated, be alert to any fever, which may indicate that the wound has become infected.

Professional Treatment

After examining the break, the doctor will order X-rays to determine the extent of the damage. If the doctor suspects that the bone's growth plate is affected, or if the bones are out of line, an orthopedic consultation will be necessary. Because children's bones heal rapidly and well, a plaster or fiberglass cast, or sometimes just an immobilizing splint, is all that is needed for most minor fractures. For a displaced fracture, where the bones aren't aligned properly, an orthopedic surgeon may have to realign the bones. This may be done without surgery, with an orthopedic surgeon manipulating the bones until they're straight (closed reduction), and then applying a cast. If an open reduction is necessary, this can occur in the emergency department with medication given to your child for pain and to relax him, or he can be put to sleep under general anesthesia in the operating room. After the surgical reduction, a cast will be used until the bone has healed, which usually takes about half the time that adult bones require, or less, depending on the child's age. The nice

thing about young bones is that they don't have to be in perfect alignment for them to remodel as they grow. Your pediatrician may order periodic X-rays while the bone is healing, just to make sure they are aligning properly.

Usually casting brings rapid relief or at least a decrease in pain. Your child may experience pain for the first two to three days after the injury or after setting or surgery. Typically, this can be treated with over-the-counter medications, as well as activities to distract your child from the pain. If your child has an increase in pain, numbness, or pale or blue fingers or toes, call your doctor immediately. These are signs that the extremity has swollen and requires more room within the cast. If the cast is not adjusted, the swelling may press on nerves, muscles, and blood vessels, which can produce permanent damage. To relieve the pressure, the doctor may split the cast, open a window in it, or replace it with a larger one.

Also let the doctor know if the cast breaks or becomes very loose, or if the plaster gets wet and soggy. Without a proper, secure fit, the cast will not hold the broken bone in position to mend correctly. Often, bones that have been broken will form a hard knot, known as a callus, at the site of the break during the healing process. Especially with a broken collarbone, this may look unsightly, but there is no treatment for this, and the knot will not be permanent. The bone will remodel and resume its normal shape in a few months.

Head Injury/Concussion

It's almost inevitable that your child will hit her head every now and then, especially when she's a toddler— falling off playground equipment or a bed, for example. These blows may upset you, but your anxiety is usually worse than the bump. Most head injuries are minor, causing no serious problems. Even so, it's important to know the difference between a head injury that warrants medical attention and one that needs only a comforting hug.

By definition, a concussion is a hard strike to the head resulting in temporary confusion or a change in behavior, and sometimes with a loss of consciousness. Particularly if a child has significant memory loss, disorientation, altered speech, visual changes, seizure, or nausea and vomiting after a head injury, call 911 and contact your pediatrician. In fact, if your child experiences head trauma with persistent pain or any other symptoms, your child should be examined by her doctor.

Treatment

If a child's head injury has been mild, she'll remain alert and awake after the incident, and her color will be normal. She may cry out due to momentary pain and fright, but the crying should last no more than ten minutes and then she'll go back to playing as usual.

If the injury seems minor and there's not a significant cut (one that's deep and/or actively bleeding) that might require immediate medical attention or possibly stitches (see *Cuts and Scrapes*, page 701), you may be able to treat your child at home. Just wash the cut with soap and water. If there's a bruise, apply a cold compress. This will help minimize the swelling if you do it in the first few hours after the injury. Even in these cases, however, it may be wise to call your pediatrician and explain the circumstances and your child's condition.

Even after only a minor head injury, you should observe your child for twenty-four to forty-eight hours to see if she develops any signs that the injury was more severe than it first appeared. Although it's very rare, children can develop a serious brain injury after a seemingly minor bump on the head that causes no immediate obvious problems. If your child develops any of the following symptoms, be sure to consult your pediatrician immediately or seek prompt attention from the nearest emergency room:

■ *She seems excessively sleepy or lethargic* during her usual wakeful hours, or you cannot awaken her while she's asleep at night. It is normal for children to seem tired or less active after a head injury, but this should improve within a few hours; seek medical attention if it doesn't.

■ *She vomits or has a headache that won't go away* (even with acetaminophen). Headache and vomiting occur commonly after head trauma, but they are usually mild and last only a few hours. (Small children may not be able to let you know that they have a headache, so they may cry or be inconsolable.) Vomiting that occurs more than four to six hours after the head trauma is less common, so call your doctor or take your child to the emergency department for an evaluation.

■ *She's persistently or extremely irritable.* With an infant who cannot tell you what she's feeling, this may indicate a severe headache.

■ *Any significant change* in your child's mental abilities, coordination, sensation, or strength warrants immediate medical attention. Worrisome changes would include weakness of arms or legs, clumsy walking, slurred speech, crossed eyes, or difficulty with vision.

■ *She becomes unconscious again* after being awake for a while, or she has a seizure (convulsion) or starts to breathe irregularly.

If your child loses consciousness *at any time* after hitting her head, notify the pediatrician. If she doesn't awaken within a few minutes, she needs *immediate medical attention.* Call 911 for help while you follow these steps.

1. Move your child as little as possible. **If you suspect that she might have injured her neck, do not attempt to move her. Changing the position of her neck might make her injuries worse.** One exception: move her if she's in danger of being injured further where she is (e.g., on a ledge or in a fire), but try to avoid bending or twisting her neck.

2. Check to see if she's breathing. If she isn't, perform CPR (see page 699).

3. If she's bleeding severely from a scalp wound, apply direct pressure with a clean cloth over the wound.

4. After calling 911, wait for the ambulance's arrival rather than taking your child to the hospital yourself.

Loss of consciousness following a head injury may last only a few seconds or as long as several hours. If you find the child after the injury happened and you are not sure if she lost consciousness, notify the pediatrician. (An older child who has had a concussion may say that she can't remember what happened just prior to and just after the injury.)

Most children who lose consciousness for more than a few minutes will be observed in the emergency department, and some may be hospitalized overnight for observation. Hospitalization is essential for youngsters with severe brain injury and irregular breathing or convulsions. Fortunately, with modern pediatric intensive care, many children who have suffered serious head injury—and even those who have been unconscious for several weeks—eventually may recover completely.

Poisoning

About 2.2 million people swallow or have contact with a poisonous substance each year. More than half of these poison exposures occur in children under six years of age. Most children who are poisoned are not permanently harmed, particularly if they receive immediate treatment. If you think your child has been poisoned, stay calm and act quickly. You should suspect poisoning if you ever find your child with an open or empty container of a toxic substance, especially if she is acting strangely. Be alert for these other signs of possible poisoning:

- Unexplained stains on her clothing

- Burns on her lips or mouth

- Unusual drooling, or odd odors on her breath

- Unexplained nausea or vomiting

- Abdominal cramps without fever

- Difficulty in breathing

- Sudden behavior changes, such as unusual sleepiness, irritability, or jumpiness

- Convulsions or unconsciousness (only in very serious cases)

Treatment

If there's an emergency and you cannot find the Poison Help number, dial 911 or directory assistance and ask for the number. Keep the Poison Help number in your cellphone (1-800-222-1222). Poison Help will provide the immediate information and guidance you need. These centers are staffed twenty-four hours a day with experts who can tell you what to do without delay. (Anytime your child has been exposed to a poison of any kind, you should notify your pediatrician as well.) The immediate action you need to take will vary with the type of poisoning. Poison Help can give you specific instructions if you know the particular substance your child has swallowed. However, carry out the following instructions before calling them.

(For more information about poisoning, see *Food Poisoning and Food Contamination* in Chapter 16, page 544.)

POISON IN THE EYE

Flush your child's eye by holding her eyelid open and pouring a steady stream of lukewarm water into the inner corner. A young child is sure to object to this treatment, so get another adult to hold her while you rinse the eye. If that's not possible, wrap her tightly in a towel and clamp her under one arm so you have one hand free to hold the eyelid open and the other to pour in the water.

Continue flushing the eye for fif-

Poison-Proofing Your Home

- Store drugs and medications in a medicine cabinet that is locked and out of reach. Do not keep toothpaste, soap, or shampoo in the same cabinet. If you carry a purse, keep potential poisons out of your purse, and keep your child away from other people's purses.

- Buy and keep medications in their own containers with child safety caps. (Remember, however, that these caps are child-resistant, not childproof, so keep the containers in a locked cabinet.) Safely dispose of leftover prescription medicines when the illness for which they were prescribed has passed. Many pharmacies and municipalities accept leftover medications and will dispose of them safely.

- Do not take medicine in front of small children; they may try to imitate you later. Never tell a child that a medicine is candy in order to get him to take it.

- Check the label every time you give medication, to be sure you are giving the right medicine in the correct dosage. Mistakes are most likely to occur in the middle of the night, so always turn on the light when handling any medication.

- Read labels on all household products before you buy them. Try to find the safest ones for the job, and buy only what you need to use immediately.

- Store hazardous products in locked cabinets that are out of your child's reach. Do not keep detergents and other cleaning products under the kitchen or bathroom sink unless they are in a cabinet with a safety latch that locks every time you close the cabinet. (Most hardware stores and department stores sell these safety latches.) Newer detergent products packaged in single-load packets or "pods" offer convenience but often resemble candy or gummy treats and are tempting for children to put in their mouth. This can make them violently ill very quickly and lead to serious breathing or stomach problems, coma, and even death. It is best to use traditional liquid or powder detergent products until all children in the household are at least six years of age. If you do use concentrated detergent packets, keep them locked up out of sight and reach of children.

- Never put poisonous or toxic products in containers that were once used for food, especially empty drink bottles, cans, or cups.

- Always open the garage door before starting your car, and never run the car in a closed garage. Be sure that coal, wood, or kerosene stoves are properly maintained. If you smell gas, turn off the stove or gas burner, leave the house, and then call the gas company.

■ Post the Poison Help number, 1-800-222-1222, near every telephone in your home and in your cellphone contacts, along with other emergency numbers. Be sure that your childcare provider and anyone else caring for your child knows when and how to use these numbers.

Keep in mind that these guidelines should apply not only to your home but also to any other settings where your child visits, including the homes of grandparents and babysitters.

teen minutes. Then call Poison Help, 1-800-222-1222, for further instructions. Do not use an eyecup, eye drops, or ointment unless Poison Help tells you to do so. If there is any question of continued pain or severe injury, seek emergency assistance immediately.

POISON ON THE SKIN

If your child spills a dangerous chemical substance on her body, remove her clothes and rinse the skin with lukewarm—not hot—water. If the area shows signs of being burned, continue rinsing for at least fifteen minutes, no matter how much your child may protest. Then call Poison Help for further advice. Do not apply ointments or grease.

POISONOUS FUMES

In the home, poisonous fumes are most likely to be produced by an idling automobile in a closed garage; leaky gas vents; wood, coal, or kerosene stoves that are improperly vented or maintained; or space heat-

ers, ovens, stoves, clothes dryers, or water heaters that use gas. If you have any of these appliances, you should also have carbon monoxide detectors in your home, since carbon monoxide has no odor. If your child is exposed to fumes or gases from these or other sources, get her into fresh air immediately. If she is breathing, call Poison Help, 1-800-222-1222, for further instructions. If she has stopped breathing, start CPR (see pages 902-3), and don't stop until she breathes on her own or someone else can take over. If you can, have someone call 911 for emergency medical help immediately; otherwise, try one minute of CPR and then call for emergency assistance.

SWALLOWED POISON

First, get the poisonous substance away from your child. If she still has some in her mouth, make her spit it out, or remove it with your fingers. Keep this material along with any other evidence that might help determine what she swallowed.

Next, check for these signs:

- Severe throat pain

- Excessive drooling

- Breathing difficulty

- Convulsions

- Excessive drowsiness

If any of these are present, or if your child is unconscious or has stopped breathing, start emergency procedures such as CPR and get medical help immediately by calling 911. Take the poison container and remnants of material with you to help the doctor determine what was swallowed. *Vomiting may be dangerous, so do not make your child vomit*—even if the label on the container suggests it—as this may cause further damage. Strong acids (e.g., toilet bowl cleaner, bleach) or strong alkalis (e.g., lye, drain or oven cleaner, or dishwasher detergent) can burn the throat, and vomiting will only increase the damage by bringing these fluids back up into the esophagus and throat. Syrup of ipecac is a drug that was used in the past to make children vomit after they swallowed a poison; although this may seem to make sense, it is no longer considered a good poison treatment. If you have syrup of ipecac in your home, properly dispose of it and throw away the container. Do not make a child vomit by any means, whether by giving him syrup

of ipecac, making him gag, or giving him salt water. Instead, you may be advised to have the child drink milk or water.

If your child is not showing these serious symptoms, call Poison Help, 1-800-222-1222, which will direct your call to your regional poison center. The person answering the phone will need the following information in order to help you:

- Your name and phone number.

- Your child's name, age, and weight. Also be sure to mention any serious medical conditions she has or medications she is taking.

- The name of the substance your child swallowed. Read it off the container, and spell it if necessary. If ingredients are listed on the label, read them, too. If your child has swallowed a prescription medicine and the drug is not named on the label, give the center the name of the pharmacy and its phone number, the date of the prescription, and its number. Try to describe the color and shape of the tablet or capsule, and mention any imprinted numbers on it. If your child swallowed another substance, such as a part of a plant, provide as full a description as possible to help identify it.

- The time your child swallowed this poison (or when you found her), and the amount you think she swallowed.

If the poison is extremely dangerous, or if your child is very young, you may be told to take her directly to the nearest emergency department for medical evaluation. Otherwise, you will be given instructions to follow at home.

Prevention

Young children, especially those between ages one and three, are commonly poisoned by things in the home such as medications—even those sold over the counter—and illegal drugs, cleaning products, plants, cosmetics, pesticides, paints, solvents, antifreeze, windshield wiper fluid, gasoline, kerosene, and lamp oil. This happens because tasting and mouthing things is a natural way for children to explore their surroundings, and because they imitate adults without understanding what they are doing.

Most poisonings occur when parents are distracted. If you are ill or under a great deal of stress, you may not watch your child as closely as usual. The hectic routines at the end of the day contribute to lapses in parental attention. So keep all poisons, medications, and toxins high out of children's sight and reach. The best way to prevent poisonings is to store all toxic substances in a locked cabinet where your child cannot possibly get to them, even when you are not directly watching her. Also, supervise her even more closely whenever you're visiting a store or a friend or relative's home that has not been childproofed. (See also Chapter 15, *Keeping Your Child Safe*.)

~ 24 ~

Environmental Health

ALL CHILDREN ARE potentially exposed to environmental toxins in the world in which we live. But while you can't protect your child from every environmental hazard that exists, whether indoors or out, you can prevent his exposure to some.

Air Pollution

The outdoor air contains several substances that could be harmful to children. One of the most worrisome is ground-level ozone, which is a colorless gas that is created when nitrogen oxides interact with volatile organic compounds. These compounds are released by cars and industry and react with sunlight to make ozone. Ground-level ozone is the main ingredient in smog. Ozone concentrations are likely to be at the highest unhealthy levels in the summer on warm, sunny days, peaking in the mid- to late afternoon. Ozone can be present at high levels in the winter, too. It can travel by wind, resulting in rural areas being affected by ozone as well. Because children spend time playing outdoors, they are particularly susceptible to ozone's effects, with breathing difficulties most likely to occur in youngsters with asthma. Children also breathe more rapidly than adults and inhale more pollutants per pound of body weight.

Other air pollutants that can cause harm include carbon monoxide, particulate matter released from cars and industry, sulfur dioxide, and other pollutants. Not all chemicals in our air are regulated by the Environmental Protection Agency. Parents and caregivers should pay attention to air alerts in the media or should assess data online before sending children out to play. Children with asthma or other chronic disease can be greatly affected by poor air quality and should be kept indoors when air quality alerts show danger.

Prevention

To protect your child from air pollution, limit his playtime outdoors when local agencies have issued health advisories or smog alerts—particularly if your child has a respiratory problem like asthma. Newspapers and TV news programs often provide information about the air quality in the community. A good site to find real-time information about air quality is airnow.gov.

To reduce the air pollution from automobiles on smoggy days, keep your car in the garage and use public transportation or car pools instead. Do not use gasoline-powered lawnmowers on high-pollution days and limit their use at other times. Turn off the car rather than letting it idle while you are waiting, as idling increases air pollution. Work with local, state, and national government to enforce and tighten air pollution laws and regulations.

Asbestos

Asbestos is a natural fiber that was widely used as a spray-on material for fireproofing, insulation, and soundproofing in schools, homes, and public buildings from the 1940s through the 1970s. It does *not* pose health risks unless it deteriorates and becomes crumbly, when it can release microscopic asbestos fibers into the air. When asbestos fibers are inhaled, they can cause chronic health problems to the lungs, throat, and gastrointestinal tract, including a rare type of chest cancer (called mesothelioma) that can occur as long as five decades after asbestos exposure.

Today, schools are mandated by law to either remove asbestos or otherwise ensure that children are not exposed to it. However, it is still in some older homes, especially as insulation around pipes, stoves, and furnaces, as well as in walls and ceilings.

Prevention

Follow these guidelines to keep your child safe from asbestos.

■ If you think there may be asbestos in your home, have a professional inspector check for it. Local health departments and regional offices of the Environmental Protection Agency (EPA) can provide the names of individuals and labs certified to inspect homes for asbestos. To locate the regional EPA office nearest you, go to epa.gov/asbestos.

■ Do not let your youngster play near any exposed or deteriorating materials that could contain asbestos.

■ If asbestos is found in your home, it may be acceptable to leave it there if it is in good condition. But if it is deteriorating, or if it might be disturbed by any renovations you're planning, have a properly accredited and certified contractor remove the asbestos, which must be taken off in a safe manner. Again, ask the local health department or the EPA for information on finding a certified contractor in your community.

Carbon Monoxide

Carbon monoxide is a toxic gas that is a by-product of appliances, heaters, and automobiles that burn gasoline, natural gas, wood, oil, kerosene, and propane. It has no color, no taste, and no odor. It can become trapped inside your home if appliances are not working efficiently, if a furnace, stove, or fireplace has a clogged vent or chimney, or if a charcoal grill is used in an enclosed area. Carbon monoxide also might enter your home when an automobile is left running in an attached garage. During power outages and storms, using electrical generators indoors increases the risk for carbon monoxide poisoning. These appliances should remain outdoors.

When your child breathes carbon monoxide, it harms the ability of his blood to transport oxygen. Although everyone is at risk for carbon monoxide poisoning, it is particularly dangerous for children because they breathe faster and inhale more carbon monoxide per pound of body weight. Symptoms may include headaches, nausea, shortness of breath, fatigue, confusion, and fainting. Persistent exposure to carbon monoxide can lead to personality changes, memory loss, severe lung injury, brain damage, and death.

Prevention

You can reduce your child's risk of carbon monoxide poisoning by:

■ Buying, installing, and periodically checking the function of carbon monoxide detectors in your home, particularly near the bedrooms, or near a furnace or woodstove

■ Never leaving your car running in an attached garage (even if the garage door is open)

■ Never using a charcoal or propane grill, hibachi, or portable camping stove indoors or in an enclosed area

■ Never using a fuel-burning electric generator inside your home, and even when using a generator outdoors, never running it near an open window or a fresh air intake vent for your home

■ Scheduling an annual inspection and servicing of oil and gas furnaces, woodstoves, gas ovens and ranges, gas water heaters, gas clothes dryers, and fireplaces

■ Never using your nonelectric oven to heat your kitchen or your house

Drinking Water

Children drink much more water for their size than adults. Most of this water comes from the tap, and the quality of this water is regulated by standards instituted by Congress, included in the Safe Drinking Water Act of 1974. Subsequent laws have set drinking water standards for chemicals that were known to be in some water supplies.

Today the drinking water in the United States is among the safest in the world, although problems can occur from time to time. Violations in water safety standards are most likely to occur in small systems that serve less than a thousand people. Also, keep in mind that private wells are not federally regulated and should be tested for nitrates and other environmental toxins if appropriate (see *Where We Stand* on page 725).

The drinking water standards for lead are not health-based standards. Thus, lead at the current standard, 15 parts per billion (ppb), may result in elevated blood lead levels if that water is the only source of liquid. This can be very important for infants who are bottle-fed with reconstituted formula. The American Academy of Pediatrics recommends that lead in water be as low as possible (a maximum of 1 ppb) in drinking water, including school drinking fountains. Pipes from the water treatment plant and within homes have been made with lead. Water companies use corrosion control measures to decrease the amount of lead that enters water from the pipes. Recent events have shown this may not occur to the extent it should. Also, the water treatment facility is not responsible for the pipes in homes, which may also be lead. Flushing the lines before use and using cold water may decrease the amount of lead exposure.

The addition of fluoride to municipal water supplies has resulted in a substantial decrease in dental caries in children. There can be too much fluoride in water, though, and care is needed to not let it get too high. However, science shows that fluoride in tap water is a safe and effective way to promote the development of healthy teeth and help prevent cavities. In many communities, tap water is better for children to drink than bottled water due to the fluoride that is added. Children who do not have access to fluoridated tap water may be at higher risk for cavities, and finding a dental home by one year of age is especially important for these children. Fluoridated tap water is safe for pregnant women to drink, and is also safe to mix with formula for an infant.

Contaminants that can cause illness in the drinking water include germs, nitrates, man-made chemicals, metals, radioactive particles, and by-products of the disinfecting process.

Plastics (Bisphenol A [BPA])

Breastfeeding is safe and the most important way to nourish your baby. Many food and liquid containers, including some baby bottles, are made of polycarbonate, or have a lining that contains the chemical bisphenol A (BPA). BPA is used to harden plastics, keep bacteria from contaminating foods, and prevent cans from rusting. Other man-made chemicals—phthalates—are used in soft, flexible plastics.

There are concerns over the possible harmful effects that BPA and phthalates may have on humans, particularly on infants and children. For example, animal studies have shown effects on endocrine function in animals related to BPA and phthalate exposure. BPA acts as a weak estrogen in animals and perhaps in humans, too. Additional and ongoing studies will determine what level of exposure to these chemicals might cause similar effects in humans.

Risk Reduction

As research continues, concerned parents can take the following precautionary measures to reduce babies' exposure to BPA:

- Avoid clear plastic baby bottles or containers with the recycling number 7 and the letters "PC" imprinted on them. Many contain BPA, although newer bottles should be BPA-free.

- Consider using certified or identified BPA-free plastic bottles.

- Glass bottles can be an alternative, but be aware of the risk of injury to you or your baby if the bottle is dropped or broken.

- Because heat may cause the release of BPA from plastic, do not heat polycarbonate bottles or other plastic food containers in the microwave and do not wash polycarbonate bottles or other plastic food containers in the dishwasher.

- Breastfeeding is another way to reduce potential exposure to unwanted chemicals. The AAP recommends exclusive breastfeeding for about six months. Breastfeeding should be continued thereafter as long as it is mutually desired by mother and infant.

- Many parents are concerned about BPA in dental sealants or fillings. Science shows that the exposure to BPA in these dental materials is very minimal, and fears over BPA should not prevent your child from receiving necessary dental care.

(continues on next page)

If you are considering switching from canned liquid to powdered formula, note that the mixing procedures may differ, so pay special attention when preparing formula from powder.

If your baby is on specialized formula to address a medical condition, you should not switch to another formula, as the known risks would outweigh any potential risks posed by BPA in particular.

Risks associated with giving infants inappropriate (homemade condensed milk) formulas or alternative (soy or goat) milk are far greater than the potential effects of BPA and phthalates.

In some communities, bottled water is being used or recommended due to contamination in the drinking water supply. It is important to note that while bisphenol A and phthalates may not be used in the manufacturing of plastics, other chemicals used to make plastic serve the same functions. These "regrettable substitutes" have resulted in less knowledge about what chemicals have entered our bodies from plastics. Additionally, fluoride is not added to bottled water, and additional fluoride treatments may be needed for children in this population.

Although bottled water can be purchased in markets, many brands are just tap water that has been bottled for sale. Bottled water is generally much more expensive than tap water, and unless there are known contamination problems in your community's water supply, it is not necessary. In summary, be careful about using bottled water with children on a regular basis.

Prevention

To ensure that your child is consuming safe drinking water, you can check the water quality by contacting the county health department, the state environment agency, or the Environmental Protection Agency's Safe Drinking Water Hotline (1-800-426-4791). Local water companies are mandated to report what is in the water on an annual basis. Well water should be tested yearly.

Other guidelines include:

■ Use cold water for cooking and drinking. Contaminants can accumulate in water heaters.

■ If you are concerned about the quality of your plumbing, run the faucet for two minutes each morning prior to using the water for cooking or drinking. This will flush the pipes and lower the likelihood that contaminants will end up in the water you consume.

■ Have well water tested for nitrates before giving it to infants under one year of age.

■ Drinking water that may be contaminated with germs should be boiled and then allowed to cool before drinking. Boil for no more than one minute. However, it is important to remember that boiling water only kills bacteria and other germs; it does *not* remove toxic chemicals. If you don't like the taste or smell of your tap water, filters made with activated carbon will remove the odd taste or smell. Such filters will also remove undesirable chemicals without removing fluoride needed to prevent tooth decay.

WHERE WE STAND

IN THE UNITED STATES, about 15 million families get their drinking water from private, unregulated wells. Studies show that a significant number of these wells have concentrations of nitrates that exceed federal drinking water standards. These nitrates are a natural component of plants and nitrate-containing fertilizers that can seep into well water and don't pose any toxic risk to humans on their own. But in the body, they can be converted to nitrites, which are potentially hazardous. In infants, they can lead to a condition called methemoglobinemia, a dangerous and sometimes fatal blood disorder that interferes with the circulation of oxygen in the blood.

Babies whose formula is prepared using well water may have a high risk of nitrate poisoning. The AAP recommends that if your family drinks well water, the well should be tested for nitrates. If the well water contains nitrates (above a level of 10 mg/L), it should not be used for infant formula or food preparation. Instead, you should prepare food or formula by using purchased water, public water supplies, or water from deeper wells with minimal nitrate levels.

How often should well water be tested? Tests should be done every three months for at least one year to determine the levels of nitrates. If these tests show safe levels, then a follow-up test once a year is recommended.

Breastfeeding is the safest way to nourish your infant, since high levels of nitrates are not passed through breast milk.

Fish

Fish is a protein-rich food that is healthy for both children and adults. It contains a good type of fat (omega-3 fatty acids), as well as nutrients such as vitamin D. It also is low in saturated fat. At the same time, a lot of attention has focused on the contaminants that may be in fish and that could pose health risks.

One of the most widely discussed contaminants is mercury, which at high levels can be toxic. It gets into oceans, rivers, lakes, and ponds, and can end up in the fish we eat. Mercury in bodies of water like lakes and streams—some of it discharged from industrial plants—can be converted by bacteria into mercury compounds such as methylmercury. As a result, certain predatory fish (including shark and swordfish) can contain high quantities of mercury, which when consumed can have a serious negative effect on a young child's developing nervous system.

Other environmental pollutants have been found in fish and other foods, including polychlorinated biphenyls (PCBs) and dioxins. Although PCBs are chemicals that were manufactured primarily for use as fire retardants and in electrical transformers, they were banned in the United States in the late 1970s. However, they have remained in the environment in water, soil, and air, and have been found in fish. PCBs have been associated with thyroid problems, lowered IQ, and memory impairment in young children.

Dioxin is another pollutant that has been detected in fish. It is the by-product of certain chemicals by incineration and can interfere with the developing nervous system and other organs, particularly when the exposure is long-term. Fortunately, PCBs and dioxins have decreased significantly in recent years.

Prevention

Certain types of fish and shellfish are lower in mercury, including canned light tuna, salmon, shrimp, cod, catfish, clams, flatfish, crab, scallops, and pollock. These are healthy choices of fish for your child to consume. Nevertheless, you should limit your child's intake of even these safer selections to less than 12 ounces per week. Government agencies are recommending that young children reduce their intake of certain fish that may contain high levels of mercury. Specifically, young children should not consume king mackerel, swordfish, shark, and tilefish.

For information about the safety of fish and shellfish caught in your area, contact state and local health departments. Also check fish advisories on the Environmental Protection Agency's website: epa.gov/water science/fish. The health department in your state can provide any advisories issued about the presence of other toxins in fish in your area.

Lead Poisoning

Lead poisoning is caused most often by touching and then mouthing dusty toys, chips of old paint, or dirt; by breathing lead in the air; or by drinking water from pipes lined or soldered with lead. There also may be lead in hobby materials such as stained glass, paints, solders, bullets, and fishing weights. It might be in miniblinds manufactured outside the United States prior to July 1997. If you buy new miniblinds, look for those that have a label that says "new formulation" or "nonleaded formula." Lead also might be in food cooked or stored in some imported ceramic dishes. Do not serve acidic substances (e.g., orange juice), hot/warm food, or liquids in these dishes, since this can cause the lead from the dishes to leach into the food. Although food cans with soldered seams could add lead to the food inside them, these cans generally have been replaced by seamless aluminum containers in the United States.

Parents may work in places where lead is used, such as battery plants, shooting ranges, or oil fields, and dust or lubricants that contain lead may come home on clothes, cars, and hair. Parents should shower and change clothes at work. Any work clothes should be laundered separately.

Other sources of lead can include candy, ethnic remedies, and alternative sources of medicine from countries like Mexico, as well as some spices, cosmetics, items used for worship, and Ayurvedic treatments from India, the Middle East, and Southeast Asia. More recently in the United States, lead has been found in charcoal-containing toothpaste and infant teething bracelets. Avoid toothpastes that are not ADA approved. Infant teething bracelets and necklaces may also present a choking and strangulation hazard. Better alternatives include a frozen banana, a teething ring, or a cold wet clean washcloth to chew on. Recalls and warnings about lead-contaminated products are available on the Consumer Product Safety Commission and FDA websites.

Lead was an allowable ingredient in house paint before 1978 and so may be on the walls, doorjambs, and window frames on many older homes. The EPA's Federal Lead Disclosure Rule outlines requirements for informing renters and buyers about the possibility of lead paint existing in a pre-1978 residential property. As the paint ages, it chips, peels, and comes off in the form of dust. Toddlers may be tempted by such bite-size pieces and will taste or eat them out of curiosity. Even if they don't intentionally eat the material, the dust can get on their hands and into their food. Sometimes the lead-containing finish has been covered with other layers of newer, safer paints. This can give you a false sense of reassurance, however, since the underlying paint still may chip or peel off with the newer layers and fall into the hands of toddlers.

There is no safe level of lead in the human body. Although there has been a decline in high lead levels in children's blood, somewhere between half a million and one million children in the United States have unacceptably high levels. Living in a city, being poor, being an immigrant, and being African American or Hispanic are all risk factors that increase the chances of having an elevated blood lead level. But even children living in rural areas or who are in well-to-do families still can be at risk.

In a child who continues consuming lead, the substance will accumulate in the body. Although it may not be noticeable for some time, ultimately it can affect many areas of the body, including the brain. Lead poisoning can cause learning disabilities and behavioral problems. Very high levels will likely cause the most severe problems, but the extent of damage for any individual child cannot be predicted. Lead also can cause stomach and intestinal problems, loss of appetite, anemia, headaches, constipation, hearing loss, and even short stature. Iron deficiency increases the risk for lead poisoning in children, which is why these two disorders are often found together in children. (See *Abdominal Pain*, page 527.)

Prevention

If your home was built after 1977, when federal regulations restricted the amount of lead in paint, the risk for having dangerous amounts of lead in the dust, paint, or soil of your residence is low. However, if your home is older, the likelihood of having dangerous amounts of lead there can be very high, especially for the oldest homes (those built before 1960). This is because of the myriad of other sources that may contain lead. It is imperative that you assess your home and goods for the possibility of lead contamination. If you think your home may contain lead, clean up any paint dust or chips using water. During this cleanup, if you add a detergent to the water, it will help bind the lead into the water. Also, keeping surfaces (floors, window

WHERE WE STAND

LEAD CAUSES SERIOUS damage to children's brains even at low levels of exposure, and the effects are difficult to overcome. The American Academy of Pediatrics supports widespread lead screening of children, as well as funding programs to remove lead hazards from the home, learning, and play environments. Primary prevention is the only way to combat lead poisoning. Knowing the environment where your child will live, learn, and play *and* removing the source of lead before your child encounters it will prevent lead exposure and the adverse effects that result from it.

areas, porches, etc.) clean may lower your child's chance of being exposed to lead-containing dust. Older windows are of particular concern since paint on wood frames frequently is damaged and the action of opening and closing windows can produce lead-containing dust. Do not vacuum the chips or dust using a regular vacuum because that will spread the dust out through its exhaust hole. The National Center for Healthy Housing, EPA, and many state agencies suggest the HEPA vacuum as an effective tool for removing lead paint chips. It's also a good idea to have your child leave his shoes at the door and wash his hands often, particularly before he eats.

Another step is to identify surfaces in your home with lead-contaminated paint, or areas with dangerous amounts of lead in the dust or dirt. A home inspection is necessary to do this, and you can get help from your local or state health department to find a lead inspector in your area.

Diagnosis and Treatment

Children who have lead poisoning rarely show any physical symptoms. However, learning and behavior problems from lead may show up in the preschool child, or they may not show up until the child reaches school age. At that point children need to learn more complicated tasks like reading or arithmetic and may have trouble keeping up with class work. Some may even seem overly active, due to the effects of the lead. For this reason, the only sure way to know if your child has been exposed

to excessive lead is to have him tested. In fact, a blood test for lead around ages one and two years is recommended for all children. The CDC's advisory committee now recommends performing interventions for children who test at 5 µg/dL or higher. This recommendation dropped the level for action from 10 µg/dL to 5 µg/dL in the last couple of years.

The most common screening test for lead poisoning uses a drop of blood from a finger prick. If the results of this test indicate that a child has been exposed to excessive lead, a second test will be done using a larger sample of blood obtained from a vein in the arm. This test is more accurate and can measure the precise amount of lead in the blood.

Children who are found to have elevated blood lead levels should receive an assessment of their home to evaluate the source. At higher levels, the child may need to stay in a lead-safe home while the original home is assessed and remediated. In rare instances, they may require treatment with a drug that binds the lead in the blood and greatly increases the body's ability to eliminate it. When treatment is necessary, usually oral medicines are used on an outpatient basis. Much less frequently, the treatment may involve hospitalization.

Some children with lead poisoning require more than one course of treatment. Unfortunately, standard treatments for lead-poisoned children produce only a short-term or marginal lowering of the child's body lead levels and do not lower the child's chance of developing lead-related behavioral or learning problems. Children who have had lead poisoning will need to have their physical health, behavior, and academic performance monitored for many years and should receive special schooling and therapy to help them overcome learning and behavior problems.

The best treatment for lead poisoning is prevention. If you are considering the purchase of an older home, have it tested first by the health department or commercial lead testing firm. In the same way, children who spend time in older buildings for daycare or other reasons may be at risk.

Pesticides/Herbicides

Pesticides and herbicides are used in a variety of settings, including homes, schools, parks, lawns, gardens, and farms. While they may kill insects, rodents, and weeds, many are toxic to people when consumed in food and water.

More research is needed to determine the short- and long-term effects of pesticides and herbicides on humans. Although some studies have found connections between some childhood cancers and an exposure to pesticides, other studies have not

ORGANIC FOODS

The US Department of Agriculture has established a certification program that requires farmers to meet government guidelines for growing and processing foods before the "organic" label can be attached to them. When foods like fruits, vegetables, and grains are organic, they are grown in soil fertilized with manure and compost, and without the use of pesticides, herbicides, dyes, or waxes; these standards prohibit the use of nonorganic ingredients for at least three years before crops are harvested. Organically produced meats must be raised free of growth hormones or antibiotics.

But does it really make a difference to buy organic? Are these foods actually safer and more nutritious—and are they worth the premium prices often charged for them?

Several studies have examined whether health risks can be reduced by limiting or eliminating exposure to pesticides. These pesticides are sprayed on crops to safeguard them from insects and molds, and their residue can be left on fruits and vegetables and then later consumed. But the fact is that any risk to children and adults when eating these foods is minimal. The traces of pesticides found on produce are usually much lower than the safety levels established by government agencies.

To complicate the issue of whether to buy organic, even organic foods may not be completely chemical-free. Although they haven't been treated with pesticides, small amounts of these chemicals can be carried by the wind or water and end up on organic crops. Similar concerns surround other chemicals as well, such as nitrates; the levels of nitrates in organically grown plant foods vary from one producer to another, and are dependent on factors like the season in which they're grown, the geographic location, and the post-harvest processing.

No matter what you decide, don't let any concerns about chemicals keep you from feeding your children a healthy diet rich in fruits, vegetables, whole grains, and low-fat dairy products, whether those are conventional or organic foods. In fact, there are greater risks in *not* making fruits and vegetables part of your child's meals, compared with any hazards posed by pesticides or herbicides.

So are there nutritional benefits of organic foods? Are these foods more nutritious for your child? Bear in mind that there is *no* convincing evidence that the nutritional content of organic foods differs in any significant way from conventional foods—in other words, there's no persuasive research showing that organic foods are more nutritious, safer, or even more tasty for your family. Remember that foods labeled as organic may still be unhealthy for other reasons, such as fruit snacks or juices that contain a lot of sugar and may cause dental cavities and which are less healthy than fresh fruit and vegetables. If you have easy access to organic foods in local farmers' markets or stores, and their higher prices fit into your budget, there is certainly little downside to choosing organic items.

reached the same conclusions. Many pesticides disrupt the nervous system of insects, and research has shown that they have the potential to damage the neurological system of children.

Prevention

Try to limit your child's unnecessary exposure to pesticides or herbicides. To reduce such exposure:

■ Minimize using foods in which chemical pesticides or herbicides were used by farmers.

■ Wash all fruits and vegetables with water before your child consumes them.

■ For your own lawn and garden, use nonchemical pest control methods whenever possible. If you keep bottles

Handwashing is an important part of a healthy lifestyle.

of pesticides in your home or garage, make sure they're out of the reach of children to avoid any accidental poisoning.

■ Consider that children and adults who eat organic foods have lower levels of pesticide metabolites in their system, so choose organic (when possible) to decrease your family's risk.

■ Avoid routinely spraying homes or schools to prevent insect infestations.

■ Integrated pest management focuses on the use of baits, and blocking the sources of entry.

Radon

Radon is a gas that is a product of the breakdown of uranium in soil and rock. It also may be in water, natural gas, and building materials.

High levels of radon are found in homes in many regions of the United States. It makes its way into homes through cracks or openings in the foundation, walls, and floors, or occasionally in well water. It does not cause health problems immediately upon inhalation. Over time, however, it can increase the risk of lung cancer. In fact, next to cigarette smoking, radon is thought to be the most common cause of lung cancer in the United States.

Prevention

To reduce your child's risk of radon exposure:

■ Ask your local health department whether radon levels are high in your community.

■ Have your home tested for radon, using an inexpensive radon detector.

(Hardware stores sell these detectors.) A certified laboratory should analyze the results of this test.

■ If the levels are too high in your home, call the Radon Hotline (operated by the National Safety Council in conjunction with the Environmental Protection Agency) at 1-800-644-6999; this is a good resource for information on reducing the radon risk in your home.

Smoke Exposure

According to the Centers for Disease Control and Prevention, about 25 percent of children ages three to eleven years old live in a household with at least one smoker. Secondhand (or environmental) cigarette smoke is exhaled smoke from burning tobacco or smoke from the mouthpiece end or filter of a cigarette, cigar, or pipe. If you or others in your home use cigarettes, pipes, or cigars, your child is being exposed to their smoke. This smoke contains thousands of chemicals, some of which have been shown to cause cancer and other illnesses, including respiratory infections, bronchitis, and pneumonia. Children exposed to cigarette smoke also have a greater likelihood of developing ear infections and asthma, and they may have a more difficult time getting over colds. They are more susceptible to headaches, sore throats, hoarseness, irritated eyes, dizziness, nausea, lack of energy, and fussiness. For these reasons, many parents have designated their homes as nonsmoking areas.

Thirdhand smoke exposure is usually defined as the smoke, residual nicotine, and other chemicals that tobacco smoke leaves behind on clothes, furniture, carpets, a person's hair, and her skin after a cigarette has already been extinguished. Newer tobacco products, including e-cigarettes and vaping devices, can also cause harm through secondhand aerosol. E-cigarette aerosol can contain substances that harm the body, such as cancer-causing chemicals and tiny particles that reach deep into the lungs.

If a parent smokes around her newborn, the baby has a greater risk of dying from sudden infant death syndrome (SIDS). In addition, nicotine and dangerous chemicals from cigarettes are in the breast milk of nursing mothers, who thus expose their babies. When children are exposed to tobacco smoke, they might develop life-threatening illnesses later in life, including lung cancer and heart disease.

One other important point: when you smoke in your home, you create a risk of fires and burns to your child and others. Children can suffer burns if they find and play with a lit cigarette or with matches or a lighter. According to a 2006 Surgeon General's report, there is no risk-free level of tobacco exposure. One study showed that when just one cigarette was smoked in a bedroom with a closed door, two hours were needed for particulates in the air to return to a threshold lower than harmful levels; even after that time, thirdhand smoke is still a risk.

As your child grows, keep in mind that you are a role model. If your child sees you smoking or using an electronic cigarette or vape product, she may want to try it as well, and you could be laying the foundation for a lifetime of tobacco addiction for your child.

Prevention

To reduce your child's exposure to environmental tobacco smoke, here are some additional steps you can take:

■ If you or other family members smoke or use electronic cigarettes, stop! If you've been unable to stop, talk to your doctor. There are a number of tobacco dependence treatment medications available that can help you to feel comfortable when not smoking. Contact 1-800-QUITNOW (1-800-784-8669) or smokefree.gov for free help to assist you in stopping smoking.

■ Don't allow anyone to smoke in your home or your car, particularly when children are present. It's important to know that smokers can also bring harmful chemicals into the house or car on their clothes after smoking. Your home and car should always remain smoke-free.

■ Store matches and lighters out of reach of children.

■ When selecting a babysitter or childcare provider, make it clear that no one is permitted to smoke around your child. In addition, nobody should leave your child unattended to go outside to smoke.

■ When you're in public places with your child, ask others not to smoke around you and your child.

Eyes

YOUR CHILD RELIES on the visual information he gathers to help him develop throughout infancy and childhood. If he has difficulty seeing properly, he may have problems in learning and relating to the world around him. For this reason it is important to detect eye deficiencies as early as possible. Many vision problems can be corrected if treated early but become much more difficult to care for later on.

Your infant should have his first eye examination at your first visit with your pediatrician. Routine vision checks then should be part of every visit to the pediatrician's office. If your family has a history of serious eye diseases or abnormalities, your pediatrician may refer your baby to an ophthalmologist (an eye specialist with a medical degree) for an early examination and follow-up visits if necessary.

If a child is born prematurely, he will be checked for a vision-threatening condition called retinopathy of prematurity (ROP), especially if he required oxygen over a prolonged period of time during his early days after birth. The risk is greater in the premature infant with a birth weight of less than 3.3 pounds (1,500 g). This condition may not be prevented even with ideal neonatal care, but in many cases, if detected early, it can be treated successfully. All neonatologists are aware of potential problems resulting from ROP and will let parents know about the necessity for evaluation by an ophthalmologist. Parents also should be told that all premature children are at greater risk for developing astig-

The Eye

matism, nearsightedness, and strabismus (these eye conditions are described later in this section) and that they therefore should be screened regularly throughout childhood.

How much does a newborn baby see? Even during the early weeks after birth, an infant can see light and shapes and can detect movement. Distance vision remains quite blurry, with the optimal viewing length being 8 to 12 inches (20.3 to 30.4 cm), which is roughly the distance from his eyes to yours as you are nursing or feeding your baby.

Until your baby learns to use both eyes together, his eyes may "wander," or move randomly. This random movement should be decreasing by two to three months of age. Around three months old, your baby should be able to focus on faces and close objects and follow a moving object with his eyes. By four months of age, he should be using his vision to detect various objects close to him, which he

probably will reach for and grasp. By six months old he should be able to visually identify and distinguish between objects.

Between one and two years of age, your child's ability to see will develop rapidly, and by ages three to five, the child with normal vision will reach typical adult visual acuity levels. By the time your child is ten, his visual system will be fully mature. At this point, many early-onset eye and vision problems may no longer be able to be reversed or corrected. This is why early detection and treatment of eye problems in children is so important and why your pediatrician will examine your baby's eyes at every routine physical examination.

Vision Screening Recommendations

Vision screening is a very important factor in identifying vision-threatening conditions. Regular eye checks during pediatric visits are done to determine if your baby's eyes are developing normally. The American Academy of Pediatrics recommends that children be screened at each well-child visit.

1. *In the newborn nursery.* Pediatricians should examine all infants prior to their discharge from the nursery to check for infections (page 739) and ocular defects, cataracts (page 739), and congenital glaucoma. If a problem is suspected, a pediatric ophthalmologist should see the newborn. All children with multiple medical problems or with a history of prematurity

should be examined by an ophthalmologist.

2. *By the age of six months.* Pediatricians should screen infants at the time of their well-baby visits to check for ocular alignment (eyes working together) and the presence of any eye disease. From six months on, photo screening may be electively performed for earlier detection of amblyopia or its risk factors.

3. *At the age of three to five years.* Vision screening by a pediatrician should be done annually during these ages. The visual acuity is checked and the eyes are examined for any other abnormality that may cause a problem with the child's educational development. Any abnormality requires referral to an ophthalmologist.

4. *At six years and older.* Pediatricians should screen children annually until the age of six, and every other year thereafter. These tests measure visual acuity and evaluate other ocular functions.

By three to four years of age, most children can follow directions and describe what they see, so visual acuity testing is reliable. Your pediatrician may use eye charts with shapes rather than letters to estimate your preschoolage child's visual acuity. By age three, visual acuity should have reached the 20/50 level in each eye, and any child with less than 20/50 vision should be referred to an ophthalmologist to determine the cause of the visual deficiency. At age four, visual acuity should be 20/40 to pass a vision screening. From age six years onward, normal visual acuity results in each eye of 20/30 or better are expected.

Your pediatrician may use a newer method for screening vision, especially in younger children, called photoscreening, in which a specially designed camera is used to help detect potential abnormalities with your child's vision. These devices are becoming an increasingly accepted method for screening infants and children, especially for those who are either too young or otherwise unable to have their vision reliably tested with a symbol or letter eye chart.

When to Call the Pediatrician

As noted above, vision screening is a very important factor in identifying vision-threatening conditions. These routine eye checks can detect hidden eye problems, but occasionally you may notice obvious signs that your child is having trouble seeing or that his eyes are not normal. Notify the pediatrician if your child shows any of the following warning signs.

■ A white appearance of the pupil (a condition called leukocoria) in one or both eyes

■ Persistent (lasting more than twenty-four hours) redness, swelling, crusting, or discharge in his eyes or eyelids

■ Excessive tearing

- Sensitivity to light, especially a change in the child's light sensitivity

- Eyes that look crooked or crossed, or that don't move together

- Head consistently held in an abnormal or tilted position

- Frequent squinting

- Drooping of one or both eyelids

- Pupils of unequal size

- Continuous eye-rubbing

- Eyes that "bounce" or "dance"

- Inability to see objects unless he holds them close

- Eye injury (see page 740)

- Cloudy cornea

You also should take your child to the pediatrician if he complains of any of the following:

- Seeing double

- Frequent headaches

- Persistent eye pain or mild headaches after doing close-up eye work (reading, watching television)

- Blurred vision

- Itching, scratching, or burning eyes

- Difficulty with color vision

Depending on the symptoms your child displays, your pediatrician probably will check for vision difficulties and/or some of the other problems discussed in the remainder of this chapter.

Amblyopia

Amblyopia, or lazy eye, is a fairly common eye problem (affecting about two out of a hundred children) that develops when a child has one eye that doesn't see well and she uses the other eye almost exclusively. In general, this problem must be detected as early as possible in order to treat and restore normal vision in the affected eye. If this situation persists for too long (past seven to ten years of age), vision is often lost permanently in the unused eye.

Once an ophthalmologist diagnoses the problems in the weaker eye, your child may need to wear a patch over the "good" eye for periods of time. This forces her to use and strengthen the eye that has become "lazy." Patching therapy will be continued for as long as necessary to bring the weaker eye up to its full potential and maintain it there. This could take weeks, months, or even a few years. As an alternative to the patch, the ophthalmologist might prescribe eye drops to blur the vision in the good eye, thereby stimulating your child to use the amblyopic eye.

Cataracts

Although we usually think of cataracts as affecting elderly people, they also may be found in infants and young children, and are sometimes present at birth. A cataract is a clouding of the lens (the transparent tissue inside the eye that helps bring light rays into focus on the retina). While rare, congenital cataracts are nonetheless a leading cause of visual loss and blindness in children.

Cataracts in children need to be detected and treated early so their vision can develop more appropriately. A cataract usually shows up as a white discoloration in the center of the child's pupil. If a baby is born with a cataract that blocks most of the light entering the eye, the affected lens has to be removed surgically to permit the baby's vision to develop. Most pediatric ophthalmologists recommend that this procedure be performed during the first month after birth. After the clouded lens is removed, the baby must be fitted with a special contact lens or with an eyeglass correction. At the age of about two years, the placement of a lens implant within the eye is recommended. In addition, visual rehabilitation of the affected eye will almost always involve use of a patch on the opposite eye until the child's eyes are fully mature (at about age ten years).

Occasionally a child will be born with a small pinpoint cataract that will not initially impede visual development. These tiny cataracts often do not require treatment; however, they need to be monitored carefully to ensure that they do not become large enough to interfere with normal vision development.

In many cases, the cause of cataracts in infants cannot be determined. Cataracts may be attributed to a tendency inherited from parents; they may result from trauma to the eye; or they may occur as a result of viral infections such as German measles and chickenpox or an infection from other microorganisms, such as those that cause toxoplasmosis and Zika. To protect the unborn child from cataracts and from other serious disorders, pregnant women should take care to avoid unnecessary exposure to infectious diseases. In addition, as a precaution against toxoplasmosis (a disease caused by parasites), pregnant women should avoid handling cat litter or eating raw meat, both of which may contain the organism that causes this disease.

Eye Infections

If the white of your child's eye and the inside of his lower lid become red, he probably has a condition called conjunctivitis. Also known as pinkeye, this inflammation, which can be painful and itchy, usually signals an infection, but may be due to other causes, such as irritation from smoke or fumes, an allergic reaction, or (rarely) a more serious condition. It's often accompanied by tearing and discharge, which is the body's way of trying to heal or remedy the situation.

If your child has a red eye, he needs to see the pediatrician as soon as possible. Eye infections typically last seven to ten days. The doctor will make the diagnosis and prescribe necessary medication if it is indicated. Never put previously opened medication or someone else's eye medication into your child's eye. It could cause serious damage.

In a newborn baby, serious eye infections may result from exposure to bacteria or viruses during pregnancy or during passage through the birth canal—which is why all infants are treated with antibiotic eye ointment or drops in the delivery room. Such infections must be treated early to prevent serious complications. Eye infections that occur after the newborn period may be unsightly, because of the redness of the eye and the yellow discharge that usually accompany them, and they may make your child uncomfortable, but they are rarely serious. If your pediatrician feels the problem is caused by bacteria, antibiotic eye drops are the usual treatment. Viral causes of conjunctivitis do not respond to antibiotics, but antibiotic eye drops may still be used if a bacterial infection is suspected.

Eye infections can be very contagious. Except to administer drops or ointment, you should avoid direct contact with your child's eyes or drainage from them until the medication has been used for several days and there is evidence of clearing of the redness. Carefully wash your hands before and after touching the area around the infected eye. If your child is in a childcare or nursery school program, you should keep him home until the pinkeye is no longer contagious, usually twenty-four hours after starting drops and/or discharge and redness have disappeared. Your pediatrician will tell you when you can safely send him back to childcare or nursery school.

Eye Injuries

When dust or other small particles get in your child's eyes, the cleansing action of tears usually will wash them out. If that fails to occur, or if a serious accident affecting the eye takes place, call your pediatrician or take your child to the nearest emergency room after heeding the following emergency guidelines.

BLACK EYE

To reduce swelling, apply a cold pack wrapped in a towel to the area for ten to twenty minutes. Then consult the doctor to make sure there is no internal damage to the eye or the bones surrounding the eye.

CHEMICALS IN THE EYE

Flush the eye extensively with water, making sure you get the water into the eye itself. Then take the child to the emergency department. (See also pages 713–15 in Chapter 23.)

CUT EYELID

Minor cuts usually heal quickly and easily, but a deep cut requires emer-

Preventing Eye Injuries

Nine out of ten eye injuries are preventable, and almost half occur around the home. To minimize the risk of such accidents in your family, follow these safety guidelines.

- Keep all chemicals out of reach and separate from medications. That includes detergents, ammonia, spray cans, superglue, and all other cleaning fluids.

- Choose your child's toys carefully. Watch out for sharp or pointed parts, especially if your child is too young to understand their danger.

- Keep your child away from darts and pellet and BB guns.

- Teach your preschooler how to handle scissors and pencils properly. If she's too young to learn, don't allow her to use them.

- Keep your child away from power lawnmowers and trimmers, which can hurl stones or other objects.

- Don't let your child near you when you're lighting fires or using tools. If you want her to watch you hammer nails, make her wear protective goggles. Safety glasses should also be worn for your safety and to set a good example for your child.

- If your child begins participating in youth sports, have her wear eye protection appropriate for her sport. Baseball is the leading cause of sports-related eye injuries in children, with many such injuries resulting from being struck by a pitched ball. Eye protection (made of polycarbonate) should be seriously considered for use as part of her batting helmet. Protective sports eye equipment (again using polycarbonate lenses) also should be worn during youth sports such as soccer or basketball, as well as other recreational sports such as skiing. Prescription sports goggles are also available and are a good way to protect the eye while providing vision help.

- Tell your child not to look directly into the sun, even with sunglasses. Doing so can cause severe and permanent eye damage. Never allow a child to look directly at an eclipse of the sun or at a laser pointer.

- Never allow your child near fireworks of any kind. The American Academy of Pediatrics encourages children and their families to enjoy fireworks at public fireworks displays rather than purchasing fireworks for home use. In fact, the Academy would support a ban on public sales of all fireworks.

gency medical attention and probably will need stitches. (See *Cuts and Scrapes*, page 701.) Cuts on the border of the eyelids by the eyelashes, or near the tear duct openings, can be of special concern. If the cut is located in these areas, call your pediatrician right away for advice on how to handle the situation.

LARGE PARTICLE IN THE EYE

If there's a particle in the eye that won't come out with tears or by flushing with water, or if your child is still complaining of pain after an hour, call your pediatrician. The doctor will remove the object or, if necessary, refer you to an ophthalmologist. Sometimes such particles cause scratches on the cornea (corneal abrasions), which are quite painful but heal rapidly with proper treatment. Corneal injuries also can be caused by blows or other injuries to the eye.

Eyelid Problems

Droopy eyelid (ptosis) may appear as a weak or heavy upper lid; if it is very slight, it may be noticed only because the affected eye appears somewhat smaller than the other eye. Ptosis usually involves only one eyelid, but both may be affected. Your baby may be born with ptosis, or it may develop later. Ptosis may be partial, causing your baby's eyes to appear slightly asymmetrical, or total, causing the affected lid to cover the eye completely. If the ptotic eyelid covers the entire pupillary opening of your child's eye,

or if the weight of the lid causes the cornea to assume an irregular shape (astigmatism), it will threaten normal vision development and must be corrected as early as possible. If vision is not threatened, surgical intervention, if necessary, is usually delayed until the child is four or five years of age or older, when the eyelid and surrounding tissue are more fully developed and a better cosmetic result can be obtained.

Most *birthmarks and growths* involving the eyelids of the newborn or young child are benign; however, because they may increase in size during the first year, they sometimes cause parents to become concerned. Most of these birthmarks and growths are not serious and will not affect your child's vision. However, any irregularity should be brought to the attention of your child's pediatrician so that it can be evaluated and monitored.

Some children will develop lumps and bumps on their lids that can impair development of good eyesight. In particular, a blood vessel tumor called a capillary or strawberry hemangioma can start out as a small swelling and rapidly enlarge. It may enlarge over the first year after birth, and then start to shrink in size without any treatment over the next few years. If it becomes large enough, it can interfere with your baby's development of good vision in the affected eye and will need to be treated. Because of their potential to cause vision problems, any child who starts to show any rapidly enlarging lumps or bumps around either eye should be evaluated by your pediatrician and perhaps an ophthalmologist as well.

A child might also be born with a flat, purple-colored lesion on her face called a port wine stain, because of its resemblance to a dark red wine. If this birthmark involves the eye, especially the upper lid, the child may be at risk for development of glaucoma (a condition where pressure increases inside the eyeball) or amblyopia (weak vision). Any child born with this birthmark needs to be examined by an ophthalmologist shortly after birth.

Small dark moles, called *nevi*, on the eyelids or on the white part of the eye itself rarely cause any problems or need to be removed. Once they have been evaluated by your pediatrician, these marks should cause concern only if they change in size, shape, or color.

Small, firm, flesh-colored bulges underneath your child's eyebrows are usually *dermoid cysts*. These cysts are noncancerous tumors that usually are present from birth. Because they tend to increase in size during early childhood, their removal is preferred in most cases before they rupture under the skin and cause inflammation.

Two other eyelid problems—*chalazia* and *hordeola (sties)*—are common but not serious. A chalazion is a cyst resulting from a blockage of an oil gland. A hordeolum, or sty, is a bacterial infection of the cells surrounding the sweat glands or hair follicles on the edge of the lid. Call your pediatrician regarding treatment of these conditions. He probably will tell you to apply warm compresses directly to the eyelid for twenty or thirty minutes three or four times a day until the chalazion or sty clears. The doctor may want to examine your child before prescribing additional treatment, such as an antibiotic ointment or drops.

Once your child has had a sty or chalazion, she may be more likely to get them again. When they occur repeatedly, it's sometimes necessary to perform lid scrubs to reduce the bacterial colonization of the eyelids and open the glands and pores in the eyelids.

Impetigo is a very contagious bacterial infection that may occur on the eyelid. Your pediatrician will advise you on how to remove the crust from the lid and then prescribe an antibiotic eye ointment and oral antibiotics. (See *Impetigo*, page 857.)

Glaucoma

Glaucoma is a serious eye disorder caused by increased pressure within the eye. It may be due to either overproduction or inadequate drainage of the fluid within the eye. If this increased pressure persists too long, it can damage the optic nerve, resulting in permanent loss of vision.

Although a child can be born with glaucoma, this is quite rare. More often it develops later in life. The earlier it is detected and treated, the better the chance of preventing permanent loss of vision. Warning signs of glaucoma in infants include:

■ Excessive tearing associated with extreme sensitivity to light (the child will turn her head into the mattress or blankets to avoid light)

■ Hazy or overly prominent appearance of either eye

■ Increased irritability (typically due to persistent eye pain and redness)

Call your pediatrician promptly if you are concerned about any of these signs.

Usually glaucoma must be treated surgically to create an alternative route for fluid to leave the eye. Any child who has this disease must be watched very carefully throughout her life so that the pressure is kept under control and the optic nerve and cornea stay as healthy as possible.

Strabismus

Strabismus is a misalignment of the eyes caused by an imbalance in the muscles controlling the eye. This condition makes it impossible for the eyes to focus on the same point at the same time. Strabismus occurs in about four out of a hundred children. It may be present at birth (infantile strabismus), or it may develop later in childhood (acquired strabismus). Strabismus can develop if your child has another visual impairment, sustains an eye injury, or develops cataracts. Always report the sudden onset of strabismus to your pediatrician immediately. Although very rare, it may indicate the development of a tumor or other serious nervous system problem. In all cases, it is important to diagnose and treat strabismus as early in your child's life as possible. If a turned eye is not treated early, the child may never develop the ability to use both eyes together (binocular vision), and if both eyes are not used together, it is common for one to become "lazy," or amblyopic (see page 738). Amblyopia often coexists with strabismus and must be treated separately with patching or the use of eye drops in the opposite eye.

Left eye turning inward

It is important to note that a newborn baby's eyes commonly and normally wander. However, within a few weeks, he learns to move his eyes together, and this strabismus should disappear within a few months. However, if this intermittent wandering continues, or if your baby's eyes don't turn in the same direction (if one turns in, out, up, or down), he needs to be evaluated by your pediatrician, and often a pediatric ophthalmologist as well.

If your child is born with strabismus and it does not resolve on its own in a few months, it's important for his eyes to be realigned as soon as possible so he can focus them together on a single object. Eye exercises alone cannot accomplish this, so the treatment usually involves eyeglasses or surgery. If your child needs an operation, this surgery is frequently done between six and eighteen months of age. The operation is usually safe and effective, although it's not uncommon for a child to need more than one procedure. Even after surgery, your child still may need glasses.

Some children look as if they have strabismus because of the way their faces are structured, but in fact their eyes may be well aligned. These children often have a flat nasal bridge and broad skin folds alongside the nose, termed *epicanthus*, which can distort the appearance of the eyes, making these youngsters appear cross-eyed when they really aren't. This condition is called pseudostrabismus. The child's vision is not affected, and, in most cases, as the child grows and the nasal bridge becomes more prominent, the child loses the appearance of crossed eyes.

Because of the importance of early diagnosis and treatment of a true misalignment (or true strabismus), if you have any suspicion that your baby's eyes may not be perfectly aligned and working together, you should bring it to the attention of your pediatrician, who can best determine whether your baby has an actual problem.

Tear (or Lacrimal) Production Problems

Tears play an important role in maintaining good eyesight by keeping the eyes wet and free of particles, dust, and other substances that might cause injury or interfere with normal vision. The lacrimal system maintains the continuous production and circulation of tears, and depends on regular blinking to propel tears from the lacrimal gland across the surface of the eye, finally draining through the tear ducts and into the nose.

This lacrimal system develops gradually over the first three or four years. Thus, while a newborn will produce enough tears to coat the surface of the eyes, it may be several months after birth before he cries real tears.

Blocked tear ducts, which are very common among newborns and young babies, can cause the appearance of excessive tearing in one or both eyes, because the tears run down the cheek instead of draining through the duct and into the nose. In newborns, blocked tear ducts usually occur when an internal membrane covering them fails to disappear around birth. Your pediatrician will demonstrate how to massage the tear duct. She'll also show you how to clean the eye with moist compresses to remove all secretions and crusting. Until the tear duct finally opens, the sticky mucous discharge may not go away. Since this is not typically a true infection or pinkeye, antibiotics are usually not necessary or helpful.

Sometimes a persistent membrane (or even a small cyst) can cause a blocked tear duct that does not resolve on its own or with massaging. When this occurs and the methods described above are unsuccessful, the ophthalmologist may decide to probe open the blocked tear duct surgically. Rarely, this procedure must be repeated more than once.

Vision Difficulties Requiring Corrective Lenses

ASTIGMATISM
Astigmatism is an uneven curvature of the surface of the cornea and/or lens. If your child has an astigmatism, vision both near and far may be blurred. Astigmatism can be corrected with either glasses or contact lenses, and, like farsightedness, may cause amblyopia if one eye is affected more than the other.

FARSIGHTEDNESS
This is a condition in which the eyeball is shorter than ideal to allow for best focusing, causing difficulty focusing on near objects. Most infants are actually born farsighted but can compensate for small amounts of it on their own. As they grow, their eyeballs get longer and the farsightedness diminishes. Glasses or contact lenses rarely are needed unless the condition is excessive. If your child has eye discomfort or frequent mild headaches related to prolonged reading, she may be suffering from a severe degree of farsightedness and should be examined by your pediatrician or pediatric ophthalmologist. Excessive farsightedness also may lead to crossed eyes (see *Strabismus*, page 744) and amblyopia (see page 738), both of which require treatment in addition to glasses.

NEARSIGHTEDNESS
The inability to see distant objects clearly is the most common visual problem in young children. This inherited trait occasionally is found in newborns, especially premature infants, but it more often develops after six to nine years of age.

Contrary to popular belief, reading too much, reading in dim light, or poor nutrition cannot cause or affect nearsightedness. That said, recent research shows that increasing time spent outdoors can reduce the risk of developing myopia and/or slow its progression. Usually nearsightedness is the result of an eyeball that is longer in shape, causing the image to be focused improperly. Less frequently, it is due to a change in the shape of the cornea or lens.

The treatment for nearsightedness is corrective lenses—either eyeglasses or contact lenses. Keep in mind that when your child grows, so do his eyes, so he may need new lenses as often as every six to twelve months. Nearsightedness usually changes rapidly for several years and then stabilizes during or after adolescence.

~ 26 ~

Family Issues

Adoption

IF YOU ARE about to adopt or have just adopted a child, you are likely experiencing a mix of emotions. Along with excitement and delight, you also may feel some anxiety and apprehension. These are emotions common to all parents, regardless of whether a child joins their family by birth or by adoption. Choosing an understanding, supportive, and collaborative pediatrician will be helpful as you begin your new job as a parent. Even before a child joins your family, a pediatrician can discuss your feelings about impending parenthood. If you are adopting a child internationally or domestically, a pediatrician will also be able to address any medical issues that may arise.

Once your child is home with you, schedule a visit to a pediatrician as soon as possible. Similar to an initial newborn exam, this initial postadoptive visit can provide an opportunity to ask any questions you have about your child's physical and mental health and development. Schedule future exams as required by the child's age and medical needs. Many families find that they benefit from additional visits with their pediatrician during the first year or so to help address concerns that may arise as parents and child start to develop a relationship.

In addition to the typical challenges of parenting, adoptive parents also face several issues and questions that nonadoptive parents do not.

HOW AND WHEN SHOULD I TELL MY CHILD SHE IS ADOPTED?

Your child should learn the truth about her birth family and her adoptive family as early as she is able to understand, which probably will be between ages two and four. It is important to adjust the information to her maturity level, so that she can make sense of it. For example: "Your birth parents loved you very much, but they knew they could not take care of you. So they looked for someone who also loved little children and wanted to have a bigger family." As she gets older and asks more specific questions, give her honest answers, but do not press information on her if she seems uncomfortable, fearful, or disinterested about it. Children should come to know about and understand adoption gradually, as they mature, just as they come to understand many other complicated ideas.

ARE THERE SPECIAL CONCERNS TO WATCH FOR?

Adopted children have the same problems that other children of the same age and background have. Children with a history of living in an orphanage or in foster care have often experienced significant adversity or trauma, and may benefit from specific parenting strategies to address those. They may also benefit from counseling at the time of placement, or at different times in their lives.

SHOULD I TELL OTHERS THAT MY CHILD IS ADOPTED?

If you are asked, answer the question honestly, with as much detail as seems appropriate for the situation. Recognize that the most important audience for your answer is your child. Many professionals believe that your child's adoption story is hers to own and share as she desires as she gets older. You may wish to share general information with friends and family, but hold sensitive details privately until your child is old enough to understand them and decide for herself how and with whom she would like them to be shared.

WHAT IF SHE WANTS TO FIND HER BIRTH PARENTS?

Many adoptions today include some degree of openness, or ongoing identified contact between birth parent, adoptee, and adoptive parents, and there is a lot of evidence that this arrangement is helpful to children in many ways. If your adoption is not open, though, it is still very natural for children to wonder about birth parents, and this in no way diminishes the love that your child has for you. Talking with your child about his birth parents helps him to know that you understand this, and that he can share those thoughts and feelings with you. Circumstances will vary, but let your child know that when he is old enough, you will help him to search for them if he wants to. Your adoption agency and adoption search specialists can help.

Your pediatrician may be able to help you with more detailed answers to these and other questions that arise in adoptive families.

WHERE WE STAND

INCREASING NUMBERS OF children have been adopted by gay or lesbian individuals or couples in recent years. In some states this has stimulated political debate and public policy change. A growing body of scientific literature reveals that children who grow up with one or two gay or lesbian parents will develop emotionally, cognitively, socially, and sexually just as well as children whose parents are heterosexual. Parents' sexual orientation is much less important than having loving and nurturing parents.

The American Academy of Pediatrics recognizes the diversity of families. We believe that children who are born to, or adopted by, one member of a gay or lesbian couple deserve the security of two legally recognized parents. Therefore, we support statutory and legal means to enable children to be adopted by the second parent or coparent in families headed by gay and lesbian couples.

Child Abuse and Neglect

Child abuse, also known as child maltreatment (a term that encompasses both abuse and neglect) is common. Child maltreatment is defined as "behavior toward a child that is outside the norms of conduct and entails a substantial risk of causing physical or emotional harm." The types of child maltreatment generally recognized are physical abuse, sexual abuse, and neglect including emotional maltreatment. It is important to understand and reduce the risks of abuse for your child and familiarize yourself with the signs of abuse. Recent statistics show that there are about four million reports of suspected child maltreatment, involving almost seven million children, per year. The highest rate of child abuse is in babies less than one year of age, and 25 percent of victims are less than three. There is considerable overlap among children who are abused, with many suffering a combination of physical abuse, sexual abuse, and/or neglect. The majority of cases reported to child protection agencies involve neglect, followed by physical and sexual abuse.

According to Prevent Child Abuse, "Neglect occurs when children's basic needs are not adequately met, resulting in actual or potential harm. Child neglect can harm children's physical and mental health as well as their social and cognitive development in many different ways." Child neglect can include physical neglect (failing to provide food, clothing, shelter, or other physical necessities), emotional neglect (failing to provide love, comfort, or affection), medical neglect (failing to provide needed medical care), educational neglect (failing to give access to education), or supervisory neglect (failure to appropriately supervise). Psychological or emotional abuse results from all of the above but also can be associated with verbal abuse, which can harm a child's self-worth or emotional well-being.

Physical abuse occurs when a child's body is injured as a result of hitting, kicking, shaking, burning, or other show of force. One study suggests that about one in twenty children has been physically abused in their lifetime. Sexual abuse is any sexual activity that a child cannot comprehend or give consent to. It includes acts such as fondling, oral-genital contact, genital and anal intercourse, exhibitionism, voyeurism, and exposure to pornography. Studies have suggested that up to one in five girls and one in twenty boys have been sexually abused before the age of eighteen. More than 90 percent of child sexual abuse victims know their abuser, and most of the abuse occurs within the family, which may make it difficult for a child to disclose the abuse. Teach your child that it is not OK for adults to touch his body if he does not want them to or if it makes him feel uncomfortable, and teach him to always tell a trusted grown-up if something like that happens.

Risk factors for child maltreatment include parental depression or other mental health issues, a parental history of childhood abuse or neglect, parental substance abuse, and domestic violence. Child neglect and other forms of maltreatment are also more common in families living in poverty, among teenage parents, and among those who abuse drugs or alcohol.

Signs and Symptoms

It is not always easy to recognize when a child has been abused. Children who have been maltreated are often afraid to tell anyone, fearing they will be blamed or that no one will believe them. Sometimes they remain quiet because the person who abused them is someone they love very much, or because of fear, or both. Parents also tend to overlook signs and symptoms of abuse, because it is hard to believe it could happen or they are fearful of repercussions. A child who has been abused needs special support and treatment as early as possible. The longer children continue to be abused or are left to deal with the situation on their own, the harder it is for them to be able to heal and develop optimally physically and mentally.

Parents should always be alert to any unexplainable changes in the child's body or behavior. While injuries are often specific for an incident of physical abuse, behavioral change tends to reflect the anxiety that results from a variety of acute and chronic stressful situations including child abuse and neglect. There are no behaviors that specifically relate to a particular type of child abuse or neglect. Here is a short list of physical signs and behavioral changes that may indicate a child has experienced abuse or neglect:

Physical Signs

■ Non-mobile infant with any injury

■ Bruises to the torso, ears, or neck in a child less than four years of age

■ Any injury (bruise, burn, fracture, or abdominal, chest, or head injury) that is not consistent with the way the injury is said to have happened, that cannot be adequately explained, or that is inconsistent with the child's developmental capabilities

■ The child discloses abuse or neglect

■ Failure to gain weight (especially in infants) or sudden dramatic weight gain

■ Genital pain, bleeding, or discharge

■ A sexually transmitted disease

BEHAVIORAL AND MENTAL HEALTH CHANGES THAT RAISE CONCERN ABOUT POSSIBLE ABUSE OR NEGLECT

It is important to remember that the following changes are seen in many children as a result of many different kinds of stressful situations and are not specific to child abuse and neglect. The reason for the appearance of these behaviors should always be investigated.

■ Fearful behavior (nightmares, depression, unusual fears)

■ Unexplained abdominal pain, sudden onset of bed-wetting, or regression in toileting (especially if the child has already been toilet trained)

■ Attempts to run away

■ Extreme sexual behavior that seems developmentally inappropriate for the child's age

■ Sudden change in self-confidence

■ Headaches or stomachaches with no medical cause

■ School failure

■ Extremely passive or aggressive behavior

■ Desperately affectionate behavior or social withdrawal

■ Big appetite and stealing food

LONG-TERM CONSEQUENCES

In most cases, children who are abused or neglected suffer from greater long-term mental health issues than physical health damage. Emotional and psychological abuse, physical abuse, and neglect deny the child the tools needed to cope with stress and the opportunity to learn the skills needed to become resilient, strong, and successful. A child who is maltreated or neglected may have a wide range of reactions and may even become depressed or develop withdrawn, suicidal, or violent behavior. As he gets older, he may display learning difficulties, use drugs or alcohol, try to run away, refuse discipline, or abuse others. As an adult, he may develop marital and sexual difficulties, criminal behaviors, depression, or suicidal behavior. Identifying a child victim as early as possible is the first step to helping him recover. Recognizing the important influence of early trauma on future development is crucial to assisting the child.

Not all children who are abused have severe reactions. Usually the younger the child, the longer the abuse continues, and the closer the child's relationship with the abuser, the more serious the mental health effects will be. A close relationship with a very supportive adult can increase resiliency, reducing some of the impact.

Getting Help

If you suspect your child has been abused, get help immediately through your pediatrician or a local child protection agency. Physicians are *legally obligated* to report all suspected cases of abuse or neglect to state authorities. Your pediatrician will also examine your child to detect and treat any medical injuries or conditions, recommend a therapist, and provide necessary information to investigators. The doctor also may testify in court if necessary to obtain legal protection for the child or criminal prosecution of the person suspected of perpetrating the abuse or neglect.

If he has been abused, your child will benefit from services including mental health professionals, speech and other therapists, and/or a developmental or behavioral pediatrician depending on the child and situation. You and other members of the family may be advised to seek counseling so that you'll be able to provide the support and comfort your child needs. If someone in your family is responsible for the abuse, a mental health professional may be able to help that person as well.

If your child has been abused, you may be the only person who can help him. Many times this is a complicated process due to multiple family dynamics, such as emotional and financial support of the abuser. Discuss the situation with a professional, such as your pediatrician, teacher, or religious leader, who can then assist and support you through this process. Failure to report can also make it appear you are failing to protect your child and decreases your child's chance for optimal physical and mental health. In any case of abuse or neglect, the child's safety is of primary concern. He needs to be in a safe environment free of the potential for continuing abuse and neglect.

Preventing Abuse and Neglect

The major reasons for physical and psychological maltreatment of children within the family are parental feelings of isolation, stress, and frustration. Parents need support and as much information as possible in order to raise their children responsibly. They need to be taught how to cope with their own feelings of frustration and anger without venting them on children. They also need the companionship of other adults who will listen and help during times of crisis. Support groups through local community organizations often are helpful first steps to diminish some of the isolation or frustration parents may be feeling. Parents who were themselves abused as children are in particular need of support. Confronting, addressing, and healing parental mental and emotional health takes uncommon courage and insight, but this is often the best way to reduce the chances that past abuse is not passed on to the next generation of children.

Personal supervision of and involvement in your child's activities are the best ways to prevent physical and sexual abuse outside the home. Any school or childcare program you select for your child should allow unrestricted and unannounced parental visits without prearrangement. Parents should be allowed to help in the classroom on a volunteer basis and be informed about the selection of or changes in staff members. Parents should pay careful attention to their child's reports about and reactions to his experiences at childcare and school. Always investigate if your child tells you he's been maltreated or if he undergoes a sudden unexplained change in behavior.

Although you don't want to frighten your child, you can teach him some basic rules of safety in a non-threatening manner. Teach him to keep his distance from strangers, not to wander away from you in unfamiliar territory, to say "no" when someone asks him to do something against his will, and always to tell you if some-one hurts him or makes him feel bad, even if that person is someone he knows. Always remember that open, two-way communication with your child provides the best chance that you will know early if a problem occurs. Emphasize that he will not get in trouble if he tells you about abuse or other confusing events. Emphasize that you need to know this to be able to keep him safe and that he will be OK if he tells you. Instead of teaching him that he's surrounded by danger, teach him that he is strong, capable, and can count on you to keep him safe, as long as he can tell you about it.

Divorce

Every year over one million children in the United States are involved in a divorce. Even those children who lived with parental conflict and unhappiness for a long time may find the changes that follow divorce more difficult than anything they have experienced before. At the very least, the child must adjust to living apart from one parent or, if in shared custody, to dividing her life between two homes. Because of financial changes, she also may have to move to a smaller home and a different neighborhood. A parent who stayed at home before now may have to go to work. Even if the parent doesn't have to go to work, the stress and depression that often accompany divorce may make some parents less attentive to and loving with their children.

No one can predict specifically

how divorce will affect your child. Her response will depend on her own sensitivity, the quality of her relationships with each parent, and the parents' ability to work together to meet her emotional needs during this time. It also will depend to some extent on her age and on the resiliency or vulnerability that her previous life experiences have given her. In a very general way, you can anticipate how your child will react to divorce based on her age at the time it occurs:

Children under two often revert to more infantile behavior. They may become unusually clingy, dependent, or frustrated. They may refuse to go to sleep and may suddenly start waking up during the night. Under the age of three, they may show signs of sadness and fear of others. They may have angry outbursts and tantrums, lose interest in eating, and have problems with toilet training.

Children between three and five years may act more like infants. They may feel that they are responsible for their parents' breakup. At this age, children do not fully understand that their parents' lives are separate from their own. They believe that they are the center of their family's universe and therefore blame themselves when significant events happen in their lives. Children may become more aggressive and defiant toward one parent. The less contact the child has with the noncustodial parent, or the more tense the postdivorce relationship, the more serious these reactions are likely to be. In the process, the child's self-worth may be impacted negatively.

Your child's response to the divorce probably will be most intense during and immediately following the physical separation. As she grows older, she may continue to think about the past and struggle to understand why her parents separated. For years she may have some sense of loss, which might become especially painful during holidays and on special occasions like birthdays and family reunions.

Most children of divorce wish desperately for their parents to get back together. However, it is much more difficult for them if the parents repeatedly attempt to reconcile and then part again than if the initial separation is final. When the parents act indecisively, the child is likely to become suspicious, confused, and insecure.

In some cases, a child's behavior and self-esteem actually improve after the parents' divorce. Sometimes this is because the parents are relieved of the tension and sadness of an unhappy marriage and now can give the child more affection and attention. Sometimes it is because the divorce ends an emotionally or physically abusive situation. Often, however, even children who have been abused by a parent still yearn for that abusive parent's love and for the family to be restored.

In summary, some children have serious and lasting psychological aftereffects from a divorce, but many others do well once the initial impact has been experienced and coped with and the child and other family members have learned how to successfully adapt and support each other with their new life circumstances.

How Parents Can Help the Child

A child integrates and mirrors her parents' emotions. If her parents are angry, depressed, or violent during the separation process, a child is likely to absorb these disturbing feelings and may turn them against herself. If the parents argue about her, or if she hears her name during their disputes, she may believe even more strongly that she is to blame. Secrecy and silence probably won't make her feel much better, however, and actually may intensify the unhappiness and tension she feels around her. If you're divorcing, the best approach is to be honest about your feelings but make a special effort to be loving and reassuring with your child. She will have to accept that her parents no longer love each other—and you shouldn't try to pretend otherwise—but make sure she understands and feels that both parents love her just as much as ever and want to help her through this process.

When parents are sensitive to what their child is going through, the child has a greater likelihood of coping and rebounding from the uncertainty and anxiety that are often present due to the divorce. But each child is different. Children have their own way of reacting to the situations around them—some respond with resilience and a sense of optimism, while others tend to think negatively and disastrously about the present and the future. One of your tasks is to help your child deal with the divorce realistically and help her avoid any thoughts that these major life changes will negatively impact her life.

To help in the adjustment process, emphasize and reemphasize that even though your child may be spending time in two homes now, she will continue to be loved just as much as always by both parents. She will continue to be safe. In fact, explain that you and your spouse will each have more special time to devote to her. Also, point out that you and your spouse expect to be happier because of the divorce, and the household will be a more pleasant place.

In the weeks, months, and years after a divorce, keep the dialogue with your child open and appropriate for her age level. Repeatedly encourage her to talk about her feelings. Respond to her questions with clear and simple answers, and don't hesitate to bring up issues that she may have never raised on her own but are common among children of divorce. (She may be thinking, "Is it my fault that my parents are going to be apart?" or "If I'm a good girl, will my parents get together again?" or "Will my parents always love me?")

If your child is younger than two years, you can't get these messages across very well with words. You will have to convey them through your actions. When you are with your child, try to put your own issues and worries aside and concentrate on her needs. Keep the daily routine as consistent as possible, and do not expect her to make any other major changes (e.g., toilet training, moving from a crib to a bed, or, if avoidable, adjusting to a new care provider or home arrangement) during this transitional period. In the beginning, try to be understanding and patient if your child's behavior regresses, but if this regression continues even after the divorce is completed and your life has settled back into a regular routine, ask your pediatrician for advice.

If your child is older, she needs to feel that both of her parents care about her and that they are willing to put their differences aside when it comes to her welfare. This means that you both must maintain an active involvement in her life. In the past, many fathers gradually withdrew from their children following divorce. Today courts and psychologists are trying to correct this pattern, in part by making a distinction between physical and legal custody. In this way, one parent can be granted physical custody, so that the child can have a home base, while legal custody can be awarded jointly, so that both parents remain involved in decisions about the child's education, medical care, and other basic physical, mental, and social needs. The child can visit regularly with the parent who does not have physical custody.

It is also possible to have both joint physical custody and joint legal custody. This arrangement has the advantage of keeping both parents fully involved with the child. However, it also may have serious drawbacks. Especially if they are under ten, the children may feel split between two homes, two sets of friends, and two routines. Many parents who have joint physical custody find it difficult to manage all the day-to-day decisions about scheduling, birthday parties, lessons, and schoolwork. Unless both parents are fully committed to making this arrangement work, it can lead to more conflict, confusion, and stress for the child. Any custody arrangement should give a high priority to the child's mental health, as well as her emotional and developmental needs.

Whatever your custody arrangement, both of you, as your child's parents, will continue to play key roles in her life. Try to support each other in these roles. As much as possible, avoid criticizing each other in front of your child. There's no place for your child to witness anger and hostility between you and your spouse or choose sides in an argument; it can only confuse and upset her. Your child needs reassurance that it is still OK for her to love both of you. She needs you to help her feel that she's safe with either of you and that there is no need for secrets or guilt.

If you and her other parent cannot actively cooperate, at least be tolerant of each other's routines, rules, and plans, even if you have minor reservations. Under the circumstances, arguments over how much television your child watches or what foods she eats can cause her far more damage than will the TV or the snacks. If necessary, discuss your concerns when your child is not around. Your pediatrician can provide guidance about sleep,

Helping Your Child Move Forward

To ease your child through the divorce, here are some suggestions:

- Talk with your child on an ongoing basis, and make her feel safe despite her fears and worries.

- Be honest, but keep things simple ("Your daddy and I are having trouble getting along").

- Show patience with your child, who may ask questions like "Why is Daddy moving away?" "How often will I see Daddy?" "When is he moving back?" "Where am I going to live?"

- Make it clear that your child did not cause your marital problems.

- Do not blame your spouse or express any anger in front of your child.

- Reassure your child that despite the divorce, both you and your spouse love her and will not abandon her. Let her experience demonstrations of love from both parents.

- Keep your child on simple schedules and routines. Keep activities, meals, and bedtime at regular times to give her stability and comfort, and so that she knows what to expect each day.

food, and discipline to help inform these conversations. If a child hears you trying to undermine each other's authority, she may come to feel that she cannot trust either of you or that she can't talk about her feelings openly. An atmosphere of hostility may make it hard for her to feel secure and comfortable about her relationships with her parents and with others in her life.

As your child reaches age four or five, her life will broaden to include school and neighborhood activities, and she will develop much more complex feelings about her place in the world. You and your former spouse should discuss how she behaves and what she talks about when she is with each of you. Even though you are no longer in a personal relationship with each other, you still share responsibility for your child, and you need to work together to resolve any emotional or behavioral problems she may develop. Be especially alert for any signs of low self-esteem, unusual moodiness or depression, or excessive apologizing or self-criticism. These signs may indicate that she is blaming herself for the divorce. If this is the case and you cannot convince her that she is blameless, talk to your pediatrician. She may advise you to consult a child psychiatrist or psychologist or other mental health professional.

If you feel very depressed or disturbed after your divorce and cannot seem to regain control of your life, you will not be able to give your child the nurturing and support she needs and that you wish to provide. For everyone's sake, it is very important for you to consult with a professional for psychological counseling for yourself as soon as you realize you are having difficulty.

Although there are always difficult moments in any divorce, you and your spouse can help your child adjust by making an effort to keep the divorce as nonconfrontational as possible. Consider using a "collaborative law" approach or mediation, where couples reach a settlement outside of the court system. Although each partner often hires his or her own lawyer, both sides have the same goal—namely, to reach an agreement that is acceptable to everyone, with the intent to cooperate and avoid rivalry, for their own sake and the sake of their children. A growing number of divorce lawyers now specialize in this collaborative law; your attorney is an advocate on your behalf but is trained to minimize problems and reach a resolution that everyone finds acceptable.

If your divorce is full of tension and anger, you may worry that the battles will never end and that your child will not be able to experience good physical and mental health and well-being. Although it is true that some of the emotional effects of divorce may remain with your child permanently, she will have every chance to grow up healthy and happy if she receives the love, affection, and support she needs from her parents and other caregivers. With time, most children accept the changes that occur because of the divorce, and in many families, children become much closer to both parents.

(See also *Single-Parent Families*, page 766; *Stepfamilies*, page 769.)

Grief Reactions

Losing a parent is one of the most traumatic events that can happen to any child, and grief is the natural response. Your child may experience grief not only if a parent dies but also if one becomes chronically or seriously ill or if there is a divorce. (Even if he remains in touch with both parents following divorce, he may mourn the loss of the family as he's known it.) Children also may grieve for siblings, grandparents, a beloved caregiver, or a pet.

WHEN A CHILD LOSES A PARENT

For a young child, losing a parent is an overwhelming crisis that is impossible for the child to understand. Children under five developmentally cannot grasp the permanence of death. Because of this, the first stage of grief is often a period of protest and hope that the lost parent will return. Many children will try to use fantasy to make this happen, imagining the missing parent in familiar situations or places.

Once the child begins to realize that his parent is truly gone forever, despair sets in. Infants, with their limited communication skills, generally express their distress by crying, feeding poorly, and being difficult to console. Toddlers will cry and be easily excitable and uncooperative, and may regress to infantile behavior. Older children may become withdrawn. A preschooler might have a sad look on his face, or be less creative and less enthusiastic about play during this period. The more anguished or emotionally distant the other members of the family are, the more intense a young child's despair is likely to be.

Eventually he will emerge from this mood of despair and begin to shift his love and trust to others. This does not mean that he's forgotten the missing parent or that the hurt has gone away. Throughout his life there will be times when he will experience conscious and unconscious feelings of loss, especially on birthdays and holidays, during special occasions such as a graduation, and when he's ill. At these times the child may voice his sadness and ask about his missing parent.

If the deceased parent was the same sex as the child, these questions probably will come up frequently between ages four and seven, when he is struggling to understand his own gender identity. In the best of outcomes, these remembrances will be brief and positive and will not create serious distress. If they are prolonged or if they noticeably disturb the child, you should discuss them with the pediatrician.

WHEN A CHILD LOSES A SIBLING

Losing a sibling also is a devastating experience. Many children, even those old enough to understand how their sibling died, may feel that in some way they are to blame. These feelings may be intensified if parents, deep in their own feelings, become withdrawn or angry and unwittingly shut themselves off from the child.

The surviving sibling often watches helplessly as his parents go through the same agony of grief that he would experience if he'd lost them. First he will see the shock and emotional numbness, then denial, then anger that such a thing could possibly happen. Through it all, he is likely to hear guilt in his parents' words and voices. He may interpret this guilt to mean that they were devoting time or attention to him that should have been given to his lost sibling.

His parents may feel driven to talk about their lost child, how the death occurred, and what they could have done to prevent it. The surviving child may try to comfort his parents even though that is not an appropriate role for him and it is more appropriate for him to work on learning to cope effectively with what has happened. The realization that the surviving child cannot make his parents happy, no matter what he does, may seriously damage his own feelings of security and self-esteem. If parents unwittingly react by becoming restrained, short-tempered, and preoccupied with distractions outside the family, the surviving sibling may feel frightened and rejected by them.

In a household where one parent intensively feels the need to talk and the other avoids talking, the essential mutual support and understanding they each need is difficult to achieve. As a result, the relationship between the parents may suffer. The surviving child feels this stress as keenly as his grief for the sibling he's lost, and may assume that he's responsible for his parents' disputes as well as for his sibling's death. The entire family will benefit from professional counseling after a child dies. Your pediatrician can recommend a qualified family therapist, psychologist, or child psychiatrist to help you all cope with your grief and help your family learn to cope, heal, and rebuild healthy and supportive relationships and interactions.

HELPING YOUR GRIEVING CHILD

When you are grieving for your spouse or your child, it is easy to overlook your surviving child's needs. The following suggestions can help you provide the love, comfort, and trust your child needs during and after the grieving process.

1. Maintain your child's familiar day-to-day routine as much as possible. Ask the people he loves and trusts—family members, familiar care providers, or preschool teachers—to be there for him when you are unavailable.

2. Offer frequent, calm explanations, keeping in mind your child's level of understanding and possible feelings of guilt. Keep the explanations as simple as possible, but be truthful. Do not construct fairy tales that will leave him more confused or hopeful that the death can be reversed. If your child is older than three, reassure him that nothing he did or thought caused the death and that no one is angry with him. To help ensure that he understands, it may help to ask him to repeat what you've said.

3. Get help from loved ones. It is difficult to give your grieving child all the attention and support he needs when you are grief-stricken yourself. Close friends and family members may be able to give you some relief while at the same time providing a comforting sense of family and community when he may feel alone and lost. If you have lost a child, it is especially important for the family's sake that you and your spouse try to be mutually supportive during this time.

4. Be open to discussions about the loss over the ensuing weeks, months, and years. Even if your child appears to recover from grief faster than you do, his grieving process will go on below the surface for many years—possibly, in a quiet way, for a lifetime. He will need your continuing support and understanding as he tries to come to terms with his loss. As he grows older, he will ask more sophisticated questions about the circumstances and reasons for the death. As painful as it may be for you to recall these events, try to answer him honestly and directly. The more he understands what happened, the easier it will be for him to make his peace with it.

SHOULD YOUR PRESCHOOLER ATTEND THE FUNERAL?

Whether a young child attends a funeral for a loved one depends on the child's individual level of understanding, emotional maturity, and desire to participate in this ritual. If he seems very fearful and anxious, and cannot understand the purpose of the ceremony, then he probably should not attend. On the other hand, if he seems able to understand the situation to some degree and wishes to be there to say goodbye one last time, attending may be consoling and actually help him deal with his grief.

If you decide to have him at the funeral, prepare him for what will happen. Also, make arrangements ahead of time for a close family member or caregiver to take the child if he needs to leave, so you can remain at the funeral. Having this extra help also will free you to meet your own emotional needs during the ceremony.

If you decide not to have your child at the funeral, you might arrange a private, less formal visit later to the gravesite. Although this, too, will be stressful, it may make it easier for him to understand what has happened. If there is one, you might also consider having him attend a family gathering afterward, where he may find it comforting to be around family members.

When to Get Professional Help

You may want to consult your pediatrician for advice soon after the death has occurred. With the experience and knowledge to help you guide your child through the grieving process, the physician can help you decide how and what to tell your child, and can discuss how your child may be feeling and behaving in the months to come.

It is not possible to say how long your child will continue to grieve. Ordinarily, a grieving child will show signs of gradual recovery; eventually there will be hours, then days, and eventually weeks when he acts pretty much as he did before the death. If he does not start to have these periods of normalcy within four to six weeks, or if you feel that his initial feelings and behaviors are too intense or are lasting too long, talk with your pediatrician.

Although it is normal for a child to miss a deceased parent or sibling at times, it is not normal for the preoccupation to overshadow the child's entire life for years to come. If your child seems to be thinking constantly about the death, with his grief dominating every family occasion and interfering with his social and psychological development, he needs psychological counseling. Your pediatrician can refer you to a qualified mental health professional. If a dying relative is in hospice care, the facility or program often has grief counseling expertise that would be of help to parents and to children.

Your child also needs you to return gradually to normal functioning. After you have lost a child or your spouse, it may take many months before you are able to return to your usual daily routine and much longer before your strong sad feelings begin to subside. If a year has passed since the death and you still do not feel that you can resume your former activities, or if your grieving is replaced by ongoing depression, it's good to seek help from a mental health professional, not only for your benefit but for your child's as well.

Sibling Rivalry

If you have more than one child, you almost certainly will have to deal with some amount of sibling rivalry. Competition between youngsters in a family is natural. All children want parental affection and attention, and each child believes he should receive all of yours. Your child does not want to share you with his brother or sister, and when he realizes he has no choice in the matter, he may become jealous, possibly even violent, toward his sibling.

Sibling rivalry between younger children tends to be most troublesome when the age difference is from one and a half to three years. This is because the preschool child is still very dependent on his parents and has not yet established many secure relationships with friends or other adults. However, even when the spread is as much as nine years or more, the older child still needs parental attention and affection. If he feels that he is being left out or rejected, he likely will blame the baby. In general, the older the child, the less jealousy he will feel toward his younger sibling. The jealousy is often most intense for preschoolers when the sibling is a newborn.

There may be days when you're convinced your children really do hate each other, but these emotional outbursts are only temporary. Despite their feelings of resentment, siblings usually have true affection for one another. You may have difficulty seeing this, however, since they may reserve their worst behavior for moments when you are around and they are competing directly for your attention. When you are absent, they may be fine companions. As they get older and their need for your complete and undivided attention decreases, their feelings of affection probably will overcome their jealousy of each other. Intense sibling rivalry that begins in early childhood rarely lasts into adulthood.

What to Expect

You may notice the first signs of sibling rivalry even before your younger child is born. As the older one watches you preparing the nursery or buying baby equipment, he may demand gifts for himself. He may want to wear diapers again or drink from a bottle "like the baby." If he senses that you're preoccupied with the baby, he may misbehave or act out in order to get your attention.

This unusual or regressive behavior may continue after the baby is home. Your older child may cry more frequently, become more clingy and demanding, or simply withdraw. He may imitate the baby by asking for his old baby blanket, sucking on a pacifier, or even demanding to nurse. School-age children often appear very interested and affectionate toward the baby, but may be aggressive or misbehave in other ways to get attention. Among all siblings, the demand for attention is usually greatest when the parents are actively and intimately involved with the baby—for example, during breastfeeding or bath time.

As your younger child gets older and becomes more mobile, quarrels will erupt over the older child's toys and other possessions. The toddler will go straight for what he wants, without caring who owns it, while your preschooler will guard his own territory jealously. When the toddler intrudes on this space, the older child usually reacts strongly.

Sometimes, particularly when the children are several years apart, the older one is accepting and protective of the younger sibling. However, as the younger one grows and begins to develop more mature skills and talents (e.g., in schoolwork, athletics, talking, singing, or acting), the older child may feel threatened or embarrassed by "being shown up." He may then become more aggressive or irritating, or start to compete with the younger sibling. The younger child, too, may experience jealousy about the privileges, talents, accomplishments, or advantages that his older sibling accumulates as he gets older. Often it is almost impossible to tell which child is contributing more to the rivalry.

How Should Parents React?

It is important not to overreact to jealousy between your children, especially if the older child is a preschooler. Feelings of resentment and frustration are understandable—no child wants to give up the spotlight of parental affection. It takes time for a child to discover that his parents don't love him any less because they have a second child.

If your older child starts imitating the baby, do not ridicule or punish him. You can indulge him briefly by allowing him to drink from a bottle or climb into the crib or play yard, but only once or twice at the most, and don't reward this behavior by giving him extra attention. Make it absolutely clear that he does not have to behave like a baby to gain your approval, love, or affection. Praise him when he acts "grown-up," and give him plenty of opportunities to be a "big brother" (or, in the case of a girl, a "big sister"). If you intentionally try to catch him being good, it should not take long for him to realize that he benefits more by acting maturely than by behaving like a baby.

If your older child is between three and five years old, try to minimize conflicts over space by guaranteeing some secure, protected area. Separating his private possessions from shared ones will help reduce quarreling. It is natural for parents to compare their children, but do not do this in front of them. Each child is special and should be treated as such. Comparisons inevitably make one child feel inferior to the other. A statement such as "Your sister is always so much neater than you," for example, will make a child resent both you and his sister, and actually may encourage him to be messy.

When your children get into an argument, usually the best strategy is to stay out of it. Left alone, they probably will settle it peacefully. If you get involved, you may be tempted to take sides, making one child feel triumphant and the other betrayed. Even if they bring their fight to you, try to be impartial and tell them to settle it peacefully on their own. Instead of blaming either one, explain that they're both responsible for creating the dispute and for ending it. Doing so encourages them to problem-solve together, a social skill that will serve them well in the future.

Obviously, you must intervene if the situation becomes violent, especially if the older child might harm the younger one. In this case you must first protect the younger child. Make sure the older child understands that you will not tolerate any abusive behavior. If the age difference is large or if there is any reason to suspect that violence may erupt, supervise them closely when they are together. Preventing aggressive behavior is always better than punishment, which all too often increases rather than decreases the older child's feelings of rivalry.

It is important to spend time separately with each child. Even as little as ten to fifteen minutes daily of one-on-one time without electronics, doing an activity your child chooses, often makes a huge difference. Finding the right balance of attention is not always easy, but if your older child's acting out is becoming extreme, it could be a signal that he needs more of your time. If the older sibling remains extremely aggressive, or if you feel that you don't know how to handle the situation, consult your pediatrician, who can determine whether this is normal sibling rivalry or a problem that requires special attention. The pediatrician also can suggest ways to ease the tensions. If necessary, she will refer you to a qualified mental health professional.

(See also *Preparing Your Other Children for the Baby's Arrival*, page 38.)

Single-Parent Families

Single-parent families are becoming more common. Most children of divorce spend at least some years in single-parent households. Another increasingly large group of children live with single parents who were never married or involved in a long-term relationship. A smaller number of children have widowed parents.

From a parent's viewpoint, there are some benefits to being single. You can raise the child according to your own beliefs, principles, and rules, with no need for conflict or resolving differences. Single parents often develop closer bonds with their children. When the father is the single parent, he may become more nurturing and more active in his child's daily life than some fathers in two-parent households. Children in single-parent households may become more independent and mature because they have more responsibility within the family.

Single parenthood is not easy, for parents or for children. If you can't arrange or afford childcare, getting and holding a job may be difficult. (See Chapter 14, *Early Education and Childcare*.) Without another person to share the day-in, day-out job of raising the child and maintaining the household, you may find yourself so busy that you become socially isolated. When you are under stress, the child may sense and share this stress. You can easily become too tired and distracted to be as emotionally supportive or consistent about rules and discipline as you would like to be. This can lead to distress and behavior problems for the child. Some single parents worry that the lack of a same-sex parent may deprive their son or daughter of a potential role model.

Here are some suggestions that may help you meet your own emotional needs while providing your child with the guidance she needs.

■ Take advantage of all available resources in finding help in caring for your child. Use the guide to childcare in Chapter 14.

■ Maintain your sense of humor as much as possible. Try to see the positive or funny side of everyday surprises and challenges.

■ For your family's sake as well as your own, take care of yourself. See your doctor regularly, eat properly, and get enough rest, exercise, and sleep.

■ Set a regular time when you can take a break without your child. Relax with friends. Go to a movie. Pursue hobbies. Join groups. Do things that interest you. Pursue a social life of your own.

■ Do not feel guilty because your child has only one parent. There are plenty of families in the same situation. You didn't "do it to her," and you don't need to penalize yourself or spoil her to make amends. Feeling and acting guilty won't help anyone.

■ Do not look for problems where none exist. Many children grow up very well in single-parent homes, while others have a great many problems in two-parent homes. Being a single parent does not necessarily mean you'll have more problems or have more trouble resolving them.

■ Set firm but reasonable limits for your children, and do not hesitate to enforce them. Children feel more secure and develop responsible behavior better when limits are clear and consistent. Expand these limits as the child demonstrates the ability to accept increased responsibility.

■ Find some time each day to spend with your child—playing, talking, reading, helping with homework, or watching television.

Parenting in Military Families

Being a parent in the military can present unique challenges, particularly in times of deployment or military conflict, when the stresses of being away from a child can be difficult for the entire family. Young children may demonstrate a number of behaviors in response to being separated from a parent, such as clinginess to the other parent and/or a caregiver, regressive behaviors (e.g., bed-wetting after having been toilet trained), anxiety over new people or circumstances, and being quiet and pulling away from others.

If you're the parent remaining at home with your child, try to keep things as normal as possible, including maintaining usual daily routines. Answer questions as honestly as possible (keeping in mind his level of understanding), and reassure him that the deployed parent is fine and doing well. Try to maintain as much communication as possible with the absent parent, letting your child communicate by phone, letter, email, or videoconferencing. If your child seems to be in particular distress, talk with your pediatrician, who might make a referral to a mental health professional. Also, there is a website for all military spouses to access mental health services, regardless of location, at MilitaryOneSource.com.

The AAP's Deployment and Military Medical Home Resources webpage has been designed to support youth in military families, other family members, and the professionals caring for this population. Please spend some time on the site to learn more about what military pediatricians and other youth-serving professionals are doing to help these children and adolescents every day: aap.org/en-us/advocacy-and-policy/aap-health-initiatives/Pages/Deployment-and-Military.aspx.

■ Praise your child often, showing genuine affection and unconditional, positive support.

■ Create as large a support network for yourself as possible. Keep active lists of relatives, friends, and community services that can help with childcare. Establish friendships with other families who will let you know of community opportunities (sports leagues, cultural events, etc.) and are willing to exchange babysitting.

■ Talk to trusted relatives, friends, and professionals such as your pediatrician about your child's behavior, development, and relationships within the family.

Stepfamilies

A single parent's remarriage can be a blessing for the parent and child alike, restoring the structure and security that were lost through divorce, separation, or death. Benefits may include additional love and companionship for a parent as well as the children. Often a stepparent becomes another adult role model and may take on some responsibilities of the former spouse. In addition, there may be financial benefits from having another caregiver in the house.

But creating a stepfamily also requires many adjustments and can be very stressful. If the stepparent is introduced as a substitute for your child's absent parent, the child may feel torn by her loyalty to her biologic parent and may reject the stepparent immediately. There is often a great deal of jealousy between stepparents and stepchildren, as well as competition for the love and attention of the parent who has brought them together. If a child feels that her new stepparent is coming between her and her parent, she may reject the stepparent and act out in order to regain her parent's attention. The situation becomes even more complex and stressful when there are children on both sides who are suddenly expected to accept each other's parents and get along as siblings. With time, most blended families do manage to sort through these conflicts, but it requires a great amount of patience and commitment on the part of the adults, as well as the willingness to get professional help early to prevent significant problems from developing.

As difficult as the transition may seem at first, try to keep in mind that relationships between stepparents and stepchildren tend to develop gradually over a period of one to several years, rather than over weeks or months. An important factor in the development of the step-relationship may be support from the other biological parent. The child may resent a relationship with a biological parent that prevents closeness to the stepparent and may feel guilty whenever she is emotionally drawn to the stepparent. Good communication among all three (or four) parents can minimize this guilt, as well as reduce the confusion that a child could feel when she tries to adjust to the values and expectations of several adults. For this reason, when a child is spending time in two households, occasional meetings with all of the parents, if possible, may be very helpful. Sharing perspectives on rules, values, and scheduling tells the child that all her parents can talk with one another, are mutually respectful, and have her health and well-being as a central priority.

In an atmosphere of mutual respect between biological and stepparents, the child is more likely to have the benefits of stepfamilies mentioned earlier. The child again has the opportunity of living in a household with two parents. The remarried parent often is happier and thus better able to meet the child's needs. As the child gets older, her relationship to the step-

Suggestions for Stepfamilies

Making a smooth transition from a single-parent family to a successful stepfamily requires special sensitivity and effort from the biological parent and stepparent. Here are some suggestions that may help.

- Inform your former spouse of your marriage plans, and try to work together to make the transition as easy as possible for your child. Make sure everyone understands that the marriage will not change your former spouse's role in your child's life.

- Give your child time to get to know the stepparent (and stepsiblings, if any) before you begin living together. Doing this will make the adjustment easier for everyone and will often eliminate much of your child's anxiety about the new arrangement.

- Watch for signs of conflict, and work together to correct them as early as possible.

- Parent and stepparent should decide together what will be expected of the child, where and how limits will be set, and what forms of discipline are acceptable.

- Parent and stepparent need to share the responsibilities of parenthood. This means that *both* will give affection and attention and that *both* will have authority in the household. Deciding together how the child should be disciplined, and supporting each other's decisions and actions, will make it easier for the stepparent to assume a role of authority without fear of disapproval or resentment.

- If a noncustodial parent visits the child, these visitations should be arranged and accepted so that they do not create disagreement within the stepfamily.

- Try to involve both biological parents and stepparent(s) in all major decisions affecting a child. If possible, arrange for all the adults to meet together to share insights and concerns; doing this will let the child know that the grown-ups are willing to overcome their differences for his benefit.

- Be sensitive to your child's wishes and concerns about his role within the stepfamily. Respect his level of maturity and understanding when, for example, you help him decide what to call the stepparent or introduce him to the stepparent's relatives.

parent may give her additional support, skills, and perspectives. These benefits, together with the economic advantages of the stepfamily situation, may give the child a broader range of opportunities.

Multiples

Having twins (or other multiples, such as triplets) means much more than simply having two or more babies at once, and the challenges go beyond having twice or three times the work or pleasure. Twins and other multiples quite frequently are born earlier than single-born babies and so tend to be smaller than the average newborn; you may need to consult your pediatrician more frequently than you would with a single baby. It is possible that after birth your multiples may need extra time in the hospital's neonatal intensive care unit (NICU). Feeding twins and other multiples, whether by breast or bottle, also requires some special strategies, and the pediatrician and lactation consultant can provide advice and support. There may be added financial pressures upon the family as well, requiring more diapers, clothing, food, car safety seats, and dozens of other items—and perhaps needing a larger family car or even a larger home. (See Chapter 1.)

Currently, the twin birth rate in the United States is just over 3 percent, and the number of multiple births has risen in recent years: it has increased 42 percent since 1990 and 70 percent since 1980. Some researchers have attributed much of this increase to the more frequent use of infertility treatments and procedures such as in vitro fertilization. In vitro fertilization may involve implanting more than one fertilized egg into the uterus, while using infertility drugs can stimulate the ovaries to release two or more eggs.

This section is written primarily with twins in mind, but most of the same information and guidelines apply to triplets and higher-order multiple births. (For more information on multiples, check out *Raising Twins: Parenting Multiples From Pregnancy Through the School Years* by Shelly Vaziri Flais [AAP, 2020].)

Raising Multiples

You should care for your healthy multiples just like any other infants. From the very beginning, it is important that you recognize that your babies are separate individuals. If they are identical, it is easy to treat them as a "package," providing them with the same clothing, toys, and quality of attention. But as similar as they may appear physically, emotionally, behaviorally, and developmentally, they are two different people, and in order to grow up happy and secure as individuals, they need you to support their differences. As one twin explained, "We're not twins. We're just brothers who have the same birthday!"

Identical twins come from the same egg, are always the same sex, and look very much alike. Fraternal twins come from two separate eggs that are fertilized at the same time. They may or may not be the same sex. Whether identical or fraternal, all twins have their individual personalities, styles, and temperaments. Both identical and fraternal twins may become either competitive or interdependent as they grow. Sometimes one twin acts as the leader and the other as the follower. Whatever the specific quality of their interaction, most twins develop very intense relationships early in life simply because they spend so much time with each other.

If you also have other children, your twin newborns may prompt more than the usual sibling rivalry. They will require a large amount of your time and energy, and will attract a great deal of extra attention from friends, relatives, and strangers on the street. You can help your other children accept, and perhaps even take advantage of, this unusual situation by offering them "double rewards" for helping with the new babies and encouraging even more involvement in the daily baby care chores. It also becomes even more essential that you spend some special time each day alone with your other children, reading books or doing their favorite activities.

As your twins get older, particularly if they are identical, they may choose to play only with each other, and other siblings may feel left out. To discourage the twins from forming such exclusive bonds, urge them to play individually (not as a unit) with other children. Also, you or a babysitter might play with just one twin while the other plays with a sibling or friend.

You may find that your twins do not develop in the same pattern as do other children their age. Some twins seem to "split the work," with one concentrating on motor skills while the other advances in social or communication abilities. Because they spend so much time together, many twins communicate better with each other than with other family members or friends. They learn how to read each other's gestures and facial expressions, and occasionally they even have their own verbal language that no one else can understand—this is particularly true of identical twins. This unique developmental pattern does not represent a problem, but it does make it very important to separate your twins on a regular basis and expose them individually to other playmates and learning situations.

Twins are not always happy about being apart, especially if they have established strong play habits and preferences for each other's company. For this reason, it is important to begin separating them occasionally as early as possible. If they resist strongly, try a gradual approach using very familiar children or adults to play with them individually but in the same room or play area. Being able to separate will become increasingly important as the twins approach school age. In preschool most twins can stay together in the same room, but many elementary schools prefer twins to be in separate classes.

Transporting Your Newborn Multiples

In many cases, infant twins and higher-order multiples are smaller and weigh less than the average newborn. When bringing your babies home from the hospital and for subsequent trips in the car, keep the same guidelines in mind for choosing and using car safety seats. That means choosing rear-facing car safety seats and relying on them until your babies have outgrown the rear-facing weight or height limit for their seats, which will likely be well past the second birthday. Rear-facing-only seats have carrying handles and may be sold with a base that can stay in your car. Convertible seats are larger than rear-facing-only seats and can be used both rear-facing and forward-facing, so some parents choose to use a convertible seat from birth.

But here's a very important point to keep in mind if your babies were born prematurely: rear-facing *convertible* car seats may be too large to fit your preemies appropriately. Before your newborns are discharged from the hospital, make sure they are tested to determine if they can ride safely while reclining in a car safety seat. The hospital calls this the "car seat test." If they have certain medical issues related to breathing or heart rate, they may not be able to ride in a semireclined position. In these instances, preemies should lie flat when they're riding in a car, and you will need a crash-tested car bed. (In most cases, the car bed will be purchased through the hospital, and your babies should be tested in the car beds before being sent home.) Always use the harnesses and buckle that are part of the car beds, and install the beds lengthwise in the backseat; position your babies so their heads are toward the center of the car. After they've had additional time to grow bigger and stronger, your babies should be tested again in their car safety seats to make sure they are ready to make the switch to a regular semi-reclined rear-facing seat.

As much as you appreciate the individual differences between your twins, you no doubt will have certain feelings for them as a unit. There is nothing wrong with this, since they do share many similarities and are themselves bound to develop a dual identity—as individuals and as twins. Helping them understand and accept the balance between these two identities is one of the most challenging tasks facing you as the parent of twins.

Your pediatrician can advise you on how to cope with the special parenting challenges with twins. He also can suggest helpful reading material or refer you to organizations that help parents with multiples. It is enormously helpful to connect with other families who are experiencing similar challenges to yours. One organization to look for in your area may be Multiples of America, which has local chapters nationally.

At the same time, take care of yourself, and get as much rest as possible. Many parents find that raising twins and other multiples is much more physically demanding and emotionally stressful than having just one baby. So make an effort to catch up on your own sleep whenever you can. Take turns with your partner on who's going to handle the middle-of-the-night feedings and who will bathe and feed the babies. Consider one parent taking the "early shift" of nighttime feeds and a second caregiver taking the "late shift," affording you both a longer stretch of sleep. If your budget can afford it, get some extra help for routine tasks like bathing the newborns and grocery shopping—or ask friends and family members for assistance. An extra set of hands, especially when there are more than twins, even for just a few hours a week, can make an enormous difference, and can give you not only more time to enjoy your babies, but also more time for yourself.

~ 27 ~

Fever

YOUR CHILD'S NORMAL temperature will vary with his age, activity, and the time of day. Infants tend to have higher temperatures than older children, and everyone's temperature is highest between late afternoon and early evening and lowest between midnight and early morning. Ordinarily, a rectal reading of 100.4 degrees Fahrenheit (38 degrees Celsius) and higher indicates fever. When other sites are used for temperature taking, such as oral, tympanic (ear), and temporal artery (side of forehead), you should still generally use 100.4 degrees or more as the cutoff for a true fever, while axillary (underarm) measurements may have a lower cutoff. A rectal reading is the gold standard for infants, especially those under three months of age. When-ever you think your child has a fever, take his temperature with a thermometer. (See *Best Ways to Take a Temperature* on page 778.) Feeling the skin (or using temperature-sensitive tape also referred to as "fever strips") is not accurate, especially when the child is experiencing a chill.

By itself, fever is *not* an illness. Rather, it is a sign or symptom of sickness. In fact, usually it is a positive sign that the body is fighting infection. Fever stimulates certain defenses, such as the white blood cells, which attack and destroy invading bacteria and viruses. The fever may actually be important in helping your child fight his infection. However, fever is often associated with discomfort. It increases his need for fluids and makes his heart rate and breathing rate faster.

Fever may accompany any infection. This includes respiratory illnesses such as croup or pneumonia, ear infections, influenza (flu), colds, and sore throats. Fever may occur with infections of the bowel, blood, urinary tract, or brain and spinal cord (meningitis), and with most viral illnesses.

In children between six months and five years, fever can trigger seizures (called febrile convulsions), although they happen only rarely. These convulsions tend to run in families and usually happen during the first few hours of a febrile illness. Children may look "peculiar" for a few moments, then stiffen, twitch, and roll their eyes. They will be unresponsive for a short time, and their skin may appear to be a little darker than usual during the episode. The entire convulsion usually lasts less than one minute, and may be over in a few seconds, but it can seem like a lifetime to a frightened parent. Although uncommon, convulsions can last for up to fifteen minutes. It is reassuring to know that febrile convulsions almost always are harmless—they do not cause brain damage, nervous system problems, paralysis, intellectual disability, or death—although they should be reported promptly to your pediatrician. If your child is having trouble breathing or the convulsion (also referred to as a seizure) does not stop within fifteen minutes, call 911.

Children younger than one year at the time of their first simple febrile convulsion have approximately a 50 percent chance of having another such seizure, while children over one year of age when they have their first seizure have about a 30 percent chance of having a second one. Nevertheless, febrile convulsions rarely happen more than once within a twenty-four-hour period. Although many parents worry that a febrile convulsion will lead to epilepsy, keep in mind that epileptic seizures are not caused by a fever, and children with a history of fever-related convulsions have only a slightly higher likelihood of developing epilepsy by age seven. Ironically, working extra-hard to control fevers does not prevent future febrile seizures, so do not go to extremes trying to keep a child's temperature down just because he has had a febrile seizure in the past.

Treating a Febrile Seizure

If your child has a febrile seizure, take the following steps immediately to prevent injury:

■ Place him on the floor or bed away from any hard or sharp objects.

■ Turn his head to the side so that any saliva or vomit can drain from his mouth.

■ Do not put anything into his mouth; he will not swallow his tongue.

■ Call your pediatrician.

■ Call 911 if the seizure lasts longer than fifteen minutes.

What Type of Thermometer Is Best?

The American Academy of Pediatrics no longer recommends mercury thermometers because these glass thermometers may break and, as their mercury vaporizes, it can be inhaled, resulting in toxic levels. Digital electronic thermometers are better choices.

■ *Digital devices* can measure temperatures in your child's mouth, armpit, or rectum. As with any device, some digital thermometers are more accurate than others. Follow the manufacturer's instructions carefully, and be sure the thermometer is calibrated as recommended by the manufacturer.

■ *Ear (tympanic) thermometers* are another acceptable choice. Their accuracy depends on the ability of the beam emitted by the device to reach the eardrum. Thus, some of these devices may not be as reliable because of earwax or a small or curved ear canal. For that reason, most pediatricians prefer that parents use digital electronic thermometers.

■ *Temporal artery thermometers* are also available. They use an infrared scanner to determine the temperature of the temporal artery, which runs across the forehead just below the skin. They are most useful in children three months and older, although recent research shows that they are reliable in babies younger than three months as well. They also are simple to use, even while your child is asleep.

When to Call the Pediatrician

If your child is two months or younger and has a rectal temperature of 100.4 degrees Fahrenheit (38 degrees Celsius) or higher, call your pediatrician immediately. *This is an absolute necessity.* The doctor will need to examine the baby to rule out any serious infection or disease.

You also may need to notify the doctor if your child is between three and six months and has a fever of 101 degrees Fahrenheit (38.3 degrees Celsius) or greater, or is older than six months and has a temperature of 103 degrees Fahrenheit (39.4 degrees Celsius) or higher. Such a high temperature may indicate a significant infection or dehydration, which may require treatment. However, in most cases, your decision to call the pediatrician for an older child's fever should depend on associated symptoms, such as a sore throat, an earache, a cough, unexplained rash, or repeated vomiting or diarrhea. Also, if your child is very fussy or sleeping more than usual, call your doctor. In fact, your child's activity level tends to be a more important indicator than the height of the fever. Again, fever in and of itself is not a sickness; it is a sign of sickness.

If your child is over one year of age, is eating and sleeping well, and has playful moments, there usually is no need to call the doctor immediately. If a high fever (as defined earlier) persists for more than twenty-four hours, however, it is best to call even if there are no other complaints or findings.

Best Ways to Take a Temperature

There are several ways to take your child's temperature. A digital thermometer (which shows the temperature in numbers in a small window) reads the body temperature when its sensor, located in the tip of the thermometer, touches the part of the body where it is used—in the mouth, under the arm, or in the rectum. A tympanic (ear) thermometer or a temporal artery thermometer can also be used. (See page 777 for more information about different types of thermometers.) Whatever approach you use, clean the thermometer as directed—usually with lukewarm soapy water or rubbing alcohol—before each use, and then rinse with cool water. There's no need to add or subtract a degree depending on the device used or how the temperature was taken.

Here are some other guidelines to keep in mind:

- To take the temperature in your child's bottom (rectally), turn on the digital thermometer and then put a small amount of lubricant, such as petroleum jelly, on the end of the thermometer that will be inserted into your baby. Place your child across your lap or on something firm, either face-up or facedown (if he's facedown, put one hand on his back; if he's face-up, bend your child's leg to his chest, resting your free hand on the back of his thighs).Then gently insert the small end of the thermometer into your child's bottom (or rectum), putting it in about ½ inch to 1 inch (1–2 cm). Hold the thermometer in place for about one minute or until the device signals that it's done (by beeping or lighting up). Remove it and read the number.

- Taking a rectal or oral temperature is more accurate than taking it under your child's arm. Also, in your household, label one digital thermometer "oral" and another one "rectal." Don't use the same thermometer in both places.

- At ages four or five years old, you also can take your child's temperature by placing the thermometer in his mouth (orally). After turning on the thermometer, place the small end under your child's tongue, toward the back of his mouth. Ask him to close his mouth around the thermometer and hold it in place. After about a minute, you should hear the thermometer beep or see it light up. Remove it and read the number.

- Tympanic (ear) and temporal artery (side of forehead) thermometers are increasingly popular among parents and healthcare providers, and appear to be quite accurate when used correctly.

Heat-Related Illness

A rare but serious problem that is easily confused with fever is heat-related illness, or heatstroke. This is caused not by infection or internal conditions, but by surrounding heat. It can occur when a child is in a very hot place—for example, a hot beach in midsummer or an overheated closed car on a summer day. Leaving children unattended in closed cars is the cause of several deaths a year; *never* leave an infant or child unattended in a closed car, even for a few minutes. Heatstroke also can occur if a baby is overdressed in hot, humid weather. Under these circumstances, the body temperature can rise to dangerous levels (above 105 degrees Fahrenheit [40.5 degrees Celsius]), which must be reduced quickly by removing some of the clothing, cool-water sponging, fanning, and removal to a cool place. Call 911. Children experiencing heatstroke must be taken to the emergency department right away. Heatstroke is an emergency condition.

If your child becomes delirious (acts frightened, "sees" objects that are not there, talks strangely) while he has a high fever, call your pediatrician, particularly if this has not occurred before. These unusual symptoms probably will disappear when the temperature returns to normal, but the doctor may want to examine your child and determine it is not caused by something more serious, such as an inflammation of the brain (encephalitis) or of the membranes covering the brain and spinal cord (meningitis).

Home Treatment

Fevers generally do not need to be treated with medication unless your child is uncomfortable. Even higher temperatures are not in themselves dangerous or significant unless your child has a chronic disease. If your child has a history of a fever-related convulsion, treating the fever with medication has not been shown to be an effective strategy to prevent this kind of seizure. It is more important to watch how your child is behaving. If he is eating and sleeping well and has periods of playfulness, he probably doesn't need any treatment. You should also talk with your pediatrician about when to treat your child's fever. A good time to do this is at well-child visits. When your child has a fever and seems to be quite bothered by or uncomfortable from it, you may treat it with the following approaches.

MEDICATION

Several medications can reduce body temperature by blocking the mecha-

Acetaminophen Dosage Chart

Dosages may be repeated every four hours, but should not be given more than five times in twenty-four hours. (*Note:* Use only a syringe or accurate measuring device that measures in milliliters [ml], not household teaspoons, which can vary in size.) Be sure to read the label to make sure you are using the right product.

Age*	Weight**	Infant/Children's Oral Suspension (160 mg per 5 ml)	Chewable Tablets (80 mg tabs)***
6–11 mos.	12–17 lbs. (5.5–7.7 kg)	2.5 ml	1 tab
1–2 yrs.	18–23 lbs. (8.2–10.5 kg)	3.75 ml	1½ tabs
2–3 yrs.	24–35 lbs. (10.9–15.9 kg)	5 ml	2 tabs
4–5 yrs.	36–47 lbs. (16.3–21.4 kg)	7.5 ml	3 tabs

* Age is provided as a convenience only. Dosing for fever should be based on current weight.
** Weight given is representative of the age range.
*** Make sure, when using chewable tablets, to refer to the 80 mg chewable dosage.

We do not recommend using aspirin to treat a simple fever in infants, children, or teens.

nisms that cause a fever. These antipyretic agents include acetaminophen, ibuprofen, and aspirin. All three of these over-the-counter drugs appear to be equally effective at reducing fever. *However, because aspirin may cause or be associated with Reye syndrome, the American Academy of Pediatrics does not recommend using aspirin to treat a fever in children.* Acetaminophen can be given without a doctor's advice once your child is older than three months, and ibuprofen can be given to children older than six months of age. However, if your child has a disease affecting his liver, ask your doctor if acetaminophen is safe to use. Similarly, if your child has kidney disease, an ulcer, or other chronic illness, ask your doctor first if ibuprofen is safe. If your child is dehydrated or vomiting, ibuprofen should be given only under the supervision of a doctor due to risk of kidney damage.

Ideally, the doses of acetaminophen and ibuprofen should be based on a child's weight, not his age. (See the dosage charts above and on page 781.)

Ibuprofen Dosage Chart

Dosages may be repeated every six to eight hours, but should not be given more than four times in twenty-four hours. (*Note:* Use only a syringe or accurate measuring device that measures in milliliters [ml], not household teaspoons, which can vary in size.) Be sure to read the label to make sure you are using the right product.

Age*	Weight**	Infant Drops (50 mg per 1.25 ml)	Children's Suspension (100 mg per 5 ml)	Chewable Tablets (100 mg tabs)
6–11 mos.	12–17 lbs. (5.5–7.7 kg)	1.25 ml	2.5 ml	½ tab ·
1–2 yrs.	18–23 lbs. (8.2–10.5 kg)	1.875 ml	3.75 ml	½ tab
2–3 yrs.	24–35 lbs. (10.9–15.9 kg)	2.5 ml	5 ml	1 tab
4–5 yrs.	36–47 lbs. (16.3–21.4 kg)	—	7.5 ml	1½ tabs

* Age is provided as a convenience only. Dosing for fever should be based on current weight.
** Weight given is representative of the age range.

We do not recommend using aspirin to treat a fever. Aspirin should only be used in special circumstances as recommended by your pediatrician for specific rare conditions.

However, the dosages listed on the labels of acetaminophen bottles (which are usually calculated by age) are generally safe and effective unless your child is unusually light or heavy for his age. Keep in mind that at too-high doses of acetaminophen, a toxic response in the liver can develop, although it happens only rarely. When a toxic reaction does occur, the symptoms may include nausea, vomiting, and abdominal discomfort.

As a general guideline, read and follow the instructions on the manufacturer's label when using *any* medication. Following the instructions is important to ensure that your child receives the proper dosages, and only use the measuring device that comes with the medication you are using. Also, other over-the-counter medications, such as cold and cough preparations, may contain acetaminophen, and using more than one acetaminophen-containing product can result in a dangerously high dosage; read all medication labels to ensure that your child is not receiving multiple doses of the same medicine. Also, as a general rule, do not give a child under two months old either acetaminophen or any other medication without the advice of your pediatrician.

Some parents have tried alternating between giving acetaminophen and ibuprofen when their child is running a fever. This approach, however, can theoretically cause medication errors—"Which medicine am I supposed to give him next?"—and could lead to potential side effects. So if your child is uncomfortable with a fever, choose which medicine to give, and then give it according to the dosing recommendations and only if your child still needs it. Either ibuprofen or acetaminophen is effective in reducing fever and making your child feel better. Always consult your doctor before changing the dose schedule or using these medicines in combination.

Also keep in mind that over-the-counter cough and cold medicines should *not* be given to infants and children under six years of age because of potentially serious side effects. Studies also have shown that these cough and cold products are not effective in treating the symptoms of young children and may even pose health risks.

OTHER TREATMENT SUGGESTIONS FOR FEVER

■ Keep your child's room and your home comfortably cool, and dress him lightly.

■ Encourage him to drink extra fluid or other liquids (water, diluted fruit juices, commercially prepared oral electrolyte solutions, Popsicles, etc.).

■ If the room is warm or stuffy, place a fan nearby to keep cool air moving.

■ Your child does not have to stay in his room or in bed when he has a fever. He can be up and about the house, but should not run around and overexert himself.

■ If the fever is a symptom of a highly contagious disease (e.g., chickenpox or the flu), keep your child away from other children, elderly people, or people who may not be able to fight infection well, such as those with cancer.

~ 28 ~

Genital and Urinary Systems

Blood in the Urine (Hematuria)

IF YOUR CHILD'S urine has a red, orange, or brown color, it may contain blood. When the urine specifically contains red blood cells, doctors use the medical term "hematuria" to describe this condition. Many things—such as a physical injury, inflammation, or an infection in the urinary tract—can cause it. Hematuria also is associated with some general medical problems, such as defects of blood clotting, exposure to toxic materials, hereditary conditions, or immune system abnormalities.

Sometimes there may be such small amounts of blood in the urine that you cannot see any color change, although it may be detected by a urine test performed by the pediatrician. In some cases the reddish color is not associated with hematuria at all, and may be due to something your child has eaten or swallowed. Beets, blackberries, red food coloring, phenolphthalein (a chemical sometimes used in laxatives), pyridium and phenazopyridine (medicines used to relieve bladder pain), and rifampin (a medication used to treat tuberculosis) may cause the urine to turn red or orange. Anytime you are not certain that one of these substances is responsible for the change in the color of your child's urine, call your pediatrician. When blood in the urine is accompanied by protein (albumin), it is usually due to nephritis, or inflammation of the filtering membranes of the kidney. Your doctor may recommend further tests to distinguish among several different kinds of nephritis.

Treatment

Your pediatrician will ask you about any possible injury, foods, or health symptoms that might have caused the change in urine color. Helpful information may include the presence or absence of pain with urination that could indicate a urinary tract infection. Also, the timing of blood in the urine stream can help to localize where in the urinary tract blood is coming from (i.e., blood throughout the whole stream, versus just at the end of the stream). He will perform a physical exam, checking particularly for any increase in blood pressure, tenderness in the kidney area, or swelling (particularly of the hands or feet or around the eyes) that might indicate kidney problems. He also will conduct tests on a sample of urine and may order blood tests, imaging studies (such as an ultrasound scan or X-rays), or perform other examinations to check your child's kidneys, bladder, and immune system. If none of these reveals the cause of the hematuria and it continues to occur, your pediatrician may refer you to a children's kidney specialist, who will perform additional tests. (Sometimes these tests include examining a tiny piece of kidney tissue under the microscope, a procedure known as a biopsy. This tissue may be obtained by surgery or by performing what's called a needle biopsy.)

Once your pediatrician knows more about what is causing the hematuria, a decision can be made whether treatment is necessary. Often no treatment is required, indicating that there is nothing to worry about. Occasionally medication is used to suppress the inflammation that is the hallmark sign of nephritis. Whatever the treatment, your child will need to return to the doctor regularly for repeat urine and blood tests and blood pressure checks. This is necessary to make sure that she isn't developing chronic kidney disease, which can lead to kidney failure.

Occasionally hematuria is caused by kidney stones or, rarely, by an abnormality of the urinary tract that

Kidney

Ureter

Bladder
Urethra
Vagina

Genitourinary System

will require surgery. If this is the case, your pediatrician will refer you to a pediatric urologist (a bladder and kidney surgeon) who can perform such procedures.

Proteinuria

A child's urine sometimes contains abnormally high amounts of protein. Although the body needs proteins to perform essential functions, such as guarding against infections and helping the blood to clot, only a minimal amount of these proteins should leak into the urine. If high amounts of protein are detected in the urine, this may indicate that the kidneys are not working properly and are allowing proteins (which are large molecules) to leak out into the urine. This leakage of protein may be due to various abnormalities of the kidney's filtering membranes.

Diagnosis

Proteinuria often causes no symptoms. But when high levels of protein are in the urine, blood protein levels may drop and your child could develop swelling in the legs, ankles, abdomen, or eyelids. At the same time, the blood pressure may be elevated, another sign of likely kidney disease. Your pediatrician can detect proteinuria using a simple test in which a chemically treated paper strip is dipped into the urine and will change colors if protein is present. She may recommend that you collect urine samples from your child just after awakening in the morning (if the proteinuria disappears, the condition is benign or normal), that the urine specimens be examined in the laboratory, or that your child have some blood tests. In some children, a small amount of protein may be found in the urine for a short time and later disappear without any consequences.

At times, your pediatrician may decide to have your child seen by a kidney specialist (nephrologist), who might recommend further testing that may include a kidney biopsy. During a kidney biopsy, a needle is used to remove a small amount of kidney tissue for examination in the laboratory. Your child will be sedated for this procedure and the area over the kidney will be made numb by injecting a local anesthetic.

Treatment

Medication can be given to treat some underlying kidney problems associated with proteinuria. Your pediatrician might recommend that your child consume less salt, to curtail the swelling associated with proteinuria. Children who have had proteinuria, even if it appears to be one of the harmless varieties, probably will be monitored over time with regular urine tests.

Circumcision

Circumcision is a common procedure performed in many infant boys. It involves removing the foreskin covering the tip of the penis. There are benefits and risks to circumcision, and you should discuss them with your pediatrician or obstetrician and your spouse or partner before your baby is born. Although it is not routinely recommended for all newborn boys, there may be cultural, religious, medical, and other reasons why you may decide that it is appropriate for your son. Circumcision is discussed in detail on pages 28–30 and 143–44. The choice to circumcise or not to circumcise is completely that of the parent, as circumcision is not necessary to have a healthy child; however, current data has shown that the benefits outweigh the risks.

Hypospadias and Chordee

In boys, the opening through which urine passes (the urethral meatus) is located at the tip of the penis. A condition known as hypospadias is an abnormality in penile development, in which this opening is on the underside of the penis. There also may be an abnormal downward bending of the penis called chordee, which may cause sexual problems in adulthood. The meatus may direct the urinary stream downward and cause the stream to spray, making standing to urinate difficult or impossible. A concern of many parents is the abnormal appearance of the penis in severe hypospadias, which can be a source of embarrassment to boys as they grow older.

Treatment

After detecting hypospadias or chordee in your newborn, your pediatrician probably will advise against circumcision until after consultation with a pediatric urologist or surgeon. This is because the foreskin may be used for future surgical repair, and circumcision may make that repair more difficult.

Mild hypospadias may require no treatment, but treatment for moderate or severe forms may include surgical repair. Most children with hypospadias undergo outpatient surgery at around six months of age, but each family should decide for themselves if the risk of anesthesia and surgery is in the best interests of their child. It may help to discuss with a multidisciplinary health team, and other families or older patients who have been through similar surgeries, in order to consider timing and impact of each procedure. Often, hypospadias and chordee can be repaired in conjunction with circumcision in one procedure. In severe cases, more than one operation may be needed to repair the condition completely. Surgery can impact appearance of the penis, urinary stream, and adult sexual functioning. The goal of surgery is to allow your child to urinate normally, have normal sexual function as an adult, and have an acceptable cosmetic result.

Meatal Stenosis

Sometimes, particularly in circumcised boys, irritation of the tip of the penis causes scar tissue to form around the urethral meatus, making it smaller. This narrowing, called meatal stenosis ("opening"), may develop at any time during childhood, but is most commonly found between ages three and seven. Boys with meatal stenosis have a narrowed and abnormally directed urinary stream. The stream is directed upward (toward the ceiling), making it difficult to urinate into the toilet without pushing the penis down between the legs. Your son may take longer to urinate and have difficulty emptying his bladder completely.

Treatment

If you notice that your son's urinary stream is very small or narrow, if he strains to urinate, or if he dribbles or sprays urine, discuss it with your pediatrician. Meatal stenosis is not a serious condition, but it should be evaluated to see if it needs treatment. If an operation is needed, this surgery is very minor. Your child will have some minor discomfort after the procedure, but this should disappear after a very short period of time.

Labial Adhesions

Ordinarily the lips of skin (labia) surrounding the entrance to the vagina and urethra are separated. Sometimes they grow together to partially or completely block the opening. This condition, called labial adhesions (sticking together of labia), may occur in the early months or later on if there is constant irritation and inflammation in the diaper area. The problem is usually traceable to diaper irritation, contact with harsh detergents, or underwear made with synthetic fabric. Usually labial adhesions do not cause symptoms, but sometimes they can

Normal labia

Labia with adhesions

lead to difficulty with urination and increase a girl's susceptibility to urinary tract infections. If the vaginal opening is significantly blocked, urine and/or vaginal secretions will sometimes build up behind the obstruction.

Treatment

If the opening of your daughter's vagina appears to have closed or looks partially blocked, notify your pediatrician. He will examine your child and advise you whether any treatment is necessary. The majority of such adhesions require no treatment and resolve on their own as the child gets older. In general, if your daughter is not having symptoms like dribbling incontinence after urination or urinary tract infections, no treatment is needed.

Treatment options for labial adhesions include watchful waiting or observation, treatment with estrogen cream applied a few times daily at home, or manual separation of the adhesions in the office or the operating room with the use of numbing medication.

If estrogen cream is needed, your doctor will instruct you on exactly how and where to apply the cream. Good hygiene, such as giving your child daily sitz baths, is also important in the treatment and prevention of labial adhesions. You may want to apply a lubricant along the edges to prevent them from sticking back together. It is important to keep in mind that the estrogen cream may result in temporary changes in the appearance of the hymen (tissue at the opening of the vagina) or withdrawal bleeding (akin to a period). These will resolve after discontinuation of the estrogen cream. As the adhesion opens up, the area may take on a bruised appearance that can be mistaken for trauma. This will also go away.

Posterior Urethral Valve

Urine leaves the bladder through a tube called the urethra, which in boys passes through the penis. Rarely, a small membrane forms across the urethra in boys early in pregnancy, and it can block the flow of urine out of the bladder. This problem, posterior urethral valve, can have life-threatening consequences by causing blockage of normal urine flow, thus interfering with development of the bladder and kidneys. If there is abnormal kidney development in utero, there can also be abnormal development of the lungs.

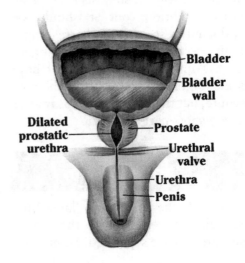

The severity of posterior urethral valve can vary widely. Most cases are diagnosed before birth with a screening ultrasound. This condition may be suspected in boys if there appears to be a decrease in the amount of amniotic fluid. Consulting a pediatric urology specialist is always advisable before the baby is born. In boys who are not diagnosed before birth with posterior urethral valve, sometimes the newborn exam may reveal that the baby's bladder is distended and enlarged. Other warning signals include a continual dribbling of urine and a weak stream during urination. More commonly, though, posterior urethral valve is diagnosed in the first year when the boy develops a urinary tract infection with fever and poor feeding. If you notice these symptoms, notify your pediatrician at once.

Posterior urethral valve requires immediate medical attention to prevent serious urinary tract infections or damage to the kidneys. If the blockage is severe, the urine can back up through the ureters (the tubes between the bladder and the kidneys), creating pressure that can damage the kidneys.

Treatment

If your child has posterior urethral valve, your pediatrician may pass a small tube (catheter) into the bladder to relieve the obstruction temporarily and allow the urine to flow out of the bladder. He will obtain imaging of the bladder and kidneys. Your pediatrician will consult with a pediatric urologist, who may recommend surgery to remove the obstructing valve and prevent further infection or damage to the kidneys or urinary system. Bloodwork will be done to look at the level of kidney function, and a pediatric nephrologist will likely be consulted as well.

Undescended Testicles (Cryptorchidism)

During a woman's pregnancy, the baby boy's testes develop in his abdomen. As he nears birth, they descend through a tube (the inguinal canal) into the scrotum. In a small number of boys, especially those who are premature, one or both testicles fail to descend by the time of birth. In many of these boys, descent will occur during the first few months after birth. In some, however, this does not happen.

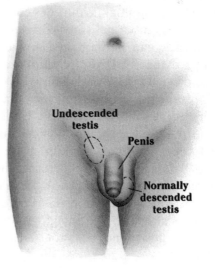

Undescended testis

Penis

Normally descended testis

Most boys will have a normal retraction of the testes under certain situations, such as while sitting in cold water (i.e., the testes "disappear" temporarily up into the inguinal canal) or when being examined by your pediatrician. However, in general, when the boy is warm and relaxed, testes should be low in the scrotum. The cause of most cases of undescended testicles is unknown.

If your child has undescended testicles, his scrotum may be small and appear underdeveloped. If only one testicle is undescended, the scrotum may look asymmetrical (full on one side, empty on the other). If the testicles sometimes are in the scrotum and at other times (e.g., when he is cold or excited) are absent and located above the scrotum, they are said to be retractile. This condition usually self-corrects as a boy grows older.

Rarely the undescended testicle may be twisted, and in the process, its blood supply may be stopped, causing pain in the inguinal (groin) or scrotal area. If this situation is not corrected, the testicle can be damaged severely and permanently. If your child has an undescended testicle and complains of pain in the groin or scrotal area, call your pediatrician immediately. Undescended testicles should be reevaluated at each regular checkup. If they do not descend into the scrotum by six months of age, treatment should be considered. The diagnosis is made by physical exam, and imaging studies like ultrasound are not usually helpful.

Treatment

Undescended testicles are treated with surgery to bring the testicle into the proper location in the scrotum. Many children with true undescended testes will also have an inguinal hernia (see page 552), and the hernia will be repaired at the same time that the undescended testis is surgically moved to the scrotum. If your son's undescended testicle is allowed to remain in that position for more than two years, he may have a higher than average risk of being unable to father children (infertility). This is especially true if both testes are undescended. Undescended testes are also at higher risk of developing testicular tumors in adult life. The risk is small but is still present even after the testis is surgically brought into the scrotum. Therefore it is important that children with an undescended testis be taught the importance of testicular self-exam when they are going through puberty.

Urinary Tract Infections

Urinary tract infections are common among young children, particularly girls. They generally are caused by bacteria that enter through the urethra. In infants, though, they may also rarely be caused by bacteria carried through the bloodstream to the kidneys from another part of the body. As the bacteria move through the urinary tract, they may cause an infection in various locations. Urinary tract infection (UTI) is a general term used for all the following specific infections.

- *Cystitis:* infection of the bladder

- *Pyelonephritis:* infection of the kidney

- *Urethritis:* infection of the urethra

The bladder is the area most commonly infected. Usually cystitis is caused by bacteria that get into the urinary tract through the urethra. The urethra is very short in girls, so bacteria that live on the skin, in the colon, and in the vagina can get into the bladder easily. Fortunately, these bacteria normally wash out when urinating.

Cystitis can cause lower abdominal pain, vomiting, tenderness, pain during urination, frequent urination, blood in the urine, recurrence of day- or nighttime wetting in a previously toilet-trained child, and a low-grade fever. Infection of the upper urinary tract (the kidneys) will cause more general abdominal pain and a higher fever, but is less likely to cause frequent and painful urination. In general, urinary tract infections in infants and young children (up to two years of age) may have few recognizable signs or symptoms other than a fever; they also have a greater potential for causing kidney damage than those occurring in older children.

Urinary tract infections must be treated with antibiotics as quickly as possible, so you should notify your pediatrician promptly if you suspect your child has developed one. This is especially the case for infants, in whom an unexplained high fever (that is, not explained by a respiratory infection or diarrhea) may be the only indicator of a urinary tract infection. If your infant has a fever with no other symptoms for more than three days, make sure to talk to your pediatrician, as an evaluation may be indicated.

Diagnosis/Treatment

When a urinary tract infection is suspected, particularly in a child with symptoms, your pediatrician will measure her blood pressure (since an increase in blood pressure can be a sign of a related kidney problem) and examine her for lower abdominal tenderness that might indicate a UTI. Your doctor will want to know what your child has been eating and drinking, because certain foods can irritate the urinary tract, causing symptoms similar to those of an infection.

Your pediatrician also will want a urine sample from your child for analysis. This must be collected by using a catheter in infants and small children who are not toilet trained. In toilet-trained children, the urine can be collected by the "clean catch" method. First, you'll use soap and water or special wipes provided by your pediatrician to cleanse the urethral opening (with an uncircumcised boy, hold the foreskin back). Then allow your child to start to urinate, but wait just a moment before you start to collect the sample in the special container provided by the doctor. In this way, any bacteria around the outside of the urethral opening will be washed away by the early urine voided and won't contaminate the specimen. In rare cases, a doctor may perform a suprapubic tap, in which a small needle is inserted through the skin of the lower abdomen into the bladder. The urine that is collected will be examined for any sign of blood cells or bacteria, and special tests (cultures) will be done to identify the bacteria. An antibiotic will be started if an infection is suspected, although depending on what the final results of the culture show, the particular antibiotic may need to be changed.

In agreement with guidelines for the treatment of UTI in infants and children (up to age twenty-four months), your pediatrician may prescribe antibiotics for a total of seven to fourteen days. Prompt treatment is important in order to eliminate the infection and prevent its spread, and also to reduce the chances of kidney damage. *It is important to take the full course of antibiotics, even if the discomfort resolves after a few days of treatment.* Otherwise the bacteria may grow again, causing further infection and more serious damage to the urinary tract.

The American Academy of Pediatrics recommends that imaging tests (such as ultrasound, X-rays, or renal scans) may be done in children depending on their age and how many urinary tract infections they have had. Some imaging studies may not be necessary following a first urinary tract infection if prenatal ultrasound stud-ies have adequately visualized the structure of the infant's urinary tract. Your pediatrician may conduct other tests to check the functioning of the kidneys. If any of these examinations indicate an anatomical abnormality of the bladder, ureters, or kidneys that should be corrected, your doctor will recommend that your child see a pediatric urologist or nephrologist.

In most cases, the AAP does *not* currently recommend after a course of antibiotics that additional antibiotics be given as a preventive (prophylactic) measure to prevent a recurrence of the infection, since research shows that this does not prevent future UTIs.

Wetting Problems or Enuresis

After your child is toilet trained (usually between ages two and four), it is not uncommon for him to wet the bed at night. This may happen as often as two to three times per week early in this period, and gradually become less and less frequent until it is completely gone at around age five in most children. The exact cause of this incontinence (wetting) is not known. The best way to approach it is to consider it to be something natural and unimportant, and never to scold or punish your child.

Some children continue to wet at night past the age of five. When wetting occurs only during sleep, it is called nocturnal (nighttime) enuresis, or bed-wetting. It affects one out of every four children at age five, one in five at age seven years, and about one in twenty at age ten years. Boys make up two-thirds of this group, and often there is a family history of bed-wetting (usually in the father). Although the reasons for bed-wetting are not fully understood, it may be related to the time it takes different children to develop control over the nervous and muscular aspects of responding to the sensation of a full bladder during the nighttime. Bed-wetting generally is *not* associated with other physical or emotional problems. It is important to realize that children have no conscious control of their bladders when they are sleeping. Thus, they should never be made to feel that the bed-wetting is something that they can consciously control and stop on their own.

A much smaller number of children over age five have daytime wetting problems, and an even smaller group is unable to hold their urine both day and night. When incontinence does occur during both the day and night, it may signal a more complicated problem with the bladder or the kidneys.

If your child wets at night, here are some possible causes:

■ Difficulty waking up when the bladder is full

■ Constipation, which can cause extra pressure on the bladder from the rectum

■ An abnormality of the spinal cord affecting nerves to the bladder

■ An early sign of diabetes mellitus (see page 632), a urinary tract infection (see page 790), or emotional distress caused by an upsetting event or unusual stress—but only if wetting began suddenly after an extended dry period.

Signs of a Problem

When your child is starting toilet training, he is sure to have "accidents." Therefore, you shouldn't be concerned about wetting until at least six months to a year after the training is successful. Even then, it is still normal for him to have some accidents, but they should decrease in number, so that by six months after toilet training is achieved, he should have only occasional accidents during the day, with perhaps a few more at night. If your child continues to wet frequently, or if you notice any of the following signals, talk with your pediatrician.

■ Wet underpants, nightclothes, and bed linens, even when the child regularly uses the toilet

■ Unusual straining during urination, a very small or narrow stream of urine, or dribbling after urination

■ Cloudy or pink urine, or blood-stains on underpants or nightclothes

■ Redness or rash in the genital area

■ Hiding underwear to conceal wetting

- Daytime as well as nighttime wetting

- Hard or infrequent stools

Treatment

Up to about the age of five years old, it is perfectly normal for your child to have occasional nighttime wetting or daytime accidents when she is laughing, engaged in physical activity, or just too busy playing; in these cases, you should not be concerned. Although annoying to you and perhaps embarrassing for your child, these episodes should stop on their own. There probably is no need for a medical investigation. However, your pediatrician will want to know the answers to the following questions.

- Is there a family history of wetting?

- How often does your child urinate, and at what times of the day?

- When do the accidents occur?

- Do accidents happen when your child is very active or upset, or when she's under unusual stress?

- Does your child tend to have accidents after drinking a lot of fluids or eating a lot of salty foods?

- Is there anything unusual about your child's urination or the way her urine looks?

If your pediatrician suspects a problem, he may check a urine sample for signs of a urinary tract infection (see page 790). If there is an infection, the doctor will treat it with antibiotics, and this may cure the wetting problems. Usually, however, an infection is not the cause.

If there are other indications that wetting is due to more than just slow development of the ability to respond to a full bladder, and the wetting persists well beyond age five, your pediatrician may request additional tests, such as an X-ray of the abdomen or an ultrasound of the kidneys. If an abnormality is found, the doctor may recommend that you consult a specialist.

If no physical cause can be found in a child who wets and is over five years of age, and the wetting is causing significant family disruption, your pediatrician may recommend a home treatment program. The program will vary, depending on whether your child wets during the day or the night.

HOME TREATMENT FOR DAYTIME WETTING AFTER TOILET TRAINING

1. *Prevent skin irritation* in the genital area by avoiding harsh detergents or underclothing, as well as bubble-making products in the bathwater. Also, choose mild soaps for bathing, and apply petroleum jelly to protect the affected areas from further irritation from the water and urine.

2. *Prevent constipation* or treat it if it occurs (see page 534). Sometimes treatment of constipation can completely cure daytime wetting.

3. *Try using a timed voiding program,* reminding your child to empty his bladder every few hours rather than waiting until he "has to go"—which by then may be too late. "Potty watches" can be useful tools to help with timed voiding and can be purchased online.

4. *Encourage good toilet posture.* This is especially important for girls in order to get all of the urine in the bladder out. Children should sit with a stool under their feet if their feet do not touch the bathroom floor. Legs should be relaxed and slightly spread to encourage pelvic floor muscles to relax.

HOME TREATMENT FOR NIGHTTIME BED-WETTING OVER THE AGE OF FIVE

The following plan usually is helpful, but you should discuss it with your pediatrician before beginning.

1. Explain the problem to your child, emphasizing that you understand and know it's not his fault.

2. Discourage him from drinking fluids during the two hours before bedtime.

3. Treat constipation if it is present.

If your child is still wetting after one to three months on this plan, your pediatrician may recommend using a bed-wetting alarm device. This alarm will awaken your child automatically as soon as he begins to wet, so he can get up and complete his urination in the toilet. Oftentimes, children will sleep through the alarm and not wake up when it goes off. When this occurs, parents will need to be able to hear the alarm so they can assist in waking the child up. When used consistently and according to your pediatrician's guidelines, this bladder-conditioning method is successful for more than half of the children who try it, and the relapse rate is low. However, it may take up to four months to work. It is important to follow your pediatrician's directions carefully in order to give this device the best chance to work.

Another option may be oral medications. These work in about half to two-thirds of the children who use them, and side effects are rare. However, relapse rates are high. Oral medications can also be used intermittently for camp, sleepovers, and other similar situations. It is important to limit drinking water before bedtime when on certain oral medications. This should be discussed with your doctor.

If None of the Treatments Work

A small number of children with bed-wetting simply do not respond to any treatment. However, almost all will outgrow the problem by adolescence. Until your child outgrows his wetting problem, he may need some emotional support from the family, and he also may benefit from speaking with his pediatrician about this condition, or receiving counseling with a child mental health professional.

Because bed-wetting is such a common problem, you may see advertisements for many treatment programs. You should be wary of them, however, as many false claims and promises are made. Your pediatrician is still your most reliable source for advice, and you should ask him for it before enrolling in or paying for any treatment program.

Read more about bed-wetting. A recommended book is *Waking Up Dry: A Guide to Help Children Overcome Bedwetting* by Howard J. Bennett (Elk Grove Village, IL: AAP, 2015).

~ 29 ~

Head, Neck, and Nervous System

Meningitis

Meningitis is an inflammation of the tissues that cover the brain and spinal cord. The inflammation sometimes affects the brain itself. With early diagnosis and proper treatment, a child with meningitis has a reasonable chance of a good recovery, though some forms of bacterial meningitis develop rapidly and have a high risk of complications.

Thanks to vaccines that protect against serious forms of bacterial meningitis, today most cases of meningitis are caused by viruses. The viral form usually is not very serious, except in infants less than three months of age and with certain viruses such as herpes simplex, which typically causes another serious infection. Once meningitis is diagnosed as being caused by a virus, there is no need for antibiotics and recovery should be complete.

Bacterial meningitis (several types of bacteria are involved) is a very serious disease. It occurs rarely in developed countries (because of the success of vaccines), but when it does occur, children under the age of two are at greatest risk.

The bacteria that cause meningitis often can be found in the mouths and throats of healthy children. But this does not necessarily mean that these children will get the disease. That doesn't happen unless the bacteria get into the bloodstream.

We still don't understand exactly why some children get meningitis and others don't, but we

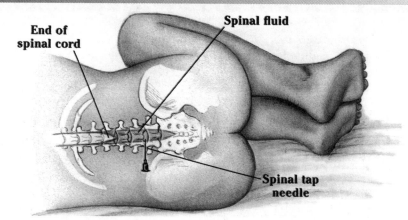

A spinal tap is taken from the space below the spinal cord so that the needle will not touch the spinal cord.

do know that certain groups of children are more likely to get the illness. These include the following:

■ Babies, especially those under two months of age (because their immune systems are not well developed, the bacteria can get into the bloodstream more easily)

■ Children with recurrent sinus infections

■ Children with recent serious head injuries and skull fractures

■ Children who have just had brain surgery

■ Children with cochlear implants

With prompt diagnosis and treatment, seven out of ten children who get bacterial meningitis recover without any complications. However, bear in mind that meningitis is a potentially fatal disease, and in about two

out of ten cases, it can lead to serious nervous-system problems, deafness, seizures, paralysis of the arms or legs, or learning difficulties. Because meningitis progresses quickly, it must be detected early and treated aggressively. This is why it's so important for you to notify your pediatrician immediately if your child displays any of the following warning signs.

If your child is less than two months old: A fever, decreased appetite, listlessness, or increased crying or irritability warrants a call to your doctor. At this age, the signs of meningitis can be very subtle and difficult to detect. It's better to call early and be wrong than to call too late.

If your child is two months to two years old: This is the most common age for meningitis. Look for symptoms such as fever, vomiting, decreased appetite, excessive crankiness, or excessive sleepiness. (His cranky periods might be extreme and his sleepy periods might make it impossible to arouse him.) Seizures along with a fever may be the first signs of meningitis, although most brief, generalized (so-called tonic-clonic) convulsions turn out to be simple febrile seizures, not meningitis. (See *Seizures, Convulsions, and Epilepsy*, page 803.) A rash also may be a symptom of this condition.

If your child is two to five years old: In addition to the above symptoms, a child of this age with meningitis may complain of a headache, pain in his back, or a stiff neck. He also may object to looking at bright lights.

Treatment

If, after an examination, your pediatrician is concerned that your child may have meningitis, she will order a blood test to check for a bacterial infection and also will want to obtain some spinal fluid by performing a spinal tap, or lumbar puncture (LP). This simple procedure involves inserting a special needle into your child's lower back to draw out spinal fluid. This is usually a safe technique in which fluid is sampled from the bottom of the sac surrounding the spinal cord. Signs of infection in this fluid will confirm that your child has bacterial meningitis. In that case he'll need to be admitted to the hospital for intravenous antibiotics and fluids and for careful observation for complications. During the first days of treatment, your child may not be able to eat or drink, so intravenous fluids will provide the medicine and nutrition he needs. For bacterial meningitis, intravenous antibiotics may be necessary for seven to twenty-one days, depend-

ing on the age of the child and the bacteria identified. If prolonged antibiotics are needed, your child may be able to continue receiving medication in the comfort of your own home. Most children with viral meningitis improve within seven to ten days without antibiotics. Children will typically recover at home with rest, fluids, and over-the-counter pain medications, although some might need to be treated in the hospital.

Prevention

Some types of bacterial meningitis can be prevented with vaccines. Ask your pediatrician about the following.

HIB (*HAEMOPHILUS INFLUENZAE* TYPE B) VACCINE

This vaccine will decrease the chance of children becoming infected with *Haemophilus influenzae* type b (Hib) bacteria, which was the leading cause of bacterial meningitis among young children before this immunization became available. The vaccine is given by injection to children at two months, four months, and six months, and then again between twelve and fifteen months of age. (Some combined vaccines may allow your doctor to omit the last injection.)

MENINGOCOCCAL VACCINE

There are two kinds of meningococcal vaccines available in the United States, but the preferred vaccine for children is called the meningococcal conjugate vaccine (MCV4). Although it can prevent four types of meningococcal disease, it is not routinely recommended for very young children; rather, it is given to young adolescents (eleven to twelve years of age), or teenagers at the time they start high school (or at fifteen years old).

PNEUMOCOCCAL VACCINE

This vaccine is effective in preventing many serious infections caused by the pneumococcus bacteria, including meningitis as well as bacteremia (an infection of the bloodstream) and pneumonia. It is recommended starting at two months of age, with additional doses at four, six, and between twelve and fifteen months of age. Some children who have an increased susceptibility to serious infections (these high-risk children include those with abnormally functioning immune systems, sickle cell disease, certain kidney problems, and other chronic conditions) may receive an additional pneumococcal vaccine between ages two and five years.

Motion Sickness

Motion sickness occurs when the brain receives conflicting signals from the motion-sensing parts of the body: the inner ears, the eyes, and nerves in the extremities. Under usual circumstances, all three areas respond to any motion. When the signals they receive and send are inconsistent—for example, if you watch rapid motion on a movie screen, your eyes sense the motion, but your inner ear and joints do not—the brain receives conflicting signals and activates a response that can make you feel sick. The same thing can happen when a child is sitting so low in the backseat of a car that she cannot see outside. Her inner ear senses the motion, but her eyes and joints do not.

Motion sickness usually starts with a vague feeling of stomach upset (queasiness), a cold sweat, fatigue, and loss of appetite. This usually progresses to vomiting. A young child may not be able to describe queasiness but will demonstrate it by becoming pale and restless, yawning, and crying. Later she may lose interest in food (including her favorite ones) and even vomit. This response can be affected by previous car trips that made her sick, but it usually improves over time.

We do not know why motion sickness happens more often in some children than others. Since many of these children years later experience occasional headaches, there is a belief that motion sickness may be an early form of migraine. Motion sickness occurs most often on a first boat or plane ride, or when the motion is very intense, such as that caused by rough water or turbulent air. Stress and excitement also can start this problem or make it worse.

What You Can Do

If your child starts to develop motion sickness, the best approach is to stop the activity that is causing the problem. If it occurs in the car, stop as soon as safely possible and let her get out and walk around. If you are on a long car trip, you may have to make frequent short stops, but it will be worth it. If this condition develops on a swing or merry-go-round, stop the motion promptly and get your child off the equipment.

Since car sickness is the most common form of motion sickness in children, many preventive measures have been developed. In addition to frequent stops, try the following.

■ If she has not eaten for three hours, give your child a *light* snack before the trip—which also helps on a boat or plane. This relieves hunger pangs, which seem to add to the symptoms.

■ Try to focus her attention away from the queasy feeling. Listen to the radio, sing, or talk.

■ Have her look at things outside the car, not at books, games, or screens in her lap.

If none of the above works, stop the car, remove her from her car safety seat, and have her lie on her back for a few minutes with her eyes closed. A cool cloth on the forehead also tends to lessen the symptoms.

If you are going on a trip and your child has had motion sickness in the past, you might want to give her medication ahead of time to prevent problems. Some of these medications are available without a prescription, but ask your pediatrician before using them. Although they can help, they often produce side effects, such as drowsiness (which means that when you get to your destination your child might be too tired to enjoy it), dry mouth and nose, or blurred vision. Using nondrowsy versions usually cause fewer side effects.

If your child has symptoms of motion sickness at times when she is not involved with a movement activity—particularly if she also has a headache; has difficulty hearing, seeing, walking, or talking; or stares off into space—tell your pediatrician about it. These may be symptoms of problems other than motion sickness.

Mumps

Mumps is a viral infection that usually causes swelling of the salivary glands (the glands that produce the digestive juices in the mouth). Thanks to the MMR (measles, mumps, and rubella) vaccine given at twelve to fifteen months with a booster at age four to six years, most children in developed countries will never get this disease. The American Academy of Pediatrics recommends that if your child has not been immunized with the MMR vaccine in early childhood as suggested, your child (eighteen years old and younger) should be given two doses of MMR, separated by four weeks.

While the administration of the MMR vaccine is very important, if a child has not been immunized, the parent should know how to identify mumps and distinguish it from similar ailments. The parotid gland, located in front of the ear at and above the angle of the jaw, is the one most often affected by mumps. The swelling can be on one or both sides of the face. However, other salivary glands in and around the face may be involved. Symptoms normally last seven to ten days. Not all children with mumps appear swollen, as some have a milder case. Anyone who has the virus in his system, whether symptoms were mild or severe, will become immune to it and be protected for life.

The mumps virus is transmitted when an infected individual coughs droplets containing the virus into the air or onto his hands. A nearby child can inhale these particles, and the virus can pass through his respiratory system into his bloodstream, finally settling in his salivary glands. At this point, the virus usually causes swelling of the glands along the side of one or both cheeks.

Parotid gland   Salivary glands
Sublingual
Submandibular

Other symptoms of mumps may include swelling and pain in the joints and, in boys, swelling of the testes. In extremely rare cases, the virus can cause swelling of the ovaries in girls or swelling of the brain in boys or girls.

It's important to note that salivary gland swelling can be caused by infections other than mumps. This explains why some parents are convinced that their children have had the disease more than once. If your child has been immunized or already has had mumps and his cheeks become swollen, consult your pediatrician to determine the cause.

Treatment

There is no specific treatment for mumps, aside from making the child as comfortable as possible with rest, lots of fluids, and acetaminophen for fever. Although a child with the disease may not be too eager to take fluids, you should keep a glass of water or noncitrus juice nearby, and encourage him to take frequent sips. Sometimes a warm compress over the swollen gland will give some short-term relief.

If your child's condition worsens, or if he develops complications such as painful testes, severe abdominal pain, or extreme listlessness, contact your pediatrician right away. Complications are extremely rare, but the doctor will want to examine your child to see if he needs more extensive medical treatment.

Seizures, Convulsions, and Epilepsy

Seizures are sudden temporary changes in consciousness, physical movement, sensation, or behavior caused by abnormal electrical impulses in the brain. Depending on what part(s) of the body are affected by the abnormal electrical impulses, a seizure may cause sudden stiffening of the body, rhythmic shaking, isolated body jerks, complete relaxation of the muscles (which can make a person appear to be paralyzed temporarily), or staring spells. Sometimes these seizures are referred to as "fits" or "spells." The terms "convulsion" and "seizure" are often used interchangeably.

A convulsion that involves the whole body (sometimes called a generalized tonic-clonic or grand mal seizure) is the most dramatic type of seizure, causing rapid, violent movements and loss of consciousness. Convulsions occur in about five out of every hundred people at some time during childhood. By contrast, absence seizures (previously called petit mal seizures) are momentary episodes with a vacant stare or a brief (one- or two-second) lapse of attention. These occur mainly in young children and may be so subtle that they aren't noticed until they begin affecting schoolwork.

Febrile convulsions (seizures caused by high fever in the absence of acute or chronic neurological disease) occur in three or four out of every hundred children between six months and five years of age, but most often around twelve to eighteen months old. Children younger than one year at the time of their first simple febrile seizure convulsion have approximately a 50 percent chance of having another, while children over one year of age when they have their first seizure have about a 30 percent chance of having a second one. Nevertheless, only a very small number of affected children will go on to develop epilepsy (chronic seizures without a fever). A febrile convulsion can cause reactions as mild as a rolling of the eyes or stiffening of the limbs, or as startling as a generalized convulsion with twitching and jerking movements that involve the whole body. Febrile convulsions usually last less than one minute, but although uncommon, can last for up to fifteen minutes, and ordinarily the child's behavior shortly returns to normal.

The term "epilepsy" is used to describe seizures that occur repeatedly over time without an acute illness (like fever) or other trigger. Sometimes the cause of the recurring seizures is known (symptomatic epilepsy), and sometimes it is not (idiopathic epilepsy). Some children experience sudden episodes that might masquerade as or imitate seizure but are really not. Examples include breath holding, fainting (syncope), facial or body twitching (myoclonus), and unusual sleep disorders (night terrors, sleepwalking, and cataplexy). They may occur just once or may recur over a limited time period. Again, although these episodes may resemble epilepsy or true seizures, they are not, and they require quite different treatment.

Treatment

Most seizures will stop on their own and do not require immediate medical treatment. If your child is having a convulsion, protect her from injuring herself by laying her with her head turned to the side, so she will not choke if she vomits.

If the convulsion does not stop within two or three minutes or is unusually severe (difficulty breathing, choking, blueness of the skin, having several in a row), call 911 for emergency medical help. Do not leave your child unattended. After the seizure stops, call the pediatrician immediately and arrange to meet in the doctor's office or the nearest emergency department. Also call your doctor if your child is on an anticonvulsant medication, since this may mean that the dosage must be adjusted.

If your child has a fever, the pediatrician will check to see if there is an infection. If there is no fever and this was your child's first convulsion, the doctor will try to determine other possible causes by asking if there is a family history of seizures or if your child has had any recent head injury. He will examine your child and also may order blood tests or testing with an electroencephalogram (EEG), which measures the electrical activity of the brain. In some cases, your child may require imaging of the brain using computed tomography (CT or CAT scan) or magnetic reso-nance imaging (MRI). Sometimes a spinal tap will be performed to obtain a specimen of spinal fluid that can be examined for some causes of convulsions such as meningitis, an infection of the covering of the brain (see page 797). If no explanation or cause can be found for the seizures, the doctor may consult a pediatric neurologist, a pediatrician who specializes in disorders of the nervous system.

If your child has had a febrile convulsion, some parents may try controlling fever using fever-reducing medications (acetaminophen, ibuprofen) or lukewarm baths. However, these approaches do *not* prevent future febrile seizures, but only make the child more comfortable. If a bacterial infection is present, your doctor will probably prescribe an antibiotic. If a serious infection such as meningitis is responsible for the seizure, your child will have to be hospitalized for further treatment. Also, when seizures are caused by abnormal amounts of sugar, sodium, or calcium in the blood, hospitalization may be required so that the cause can be found and the imbalances corrected.

If epilepsy is diagnosed, your child usually will be placed on an anticonvulsant medication. When the proper dosage is maintained, the seizures are often well controlled. Your child may need to have her blood checked periodically after starting some medications to make certain there is an adequate amount of medication in her system. She also may need periodic EEGs. Medication usually is continued until there have been no seizures for a year or two.

As frightening as seizures can be, it's encouraging to know that the likelihood that your child will have another one drops greatly as she gets older. (Only one in a hundred adults ever has a seizure.) Unfortunately, a great deal of misunderstanding and confusion about seizures still exists, so it is important that your child's friends and teachers become educated about her condition. (If you need additional support or information, consult with your pediatrician or contact your local or state branch of the Epilepsy Foundation, epilepsy.com; 1-800-332-1000.)

Head Tilt (Torticollis)

Head tilt is a condition that causes a child to hold her head or neck in a twisted or otherwise abnormal position. She may lean her head toward one shoulder and, when lying on her stomach, always turn the same side of her face toward the mattress. This can cause her head to flatten on one side and her face to appear uneven or out of line. If not treated, head tilt may lead to permanent facial deformity or unevenness and to restricted head movement.

Most cases of head tilt are associated with a condition called torticollis, although in rare instances a head tilt can be due to other causes such as hearing loss, misalignment of the eyes, reflux (a flowing back of stomach acid into the esophagus), a throat or lymph node infection, or, very uncommonly, a brain tumor.

ACQUIRED TORTICOLLIS (DUE TO INJURY OR INFLAMMATION)

This is more likely to occur in older children, up to the age of nine or ten. This type of torticollis usually results from an inflammation of the throat caused by an upper respiratory infection, a sore throat, an injury, or some unknown factor. The swelling, for reasons still not known, causes the tissue surrounding the upper spine to loosen, allowing the vertebral bones to move out of normal position. When this happens, the neck muscles go into spasm, causing the head to tilt to one side. Onset of this condition is typically sudden and very painful.

CONGENITAL MUSCULAR TORTICOLLIS

By far the most common cause of head tilt among children under age five is congenital torticollis. This condition commonly occurs due to positioning while the baby is still in the womb and rarely may occur during birth (particularly breech and difficult first-time deliveries). Whatever the cause, this condition usually is detected in the first six to eight weeks after birth, when the pediatrician notices tightness in one of the muscles of the neck. About half the time there may be a small lump in the muscle. The affected muscle is the sternocleidomastoid muscle, which connects the breastbone, head, and neck. Later the muscle contracts and causes the head to tilt to one side and look toward the opposite side.

Treatment

Each type of head tilt requires different treatment. It is very important to seek such treatment early, so that the problem is corrected before it causes permanent deformity. Your pediatrician will examine your child's neck and may order X-rays of the area in order to identify the cause of the problem. X-rays or ultrasound of the hip also may be ordered, as some children with congenital muscular torticollis also have an abnormality known as developmental dysplasia of the hip. If the doctor decides that the problem is congenital muscular torticollis, you will learn an exercise program to stretch the neck muscles. The doctor will show you how to gently move your child's head in the opposite direction from the tilt. You'll need to do this several times a day, very gradually extending the movement as the muscle stretches.

When your child sleeps, it is best to place her on her back, with her head positioned opposite to the direction of the tilt. In rare instances, your pediatrician may suggest adjustments to her sleep position. When she is awake, position her so those things she wants to look at (windows, mobiles, pictures, and activity) are on the side away from the injury. In that way, she'll stretch the shortened muscle while trying to see these objects. Your pediatrician may also recommend placing her on her stomach while awake and turning her face away from the affected side. These simple strategies cure this type of head tilt in the vast majority of cases, preventing the need for later surgery. (Your pediatrician may refer your child to a physical therapist to help work on this condition.)

If the problem is not corrected by exercise or position change, your pediatrician will refer you to a pediatric neurologist or orthopedist. In some cases it may be necessary to lengthen the involved tendon surgically. If your child's head tilt is caused by something other than congenital muscular torticollis and the X-rays show no spinal abnormality, other treatment involving rest, a special collar, gentle stretching, massage, traction, application of heat to the area, medication, or, rarely, further imaging or surgery may be necessary. For treating torticollis due to injury or inflammation, your doctor may recommend applying heat, as well as using massage and stretching to ease head and neck pain. Your pediatrician can refer you to a specialist for a definitive diagnosis and treatment program.

~ 30 ~

Heart

Arrhythmias

YOUR CHILD'S HEART rate normally will vary to some degree. Fever, crying, exercise, or other vigorous activity makes any heart beat faster. The younger the child, the faster the normal heart rate. As your child gets older, the heart rate will slow down. A resting heart rate of 130 to 150 beats per minute is normal for a newborn infant, but it is too fast for a five-year-old child at rest. In a very athletic teenager, a resting heart rate of 50 to 60 beats per minute may be normal.

The heart's regular rhythm or beat is maintained by a small electrical circuit that runs through nerves in the walls of the heart. When the circuit is working properly, the heartbeat is quite regular; but when there's a problem in the circuit, an irregular heartbeat, or arrhythmia, can occur. Some children are born with abnormalities in this heart circuitry, but arrhythmias also can be caused by infections or chemical imbalances in the blood. Even in healthy children, there can be other variations in the rhythm of the heartbeat, including changes that occur just as a result of breathing. Such a fluctuation is called sinus arrhythmia, and requires no special evaluation or treatment because it is normal.

So-called premature heartbeats are another form of irregular rhythm that requires no treatment. If these occur in your child, she might say that her heart "skipped a beat" or did a "flip-flop." Usually these symptoms do not indicate the presence of significant heart disease.

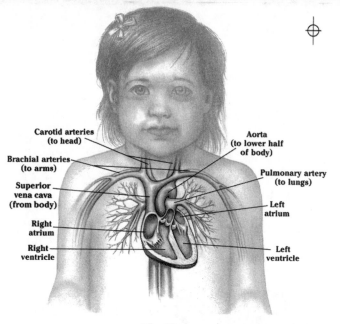

Carotid arteries
(to head)

Brachial arteries
(to arms)

Superior
vena cava
(from body)

Right
atrium

Right
ventricle

Aorta
(to lower half
of body)

Pulmonary artery
(to lungs)

Left
atrium

Left
ventricle

The Heart

If your pediatrician says that your child has a true arrhythmia, it could mean that her heart beats faster than normal (tachycardia), very fast (flutter), fast and with no regularity (fibrillation), slower than normal (bradycardia), or that it has isolated early beats (premature beats). While true arrhythmias are not very common, when they do occur they can be serious. On rare occasions they can cause fainting or even heart failure. Fortunately, they can be treated successfully, so it's important to detect arrhythmias as early as possible.

Signs and Symptoms

If your child has a true arrhythmia, your pediatrician may discover it during a routine visit. But should you notice any of the following warning signs between pediatric visits, notify your doctor immediately.

■ Your infant suddenly becomes pale and listless; the body feels limp.

■ Your child complains of her heart beating fast while at rest.

■ She tells you she feels uncomfortable, weak, or dizzy.

■ She blacks out or faints.

It's unlikely that your child will ever experience any of these symptoms, but if she does, your pediatrician will perform additional tests and perhaps consult with a pediatric cardiologist. In the process the doctors may do an electrocardiogram (ECG) to better distinguish a normal sinus arrhythmia from a true arrhythmia. An ECG is the recording of the electrical activity of the heart, and it will allow the doctor to observe any irregularities more closely.

Sometimes your child's unusual heartbeats may occur at unpredictable times, often not when the ECG is being taken. In that case the cardiologist may suggest that your child carry a small portable recorder called a Holter monitor that continuously records her heartbeat over a one- to two-day period. During this time you'll be asked to keep a log of your child's activities and symptoms. Comparing the ECG with your observations will help make a diagnosis. For example, if your child feels her heart "flutter" and becomes dizzy at 2:15 p.m. and the ECG shows her heart suddenly beating faster at the same time, the diagnosis of arrhythmia will probably be established.

Occasionally irregular heartbeats will occur only during exercise. If that's the case with your child, the cardiologist may have her ride a stationary bicycle or run on a treadmill while her heartbeat is being recorded. When your child is old enough to participate in sports, ask your pediatrician if any special tests or restrictions are necessary.

Heart Murmur

Technically, a heart murmur is simply a noise heard between the beats of the heart. When a doctor listens to the heart, she hears a sound something like *lub-dub, lub-dub, lub-dub*. Most often, the period between the *lub* and the *dub* and between the *dub* and the *lub* is silent. If there is any sound during this period, it is called a murmur. Heart murmurs are extremely common, and are usually "functional" or "innocent" (that is, the sounds are caused by a healthy heart pumping blood normally). In preschool and school-age children, heart murmurs are almost never a concern. Most children with a murmur require no special care, and the sound eventually disappears.

If your child has such a murmur, it probably will be discovered between the ages of one and five years during a routine examination. The doctor then will listen carefully to determine if this is a functional heart murmur or one that might indicate a problem. Usually, just by listening to its sound, the pediatrician will be able to tell if a murmur is innocent (normal blood flow through a normal heart). If necessary, she will consult a pediatric cardiologist to be certain, but additional tests are usually not needed. On rare occasions, a pediatrician will hear a murmur that sounds abnormal enough to indicate that something might be wrong with the heart. If the doctor suspects this, your child will be referred for an echocardiogram (ultrasound exam of the heart) or to a pediatric cardiologist to enable a precise diagnosis to be made.

Although some murmurs are normal and do not mean there is any underlying abnormality of the heart, other murmurs are more concerning.

Such abnormal murmurs are *not* functional or innocent, and most likely they will require the attention of a pediatric cardiologist immediately. They may be due to abnormal connections between the pumping chambers (septal defects) or the major blood vessels coming from the heart (e.g., transposition of vessels). Your infant will be observed for changes in skin color (turning blue), as well as breathing or feeding difficulties. He also may undergo additional tests, such as a chest X-ray, electrocardiogram (ECG), and an ultrasound of the heart (echocardiogram). This echocardiogram creates a picture of the inside of the heart by using sound waves. The cardiologist and pediatrician together will make a decision as to next steps depending on the results of these tests. If all of these tests prove normal, then it is safe to conclude that the baby has an innocent murmur and he will not need to be seen again by a cardiologist.

When a specific condition called patent ductus arteriosus (PDA) occurs, it is often detected shortly after birth, most commonly in premature babies. In infants with PDA, blood circulates abnormally between the two major arteries that come off the heart. In most cases, the only symptom of PDA is a heart murmur until the ductus closes on its own shortly after birth, which often happens in otherwise healthy, full-term newborns. Sometimes, especially in premature babies, it may not close on its own, or it may be large and permit too much blood to pass through the lungs, which can place extra strain on the heart, forcing it to work harder and causing a rise in pressure in the arteries of the lungs.

Treatment

Functional or innocent heart murmurs are normal and therefore require no treatment. Children with this type of heart murmur do not need repeated evaluations or long-term follow-up care from cardiologists, nor do they require restrictions on sports or other physical activities. Innocent heart murmurs generally disappear by midadolescence. Cardiologists don't know why they go away, any more than we know why they appear in the first place. In the meantime, don't be discouraged if the murmur is softer on one visit to the pediatrician and loud again on the next. This may simply mean that your child's heart is beating at a slightly different rate each time. Most likely, this normal murmur will go away eventually.

Patent ductus arteriosus is a self-correcting problem in some cases; in others, medications can be used to close a PDA. But if the ductus arteriosus remains open, it may need to be corrected surgically or with a catheter.

If other, more serious, heart conditions are diagnosed from birth or shortly thereafter, and the evaluation reveals more serious defects, the pediatric cardiologist and pediatrician will consult a pediatric cardiac surgeon, often at a children's hospital or large university hospital where complete pediatric cardiac diagnostic and intervention capabilities exist.

Hypertension/High Blood Pressure

We usually think of high blood pressure, or hypertension, as a problem that affects adults. But, in fact, this condition can occur at any age, even in infancy. About ten of every hundred children have higher than normal blood pressure, although only about three to four of those have actual hypertension.

The term "blood pressure" actually refers to two separate measurements: *Systolic* blood pressure is the highest pressure reached in the arteries as the heart pumps blood out for circulation through the body; *diastolic* blood pressure is the lower pressure that occurs in the arteries when the heart relaxes between beats. If either or both of these measurements are above the range found in healthy people of the same age and sex, it's called hypertension.

In many cases, hypertension seems to develop with age. As a result, your child may show no signs of high blood pressure as an infant, but may develop the condition as she grows. Children who have overweight are much more prone to have hypertension (as well as other health problems). Thus, healthy eating habits (getting important nutrients without overeating) and plenty of physical activity are important throughout the early years of childhood (and for the rest of her life).

In most instances of high blood pressure, other than those cases caused or made worse by obesity, no known cause can be identified. However, in certain children, hypertension may be a symptom of another serious problem, such as kidney disease or abnormalities of the heart or of the nervous or endocrine (gland) system.

Most often, this condition causes no noticeable discomfort, but any of the following symptoms may indicate high blood pressure:

- Headache

- Dizziness

- Shortness of breath

- Visual disturbances

- Fatigue

- Swelling around the ankles

Fortunately, high blood pressure in children rarely causes the serious problems that can occur in adults with hypertension. Usually hypertension in children can be controlled through dietary changes, medication, or a combination of the two. However, if hypertension is allowed to continue or become worse over many years, the prolonged extra pressure can lead to heart failure or stroke in adulthood. Also, long-term hypertension causes changes in blood vessel walls that may result in damage to the kidneys, eyes, and other organs. For these reasons it's important for children with hypertension to have their blood pressure checked regularly by their pediatrician, and for you to follow the doctor's treatment advice carefully.

Treatment

Starting at the age of three, your child's blood pressure will be measured as part of their yearly well-child checkup. This is how hypertension is usually discovered. If the blood pressure reading is high, you will be asked to return to have it repeated. If it is still high after several visits, your child may be asked to have a special test called twenty-four-hour ambulatory blood pressure monitoring to confirm that the blood pressure is high not just in the doctor's office, but throughout the day and night.

If your child still has high blood pressure after these repeat measurements, your pediatrician will order tests to see if there is an underlying medical problem. These tests include examining the urine and blood. Sometimes an ultrasound is used to examine the kidneys. If no medical problem can be found, your child will be diagnosed with *primary hypertension*. If there is an underlying cause found, your child will need to be sent to the appropriate pediatric specialist so that

High-Sodium (Salt) Foods

(more than 400 mg/serving)

Seasonings: bouillon, salted meat tenderizers, salted spices (e.g., garlic salt, onion salt, seasoned salt), soy sauce, teriyaki sauce

Snack foods, processed foods in boxes or bags: salted pretzels, crackers, chips, and popcorn

Commercially prepared foods: most frozen dinners and commercially prepared entrees; dry and canned soups

Canned or processed vegetables: any vegetables prepared in brine (e.g., olives, pickles, sauerkraut); vegetable juices (e.g., tomato juice)

Cheeses: processed cheese foods, some types of cheeses including American cheese, blue cheese, cottage cheese, and Parmesan cheese

Processed or packaged meat: any smoked, cured, pickled, or processed products (e.g., corned beef, bacon, dried meat and fish, ham, luncheon meats, sausages, and frankfurters)

your child receives the right kind of care for that condition.

What will the doctor tell you to do? If obesity is the cause, the first step may be to have your child lose weight. This will need to be very closely monitored by your pediatrician. Not only will weight loss lower blood pressure, it can provide many other health benefits as well. The next step toward reducing your child's blood pressure is to make dietary changes. These include increasing the number of servings of fruits and vegetables, and reducing the salt in her diet. (See box opposite, *High-Sodium [Salt] Foods.*) Be cautious when shopping for packaged foods; some canned and processed foods contain a great deal of salt, so learn to read labels and check labels carefully to make sure the items have little or no salt added. Fast food and other types of restaurant foods are often high in salt, so minimize their intake. Cooking fresh foods at home is always healthier than eating out. Your pediatrician may have you speak with a dietitian to help you learn the best eating plan for your child. Your pediatrician will suggest that your child get more exercise and limit the amount of time spent in sedentary activities like watching TV. Physical activity seems to help regulate blood pressure, may help control weight, and thus can help reduce mild hypertension.

Once your pediatrician knows your child has high blood pressure, he'll want to check it frequently to make sure the hypertension is not becoming more severe. Depending on how high the blood pressure is, he may refer your child to a child hypertension specialist, usually a pediatric nephrologist (kidney specialist) or pediatric cardiologist (heart specialist). If it does become worse, it may be treated with medication as well as diet and exercise. Many types of medications are available, which work in different ways. When your child's blood pressure is brought under control with diet or medication, it is important to continue the treatment according to your doctor's recommendations, including changes in diet, or the hypertension will return.

Prevention

It's very important to detect hypertension early. Uncontrolled long-standing hypertension can have damaging effects on several other organs in the body such as the heart, kidneys, and brain. It is recommended that all children have their blood pressure checked at their well-child visits beginning at age three, sooner for those at high risk. These include infants who were preterm, or of low birth weight, or who had a difficult or prolonged hospital stay. It also includes children who have congenital heart disease, who are receiving medications that might increase blood pressure, or who have any other condition that might lead to high blood pressure.

Because children with overweight are more likely to develop hypertension (as well as other health problems), watch your child's caloric intake, teach your children about healthy food choices, and make sure she gets plenty of exercise. Even relatively small decreases in weight or small increases in physical activity can make a big difference and may prevent hypertension in children with overweight.

Kawasaki Disease

Kawasaki disease is a rare systemic process where blood vessels throughout the body become inflamed. It is a potentially serious and perplexing disease, the cause of which is unknown. One sign of this disease includes fever, usually quite high, that lasts for at least five days and doesn't respond to antibiotics and does not have an alternative cause. Fever should be present to consider a diagnosis of Kawasaki disease in the ill child; in addition, other signs must be present on examination. Most often, four of the six following signs appear in the first week of a typical case:

1. Rash over some or all of the body, often more severe in the diaper area, especially in infants under twelve months of age

2. Redness and swelling of the palms of the hand and the soles of the feet; in the later stage, peeling of the skin around the base of the nails

3. Red, swollen, and cracked lips and/or a strawberry tongue (red and bumpy)

4. Red, inflamed eyes, involving the sclerae (white part)

5. A single swollen lymph gland, particularly on one side of the neck

6. Irritability (crankiness) or listlessness (lethargy); complaints of abdominal pain, headache, and/or joint pain

When Kawasaki-disease-associated inflammation of the blood vessels occurs, it often involves the arteries of the heart (the coronary arteries); this can be present in up to 25 percent of cases. Blood tests are used to demonstrate inflammation, and a heart ultrasound (echocardiogram) will be used to evaluate the coronary arteries in the child with Kawasaki disease. The echocardiogram can identify inflammation, which can weaken the walls of the blood vessels. In some cases this weakening may even balloon out, causing aneurysms (blood-filled swellings of the blood vessels). In most cases the inflammation in the blood vessels appears to resolve after several months to years, but in some cases, the coronary artery may become stenotic (narrow).

Kawasaki disease occurs most frequently in Japan and Korea and in individuals of Japanese and Korean ancestry, but it can be found among all racial groups and on every continent. The exact number of cases is not known, but it is probably between five thousand and ten thousand per year in the United States, typically occurring in infants between eighteen and twenty-four months of age and in preschoolers. Kawasaki disease occurs rarely in infants between six weeks and six months of age; in this age group, unremitting fever may be the only sign noted. The peak age of occurrence in the United States is between six months and five years.

Kawasaki disease is not contagious. It is extremely uncommon for two children in the same household to get the disease. Likewise, it does not spread among children in childcare programs, where there is daily close contact. Although Kawasaki disease can occur in community outbreaks, particularly in the winter and early spring, no one knows the cause. Despite intensive research, no bacterium, virus, or toxin has been identified as a cause of the disease. No specific test makes the diagnosis. The diagnosis is made based on the signs of illness mentioned previously and by excluding other possible diseases.

Treatment

Kawasaki disease can be treated but not prevented. If it is diagnosed early enough, intravenous immunoglobulin (a mixture of human antibodies), also known as IVIG, can greatly reduce the risk of a child developing coronary aneurysms. If your child receives IVIG, this may impact the routine immunization schedule for so-called live virus vaccines (varicella and MMR vaccine), so parents should check with their pediatrician. However, all inactivated vaccines, including influenza vaccine, should be given on schedule.

In addition to IVIG, the child with Kawasaki disease will receive aspirin, initially in high doses during the first stage of Kawasaki disease and in low doses during the recovery stage, until your pediatrician tells you it is OK to stop. Aspirin can decrease the tendency of blood to clot in damaged blood vessels, and it is used to prevent clots from developing in the coronary arteries. Although it's appropriate to use aspirin to treat Kawasaki disease, aspirin should not be used to treat children with minor illnesses (e.g., a cold or influenza), as it has been linked with a serious disease called Reye syndrome (see page 555). If a child is treated with aspirin for Kawasaki disease and exposed to influenza or chickenpox, the aspirin should be stopped and parents should discuss a suitable temporary substitute medicine with their pediatrician.

~ 31 ~

Immunizations

IMMUNIZATIONS HAVE HELPED children stay healthy for more than a century. Routine vaccines have become one of the best weapons available to protect your child against major childhood diseases.

Immunizations, in fact, are one of the greatest public health success stories of our times. Many diseases that were once a routine part of growing up, some of them life-threatening, are now preventable and relatively rare, thanks to improvements in sanitation, better nutrition, less crowded living conditions, antibiotics—and, most important, vaccines. At one time, most people did not reach adulthood without someone in their family or circle of friends being touched by a very serious illness or death caused by an infec-

tious disease. But now those same diseases are at record low levels in the United States as well as many other countries in the world—and that's because immunization rates are at record highs. Routine immunization against sixteen infectious diseases is now recommended between birth and eighteen years of age as well as annual immunization against influenza. Vaccines work extremely well—most are more than 90 percent effective in preventing diseases—so they are valuable tools for keeping children safe and healthy. When parents learn of the risks of these infections—for example, whooping cough causing seizures, brain disease, and even death—the argument in favor of childhood immunizations is persuasive. Although chickenpox, for example, is usually a mild disease, before the vaccine was available more than eleven thousand children were hospitalized each year when chickenpox sores became infected. Before the vaccine, about a hundred people per year died of chickenpox complications, and untold numbers were scarred each year. But now this disease can be prevented.

Important and Safe

Because many parents (and even some doctors) have never seen a child with whooping cough, diphtheria, tetanus, polio, or measles, mothers and fathers sometimes ask their pediatrician whether their child really needs vaccines at all. But while many of the illnesses that once caused lifelong disabilities or even death are now uncommon, they haven't been wiped out completely. Yes, they are preventable, but the germs that cause many of them are still around, and are regularly brought into the country by international travelers.

Just consider the case of the *Haemophilus influenzae* type b (Hib) vaccine. It protects children from serious childhood diseases like meningitis (an inflammation of the tissues that cover the brain and spinal cord) and throat infections that can block the airway (epiglottitis). Before this vaccine became available in the 1980s, there were about twenty thousand cases of Hib disease in the United States every year. *H. influenzae* type b was the most common cause of bacterial meningitis in the United States, and it was a major cause of intellectual disability and deafness. It caused about twelve thousand cases of meningitis each year in children younger than five years of age—especially in babies six to twelve months old. Of those children infected, one in twenty died from this disease, and one in four developed permanent brain damage. Today, because most Hib disease is prevented by immunization, there are fewer than one hundred cases annually in the United States.

At the same time, vaccines are very safe—but they're not perfect. Like medications, they can cause occasional reactions, but usually these are mild (see *More About Immunizations* on page 819). Side effects like redness or discomfort at the site of the injection can happen in as many as one out of four children. They appear soon after the shot is given, and then usually go away within a day or two. Your child also may be fussy for a day or two following immunization. Although more severe reactions can occur, they are much less common. A very small number of children with certain health conditions should not receive certain vaccines. Talk to your doctor if your child had a serious reaction to a previous vaccine, is allergic to a vaccine component, has a problem fighting infections, or is sick on the day of the appointment. This type of information can help your doctor determine if your child should postpone or not receive some vaccines. In years past, some critics of immunizations have pointed to a preservative called thimerosal, which for decades had been added to some vaccines to prevent contamination of vaccines by bacteria. Thimerosal has a small amount of organic mercury in it, which worried some parents. They were concerned about a link between disorders such as autism and vaccines that contain thimerosal. Numerous rigorous scientific studies in multiple countries have shown there is no link between thimerosal in vaccines and autism. There is no credible evidence linking vaccines, or any component of them, to autism. In addition, all vaccines manufactured for infants and almost all for older children and adults in the United States are thimerosal-free or contain only trace amounts.

More About Immunizations

When you have your children immunized:

- You protect them from dangerous and potentially fatal diseases.

- You reduce the severity of the disease if your children happen to get it.

- You cut down the chances that contagious diseases will spread.

- You safeguard other people in your community who are too young to receive the vaccine or cannot receive vaccinations due to medical issues.

Also of Note

- After receiving a vaccine, some children experience mild symptoms such as a low fever and fussiness, as well as tenderness, swelling, or redness where the shot was given. They also may sleep a little longer than usual in the day or two after receiving the shot.

- On very rare occasions, children may react to a vaccine with a more concerning response, such as a seizure, rash, or high fever. Call your pediatrician if your child develops a fever over 103 degrees Fahrenheit (39.4 degrees Celsius), a rash all over the body (including hives), a large amount of swelling in the limb where the shot was given, or any other symptoms that worry you. These guidelines apply to all of the immunizations described in this chapter.

While some parents also worry that their child is receiving "too many vaccines" at one time, there is plenty of research showing that multiple childhood vaccines can be given at the same time safely. In fact, a vaccine cannot be licensed by the FDA and recommended until the manufacturers show that it can be given safely with other recommended vaccines. And although children receive more vaccines than in years past, the ones they're receiving have been improved, so children are actually receiving fewer antigens (substances that help a body build up an immunity) with each shot than in previous years. These shots are effective and safe when they're given according to the guidelines recommended by the American Academy of Pediatrics.

The important point to remember is that getting these vaccine-preventable diseases is much more dangerous than getting the vaccines. If you have questions or concerns about immunizations, talk with your pediatrician.

Easing the Hurt

Shots can hurt. When your child receives a vaccine, she can be uncomfortable and may cry for several minutes. But fortunately, any pain is very short-lived. At the moment the immunization is given, you may be able to soften the experience by distracting your child. Talk soothingly, and make eye contact with her. Afterward, comfort and play with her for a while.

If your child develops side effects, you may be able to ease any fever or irritability by giving her acetaminophen or ibuprofen. Be sure to discuss the use and proper dosage of these medicines with your pediatrician or Poison Help at 1-800-222-1222. If your child has pain at the site where the shot was given, your doctor might recommend applying cool compresses to lessen the discomfort. Certainly, if any reaction makes your child uncomfortable for more than four hours, notify your pediatrician, who will want to note it in your child's records and advise you on what to do.

Before immunizing your child, it's a good idea to talk with your doctor about what reactions could occur, if any. If unusual or severe reactions (like a fever or changes in behavior) happened in the past, you and your pediatrician should discuss the pros and cons of whether it's appropriate to give another dose of the same vaccine at the scheduled time.

As painful as it may be for you to watch your child experience the discomfort of a shot, don't lose sight of the fact that you're doing enormous good for her by making sure she is protected from the diseases that vaccines can prevent.

What Shots Does Your Child Need?

Your child should be vaccinated according to the schedule of immunizations recommended by the American Academy of Pediatrics. The entire schedule appears in the Appendix, and includes the immunizations described below for young children. Please refer to the chart often for information on the immunizations your child needs and when they should be given. Also, recommendations change as vaccines are improved and new ones are developed, so be sure to speak with your pediatrician or visit aap.org for the most current immunization schedule.

DIPHTHERIA, TETANUS, AND PERTUSSIS

The DTaP vaccine protects your child against diphtheria (D), tetanus (T), and pertussis (aP). The diphtheria portion of this vaccine guards against a throat infection that can trigger breathing difficulties, paralysis, or heart failure. The tetanus portion pro-

tects against a disease that causes the tightening or "locking" of all of the muscles in the body, especially the jaw, and is potentially fatal. The vaccine for pertussis (also called whooping cough) prevents bacteria from causing severe and violent coughing spells in infants that can make breathing and eating difficult.

What about expected side effects? Redness and tenderness may occur with the diphtheria and tetanus portions of the vaccine. Severe, but very rare, problems that have been reported after the DTaP vaccine include long-term seizures, coma, and permanent brain damage. These are so rare that it is hard to tell if they are caused by the vaccine. Don't keep your child from getting this—or any—vaccine without first speaking with your pediatrician. He can address any concerns you may have. For the vast majority of children, the dangers of the diseases themselves far outweigh any risks of the shots. Keep in mind, for example, that two out of ten people who get a tetanus infection die from it, one out of a hundred

WHERE WE STAND

THE AMERICAN ACADEMY OF PEDIATRICS believes that immunizations are the safest and most cost-effective way of preventing disease, disability, and death. We urge parents to make sure that their children are immunized against dangerous childhood diseases, since it is always better to prevent a disease than to have to treat it or live with the consequences of having it.

babies under two who get a pertussis infection die, and more than one out of ten children who get a diphtheria infection die of complications. Immunizations are very important to protect your child from these diseases. To fully protect the newborn, pregnant mothers should receive a dose of the adult version of the vaccine, Tdap, during the third trimester of pregnancy.

MEASLES, MUMPS, AND RUBELLA (MMR)

The measles portion of this vaccine protects against an infection that causes an extensive red or brownish blotchy rash, as well as flu-like symptoms; measles can lead to severe complications such as pneumonia, seizures, and brain damage. The mumps vaccine gives your child protection against a virus that causes swollen salivary glands, a fever, and headaches, and can lead to deafness, meningitis, and painful swelling of the testicles or ovaries. The rubella (German measles) vaccine guards against an infection of the skin and lymph nodes, in which the child may have a pink rash and swollen, tender glands at the back of the neck. In addition, the vaccine protects pregnant women from passing the rubella virus to the developing fetus.

There was considerable media attention in the past about a possible connection between the MMR vaccine and autism. In fact, extensive research has shown that there is no connection. There has been confusion because autism is often diagnosed at about the age at which children receive the MMR vaccine. This has led to the erroneous conclusion that the vaccine somehow causes autism. But, in fact, studies now clearly show that autism actually begins before a baby is born and vaccines play no role.

Use of the MMR vaccine was once discouraged for children who had an allergy to eggs. But because the MMR vaccine now contains only trace amounts of egg protein and research has shown that the vaccine can be safely administered to egg-allergic children without special precautions, the recommendation has been adjusted. However, if your child is taking any medication that interferes with the immune system, or if her immune system is weakened for any reason, she generally should not receive this immunization. As for side effects, sometimes, around seven to twelve days after the MMR vaccine, a child may develop mild swelling of the glands in the cheeks or neck, and a fever or mild rash. If this mild vaccine side effect does occur, it is important to note that it is not dangerous or contagious and will resolve on its own. Such findings occur less often after the second dose. Severe problems such as seizures caused by fever occur in one out of three thousand doses. Serious allergic reactions are very rare (about one out of a million doses).

CHICKENPOX (VARICELLA)

The vaccine to protect against the varicella virus became available in 1995, and not only protects against chickenpox but also reduces the risk of shingles in later life. Natural chickenpox infection can cause a fever and an itchy, blister-like rash all over the body. There may be as many as 250 to 500 of these blisters. Sometimes the infection causes serious complications, including skin infections, brain swelling, and pneumonia.

Varicella vaccine is safe. Reactions to the vaccine are generally mild. About 20 percent will develop mild pain, redness, or swelling at the injection site. If your child has a weakened immune system, or is taking steroids or other drugs that can affect the immune system, check with your doctor before she gets the chickenpox immunization.

Two doses of the vaccine provide more than 90 percent protection against infection. Currently if someone who has been vaccinated does get chickenpox, it is usually very mild. They will have few spots, are less likely to have a fever or serious complications, and will recover faster.

INFLUENZA

Influenza (the flu) is a respiratory illness caused by a virus. This infection leads to symptoms such as a high fever, muscle aches, sore throat, and cough, and it may take your child several days of rest to recover. There are often two types of influenza vaccine available to protect your child:

■ The inactivated (killed) vaccine, given by injection (flu shot)

■ The live attenuated (weakened) vaccine, sprayed into the nostrils (flu mist)

All children six months of age and older—including all children, adolescents, young adults, and those caring for a child too young to receive a vaccine (such as a newborn)—should receive the annual seasonal influenza vaccine unless there is a specific and uncommon contraindication to this vaccine. Special efforts should be made to vaccinate those who have chronic medical conditions that increase their risk of severe influenza complications (such as asthma, diabetes, immunosuppression, or neurological disorders). The formulation of the influenza vaccine changes yearly, depending on the expected prevalence of the various influenza strains. This is one reason the influenza vaccine must be administered every year. It is also important to be sure that all individuals caring for young children and for children with chronic medical conditions receive an annual flu vaccine.

POLIO

The polio vaccine provides protection from the virus that causes polio. While some infections with the polio virus cause no symptoms, it can cause paralysis and death in other cases. Before the polio vaccine was available, millions of children throughout the world were left paralyzed from polio.

Today, all children need four doses of the polio vaccine before they start school, starting with shots at two months of age. The inactivated polio vaccine is given as shots, and there is no risk of the vaccine causing the disease. An oral form of the vaccine is no longer available in the United States.

HIB (*HAEMOPHILUS INFLUENZAE TYPE B*)

The Hib vaccine protects your child from the bacterium that (before the vaccine became available) was the leading cause of meningitis. This serious disease occurs most often in children from ages six months to five years, leading to symptoms such as fever, seizures, vomiting, and a stiff neck. Meningitis also can cause hearing loss, brain damage, and death. These same bacteria can also lead to a rare but serious inflammation of the throat called epiglottitis.

The first Hib vaccine should be given at two months of age, with additional doses to follow. It is important to have your child immunized with this vaccine in order to lower her risk of getting Hib diseases during the early years, when she is most vulnerable to these infections. There are no reasons to withhold this vaccine from your child unless she has had a rare life-threatening allergic reaction to a previous dose of the vaccine.

HEPATITIS B

The hepatitis B vaccine offers protection against a liver disease that can be spread by infected blood and body fluids. The infection is caused by the hepatitis B virus, and can lead to cirrhosis and liver cancer. The infection can be passed from an infected mother to her baby at the time of birth, or from one household member to another.

The first hepatitis B shot should be given within twelve hours after birth, even before your baby is discharged from the hospital. A second dose should be given at one to two months of age, and a third dose when the child is six to eighteen months old. The hepatitis B vaccine is very safe. Severe problems are rare. Possible mild reactions include soreness where the shot was given, and in one out of fifteen people, a temperature of 99.9 degrees Fahrenheit (37.7 degrees Celsius) or higher.

HEPATITIS A

Like the hepatitis B vaccine, the hepatitis A immunization protects against a common liver disease, which your child can catch by eating food or drinking water contaminated with the hepatitis A virus. This common infection can sometimes be spread in childcare settings when caregivers do not follow good handwashing procedures.

The hepatitis A vaccine is very safe. The first dose is given at twelve months of age, followed by a second dose six to twelve months later. Reactions to this vaccine are very uncommon and usually are nothing more than soreness where the shot was given.

PNEUMOCOCCAL VACCINE

The pneumococcal conjugate vaccine protects your child from meningitis, as well as common forms of pneumonia, blood infections, and certain ear infections. Four doses are recommended starting at two months of age. A pneumococcal infection is one of the most common causes of vaccine-preventable deaths in children. Only mild reactions are associated with the vaccine. Some children become fussy or drowsy, lose their appetite, or develop a fever.

ROTAVIRUS

The rotavirus vaccine protects against a potentially serious stomach virus (often referred to as the "stomach flu"), which can cause vomiting, diarrhea, and related symptoms in children. Before the vaccine was available, rotavirus was the most common cause of severe diarrhea in children under the age of two years. In the United States before the rotavirus vaccine was given, about fifty thousand children under five years of age were hospitalized each year because of rotavirus infection.

The rotavirus vaccine is an oral vaccine, given in a two- or three-dose series, starting at two months of age.

Some children may experience mild, temporary diarrhea or, rarely, vomiting within seven days of getting a dose of the rotavirus vaccine. There are no severe reactions associated with this vaccine. As with some other vaccines mentioned earlier, talk with your doctor before getting the rotavirus vaccine if your child's immune system might be weakened by conditions like HIV or steroid use.

MENINGOCOCCAL VACCINE

The meningococcal vaccine that is recommended for all preteens and teens may be recommended for younger children with an increased risk of infection. Check with your pediatrician about when the vaccine should be administered if your child has a weakened immune system or other condition that might make her at high risk for this infection.

~ 32 ~

Media

TECHNOLOGIES SUCH AS TV, mobile devices, and Internet-related games offer entertainment, culture, and education to our children. They are an important part of the average daily lifestyle. While it may offer many benefits, media use has also been associated with the risk of obesity, sleep issues, aggressive behaviors, and attention issues in preschool- and school-age children. When it comes to incorporating technology into your child's daily routine, she needs your experience, judgment, and supervision.

Development and Learning

Children younger than fifteen months to eighteen months of age may be fascinated by electronic screens. Starting as soon as their vision permits (around six months of age), they will stare at the colors and patterns on the screens, and they may even swipe and tap around as much as their limited motor skills allow. Parents can easily misinterpret this activity as a child understanding what she sees in the way that older children and adults do. Children in this age range, however, do not have the mental skills to make sense of screen programming. They can be distracted by screens, but research shows they learn nothing from them, no matter what the program or app suggests.

Instead, babies and toddlers learn by exploring their worlds physically, usually in the company of a parent or other caring adult. Children learn through reading, singing, rocking, clapping, and playing. Anything that distracts from these activities, including screen media, can interfere with learning. For this reason, the American Academy of Pediatrics discourages screen time for children under eighteen months of age with the exception of live video chatting, usually used to keep children in touch with distant loved ones.

Starting around fifteen months of age, children may be able to learn from some screen content, but only when a parent is helping them process and understand the content. High-quality screen programming may be useful for children over age eighteen months, but it should be used as a companion to in-person learning, not as a substitute. Children over three years of age can learn numbers, letters, words, and even the concept of kindness from well-crafted programming. Programming that is more interactive functions as a better teacher than programs that are passively viewed. Viewing with a parent helps even more, so take time to view or play with your child and research whether the programming you're choosing for her has proven educational benefit. Of the thousands of apps that promise to help teach children, very few have been rigorously studied.

Young children with heavy media use are at risk for delays in language development once they start school, as they may experience less "talk time" with adults when screens are on, even in the background. Research shows that this talk time is valuable for children's emerging language development. And when parents are watching their own programs and using mobile devices or computers, they may be dis-

WHERE WE STAND

THE AAP RECOMMENDS that parents and caregivers minimize or eliminate altogether media exposure for children under the age of eighteen months. For older preschool-age children, media limits are very appropriate, and parents should have a strategy for managing electronic media when choosing to maximize its benefits. Remember that supervised independent play for infants and young children has been shown to have benefits superior to the use of screen media when you cannot sit down and actively engage in play with your child. For example, have your child play with nesting cups on the floor nearby while you prepare dinner. Also avoid placing a television set in your child's bedroom. And recognize that your own media use can have a negative effect on children.

tracted and engage in less parent-child interaction. Parents using mobile devices in their children's presence pay considerably less attention to their children, and may display less patience and more frustration with their children's behavior.

Background media may also interfere with a young child's learning from play and activities. Research shows that even when a show is not intended for a child audience, a child will glance up at the screen three times every minute. It disrupts a child's concentration when he is "at work" (playing). Children are less focused and more likely to move on to a new toy more quickly when a screen is on.

Children who are inadvertently exposed to adult content may absorb some negative messages if present. A child watching a show with adult content may observe characters engaging in violence or using inappropriate language. These types of programs may also present sexuality, drugs, and alcohol to children who are too young to understand the reality of these is-

WHERE WE STAND

ALTHOUGH THE AMERICAN ACADEMY OF PEDIATRICS does not hold media solely responsible for violence in our society, we believe that violence in television, movies, or videogames has a clear effect on the behavior of children and contributes to the frequency with which violence is used to resolve conflict. Entertainment media also distort reality on matters such as drugs, alcohol, tobacco, sexuality, and family relations.

We encourage parents to manage both the quantity and the quality of their family's screen time. Parents can create a healthy media diet and lead by example. Children's TV programming is supported by commercial advertisers whose primary motivation is to sell products. Young children are not prepared to distinguish between programs and the commercials that interrupt them, nor do they understand that commercials are designed to sell them (and their parents) something.

Together, parents, broadcasters, programmers, and advertisers must be held responsible for the media that children consume. The American Academy of Pediatrics strongly supports legislative efforts to improve the quality of children's programming. We urge parents to limit and monitor the amount of screen time (including television, videos, computer, and videogames) for their children, to monitor what their children are watching, and to watch media with them to help them learn from what they see.

sues. In addition, a great deal of screen time perpetuates myths and stereotypes of certain gender tasks and racial associations that will serve as poor influences on children. Children view social interactions on video programs as a glimpse of the "real world" when in fact they are often far from reality. This is why it is important for parents to preview or watch programs with their child to discuss what is happening on the screen and answer questions.

Childhood Obesity

Research shows that time spent watching TV programming (regardless of the device) contributes to childhood obesity. The effect seems to come more from advertising for unhealthy foods and sweetened beverages than from children's decreased activity levels; however, children do tend to ignore cues that they are full if they eat while watching TV. Help children develop healthy eating habits early by keeping screens off for the family during mealtimes. Also, keep track of what they're watching and playing, and consider choosing different content if it exposes them to advertising for unhealthy foods and beverages.

All children need active play, not only for the physical exercise but also for proper mental and social development. Most media use is passive. Sitting and watching TV all the time, for example, does not help your child acquire the most important skills and experiences she needs at this age, such

as communication, creativity, fantasy, judgment, and experimentation. The more time your child spends in front of a screen, the less time there is to spend on the wide variety of activities that create a fun and memorable childhood. While there may be some educational benefits to screens, children need a healthy variety of daily activities. Independent play encourages creativity. Playing with other children fosters social skills and problem-solving. And physical activity is critical for a healthy lifestyle. This is why children need a balance of activities in their day.

Sleep

Many parents may use screen media to help their children settle down in the evening. However, screens typically emit a lot of light with wavelengths at the bluer end of the spectrum, and blue light has been proven to interfere with sleep. Screen use in early childhood contributes to shorter and poorer quality sleep. Poor sleep habits have adverse effects on mood, behavior, weight, and learning.

Ideally, screens should be off for at least sixty minutes prior to bedtime, and screen use should never interfere with or take the place of bath time, stories, puzzles, or drawing. If your child needs sound to drown out household noises, consider buying a specialized sound machine or even a box fan to create white noise. Keep the volume low, however, because young children are very susceptible to hearing loss from prolonged noise exposure.

Monitoring Technology Use

In a fast-changing, increasingly technological world, children will naturally become adept at using various forms of technology as they grow older. Carefully monitoring your child's usage will lead to a safe and fun experience.

If your child chooses to play games on a tablet, mobile device, or family computer, ensure that she plays games that are suited to her age. If the game requires using the Internet, check that it is housed on a safe, kid-friendly website, and assess whether it includes direct advertising or advertising that is integrated into the content ("advergaming"). This will limit the possibility of her encountering inappropriate material inadvertently. Furthermore, the American Academy of Pediatrics recommends using the parental controls on your computer's or mobile device's operating system, which can block or filter Internet content. Many Internet service providers have software for the same purpose, generally free of charge. Parents can choose to purchase a separate software program or app that can block and track inappropriate or unwanted websites, and lock parts of the device to prevent your child from viewing other areas. There are also apps that can report on and control the *length* of time a child is on a screen.

TV shows and movies often come with a rating that indicates the type of content included in the program. These are usually located in the TV listings or TV guide. News programs do not have ratings, and certain information presented may not be suitable

Special-Needs Children and Computers

If your child has special needs, you can get equipment that makes it easier for her to use computers. For example, special screens, keyboards, joysticks, and computerized voice programs allow children with disabilities to enjoy using a computer.

For additional information, contact:

- ERIC (Institute of Education Sciences 1-800-538-3742; eric.ed.gov). This resource is an online digital library of education research and information.

- The Starlight Children's Foundation (1-310-479-1212; starlight.org). Another excellent resource, this organization is dedicated to developing projects that empower seriously ill children to face their day-to-day challenges.

for children to hear. Be firm with your child about what is appropriate material for her to view.

In addition, your child should clearly understand that people online are not always who they say they are, and may not be the "friends" they claim to be.

Guidelines for Media Use

■ Avoid digital media use (except video chatting) by children younger than eighteen months.

■ For children eighteen months to twenty-four months of age, parents can introduce digital media, choosing high-quality programming. Avoid solo media use at this age.

■ Do not feel pressured to introduce technology early; interfaces are so intuitive that children will figure them out quickly once they start using them at home or in school.

■ For children two years to five years of age, limit screen use to one hour per day of high-quality programming. Help children understand what they are viewing and how they can apply what they learn to the world around them.

■ Avoid fast-paced programs (young children do not understand them as well), apps with lots of distracting content, and any violent content.

■ Turn off televisions and other devices when not in use.

■ Avoid using media as the only way to settle your child. Although there are intermittent times (i.e., medical procedures, airplane flights) when media is useful as a soothing strategy, there is concern that using media as a calming strategy could lead to problems with overuse or the inability of children to develop their own emotional self-regulation. Ask your pediatrician for help if needed.

■ Monitor children's media content and what apps are used or downloaded. Test apps before your child uses them, then use them together, and ask your child what he or she thinks about the app.

■ Keep bedrooms, mealtimes, and parent-child playtimes screen free for both children and parents. Parents can set a "do not disturb" option on their devices during these times.

■ Avoid screens for one hour before bedtime, and keep devices and screens out of bedrooms.

■ Consult the American Academy of Pediatrics Family Media Use Plan at healthychildren.org/MediaUsePlan.

A Message to Parents

Teach your child that screen time means television, movies, and digital gaming, and that these are privileges that one can enjoy but that also come with responsibilities.

Be media-smart by:

■ Setting limits and offering guidance for your child's media time

■ Helping your child to plan which programming and movies to watch and when

■ Turning the screen off when the show is over or they have reached their maximum allowed usage time

■ Being mindful of times when you use media as a "babysitter"

■ Keeping TV, DVD players, video games, and computers out of your child's bedroom and in open family areas of your home

■ Watching TV with your child to help educate her about advertising and commercials

To increase her interest in other activities that don't involve forms of media, invite her to join you in reading, playing board or outdoor games, coloring, cooking, building, or visiting with friends. Praise her when she entertains herself without relying on television or the computer, and present a good model by restricting your own media time. You are your child's best role model. You have to show her that you value human interactions and that you also have limits on your screen time. And *do not* use television as a reward or withhold it as a punishment, as that will only make it seem more enticing. Set up the ground rules and be consistent. Maybe your house rules are "no videos or TV shows on school nights" or "up to one hour of recreational screen time after homework is done"—media is earned after the homework is done. No matter what your family's rules are, having and enforcing rules is the key.

Monitoring your children's "media diet" is important to establish at an early age. Media education can lead to a better understanding of the pros and cons of all types of media, and how best to introduce and use it in your home.

~ 33 ~

Musculoskeletal Problems

Arthritis

Arthritis involves inflammation of the joints that produces swelling, stiffness, redness, heat, tenderness, and pain with motion. Although arthritis is typically thought of as a condition of the elderly, children can also develop arthritis. The four most common forms of childhood arthritis are as follows:

BACTERIAL INFECTION OF A JOINT (SEPTIC ARTHRITIS) OR BONE (OSTEOMYELITIS)

When a joint or bone becomes infected with bacteria, it becomes very painful, hot, swollen, and stiff. An affected child will often walk with a limp, refuse to bear weight, or have decreased movement in an arm. An affected child also will typically have a fever, and very young children may simply be irritable and refuse to walk or use an extremity. Notify your pediatrician immediately if these signs or symptoms appear, as rapid treatment can prevent joint or bone damage. If infection involves the hip or other deep and inaccessible joints or bones, it can be difficult to diagnose; and infection of the large weight-bearing joints and bones is a very serious condition that needs to be properly diagnosed and treated by a specialist (usually an orthopedist). Treatment may include imaging such as X-ray or ultrasound, needle aspiration or surgical drainage of the infected joint or bone, and intravenous (IV) antibiotics.

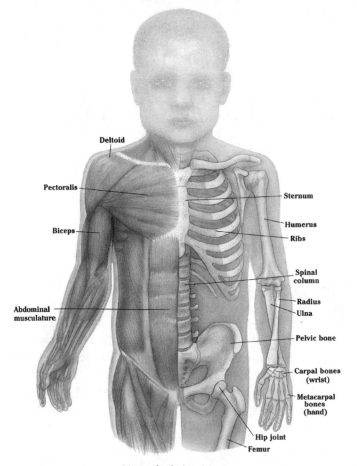

Deltoid

Pectoralis

Biceps

Abdominal
musculature

Sternum

Humerus

Ribs

Spinal
column

Radius

Ulna

Pelvic bone

Carpal bones
(wrist)

Metacarpal
bones
(hand)

Hip joint

Femur

Musculoskeletal System

LYME DISEASE

An infection transmitted by the deer tick can cause a form of arthritis known as Lyme disease. It is called this because it was first diagnosed in a child in Old Lyme, Connecticut. This infection often starts with a red mark that is surrounded by a light ring or halo (having the appearance of a red and white target) at the site where your child was bitten by a deer tick. Later, a similar but smaller rash may appear on other areas of the body.

Your child also may develop flu-like symptoms such as headache, fever, swollen lymph nodes, fatigue, and muscle aches. More rarely, Lyme disease can cause symptoms involving the nerves, eyes, or heart. Arthritis then typically develops weeks to months after the skin rash. If arthritis is severe, medications can be prescribed to control inflammation and pain until the condition gradually resolves on its own.

Symptomatic Lyme disease is treated

with antibiotics. However, the American Academy of Pediatrics does not recommend routinely taking antibiotics after a tick bite in an effort to *prevent* Lyme disease, for several reasons: most tick bites do not transmit the germ that causes Lyme disease; the possible side effects of antibiotics; the cost of treatment; and the risk of promoting antibiotic-resistant bacteria. The Academy also does not recommend testing your child's blood for Lyme disease shortly after a tick bite, since it takes quite a while for antibodies to show up in the blood even with an infected tick bite. To prevent Lyme disease, your child should avoid tick-infested areas such as wooded regions, high grasses, or marshes. Children also can protect themselves from ticks by wearing long-sleeved shirts, tucking their pants into their socks, and using an insect repellent that has DEET as the active ingredient when outside. (See page 580 for more information on DEET.) Almost all cases of Lyme disease can be readily treated with antibiotics, even if arthritis develops.

JUVENILE IDIOPATHIC ARTHRITIS (JIA)

Juvenile idiopathic arthritis (JIA, previously referred to as juvenile rheumatoid arthritis or juvenile chronic arthritis) is the most common form of chronic joint inflammation in children. JIA is a puzzling disorder that is often difficult to diagnose and challenging for families to understand. Common symptoms include persistent joint stiffness and swelling, and pain with motion of affected joints. If your

How to Remove a Tick

1. Gently cleanse the area with an alcohol-soaked sponge or cotton ball.

2. Using forceps, tweezers, or fingers (protected by a tissue or cloth), grasp the tick as near to the mouth parts and as close to the child's skin as possible.

3. Using gentle but steady tension, pull the entire tick up and out.

4. Be sure the tick is dead before disposing of it. Removal and disposal of ticks should be done with a protective barrier (tissue or cloth) so you do not get exposed to any bacteria or infectious agents that could be spread by a tick.

5. After the tick is out, cleanse the bitten area thoroughly with alcohol or other cleansing (soap) agent.

child has these symptoms, and/or an unusual pattern of walking, especially in the morning or after naps, call your pediatrician to have your child evaluated. Surprisingly, many children with JIA do not complain of much pain; stiffness and swelling are often the most prominent signs of arthritis.

JIA can occur at almost any age, but it is very uncommon before the first birthday. Particular types of JIA are common before the age of six or around the time of puberty. Although this condition can be disabling, and many children with JIA require long-term treatment with medications, with appropriate therapy most children have good outcomes. The exact cause of JIA is unknown. JIA may be triggered by an infection that in a genetically predisposed person causes an abnormal response of the immune system, which leads to joint inflammation.

Signs, symptoms, and long-term consequences vary depending on the subtype of JIA. A form of JIA known as systemic JIA involves not only arthritis, but also inflammation throughout the body, with associated fever and rash, and possible effects on other organs. For example, a child with systemic JIA can develop pericarditis (inflammation of the sac that surrounds the heart), pleuritis (an inflammation of the inner lining of the chest), pneumonitis (inflammation of the lungs), or enlargement of the liver, spleen, or lymph nodes. Other subtypes of JIA include oligoarthritis, polyarthritis–rheumatoid factor nega-

tive, polyarthritis–rheumatoid factor positive, psoriatic arthritis, enthesitis-related arthritis, and undifferentiated arthritis. Oligoarticular JIA affects no more than four joints and most commonly starts in preschool girls. The two forms of polyarticular JIA affect at least five joints, and the rheumatoid factor positive subtype is similar to adult rheumatoid arthritis. Psoriatic JIA occurs in children with the skin condition of psoriasis or children who have typical features of psoriatic JIA (swelling of entire fingers or toes, nail changes, or first-degree relative with psoriasis). Enthesitis-related arthritis involves both arthritis and enthesitis (inflammation of sites where tendons and ligaments attach to bone). This subtype of JIA is often associated with a gene, HLA-B27, and is the only form of JIA that is more common in boys. Undifferentiated JIA does not fit neatly into one of the other categories, or it has features of more than one JIA subtype.

There is no perfect blood test for diagnosing JIA. JIA is diagnosed when a doctor finds evidence of arthritis in the child's joints on a physical exam (such as swelling, pain with range of motion, limited range of motion, or deformities), the child has had persistent symptoms of arthritis for at least six weeks, and there is no other underlying cause. Blood tests can help the doctor and family better understand the prognosis of a child with JIA. In particular, some children with JIA can have inflammation in the front of the eye, called uveitis, that can cause damage to the eye and eventual blindness if not treated. Uveitis is most common in JIA patients who have a positive ANA blood test. All children with JIA should be evaluated by an ophthalmologist early in the course of the disease. The results of the ANA test help determine how often eye exams are needed.

Great strides have been recently made in the treatment of JIA. Treatment varies depending on the severity and location of arthritis, but it often includes both medications and exercise. Children with JIA should be treated by a doctor with special training in arthritis, called a rheumatologist. It is important to follow the treatment plan that is recommended by your rheumatologist to ensure the best outcome for the child.

The main goal of medical treatment of JIA is reduction of joint inflammation. Nonsteroidal anti-inflammatory drugs (NSAIDs) are often used initially to decrease pain and stiffness. Commonly used NSAIDs include ibuprofen, naproxen, and meloxicam. NSAIDs work quickly, but they can cause stomach upset and should always be taken with food. Call your doctor if a child taking NSAIDs complains of abdominal pain or loses appetite. Children with an inadequate response to NSAIDs may be treated with more effective medications, including methotrexate and newer biologic medications such as etanercept, adalimumab, abatacept, and tocilizumab. These medications have more risks that require monitoring by a rheumatologist, but

they can also make a huge difference in the lives of children with arthritis. Another treatment that is commonly used when only one or a few joints have arthritis is injection of a long-acting steroid directly into affected joints, which can control inflammation and rapidly restore function in even severely affected joints.

Exercise plays an important role in slowing progression of JIA and preventing joints from getting too stiff. Although exercise may be uncomfortable at times, especially when a child's joints are already sore, it is important for families to help their child work through the discomfort for the long-term benefits. Physical and occupational therapists can help to design a stretching and exercise program. For patients with severe arthritis, therapists sometimes use strategic splinting to prevent progression of deformities. In general, however, joint immobilization should be avoided in patients with arthritis, as it can make stiffness worse.

Living with JIA requires a great deal of adjustment and dedication, not only for affected children but also for their families. Working as a team with your healthcare providers can help decrease the risk of a child with JIA having long-term problems or disabilities.

TRANSIENT SYNOVITIS (INFLAMMATION) OF A HIP

This is the most common form of arthritis in children. It typically develops suddenly between two and ten years of age, and then it resolves after a short period of time (days to weeks), with no serious lasting effects. The most common cause involves the immune system's overreaction to a virus, so it is frequently seen after a viral infection like a cold. Treatments include rest and anti-inflammatory medications (such as ibuprofen), which may help symptoms go away faster.

Bowlegs and Knock-Knees

Toddlers' legs often have a bowed appearance. In fact, many children have bowing of the legs until they are about two years old. After this age, they often will look progressively knock-kneed until they are about six years of age; afterward this returns to normal. At times, children may not have straight lower legs until they are nine or ten years old.

Bowlegs and knock-knees usually are variations of normal and typically require no specific treatment. In most cases a child's legs will straighten naturally by the teen years, but treatment may become necessary if there is a severe deformity or the deformity occurs during the teen years. Bracing, corrective shoes, and special exercises are rarely helpful except for severe deformities, and they may hinder a child's physical development and cause unnecessary emotional stress. Rarely, bowlegs or knock-knees are the result of a disease. Arthritis, injury to the growth plate around the knee (see *Fractures/Broken Bones*, page 708), infection, tumor, Blount's

disease (a growth disorder of the knee and shinbone), and rickets (caused by vitamin D deficiency) all can cause changes in the curvature of the legs.

Here are some signs that suggest a child's bowlegs or knock-knees may be caused by a serious problem:

- The curvature is extreme.

- Only one side is affected.

- The bowlegs get worse after age two.

- The knock-knees persist after age seven.

- Your child also is unusually short for his age.

- Your child has trouble walking, running, or often stumbles and falls.

If your child shows any of these signs, talk to your pediatrician. In some cases, treatment, including referral to a pediatric orthopedist, may be needed.

Elbow Injuries

A pulled elbow (also known as nursemaid's elbow) is a common, painful injury generally among children under four years old but occasionally older. It occurs when the tissue of the outer part of the elbow slips between the bones of the joint. This happens because the child's elbow joint is loose enough to separate slightly when her arm is pulled to full length (while being lifted, yanked, or swung by the hand or wrist, or if she falls on her outstretched arm). The nearby tissue slides into the space created by the stretching and becomes trapped after the joint returns to its normal position.

A nursemaid's elbow injury usually doesn't cause swelling, but the child will complain that the elbow hurts, or cry when his arm is moved. A child will typically hold his arm close to the side, with the elbow slightly bent and the palm turned toward the body. If someone tries to straighten the elbow or turn the palm upward, the child will resist because of the pain.

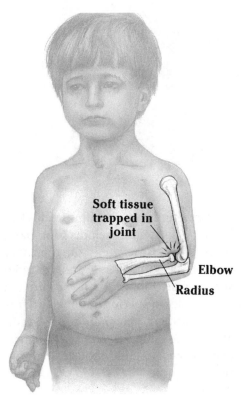

Soft tissue trapped in joint

Elbow

Radius

Treating Nursemaid's Elbow

This injury should be treated by a pediatrician or other trained healthcare provider. Since elbow pain can also be due to a fracture, your pediatrician may need to consider this before the elbow is "reduced" or put back into place.

Your doctor will check the injured area for swelling and tenderness and any limitation of motion. If an injury other than nursemaid's elbow is suspected, X-rays may be taken. If no fracture is noted, the doctor will move and twist and flex the arm gently to release the trapped tissue and allow the elbow to return to its normal position. Once he has moved the elbow back in place, the child will generally feel immediate relief and within a few minutes should be using her arm normally without any discomfort. Occasionally, the doctor may recommend a sling for comfort for two or three days, particularly if several hours have passed before the injury is treated successfully. If the injury occurred several days earlier, a hard splint or cast may be used to protect the joint for one to two weeks. Persisting pain after a reduction may mean that a fracture occurred that may not have been apparent at the time of initial X-rays.

Prevention

Nursemaid's elbow can be prevented by not pulling or lifting your child by the hands or wrists, or swinging her by the arms. Instead, lift your child by grasping her body under the arms.

Flat Feet/Fallen Arches

Babies are often born with flat feet, which may persist well into childhood. This occurs because children's bones and joints are flexible, causing their feet to flatten when they stand. Young babies also have a fat pad on the inner border of their feet that hides the arch. You still can see the arch if you lift your baby up to stand on the tips of the toes, but it may disappear when he's standing normally. The foot may also turn out, increasing the weight on the inner side and making it appear even more flattened.

Normally, flat feet disappear by age six as the feet become less flexible and the arches develop with increased leg muscle strength. Only about one or two out of every ten children will continue to have flat feet into adulthood. For children who do not develop an arch, treatment is not recommended unless the foot is stiff or painful, which may mean that there is a possible connection between some of the small foot bones called a tarsal coalition (fused or connected bones), in which case an X-ray is indicated. Shoe inserts won't help your child develop an arch, and may cause more problems than the flat feet themselves.

However, certain forms of flat feet may need to be treated differently. For instance, a child may have tightness of the heel cord (Achilles tendon) that limits the motion of his foot. This tightness can result in a flat foot, but it usually can be treated with special stretching exercises to lengthen the heel cord. Rarely, a child will have truly rigid flat feet due to a tarsal coalition (fused or connected bones), a condition that can cause problems. These children have difficulty moving the foot up and down or side to side at the ankle. The rigid foot can cause pain and, if left untreated, can lead to arthritis. This rigid type of flat foot is seldom seen in an infant or very young child. (More often, rigid flat feet develop during the teen years and should be evaluated by your child's pediatrician.)

Symptoms that should be checked by a pediatrician include foot pain, sores or pressure areas on the inner side of the foot, a stiff foot, limited side-to-side foot motion, or limited up-and-down ankle motion. For further treatment you should see a pediatric orthopedic surgeon or podiatrist experienced in childhood foot conditions.

Limp

Limping can be caused by something as simple as a pebble in your child's shoe, a blister on her foot, or a pulled muscle. But a limp also can be a sign of more serious trouble, such as a broken bone, arthritis, infection, or hip dysplasia. For that reason, it's important to have your pediatrician examine a child with a limp to make sure that no serious problems exist.

Some children limp when they first learn how to walk. Early limping can be caused by neurological damage (such as cerebral palsy; see page 648). But any limp around the time your child begins to walk needs to be investigated as soon as possible, since the longer it goes untreated, the more difficult it may be to correct. Once walking is well established, significant sudden limping usually indicates one of several conditions:

■ A "toddler fracture"

■ Hip injury or inflammation (synovitis)

■ Previously undiagnosed developmental dysplasia (abnormal development) of the hip (DDH)

■ Infection in the bone or joint

■ Kohler's disease (loss of blood supply to a bone in the foot)

■ Juvenile idiopathic arthritis

A "toddler fracture" is a spiral fracture of the tibia (one of the leg bones that extends from the knee to the ankle; see *Fractures/Broken Bones*, page 708). It can occur with minor accidents such as when children trip, jump, or fall, or when they go down a slide in an older child's or an adult's lap with their feet tucked under them. Sometimes children can explain how the injury occurred, but usually they have difficulty recalling exactly what happened. At times an older sibling or childcare provider can solve the mystery.

Hip problems that cause a limp at this age usually are due to a viral joint infection causing transient synovitis and should be evaluated by your pediatrician. When a child has an infection in the bone or joint, she usually experiences a fever, swelling of the joint, and redness. If the infection is in the hip joint, she will hold her leg flexed or bent at the hip and be extremely irritable and unwilling to move the hip and leg in any direction, although swelling and redness may not be obvious in this deep joint.

Sometimes a child is born with a hip problem (developmental dysplasia of the hip, DDH) that may not be noticed until she starts to walk. As one limb is shorter, the hip is less stable, and the buttock muscles are weaker than the other side, the child may walk with an obvious limp.

Perthes disease is another disorder that causes children to limp and that is most often *not* associated with any pain complaints. It is usually only a minor problem in children younger than six years, but in older children, usually older than ten years of age, it can be a significantly disabling problem.

Limping is a major reason that parents of children with juvenile idiopathic arthritis (see page 837) seek medical care. In a typical case, a child will not complain of being in pain. But she limps nevertheless, with this limping at its worst after waking in the morning or from a nap, and becoming less noticeable with activity.

Treatment

With minor injuries, such as a blister, cut, or sprain, simple first-aid treatment can be performed at home. However, if your child has just started walking and is constantly limping, your pediatrician should evaluate her. It is all right to wait twenty-four hours if your older child develops a limp, since sometimes the problem will disappear overnight. But if your child is still limping the next day, or is in extreme pain or has a high fever, see your pediatrician.

X-rays of the hip or the entire leg may be necessary to make the diagnosis. If there is an infection, antibiotics should be started and hospitalization may be required. Intravenous (IV) antibiotics may be given in high doses to allow them to get to the joint and bone. If a bone is broken or dislocated, the limb will be placed in a splint or cast and the child will be referred to an orthopedist for evaluation and further management. It is also advisable to see a pediatric orthopedist if a congenital dislocated hip (DDH) or Perthes disease is diagnosed.

Pigeon Toes (Intoeing)

Children who walk with their feet turned in are described as being "pigeon-toed" or having "intoeing." This is a very common condition that may involve one or both feet, and it occurs for a variety of reasons.

INTOEING DURING INFANCY
Infants are sometimes born with their feet turning in. If this turning occurs from the front part of their foot only, it is called metatarsus adductus (see figure). Most commonly it is due to the foot being positioned in a certain way inside the uterus before the baby is born.

You can suspect that metatarsus adductus may be present if:

■ At rest, the front portion of your infant's foot turns inward.

■ The outer side of the child's foot is curved like a half-moon.

Appearance of foot in metatarsus adductus

This condition is usually mild and will resolve before your infant's first birthday. Sometimes it is more severe, or accompanied by other foot deformities that result in a problem called clubfoot. This condition requires a consultation with a pediatric orthopedist, and there is extremely effective nonoperative treatment with early casting or splinting.

Internal tibial torsion

INTOEING IN LATER CHILDHOOD

When a child is intoeing during her second year, this is most likely due to inward twisting of the shinbone (tibia). This condition is called internal tibial torsion (see figure). When a child between ages three and ten has intoeing, it is probably due to an inward turning of the thighbone (femur), a condition called medial femoral torsion. Both of these conditions tend to run in families.

Treatment

Some experts feel no treatment is necessary for intoeing in an infant under six months of age. For severe metatarsus adductus in infancy, early casting may be useful. Studies show that most infants who have metatarsus adductus in early infancy will outgrow it with no treatment necessary. If your baby's intoeing persists after six months, or if it is rigid and difficult to straighten out, your doctor may refer you to a pediatric orthopedist, who may recommend a series of casts applied over a period of three to six weeks. The main goal is to correct the condition before your child starts walking.

Intoeing in early childhood often corrects itself over time, and usually requires no treatment. But if your child has trouble walking, discuss the condition with your pediatrician, who may refer you to an orthopedist. In the past, a night brace (special shoes with connecting bars) was used for this problem, but it hasn't proven to be an effective treatment. Because intoeing often corrects itself over time, it is very important to avoid nonprescribed "treatments" such as corrective shoes, twister cables, daytime bracing, exercises, shoe inserts, or back manipulations. These do not resolve the problem and may be harmful because they interfere with normal play or walking. Furthermore, a child wearing these braces may face unnecessary emotional strain from her peers. Nevertheless, if a child's intoeing remains by the age of nine or ten years old, surgery may be required to correct it.

Sprains

Sprains are injuries to the ligaments that connect bones to one another. A sprain occurs when a ligament is stretched excessively or torn. Sprains are less common in young children, because their ligaments are usually stronger than the growing bones and cartilage to which they are attached. Therefore, the growing part of the bone might separate or tear away before the ligament is injured.

In young children, the ankle is the most commonly sprained joint, followed by the knee and wrist. In a mild sprain (grade 1), the ligament simply is overstretched, while more severe sprains can involve partial tearing of the ligament (grade 2) or complete tearing (grade 3).

Call your child's pediatrician if your child has a joint injury and is unable to bear weight or has excessive swelling or pain. Often the doctor will want to examine your child. In some instances, special X-rays may be ordered to rule out a fracture (a break in the bone). If there is a fracture, your pediatrician may consult with or refer you to an orthopedist or sports medicine specialist. When a sprain is diagnosed, treatment usually involves compression using an elastic bandage or immobilization with a splint. A walking cast or removable device may be necessary if the ankle or foot injury has been severe.

Most grade 1 sprains will heal within two weeks without subsequent complications. Your child's physician should be called anytime a joint injury fails to heal or swelling recurs. Ignoring these signs could result in serious damage to the joint and long-term disability.

~ 34 ~

Skin

SKIN PROBLEMS IN children often get the attention of parents—and sometimes raise their anxiety levels. After all, skin conditions are immediately visible, and while the overwhelming majority are not serious, they may still be a source of worry. In this chapter, you'll find an alphabetical description of common skin problems. Other related skin conditions (specifically eczema, hives, and insect bites and stings) are discussed in Chapter 17, *Allergies*.

Birthmarks and Hemangiomas

Dark-Pigmented Birthmarks (Nevi or Moles)

Nevi, or moles, are either congenital (present at birth) or acquired. Composed of so-called nevus cells, these spots range in color from light tan to dark brown or black.

CONGENITAL NEVI

Small nevi appear at birth and are relatively common, occurring in about one out of every hundred newborns. They tend to grow with the child and usually don't cause any problems. Rarely, however, these moles may develop into a type of serious skin cancer (melanoma) at some later time. Therefore, while you don't have to worry about them right away, it's a good idea to watch them carefully and have them checked by your pediatrician at regular intervals or if there is any change in appearance (color, size, or shape). She may refer you to a pediatric dermatologist, who will advise you on removal and any follow-up care.

A much more serious type of nevus is a large congenital one that is over 7⅞ inches (20 cm) in diameter. It might be flat or raised, may have hair growing from it (although small, insignificant nevi sometimes also have hair), and can be so large that it covers an arm or a leg. Fortunately, these nevi are very rare (occurring in one out of every twenty thousand births). However, they are more likely than the smaller ones to develop into a melanoma (maybe up to 5 percent do), so early consultation with a pediatric dermatologist and regular mole checks are advisable.

ACQUIRED NEVI, OR MOLES

Most light-complected people develop ten to thirty pigmented nevi, or moles, throughout the course of their lives. They usually occur after the age of five, but sometimes develop earlier. These acquired moles are seldom a cause for worry. However, if your child develops one that's irregularly shaped (asymmetrical), has multiple colors within its structure, and is larger than a pencil eraser, ask your pediatrician to examine it.

One final note: Probably the most common acquired dark spots on the skin are freckles. They can appear as early as ages two to four years, are found more often on parts of the body exposed to the sun, and tend to run in families. They often become darker or larger during the summer and are less prominent in the winter. Although they represent no danger, they may be an indicator of excessive sun exposure. They are also an important reminder to keep kids out of the sun when possible and to use UV protective clothing, hats, sunglasses, and sunscreen to protect their skin.

Blood Vessel Birthmarks on the Skin

Your baby has a flat red patch on the back of the neck at birth and then at two to three weeks of age develops a new red raised bump on the forehead. They're unsightly, but are they harmful?

Although some of these blood vessel or vascular marks are usually innocent and do not cause trouble, it's important to recognize the difference between the marks that are not concerning and those that may be associated with medical complications. Your pediatrician will also evaluate such birthmarks at each visit.

CAPILLARY MALFORMATIONS (SALMON PATCHES AND PORT WINE BIRTHMARKS)

Capillary malformations are recognized as flat red patches in the newborn and include salmon patches (most common) and port wine birthmarks (less common). Salmon patches occur in more than 80 percent of infants and most commonly involve the back of the neck, the mid-forehead, the upper eyelids, the sides of the nose, and the middle of the upper lip. Although they fade during the first few years and are not associated with any serious medical problems, they may still be noticeable when children are overheated or having a temper tantrum, because the blood vessels dilate, making the skin lesion look more prominent, especially in light-complected individuals.

Port wine birthmarks occur in other areas of the skin, tend to be darker at birth, do not fade, and usually gradually darken with increasing age. They may be associated with other birth defects, including abnormalities of the underlying veins and arteries in the involved skin. When a port wine birthmark involves the skin around the eye, forehead, or scalp, it may be associated with abnormalities of the eye and brain known as Sturge-Weber syndrome. Affected children should be checked for glaucoma and other eye defects as well as abnormalities of the brain. This evaluation may be performed by your pediatrician in collaboration with a pediatric neurologist, ophthalmologist, and dermatologist or in a center specializing in Sturge-Weber syndrome.

Since port wine birthmarks usually intensify during childhood and adult life, treatment with a pulsed dye laser, which involves multiple treatments spaced six to twelve weeks apart, could be considered in infancy or early childhood if desired by the family. Special medical makeup can also be used to camouflage these marks.

HEMANGIOMAS OF INFANCY (HOI)

Hemangiomas of infancy (often referred to by parents as strawberry marks) occur in 10 percent of babies by two months of age, with most ap-

pearing by two to three weeks of age. They often are not present at birth or are only noted as subtle flat red spots that may be mistaken for bruises. They can involve any part of the body, but there is a predilection for the head and neck. Most children have a single HOI, but in rare cases some infants have hundreds. For reasons that are not well understood, two-thirds to three-fourths occur in girls. HOI are also much more common in premature infants, especially in infants of low birth weight. HOI usually peak in size by three to four months of age, often looking reddish-purplish in appearance, followed by slow but steady regression, often without treatment.

If your infant develops a hemangioma, have your pediatrician examine it so he can follow its course from the start. Newer non-invasive treatments are available to help treat the hemangioma and prevent any future scarring. However, since the vast majority will gradually shrink in size without treatment, sometimes the best course of action is to leave it alone. Studies have shown that when this type of hemangioma is left untreated, few complications or cosmetic problems result.

At times, hemangiomas may need to be treated or removed—namely, when they are large, on the face, or in an exposed area where they can be easily seen, as well as if the hemangioma occurs close to vital structures, such as the eye, throat, or mouth; when they seem to be growing much faster than usual; or when they are likely to bleed profusely or become infected. Such conditions are uncommon but require careful evaluation and management by your pediatrician and pediatric dermatologist, ENT, cardiologist, or plastic surgeon. Several treatment options are available, including oral medications to help shrink the hemangioma, drops that can be placed directly on the skin, and, rarely, surgical removal.

Very rarely, HOI are found in large numbers widely scattered over the skin surface. In some of these infants, HOI may also be located on organs inside the body. If this is suspected, your pediatrician may need to conduct further tests. When large HOI are present in certain locations (such as the head and neck, the chin in a beard-type distribution, and the lower spine), they may be associated with problems in underlying bony structures and soft tissues and may require additional evaluation by your pediatrician.

(See also *How Your Newborn Looks*, page 140.)

Chickenpox (Varicella)

Chickenpox was once one of the most common childhood illnesses. But thanks to the varicella vaccine, far fewer children now get this disease. Chickenpox is a highly contagious infection causing an itchy, blister-like rash that can cover most of the body. Children often get a mild fever along with the rash.

The chickenpox rash is usually seen approximately two weeks after exposure to the virus that causes chickenpox. Small blisters, which may have a red area around them, will begin to appear on the body and scalp, then spread to the face, arms, and legs. There may be as many as 250 to 500 of these blisters. Normally the blisters will crust over and heal, but tiny sores and possibly small scars may develop if your child scratches them and they become infected. The skin around some of the blisters may become darker or lighter, but this change in coloring will disappear gradually after the rash is gone. Blisters may also appear on the inside of your child's mouth or other mucosal surfaces.

Treatment

Chickenpox can be very itchy and uncomfortable, but try to discourage your child from scratching, which can lead to additional infection by bacteria. Acetaminophen or ibuprofen (in the appropriate dose for your child's age and weight) may decrease the discomfort from the rash or fever. Trimming fingernails and bathing daily with soap and water also can help prevent secondary bacterial infection. Oatmeal baths, available without prescription from your pharmacy, will ease the itch. Antihistamines can also be used to decrease the itch. (Be sure to follow the dosing instructions carefully.) A prescription medicine (acyclovir or valacyclovir) can modestly decrease the severity of the symptoms if started within twenty-four hours of the onset of the disease. This medicine should be considered for those at risk for moderate to severe disease (e.g., children with weakened immune systems or those with certain skin disorders such as eczema), but it is not recommended for healthy children younger than twelve years of age.

Do not give your child aspirin or any medication that contains aspirin or salicylates when she has chickenpox. These products increase the risk of Reye syndrome (see page 555), a serious illness that involves the liver and brain. You should avoid steroids and any medicines that interfere with the immune system. If you are not sure about what medications you can safely use at this time, ask your pediatrician for advice.

Because chickenpox is now rare, many doctors will want to see your child to confirm whether your child actually has the illness, but because it is so contagious, you should call and discuss whether your child needs to be seen before you make a trip to the doctor's office. Many times what looks like possible chickenpox may be another virus. If your child develops a complication such as a skin infection, trouble breathing, or a fever that rises above 102 degrees Fahrenheit (38.9 degrees Celsius) or lasts longer than four days, be sure to call your pediatrician immediately. Let the pediatrician know if areas of the rash become very red, warm, or tender, as this may indicate a bacterial infection. Be sure to call your pediatrician *immediately* if your child develops any signs of Reye syndrome or encephalitis: vomiting, nervousness, confusion, convulsions, lack of respon-

siveness, increasing sleepiness, or poor balance.

If your child does have chickenpox, you should mention it to parents whose children may have been exposed, especially infants too young to be vaccinated or anyone with a compromised immune system. Your child may be contagious one to two days before the rash starts and for twenty-four hours after the last new blister appears (usually five to seven days). In some cases, the contagious period lasts until all the blisters are dry and crusted over. After she's recovered from the chickenpox, your child usually will be immune to chicken pox for the rest of her life, but can get Shingles later on in life since the virus stays in the nerve cells and can reactivate as Shingles.

Prevention

A vaccine to protect against chickenpox is recommended for all healthy children, with the first dose given between twelve and fifteen months of age, plus a second (booster) dose given between four and six years of age. Until your child has received this vaccine, the only sure way to protect her is to avoid exposure to the chickenpox virus. Protection from exposure is important for newborn infants, especially premature babies, in whom the disease can be more severe.

Most infants whose mothers have had chickenpox or have been vaccinated are immune to the disease for the first few months after birth, since mothers pass short-lived protective antibodies to their infants. Susceptible children who have diseases affecting the immune system (e.g., cancer) or who are using certain drugs (e.g., prednisone) should avoid being exposed to chickenpox. If these children are exposed, they may be eligible for a special medication that will provide protection against the disease for a limited period. It's important to remember that since the varicella vaccine is a live virus vaccine, children who have a weakened immune system may not have a normal response to it and may not be able to receive the vaccine.

Cradle Cap and Seborrheic Dermatitis

Your beautiful one-month-old baby has developed a scaly rash on his scalp. You're concerned and think maybe you shouldn't shampoo as usual. You may also be concerned if you see some redness in the creases of his neck and armpits and behind his ears. What is it and what should you do?

When this rash occurs on the scalp alone, it's known as cradle cap. Although it may start as scaling and/or redness of the scalp, it also can be found later in the other areas just mentioned. It can extend to the face, body, and diaper area, too. When it extends beyond the scalp, pediatricians call it seborrheic dermatitis. Seborrheic dermatitis is a noninfectious skin condition that's very common in infants, usually beginning in the first weeks after birth and slowly disap-

pearing over a period of weeks or months. Unlike eczema or contact dermatitis (see pages 568–69), it's rarely uncomfortable or itchy.

Doctors think that seborrheic dermatitis is caused by a reaction that the skin has to certain common fungi that live on all human skin. Some doctors have speculated that it may be influenced by the mother's hormonal changes during pregnancy, which stimulate the infant's oil glands. This overproduction of oil may have some relationship to the scales and redness of the skin.

Treatment

If your baby's seborrheic dermatitis is confined to his scalp (and is therefore just cradle cap), you can treat it yourself. Don't be afraid to shampoo the hair; in fact, you should wash it (with a mild baby shampoo) more frequently than before. This, along with soft brushing, will help remove the scales. Stronger medicated shampoos (antidandruff or anti-seborrhea shampoos, such as those containing selenium sulfide, sulfur, salicylic acid, ketoconazole, or coal tar) may loosen the scales more quickly, but since they also can be irritating, use them only after consulting your pediatrician.

Some parents have found using petroleum jelly, ointments, or oils can help soften the scales and make them easier to remove. In some cases, especially if the seborrhea has spread to other areas of the body, your pediatrician may also recommend hydrocortisone cream or antifungal cream to help it clear. Once the condition has improved, in most cases you can prevent it from recurring by continuing with frequent hair washing with a mild baby shampoo. Fortunately, most babies' conditions clear up during the second half of the first year, so prolonged treatment is usually unnecessary.

Sometimes yeast infections occur on the affected skin, most likely in the crease areas rather than on the scalp. If this occurs, the area will become extremely reddened and quite itchy. In this case, your pediatrician might prescribe a medication such as an anti-yeast cream. Rest assured that seborrheic dermatitis is not a serious condition. Nor is it an allergy to something you're using, or due to poor hygiene. It will go away without any scars.

Fifth Disease (Erythema Infectiosum)

Rosy cheeks are often considered a sign of good health, but if your child suddenly develops bright-red patches on her cheeks that are also raised and warm, she may have a viral illness known as fifth disease. Like so many other childhood illnesses, this one is spread from person to person. The virus causing this disease is called a parvovirus. Once your child is exposed to the virus, it usually takes four to fourteen days for symptoms to appear.

This is a mild disease, and most children feel well even when the rash appears. However, fifth disease can occur with mild cold-like symptoms, such as sore throat, headache, pinkeye, fatigue, a mild fever, or itching. In rare cases there may be aches in the knees or wrists. The disease process may be more severe in children with abnormal hemoglobin or red blood cells, such as sickle cell anemia, and in children with cancer.

The rash usually begins on the cheeks, causing them to look as if they've been slapped. During the next few days, the arms and then the trunk, thighs, and buttocks will develop a pink, slightly raised rash that has a lacy pattern. Fever is usually absent or mild. After five to ten days the rash will fade, with the face clearing first, followed by the arms, and then the trunk and legs. Interestingly, the rash may reappear briefly weeks or months later, particularly if your child becomes hot from bathing, exercise, or sunlight, or spends time in the sun.

Treatment

For most children, fifth disease is not serious. The rash, however, may look similar to other rashes that may be more serious, as well as certain drug-related rashes; as a result, it's important to discuss the rash with your pediatrician and let him know about any medications your child may be taking. When you describe the symptoms over the phone, the doctor may suspect fifth disease, but he still may want to examine your child to be certain.

There is no specific medicine for fifth disease; treatment is geared to providing relief of the symptoms. For instance, if your child has a fever or aches and pains, you can treat her with acetaminophen or ibuprofen. If she exhibits new symptoms, feels sicker, or develops a high fever, call your pediatrician.

A child with fifth disease is contagious when she is suffering from the cold-like symptoms that *precede* the rash. But by the time she demonstrates a rash, she is no longer contagious. Nevertheless, as a rule, whenever your child has a rash or a fever, you should keep her away from other children until your doctor identifies the illness. As a precaution, wait until she no longer has a fever and is feeling normal before allowing her to play with other children. Also, it is important to keep your child away from pregnant women (particularly in their first trimester), since the virus that causes this disease may cause serious illness or even death in the fetus if the mother becomes infected.

Hair Loss (Alopecia)

Almost all newborns lose some or all of their hair. This is normal and to be expected. The baby hair falls out at three to five months of age and is gradually replaced by the mature hair. So hair loss occurring in the first six months in this pattern is not a cause for concern.

Very commonly, a baby loses her hair where she rubs her scalp against the mattress or as a result of a head-banging habit. As she starts to move more and sit up or outgrows this head-rubbing or -banging behavior, this type of hair loss will correct itself. Many babies also lose hair on the back of the scalp at age four months, as their hair grows at varying times and rates.

In very rare cases, babies may be born with alopecia (hair loss), which can occur by itself or in association with certain abnormalities of the nails and the teeth. Later in childhood, hair loss may be due to other reasons, including medications, a scalp injury, or a medical or nutritional problem.

An older child may also lose her hair if it's braided too tightly or pulled too hard when combing or brushing. Some children (under age three or four) twirl their hair as a comforting habit and innocently break it off or pull it out. Other children (usually older ones) may pull their hair out on purpose but deny doing so, or they simply may be unaware that they are doing it; this often is a signal of emotional stress, which you should discuss with your pediatrician.

Alopecia areata, a condition common in children and teenagers, seems to be an allergic reaction to one's own hair. In this disorder, children lose hair in a circular area, causing a bald spot. In general, when it's limited to a few patches, the outlook for complete recovery is good. But when the condition persists or worsens, steroid creams and even steroid injections and other forms of therapy at the site of the hair loss often are used. Unfortunately, if the hair loss is extensive, it may be difficult to renew its growth.

Because alopecia and other types of hair loss can be a sign of other medical or nutritional problems, bring these conditions to your pediatrician's attention whenever they occur after the first six months of age. The doctor will look at your child's scalp, determine the cause, and prescribe treatment. Sometimes a referral to a pediatric dermatologist is necessary.

Head Lice

Head lice, *Pediculus humanus capitis*, commonly occur in young children who play together, share clothing, hats, or hairbrushes, or are generally in close contact. Although often misunderstood and embarrassing to parents, head lice are neither painful nor a serious medical problem. Head lice do not transmit diseases or cause permanent problems. Many parents with children in school or childcare have received a note informing them of a case of head lice in their child's classroom. This condition occurs in all socioeconomic groups, is most common in children ages three to twelve, and only rarely occurs in African American children.

Usually you first become aware of head lice by noticing that your child has an extremely itchy scalp. On close inspection, you may see little white dots in the hair or on the neck at the hairline. Sometimes you may confuse this with dandruff or seborrhea. Dandruff generates larger flakes, however, while lice infestation results in more discrete dots that usually are stuck onto the shaft of the hair near the scalp. These are the eggs of the lice. In addition, you may find living lice in the hair. They avoid light and will move rapidly to get out of the light, so living lice can be hard to see. Also, the itchiness of the scalp is usually far more uncomfortable with lice than with seborrhea or dandruff.

Try not to overreact when you first realize this or when your child's school phones or sends home a note. It is a very common condition that should not reflect negatively on your family's personal hygiene. It is merely the result of having your child in contact with other children infected with head lice. Because children in the same family spend so much time together in such close proximity, it is not unusual for lice to be spread from one sibling to another.

Treatment

Once you recognize that your child has head lice, there are several treatments available (both over-the-counter and by prescription). They come in a variety of forms such as cream rinse, shampoo, gel, and mousse. Most should be applied to dry hair because wet hair can dilute the chemicals in the treatment, and they should be kept on the hair for the full amount of time recommended on the product label. While the treatments are effective at killing live lice, they may not always kill all of the eggs, and thus a second treatment is usually needed seven to ten days after the first one.

Some available medications to

help remove or kill lice are chemical-free and nontoxic, while others are potentially dangerous insecticides. Therefore, always use these medications strictly according to the package instructions and with your pediatrician's recommendations. Your pediatrician may recommend use of a prescription medication if an over-the-counter product doesn't work.

Some parents also try home remedies for head lice, which often involve "washing" their child's hair with thick or oily substances like petroleum jelly, olive oil, tub margarine, or mayonnaise, and then leaving these products on the hair overnight. Proponents of these approaches believe that coating the hair will smother and kill the lice. However, there is no scientific proof that they work, even though they won't hurt your child if you decide to try them. On the other hand, certain home treatments must be avoided, particularly coating the hair with toxic or highly flammable substances such as gasoline or kerosene, or using products that are manufactured for use on animals.

After using one of the over-the-counter or prescription medications, carefully combing the hair with a fine-tooth comb can remove the dead egg cases (nits) and any eggs that have survived treatment. Combing is often tedious, but it is a good idea to remove any eggs or nits. Most pediatricians recommend combing once a day until no more are found and then every few days for a week or two. In most cases, as noted, a child must be retreated seven to ten days later.

To prevent reinfection, wash all bedclothes and clothing (including hats) that have been in contact with the child for the forty-eight hours immediately preceding your noticing the head lice. Use the hot cycle to wash the clothes, or have them dry-cleaned if you prefer. Items like stuffed animals that cannot be washed should be bagged up for forty-eight hours. Head lice and nits cannot survive away from the scalp for longer than that, so after that time they should be safe to use again.

You can wash combs and brushes in a shampoo specific against lice, or soak in boiling water for five to ten minutes. In addition, if your child has lice, it's important to inform the child-care center or school. However, the American Academy of Pediatrics believes that no healthy child should be excluded from or allowed to miss school because of head lice. The Academy also discourages "no nit" policies that require the absence of nits in order for a child to return to school. A child with an active head lice infestation likely has had this outbreak for a month or more by the time it is discovered. So because he poses little risk to others, he should remain in class while trying to avoid direct head contact with other children. Also, to prevent your child from contracting head lice, teach him not to share personal items such as hats, combs, and brushes. If your active, engaging three-year-old has head lice, someone else in the group probably does, too. Because head lice are very contagious, *other family members also may need to be examined and treated* and have their clothing and bedding laundered.

Impetigo

Impetigo is a contagious bacterial skin infection that often appears around the nose, mouth, and ears. More than 90 percent of impetigo cases are caused by staphylococcal bacteria, while the rest are caused by the streptococcal bacteria (which also are responsible for strep throat and scarlet fever).

If staphylococcal bacteria are to blame, the infection may cause blisters filled with clear or yellow fluid. These can break easily, leaving a raw, glistening area that soon forms a scab with a honey-colored crust. By contrast, infections with strep bacteria usually are not associated with blisters, but they do cause crusts over larger sores and ulcers.

Treatment

Impetigo needs to be treated with antibiotics, either topically or by mouth. Rarely your pediatrician may order a culture in the lab to determine which bacteria are causing the rash. Make sure your child takes the medication for the full prescribed course, or the impetigo could return.

One other important point to keep in mind is that impetigo is contagious until the rash clears, or until at least two days of antibiotics have been given and there is evidence of improvement. Your child should avoid close contact with other children during this period, and you should avoid touching the rash. If you or other family members do come in contact with it, wash your hands and the exposed site thoroughly with soap and water. Also, keep the infected child's washcloths and towels separate from those of other family members.

Prevention

The bacteria that cause impetigo thrive in breaks in the skin. The best ways to prevent this rash are to keep your child's fingernails clipped and clean and to teach him not to scratch minor skin irritations. When he does have a scrape, cleanse it with soap and water, and apply an antibiotic cream or ointment. Be careful not to use washcloths or towels that have been used by someone else who has an active skin infection.

When certain types of streptococcal bacteria cause impetigo, a rare but serious complication called glomerulonephritis can develop. This disease injures the kidneys and may cause high blood pressure and blood to pass in the urine. Therefore, if you notice any blood or dark brown color in your child's urine, let your pediatrician know so he can evaluate it and order further tests if needed.

Measles

Thanks to vaccinations, cases of measles were on the decline. But unfortunately they have been on the rise in the

United States recently, with multiple outbreaks occurring in several states. According to the Centers for Disease Control and Prevention, eleven states reported approximately 206 measles cases in the United States from January 2019 to February 2019. The majority of these cases were in people younger than twenty years old who were unvaccinated or whose vaccination status was unknown. Most cases that occur now are in travelers who have not been immunized bringing measles back to the United States after traveling to a country where there is a reported outbreak. If your child has never been immunized or had the measles, he can get the disease if he is exposed. The measles virus is highly contagious and passed through the air via droplets transmitted by an infected person. The virus can live up to nearly two hours in the air where an infected person coughed or sneezed. Almost everyone who breathes the droplets and is not immune to the disease will become infected.

Signs and Symptoms

For the first eight to twelve days after being exposed to the measles virus, your child will probably have no symptoms; this is called the incubation period. Then he may develop an illness that seems like a common cold, with a cough, runny nose, and pinkeye (conjunctivitis; see pages 739–40). The cough may be severe at times and will last for about a week, and your child probably will feel miserable.

During the first one to three days of the illness, the cold-like symptoms will become worse, and he'll develop a fever that may run as high as 103 to 105 degrees Fahrenheit (39.4–40.5 degrees Celsius). The fever will last until two to three days after the rash first appears.

After two to four days of illness, the rash will develop. It usually begins on the face and neck, then spreads down the trunk and out to the arms and legs. It starts as very fine red bumps, which may join together to form larger splotches. If you notice tiny white spots, like grains of sand, inside his mouth next to his molars, you'll know the rash will follow soon. The rash will last five to eight days. As it fades, the skin may peel a little.

Treatment

Although there is no treatment for the disease, it is important that the pediatrician examine your child to determine that measles is, in fact, the cause of the illness. If the illness is measles, a dose of vitamin A may be indicated, as treatment of children who have measles with vitamin A has been found to lessen the chances of the associated complications and death due to the infection. Your pediatrician will advise you on the correct dose of vitamin A.

Many other conditions can start in a similar way, so when you call the pediatrician's office, describe the fever and rash, so that the doctor knows you suspect measles. When you visit the office, the staff will want to separate your child from other patients, so that the virus is not transmitted to them.

Your child is contagious from several days before the rash breaks out until the fever and rash are gone. During this period he should be kept at home (except for the visit to the doctor) and away from anyone who is not immune to the illness. At home, make sure your child drinks plenty of fluids, and give acetaminophen in the proper dose if your child is uncomfortable due to the fever. The conjunctivitis that accompanies measles can make it painful for the child to be in bright light or sunshine, so you may want to darken his room to a comfortable level for the first few days.

Sometimes infections develop as a complication of the measles. These most often include pneumonia (see page 612), middle ear infection (see page 670), or encephalitis (inflammation of the brain). In these cases, your child must be seen by the pediatrician, who may prescribe antibiotic treatment or admit your child to the hospital.

Prevention

Almost all children who receive two doses of the MMR (measles, mumps, rubella) vaccine after their first birthday are protected against measles for life. The first dose of the vaccine should be administered between ages twelve and fifteen months, and the second one between ages four and six years old, although it can be given at a younger age as long as at least twenty-eight days have passed since the first dose. Because up to 5 percent of children may not have an adequate immune response to the initial vaccination, the second (booster) dose is recommended for all children. (See Chapter 31, *Immunizations*.)

If your unimmunized child has been exposed to someone who has the measles, or if someone in your household has the virus, notify your pediatrician at once. The following steps can help keep your child from getting sick.

1. If he is under one year old or has a weakened immune system, he can be given immune globulin (gamma globulin) up to six days following exposure. This may temporarily protect him from becoming infected, but it will not provide extended immunity.

2. An infant six through eleven months of age may receive the measles vaccine if he is exposed to the disease or if he is living in a community where exposure is highly likely or in an epidemic situation. If doses are given during these months, your child still may need additional doses to be fully immunized.

3. If your child is otherwise healthy and over one year old, he can be vaccinated. The vaccine may be effective if given within seventy-two hours of his exposure to an infected person, and *will* provide extended immunity. If your child has previously received one dose of the measles vaccine and at least twenty-eight days have elapsed since that dose, he may be given a second dose after exposure.

Molluscum Contagiosum

Molluscum contagiosum is a common skin infection in young children that is caused by a virus. The tiny raised lesions look like shiny flesh-colored or pinkish dome-shaped bumps or nodules on the skin with an indentation in the center. Some kids get a few, while others may get twenty or more on their body. They are found most often on the face, trunk, and extremities, but may develop anywhere on the body except the palms of the hands and soles of the feet. They are painless, harmless, and noncancerous growths in the skin's top layers. The most annoying part is that they last for several months to a few years and sometimes spread to other areas of the body.

The disease is spread by direct contact with the skin of an infected person or sharing towels with someone who has the disease. Outbreaks have occasionally been reported in childcare centers. The incubation period varies between two and seven weeks, although it is sometimes much longer (up to six months).

Most often, molluscum nodules go away on their own without treatment. This means that children with just one or a few widely scattered lesions do not need any special care. However, if the lesions are extensive, or if you and your child desire, your pediatrician or dermatologist may recommend topical medications to help the molluscum resolve sooner, or the bumps can be removed by a scraping procedure with a sharp instrument (curette) or by using peeling agents or freezing techniques (such as liquid nitrogen).

Mosquito-Borne Illnesses (Zika and West Nile)

There are many infections that spread to humans through the bite of an infected mosquito. Mosquitoes become carriers of the viruses by feeding on infected people or animals. Once the virus has been transmitted to a human through a bite, it can multiply in an individual's bloodstream and in some cases cause illness.

WEST NILE

The first outbreak of West Nile virus occurred in the United States in 1999. Although some children have become ill when infected with West Nile virus, most have mild or no symptoms at all. About one in five people with West Nile virus develop mild flu-like symptoms (fever, headaches, and body aches) and at times a skin rash. These symptoms tend to last only a few days. In fewer than one out of a hundred infections, a severe illness can occur (West Nile encephalitis or meningitis), with symptoms such as a high fever, a stiff neck, tremors, muscle weakness, convulsions, paralysis, and loss of consciousness.

ZIKA

In children, Zika virus is rarely dangerous. In fact, as long as you aren't pregnant or of childbearing age, Zika is of little concern. Only one in five people infected with Zika virus have symptoms of illness. Because the disease affects people differently, some may have a rash, fever, pinkeye (conjunctivitis), joint and/or muscle pain, or headache. Symptoms usually clear up in less than a week, are mild, and rarely require hospitalization.

Zika virus is particularly dangerous, however, for women who are pregnant or who are planning to become pregnant, because the virus affects the developing fetus in the womb. Zika virus can also be sexually transmitted to a pregnant woman or woman of childbearing age and affect a developing or future fetus. Federal health officials have confirmed the Zika virus can cause microcephaly (babies born with a small head) and other brain and physical abnormalities in infants. Because the Zika virus can affect the fetus's developing brain and cause long-lasting negative consequences, prevention is critical.

Prevention of Mosquito-Borne Infections

Risk of contracting Zika or West Nile virus comes mostly from mosquito bites. The disease cannot be transmitted through casual person-to-person contact.

There is currently no vaccine available in the United States to protect from such viruses. But you can reduce the likelihood of developing the disease by taking steps to reduce the chance of a bite from a mosquito that could be carrying the virus. Here are some strategies to keep in mind. (Some of them are described in the *Insect Bites and Stings* section on page 577.)

■ Apply insect repellent to you or your child, using just enough to protect the exposed skin. (See the chart *Types of Insect Repellents* on page 862.) Wash the repellent off with soap and water when it is no longer needed to protect the skin.

■ Avoid products that include insect repellent and sunscreen together because the sunscreen needs to be applied more frequently than insect repellent.

■ Do not use DEET preparations on infants under two months of age. In older children, apply it sparingly around the ears, and don't use it on the mouth or the eyes. Don't put it over cuts.

■ Whenever possible, dress your child in long sleeves and long pants while she's outside. Use mosquito netting over a baby's infant carrier.

■ Keep your child away from locations where mosquitoes are likely to congregate or lay their eggs, such as standing water (e.g., in birdbaths and pet water dishes).

■ Because mosquitoes are more likely to bite humans at certain times of day—most commonly at dawn, at dusk, and in the early evening—consider limiting the amount of time your child is outdoors during those hours.

■ Repair any holes in your window screens.

AVAILABLE INSECT REPELLENTS

What's available	How well it works	How long it protects	Special precautions
Chemical repellents with DEET (N, N-diethyl-3-methylbenzamide)	Considered the best defense against biting insects.	About 2 to 5 hours depending on the concentration of DEET in the product.	Caution should be used when applying DEET to children.
Picaridin	In April 2005, the Centers for Disease Control and Prevention (CDC) recommended other repellents that may work as well as DEET: repellents with picaridin and repellents with oil of lemon eucalyptus or 2% soybean oil. Currently these products have a duration of action that is comparable to that of about 10% DEET.	About 3 to 8 hours depending on the concentration.	Although these products are considered safe when used as recommended, long-term follow-up studies are not available. Also, more studies need to be done to see how well they repel ticks.
Repellents made from essential oils found in plants such as citronella, cedar, eucalyptus, and soybean		Usually less than 2 hours.	Allergic reactions are rare, but can occur when using repellents made from essentials oils.
Chemical repellents with permethrin	These repellents kill ticks on contact.	When applied to clothing, it lasts even after several washings.	Should only be applied to clothing, not directly to skin. May be applied to outdoor equipment such as sleeping bags and tents.

Types of Insect Repellents

Insect repellents come in many forms, including aerosols, sprays, liquids, creams, and sticks. Some are made from synthetic chemicals, and some have natural ingredients. Insect repellents prevent bites from biting insects but not stinging insects. Biting insects include mosquitoes, ticks, fleas, chiggers, and biting flies. Stinging insects include bees, hornets, and wasps.

MRSA Infections

Methicillin-resistant *Staphylococcus aureus* (MRSA) is the name of a staphylococcal bacterium that can cause infections not only on the surface of the skin, but also into the soft tissue, where a boil or abscess can form. In recent years, MRSA has become a major public health problem because this bacterium has become resistant to antibiotics called beta-lactams, which include methicillin and other commonly prescribed antibiotics. This resistance has made treating these infections more difficult. While MRSA was once limited to hospitals and nursing homes, it has spread into the community in schools, households, and childcare centers, among other places. It can be transmitted from person to person through skin-to-skin contact, particularly through cuts and abrasions.

If your child has a wound that appears to be infected—specifically, if it is red, swollen, hot, and oozing pus—have it checked by your pediatrician. He may drain the infection and prescribe topical and/or oral antibiotics. The most serious MRSA infections may cause pneumonia and bloodstream infections. Even though MRSA infections are resistant to some antibiotics, they are treatable with other medications.

To prevent your child from getting MRSA at school or other public places, the following strategies can be helpful:

■ Follow good hygiene practices. Your child should wash his hands frequently with soap and warm water, or use alcohol-based hand sanitizers.

■ Use a clean dry bandage to cover any cuts, scrapes, or breaks in your child's skin. These bandages should be changed at least daily.

■ Don't let your child share towels, washcloths, or other personal items (including clothing) with anyone else.

■ Frequently clean and disinfect surfaces that your child touches.

Pinworms

Fortunately, the most common type of worm infesting children, the pinworm, is essentially harmless. The pinworm is unpleasant to look at and may cause rectal itching and, in girls, vaginal itching and discharge, but it is not responsible for more serious health concerns. Pinworms cause more social concern than medical problems.

Pinworms are spread easily from one child to another by the transfer of eggs. Often an infected child scratches her anal area, picking up an egg, and then plays in the sandbox or touches a toilet seat, where another child unknowingly picks up the egg and later transfers it to his mouth. The eggs are swallowed and later hatch, and the pinworm makes its way to the anus to again deposit its eggs. Pinworms usually present with itching around your child's behind at night. Girls may also have vaginal itching. If you take a look at the skin around the anus first thing in the morning before the child has gotten up from bed, you may see the adult worms, which are whitish gray and threadlike, measuring about ¼ to ½ inch (0.63–1.27 cm) long. Your pediatrician might collect some of the worms and eggs by applying the sticky side of a strip of clear cellophane tape to the skin around the anus. The tape can be examined under a microscope to confirm the presence of the parasite. Alternatively, your pediatrician may decide to treat your child based on history alone.

Treatment

Pinworms can be treated easily with an over-the-counter or prescription oral medication, taken in a single dose and then repeated in one to two weeks. This medication causes the mature pinworms to be expelled through bowel movements. Some pediatricians may advise treating the other family members as well, since one of them may be a carrier without having any symptoms. Also, when the infection is resolved, the child's underclothes, bedclothes, and sheets should be washed carefully to reduce the risk of reinfection.

Prevention

It is very difficult to prevent pinworms, but here are some hints that might be helpful.

■ Encourage your child to wash her hands after using the bathroom.

■ Encourage your child to wash her hands after playing in the sandbox.

■ Encourage her sitter or childcare provider to wash shared toys frequently, particularly if pinworms have been detected in one or more of the children.

■ Encourage your child to wash her hands after playing with a house cat or dog, since these pets can carry the eggs in their fur.

Poison Ivy, Poison Oak, and Poison Sumac

Poison ivy, poison oak, and poison sumac commonly cause skin rashes in children during the spring, summer, and fall seasons. An allergic reaction to the oil in these plants produces the rash. The rash occurs from several hours to three days after contact with the plant and begins in the form of blisters, accompanied by severe itching.

Contrary to popular belief, it is not the fluid in the blisters that causes the rash to spread. This spreading occurs when small amounts of oil remain under the child's fingernails, on her clothing, or on a pet's hair that then comes in contact with other parts of her body. The rash will not be spread to another person unless the oil that remains also comes in contact with that person's skin.

Poison ivy is a three-leafed green weed and grows in vine-like form in all parts of the country except the Southwest. Poison sumac is a shrub, not a vine, and has seven to thirteen leaves arranged in pairs along a central stem. Not nearly as abundant as poison ivy, it grows primarily in the swampy areas of the Mississippi River region, and it is seen primarily on the West Coast. All three plants produce similar skin reactions. These skin reactions are forms of contact dermatitis. (See *Eczema*, page 568.)

Treatment

Treating reactions to poison ivy—the most frequent of these forms of contact dermatitis—is a straightforward matter.

■ Prevention is the best approach. Know what the plant looks like and teach your children to avoid it.

■ If there is contact, wash all clothes and shoes in soap and water. Also, wash the area of the skin that was exposed with soap and water for at least ten minutes after the plant or the oil has been touched.

■ If the eruption is mild, apply calamine lotion three or four times a day to cut down on the itching. Avoid preparations containing anesthetics or antihistamines, as often they can cause allergic eruptions themselves.

■ Apply 1 percent hydrocortisone cream to the affected skin to decrease the inflammation.

■ If the rash is severe, on the face, genitals, or on extensive parts of the body, the pediatrician may need to place your child on a high-potency topical steroid or oral steroids. These will need to be given for about ten to fourteen days, often with the dose tapering on a specific schedule determined by your pediatrician. This treatment should be reserved for the most severe cases.

Call the pediatrician if you notice any of the following:

■ Severe eruption not responsive to the previously described home methods

■ Any evidence of infection, such as redness or oozing

■ Any new eruption or rash

■ Severe poison ivy on the face or genital area

■ Fever

Ringworm (Tinea)

If your child has a scaly round patch on his scalp or elsewhere on his skin, and he seems to be losing hair in the same area of the scalp, the problem may be a contagious infection known as ringworm.

This disorder is caused not by worms but by a fungus. It's called ringworm because the infections tend to form round or oval spots that, as they grow, become smooth in the center but keep an active red scaly border.

Scalp ringworm is spread from person to person, sometimes when sharing infected hats, combs, brushes, and barrettes. If ringworm appears elsewhere on your child's body, he may have the type spread by infected dogs or cats. The first signs of infection on the body are red, scaly patches. They may not look like rings until they've grown to ½ inch (1.25 cm) in diameter, and they generally stop growing at about 1 inch (2.5 cm).

Your child may have just one patch or several. These lesions may be mildly itchy and uncomfortable.

Scalp ringworm starts the same way the body variety does, but as the rings grow, your child may lose some hair in the infected area. Certain types of scalp ringworm produce less obvious rings and are easily confused with dandruff or cradle cap. Cradle cap, however, occurs only during infancy. If your child's scalp is continually scaly and he's over a year old, you should suspect ringworm and notify your pediatrician.

Treatment

A single ringworm patch on the body can be treated with an over-the-counter cream recommended by your pediatrician. The most frequently used ones are clotrimazole, tolnaftate, or miconazole. A small amount is applied two or three times a day for at least a week, during which time some clearing should begin. If there are any patches on the scalp or more than one on the body, or if the rash is getting worse while being treated, check with your pediatrician again. She will prescribe a stronger medication and, in the case of scalp ringworm or widespread body ringworm, will use an oral antifungal preparation. Your child will have to take medicine for several weeks depending on the medication to clear the infection.

You also may need to wash your child's scalp with a special shampoo when he has scalp ringworm. If there's any possibility that others in the family have caught the infection, they also should use this shampoo and be examined for possible signs of infection. Do not allow your child to share combs, brushes, hair clips, barrettes, or hats.

Prevention

You can help prevent ringworm by identifying and treating any pets with the problem. Look for scaling, itchy, hairless areas on your dogs and cats, and have them treated right away. Any family members, playmates, or schoolmates who show symptoms also should be treated.

Roseola Infantum

Your ten-month-old doesn't look or act very ill, but she suddenly develops a fever between 102 degrees Fahrenheit (38.9 degrees Celsius) and 105 degrees Fahrenheit (40.5 degrees Celsius). The fever lasts for three to seven days, during which time your child may have less appetite, mild diarrhea, a slight cough, and a runny nose, and seems mildly irritable and a little sleepier than usual. Her upper eyelids may appear slightly swollen or droopy. Finally, *after her temperature returns to normal,* she gets a slightly raised, spotty pink rash on her trunk, which spreads only to her upper arms and neck and fades after just twenty-four hours. What's the diagnosis? Most likely it's a disease called roseola—a contagious viral illness that's most common in children under age two. Its incubation period is thought to be nine to ten days. The key to this diagnosis is that the rash appears *after* the fever is gone. We now know that a specific virus (parvovirus B19) causes this condition.

Treatment

Whenever your infant under three months of age has a fever of 100.4 degrees Fahrenheit or higher, call your pediatrician. For infants over three months of age, if the fever is 102 degrees Fahrenheit (38.9 degrees Celsius) or higher for more than twenty-four to seventy-two hours, call your pediatrician, especially if there are no other symptoms. If the doctor suspects the fever is caused by roseola, he may suggest ways to control the temperature and advise you to call again if your child becomes worse or the fever lasts for more than three or four days. For a baby under three months of age, or a child who has other symptoms or appears more seriously ill, the doctor may order a blood count, urinalysis, or other tests.

Since illnesses that cause fever can be contagious, it's wise to keep your child away from other children, at least until you've conferred with your pediatrician. Once her fever is gone for twenty-four hours, even if the rash has appeared, your child can return to childcare or preschool and resume normal contact with other children. While your child has a fever, dress her in lightweight clothing. If she is very uncomfortable because of the fever, you can give her acetaminophen in the appropriate dose for her age and weight. (See Chapter 27, *Fever.*) Don't worry if her appetite is decreased, and encourage her to drink extra fluids.

Although this disease rarely is serious, be aware that early in the illness, when fever climbs very quickly, there's a chance of a seizure (see *Seizures, Convulsions, and Epilepsy*, page 803). There may be a seizure regardless of how well you treat the fever, so it's important to know how to manage this, even though seizures that occur with roseola are usually quite mild and brief, if they occur at all.

Rubella (German Measles)

Although some of today's parents had rubella, or German measles, during their childhood, it is a rare illness now, thanks to an effective vaccine. Even when it was prevalent, however, rubella was usually a mild disease—unless contracted by a pregnant woman, in whom it can cause serious illness and long-term problems in the developing baby.

Rubella is characterized by a mild fever (100–102 degrees Fahrenheit [37.8–38.9 degrees Celsius]), swollen glands (typically on the back of the neck and base of the skull), and a rash. The rash, which varies from pinhead size to an irregular redness, is raised and usually begins on the face. Within two to three days it spreads to the neck, chest, and the rest of the body as it fades from the face.

Once exposed to rubella, a child usually will develop the disease in fourteen to twenty-one days. The contagious period for rubella begins several days before the rash appears and continues for five to seven days after it develops. Because the disease can be so mild, it goes unrecognized in about half the children who contract it.

Before the rubella vaccine was developed, this illness tended to occur in epidemics every six to nine years. Since the vaccine was introduced in 1968, there have been no significant epidemics in the United States. Even so, the disease still occurs. Each year unvaccinated and susceptible teenagers, often in college campus settings, develop the illness. Fortunately, except for causing fever, discomfort, and occasional pain in the joints, these small epidemics are of little consequence.

What You Can Do

If your pediatrician diagnoses rubella in your child, you may be able to make him more comfortable by giving him extra fluids, encouraging bed rest (if he's fatigued), and giving acetaminophen if he has a fever. Keep him away from other children or adults unless you are sure that they're immunized. As a general rule, children with rubella should not be in childcare or any other group setting for seven days after the rash first appears. In particular, make a special effort not to expose pregnant women to rubella.

If your child is diagnosed as having the congenital form of rubella, your pediatrician can advise you on the best way to manage his complex and difficult problems. Infants born with congenital rubella are often infectious for a year after birth and therefore should be kept out of any group childcare setting, where they could expose other susceptible children or adults to the infection.

When to Call the Pediatrician

If your child has a fever and a rash and appears uncomfortable, discuss the problem with your pediatrician. If rubella is diagnosed, follow the guidelines suggested earlier for treatment and isolation.

Prevention

Being immunized is the best way to prevent rubella, or German measles. The vaccine usually is administered as part of a three-in-one shot called MMR (measles, mumps, rubella), given when the child is twelve to fifteen months old. A booster dose needs to be given as well. (See Chapter 31, *Immunizations.*)

A child can be immunized even if his mother is pregnant at the time. However, a susceptible pregnant woman should not be immunized herself. She also should be extremely careful to avoid contact with any child or adult who may be infected with the virus. After delivery, she should be immunized immediately.

Scabies

Scabies is caused by a microscopic mite that burrows under the top layers of skin and deposits its eggs. The rash that results from scabies is actually a reaction to the mite's body, eggs, and excretions. Once the mite gets into the skin, it takes two to four weeks for the rash to appear.

In an older child, this rash appears as numerous itchy, fluid-filled bumps that may be located under the skin next to a reddish burrow track. In an infant, the bumps may be more scattered and isolated and often are found on the palms and soles. Because of scratch marks, crusting, or a secondary infection, this annoying rash often is difficult to identify except in infants who usually demonstrate distinct burrows.

According to legend, when Napoleon's troops had scabies, one could hear the sound of scratching at night from over a mile away. A bit of exaggeration perhaps, but it illustrates two key points to remember if you think your child has scabies: it's very itchy, and it's very contagious. Scabies is spread only by person-to-person contact, and this happens extremely easily. If one person in your family has the rash, the others may get it, too.

Scabies can be located almost anywhere on the body, including the area between the fingers. Older children and adults usually don't get the rash on their palms, soles, scalp, or face, but babies may.

Treatment

If you notice that your child (and possibly others in the family) is scratching constantly, suspect scabies and call the pediatrician, who will examine the rash. The doctor may gently scrape a skin sample from the affected area and look under the microscope for evidence of the mite or its eggs. If scabies turns out to be the diagnosis, the doctor will prescribe one of several anti-scabies medications. Most are lotions that are applied over the entire body—from the scalp to the soles of the feet—and are washed off after several hours. You may need to repeat the application one week later.

Most experts feel the whole family must be treated—even those members who don't have a rash. Others feel that although the entire family should be examined, only those with a rash should be treated with anti-scabies medications. Any live-in help, overnight visitors, or frequent babysitters also should receive care.

To prevent infection caused by scratching, cut your child's fingernails. If the itching is very severe, your pediatrician may prescribe an antihistamine or other anti-itch medication. If your child shows signs of bacterial infection in the scratched areas, notify the pediatrician. She may want to prescribe an antibiotic or another form of treatment.

Following treatment, the itching could continue for two to four weeks, because this is an allergic rash. If it persists past four weeks, call your doctor, because the scabies may have returned and need retreatment.

Incidentally, there is some controversy over the possible spread of scabies from clothing or linen. Evidence indicates that this occurs very rarely. Thus, there's no need for extensive washing or decontamination of the child's room or the rest of the house, since the mite usually lives only in people's skin.

Scarlet Fever

When your child has strep throat (see page 681), there's a chance that he'll get a rash. This is known as scarlet fever. The symptoms of scarlet fever begin with a sore throat, a fever of 101–104 degrees Fahrenheit (38.2–40 degrees Celsius), and headache. This is followed within twenty-four hours by a red rash covering the trunk, arms, and legs. The rash is slightly raised, which makes the skin feel like fine sandpaper. Your child's face may turn red, too, with a pale area around his mouth. This redness will disappear in three to five days, leaving peeling skin in the areas where the rash was most intense (neck, underarms, groin, fingers, and toes). He may also have a white-coated, then reddened, tongue, and mild abdominal pain.

Treatment

Call your pediatrician whenever your child complains of a sore throat, especially when a rash or fever also is present. The doctor will examine him and swab his throat to check for streptococcal bacteria. If the streptococcal bacteria are found, an antibiotic (usually penicillin or amoxicillin) will be given. If your child takes the antibiotic by mouth instead of as an injection, it's extremely important to complete the entire course because shorter treatment sometimes results in a return of the disease.

Most children with streptococcal throat infections respond very quickly to antibiotics. The fever, sore throat, and headache usually are gone within twenty-four hours. The rash, however, will remain for about three to five days. If your child's condition does not seem to improve with treatment, notify your pediatrician. If other family members develop a fever or sore throat at this time—with or without a rash—they, too, should be examined and tested for strep throat.

If not treated, scarlet fever (like strep throat) can lead to ear and sinus infections, swollen neck glands, and pus around the tonsils. The most serious complication of untreated streptococcal throat is rheumatic fever, which results in joint pain and swelling and sometimes heart damage. Very rarely, the streptococcal bacteria in the throat can lead to glomerulonephritis, or inflammation of the kidneys, causing blood in the urine and sometimes high blood pressure.

Sunburn

While those with darker skin coloring tend to be less sensitive to the sun, everyone is at risk for sunburn and its associated disorders. Children especially need to be protected from the sun's burning rays, since most sun damage occurs in childhood. Like other burns, sunburn will leave the skin red, warm, and painful. In severe cases it may cause blistering, fever, chills, headache, and a general feeling of illness.

Your child doesn't actually have to be burned, however, in order to be harmed by the sun. The effects of exposure build over the years, so even moderate exposure during childhood can contribute to wrinkling, toughening, freckling, and even cancer of the skin in later life. Also, some medications can cause a skin reaction to sunlight, and some medical conditions may make people more sensitive to the sun.

Treatment

The signs of sunburn usually appear six to twelve hours after exposure, with the greatest discomfort during the first twenty-four hours. If your child's burn is just red, warm, and painful, you can treat it yourself. Apply cool compresses to the burned areas or bathe the child in cool water. You also can give acetaminophen to help relieve the pain. (Check the package for appropriate dosage for her age and weight.)

If the sunburn causes blisters, fever, chills, headache, or a general feeling of illness, call your pediatrician. Severe sunburn must be treated like any other serious burn, and if it's very extensive, hospitalization sometimes is required. In addition, the blisters can become infected, requiring treatment with antibiotics. Sometimes extensive or severe sunburn also can lead to dehydration (see *Diarrhea*, page 537, for signs of dehydration)

and, in some cases, fainting (heatstroke). Such cases need to be examined by your pediatrician or the nearest emergency facility.

Prevention

Many parents incorrectly assume that the sun is dangerous only when it's shining brightly. In fact, it's not the visible light rays but rather the invisible ultraviolet rays that are harmful. Your child actually may be exposed to more ultraviolet rays on foggy or hazy days because she'll feel cooler and therefore stay outside for a longer time. Exposure is also greater at higher altitudes. Even a big hat or an umbrella is not absolute protection because ultraviolet rays reflect off sand, water, snow, and many other surfaces.

Try to keep your child out of the sun when the peak ultraviolet rays occur (between 10 a.m. and 4 p.m.). In addition, follow these guidelines.

■ Always use a sunscreen to block the damaging ultraviolet rays. Choose a sunscreen made for children with a sun protection factor (SPF) of 30 or higher and with broad-spectrum coverage for UVA and UVB light. (Check the label.) Apply the protection half an hour before going out. Keep in mind that *no* sunscreens are truly waterproof, and thus they need to be reapplied every one and a half to two hours, particularly if your child spends a lot of time in the water. Consult the instructions on the bottle, and choose a product that is labeled "water resistant."

■ Dress your child in lightweight cotton clothing with long sleeves and long pants. SPF-rated clothing and hats are also a good idea to protect your child's skin when she's outdoors.

■ Use a beach umbrella or similar object to keep her in the shade as much as possible.

■ Have her wear a hat with a wide brim.

■ Babies under six months of age should be kept out of direct sunlight. If adequate clothing and shade are not available, sunscreen may be used on small areas of the body, such as the face and the backs of the hands.

(See also *Burns*, page 697.)

Warts

Warts are caused by a virus—the human papillomavirus (HPV). These firm bumps (although they also can be flat) are yellow, tan, grayish, black, or brown. They usually appear on the hands, on the toes, around the knees, and on the face, but can occur anywhere on the body. When they're on the soles of the feet, doctors call them plantar warts. Although warts can be contagious, they appear infrequently in children under the age of two.

Treatment

Your pediatrician can give you advice on treating warts. Sometimes he will recommend an over-the-counter medication that contains salicylic acid or even treat them in the office using a liquid-nitrogen-based solution or spray. If any of the following are present, he may refer you to a dermatologist:

■ Multiple, recurring warts

■ A wart on the face or genital area

■ Large, deep, or painful plantar warts (warts on the soles of the feet)

■ Warts that are particularly bothersome to your child

Some warts will just go away by themselves. Others can be removed using prescription or nonprescription preparations. However, surgical removal by scraping, cauterizing, or freezing is sometimes necessary with multiple warts, those that continue to recur, or deep plantar warts. Although surgery or laser treatment might help, there are no good, well-controlled studies showing that painful, destructive treatments are any better than no treatment at all. Fortunately, most children develop immunity against warts within two to five years, resulting in clearing of warts even without treatment.

~ 35 ~

Your Child's Sleep

SLEEP IS AN essential, healthy part of your child's life. In the same way that good nutrition is important for the development of his body, sleep is crucial for the development of his brain. When kids don't get enough sleep, it can affect their behavior, their health, and how they learn. In turn, how much your child sleeps will also affect *your* sleep and *your* health. As your young child establishes and maintains a regular sleep schedule, he is more likely to sleep longer and less likely to awaken during the night, with all the health benefits of that kind of sound sleep. The sleeping brain is not a resting brain, but rather is functioning in a different manner. When you provide your child's growing brain with sufficient sleep, your child will be better able to concentrate and his temperament will be more even.

(While this chapter focuses on your baby's sleep needs, sleep training, implementing a sleep plan, and maintaining your baby's bedtime routine, more detailed information and specific guidance on sleep for particular age groups such as safe sleep tips, can be found in various chapters in Part I of the book, including pages 64, 217, 246, 286, 322, 360, 395, and 425.)

How Much Sleep Does My Baby Need?

Not surprisingly, many parents worry about the sleep habits and behaviors of their child: "Is he getting too little sleep? Or too much? How important are naps, and how many hours of napping are enough? Should I let him cry himself to sleep at night, or should I pick him up when he's in tears? Why does he seem to go to sleep later—or earlier—than other children of the same age?"

Even though many parents are anxious about their child's sleep patterns, the good news is that many of their concerns can easily be addressed. Many moms and dads may be unclear about the optimal sleep schedule for a child at different ages. While there are normal variations in sleep patterns between children, the following are specific recommendations on how many hours of sleep a child needs.

The American Society of Sleep Medicine and the AAP recommend the following amounts of sleep:

■ *Infants (4 months to 12 months):* 12 to 16 hours per 24 hours (including naps) on a regular basis to promote optimal health.

■ *Children (1 year to 2 years):* 11 to 14 hours per 24 hours (including naps) on a regular basis to promote optimal health.

■ *Children (3 years to 5 years):* 10 to 13 hours per 24 hours (including naps) on a regular basis to promote optimal health.

The first question many parents have is "When will my baby sleep through the night?" Great question, but the answer isn't the same for all infants. After all, not all children are alike, and there are normal variations from one child to another. Some babies may develop regular sleep rhythms in the first six to eight weeks, and they may sleep for many hours at a time; others, however, may have unpredictable sleep behaviors that stay that way for many months—or longer.

In most cases, though, your baby will learn to stretch out his nighttime feeds over the first few months, and by four to six months of age, he will likely no longer need to feed in the middle of the night. You can help your infant achieve this by having a consistent bedtime routine, such as bath, breast or bottle, book, and bed (placed on his back to sleep). Also, allow him to soothe himself to sleep at night, keep the room dark and quiet, and ensure that he gets plenty of time outdoors (weather permitting) and feeds well during the day.

As an infant gets older, he will continue to stretch out his nighttime sleep, as long as you let him. Your infant's unique genetics has a powerful influence on sleep; whether he takes long naps or short ones, his genetic makeup may be the reason. Or his distinctive temperament could be influencing his sleep behavior. Also, family circumstances can vary, affecting when, how long, and how well a child sleeps. In general, as long as you have a good sleep routine, your child will adjust on those evenings where the routine changes, such as sleeping at a different house or being woken early for a sibling playdate.

Scenario #1

The mother of a four-month-old baby complained to friends that while her infant had slept extremely well in the first week of his life, his sleep patterns seemed to have unraveled after that. More than anything, his sleep times were erratic and unpredictable. She conceded that she tried to keep her baby awake well into the evening so her husband could play with the infant upon returning home from work between 8:00 and 8:30 p.m. But before his arrival, her baby would often fuss and cry. Even though he seemed drowsy at times, she would try keeping him awake for a little while longer, awaiting her husband's arrival. But more often than not, the infant had become so overtired that he just couldn't be consoled.

Mother and father were conflicted over what to do: Dad seemed comfortable with the baby crying until he arrived home, while Mom worried they were being heartless. Sometimes she would try putting him down for a brief nap in the very late afternoon, but he would still become cranky later that night, and tension escalated between husband and wife.

They decided to ask their pediatrician for advice. The doctor explained the importance of being respectful of the child's evolving sleep schedule. For a typical four- to eight-month-old, a healthy nightly bedtime is between 6 and 8 p.m. Keeping the child up longer to greet his father would leave him overtired and out of sync with his own biological rhythms.

Always be mindful of your own child's sleep needs. His biological clock is evolving, and when he feels the need to sleep, he should be allowed to do so. If his sleep-wake schedule is artificially disrupted, he will probably become moody and less attentive when he is awake. If he goes to bed earlier, he may get up a *little* earlier, but his total night sleep will be longer. This will allow more time for a working parent to spend with his or her child in the morning. If any adjustments in schedules need to be made, they should begin with Mom and Dad, who should find a way to be available to their child when he's awake and alert.

Getting Sleep in Sync

Despite parental concerns—or in some cases, perhaps because of them—moms and dads sometimes unknowingly disrupt the sleep of their children. For example, even though parents want to do what's healthy for their child, they don't always appreciate the effect that their own busy schedules and family decision-making may have on their child's sleep.

Most commonly, parents may not recognize the importance of adopting a lifestyle that keeps their child in sync with his emerging biological system. When it comes to sleep, timing is everything, or nearly so. It is important to understand that *when* your children sleep is probably more important than *how long* they sleep. The quality of a child's sleep, which can restore alertness and maintain an even temperament, depends largely on when sleep occurs. That means encouraging him to sleep in rhythm with his own biological clock. A consistent bedtime that is in sync with his biological clock will typically result in restful and prolonged sleep.

Pay attention to your child, and you'll find that, just like adults, he has drowsy times during the day. If he sleeps during these drowsy periods, the quality of that sleep will be better than sleep that occurs out of phase with his biological cycles. But if you wait to put him down for sleep until well after he's shown signs of drowsiness, he's likely to be overtired by then, which may make it more difficult for him to fall asleep.

THE FIRST YEAR

As a parent, you need to nurture and support your child's need to sleep. As much as possible, encourage him to sleep during those times of the day when he's likely to benefit the most from it. However, adopting an optimal sleep schedule won't happen overnight. For infants, it takes a while for a baby's biological (circadian) rhythms to develop, with your ultimate goal of getting his sleep patterns to match his internal mechanisms. Give it time, and it will develop naturally. Your challenge as a parent is to be sensitive to those moments when his body is telling him (and you) that he's ready for sleep. Otherwise, you may be putting him down in his crib or bed way too early or way too late, and the ease with which he falls asleep—and the restorative capacity of that sleep—will be affected.

YOUR TODDLER OR PRESCHOOL-AGE CHILD

For clues on whether your older child is getting enough sleep—particularly quality sleep—observe him at the end of the day. Is he sweet, adaptable, friendly, cooperative, independent, and engaging? Or is he whiny, crabby, excitable, wired, and irritable? He may be running out of steam as the day draws to a close, all because of mild but chronic sleep deprivation. So pay attention to him, and you'll find that, just like with adults, he experiences a drowsy time during the day. If he's consistently melting down, you may need to make some adjustments in the times when you put him to sleep. He may need to go to bed earlier. The earlier bedtime will get rid of his unpleasant behavior near the end of the day.

Also keep the following caveat in mind: when parents move their baby's bedtime earlier, they may see no improvement in the baby's pre-sleep behavior. In cases like this, the earlier bedtime may still be too late, and needs to be adjusted further, so that it is even earlier.

Sleep Routines and Dealing with Crying

Some babies cry every night when they're placed in their crib for sleep; others almost never do. For many parents, it can be gut-wrenching when a child cries in his crib for long periods of time. As your baby cries, your heart may be breaking, and it can be anguishing to keep your distance while you wait for him to fall asleep. Or you might feel frustration or anger at his apparent unwillingness or inability to quiet down and sleep. Even just a few minutes of tears can seem like an eternity.

Often concerned about why their baby is crying, parents may wonder whether the infant is simply letting off steam, is feeling lonely, or is really in distress. Many parents just give in and rush to their infant's side, unable to bear the sound of the sobs. Not surprisingly, some of the most common questions asked of pediatricians are "Should I let my baby cry himself to sleep, or should I pick him up and comfort him?" and the more fundamental question "How much sleep should he really be getting?" To a large degree, the answers to these questions depend on the age of the child.

THE FIRST MONTH

During this period, your baby will spend most of his time asleep. When you place him on his back in his crib for sleep, or when he awakens, try to avoid letting him cry. Instead, respond to those tears, and do whatever you can to soothe your baby, such as singing quietly, talking to him quietly, playing soft music, keeping the lights dim, and/or rocking him gently. Pick him up if necessary, placing him back in the crib again five to ten minutes later. By minimizing his discomfort in whatever way works, you'll maximize his sleep time and its quality. (For additional information about soothing a crying baby, see the information later in this section, as well as pages 880 and 881 later in this chapter.)

When is an infant of this age ready for sleep, whether or not he's in tears? In general, after he has been awake for one to two hours, he needs sleep. Sometimes he may need to fall asleep even before an hour goes by, and rarely he may stay awake for three hours. If he is a little fussy or has some low-level crying, wait to see if it escalates once you place him back in the crib, and if it does, then of course pick him up. But he just might drift off to sleep.

Generally, no matter what the circumstances, he will begin to show signs of being overtired and irritable if he doesn't get his nap when he needs it. So start soothing him to sleep. After he's been awake for an hour or two, he may need to be soothed. Place him in his crib when he's drowsy but still awake (this approach will be particularly helpful for daytime napping). If you wait too long, he's likely to become cranky and have even more difficulty falling asleep. (For more information on crying and colic, see page 167.)

Sharing the Bedtime Routine

During these early weeks after birth, it is also important to get other adults, such as your spouse or partner, a grandparent, a sitter, or a nanny, involved in bedtime rituals. When you are the only one participating in getting him into bed, he will associate only you with putting him to sleep. The more people who are involved, the less likely it is that your baby will associate a certain scenario with falling asleep. This notion is sometimes called "many hands."

Parent Sleep Deprivation

In your baby's first weeks after birth, another issue may surface: Mom or Dad may be sleep deprived. A newborn's sleep schedule may leave your spouse anxious and overwhelmed, particularly if she feels that there are more responsibilities added to her life when she herself is feeling so sleep deprived and exhausted. You should support each other, and when necessary provide the primary caregiver with additional periods when she can take a break to catch a nap or find another way to recharge her batteries.

IMPLEMENTING A SLEEP PLAN

It is important that both you and your spouse/partner agree to a sleep plan for your child. If only one parent is on board, the plan is unlikely to succeed. Decide together whether to adopt any new steps gradually or quickly. Many pediatricians advise small, simple steps first, making it a little easier for both parent and child to adjust. A slightly earlier bedtime, for example, may improve your child's mood and lead to less disappointment.

Whenever a change is made, wait and watch for a while to see how successful it is. Do not make your evaluation on a day-by-day (or night-by-night) basis. Try a new approach for at least several days before concluding that the change is worth continuing.

■ *At about six weeks of age (counting from the baby's due date for an infant born prematurely):* Your baby's sleep-wake schedule will start to settle into more of a routine at this time. He will begin to sleep longer at night, and may exhibit signs of drowsiness (and perhaps some crying) earlier in the evening. For example, while he may have once been ready for sleep between 9 and 11 p.m., he may start to need sleep somewhat earlier—perhaps between 6 and 8 p.m. His longest sleep period will be in the late evening, lasting for three to five hours.

Variations exist, of course, so be sensitive to your own baby's needs and anticipate that he may require an earlier bedtime—no longer at 11 p.m. but rather at 8 p.m. So to minimize crying, put your child to sleep earlier, spend some time soothing him if needed (although if he fusses a little, it won't cause any harm), and let his own biological rhythm dictate whether it will turn into a thirty-minute nap or a four-hour snooze.

As you and your baby get in tune with his rhythms, he'll gradually learn to soothe himself to sleep when you put him down. As that happens, there will be little or no crying. By about three months of age, most babies sleep six to eight hours during the night without waking their parents up. If he awakens too early, you might be able to encourage him to go back to sleep by soothing him, and keeping the lights off and the shades drawn. Avoid picking him up or feeding him, if possible.

■ *Four to twelve months of age:* With a four-month-old, and continuing into the weeks and months ahead, keep working at being sensitive to your baby's bodily rhythms, which will minimize episodes of crying. From four months through the rest of the first year, most infants need at least two naps, one at midmorning and the other at midday; some children may nap a third time later in the afternoon. Try to get him on a schedule of napping at about 9 a.m., then at 1 p.m., and finally a late afternoon nap if he needs it. Most parents hate to awaken a young child from a nap because sleep is precious for him. Let him nap for as long as he wishes unless he has difficulty falling asleep at night; in that case, talk to your pediatrician about awakening him from his afternoon nap a little earlier than he might wake up on his own. If he takes late and lengthy naps, it might be because his bedtime is too late, and he is partially compensating for lost sleep at night by taking long naps. Skipping

the third nap and having an earlier bedtime might be warranted. By about nine months of age, try to dispense with late afternoon naps so he'll be ready for bedtime for the night at an earlier time than if those late afternoon naps continued.

At this age, a child's nighttime sleep will be his longest sleep period of the day, and by about eight months old, it should last from ten to twelve hours without him awakening for a nighttime feeding. But if a child of this age seems overtired and he cries at the mere sight of his bed, his naps may be too short (less than thirty minutes long), his naps may not be occurring with his sleep rhythms, or perhaps you're putting him to bed too late at night. In the latter case, place him in bed much earlier, at least temporarily—perhaps at 5:30 or 6 p.m.—to respond to his excessive tiredness. If he cries, check on him and console him with a few comforting words. Change his diaper if needed, make sure he is comfortable, but keep the lights dim and don't arouse him more fully by picking him up and walking with him. Then leave the room quietly. As the days and weeks pass, gradually give him less attention at night; this will help him stop anticipating that you'll show up whenever he cries or calls out for you, and he'll be more likely to learn self-soothing techniques such as sucking on his hand, rocking his head, or rubbing the sheet.

It's important to keep in mind that there are times when you may need to let your baby cry himself to sleep; it

Scenario #2

A mother and father brought their five-month-old daughter to the pediatrician, and explained that her napping (or lack of it) had become a serious problem that affected the entire family. They would put their child down for a daytime nap, but she would awaken about thirty-five to forty minutes later, ready to continue her day, at least for a while. They agreed that their baby needed lengthier naps, but were frustrated in their attempts to make them longer. They had tried leaving their baby in her crib for twenty more minutes after awakening, but she would cry nonstop and resisted returning to sleep.

Their pediatrician explained that in infants four to five months old, it can be challenging to initiate a regular nap schedule because their biological rhythms are continuing to change and mature; nap times may not become well established for about another month or two. The doctor suggested that they could try extending the naps by responding promptly when the child first makes noises or calls out for attention. When that happens, they can try gently patting their baby or give her a massage for a short time. With this approach, many children will fall back asleep for another twenty to thirty minutes, providing a truly restorative nap that leads to greater alertness and attention spans later in the day.

As a child becomes older, however, these particular approaches can become more stimulating than soothing in some children, and thus become counterproductive. After discussing the matter further with the parents, the pediatrician felt there were a couple of factors at play. The child's bedroom might not be dark enough and the apartment might not be quiet enough to encourage sleep. But more important, the timing of the child's naps was likely not in sync with her natural rhythms. He recommended that they adjust the sleep environment to make it more conducive to napping, and to be patient until their child's biological rhythms made her body more agreeable to predictable daytime napping.

won't cause any harm, and there's no need to worry about the possible messages behind those tears. Remember, you have all day to show your infant how much you love him and care for him. At night, he'll get the message that nighttime is for sleeping, and on those nights when you let him cry, you're helping him learn to soothe himself. He won't be thinking that you're abandoning him or that you don't love him anymore; he knows by your daytime behaviors that this isn't the case at all. In other words, there's no need to worry. However, if the crying is prolonged, do check on your child; the goal with sleep training is to teach your child to fall asleep on his own, not to make him more upset.

Daytime Nap Evolution

■ *About ages ten to twelve months:* The baby's morning nap will begin to taper off in the minority of children around ten to twelve months. Around twelve months of age, some babies may drop their morning nap altogether. As that happens, you can start moving his nighttime bedtime somewhat earlier (perhaps by about twenty to thirty minutes); the afternoon nap can be started a little sooner, too. The time when you put your baby down for nighttime sleep may vary for a while, depending on factors such as how tired your child seems and the quality of his daytime napping.

Scenario #3

Many parents recognize the importance of bedtime routines—but for some parents, these routines don't always work. One mother tried out many she had heard about, including bathing her baby, massaging her after the bath, singing soft lullabies, and swaddling the baby, but none was effective. In fact, her baby often became *more* irritable with these approaches.

When this mother expressed her frustration to her pediatrician, he offered some pointers to make these bedtime routines more effective. He told her to begin using them early, *before* the child is already overtired and becoming crabby. He also urged her to be consistent, using the same bedtime routines day after day until the child begins to associate them with sleep. He stressed persistence, explaining that changes don't happen overnight, and that routines need to be relied on over time to have a positive effect.

The pediatrician had another suggestion. He asked the parents to place the infant in the crib for a nap about twenty to thirty minutes *before* they thought the nap should actually begin. As the baby relaxed in her crib, she almost always had a bowel movement within ten to twenty minutes, which prompted her to cry. But then once her diaper was changed, she was now in the correct biological time frame for her nap to begin. Her parents soothed her, and she fell asleep for a lengthy nap.

■ *Thirteen to twenty-three months of age:* The amount of time that your child spends napping will begin to change during this time of life. By age fifteen months, about half (but certainly not yet all) children will be taking only one nap a day, typically in the afternoon. The morning nap may simply fade away on its own, although there could be some rough periods as this transition to a single daily nap takes place. Even so, for most children, the morning nap will gradually disappear. As that happens, if you put your child to bed earlier for the night, he'll actually be less likely to miss those morning naps, and he's more likely to wake up rested.

■ *Twenty-four months of age:* By this time, nearly all children have transitioned to just a single afternoon nap, although this napping remains biologically important for them to function well during the rest of the day.

■ *Between two and three years old:* Most children continue needing one daytime nap so that they're not irritable and fussy by late afternoon. By about three years old, the average child will sleep about two hours during the daytime. However, some will sleep more and others less (as little as an hour in some cases). Try to make the timing of naps and nighttime sleep regular, although the need for some flexibility is inevitable. Some children will go through periods where they resist napping, even though their body is telling them (and you) that they need a nap; in those in-stances, try out an earlier or later bedtime at night, and see if that helps your child rest better during the day.

The best rule of thumb about the length of napping is that your child's naps should be long enough to be restorative. There is some evidence that longer naps tend to improve a child's attention span and his ability to learn. Conversely, if he's having very brief mini-naps that are just a few minutes in length, they simply won't sustain him through the day. A child's need for an afternoon nap about one to two hours in length tends to persist until he is about three years old, and then the length will shorten after that. Research shows that 90 percent of three-year-olds are still napping.

■ *Three to five years of age:* Most children in this age range are ready for nighttime sleep between 7 and 9 p.m., or earlier if naps are brief or absent, and they'll sleep through the night until about 6:30 to 8 a.m. Naps tend to become less common in some children by age three or four.

During this age, get in tune with your child's need for sleep, and set a regular bedtime. With less napping time and greater physical activity, the sleep needs at night actually increase in some children.

Getting the Most Out of Sleep

So how do you prepare and soothe your child to sleep? Soothing techniques may vary based on the age of your child. Some gentle rubbing of his back can help at almost any age. For young infants, so can touching your own cheek to his in a rhythmic pattern that coincides with his own breathing. Patting him, kissing his forehead, or encouraging sucking behavior with a pacifier or finger may also be useful for young infants.

Bedtime routines can start as early as four to six months of age, and they'll help get your child ready for rest, particularly as he starts to associate them with sleep. Try reading him a story. Or give him a warm bath or a massage, sing him a lullaby, or play soothing music. Cut down on your playtime with him right before bedtime, close the curtains, dim the lights, and avoid using your mobile phones.

More important than your choice of a specific routine or ritual, you need to continue to stay in rhythm with your child's circadian clock. When it's time to sleep, keep your child away from situations where there is a lot of stimulation, which can lead to crankiness and make sleep difficult. Family activities with the baby before bedtime should be low-key, so as not to overstimulate him. Remember, timing is the key to healthy sleep. So while it's fine to sit quietly with your child for ten to twenty minutes and read him a story, what you choose to do is usually of less importance than the time you choose to do it.

With this in mind, many mothers and fathers try to change their own behaviors to encourage better sleep in their children. If possible, parents can create a parenting plan, similar to creating a sleep or bedtime routine. While one parent stays home with a child, the other parent is able to run errands or visit friends, and vice versa. This type of schedule can be implemented into a daily, weekly, or monthly routine in a way that works best with the family. Once your baby adopts a regular schedule in sync with his own internal clock, it can be liberating for Mom and Dad. You can take your child out for special events, and he won't fuss or cry. If your baby sticks to a routine for at least 80 percent of the time, the other 20 percent may not be a problem if you need to adjust his sleep schedule.

If your infant is in childcare during the first year, ask his caregivers to keep him on a regular napping schedule as much as possible. It should be the same schedule that you follow at home to minimize disruptions. Sometimes you may not even notice if he is overtired because he is so excited to see you when you pick him up at the childcare facility, and you are so enthusiastic to see him. But pay attention to what he's experiencing. The staff's willingness to adapt to your own preferences for napping may be an important factor when you're choosing a facility.

Of course, many (but not all) childcare facilities are willing and able to make the timing of napping a priority. However, depending on where your child is being cared for, there may not be a dark, quiet room for napping, which can make sleeping difficult. Your child may be ready for

SCENARIO #4

A father called the family's pediatrician with a problem that he and his wife were trying to solve. They understood the value of keeping their nine-month-old infant on a sleep schedule. At the same time, however, they had two older children with activities that didn't always fit in with the parents' commitment to be protective of their baby's need to nap.

Their pediatrician recommended that the parents work hard at finding a balance between the older children's social needs, and the baby's biologic requirement to nap during the day. Noting that they may not always find the perfect solution that meets the needs of everyone, the doctor added that compromises may be necessary. "Sometimes," he said, "you may have to tell an older child, 'You'll be a little late to your playdate because we're going to wait a few extra minutes until Owen finishes sleeping.' But other times, when the older child has a special event, you may decide to wake up the infant to make sure the older brother or sister gets to where he or she needs to go on time."

It's true that, in most cases, you should try to avoid awakening a sleeping baby. But a slightly shorter nap now and then won't cause harm, as long as it doesn't become a regular pattern.

a nap between 9 and 10 a.m. and then again between 1 and 3 p.m.—but the childcare environment may not be conducive to napping at those times. There might be too much light, or lots of noise (including crying) from other children. As a result, he may not get the sleep he needs at the time when he most needs it. When that happens, he could be overtired when you pick him up at the end of your workday, and it may be particularly hard to keep him on a regular schedule. Your own time spent with the baby, bathing, feeding, and dressing him in the morning, can help make up for any time lost later in the day.

Try your best to continue the weekday schedule on the weekends and during vacations for consistency of sleep for your child. Nevertheless, some disruptions in sleep schedules are inevitable. Holidays, vacations, or a family gathering can keep your child from napping or getting to bed on time. Because the temperament of children varies, some are much more adaptable to changes like these than others; while one child will adjust to changing circumstances very easily, others may not.

As much as possible, respect your child's nature, and try to maintain normal sleep routines. At the same time, if you know that a disruption of his sleep schedule is on the horizon, he will fare better and adapt more successfully, and have a cheerier disposition, if he is more rested ahead of time. So when you look ahead to a family party, for example, try to keep your child well rested in the preceding day or two so that this intrusion into his sleep schedule will unfold as smoothly as possible. The more rested your child is, the better his temperament and the more adaptable he will be to changes in his environment—and the better he will sleep.

How often can you disrupt your child's sleep schedule? Exceptions to sleep routines, when you can adjust naps and bedtimes, can occur once or twice a month, so you and your baby can enjoy holidays, birthdays, and other special events. Most well-rested children adapt to these occasional events. But do not overdo it with disruptions once or twice a week.

If your baby does get off schedule—perhaps because of a grandparent's visit, or when an unexpected illness occurs—think of the notion of a "reset" that lasts just one night. For this night of readjustment, put your child to bed very early, ignoring protest crying related to the sleep debt he has accumulated. A more gradual approach often fails due to the child's overtiredness and his battle to get extra attention. It can be frustrating for parents, but a single "reset" night should resolve the problem. The key here is to get back to the normal bedtime routine.

Dealing with Other Sleep Concerns

Sometimes family issues can also affect and disrupt your child's sleep. For example, if you have trouble setting limits during the day, if you and your spouse aren't on the same page, or you've had an exhausting day at work, all of this can make sleep in your home more challenging for everyone, especially your child. Dealing effectively with everyday problems can help your entire family get appropriate sleep.

Also, does your child have health issues that make sleeping difficult, such as colic, severe eczema, or sleep apnea? (Colic is a frequent cause of sleep-disrupting fussiness in very young babies; see page 167 for more information and guidance.) Or your child could have a short-term health problem like an ear infection that is causing pain and keeping him awake. Tend to his immediate needs, following your pediatrician's instructions on how to manage the problem and ease your child's discomfort.

Putting Sleep in Perspective

When it comes to your child's sleep, do the best you can, but don't feel bad if things don't always go smoothly. Make a concerted effort to get your child to bed on time for naps and at night. If your baby spends time at childcare or with a nanny and you're simply not present to put him to sleep at nap time, make sure that his caregivers understand and are trying to comply with your own preferences about your child's sleep schedule. But you also need to set aside any anxiety and blame you might feel if you aren't doing everything perfectly. Inevitably, there will be days and nights when your child doesn't sleep well. Don't beat yourself up if your child goes to bed a little late for a night or two (or more). Just get back on track as soon as possible, and help him return to a normal sleeping routine. Dealing effectively with your child's sleeping problems is important, not only for your child, but also because his sleep difficulties can interfere with your own need to rest. Meeting your own sleep needs (as well as those of your partner) is important to effectively care for your baby and the rest of your family. Chronically overtired parents also have a greater risk of becoming depressed.

As we mentioned earlier, sleep is an essential, healthy part of your child's life. Helping your child sleep can be one of parenting's biggest challenges. But it can have an enormous payoff in terms of your child's health, now and in the future. Many adults are chronically poor sleepers because of patterns that may have begun during their own childhood. Sleeping poorly is a learned behavior, and when a child doesn't get quality sleep, he may not learn how to sleep well. In many cases, such sleep issues are likely to become part of his life for many years. The younger your child is when you begin to deal with his sleep problems, the more likely you are to resolve them. Remember that your pediatrician can be an ongoing source of support, advice, and reassurance. Additionally, many pediatric medical centers have individuals who specialize in helping children sleep better.

~ APPENDIX ~

Recommendations for Preventive Pediatric Health Care
Bright Futures/American Academy of Pediatrics

Each child and family is unique; therefore, these Recommendations for Preventive Pediatric Health Care are designed for the care of children who are receiving competent parenting, have no manifestations of any important health problems, and are growing and developing in a satisfactory fashion. Developmental, psychosocial, and chronic disease issues for children and adolescents may require frequent counseling and treatment visits separate from preventive care visits. Additional visits also may become necessary if circumstances suggest variations from normal.

		INFANCY							EARLY CHILDHOOD					
AGE[1]	Prenatal[2]	Newborn[3]	3-5 d[4]	By 1 mo	2 mo	4 mo	6 mo	9 mo	12 mo	15 mo	18 mo	24 mo	30 mo	3 y
HISTORY Initial/Interval	●	●	●	●	●	●	●	●	●	●	●	●	●	●
MEASUREMENTS														
Length/Height and Weight		●	●	●	●	●	●	●	●	●	●	●	●	●
Head Circumference		●	●	●	●	●	●	●	●	●	●	●		
Weight for Length		●	●	●	●	●	●	●	●	●	●			
Body Mass Index[5]												●	●	●
Blood Pressure[6]		★	★	★	★	★	★	★	★	★	★	★	★	●
SENSORY SCREENING														
Vision[7]		★	★	★	★	★	★	★	★	★	★	★	★	●
Hearing		●[8]	●[9]——→			★	★	★	★	★	★	★	★	★
DEVELOPMENTAL/BEHAVIORAL HEALTH														
Developmental Screening[11]								●			●		●	
Autism Spectrum Disorder Screening[12]											●	●		
Developmental Surveillance		●	●	●	●	●	●		●	●	●			●
Psychosocial/Behavioral Assessment[13]		●	●	●	●	●	●	●	●	●	●	●	●	●
Tobacco, Alcohol, or Drug Use Assessment[14]														
Depression Screening[15]														
Maternal Depression Screening[16]				●	●	●	●							
PHYSICAL EXAMINATION[17]		●	●	●	●	●	●	●	●	●	●	●	●	●
PROCEDURES[18]														
Newborn Blood		●[19]	●[20]——→											
Newborn Bilirubin[21]		●												
Critical Congenital Heart Defect[22]		●												
Immunization[23]		●	●	●	●	●	●	●	●	●	●	●	●	●
Anemia[24]						★			●	★	★	★	★	★
Lead[25]							★	★	● or ★[26]		★	● or ★[26]		★
Tuberculosis[27]			★				★		★			★		★
Dyslipidemia[28]												★		
Sexually Transmitted Infections[29]														
HIV[30]														
Cervical Dysplasia[31]														
ORAL HEALTH[32]							●[33]	●[33]	★		★	★	★	★
Fluoride Varnish[34]							←				●		→	
Fluoride Supplementation[35]							★	★	★		★	★	★	★
ANTICIPATORY GUIDANCE	●	●	●	●	●	●	●	●	●	●	●	●	●	●

KEY: ● = to be performed   ★ = risk assessment to be performed with appropriate action to follow, if positive

◄———— ● ————► = range during which a service may be provided

American Academy of Pediatrics
DEDICATED TO THE HEALTH OF ALL CHILDREN®

Bright Futures.
prevention and health promotion for infants,
children, adolescents, and their families™

These recommendations represent a consensus by the American Academy of Pediatrics (AAP) and Bright Futures. The AAP continues to emphasize the great importance of continuity of care in comprehensive health supervision and the need to avoid fragmentation of care.

Refer to the specific guidance by age as listed in the *Bright Futures Guidelines* (Hagan JF, Shaw JS, Duncan PM, eds. *Bright Futures: Guidelines for Health Supervision of Infants, Children, and Adolescents.* 4th ed. Elk Grove Village, IL: American Academy of Pediatrics; 2017).

	MIDDLE CHILDHOOD						ADOLESCENCE											
y	6 y	7 y	8 y	9 y	10 y	11 y	12 y	13 y	14 y	15 y	16 y	17 y	18 y	19 y	20 y	21 y

The recommendations in this statement do not indicate an exclusive course of treatment or standard of medical care. Variations, taking into account individual circumstances, may be appropriate.

1. If a child comes under care for the first time at any point on the schedule, or if any items are not accomplished at the suggested age, the schedule should be brought up-to-date at the earliest possible time.

2. A prenatal visit is recommended for parents who are at high risk, for first-time parents, and for those who request a conference. The prenatal visit should include anticipatory guidance, pertinent medical history, and a discussion of benefits of breastfeeding and planned method of feeding, per "The Prenatal Visit" (http://pediatrics.aappublications.org/content/124/4/1227.full).

3. Newborns should have an evaluation after birth, and breastfeeding should be encouraged (and instruction and support should be offered).

4. Newborns should have an evaluation within 3 to 5 days of birth and within 48 to 72 hours after discharge from the hospital to include evaluation for feeding and jaundice. Breastfeeding newborns should receive formal breastfeeding evaluation, and their mothers should receive encouragement and instruction, as recommended in "Breastfeeding and the Use of Human Milk" (http://pediatrics.aappublications.org/content/129/3/e827.full). Newborns discharged less than 48 hours after delivery must be examined within 48 hours of discharge, per "Hospital Stay for Healthy Term Newborns" (http://pediatrics.aappublications.org/content/125/2/405.full).

5. Screen, per "Expert Committee Recommendations Regarding the Prevention, Assessment, and Treatment of Child and Adolescent Overweight and Obesity: Summary Report" (http://pediatrics.aappublications.org/content/120/Supplement_4/S164.full).

6. Screening should occur per "Clinical Practice Guideline for Screening and Management of High Blood Pressure in Children and Adolescents" (http://pediatrics.aappublications.org/content/140/3/e20171904). Blood pressure measurement in infants and children with specific risk conditions should be performed at visits before age 3 years.

7. A visual acuity screen is recommended at ages 4 and 5 years, as well as in cooperative 3-year-olds. Instrument-based screening may be used to assess risk at ages 12 and 24 months, in addition to the well visits at 3 through 5 years of age. See "Visual System Assessment in Infants, Children, and Young Adults by Pediatricians" (http://pediatrics.aappublications.org/content/137/1/e20153596) and "Procedures for the Evaluation of the Visual System by Pediatricians" (http://pediatrics.aappublications.org/content/137/1/e20153597).

8. Confirm initial screen was completed, verify results, and follow up, as appropriate. Newborns should be screened, per "Year 2007 Position Statement: Principles and Guidelines for Early Hearing Detection and Intervention Programs" (http://pediatrics.aappublications.org/content/120/4/898.full).

9. Verify results as soon as possible, and follow up, as appropriate.

10. Screen with audiometry including 6,000 and 8,000 Hz high frequencies once between 11 and 14 years, once between 15 and 17 years, and once between 18 and 21 years. See "The Sensitivity of Adolescent Hearing Screens Significantly Improves by Adding High Frequencies" (http://www.jahonline.org/article/S1054-139X(16)00048-3/fulltext).

11. See "Identifying Infants and Young Children With Developmental Disorders in the Medical Home: An Algorithm for Developmental Surveillance and Screening" (http://pediatrics.aappublications.org/content/118/1/405.full).

12. Screening should occur per "Identification and Evaluation of Children With Autism Spectrum Disorders" (http://pediatrics.aappublications.org/content/120/5/1183.full).

13. This assessment should be family centered and may include an assessment of child social-emotional health, caregiver depression, and social determinants of health. See "Promoting Optimal Development: Screening for Behavioral and Emotional Problems" (http://pediatrics.aappublications.org/content/135/2/384) and "Poverty and Child Health in the United States" (http://pediatrics.aappublications.org/content/137/4/e20160339).

14. A recommended assessment tool is available at http://www.ceasar-boston.org/CRAFFT/index.php.

15. Recommended screening using the Patient Health Questionnaire (PHQ)-2 or other tools available in the GLAD-PC toolkit and at http://www.aap.org/en-us/advocacy-and-policy/aap-health-initiatives/Mental-Health/Documents/MH_ScreeningChart.pdf.

16. Screening should occur per "Incorporating Recognition and Management of Perinatal and Postpartum Depression Into Pediatric Practice" (http://pediatrics.aappublications.org/content/126/5/1032).

17. At each visit, age-appropriate physical examination is essential, with infant totally unclothed and older children undressed and suitably draped. See "Use of Chaperones During the Physical Examination of the Pediatric Patient" (http://pediatrics.aappublications.org/content/127/5/991.full).

18. These may be modified, depending on entry point into schedule and individual need.

19. Confirm initial screen was accomplished, verify results, and follow up, as appropriate. The Recommended Uniform Screening Panel (https://www.hrsa.gov/advisory-committees/heritable-disorders/rusp/index.html), as determined by The Secretary's Advisory Committee on Heritable Disorders in Newborns and Children, and state newborn screening laws/regulations (http://genes-r-us.uthscsa.edu/home) establish the criteria for and coverage of newborn screening procedures and programs.

20. Verify results as soon as possible, and follow up, as appropriate.

21. Confirm initial screening was accomplished, verify results, and follow up, as appropriate. See "Hyperbilirubinemia in the Newborn Infant ≥35 Weeks' Gestation: An Update With Clarifications" (http://pediatrics.aappublications.org/content/124/4/1193).

22. Screening for critical congenital heart disease using pulse oximetry should be performed in newborns, after 24 hours of age, before discharge from the hospital, per "Endorsement of Health and Human Services Recommendation for Pulse Oximetry Screening for Critical Congenital Heart Disease" (http://pediatrics.aappublications.org/content/129/1/190.full).

23. Schedules, per the AAP Committee on Infectious Diseases, are available at http://redbook.solutions.aap.org/SS/Immunization_Schedules.aspx. Every visit should be an opportunity to update and complete a child's immunizations.

24. Perform risk assessment or screening, as appropriate, per recommendations in the current edition of the AAP *Pediatric Nutrition: Policy of the American Academy of Pediatrics* (Iron chapter).

25. For children at risk of lead exposure, see "Prevention of Childhood Lead Toxicity" (http://pediatrics.aappublications.org/content/138/1/e20161493) and "Low Level Lead Exposure Harms Children: A Renewed Call for Primary Prevention" (http://www.cdc.gov/nceh/lead/ACCLPP/Final_Document_030712.pdf).

26. Perform risk assessments or screenings as appropriate, based on universal screening requirements for patients with Medicaid or in high prevalence areas.

27. Tuberculosis testing per recommendations of the AAP Committee on Infectious Diseases, published in the current edition of the AAP *Red Book: Report of the Committee on Infectious Diseases*. Testing should be performed on recognition of high-risk factors.

28. See "Integrated Guidelines for Cardiovascular Health and Risk Reduction in Children and Adolescents" (http://www.nhlbi.nih.gov/guidelines/cvd_ped/index.htm).

29. Adolescents should be screened for sexually transmitted infections (STIs) per recommendations in the current edition of the AAP *Red Book: Report of the Committee on Infectious Diseases*.

30. Adolescents should be screened for HIV according to the USPSTF recommendations (http://www.uspreventiveservicestaskforce.org/uspstf/uspshivi.htm) once between the ages of 15 and 18, making every effort to preserve confidentiality of the adolescent. Those at increased risk of HIV infection, including those who are sexually active, participate in injection drug use, or are being tested for other STIs, should be tested for HIV and reassessed annually.

31. See USPSTF recommendations (http://www.uspreventiveservicestaskforce.org/uspstf/uspscerv.htm). Indications for pelvic examinations prior to age 21 are noted in "Gynecologic Examination for Adolescents in the Pediatric Office Setting" (http://pediatrics.aappublications.org/content/126/3/583.full).

32. Assess whether the child has a dental home. If no dental home is identified, perform a risk assessment (http://www2.aap.org/oralhealth/docs/RiskAssessmentTool.pdf) and refer to a dental home. Recommend brushing with fluoride toothpaste in the proper dosage for age. See "Maintaining and Improving the Oral Health of Young Children" (http://pediatrics.aappublications.org/content/134/6/1224).

33. Perform a risk assessment (http://www2.aap.org/oralhealth/docs/RiskAssessmentTool.pdf). See "Maintaining and Improving the Oral Health of Young Children" (http://pediatrics.aappublications.org/content/134/6/1224).

34. See USPSTF recommendations (http://www.uspreventiveservicestaskforce.org/uspstf/uspsdnch.htm). Once teeth are present, fluoride varnish may be applied to all children every 3–6 months in the primary care or dental office. Indications for fluoride use are noted in "Fluoride Use in Caries Prevention in the Primary Care Setting" (http://pediatrics.aappublications.org/content/134/3/626).

35. If primary water source is deficient in fluoride, consider oral fluoride supplementation. See "Fluoride Use in Caries Prevention in the Primary Care Setting" (http://pediatrics.aappublications.org/content/134/3/626).

Summary of Changes Made to the
Bright Futures/AAP Recommendations for Preventive Pediatric Health Care
(Periodicity Schedule)

This schedule reflects changes approved in December 2018 and published in March 2019.
For updates and a list of previous changes made, visit www.aap.org/periodicityschedule.

CHANGES MADE IN DECEMBER 2018

BLOOD PRESSURE

- Footnote 6 has been updated to read as follows: "Screening should occur per 'Clinical Practice Guideline for Screening and Management of High Blood Pressure in Children and Adolescents' (http://pediatrics.aappublications.org/content/140/3/e20171904). Blood pressure measurement in infants and children with specific risk conditions should be performed at visits before age 3 years."

ANEMIA

- Footnote 24 has been updated to read as follows: "Perform risk assessment or screening, as appropriate, per recommendations in the current edition of the AAP *Pediatric Nutrition: Policy of the American Academy of Pediatrics* (Iron chapter)."

LEAD

- Footnote 25 has been updated to read as follows: "For children at risk of lead exposure, see 'Prevention of Childhood Lead Toxicity' (http://pediatrics.aappublications.org/content/138/1/e20161493) and 'Low Level Lead Exposure Harms Children: A Renewed Call for Primary Prevention' (https://www.cdc.gov/nceh/lead/ACCLPP/Final_Document_030712.pdf)."

2019 Recommended Immunizations for Children from Birth Through 6 Years Old

Birth	1 month	2 months	4 months	6 months	12 months	15 months	18 months	19–23 months	2–3 years	4–6 years
HepB	HepB			HepB						
		RV	RV	RV						
		DTaP	DTaP	DTaP		DTaP				DTaP
		Hib	Hib	Hib	Hib					
		PCV13	PCV13	PCV13	PCV13					
		IPV	IPV	IPV						IPV
					MMR					MMR
					Varicella					Varicella
					HepA§					
				Influenza (Yearly)*						

Shaded boxes indicate the vaccine can be given during shown age range.

Is your family growing? To protect your new baby against whooping cough, get a Tdap vaccine. The recommended time is the 27th through 36th week of pregnancy. Talk to your doctor for more details.

NOTE:
If your child misses a shot, you don't need to start over. Just go back to your child's doctor for the next shot. Talk with your child's doctor if you have questions about vaccines.

FOOTNOTES:
* Two doses given at least four weeks apart are recommended for children age 6 months through 8 years of age who are getting an influenza (flu) vaccine for the first time and for some other children in this age group.

§ Two doses of HepA vaccine are needed for lasting protection. The first dose of HepA vaccine should be given between 12 months and 23 months of age. The second dose should be given 6 months after the last dose. HepA vaccination may be given to any child 12 months and older to protect against hepatitis A. Children and adolescents who did not receive the HepA vaccine and are at high risk should be vaccinated against hepatitis A.

If your child has any medical conditions that put him at risk for infection or is traveling outside the United States, talk to your child's doctor about additional vaccines that he or she may need.

See back page for more information on vaccine-preventable diseases and the vaccines that prevent them.

For more information, call toll-free **1-800-CDC-INFO** (1-800-232-4636) or visit **www.cdc.gov/vaccines/parents**

U.S. Department of Health and Human Services
Centers for Disease Control and Prevention

American Academy of Pediatrics
DEDICATED TO THE HEALTH OF ALL CHILDREN®

AAFP
AMERICAN ACADEMY OF FAMILY PHYSICIANS

Vaccine-Preventable Diseases and the Vaccines That Prevent Them

Disease	Vaccine	Disease spread by	Disease symptoms	Disease complications
Chickenpox	Varicella vaccine protects against chickenpox.	Air, direct contact	Rash, tiredness, headache, fever	Infected blisters, bleeding disorders, encephalitis (brain swelling), pneumonia (infection in the lungs)
Diphtheria	DTaP* vaccine protects against diphtheria.	Air, direct contact	Sore throat, mild fever, weakness, swollen glands in neck	Swelling of the heart muscle, heart failure, coma, paralysis, death
Hib	Hib vaccine protects against *Haemophilus influenzae* type b.	Air, direct contact	May be no symptoms unless bacteria enter the blood	Meningitis (infection of the covering around the brain and spinal cord), intellectual disability, epiglottitis (life-threatening infection that can block the windpipe and lead to serious breathing problems), pneumonia (infection in the lungs), death
Hepatitis A	HepA vaccine protects against hepatitis A.	Direct contact, contaminated food or water	May be no symptoms, fever, stomach pain, loss of appetite, fatigue, vomiting, jaundice (yellowing of skin and eyes), dark urine	Liver failure, arthralgia (joint pain), kidney, pancreatic and blood disorders
Hepatitis B	HepB vaccine protects against hepatitis B.	Contact with blood or body fluids	May be no symptoms, fever, headache, weakness, vomiting, jaundice (yellowing of skin and eyes), joint pain	Chronic liver infection, liver failure, liver cancer
Influenza (Flu)	Flu vaccine protects against influenza.	Air, direct contact	Fever, muscle pain, sore throat, cough, extreme fatigue	Pneumonia (infection in the lungs)
Measles	MMR** vaccine protects against measles.	Air, direct contact	Rash, fever, cough, runny nose, pink eye	Encephalitis (brain swelling), pneumonia (infection in the lungs), death
Mumps	MMR**vaccine protects against mumps.	Air, direct contact	Swollen salivary glands (under the jaw), fever, headache, tiredness, muscle pain	Meningitis (infection of the covering around the brain and spinal cord), encephalitis (brain swelling), inflammation of testicles or ovaries, deafness
Pertussis	DTaP* vaccine protects against pertussis (whooping cough).	Air, direct contact	Severe cough, runny nose, apnea (a pause in breathing in infants)	Pneumonia (infection in the lungs), death
Polio	IPV vaccine protects against polio.	Air, direct contact, through the mouth	May be no symptoms, sore throat, fever, nausea, headache	Paralysis, death
Pneumococcal	PCV13 vaccine protects against pneumococcus.	Air, direct contact	May be no symptoms, pneumonia (infection in the lungs)	Bacteremia (blood infection), meningitis (infection of the covering around the brain and spinal cord), death
Rotavirus	RV vaccine protects against rotavirus.	Through the mouth	Diarrhea, fever, vomiting	Severe diarrhea, dehydration
Rubella	MMR** vaccine protects against rubella.	Air, direct contact	Sometimes rash, fever, swollen lymph nodes	Very serious in pregnant women—can lead to miscarriage, stillbirth, premature delivery, birth defects
Tetanus	DTaP* vaccine protects against tetanus.	Exposure through cuts in skin	Stiffness in neck and abdominal muscles, difficulty swallowing, muscle spasms, fever	Broken bones, breathing difficulty, death

* DTaP combines protection against diphtheria, tetanus, and pertussis.
** MMR combines protection against measles, mumps, and rubella.

Last updated January 2019 · CS300526-A

Birth to 24 months: Boys
Length-for-age and Weight-for-age percentiles

NAME _____

RECORD # _____

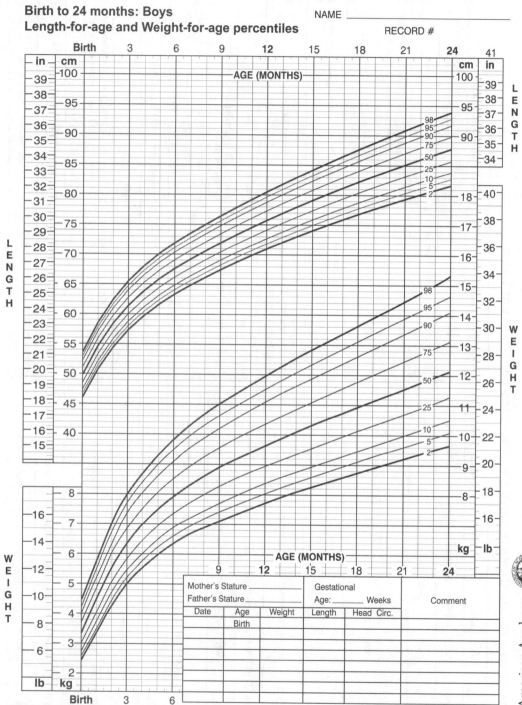

Published by the Centers for Disease Control and Prevention, November 1, 2009
SOURCE: WHO Child Growth Standards (http://www.who.int/childgrowth/en)
SAFER · HEALTHIER · PEOPLE™
Additional copies are available for purchase in quantities of 100. To order, contact:
American Academy of Pediatrics · 345 Park Blvd. Itasca, IL 60143 Web site—http://www.aap.org.
Web site—http://www.aap.org · Minimum order 100.   HE0510

Reprinted by the American Academy of Pediatrics
The recommendations in this publication do not indicate an exclusive course of
treatment or serve as a standard of medical care. Variations, taking into account
individual circumstances, may be appropriate.
© 2011 American Academy of Pediatrics   9-283/REP1018

American Academy
of Pediatrics

DEDICATED TO THE HEALTH OF ALL CHILDREN®

Birth to 24 months: Girls
Length-for-age and Weight-for-age percentiles

NAME _____

RECORD # _____

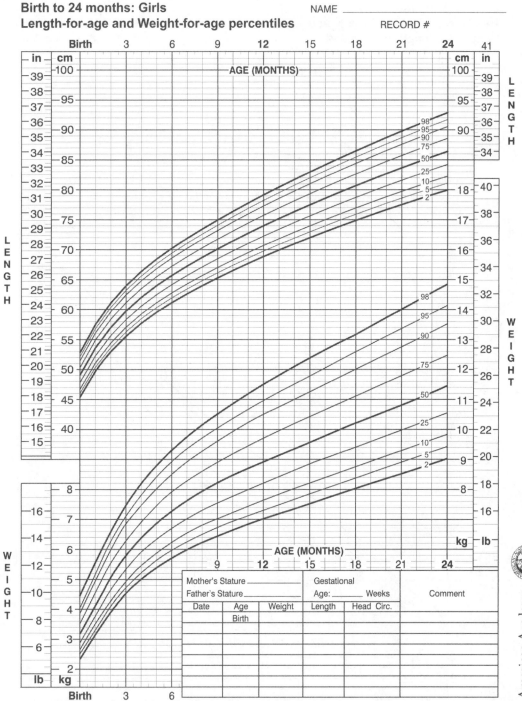

Published by the Centers for Disease Control and Prevention, November 1, 2009
SOURCE: WHO Child Growth Standards (http://www.who.int/childgrowth/en)

Reprinted by the American Academy of Pediatrics

The recommendations in this publication do not indicate an exclusive course of treatment or serve as a
standard of medical care. Variations, taking into account individual circumstances, may be appropriate.
© 2011 American Academy of Pediatrics   9-284-Rep0219

Additional copies are available for purchase in quantities of 100.

To order, contact:
American Academy of Pediatrics
345 Park Blvd
Itasca, IL 60143
Web site—http://www.aap.org. Minimum order 100.
HE0511

American Academy
of Pediatrics

Birth to 24 months: Boys
Head circumference-for-age and
Weight-for-length percentiles

NAME _____

RECORD # _____

Published by the Centers for Disease Control and Prevention, November 1, 2009
SOURCE: WHO Child Growth Standards (http://www.who.int/childgrowth/en)

Additional copies are available for purchase in quantities of 100. To order, contact:
American Academy of Pediatrics • 345 Park Blvd. Itasca, IL 60143
Web site—http://www.aap.org • Minimum order 100   HE0510

Reprinted by the American Academy of Pediatrics
The recommendations in this publication do not indicate an exclusive course of
treatment or serve as a standard of medical care. Variations, taking into account
individual circumstances, may be appropriate.
© 2011 American Academy of Pediatrics   9-283/REP1018

American Academy
of Pediatrics

DEDICATED TO THE HEALTH OF ALL CHILDREN®

Birth to 24 months: Girls
Head circumference-for-age and
Weight-for-length percentiles

NAME _____

RECORD # _____

Published by the Centers for Disease Control and Prevention, November 1, 2009
SOURCE: WHO Child Growth Standards (http://www.who.int/childgrowth/en)

Reprinted by the American Academy of Pediatrics

The recommendations in this publication do not indicate an exclusive course of treatment or serve as a
standard of medical care. Variations, taking into account individual circumstances, may be appropriate.
© 2011 American Academy of Pediatrics   9-284-Rep0219

Additional copies are available for purchase in quantities of 100.

To order, contact:
American Academy of Pediatrics
345 Park Blvd
Itasca, IL 60143
Web site—http://www.aap.org. Minimum order 100.
HE0511

American Academy
of Pediatrics
DEDICATED TO THE HEALTH OF ALL CHILDREN®

Boys, 2 to 20 years

STATURE FOR AGE AND WEIGHT FOR AGE PERCENTILES

Name _____

Record # _____

Girls, 2 to 20 years

Name _____

STATURE FOR AGE AND WEIGHT FOR AGE PERCENTILES

Record # _____

Mother's Stature _____ Father's Stature _____

Date	Age	Weight	Stature	BMI*

*To Calculate BMI: Weight (kg) ÷ Stature (cm) ÷ Stature (cm) x 10,000
or Weight (lb) ÷ Stature (in) ÷ Stature (in) x 703

Source: Developed by the National Center for Health Statistics in collaboration with the
National Center for Chronic Disease Prevention and Health Promotion (2000).
http://www.cdc.gov/growthcharts

Reprinted by the American Academy of Pediatrics

The recommendations in this publication do not indicate an exclusive course of treatment or serve as a
standard of medical care. Variations, taking into account individual circumstances, may be appropriate.

©2000 American Academy of Pediatrics

Additional copies are available for purchase in quantities of 100.

To order, contact
American Academy of Pediatrics
345 Park Blvd.
Itasca, IL 60143
Web site — http://www.aap.org
Minimum order 100.

American Academy
of Pediatrics

DEDICATED TO THE HEALTH OF ALL CHILDREN®

CDC

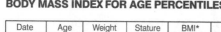

Boys, 2 to 20 years

Name _____

BODY MASS INDEX FOR AGE PERCENTILES

Record # _____

Date	Age	Weight	Stature	BMI*	Comments

*To Calculate BMI: Weight (kg) ÷ Stature (cm) ÷ Stature (cm) x 10,000
or Weight (lb) ÷ Stature (in) ÷ Stature (in) x 703

AGE (YEARS)

Source: Developed by the National Center for Health Statistics in collaboration with the
           National Center for Chronic Disease Prevention and Health Promotion (2000).
           http://www.cdc.gov/growthcharts

Reprinted by the American Academy of Pediatrics

The recommendations in this publication do not indicate an exclusive course of treatment or serve as a
standard of medical care. Variations, taking into account individual circumstances, may be appropriate.

©2000 American Academy of Pediatrics, Revised—5/01

9-8/REP0219

Additional copies are available for purchase in quantities of 100.

To order, contact:
American Academy of Pediatrics
345 Park Blvd
Itasca, IL 60143
Web site — http://www.aap.org
Minimum order 100.

HE0304

Girls, 2 to 20 years

Name _____

BODY MASS INDEX FOR AGE PERCENTILES

Record # _____

Date	Age	Weight	Stature	BMI*	Comments

*To Calculate BMI: Weight (kg) ÷ Stature (cm) ÷ Stature (cm) x 10,000
or Weight (lb) ÷ Stature (in) ÷ Stature (in) x 703

AGE (YEARS)

CDC

American Academy of Pediatrics

DEDICATED TO THE HEALTH OF ALL CHILDREN®

Source: Developed by the National Center for Health Statistics in collaboration with the National Center for Chronic Disease Prevention and Health Promotion (2000).
http://www.cdc.gov/growthcharts

Reprinted by the American Academy of Pediatrics

The recommendations in this publication do not indicate an exclusive course of treatment or serve as a standard of medical care. Variations, taking into account individual circumstances, may be appropriate.

©2000 American Academy of Pediatrics. Revised—5/01

9-10/REP0918

Additional copies are available for purchase in quantities of 100.
To order, contact
American Academy of Pediatrics
345 Park Blvd.
Itasca, IL 60143
Web site — http://www.aap.org
Minimum order 100.

HE0306

CHOKING/CPR

LEARN AND PRACTICE CPR (CARDIOPULMONARY RESUSCITATION).

IF ALONE WITH A CHILD WHO IS CHOKING...

1. SHOUT FOR HELP. 2. START RESCUE EFFORTS. 3. CALL 911 OR YOUR LOCAL EMERGENCY NUMBER.

START FIRST AID FOR CHOKING IF	DO *NOT* START FIRST AID FOR CHOKING IF
• The child cannot breathe at all (the chest is not moving up and down). • The child cannot cough or talk or looks blue. • The child is found unconscious/unresponsive. (Go to CPR.)	• The child can breathe, cry, or talk. • The child can cough, sputter, or move air at all. The child's normal reflexes are working to clear the airway.

FOR INFANTS YOUNGER THAN 1 YEAR

INFANT CHOKING

If the infant is choking and is unable to breathe, cough, cry, or speak, follow these steps. Have someone call 911.

1 GIVE 5 BACK BLOWS (SLAPS).

ALTERNATING WITH

2 GIVE 5 CHEST COMPRESSIONS.

Alternate back blows (slaps) and chest compressions until the object is dislodged or the infant becomes unconscious/ unresponsive. If the infant becomes unconscious/ unresponsive, begin CPR.

INFANT CPR

To be used when the infant is UNCONSCIOUS/UNRESPONSIVE or when breathing stops. Place infant on flat, hard surface.

1 START CHEST COMPRESSIONS.
- Place 2 fingers of 1 hand on the breastbone just below the nipple line.
- Compress chest at least 1/3 the depth of the chest, or about 4 cm (1.5 inches).
- After each compression, allow chest to return to normal position. Compress chest at rate of at least 100 times per minute.
- Do 30 compressions.

2 OPEN AIRWAY.
- Open airway (head tilt–chin lift).
- If you see a foreign body, sweep it out with your finger. Do NOT do blind finger sweeps.

3 START RESCUE BREATHING.
- Take a normal breath.
- Cover infant's mouth and nose with your mouth.
- Give 2 breaths, each for 1 second. Each breath should make the chest rise.

4 RESUME CHEST COMPRESSIONS.
- Continue with cycles of 30 compressions to 2 breaths.
- After 5 cycles of compressions and breaths (about 2 minutes) and if no one has called 911 or your local emergency number, call it yourself.

If at any time an object is coughed up or the infant/child starts to breathe, stop rescue breaths and call 911 or your local emergency number.

Ask your pediatrician for information on choking/CPR instructions for children older than 8 years and for information on an approved first aid or CPR course in your community.

CHOKING/CPR

LEARN AND PRACTICE CPR (CARDIOPULMONARY RESUSCITATION).

IF ALONE WITH A CHILD WHO IS CHOKING...

1. SHOUT FOR HELP. 2. START RESCUE EFFORTS. 3. CALL 911 OR YOUR LOCAL EMERGENCY NUMBER.

START FIRST AID FOR CHOKING IF	DO *NOT* START FIRST AID FOR CHOKING IF
• The child cannot breathe at all (the chest is not moving up and down). • The child cannot cough or talk or looks blue. • The child is found unconscious/unresponsive. (Go to CPR.)	• The child can breathe, cry, or talk. • The child can cough, sputter, or move air at all. The child's normal reflexes are working to clear the airway.

FOR CHILDREN 1 TO 8 YEARS OF AGE

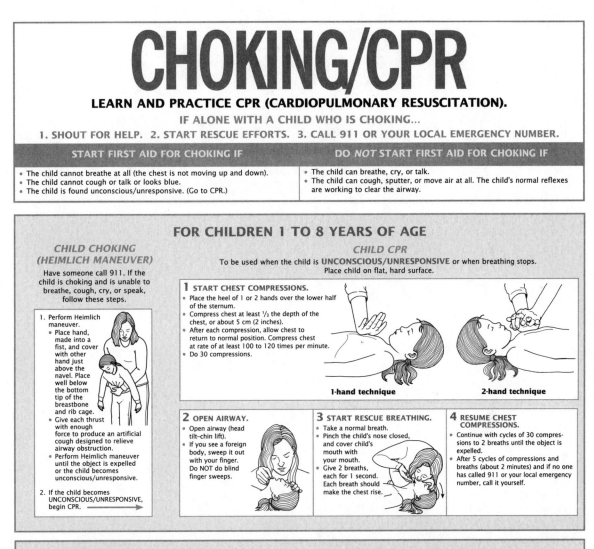

CHILD CHOKING (HEIMLICH MANEUVER)

Have someone call 911. If the child is choking and is unable to breathe, cough, cry, or speak, follow these steps.

1. Perform Heimlich maneuver.
   • Place hand, made into a fist, and cover with other hand just above the navel. Place well below the bottom tip of the breastbone and rib cage.
   • Give each thrust with enough force to produce an artificial cough designed to relieve airway obstruction.
   • Perform Heimlich maneuver until the object is expelled or the child becomes unconscious/unresponsive.
2. If the child becomes UNCONSCIOUS/UNRESPONSIVE, begin CPR.

CHILD CPR

To be used when the child is UNCONSCIOUS/UNRESPONSIVE or when breathing stops. Place child on flat, hard surface.

1 START CHEST COMPRESSIONS.
• Place the heel of 1 or 2 hands over the lower half of the sternum.
• Compress chest at least $\frac{1}{3}$ the depth of the chest, or about 5 cm (2 inches).
• After each compression, allow chest to return to normal position. Compress chest at rate of at least 100 to 120 times per minute.
• Do 30 compressions.

1-hand technique   2-hand technique

2 OPEN AIRWAY.
• Open airway (head tilt–chin lift).
• If you see a foreign body, sweep it out with your finger. Do NOT do blind finger sweeps.

3 START RESCUE BREATHING.
• Take a normal breath.
• Pinch the child's nose closed, and cover child's mouth with your mouth.
• Give 2 breaths, each for 1 second. Each breath should make the chest rise.

4 RESUME CHEST COMPRESSIONS.
• Continue with cycles of 30 compressions to 2 breaths until the object is expelled.
• After 5 cycles of compressions and breaths (about 2 minutes) and if no one has called 911 or your local emergency number, call it yourself.

If at any time an object is coughed up or the infant/child starts to breathe, stop rescue breaths and call 911 or your local emergency number.

Ask your pediatrician for information on choking/CPR instructions for children older than 8 years and for information on an approved first aid or CPR course in your community.

Page numbers in italics refer to illustrations.

abdomen and gastrointestinal
    tract, 84, 88, 90, 339,
    527–59, *528*
    abdominal pain, 72, 527–31
    appendicitis, 529, 531–33
    celiac disease, 533–34
    child abuse, 753
    colic, *528*
    communicating hydrocele,
        552–54
    constipation, 529, 534–37
    cramps, poisoning, 713
    diarrhea, 537–44
    emotional upset, 529–30
    food allergies, 530, 571
    food poisoning, 544–49
    hepatitis, 549–51
    infants, 143, 154, 527–29
    inguinal hernia, 552
    intussusception, 528–29
    lead poisoning, 530
    malabsorption, 554–55
    mumps, 802
    Reye syndrome, *555*
    strep throat, 530–31
    swollen abdomen, 541, 558
    urinary tract infections, 531
    vomiting, 555–59
abdominal wall defects, 13
abusive head trauma, 169–70
academic skills, 398
acetaminophen, 220, 224, 550,
        605, 610, 669, 672, 678,
        688, 802, 804
    dosage chart, 780–81
    toxic reaction, 781–82
acne, 160
activity center, 264, 293, 491
address, knows own, 411
adenoidectomy, 684–85
adenoids, 683–85, *683*
adenoviruses, 557, 608
adoption, 116, 749–51
affection, 239, 324, 370, 583
aggressive behavior, 581–85
    autism, 645
    bullying, 431
    child abuse, 753
    effective discipline, 583–84,
        593
    fear for safety of others,
        585

four- and five-year-old and,
    417, 431, 435
    grandparents and, 333
    modeling and, 584
    one-year-old and, 309
    physical punishment and, 325,
        348
    school and, 585
    screen time and, 348
    three-year-old and, 386
    time-outs, 584
    two-year-old and, 346, 348
air contrast enema, 529
air pollution, 563, 654, 719–20
albuterol, 565, 567
alcohol, 488, 517
    breastfeeding, 100
    pregnancy, 4–6, 146, 654, 665
allergens, 563, 569, 573–76
allergies, 561–80
    anaphylaxis and, 572, 576–77
    asthma, 561–68
    blood test for, 572–73
    breastfeeding, 30, 88–90, 119
    coughs, 606, 607–8
    ear infections, 674–75
    eczema, 568–70
    food, 571–73
    hives, 576–77
    insect stings, 575–80
    medical identification bracelet,
        577
    nasal, 573–76
    patch test for, 570
    probiotics, 539
    skin prick test, 572
alopecia, 854–55
alternative therapies, 623, 651
amblyopia, 651, 738, 743–44
American Academy of Pediatric
    Dentistry, 247, 356–57
American Academy of Pediatrics
    (AAP) policy, 5, 6, 29, 67,
        88, 129, 133, 149, 320, 329,
        466, 487, 506, 514, 623,
        636, 647, 658, 725, 728,
        751, 821, 828, 829
American Association on
    Intellectual and
    Developmental Disabilities,
        665
American Board of Pediatrics, 20

American College of
    Obstetricians and
    Gynecologists, 57, 649
American Diabetes Associations,
        633, 634
American Heart Association,
        699
American Midwifery
    Certification Board, 10,
        17–18
American Red Cross, 182, 699
American Society of Sleep
    Medicine, 874
amniotic fluid, 13, 46–47
ANA blood test, 839
anaphylaxis, 572, 576–77
anemia, 331, 627–30
    acute vs. chronic, 627–28
    prematurity and, 59
    sickle cell disease and, 638
anesthesia, 44, 49
aneurysms, 814, 815
anger, 581–85
    acknowledging, 348
    effective discipline, 582–84
    four- and five-year-old and,
        413
    physical punishment, 325
    post-traumatic stress, 587
    three-year-old and, 386
animals. *See also* pets
    allergies and, 574–75
    bites, 695–96
    safety, 517–18
    swollen glands and, 688
antibiotic ointment, 569, 702, 704
antibiotics, 545–46, 578, 613,
        617, 631, 639, 661, 668, 676,
        682, 689, 792
    animal bites, 696
    breastfeeding, 30, 115
    diaper rash, 71
    diarrhea, 538, 542
    ear infection, 24, 220, 672–74
    four- to seven-month-old and,
        253–54
    intravenous, 844
    Lyme disease, 837
    newborn eyes, 51
    pregnancy, 15
    resistance, 254, 673, 862–63
    when and how to use, 254

antibodies, 120, 572
anticonvulsant medication, 804
antidiarrheal medications, 539
antifungal cream, 852
antihistamines, 6, 547, 570, 574,
    576, 578, 661, 675
anti-HIV therapy, 635, 636
anti-inflammatory medications,
    567
anti-retroviral (ARV), 635
antiseptics, 703–4
antiviral medications, 254,
    550–51, 611, 678
Apgar scores, 51–53
appendicitis, 528, 529, 531–33,
    532, 558
appetite, 532
    four- and five-year-old and, 424
    four- to seven-month-old and,
        255
    one- to three-month-old and,
        224
    one-year-old and, 309
    post-traumatic stress, 587
applied behavior analysis, 647
arachidonic acid (ARA), 11, 122
areola, 47, 92–97, 93, 96, 98
    inverted nipple and, 94
arrhythmias, 807–9
arthritis, 835–40
    juvenile idiopathic (JIA),
        837–39
    Lyme disease, 836–37
    osteomyelitis, 835
    septic, 835
    swaddling, 68
    transient synovitis of hip,
        839–40
arts and crafts, 379–80, 410,
    413. See also drawing
asbestos, 720–21
Asperger disorder, 643
aspirin, 6, 220, 224, 550, 610,
    672, 851
    acetaminophen vs., 780
    asthma, 563
    Kawasaki disease, 815
    Reye syndrome, 555, 610
assertiveness, 278, 295–96, 305
asthma, 5, 119, 561–68, 562,
    675, 719, 733, 823
    action plan, 565, 567
    breastfeeding, 30, 88, 90
    chronic nature of, 619–20
    controller medications, 565–68

coughs, 606–8
    immediate medical attention
        for, 564
    influenza, 611
    pneumonia, 612
    probiotics, 123
    quick relief medications,
        564–65
    triggers, 561–63, 567–68
astigmatism, 735–36, 746
ASTM F406 safety standard,
    490
atopic dermatitis, 222, 568, 569
attachment, 248, 278, 645
attention
    brain development, 166
    effective discipline, 593
    four- to seven-month-old and,
        240
    giving too much, 288–89
    one-year-old and, 324, 328,
        330
    three-year-old and, 386
    physical punishment, 325
    siblings and, 217–19, 290, 330
attention-deficit hyperactivity
    disorder (ADHD), 590–94,
    641
    autism, 643
    tic disorders, 600
    trauma vs., 590
attention span, 236, 269–70,
    339–40, 342, 349
auditory brainstem response
    (ABR), 660
autism spectrum disorder (ASD),
    350, 383, 641, 643–48
    vaccines, 819, 822
autosomal inheritance, 653

babbling, 209, 213, 235–36, 240,
    269
baby carriers, 169, 507–8
baby equipment, 488–95, 521
baby foods, 243
baby-led weaning, 243
baby monitors, 36, 286, 479
baby nurse, 181
baby powder, 69, 479
babysitter. See also childcare
    provider
    allergies, 692
    choosing, 182, 438, 519
    chronic health conditions, 626

CPR classes for, 182
    crying baby, 64
    eight- to twelve-month-old
        and, 277
    emergencies and, 182, 692,
        715
    four- to seven-month-old and,
        228, 249
    grandparents as, 250, 370
    older sibling as, 369
    one- to three-month-old and,
        211
    smoking, 734
    two-year-old and, 351–52
baby walkers, 264, 293, 491
bacteria, 9, 120, 543–44
bacterial infection, 114–15,
    253–54, 529, 538–39, 557,
    559, 673
ball skills, 267, 279, 299–300,
    315, 340–42, 349, 377–78,
    391, 420, 475
bassinet, 33, 35, 37, 67, 149, 193
bathing, 33–34, 76, 197, 252
baths
    bedtime, 65, 78, 246, 322,
        425
    dilute bleach, 570
    drowning in, 257, 293, 483,
        693, 705
    eczema, 570
    first month, 197
    four- and five-year-old and,
        408, 433
    four- to six-month-old and,
        248
    frequency of, 75
    newborn, 33–34, 65, 75–78
    one- to three-month-old and,
        219, 222
    rashes, 222
    safety, 197–98, 257, 333, 404,
        433, 483, 514, 705
    three-year-old and, 404
    water temperature, 75, 225–26
bath seats, 483
bath toys, 77, 279, 315
batteries, 332, 486–87, 727
    button, 262, 372, 405, 469,
        486, 522
bed
    bunk beds, 480
    sharing, 37, 67, 198, 521
    switching from crib to, 40,
        331, 360–61

bedbugs, 578, 579
bedding, 33, 35–37, 66–67, 193–94, 197–98, 477–78
    allergens, 568, 575
    childcare and, 453, 470
    washing, 78
bedtime
    bathing and, 78
    choices, 361
    early, 427
    feeding, 127
    four- and five-year-old and, 425
    four- to eight-month-old and, 875
    four- to six-month-old and, 246
    juice, 133
    media, 832–33
    newborn, 65
    one-year-old and, 310, 322–23
    sharing with partner, 878
    routine, 874, 881, 883
    three-year-old and, 395
    two-year-old and, 360, 363
bed wetting, 587, 633, 753, 792–96. See also wetting problems
    siblings, 217
    three-year-old and, 394–95
    toilet training, 359–60
bee sting, 576, 578–80
behavioral parent training, 592
behavior problems, 581–601
    abuse or neglect and, 585–86, 753
    anger, aggression, biting, 581–85
    assessing true disorder, 585
    death of loved one, 588–89
    disasters and, 586–88
    divorce and, 758
    effective strategies chart, 593
    hyperactivity and, 590–94
    lead and, 730
    management program for, 585, 592
    pacifier and finger sucking, 594–96
    poisoning and, 713
    sexual, 585–86
    teeth grinding, 589–90
    temper tantrums, 348, 596–99
    tics and stereotypies, 599–601

behavior. See also aggressive behavior; behavior problems; and specific problems
    defiant, 313
    eight- to twelve-month-old and, 287–89
    expectations for, 324
    four- and five-year-old and, 416
    four- to seven-month-old and, 238, 249–52
    hyperactive, 349
    newborn, 147–48
    one-year-old and, 308–9, 323–30
    rewarding good, 288, 324, 328, 416, 585
    rule setting, 352
    shyness, 308
    sibling and, 217–18, 330, 370–71
    strange, and emergencies, 693
    trial runs, 346–47
    two-year-old and, 346–49, 352
bicycle, 433, 509–11, 518, 523, 691
bicycle helmet, 403
bilirubin, 59, 155–57
birth defects. See congenital abnormalities
birthmarks, 141–42, 742, 847–50
birth parents, 750
birth plan, 16–17
birth support personnel, 50–51
birth weight, 145–46. See also low birth weight
bisphenol A (BPA), 723–24
bites, 694–97. See also insect bites and stings
biting, 324, 457, 581–85, 645
    effective discipline and, 593
    temper tantrums and, 328, 348
bladder problems, 657
bleeding, 461, 464
    emergencies, 693–94, 701–4
    head injury, 712
    HIV/AIDS, 637
    nosebleeds, 680
blindness, 64, 169–70. See also vision
blisters, 681, 823, 857. See also rashes
blocks, 267, 273, 279, 289, 299, 300, 310, 315, 340, 342, 351, 379, 391, 410, 418

blood diseases, 15, 292, 610
blood pressure, 23
    anaphylaxis and, 572
    diastolic vs. systolic, 811
    high (hypertension), 811–14
    maternal, 5, 43–44
blood sugar, 14, 51, 194–95, 632
blood tests, 804
    allergies, 572
    celiac disease, 533
    general blood panels, 573
    lead, 530
    one-year-old and, 331
    pregnancy, 12–13
    two-year-old and, 371
    vomiting, 559
blood transfusions, 550, 639
Blount's disease, 840
blue baby, 154–55, 157
blue coloring
    anaphylaxis, 572
    coughing, 607, 609
    emergencies, 693
    lips or fingertips, 604
    lips or nails, 668
    pneumonia, 612
bonding, 30–31, 50, 90, 95, 148
bone health, 422, 835
bones, broken, 708–10
    bend fractures, 709
    greenstick fractures, 708–9
    limp, 843
    malabsorption, 554
    skull fractures, 798
    sprains vs., 846
booster seat, 497, 498–99, 503, 506
booster shots, 372
bottle-feeding, 120–33. See also formula
    amount and schedule of, 128–31
    bedtime routine, 246
    bonding, 31
    bowel movements, 73–74
    breastfeeding mixed with, 100, 106
    burping, 137
    childcare provider, 470
    demand feeding, 129
    dental decay, 126–27
    ear infections, 127, 675
    nipple hole, 137
    one- to three-month-old and, 215

bottle-feeding (*cont.*)
  pacifier, 67
  position for, 127–28
  prolonged, 285
  sleep, 64, 317
  solid foods, 241
  spitting up, 137
  weaning from, 285, 317
  weight gain, 244
  with breast milk, 91, 109–14, 216
bottles
  BPA-free, 723
  cleaning, 125
  glass, 126
  inner liners, 126
  insert bags, 112
  microwave oven, 114, 482
  nipple types, 127
  plastic, 126, 723
botulism, 544, 547, 650
bouncing, 204, 233
bowel movement (stools). *See also* constipation; diarrhea
  abdominal distension, 154
  bed-wetting, 395
  blood in, 72–73, 119, 155, 529, 535, 539, 541, 628
  bottle-feeding, 130
  breastfeeding, 178
  color of, 73, 113, 178
  cystic fibrosis and, 631
  diaper rash, 71–72
  dry or hard, 73, 178
  feeding adequacy, 108, 113
  first month, 178, 196
  four- and five-year-old and, 415
  frequency of, 74, 178
  iron supplements and, 630
  newborn and, 73–74, 155
  normal, 537
  one- to three-month-old and, 216
  soiling between, 535
  solid foods and, 244–45
  spina bifida, 657
  stool retention, 535, 537
  toilet training, 358
  variation in, 534
  vomiting, 222
bowlegs, 160, 840
boys
  ADHD, 591
  autism, 644

bed-wetting, 793
breasts enlarged, 143
ear infections, 670
gender characteristics, 306, 386–87
genetic abnormalities, 653
genitals in newborn, 143–45
growth, 160
inguinal hernia, 552, *553*
JIA arthritis, 838
language skills, 302, 343
meatal stenosis, 787
mumps, 802
penis care, 75, 84–85, 144–45
posterior urethral valve, 788–89, *788*
toilet training, 322, 358, 394
undescended testicles, 789–90, *789*
urination position, 358, 393–94
weight gain, 260
bradycardia, 58
brain, 164–67
  ADHD, 591
  cerebral palsy, 649, 650
  eight- to twelve-month-old and, 271–74
  elements of healthy, 165–67
  first month, 160
  four- to six-month-old and, 248–49
  injury, 711
  IVH and premature baby, 58–59
  marijuana, 5, 6
  mumps and, 802
  one-to-three-month-old and, 210
  shaking baby, 64, 169–70
  one- to three-month-old, 219
  one-year-old and, 310–11, 333
  surgery, 798
  two-year-old and, 337, 366–67
Braxton-Hicks contractions, 16
breast cancer, 119
breastfeeding, 89–119, 723, 725
  acceptance of bottle and, 114
  adequacy of, 215–17
  alternating breasts, 97
  amount consumed, 103
  in bed, 100
  bedtime routine, 246
  benefits of, 30–31, 87–90

bonding, 46
bowel movements, 73, 74, 178, 534, 537
  breast cancer and, 119
  breast plastic surgery, 119
  breast support during, 99
  chair for, 100
  checklist for optimal, 102
  classes, 16, 31
  colds, 223
  colic, 63–64, 118, 168
  colostrum, 47
  concerns about, 114–19
  constipation, 191, 536
  cost of, 111–12
  C-section, 50
  diaper rash, 71
  diarrhea, 73, 191, 540, 542
  discomfort, 91–92
  ear infections, 675
  eight- to twelve-month-old and, 281
  engorgement, 115
  expressing milk for bottle, 109–14
  father or partner, 186
  feeding adequacy, 108–9, 113
  feeding patterns, 106–7
  first, 46–47, 51, 95, 109
  food sensitivities, 118
  frequency of, 88, 105–9, 113
  fussiness, 117–19
  growth spurt, 117–18
  how long to continue, 89, 314
  hunger and weight gain, 117
  hyperalert infant, 118
  immune protection, 22, 47, 223
  inability to, 89
  information on, 136
  iron supplements, 245
  jaundice, 156–57
  let-down and latching on, 94–101, *96*
  mastitis, 115
  milk supply increase, 101–3
  mother's diet, 242
  mother's medications, 91
  nipple problems, *94*, 114–15
  nursing round the clock, 108
  one- to three-month-old and, 215
  oversupply, 118
  pacifier, 37, 67, 178–79
  pain, 98

position for, *95–97, 96–97,* 100–101
preparing for, 92–94
premature baby, *55–56,* 59
probiotics, 123
problems with, 92, 157
reflexes, 161–62
reflux, 118
SIDS, 193
signs baby is finished, 108
signs of successful, 97–98
smoking, 733
solid foods, 241–43
spitting up, 118
supplemental nurser and, 116–17
supplements, 103, 131–32, 245
supply, 101–3, 108–9, 216–17
support for, 88–89, 136
teeth and gums, 124, 127
thrush, 195
travel, 184
twins, 104
untimely weaning, 92
uterine contractions, 47
weaning to formula, 217
when not recommended, 91
working mothers, 115, 215–17
breast milk
baby's recognition of, 175
changes in, 92, 97–98, 101
childcare provider and, 461
donor, 56
expressing, 101, 109–15, *111*
formula vs., 120
freezing, 112–13, 251
galactosemia and, 122–23
heating, 112–14
hygiene and, 461
nutrients in, 11, 89, 92, 103, 131
prebiotics, 543
premature baby and, *55–56,* 59
supplemental nurser and, 116–17
twins and, 104
taste of, 147
thickening, 557
transitional, 101
breast pump, 95
cleaning, 112
electric, 18, 110–12
double, 112
inverted nipple, 94
manual, 110, *112*

stimulating production and, 106
breasts
alternating, 105–6
care for, 92–93, 100–102, 114–15
engorgement of, 101–3, 110, 115
hand-expressing milk, *95, 111*
leakage and, 96, 98, 110
mastitis and, 115
breathing problems
anaphylaxis, 572, 578
breastfeeding and, 90
bronchiolitis, 603–4
colds, 223–24, 668
coughing, 606–7
croup, 608
emergencies, 693–94
feeding and, 216
fever and, 776
first month, 190–91
food allergies, 571
food poisoning, 547
influenza and, 609–10
insect bites, 578
one- to three-month-old and, 222–24
periodic, 190
poisoning, 713
premature baby, 55
respiratory distress, 58, 157
RSV, 222–23
sleep position and, 66–67
smoking and, 4–5
tonsils and adenoids, 684
vomiting and, 558
when to call pediatrician, 607
breathing tests, 564
breech position, 12, 48
bronchiolitis, 89, 222, 603–6, 668
bronchitis, 5, 254, 603, 675
bronchodilators, 565, 605, 608
bronchopulmonary dysplasia, 58, 222–23, 604
bruxism (teeth grinding), 589–90
building skills, 342, 366, 379, 410, 418
bulb syringe, 157, 224, 669
bullying, 431–32
burns, 198, 225–26, 252, 257, 293, 372, 403–4, 434, 483, 488, 494, 693, 697–99
first degree, 697

second degree, 697
smoking, 733
third degree, 697–98
treatment for, 697–98
burping, 63–64, 134, *135, 557*
buttons, 379, 410, 486
B vitamins, 11, 131

caffeine, 7, 118
calcium, 11, 195, 312, 316, 355, 422, 424, 573
Campylobacter, 544–45
cancer, 30, 612, 604, 853
breastfeeding, 88, 119
capillary hemangiomas, 142, 742
capillary malformations, 848–49
carbon monoxide detectors, 198, 334, 372, 403, 485, 520, 721
carbon monoxide poisoning, 484, 719, 721–22
cardiopulmonary resuscitation (CPR), 16, 443, 449, 514–15, 691, 693, 705–7, 716
choking and, *902–3*
grandparents, 523
head injury, 712
training, 182, 400, 692, 699–700, 706
cardiorespiratory monitor, 55, 58
Caring for Our Children (NRC), 461
carrots, 243, 314, 353, 700–701
cars, 196–98, 248, 256, 292, 333–35, 373, 401, 404, 434–35, 464–66, 495–507
accidents and emergencies, 694
activities for, 434–35
airbags, 373, 503–4
air pollution, 720
backing up, 373, 484, 506–7
car-pools, 465
child alone in, 198, 292, 334–35, 373, 404, 435, 465, 502–3
child safety locks, 334, 435
locking, 335, 373, 404, 503
motion sickness, 435, 800–801
one- to three-month-old and, 219
rental, 183
running in garage, 484
seatbelt, 503, 505
strangers and, 519
twins or multiples, 773

car safety seat, 18, 66, 148–49, 180, 183–84, 196–97, 256, 292, 327, 333–34, 373, 401, 404, 434, 466, 489, 490, 495–503, 504–5, 506, 522, 773
  choosing, 496–99
  convertible, 404
  emergency information on, 694
  expiration date, 197, 497
  installing, 496–97, 499–501
  missing label, 497–98
  plane travel, 401
  premature baby and, 57
  rear-facing, 498, 504
  testing, 773
  using, 501–3
cataracts, 84, 736, 739, 744
cats, 9–10, 688, 695
celiac disease, 533–34, 554
Centers for Disease Control and Prevention (CDC), 10, 89, 125, 244, 646, 648, 665, 729, 733, 858
cephalohematoma, 142–43
cereals, 73, 242, 245, 312
cerebral palsy, 57, 611, 641, 648–52, 655, 843
Cerebral Palsy Foundation, 651
Cerebral Palsy Now Foundation, 651
cerebral spinal fluid, 59
cervix, 16, 42, 43, 46, 48
Cesarean (C-section), 9, 12–13, 17, 48–51, 184
  baby's appearance, 141
  bonding, 49
  breastfeeding, 97
  doula, 43
  emergency, 48, 49
  going home after, 148
  pain relief for, 44, 49
  probiotics, 123
changing table, 33, 69, 197, 204, 262, 479–80, 491
chemicals, 6, 522, 697, 722–23, 741
chemotherapy, 604
chest disorders, 603–18. See also lungs; and specific illnesses
chickenpox (varicella), 8, 253, 739, 817–18, 823, 850–52, 893
  Kawasaki disease and, 815

chickenpox (varicella) vaccine, 85, 291, 330, 371–72, 432, 461, 815, 817–18, 822–23, 852, 892, 893
chiggers, 580
child abductions, 518–19
child abuse and neglect, 585, 751–55
childbirth, 3, 42–59
  amniotic sac rupture, 42, 46
  antibiotics and GBs, 15
  baby's physical appearance and, 141, 143
  birth plan, 16–18
  bonding and, 50
  breastfeeding, 30–31, 94–96
  buying furniture before, 33–38
  cerebral palsy and, 649
  circumcision, 28–30
  contractions, 42
  C-section and, 48–51
  classes, 16, 43
  delivery room after birth, 51–53
  emotions after, 54
  epidural and, 43–44
  false labor, 42
  fathers, 185
  going home after, 148–49
  immunization after, 22
  induced, 43
  labor pain and, 42–44
  last-minute checklist, 17–18
  newborn screening and, 56
  rupturing membranes to start, 43
  spina bifida and, 656
  pediatrician and, 21–22, 19–31
  premature birth, 54–59
  preparing for, 15–18
  preparing home and family for, 32–44
  routine vaginal delivery, 45–48, 51–53
  umbilical cord blood and, 31
  vaginal bleeding and, 42
  when to leave hospital after, 26–27
childcare agencies, 182
Child Care Aware, 446, 448
childcare center, 438, 440, 447–55
  admission procedures, 451
  advantages of, 448–49

anaphylactic reactions and, 577
  chain, 447
  child's absences and, 452
  co-op, 449
  cost of, 451
  disadvantages of, 449
  discipline, 452
  emergencies, 452
  equipment, 453
  field trips, 451
  finding, 448–55
  first aid, 452
  "get-well room," 460
  goals of, 450
  Head Start, 448
  health certification, 451
  hours of, 451
  hygiene, 453–54, 461, 546
  illness policy, 451–52, 460
  immunizations, 451, 461
  independent for-profit, 447
  licensing, 451, 447–48
  medications, 452, 459
  nonprofit, 447–48
  parental involvement, 451
  special healthcare needs, 448
  staff and, 448–50
  state-funded pre-kindergarten programs, 448
  structural programs, 448
  toileting, 453–54, 461
  touring, 452–53
  toys, 453
  types of, 447–48
  waiting lists, 449
  weather cancellations, 452
childcare provider, 367, 437–72. See also babysitter; childcare center; family childcare; in-home childcare
  aggressive behavior by child, 585
  back-sleeping, 453
  backup arrangements, 440–41, 443
  basic conditions, 440
  breast milk and, 461
  car safety and, 464–66
  childbirth plan, 17–18
  choices and types of, 438–49
  chronic conditions and, 624
  CMV and parvovirus, 462
  colds, 462, 669–70

conflicts with, 457–58
cost of, 440
days and hours of, 440
diabetes, 634
diarrheal diseases, 462
discipline and, 429, 440
drop-off, 456–57
eight- to twelve-month-old
    and, 274, 278
emergency contact list, 715
eye infections, 463
finding, 437–38
four- to seven-month-old and,
    228, 249
head lice, 463, 856
hepatitis A and B, 463
HIV/AIDS, 464, 636, 637
hygiene, 460, 542, 551
illness, 458–64
in-home, 440–43
injury prevention, 464–66
naps and, 453, 883
one- to three-month-old and,
    202, 212, 219
one-year-old and, 311
pinworms, 863–64
qualifications, 440
quality of, 274
relationship with, 455–57
relatives and, 438
ringworm, 464
safety checklist for, 468–70
separation anxiety, 278
parents as, 438
sick-child programs, 460
size of program, 440
skin infections, 463
special needs and, 466–72,
    624
staff-to-child ratios, 443,
    449–50
structure and, 440
techniques for quieting baby,
    212
three-year-old and, 397–400
tics and stereotypies, 601
toddler and preschooler,
    438–40
toilet training, 357
topic list for, 457
transportation and, 440–41,
    443, 464–67
childhood disintegrative disorder,
    643

childproofing, 187, 251, 260,
    270, 291, 294, 324, 332,
    340, 370, 400, 476–77, 714,
    717
children, playing with other
    four- and five-year-old and,
        417
    four- to six-month-old and,
        248
    one- to three-month-old and,
        211
    one-year-old and, 304–6
    two-year-old and, 346, 347,
        351
choices, 327, 367, 390, 597–98
choking, 182, 226, 231, 247, 257,
    262, 293, 334, 353, 482,
    487, 493, 691, 700–701
    coughing and, 607
    CPR chart, 902–3
    eight- to twelve-month-old
        and, 262, 284
    emergencies, 693, 700–701
    first aid chart, 902–3
    life support skills, 284
    one-year-old and, 314
    preschool and, 400
    solid foods, 241, 243, 284
chordee, 786
chorionic villus sampling (CVS),
    13–14
chronic health conditions,
    619–40
    anemia, 627–30
    care plan and, 626
    connecting with others and,
        627
    coping with, 619–27
    cystic fibrosis, 630–32
    diabetes, 632–34
    family and, 625–27
    getting help for, 624–25
    growth, 339
    healthcare system, 621–23
    helping child adapt to, 625
    HIV/AIDS, 634–37
    lung disease, 58, 222–23
    nosebleeds, 680
    parent support groups, 623,
        627
    premature baby and, 57
    proactive treatment, 622–23
    receiving diagnosis of, 620–21
circulation problems, 571

circumcised penis, 28–30, 75, 84,
    143–44, 785–86
cirrhosis, 551
clay, 299, 379, 410
cleft palate, 84, 654
climbing, 340–41, 349, 378,
    409
climbing equipment, 403, 512
clinging, 276, 307, 391
Clostridium botulinum, 544
Clostridium perfringens, 545
clothing and dressing, 219, 248,
    275, 305–6, 388, 391, 410,
    415
    cords on, 199
    eczema, 570
    fire and, 699
    insect bites and, 580, 861
    newborn, 32, 34, 66–67,
        79–82, 149, 161, 180–81
    outdoor, 180–81, 245
    plane travel, 401
    removing own, 324, 347, 418
    sleepwear, 66–67, 193, 198
    sunburn, 872
    toilet and, 394
    washing and skin care, 78,
        222
clubfoot, 845
clutch hold, 97
cochlea, 671
cochlear implants, 662–63, 798
cognitive development
    eight- to twelve-month-old
        and, 269–72
    four- and five-year-old and,
        413–14
    four- to seven-month-old and,
        236–38
    grandparents and, 332
    one-year-old and, 302–4,
        332
    three-year-old and, 384–85
    two-year-old and, 344–46
cold medicines, 6, 782
colds, 223–24, 605–6, 667–70
    antibiotics, 254
    asthma, 561
    breastfeeding, 223
    childcare and, 458, 462
    four- to seven-month-old and,
        253
    influenza vs., 610
    nasal allergies vs., 574

colds (*cont.*)
noisebleeds, 679
RSV infections, 222–23
treatment, 668–69
cold sores, 678
colic, 63–64, 118, 122–23, 167–70, 528
colic drops, 63
collarbone, broken, 154, 710
color blindness, 653
colors and color vision, 148, 173–74, 208, 219, 233, 385, 414, 664, 738
colostrum, 47, 92
communicating hydrocele, 552–54, *553*
communication. *See also* language and speech
autism and, 350
child abuse, 755
eight- to twelve-month-old and, 267
four- to seven-month-old and, 228, 248
nonverbal, 267, 643
one- to three-month-old and, 209, 211
three-year-old and, 386
two-year-old and, 338, 350
community, 166, 518–23
community health agency, 448
computers, 412, 420, 487, 831
concussions, 711–12
conflict resolution, 386, 388, 584
congenital abnormalities, 652–59
causes of, 653–54
chromosome, 653
cystic fibrosis and, 630
combination genetic and environmental, 654
coping with, 654
Down syndrome, 655
hearing impairment and, 659
pregnancy, 4, 6–8, 654
resources for, 658–59
single-gene, 653
spina bifida, 656–59
tests for, 12–14, 56, 630
torticollis, 805
unknown causes, 654
congenital heart disease, 604, 655
conjunctivitis (pinkeye), 192, 682, 739–40, 858–59

consciousness
loss of, 572, 578, 693-94, 712-13
states of, 167
consistency, 167, 252, 288, 310, 326, 352
constipation, 73–74, 534–37
abdominal pain, 529–30
bed-wetting, 395
diarrhea and overflow, 538
first month, 191
treatment for, 536
Consumer Product Safety Commission (CPSC), 247, 403, 470, 479, 486, 488, 493–94, 507, 510, 530, 727
contact dermatitis, 568, 569–70
contractions, 13, 46
convulsions, 803–5
febrile, 803, 804
generalized tonic-clonic or grand mal seizure, 803
meningitis, 799, 804
poisoning, 713
treatment of, 804
vomiting, 558
cooing, 147, 209
cooperation, 385–86, 388, 419
cords, 198–99, 257, 294, 331, 475, 479, 486
cornea, 736, 738, 742
coronary arteries, 814
cortical visual impairment, 651
corticosteroids, 565–66, 684
cough, 604–12
asthma, 563–64, 606–7
blood in, 616
bronchiolitis, 604–5
calling pediatrician about, 604
causes of, 605–6
choking, 607
covering mouth while, 611, 670
croup, 608
cystic fibrosis, 631
feeding and, 216
influenza, 609
pneumonia, 612–13
treatment for, 607–8
tuberculosis, 616
when to call pediatrician about, 606–7, 668
whooping cough, 616
cough medicines, 608, 609, 613, 669, 782

counting, 344, 385, 413, 414, 664
Coxsackie infection, 681
CPAP (continuous positive airway pressure), 55
cradle cap, 195, 852–53, 866
cradle hold, 96, *104*
crawling
cerebral palsy, 650
eight- to twelve-month-old and, 259–60, 262, 263, 265, 270, 280, 290
first month, 171
four- to seven-month-old and, 228, 233
crayons, 300, 315, 342, 379–80, 391, 418
crib, 33, 35–36, 149, 183, 194, 197–98, 226, 234, 251, 331, 470, 477–79, 520. *See also* bedding
changing to bed from, 40, 331, 361
portable, 149
crib gyms, 36, 331, 479
Cronobacter bacteria, 125
croup, 286, 606, 608–9, 668
crying, 212, 215
abdominal pain, 527
bedtime routine, 322, 877
breastfeeding, 105, 117–19
eight- to twelve-month-old and, 286, 289
first month, 167–69, 877
illnesses, 119
newborn, 51, 62–65, 147, 155
one- to three-month-old and, 211–12, 215
parents and, 64, 169–70, 212
solid foods, 241
temperature, 64
variation in, 62–63
cryptochidism, 789–90
cryptosporidiosis, 545
CT or CAT (computed tomography) imagery, 650, 657, 804
cup, 114, 132, 279, 284–85, 305, 314, 317, 340
cuts, 693, 701–4, 707–8, 863
cystic fibrosis, 555, 604, 612, 627, 630–32, 653
Cystic Fibrosis Foundation, 632
cystitis, 791

cytomegalovirus (CMV), 462, 654, 659

dactylitis, 638
death. *See also* sudden infant death syndrome (SIDS)
　accidental suffocation, 67
　child left alone in car and, 373, 404, 502
　concept of, 346
　of loved one, 476, 530, 588–89, 760–64
　premature baby and, 57
　shaking baby and, 64, 169–70
　sleep position and (SIDS), 66–67
　water swallowing, 515
decongestants, 661
DEET, 10, 580, 837, 861, 862
dehumidifier, 575
dehydration, 633–34, 669, 679, 871
　bronchiolitis and, 604–5
　diarrhea and, 73–74, 191, 538, 540–41
　ibuprofen and, 780
　juice and, 133, 243
　symptoms of, 540, 547
　vomiting and, 558
delirium, 779
demand feeding, 105, 215
dental night guard, 590
dental sealants and fillings, 723
dentist, 247, 287, 356–57, 402. *See also* teeth
Deployment and Military Medical Home Resources, 768
depression, 353, 760
dermatiatis, 114
dermoid cysts, 743
desaturation, 58
development, 213. *See also* cognitive development; developmental disabilities; *and specific skills*
　checkups and, 85
　consequences and, 362
　eighteen months, 645–46
　eight- to twelve-month-old and, 280
　first year, 645
　four- and five-year-old and, 417, 646

　four- to seven-month-old and, 229–40
　kindergarten and, 430, 432
　media and, 827–30
　one- to three-month-old and, 202–6
　one-year-old and, 312–13
　preschool and, 398–99
　rule setting and, 362
　temper tantrums and, 328
　three-year-old and, 391, 646
　twins and, 772
　two-year-old and, 351, 646
developmental disabilities, 641–66
　autism, 643–48
　cerebral palsy, 648–52
　congenital abnormalities, 652–59
　defined, 641–42
　early identification of, 166, 177, 642, 646
　evaluation of, 642
　hearing impairment, 659–63
　intellectual disability, 663–66
developmental dysplasia of hip (DDH), 843, 844
developmental interventions, 647
dexamethasone, 565
DHA (docosahexaenoic acid), 11, 122
diabetes, 30, 88, 90, 145, 245, 611, 626–27, 632–34, 793
　pregnancy and, 14–15, 43, 654, 658
　type 1 vs. type 2, 632–34
DIA (dimeric inhibin A) level, 13
diaper bag, 183
diaper rash, 70–72
diapers, 32–34, 63–64, 68–72, 149
　blood in, 72
　breastfeeding and, 105
　childcare provider and, 400, 444, 454, 461
　cloth, 68–70
　disposable, 68–70, 72, 479
　eight- to twelve-month-old and, 262, 291
　father or partner and, 186
　grandparents and, 251, 291, 520–21
　how to's, 69
　hygiene and, 542, 551
　washing, 70, 75

diaper service, 70
diarrhea, 71, 73–74, 255, 537–44. *See also* food poisoning, 544
　abdominal pain and, 529, 541
　appendicitis and, 532
　bloody stools and, 541, 546
　breastfeeding and, 88, 89, 90
　childcare provider and, 454, 459, 462
　chronic, 541
　dehydration and, 541
　electrolyte solution and, 542
　fever and, 541
　first month and, 191
　formula and, 122
　juice and, 133, 243
　one- to three-month-old and, 220
　probiotics and, 123, 543
　treatment of, 539–42
　vomiting and, 196, 541, 559
diet. *See also* food; meals; menus; nutrition
　breastfeeding and, 106
　celiac disease and, 533
　constipation and, 529
　four- and five-year-old and, 420–22
　dental health and, 356
　eight- to twelve-month-old and, 281–85
　encouraging good, 318, 320–21, 392
　fiber and, 536–537
　four- and five-year-old and, 417
　mother's and colicky baby, 168
　one-year-old and, 312–13, 318
　prebiotics and, 543
　pregnancy and, 7, 9, 11
　preschoolers and, 423–24
　solid foods and, 242–44
　two-year-old and, 339, 353–55
digestive enzyme capsules, 631
diphtheria, 8–9, 822, *893*
diphtheria vaccine. *See* DTaP vaccine
discipline. *See also* spanking
　avoiding negative, 249–50
　childcare provider and, 440, 445
　consistency and, 326, 364

discipline (*cont.*)
  facial expression and, 324
  effective strategies, 582–84, 593
  eight- to twelve-month-old and, 287–89
  extinction technique, 365
  four- and five-year-old and, 427–29, 432
  four- to seven-month-old and, 249–52
  grandparents and, 251, 369
  limit-setting and, 582
  moving child and, 324–25
  nonphysical approaches, 432
  one-year-old and, 306, 310, 323–26
  person vs. behavior, 416
  praise and, 583
  preschooler, 362–63, 399
  punishment vs., 582
  smiling and, 583
  special needs and, 583
  strict, 597
  temper tantrums and, 327–28, 348
  three-year-old and, 396–97
  time-outs and, 288, 325–26, 364
  two-year-old and, 362–65
divorce, 346, 530, 626, 755–60
dogs, 334, 405, 518, 695–96
dolls, 279, 315, 380, 493
doors, 299, 340, 372, 486, 611
doula, 16, 43, 50–51
Down syndrome, 12–14, 653–55
drawing, 266, 299–300, 391, 342, 366, 379–80, 391, 409–10
dreams, 395–96
dress-up clothes, 315
driveways, 335, 404, 484, 506
drooling, 246, 713
drowning, 257, 293, 335, 404–5, 408–9, 433
  emergencies, 693, 705–6
  prevention of, 483, 514–18
drugs, illegal, 4–5, 100, 146, 549–50, 654
DTaP (diptheria, tetanus, pertussis) vaccine, 8–9, 85, 225, 255–56, 331, 371–72, 432, 461, 616, 618, 695, 697, 703, 821–22, 892–93
dust mites, 563, 568, 574, 575

ear canal, 671, 672, 685–86, *686*
eardrops, 686–87
eardrum, 671, 674, 675
ear infections, 24, 235, 286, 733
  antibiotics and, 254
  bottle-feeding and, 127–28
  breastfeeding and, 88–90
  checkups and, 84
  discharge and, 221, 671
  four- to seven-month-old and, 253
  inner ear, 662
  middle ear, 670–75
  one- to three-month-old and, 220–21
  pain, 668
  smoking and, 4
  swimmer's ear, 685–86
  vaccines and, 292
Early Hearing Detection and Intervention (EHDI), 660
ear, nose, and throat problems, 660–61, 667–89, *675*
  colds, 667–70
  epiglottitis, 677–78
  herpes simplex, 678–79
  middle ear infection, 670–75
  nosebleeds, 679–81
  sinusitis, 675–77
  sore throat, 681–83
  swimmer's ear, 685–87
  swollen glands, 687–89
  tonsils and adenoids, 683–85
ear wax, 220, 659
echocardiogram, 655, 809, 814
echolalia, 644
e-cigarettes, 562, 733
eczema, 222, 562, 568–70, 685
  atopic dermatitis, 119, 569
  breastfeeding and, 88, 90
  contact dermatitis, 569
  peanuts and, 241
  preventing, 75, 78
  probiotics and, 123
  treatment of, 570
eggs, 242
  allergies and, 241, 571, 573, 611, 822
  food poisoning and, 10, 545
eight- to twelve-month-old, 259–94
  cognitive milestones, 272
  hand and finger skills milestones, 266

language milestones, 269
movement milestones, 265
social and emotional milestones, 275
elbow
  fractures and, 709
  pulled, 840–41, *841*
electrical appliances, 483, 699, 706
electrical cords and outlets, 334, 372, 481, 485, 494, 693, 697, 699, 706–7
electrocardiogram (ECG), 592, 808–10
electroencephalogram (EEG), 804
electrolytes, 220, 540, 542
emergencies, 691–717
  anaphylactic reactions and, 577
  babysitter and, 182
  bites, 694–97
  breathing problems and, 609
  broken bones, 708–10
  bronchiolitis and, 605
  burns, 697–99
  calling 911 first, 692
  care plan, 657
  car-pools and, 465
  childcare provider and, 472
  contact list, 373, 465, 520, 692, 715
  choking, 700–701
  croup and, 609
  cuts, scrapes, bleeding, 701–4
  diabetes and, 634
  diarrhea and, 540
  disasters, 586–88
  drowning, 705–6
  electric shock, 706–7
  epiglottitis and, 677
  family meeting point after, 699
  fingertip injuries, 707–8
  grandparents and, 291, 520
  head injuries, 711–12
  hospitals and, 25
  injuries and true, 691–93
  managed care plans, 28
  nosebleeds and, 680
  pediatrician and, 25
  preparing for, 588, 691
  seizures and, 804
  symptoms of, 693
  what to do, 693–94

emotional development
  eight- to twelve-month-old
    and, 273–80
  four-and five-year-old and,
    407–8, 413, 416–19
  four- to seven-month-old and,
    228, 238–40
  grandparents and, 333
  one- to three-month-old and,
    210–15
  one-year-old and, 307–9, 311,
    333
  three-year-old and, 389–90
  two-year-old and, 338, 343,
    346, 350–53, 367
emotions
  autism and, 350
  abdominal pain and, 529–30
  expressing, in words, 311, 343,
    367, 396–97, 582
  mother's, in first months,
    184–85
  parent's, and colic, 169–70
  temper tantrums and, 599
encephalitis, 9, 591, 851,
    859–60
endocrines, 723
enema, 535–37
engorgement, 101, 115
enteritis, 538
enteroviruses, 608
enuresis, 792–96
environment, 719–34
  ADHD and, 591
  air pollution, 719–20
  asbestos, 720–21
  brain development and,
    164–66
  building positive, 166–67
  carbon monoxide, 721–22
  drinking water, 722–25
  fish and, 726
  lead and, 727–30
  pesticides and herbicides and,
    730–32
  radon and, 732–33
  smoking and, 733–34
Environmental Protection
    Agency (EPA), 720, 726–27,
    729, 733
  Safe Drinking Water Hotline,
    724
enzymes, 89, 220, 555, 628, 631
epicanthus, 745
epidural, 43–44, 49

epiglottitis, *608*, 677–78, *677*,
    682, 824
epilepsy, 666, 776, 803–5
epinephrine, 547, 572, 576–78
episiotomy, 17, 43, 184
ERIC (Institute of Education
    Sciences), 831
erythema infectiosum, 853–54
Escherichia coli (*E. coli*), 545
eustachian tube, 220, 659, *671*,
    675
exercise, 11–12, 420, 592, 813,
    839
exercise saucer, 264, 293
eye contact, 280, 350–51, 593,
    643, 645
eye drops, 51, 53, 574
eyelid, 160, 740–43
eyes, 84, 735–47, *736*
  allergies and, 574
  amblyopia or lazy, 738
  astigmatism, 746
  bathing and, 77
  black, 740
  cataracts, 739
  cerebral palsy and, 651
  chemicals in, 697, 740
  color of, 140–41
  conjunctivitis and, 192
  corrective lenses and, 746–47
  crossed, 147, 195, 738
  drainage, 239
  four- to seven-month-old and,
    239
  glaucoma, 743–4
  infections, 192, 221, 463,
    739–40
  inflammation and JIA, 838–39
  injuries, 495, 740–42
  itching or burning, 738
  Kawasaki disease and, 814
  one- to three-month-old and,
    213
  nasal allergies and, 574
  newborn and, 147
  particles in, 742
  poison in, 713–15
  redness or discharge, 737, 814
  red spot in whites of, 141, 160
  retinopathy of prematurity
    (ROP), 58
  sinusitis and, 676
  strabismus, 744–45
  tear problems, 745–46
  tracking and, 195–96, 206–7

  vision screening, 736–38
  wandering, 736

fainting, 803
falls, 225, 257, 262, 292–93,
    297, 372, 403, 486–87
  broken bones, 708
  bunk beds, 480
  cribs, 477–79
  emergencies, 693
  frequent, 351
  playgrounds and, 511
family, 749–74
  adoption, 749–51
  breastfeeding and, 91
  child abuse, 751–55
  chronic conditions and,
    625–27
  diabetes and, 626
  divorce, 755–60
  first month and, 181,
    184–90
  grief and, 760–64
  illness or death in, 346, 476,
    530, 588–89, 760–64
  leaving baby with, 182
  meeting point, 699
  military service and, 768
  multiples and, 771–74
  one-year-old and, 330
  photographs, 219, 251, 436
  sibling rivalry, 764–66
  single parent, 324, 766–68
  step, 769–71
  stories and, 251
  two-year-old and, 366–71
  vacations and, 416, 420
  wheelchair and, 626
family childcare, 443–47. *See
    also* childcare provider
Family-to-Family Health
    Information Center, 627
farsightedness, 746
father (partner, co-parent)
  bonding with newborn, 152
  breastfeeding and, 91
  crying baby and, 64
  C-section and, 50–51
  first month and, 185–87
  hospital label and, 52
  in-home help and, 181
  postpartum depression and,
    151, 184, 186
  preparing for childbirth, 41

fats, 11, 122, 313
fears, 280, 417, 537, 753
febrile convulsions, 776
Federal Aviation Administration (FAA), 401
Federal Lead Disclosure Rule, 727
feeding patterns, 106
feet, 163, 232, 261, 681
  blue, 161
  fallen arches, 842
  flat, 842
fencing posture (tonic neck reflex), 162–63, 203
fetal alcohol syndrome (FAS), 4–5, 591
fetal heart rate, 13, 48
fetal tests, 14
fever, 775–82
  abdominal pain and, 527
  appendicitis and, 532
  blood in diaper and, 72
  childcare provider and, 461
  convulsions and, 803–4
  coughing and, 607
  delirium, 779
  diarrhea and, 73–74, 539, 541
  ear infection, 672
  first month and, 190, 192
  food poisoning and, 544, 546
  influenza and, 609, 610
  Kawasaki disease and, 814
  medication for, 779–82
  meningitis and, 798–99
  newborn, 148
  one- to three-month-old and, 224
  pneumonia and, 613
  preschool and, 400
  rash and, 570
  roseola infantum, 866, 867
  seizures and, 776
  swollen glands and, 688
  taking rectal temperature, 82–83
  teething and, 246, 247
  treatment for, 779–82
  vomiting or diarrhea and, 196
  when to call pediatrician about, 668, 672, 777–79
fever strips, 83, 775
fiber, 536–37
fifth disease, 853–54

fine motor skills
  eight- to twelve-month-old and, 273, 290
  four- to six-month-old and, 249
  one-year-old and, 299–300
finger and thumb sucking, 97, 100, 161–62, 179, 282, 286
  discontinuing, 594–96
finger and toenails, 80, 141, 195
finger foods, 243, 275, 282, 284
finger paints, 342, 410
fingertip injuries, 707–8
fireplaces, 488, 562–63, 568
fires, 198, 465, 475, 482, 485, 520, 698–99
fire station safety days, 292
fireworks, 434, 699, 741
first aid, 400, 443, 449, 452, 461, 465, 691, 699–700, 703, 902
First Candle, 193
first month, 159–99
First Trimester Combined Test, 12–13
fish, 7, 9, 242, 544, 571, 726
fleas, 578–80
floor play, 274, 311, 367
floors, 293, 486–87
floppiness, 192, 239, 649
fluoride, 133, 243, 244, 287, 356–57, 722, 724
flu. See influenza
fly bites, 578–79
folate supplements, 630
folic acid, 11, 628, 639, 656, 658
fontanelles, 77, 143, 202
  bulging, 656–57
  sunken, 540, 547
food. See also diet; meals; menus; nutrition; solid food
  canned, 813
  child abuse and, 753
  choking and, 257, 293, 334, 700–701
  high-fiber, 536
  high-sodium chart, 812
  packaged, 813
  preferences for, 355, 392, 422
  probiotics and, 543
  red urine and, 783
  rejection of, 242–43, 312, 548
  storing, 243
  walking with, 405

food additives, 591
food allergies, 118–19, 123, 130, 241, 168, 255, 538, 562–63, 571–73, 576
Food and Drug Administration (FDA), 7, 121, 662, 727
food labels, 573, 813
food poisoning, 538, 544–49, 654
food preparation, 7, 9–10, 225, 252, 316, 454, 481, 548–49, 551, 637, 699
football hold, 97, 97, 104
foreskin, 75, 143–45, 785–86
formula-feeding, 30, 88–89, 120–33, 245, 724
  amount and schedule for, 128–31
  anti-reflux, 557
  breastfeeding vs., 90, 105
  colic and, 168
  concentrates, 124–24
  constipation and, 191, 536
  diarrhea and, 191, 220
  donor breast milk vs., 56
  eight- to twelve-month-old and, 281
  extensively hydrolyzed, 122
  hypoallergenic, 122
  jaundice and, 157
  lactose-free, 122
  low-iron, 121
  one- to three-month-old and, 215
  predigested 122
  preparing and storing, 124–27
  probiotics and, 122–23, 543
  protein hydrolysate, 168
  ready-to-feed, 124
  soy, 122–23
  spitting up and, 221
  supplementing and, 109
  warming, 114, 125
  water and, 125, 133, 722, 725
four- and five-year-old, 89, 407–36
  cognitive milestones, 414
  emotional milestones, 419
  hand and finger skills milestones, 410
  language milestones, 411
  movement milestones, 409
  sleep needed by, 874

social milestones, 415
vision screening, 737
four- to seven-month-old, 227–57
autism and, 646
cognitive milestones, 237
developmental health and,
239–40
language milestones, 236
movement milestones, 231
social and emotional
milestones, 240
vision milestones, 234
vision screening and, 737
fruits, 132–33, 242–43, 312,
353, 536, 537, 543
fungus infections, 635, 689,
865
furniture, 6, 33–34, 251, 260,
298, 486–87, 520

galactosemia, 122–23
gallbladder disease, 178
games, 299, 347, 375, 377, 386,
391, 401, 410, 420, 434–35
gamma globulin, 551, 859
garage, 335, 484, 522, 714, 721
gas appliances, 481, 714,
721–22
gastrocolic reflex, 74, 216
gastroenteritis, 529, 538. *See also*
abdomen and
gastrointestinal tract
gastroesophageal reflux (GER),
66–67, 118, 221–22,
556–57, 606
gates, 263, 291, 292, 372, 403,
485, 520
gender identity, 306, 344,
386–88
genetic blood spot test, 56
genital and urinary systems, 75,
84, 143, 232, 307, 418–19,
783–96, 784. *See also* penis;
vagina
blood in urine, 783–85
chordee, 786
circumcision, 785–86
hypospadias, 786
labial adhesions, 787, 787
meatal stenosis, 787
pain, child abuse and, 753
posterior urethral valve,
788–89, 788
proteinuria, 785

undescended testicles, 789–90,
789
urinary tract infections,
790–92
wetting problems, 792–96
German measles (rubella), 7–8,
654, 659, 739, 822, 867–68,
893
German measles vaccine. *See*
measles, mumps, rubella
(MMR) vaccine
Giardia lamblia parasite, 529
girls
ADHD and, 591
autism and, 644
bathing, 75
breasts enlarged and, 143
first month and, 160
gendered activities and, 306,
387
genitals in newborn, 143
hernia and, 553
HOI and, 849
JIA arthritis and, 838
labial adhesions, 787–88, 787
language skills, 302, 343
newborn, blood in diaper, 72
role-playing, 386–87
sex-linked abnormalities, 653
toilet training and, 322, 358
urinary tract infections and,
531
vaginal discharge in newborn,
143
weight gain, 260
glaucoma, 743–44, 849
glomerulonephritis, 857, 870
glucose, 14–15, 632, 634
gluten, 533–34
grandparents, 187–88, 190, 211,
214, 250–51, 290–91, 294,
324, 332–33, 369–70, 402,
435–36, 441, 444, 519–23,
715
grapes, 243, 284, 293, 314, 353,
700
grasping, 163, 205, 213, 228,
231, 266
grill, 514, 549, 721
growth, 84, 105, 229, 260–61,
296
delayed, 638
eight- to twelve-month-old
and, 260–61, 281
first month, 159–61

four- to seven-month-old and,
229
one- to three-month-old and,
202–3, 215
one-year-old and, 296–97
three-year-old and, 376
two-year-old and, 338–39
growth charts, 146, 160, 321,
894–901
growth spurts, 68, 117–18, 160,
215, 296, 339
gums, 11, 246–47
gun safety, 334, 487, 488, 741

Haemophilus influenzae type b
(Hib), 677, 799, 818, 824,
893
Haemophilus influenzae type b
(Hib) vaccine, 85, 225,
255–56, 330–31, 371, 461,
677–78, 799, 818, 824,
892–93
hair, 143, 160, 854–55
hand, foot, and mouth disease,
681
hand and finger skills
eight- to twelve-month-old
and, 265–67
four- and five-year-old and,
409–11
one-year-old and, 299–300
three-year-old and, 379–80
two-year-old and, 340–42
hand-eye coordination, 206, 208,
233, 249, 273
hands, 84, 172
blisters on, 681
blue, 161
flapping, 643
hand-foot syndrome, 638
one- to three-month-old and,
202, 204–6, 212, 213
redness and, 814
handwashing, 223, 306, 418,
422, 454, 460–61, 538, 542,
548–49, 551, 563, 611, 670,
729, 732, 863–64
head, neck, nervous system, 649,
797–806. *See also*
concussions
autism and, 645
floppy head, 239
fontanelles, 77, 143, 202, 540,
547, 656–57

head, neck, nervous system (*cont.*)
  injuries, 693, 711–12, 798, 804
  meningitis, 797–800
  motion sickness, 800–801
  mumps, 801–2
  seizures, 803–5
  shape of newborn, 142–43
  supporting head, 172, 178, *179*, 199, 203, *204*, 213
  torticollis, 805–6
headaches, 44, 609, 712, 738, 799
head lice, 463, 855–57
head size, 84, 160, 202, 229, 261, 296–97, 338
Head Start, 448
healthcare, 621–23. *See also* pediatrician; well-child checkups
  basic baby, 82–85, 178–84
  developmental milestones, 85
  first month and, 190–96
  four- to seven-month-old and, 253–55
  newborn and, 153–58
  one- to three-month-old and, 220–26
  preventive, *888–91*
health insurance, 21, 26–28, 111–12, 247
health maintenance organizations (HMOs), 27
HealthyChidren.org, 586
healthy lifestyle, 419–20
hearing aids, 522, 661
hearing problems, 84, 235, 236, 432–33, 494, 642, 659–63
  cerebral palsy and, 652
  conductive, 659, 661
  Down syndrome and, 655
  ear infections and, 671–72, 675
  early detection and 343–44
  first month and, 174, 194
  four- to seven-month-old and, 228, 229, 235
  language and, 343
  one- to three-month-old and, 208–10
  sensorineural, 659, 661–63
  sign language and, 663
  treatment of, 661–63
heart, 84, *808*

heart problems, 5, 13, 610, 613
  arrhythmias, 807–9
  congenital, 813
  hypertension, 811–14
  Kawasaki disease, 814–15
  murmurs, 809–11
  premature baby and, 59
heart rate, 58, 807
heatstroke, 335, 373, 779
height, 229, 260, 296, 338–39, 376
hemangiomas
  capillary, 142, 742
  of infancy (HOI), 849–50
hematuria, 783–85
hemoglobin, 331, 371, 628–29, 638
hemolytic anemia, 628–29
hemophilia, 653, 680
hepatitis, 549–51
  A, 463, 549, 551, *893*
  B, 549, 551, *893*
  C, 549–51
hepatitis A vaccine, 85, 291, 330–31, 371, 461, 549, 551, 824, *892–93*
hepatitis B vaccine, 22, 53, 85, 224–25, 255–56, 291, 371, 461, 463, 549, 551, 697, 824, *892–93*
herbal supplements, 11, 100, 191
herbicides, 514, 730–32
hernia
  abdominal, 143
  incarcerated, *552*
  inguinal, 143, *552, 553*
  treatment, *552*
  umbilical, 158
herpes simplex, 8–9, 678–79, 797
Hib. *See Haemophilus influenzae* type b
high chair, 244, 251, 474, 481, 488–89
HIPPA, 21
hips, 84–85
  cerebral palsy and, 652
  developmental dysplasia of (DDH), 84, 806, 843
  limp and, 843
  swaddling and, 68, *81*
  transient synovitis of, 839–40
hitting by child. *See also* aggressive behavior; spanking
  childcare provider and, 457

one-year-old and, 306, 324
three-year-old and, 386, 396–97
two-year-old and, 348
sibling and, 396–97
HIV/AIDS, 15, 29, 461, 464, 614, 616, 634–37
hives, 576–78
homeopathic teething tablets, 247
home. *See also* childproofing
  lead paint and, 728–29
  moving to new, 476
  safety and, 334, 476–78
honey, danger of, 544, 548
hormones, 90, 95, 143, 151, 184, 186, 339
hospital
  breastfeeding and, 30–31, 105, 109–10
  childbirth checklist and, 18
  childbirth discharge and, 26–27
  C-section and, 49
  delivery room, 53
  emergencies and, 25, 694
  going home before newborn, 57
  going home from, 148–49, 189
  labor and delivery and, 42, 44–53
  newborn screening, 56
  pediatrician and, 21, 25, 156–57
  premature birth and, 54–57
  rooming-in and, 109
  siblings and 38–39, 189
hot dogs, 10, 284, 293, 314, 353, 700
hot tub, 333, 408, 516
household chemicals, 252, 294, 334, 373, 405, 481, 563, 568, 714, 717
household chores, 17, 307, 332, 416, 611
household help, 181–82, 442
human papillomavirus (HPV), 872
humidifier, 38, 190d, 568, 575, 608, 610, 617–18, 669, 681
hydrocele, 143, *553*
hydrocephalus, 58–59, 656–57, 666
hygiene, 400, 461, 546, 548, 611, 637, 862

hyperactivity, 349, 590–94
hypertension. *See* blood pressure, high
hypertrophic pyloric stenosis, 556, *557*
hypoglycemia, 634
hypospadias, 30, 786
hypothermia, 51
hypothyroidism, 655, 665
hypotonia, 649

ibuprofen, 96, 102, 550, 563, 578, 605, 610, 669, 672, 680, 688, 804, 839
  dosage chart, 781
  when not to use, 780
imaginary friends, 389, 402
imaginative play (fantasy, make-believe, pretend), 303, 310, 315, 332, 345–46, 385–91, 402, 408, 415–17, 646
  autism, 350
  four- and five-year-old and, 418
  lack of, 350–51, 417
  reality vs. fantasy and, 346, 389–90, 408, 416–17, 419
  three-year-old and, 386
  two-year-old and, 346–47
  violence and, 418
imitation, 211, 248, 269, 303, 305–7, 313, 325, 346–47, 389, 475, 643, 646, 664
immune globulin, 859
immune system, 8, 31, 92, 124, 253, 533, 572, 614, 635, 800
immunizations, 292, 817–25, 852. *See also specific types*
  autism and, 644
  benefits of, 817–18
  catch-up, 403, 613
  childbirth and, 22
  childcare provider and, 461
  eight- to twelve-month-old and, 291–92
  emergencies and, 694, 703
  four- to seven months and, 255–56
  health conditions precluding, 818
  hepatitis, 551

importance of, 818–22
IVIG treatment, 815
list of, 821–25, *892–93*
managed care plans and, 27
multiple at same time, 820
one- to three-month-old and, 219, 224–25
one-year-old and, 330–31
pain of, 820
pediatrician and, 26, 85
pregnancy and, 8–10
school and, 430, 432
sickle cell disease and, 639
side effects of, 818–21
three-year-old and, 403
two-year-old and, 371–72
immunoglobulin E, 572, 695, 815
impetigo, 743, 857
independence, 307–8, 313, 327, 337–38, 340, 352, 385, 390, 408, 415, 427
Individualized Education Program (IEP), 432, 648
Individuals with Disabilities Education Act (IDEA), 467–68
infant care programs, 16
infant carriers, 66, 401
infant feeding device, 116–17
inflammatory bowel disease, 90, 554
influenza (flu), 10, 254, 606, 608–12, *893*
  antiviral medication for, 611
  complications from, 610–11
  four- to seven-month-old and, 253–54
  Kawasaki disease and, 815
  mastitis vs., 115
influenza vaccine, 10, 85, 254, 256, 372, 450, 461, 610–11, 823, *892–93*
  shot vs. mist and, 610, 823
inguinal hernia, 143, 552, 790
inhaler, 565–68
in-home care provider, 441–43
injuries. *See also specific types*
  aggressive behavior and, 585
  child abuse and, 753
  childcare provider and, 464–66
  emergencies, 691–92

safety and, 474–76
school buses and, 467
temper tantrums and, 599
insect bites and stings, 575–80, 688, 861–62
insecticides, 563
insect repellents, 580, 837, 861–62
insulin, 632–34
intellectual disability, 4, 6, 641, 643, 663–66, 706
intelligence (IQ), 343, 663, 726
interferon gamma release assay (IGRA), 615–16
internal tibial torsion, 845, *845*
intestines. *See also* abdomen and gastrointestinal system
  blockage in infant, 528–529
  bowel biopsy and, 533
  inflammation of, 538
  injured lining and, 538
  intussusception and, 528–29
  large, *528*, *532*
  malabsorption and, 554
  necrotizing enterocolitis, 59
  oligosaccharides and, 122
  probiotics and, 123
  small, *528*, *532*, 533, 557
intraventricular hemorrhage, 58–59
intussusception, 528–29
iodine, 704
ipecac, 716
iron deficiency anemia, 316, 331, 592, 628–29, 728
iron supplements, 11, 73, 103, 120–21, 132, 245, 316, 320, 331, 355, 629–30
itching, 570, 578, 869

jaundice, 59, 148, 155–57, 194, 541, 558, 629, 638, 649
jealousy, 40, 153, 190, 217–18, 252, 290, 330, 366–67, 397–98
joints
  contractures, 652, 657
  septic arthritis and, 835
juice, 132–33, 243, 321, 538, 541–42
Juvenile Diabetes Research Foundation, 634
juvenile idiopathic arthritis (JIA), 838–39, 843–44

Kawasaki disease, 814–15
kicking, 204–5, 341, 324, 328
kidney problems, 800
    blood in urine and, 783–84
    diabetes and, 632
    disease, 339, 610, 613, 784–85
    ibuprofen and, 780
    impetigo and, 857
    infections, 255
    spina bifida and, 657
    stones, 784
    streptococcal bacteria and, 870
kindergarten, 429–32, 448
kitchen, 260, 292, 372, 481–82, 521
knock-knees, 840
Kohler's disease, 843

labial adhesions, 787–88, 787
labor, false, 16, 42
labor pain, 43–44
lacrimal system, 745, 745–46
lactation consultant, 47, 88, 92, 94, 106, 108, 117, 118, 216
lactose intolerance, 571
    breast-feeding and, 124
    formula and, 122–23, 220, 541
La Leche League, 104, 136
Lamaze method, 16
language. See also sentences;
    speech and sounds;
    vocabulary
    anger and, 582
    autism and, 350, 643, 646
    brain development and, 165–66
    cerebral palsy and, 649
    delays, early treatment, 343–44
    eight- to twelve-month-old and, 267–69, 291
    emotions and, 582
    family mealtimes and, 241
    foreign, 219, 248, 268, 273, 311, 367
    four- and five-year-old and, 408, 411–13
    four- to seven-month-old and, 235–36, 241, 248
    grammar, 343
    hearing and, 194, 659
    inappropriate, 408, 411–12, 435
    intellectual disability and, 664

names and, 301–2
one-year-old and, 296, 300–302, 311
prepositions, 383, 417
pronouns, 302, 343–44, 383
pronunciation, 411
talking to baby and, 248
three-year-old and, 375, 381–83
two-year-old and, 338, 342–44, 350, 367
verbs, 301–2, 411, 418
larynx, 606, 608–9
last-minute activities checklist, 17–18
latching, 47, 94–101, 96, 98, 114, 117
LATCH system, 197, 256, 373, 404, 496–97, 500–501
laundry detergents, 222, 372–73, 405, 481–82
laxative, 535–37
lead poisoning, 293, 316, 331, 371, 530, 591, 666, 722, 724, 727–30
learning, 165–66, 236, 302–3, 310, 344, 412–14, 827–30
learning disorders, 5, 641, 657, 664, 728, 730
legs, 85, 204–5, 213
    bowlegs, 160, 204, 840
    knock-knees, 840
let-down, 94–98, 100–101, 118
leukemia, 31, 88, 90
light sensitivity, 173, 239, 738, 744
limits, 295–96, 324, 352, 362–64, 397, 427–29, 582, 597, 833
limp, 843–44
lips, red, swollen, 814
lithium button batteries, 405
liver, 178, 339, 528, 635
    hepatitis, 549–51
low birth weight, 4, 5, 11, 176, 245, 496
lungs, 603–15
    asthma, 562
    bronchiolitis, 603–5
    cancer, radon and, 732
    checkups and, 84
    coughs, 605–8
    croup, 608–9
    cystic fibrosis, 631
    infections, 255

    influenza, 609–12
    pneumonia, 612–14
    poor function, 5
    premature baby and, 58
    respiratory infections, 222–23
    tuberculosis, 614–16
    whooping cough, 616–18
Lyme disease, 836–37
lymph glands, 687–69
lymph nodes, 635, 688
lymphocytes, 687
lymphoma, 90

Madonna hold, 96
malabsorption, 554–55
malnutrition, 541
managed care plan, 20–21, 27–28
March of Dimes, 57, 658
marijuana, 5–6, 100
mastitis, 115
masturbation, 307, 419
matches, 403, 434, 475, 481, 699, 734
mattress, 35–36, 66, 197, 478, 480, 490
meals. See also diet; food; menus;
    nutrition
    choking and, 701
    eight- to twelve-month-old and, 282
    family, 422–23
    four- and five-year-old and, 422–25
    media and, 832
    one-year-old and, 310, 321
    playing or TV and, 424
    pregnancy and, 11, 17
    solid foods and, 241, 244
    one-year-old and, 321
measles, 253, 822, 857–59, 893
measles, mumps, rubella (MMR)
    vaccine, 85, 291, 330, 371–72, 432, 461, 801, 815, 822, 859, 867–68, 892, 893
meat, 9–10, 242, 545, 548, 812
meatal stenosis, 29, 787
meconium, 73, 155
media, 348, 389, 395, 420, 435, 586–88, 592, 827–33. See also television

medial femoral torsion, 845
Medicaid, 27
medical history, 694
medical home, 20, 622
medications
    ADHD and, 592
    asthma triggers, 563
    breastfeeding and, 91, 100
    childcare provider and, 459–60
    diarrhea and, 539, 542
    eczema and, 569
    grandparents and, 251, 370,
        520
    hives and, 576
    pregnancy and, 4, 6, 654
    safety and, 294, 334, 373, 405,
        475, 483, 714
    telehealth and, 24
melanoma, 847
memory
    discipline and, 249, 260,
        287–88
    eight- to twelve-month-old
        and, 273, 287–88
    four- to seven-month-old and,
        236, 249
    impairment, 726
    one-year-old and, 304
meningitis, 15, 89, 90, 292,
    797–800, 818
    ADHD and, 591
    bacterial, 797–800
    Hib vaccine and, 797, 818, 824
    seizures and, 804
    viral, 797–99
    vomiting and, 558
    West Nile and, 860
meningococcal vaccine, 461,
    799–800, 825
menus
    eight- to twelve-month-old
        and, 283
    one-year-old and, 313, 319
    pre-schooler and, 421
    two-year-old and, 354
mercury, 7, 726, 819
metabolic disorders, 665
metatarsus adductus, 844–45,
    844
microbiome, 124
middle ear fluid, 220, 659–61
middle ear infections, 558, 659,
    670–75, 671
milia, 142
military families, 768

milk, cow's, 73, 243, 573, 628
    celiac disease and, 534
    diarrhea and, 541–42
    formula vs., 120–21
    four- and five-year-old and,
        422, 424
    iron and, 355
    one-year-old and, 316
    raw, 10, 542, 544–45, 548
milk allergy, 122, 221, 255, 530,
    538
milk protein, 119, 168
mirrors, 206, 234, 240, 278,
    306, 315
mitochondrial diseases, 653
mobiles, 36, 38, 177, 206, 218,
    234, 331, 478–79
modeling behavior, 306–7, 324,
    326, 363, 412, 431. See also
    role models
moisturizers, 65, 75, 78, 570
mold, 563, 568, 574–75
moles, 847–48
molluscum contagiosum, 860
mononucleosis, 682, 689
monsters, 381, 390, 408
moods
    eight- to twelve-month-old
        and, 273
    four- to six-month-old and,
        248
    one- to three-month-old and,
        219
    one-year-old and, 310, 333
    two-year-old and, 350, 366
morning sickness, 11
Moro reflex, 162, 203, 213
mosquitoes, 10, 578–79,
    860–62
mother. See also breastfeeding;
    parents; working mother
    chronic diseases, 146
    child's preference for, 275–76
    colic and, 169–70
    crying and, 212
    diet of, 119, 168
    first month and, 149–52,
        184–85
    postpartum depression and,
        151, 186
    vitamins and, 103, 131
motion sickness, 435, 800–801
motor skills. See also specific
    skills
    delayed, 664

four- and five-year-old and,
    420
four- to seven-month-old and,
    228
one-year-old and, 332
two-year-old and, 340
Motrin, 605
mouth, 84
    blisters in, 678–79
    white patches in, 195
mouthing
    eight- to twelve-month-old
        and, 261
    four- to seven-month-old and,
        228, 230, 239, 252
    one- to three-month-old and,
        206, 213
mouth-to-mouth resuscitation,
    699–700
movement
    eight- to twelve-month-old
        and, 261–65
    first month, 171–75
    four- and five-year-old and,
        408–9
    four- to seven-month-old and,
        229–33
    one- to three-month-old and,
        203–6
    one-year-old and, 297–98
    rhythmic, 248
    three-year-old and, 377–78
    two-year-old and, 339–41
MRI (magnetic resonance
    imagery), 650, 657, 804
MRSA infections, 862–63
multiple deliveries, 54, 104,
    771–74
Multiples of America, 774
mumps, 801–2, 822, 893
mumps vaccine. See measles,
    mumps, rubella (MMR)
    vaccine
muscles, 84, 192, 229
muscular dystrophy, 653
musculoskeletal problems,
    835–46, 836
    arthritis, 835–40
    birth injury and, 154
    bowlegs and knock-knees,
        840
    elbow, 840–41
    fallen arches, 842
    flat feet, 842
    limp, 843–44

musculoskeletal problems (*cont.*)
pigeon toes, 844–45
spina bifida and, 657
sprains, 846
mushrooms, poisonous, 544, 546
music, 38, 63, 177, 218, 311, 315, 332, 367

nails, 78–80, 141
name
responding to own, 236, 280
saying own, 344, 411, 418
naps, 881–82
childcare and, 453, 883, 884
eight- to twelve-month-old and, 286
four- and five-year-old and, 425
four- to six-month-old and, 246
newborn and afternoon, 64
one-year-old and, 310
parenting plan and, 883
siblings and, 884
ten- to twelve-month-old and, 881
thirteen- to twenty-three-month-old and, 882
three- to five-year-old and, 882
three-year-old and, 395
toilet training and, 359, 360
twenty-four months, 882
two- to three-year-old and, 882
two-year-old and, 360
National Association for Family Child Care, 445, 446
National Association for the Education of Young Children (NAEYC), 367
National Capital Poison Center, 485
National Center for Healthy Housing, 729
National Center for Missing & Exploited Children, 519
National Center on Early Childhood Quality Assurance, 443
National Down Syndrome Congress, 658
National Highway Traffic Safety Administration, 498, 501

National Resource Center for Health and Safety in Child Care, 461
National Safety Council, 733
National Smokers' Helpline, 562
Native Americans, 57
nausea, 532, 800
nearsightedness, 736, 746–47
nebulizer, 565–67
neck, 172, 203, 655
stiff, meningitis and, 799
torticollis and, 805–6
necklaces, 198–99, 247
necrotizing enterocolitis, 55–56, 59
neonatal cephalic pustulosis, 160
neonatal death rate, 57
neonatal intensive care unit (NICU), 54–55, 176, 186, 235, 771
neonatologist, 20–21, 57–58
nephritis, 783–85, 792
neural tube defects, 13, 658
neurological development, 337, 589, 823
nevi, 743, 847–48
newborn, xxi–xxii
adjusting to, 140
antibiotic ointment for eyes, 51
Apgar scores, 51–53
appearance of, 140–45
basic day-to-day care, 61–82
basic healthcare, 82–85
bathing, 75–78
behavior of, 147–48
birth weight and, 145–47
blue skin color, 47–48, 52–53
bonding and, 46, 49–50
bowel movements and, 73–74, 155, 178
breastfeeding, 46–47, 87–101, 108–14, 117–19, 147, 178
breathing, 47–48, 51–52
clothing and, 32, 34, 80–82
communicating hydrocele, 553, 553
constipation and, 534
cord blood and, 31
coughing, 155
crying, 52, 62–64, 155
C-section and, 49
delivery room and, 51–53
diapers and, 68–72
dressing and undressing, 79, 82
eye infections, 740

feeding, 87, 108–9, 113
fever and, 148, 777
first bath, 53
first days, 139–62
first examination, 53
flu and, 10
footprint, 52
forceps marks, 155
furniture for, 33–38
genitalia, 143–45
going home, 148–49
head shape, 47, 142–43
health watch for, 153–58
hearing and, 56, 147, 174, 652, 660
heart rate, 53
hepatitis B and, 53, 549
HIV/AIDS and, 635, 636
immunizations and, 84
inability to spoil, 63
intensive medical care, 52
jaundice, 148, 155–57
lethargy and sleepiness, 157
listless, 148
meconium, 73
mother's feelings and, 149–52
partner's feelings and, 152
pediatrician and, 25, 83–85
premature, 54–59
preparing for, 3–44
probiotics and, 543
reflexes, 53, 161–63
relatives' vaccines and, 9
respiration and, 53, 157
safety and, 477
screening, 56, 123, 148, 174
shaking or hitting, 64
siblings and, 38–41, 152–53
sickle cell screen, 628
skin and nail care, 78–80
skin markings, 141–42
skin peeling, 78
skin-to-skin care, 46–47, 49, 51
sleep and, 54, 64–68
spina bifida and, 656
taking temperature, 83
talking to, 82
temperament, 139–140
tooth decay, 11
touch and, 148
umbilical cord, 158
urine, 72
vaccines and, 8–9
vision and, 147–48, 736–37

vitamin K and, 51
vomiting, 148
weight loss and, 108, 113
wrinkled skin of, 47
New Mother's Guide to Breastfeeding (AAP), 136
nightmares, 361, 381, 396, 587, 599
night terrors, 396, 425–27, 803
nighttime. *See also* bedtime
  bottle-feeding and, 127, 129–30
  breastfeeding and, 105, 106, 216, 217
  coughing and, 607–8
  eight- to twelve-month-old and, 286
  fears during, 395–96
  four- to seven-month-old and, 249
  one- to three-month-old and, 217
  one-year-old and, 322–23
  sleep behavior and, 874
  toilet training and, 359–60
911, calling, 577–78, 705, 707, 709, 712, 776, 779, 804
  emergency contact and, 692–94, 716
nipples, bottle 125, 127, 137
nipples, mother's, 92–94, 93
  cracking, sore, 102, 114–15
  inverted, 94
  thrush, 195
nitrates, 722, 725, 731
"no"
  baby responds to, 236, 269, 278
  discipline and, 252, 287, 327, 474, 598
  one-year-old and, 296, 326–27
  shaking head "no," 274
  two-year-old and, 338
nonsteroidal anti-inflammatory drugs (NSAIDS), 550, 563, 578, 639, 839
nonstress test, 13
norovirus, 538, 557
nose
  mucus, 668–69
  nasal allergies, 573–76
  nasal passages blocked, 157, 224
  nosebleeds, 679–81
  pneumonia and, 612

runny, 224, 609
  suctioning, 190, 224
nose drops, 669
nose sprays, 574, 675
nurse midwife, 10, 17–18
nurse practitioner, 19
nursery, 478–80
nursery safety, 477–80, 520–21
nursing bras, 93–94, 93
nursing pads, 110
nutrition. *See also* diet; feeding; food; meals; menus
  breast milk and, 89, 97, 120
  first year, 87
  formula and, 89, 120
  four- and five-year-old and, 420–25
  one- to three-month-old and, 219
  one-year-old and, 309–21
  pregnancy and, 11
  solid foods and, 244
  sweets and, 318
  three-year-old and, 392
  two-year-old and, 353–55
nuts, 243, 284, 314, 353. *See also* peanuts
  allergies, 571

obesity, 4, 320–21
  bottle-feeding and, 131, 244
  breastfeeding and, 90
  diabetes and, 633
  four- and five-year-old and, 420
  hypertension and, 811, 813
  media and, 392, 830
  one-year-old and, 312
  solid foods and, 244
object permanence, 237–38, 270
obsessive compulsive disorder (OCD), 600–601
obstetrician, 10, 16–18, 20, 42, 48, 50–51, 462
oligosaccharides, 122
omega-3 fatty acids, 7, 592, 726
one-month-old
  hearing milestones, 174
  movement milestones, 171
  smell-and-touch milestones, 175
  toys and, 177
  visual milestones, 173

one- to three-month-old, 201–26
  developmental warning signs, 177, 213
  emotional and social milestones and, 211
  hearing and speech milestones, 209
  movement milestones, 205
  visual milestones, 208
one-year-old, 295–335
  autism and, 643, 645
  cognitive milestones, 303
  hand and finger skills milestones, 300
  language milestones, 301
  movement milestones, 298
  sleep needed by, 874
  social and emotional milestones, 305, 313
ophthalmologist, 735, 839
organic foods, 730–32
organ transplant, 604, 614
osteomyelitis, 835
otitis media with effusion, 674
otoacoustic emissions test, 660
otoscopes, 23, 24
outdoors, 80–82, 180–81, 245, 315, 332, 335, 340, 420, 874
overfeeding, 168–69, 221, 557
overweight, 88, 244, 320–21, 376, 419–20, 422, 811, 813–14
oxygen, 58, 640, 649, 705
oxytocin, 43, 95–96
ozone, 719

pacifier, 37, 67, 68, 129, 131, 162, 169, 193, 611
  breastfeeding and, 100
  choosing, 178–80
  discontinuing, 594–96
  ear infections and, 675
  safety and, 198, 491–92
pages, turning, 299, 311, 340, 342
pain medication, 43–44, 95–96
pain. *See also specific types*
  bone fractures and, 710
  breastfeeding and, 95–96
  emergencies and, 693
  meningitis and, 799
  one- to three-month-old and, 211

paint, household, 6, 293, 484, 530
painting, by child, 299, 379, 410
PANDAS (Pediatric Autoimmune Neurophychiatric Disorder Associated with Streptococcal Infection), 600
PAPP-A blood test, 12
parainfluenza virus, 608
parasites, 529, 538–39, 545
parents, xxii. *See also* mother; father
    childcare provider and, 449
    child's media use and, 832–33
    preschool, 397–98
    chronic conditions and, 626
    consistency in rules and, 363
    death of, 588–89, 760–61
    divorce and, 346, 530
    interacting with child, 166, 275
    modeling behavior, 584
    parenting plan, 883
    sleep deprivation and, 878–81, 886
    tension between, 476
    twins and, 773–74
parent support groups, 166, 324, 623, 648, 651
parvovirus, 462, 853, 867
passivity, excessive, 352, 417, 753
patent ductus arteriosus (PDA), 810
paternity leave, 187
peanut butter, 284, 314, 353
peanuts, 700
    allergy to, 241, 571, 573
pediatrician. *See also* well-child checkups
    alternative therapies and, 623
    asking questions of, 83
    breastfeeding and, 30–31, 88, 92, 108–9
    bringing another adult to visit, 83
    call-in periods, 22
    changing, 28
    checkups and visits, 25–26, 152
    childcare provider and, 470–71
    choosing, 19–26
    chronic health conditions and, 623, 626
    circumcision and, 28–30

defined, 19
emergencies and, 25, 691, 697–98, 707, 711
fees and, 26
four- and five-year-old visits, 432–33
growth charts and, 146–47
hospital and, 21–22, 25, 148
immunizations and, 26, 84
issues to discuss with, 26–31
managed care plans and, 27–28
newborn and, 56, 83–85, 153–58
premature baby and, 57
school exam, 430
telehealth and, 22–24
three-year-old and, 402–3
training of, 19–20
two-year-old and, 371
when to call, 64, 72–74, 191–92, 194, 196, 224, 239–40, 255, 257, 527, 529, 541, 564, 604
pediatric subspecialists, 20, 27–28
peekaboo, 219, 238, 240, 262, 271, 273, 278, 332
penis
    cancer, 29
    chordee, 786
    circumcised, 84, 143–44
    hypospadias and, 786
    newborn, 143–45
    uncircumcised, 144–45
pericarditis, 838
Perthes disease, 844
pertussis. *See* whooping cough
pertussis vaccine. *See* DTaP vaccine
pervasive developmental disorder not otherwise specified (PDD-NOS), 643
pesticides, 514, 522, 730–32
pets, 279. *See also* dogs; cats
    allergies and, 574–75
    asthma and, 563, 568
    fleas and, 580
    grandparents and, 520
    loss of, 530
    pinworms and, 864
    safety, 334, 405, 517–18, 520
photoscreening, 737
phototherapy, *156*, 157
phthalates, 723–24

physical appearance
    first month and, 159–61
    four- to seven-month-old and, 229
    one- to three-month-old and, 202–3
    one-year-old and, 296–97
    three-year-old and, 376
    two-year-old and, 338–39
picaridin, 580, 862
picture books, 219, 248, 267–68, 279, 305, 345, 434
pigeon toes (intoeing), 261, 844–45
pincer grasp, 266
pinkeye. *See* conjunctivitis
pinworms, 863–64
pituitary, 95
plague, 518
plane travel, 183–84, 401–2, 674
Plantar grasp, 163
plants, 485, 513, 569
plastic bags and wrappings, 198, 478, 487
plastic containers, 723–24
play and playing. *See also* imaginative play; outdoors; toys
    autism and, 645, 646
    eating and, 424
    eight- to twelve-month-old and, 289–90
    fathers and, 187
    four- and five-year-old and, 420
    four- to seven-month-old and, 240, 248, 249
    grandparents and, 332
    mothers and, 187
    one- to three-month-old and, 211–12, 218–19
    one-year-old and, 304, 305, 332
    siblings and, 218, 289–90
    three-year-old and, 379
    tracking games, 172–73
    two-year-old and, 340, 342, 345, 366
play dates, 414
playground, 340, 402–3, 414, 469, 511–13, 523
play groups, 253, 347, 367, 375
playing house, 386–87
playmates, 304–5, 347, 385–86, 646

play yards, 37, 183, 197, 198, 234, 247, 266, 293, 324, 328, 470, 481, 490–91, 520, 765
pleuritis, 838
plurals, 344, 418
pneumococcal conjugate vaccine (PCV13), 330, 613, 824, 892, *893*
pneumococcal polysaccharide (PPV23) vaccine, 613–14
pneumococcal vaccine, 85, 225, 255, 256, 292, 331, 371, 461, 613, 800, 824–25
pneumococcus bacteria, 800, 824–25, *893*
pneumonia, 5, 89, 292, 606, 612–14, 635, 638, 668, 675, 700, 800, 859
    HIV/AIDS and, 635
    viral vs. bacterial, 613
    whooping cough and, 617
pneumonitis, 838
Poison Help number, 293, 373, 485, 692–93, 697, 713, 715
    information to provide to, 716
poison ivy, oak, sumac, 569, 864–65
poisons, 293, 373, 405. *See also* food poisoning; lead poisoning
    emergency, 693, 713–17
    plants and, 485, 513
policy, American Academy of Pediatrics. *See* American Academy of Pediatrics (AAP) policy
polio vaccine (IPV), 85, 225, 255, 256, 331, 371, 372, 432, 461, 823–24, *893*
polychlorinated biphenyls (PCBs), 726
popcorn, 284, 314, 353, 701
port wine stain, 142, 743, 848–49
positive pressure ventilation, 52
positive reinforcement, 324, 583, 584, 597
posterior urethral valve, 788–89, *788*
postnasal drip, 606
postpartum blues, 151, 184
postpartum depression, 151–52, 184, 186
postpartum hemorrhage, 51, 95
post-traumatic stress, 587

potty chairs, 322, 347, 358–59, 393, 454, 651
praise, 308, 324, 328, 352, 362, 582–84
prebiotics, 122, 543
preferred provider organizations (PPOs), 27
pregnancy, 3–6, 10, 13–16, 665
    breastfeeding, 92–93
    childcare and, 462
    congenital abnormalities and, 654
    cytomegalovirus and parvovirus, 462, 659
    fifth disease and, 854
    folic acid and, 658
    German measles and, 659, 867–68
    health and nutrition during, 4–11
    hepatitis and, 549–50
    premature birth and, 12
    HIV/AIDS and, 15, 635, 637
    infectious diseases and, 739
    older children and, 38–40
    prenatal care, 10–15
    preparing for delivery, 15–18
    safety and, 476
    spina bifida and, 656, 658
    Tdap vaccine and, 9, 822
    tests during, 12–15
    vaccines and, 8–9, 618
    Zika virus and, 10, 860–61
premature baby, 5, 54–59, 146, 245
    ADHD and, 591
    anemia of prematurity, 59
    apnea and, 58
    bottle-feeding, 55
    breastfeeding, 55–56, 88, 118
    breathing, 55, 604–5
    car safety seat and, 496, 773
    cerebral palsy and, 649
    clothing and, 82
    formula and, 123
    health of, 55, 57–59
    hearing and, 194
    heart murmurs, 59, 810
    history of, 12
    iron supplements, 132
    pediatrician and, 156
    personality and, 176
    plan for, 17
    returning home before, 57
    RSV and, 222–23, 605

supplemental nurser and, 116
    swaddling and, 81–82
    vision and, 195–96, 735–37
prenatal care, 10–16, 41, 88, 166, 630, 654
preschool, 40, 337. *See also* childcare centers
    activity programs, 413–14
    advantages of, 397–98
    anaphylactic reactions and, 577
    behavior problems and, 585
    bullying and, 431–32
    childproofing, 400
    child-to-staff ratios, 399
    choosing, 398–400
    CPR and, 400
    developmental disabilities and, 642
    discipline and, 399
    four- and five-year-old and, 429
    grandparents and, 402
    illness and, 400
    intellectual disability and, 664
    parents and, 397–400
    post-traumatic stress and, 587
    safety and, 519
    special needs and, 399
    staff and, 399–400, 438–39
    three-year-old and, 375, 390, 393, 397–400
    toilet training and, 357, 393
    two-year-old and, 367
Prevent Child Abuse, 751
probiotics, 122–23, 528, 539, 542–43
problem solving, 302, 344, 385–86
proteins, 353
proteinuria, 785
psoriasis, 838
Public Health Service, 658
pulmonary function test, 564
pulse oximetry, 23, 56, 58
punishment. *See also* discipline; spanking
    child saying "no" and, 327
    consistency and, 362
    discipline vs., 249, 252, 323, 582, 594
    four- and five-year-old and, 416
    four- to seven-month-old and, 252
    physical, 325, 348, 362, 427

pustular melanosis, 142
puzzles, 315, 344–45, 379, 664
pyelonephritis, 791
pyloric stenosis, 196, 222, 556

rabies, 517–18, 695
radon, 732–33
Raising Twins (Flais), 104
rapid eye movement (REM), 65
rash
    bottle-feeding and, 130
    bumpy or dry, 78
    capillary hemangiomas, 142
    chickenpox, 850–52
    childcare provider and, 459
    cradle cap, 195
    diaper, 195
    diarrhea and, 541
    eczema, 568–70
    erythema toxicum, 142
    fifth disease, 853
    fingernail infections, 195
    first month and, 195
    food allergies, 571
    German measles, 867–68
    hives, 576
    impetigo, 857
    infection and, 570, 578
    Kawasaki disease and, 814
    Lyme disease and, 836
    malabsorption and, 554
    measles, 858
    meningitis and, 799
    milia and miliaria, 142
    one- to three-month-old and, 222
    poison ivy, oak, sumac, 864–65
    pustular melanosis, 142
    ringworm, 865–66
    roseola infantum, 866–67
    scabies, 868–69
    sore throat and, 870
    umbilical infection, 195
    West Nile virus, 860
rattles, 218, 236, 493
reaching
    failure to, 240
    four- to seven-month-old and, 231, 239–40, 249
    one-hand only, 239
    one- to three-month-old and, 212–13

reading. *See also* picture books
    by child, 412
    to child, 65, 165, 174, 190, 209, 219, 248, 267–69, 273, 301, 311, 332, 343, 366, 395, 413
reasoning, 362, 384
rectum
    constipation and, 535, 537
    itching, 863
red blood cell disorders, 14, 630
reflexes, 84, 161–63, 202–4
reflux, 118, 556–57
repetitive behaviors, 383, 599, 643–45
respiratory problems. *See* breathing problems; coughs; lungs
respiratory syncytial virus (RSV), 222–23, 253, 603, 605, 608
responsiveness, declining, 693–94
retina, 58, 173, 736
retinopathy of prematurity, 58, 735
rewards, 249, 288, 324, 327, 362, 424, 585, 594
Reye syndrome, 220, 555, 610, 672, 780, 815, 851
rheumatic fever, 682, 870
rheumatoid factor positive arthritis, 838
rheumatologist, 839
riboflavin, 316
rickets, 103, 245, 316, 840
ringworm, 464, 865–66
rocking, 63, 68, 169, 175, 212, 246
    autism and, 643
role models, 368–71, 387, 583. *See also* modeling behavior
rolling over, 69, 84
    eight- to twelve-month-old and, 261, 262
    failure to, 240
    four- to seven-month-old and, 228–31, 240, 246
    one- to three-month-old and, 204
    sleep safety and, 66, 246
    swaddling and, 68, 81
rooting reflex, 95, 161, 163
roseola infantum, 866–67
rotavirus, 538, 557–58, 825, 893

rotavirus vaccine (RV), 85, 225, 256, 371, 461, 539, 542, 558, 825, 892–93
rubella. *See* German measles
rules
    changing, 362–63
    choices vs., 327
    deal-making and, 327
    four- and five-year-old and, 416
    media and, 833
    one-year-old and, 296, 323–24, 327
    safety and, 324, 475
    siblings, 218–19
    temper tantrums and, 598–99
    three-year-old and, 396–97
    too many, 324
    two-year-old and, 349, 352, 362
running, 298, 340–41, 349, 486
rye, 533–34

Safe Drinking Water Act, 722, 724
safety, 473–523. *See also* child-proofing; *and specific equipment; and locations*
    all rooms and, 484–88
    eight- to twelve-month-old and, 260, 264
    first month and, 196–99
    first six months and, 474
    four- and five-year-old and, 433–34
    four- to six-month-old and, 246
    one-year-old and, 311
    one- to three-month-old and, 225–26
    one- to two-year-old and, 474–75
    one-year-old and, 331–35
    reporting unsafe products, 494
    room-to-room in home, 476–77
    rules, 324, 475–76
    six- to eighteen-month-old and, 474
    three-year-old and, 403–5
    two-year-old and, 372–73
    two- to four-year-old and, 475
saline nasal drops, 157, 190, 604, 669, 681

salivary glands, *802*, 802
salmonella, 545–56
salmon patches, 141, 848–49
salt, 314, 540, 631, 812
scabies, 868–70
scalp, 77, 142–43, 157, 160
scarlet fever, 870
school, 372. *See also*
    kindergarten; preschool
    ADHD and, 590–91
    autism and, 647
    bullying and, 431
    buses, 466–67
    cafeterias, 545
    developmental disabilities and
      evaluation, 642, 647
    diabetes and, 634
    Down syndrome and, 655
    ear infections, 674
    failure, child abuse and, 753
    four- and five-year-old and,
      408, 429–32
    head lice and, 856
    HIV/AIDS and, 636, 637
    intellectual disability and, 664
    nurse, 432, 624
    special needs and, 624
    three-year-old and, 397–400
    transportation safety, 467
    twins and, 772
scoliosis, 652
scrotum, 84
    inguinal hernia, 552
    swelling in, 143
    undescended testicles and,
      790
seafood, 10, 548
seatbelts, 505
seborrheic dermatitis, 195, 685,
    852–53
security, 215, 219, 248, 308, 366
security objects, 282, 361
seizures, 195, 599, 642, 653,
    706, 803–5
    absence or petit mal, 803
    cerebral palsy and, 651
    emergencies and, 693–94
    fever and, 776, 867
    grand mal, 803
    head injury and, 712
    meningitis and, 798–99
    when to call 911, 804
self-concept
    eight- to twelve-month-old
      and, 278

one-year-old and, 306, 333
three-year-old and, 390
self-consoling, 63, 168, 212, 246,
    286
self-control, 324, 326, 370,
    375–76, 391, 582, 594
self-esteem, 166, 177, 333, 340,
    352, 385, 418, 651
self-feeding
    eight- to twelve-month-old
      and, 260, 281–82
    one-year-old and, 317–18
    solid foods and, 243
    three-year-old and, 379, 388
sensory impairments, 641–42,
    655
separation anxiety
    childcare drop-off and, 456
    eight- to twelve-month-old
      and, 276–78, 286
    four- and five-year-old and,
      417
    one-year-old and, 304–5,
      307–8, 313
    three-year-old and, 397–98
    two-year-old and, 351–52
sex-linked abnormalities, 653
sexual abuse, 389, 585–86,
    751–53
sexual behavior, 389, 418–19
sexual intercourse, 10, 187
sexually transmitted diseases
    (STDs), 29
shaking or hitting child, 64,
    169–70, 194–95, 199, 325.
    See also spanking
shaming, 249
shapes, 413
sharing, 304–5, 346, 375, 386
shellfish, 7, 9, 726
    contamination, 549
    allergies, 571
shingles, 822–23, 851
shoes, 34, 264, 306, 340, 511,
    523, 569, 729
shopping, 509, 518, 522–23
shyness, 239, 308, 346, 417
siblings
    baby's sleep and, 884
    breastfeeding and, 91
    chronic health conditions and,
      627
    congenital abnormalities and,
      654
    death of, 588–89, 761–62

eight- to twelve-month-old
    and, 289–90
    first month and, 152–53,
      189–90
    four- and five-year-old and,
      416
    four- to seven-month-old and,
      252–53
    grandparents and, 214
    including baby, 150
    not leaving alone with baby,
      253
    one- to three-month-old and,
      211, 214, 217–19
    one-year-old and, 330
    preparing, 38–41, 366–69
    privacy for, 289, 330
    regression and, 40, 153, 217
    rivalry and, 252, 330, 370,
      764–66, 772
    time for, 41
    twins and, 772
    two-year-old and, 366–71
sick-child programs, 460
sickle cell disease (SCD), 14,
    627–28, 637–40, 800, 853
    anemia (HbSS), 637, 639
    β-thalassemia, 637, 639
    hemoglobin C, 637
    influenza and, 611
    pneumonia and, 613
    treatment of, 639–40
sign language, 663
singing, 63, 65, 212, 218–19,
    248, 274, 322, 332, 366,
    434
single-gene abnormalities, 653
single-parent, 324, 766–68
sinus infections, 254, 563, 606,
    675–77, 798
sippy cup, 284
sitting up, 84, 228, 229–31, 240,
    261, 265, 650
skin prick test, 572–73
skin problems, 847–72. *See also*
    rashes
    birthmarks, 847–50
    blue, 154–55, 157
    cancer, 245
    chickenpox, 850–52
    childcare provider and, 463
    color of, 141
    cradle cap, 852–853
    fifth disease, 853–54
    first month and, 161

skin problems (*cont.*)
German measles (rubella), 867–68
hair loss (alopecia), 854–55
head lice, 855–57
hemangiomas of infancy, 849–50
impetigo, 857
measles, 857–59
molluscum contagiosum, 860
mosquito-borne illnesses, 860–62
MRSA infections, 862–63
newborn and, 78–80, 141–42, 154–55, 157
one- to three-month-old and, 222
peeling, 78, 141
pinworms, 863–64
poison ivy, oak, and sumac, 864–65
poison on, 715
preterm baby and, 55
ringworm, 865–66
roseola infantum, 866–67
scabies, 868–70
scarlet fever and, 870
sunburn, 870–72
warts, 872
wrinkled, 547
yellowish, 59, 130, 148, 155–57
skin-to-skin care, 46–47, 49–51, 55, 90, 95, 148, 164, 185–86, 219, 248, 273
sleep, 873–86
ADHD and, 592
amount needed, 873–76
bed-sharing and, 67
bedtime routine, 65, 878
blankets and, 66–67
bottle or breast, 247, 317
breastfeeding and, 105–6, 216
concerns about, 885
eight- to twelve-month-old and, 286
falling asleep on own, 68, 246, 322
family and, 875–76, 885
first month and, 877
first year, 876
four- and five-year-old and, 417, 425–27
four- to seven-month-old and, 246, 249

four- to twelve-month-old and, 879–81
getting most out of, 882–85
health issues and, 885
media and, 830
music or white noise, 38
naps and, 881–82
newborn and, 37, 64–67
nightlight and, 38
on adult chest, 66
one- to three-month-old and, 216–17
one-year-old and, 322–23
parental deprivation and, 184, 186, 878–81
phases of, 65, 167
post-traumatic stress and, 587
recommendations by age, 874
routines and crying, 877
safety, 37–38, 66–68, 109, 193–94, 198, 246, 331, 490 (*see also* sudden infant death syndrome)
schedule, 183, 322, 875, 884–85
six-week-old and, 878–79
swaddling and, 67–68, *80–81*
teeth grinding and, 589
three-year-old and, 391, 395–96
through the night, 217, 249
toddler and, 876
torticollis and, 806
travel and, 323
two-year-old and, 360–63
sleep apnea, 58, 108
sleepiness, excessive, 130, 157, 191, 224, 547, 655, 684, 668, 711, 798
sleepwalking, 803
small objects
manipulating, 351
safety and, 486, 493–94, 700–701
smiling, 84, 164, 170, 201–2, 209–11, 213, 350, 583
smoke detector, 198, 334, 372, 403, 485, 520, 698
smoke inhalation, 693, 698
smoking, 4–5, 100 146, 225, 257, 293, 450, 562, 562–63, 568, 591, 654, 733–34
quitting, 5, 562, 734
secondhand, 4, 5, 100, 223, 670, 675, 733

snacks, 317, 318, 321, 339, 401, 423
snake bites, 695
sneezes, 147, 611, 670
social development
autism spectrum disorder and, 350
communication disorders, 643
four-and five-year-old and, 414–16, 435–36
four- to seven-month-old and, 228, 240
grandparents and, 332–33
one- to three-month-old and, 210–15
one-year-old and, 304–7, 332–33
spina bifida and, 657
three-year-old and, 385–89
two-year-old and, 346–49, 367
withdrawal, 383
social skills group therapy, 648
solid foods, 30, 132, 222, 245, 251
balanced diet and, 121
bowel movements and, 71, 73
breastfeeding and, 88, 132
choking and, 257, 284
constipation and, 536
eight- to twelve-month-old and, 281, 283
four- to seven-month-old and, 241–45
sore throat, 681–83. See also strep throat; tonsillitis
abdominal pain and, 527, 530
extreme, 677
scarlet fever and, 870
swollen glands and, 689
sorting by shape and color, 303, 315, 344, 345
soy formulas, 122–23
spanking, 64, 169
aggressive behavior and, 309, 325, 363
avoiding, 288, 310, 325, 329, 348, 362, 397
effective discipline vs., 593–94
rewards vs., 249
time-outs vs., 288
special education, 432
special healthcare needs
car safety seat and, 496
childcare provider and, 52, 54–55, 447–48, 466–72

computers and, 831
discipline and, 288, 583
evaluation of, 642
getting help for, 624–25
school and, 399, 642
Special Olympics, 666
speech and sounds. *See also*
babbling; language;
sentences; vocabulary
eight- to twelve-month-old
and, 275
four- and five-year-old and,
411
four- to seven-month-old and,
233, 235, 239
head injury and, 712
hearing impairment and, 239,
248, 273, 659, 662, 663,
672
one- to three-month-old and,
202, 208–11, 213
one-year-old and, 296, 312
problems with, 296, 343,
351
three-year-old and, 383
two-year-old and, 343, 351
speech therapy, 382
spina bifida, 11, 14, 654,
656–59
Spina Bifida Association, 659
spinal block, 44, 49
spinal muscular atrophy, 653
spinal tap, *798, 799*, 804
spitting up, 118, 134–37,
221–22, 556
spleen, *528*, 614, 635
spoiling, 167, 215, 219, 288–89,
346
sports, 375, 655, 741
sprains, 846
stairs
eight- to twelve-month-old
and, 262–63, 291–92
four- and five-year-old and,
409
one-year-old and, 298
safety, 372, 485
three-year-old and, 378, 403
two-year-old and, 340–41,
351
standing
eight- to twelve-month-old
and, 261, 263, 265, 280
four- and five-year-old and,
409

four- to seven-month-old and,
233, 234, 240
inability to, 280
one- to three-month-old and,
204, 213
safety and, 491
Staphylococcus aureus, 546, 857
methicillin-resistant (MRSA),
862–63
Starlight Children's Foundation,
831
stepfamilies, 769–71
stepping reflex, 163, *164*, 204
stereotypies, 599–601
steroids, 570, 574, 578, 605, 609,
839
stiffness, 239, 649–50, 799
stomach
sleeping on, 66–67, 193–94,
198
time on, while awake, 68,
171–72, 203, 205, 229,
261
stomach flu, 610
stool retention, 535, 537. *See also*
bowel movements
stool softener, 536, 537
stool specimen tests, 539,
544–45
stories, 246, 322, 383, 385, 411,
425
strabismus, 651, 736, 744–45
stranger anxiety, 211, 228, 248,
274–75, 277–78
strangers, safety and, 519, 755
straws, 284
street safety, 335, 404, 408, 433,
467, 475, 506, 514
strep throat, 530–31, 681–82
scarlet fever and, 870
streptococcal bacteria, 857, 870
tic disorders and, 600–601
group B (GBS), 15
stress
child and, 219, 248, 311, 353,
361, 363, 395, 476, 529–30,
563, 589, 601, 793
mother and, 51, 55, 64
stridor, 191, 677
stroke, 638
strollers, 66, 180, 401, 508–9,
522
stuffed animals, 34, 37, 66, 193,
289, 315, 478, 493, 568
Sturge-Weber syndrome, 849

stuttering, 381–82
sucking reflex, 161
sudden infant death syndrome
(SIDS)
breastfeeding and, 30, 88, 90,
105
childcare and, 453
sleep and, 35, 37, 66–67, 221,
477–78
pacifier and, 67, 178, 491
preventing, 193–94
smoking and, 4, 5, 733
suffocation, 67–68, 197–98, 478,
487
sugar and sweets, 314, 318, 356,
392, 425, 538, 540–42
sun, 131, 180, 245, 848, 870–72
eye damage and, 741
sunscreen, 131, 180, 245, 861,
871
supervision, 198, 262, 318, 334,
378, 474
water and, 257, 333, 404, 409,
433–34, 514
supplemental nurser, 116–17
supplements, 245, 316, 355, 539.
See also vitamins
ADHD and, 592
bottle-feeding and, 245
breastfeeding and, 91, 245
four- to six-month-old and,
245
mineral, 11, 89, 103, 316
pregnancy and, 6, 11, 654
probiotics and, 543
swaddling, 63, 67–68, 149, 169,
171
how to do, *80–81*
swallowing problems, 576, 677,
715–16
swelling, 578, 638
swimmer's ear, 672, 685–87,
686
swimming and swimming pools
CPR and, 699
infections and, 515, 545, 549
pregnancy and, 12
safety, 257, 293, 333, 335,
404–5, 408, 433, 466,
514–17, 523, 705–6
swimming lessons, 404, 514–15,
706
swings, 66, 247, 403, 409, 511
swollen glands, 687–89, 802,
814

talents, 410–11, 413–14
talking to baby, 63, 82, 174, 208–10, 212, 219. *See also* reading
    effective discipline and, 593
    eight- to twelve-month-old and, 267–69, 271–72, 273
    four- to seven-month-old and, 238, 248
    one-year-old and, 300–301, 311
    two-year-old and, 366
Tay-Sachs disease, 14, 653
Tdap vaccine, 8–9, 618, 822
TEACCH, 647
tears and tear ducts, 192, 221, 239, 540, 737, 744–46, 745
teething, 68, 84, 246–47, 355, 491, 494
teething bracelets, 727
teething gels, 247, 355
teething rings, 246–47
teeth. *See also* dentist
    baking soda rinse, 11
    brushing, 247, 287, 306, 317, 355–56, 409, 415, 425
    eight- to twelve-month-old and, 286–87
    emergencies and, 693
    fluoride and, 133, 243
    grinding, 589–90
    inhaled corticosteroids and, 566
    iron supplements and, 630
    molars, 355
    pregnancy and, 10–11
    primary or baby, 355
    secondary or permanent, 355
    sweet beverages and, 133, 243
    two-year-old and, 355–57
telehealth, 22–24
television, 269, 273, 301, 321, 367, 420, 424–25, 447, 827–33
    children's programming, 829
    educational, 412
    monitoring content, 831–33
    nightmares and, 361
    nutrition and, 392, 420, 424
    violence and, 348, 367, 586, 588
temperament
    behavior and, 324
    easy or calm, 238–39, 328

first month, 175–77
four- to seven-month-old and, 229, 238
grandparents and, 250
high-strung, 238
safety and, 475–76
strong-willed, 238
temperature. *See also* fever; thermometer
    best ways to take, 64, 775, 778
    fever strips and, 83
    heat stroke and, 779
    newborn, 51, 64, 161, 180
    premature baby, 55
    oral, 83, 778
    rectal, 74, 82–83, 192, 220, 224, 775, 778
temper tantrums, 581–82, 596–99
    breath-holding, 329–30
    coping with, 326–30, 348
    effective discipline and, 593
    how to respond to, 598–99
    one-year-old and, 296, 323, 326–30
    post-traumatic stress and, 587
    preventing, 327–28, 597–98
    two-year-old and, 348, 351–52, 363
terrorism, 586–88
testicles, 84, 143
    communicating hydrocele, 552–54, *553*
    inguinal hernia and, 552, *553*
    mumps and, 802
    undescended, 789–90, *789*
    tumors, 790
tetanus, 8–9, 821–22, *893*
tetanus vaccine. *See* DTaP vaccine
thalassemia, 14, 628–30
thermometer
    digital, 777–78
    ear or tympanic, 777–78
    fever strips, 83
    oral, 83
    rectal, 83
    temporal artery, 777–78
thimerosal, 819
three-year-old, 375–405
    autism and, 646
    cognitive milestones, 385
    developmental health watch, 391

emotional milestones, 390
hand and finger skills milestones, 380
language milestones, 383
movement milestones, 378
sleep needed by, 874
social milestones, 388
vision screening and, 737
throat. *See also* sore throat; strep throat
    anaphylaxis and, 572, 578
    torticollis and, 805
throwing, 266–67, 270, 318, 324
thrush, 195, 635
thumb sucking. *See* finger and thumb sucking
thyroid problems, 726
ticks, 579, 580, 688, 836–37
tics, 599–601
time, sense of, 385, 414
timed voiding program, 795
time-ins, 364, 427, 432, 584
time-outs, 288, 309, 325–26, 330, 584, 593
    angry parent and, 397
    four- and five-year-old and, 415, 427, 432
    one-year-old and, 326, 330
    temper tantrums and, 328, 599
    two- to four-year-old and, 364
tinea, 464, 865–66
toes
    infections, 195
    turning inward, 261
    walking on, 298, 312
toilet, 483, 611
    childcare center and, 400, 454, 461, 637
    constipation and, 536–37
    drowning and, 293, 333, 705
    four- and five-year-old and, 410, 417
    handwashing and, 542
    HIV/AIDS and, 637
    posture, 795
toilet training, 40
    constipation and, 535, 537
    grandparents and, 370
    one-year-old and, 321–22
    regression and, 753
    temper tantrums and, 599
    three-year-old and, 375, 391, 393–94
    two-year-old and, 347, 357–601, 370

tongue, swelling, 572
tongue thrust reflex, 241
tonic neck reflex (fencing posture), 162–63, 203, 213
tonsillitis, 681, 683–85
toothbrush, 287, 356, 611
toothpaste, 247, 356, 569, 727
torticollis, 805–6
touch supervision, 705–6
Tourette's syndrome, 600
toxoplasmosis, 9–10, 518, 739
toys. *See also specific types*
  batteries and, 332, 494
  carrying, 298
  childcare provider and, 470
  digging, 315
  effective discipline and, 593
  eight- to twelve-month-old and, 267, 270, 273–74, 279
  electrical, 332, 494
  first month and, 177
  four- to seven-month-old and, 228, 232, 249
  grandparents and, 251, 333, 521–22
  limited interest in, 351
  mechanical, 345
  motorized riding, 333
  nesting, 315
  noisy, 494
  one- to three-month-old and, 206, 218, 226
  one-year-old and, 298–99, 302, 304, 310, 315, 331–33
  plane travel and, 401
  push-pull, 279, 298, 313, 315
  safety, 226, 332–33, 474, 493–95, 521, 530, 741
  special, 282
  squeeze, 279, 493
  stacking, 279, 342
  taking apart, 299
  three-year-old and, 379
  travel and, 183, 434
  two-year-old and, 342, 344–45
  washing shared, 863
trachea (windpipe), 562, 606, 608–9
Transcranial Doppler (TCD), 639
transgender, 387
transient synovitis, 839–40, 843
transitional objects, 282, 361

trauma, 219, 248, 590, 679
traumatic brain injury, 589
travel, 183–84, 323, 393, 400–401, 434–35, 573
  foreign, 551, 615
  motion sickness and, 800–801
tricycle, 315, 341, 377–78, 391, 403–4, 509–11, 523
triplets, 54, 771–74
tripod, 230
trisomy, 12–13. *See also* Down syndrome
tuberculosis, 614–16, 783
  test, 371, 430, 615–16
twins (multiples), 771–74
  breastfeeding, 104
  fraternal, 771–72
  identical, 771
  preterm birth and, 54
  transporting, 773
two-month-old
  cerebral palsy and, 649
  meningitis and, 798
two-year-old, 337–73
  autism and, 646, 648
  cognitive milestones, 345
  hand and finger skills milestones, 342
  language milestones, 344
  movement milestones, 341
  sleep needed by, 874
  social milestones, 347
Tylenol. *See* acetominophen

ultrasound, 529, 792
  pregnancy and, 12, 48
  premature baby and, 58
  spina bifida and, 656
umbilical cord
  bath and cleaning, 53, 75, 158
  bleeding, 158
  blood, storing, 31
  clamping, 46, 49, 52, 132
  first month and, 161
  fluids administered through, 52
  infections, 158, 195
umbilical granuloma, 158
umbilical hernia, 143, 158
United Cerebral Palsy Association, 651, 659
upper respiratory infections (URI), 223–24, 667–70. *See also* breathing problems; colds; lungs

urinary tract infection, 24, 29, 90, 395, 558, 788, 790–92
  abdominal pain and, 531
  probiotics and, 123
urination
  boy's position and, 393
  diabetes and, 632–33
  first month and, 196
  painful, 72, 395
  toilet training and, 358
  wetting problems, 395, 792–96
urine, 634
  blood in, 531, 783–85, 857
  color of, 72, 113
  posterior urethral valve blockage and, 788
urine tests, 15, 24, 531, 559, 791–92
uterus, 42, 46–47, 89, 95, 97
uveitis, 838–39

vaccines. *See* immunizations; *and specific illnesses; and vaccines*
vagina, 143, 539, 863
vaginal birth, 45–48, 51–53
valacyclovir, 9, 850
varicella. *See* chickenpox
vegetables, 10, 242–45, 284, 312, 353, 537, 543, 545
vegetarians and vegans, 122, 131, 316
Vehicle Safety Hotline, 498, 501
vernix, 46, 55
very-low-birth-weight babies, 58
violence, 586–88. *See also* aggressive behavior; hitting by child
  media and, 348, 367, 435, 586, 588, 829, 832
  physical punishment and, 325
  play and, 418
  post-traumatic stress and, 587
  teaching alternatives to, 584
viral infections, 191, 220
  abdominal pain and, 529
  antibiotics and, 253–54, 673
  asthma and, 563
  diarrhea and, 538–39
  hives and, 576
  vomiting and, 557–58
vision
  blurred, 738
  cerebral palsy and, 651

vision (*cont.*)
    colors and, 148, 173–74
    development of, 736–37
    distance, 234
    Down syndrome and, 655
    double, 738
    first month, 172–74, 195–96
    four- to seven-month-old and,
        228–29, 233–34
    head injury and, 712
    impairments, 642
    newborn, 147–48
    one- to three-month-old and,
        206–8
vision tests, 432–33, 736–38
visiting nurse, 181
vitamin A, 6, 316
    danger of, 129, 316
    measles and, 858
vitamin B$_{12}$, 103, 316, 592
vitamin C, 120, 129, 316, 630
vitamin D, 103, 129, 131, 245,
    316, 355, 424, 592, 726
vitamin K, 51, 53
vitamins, 103, 131–33, 355
    AAP recommendations, 129
    ADHD and, 592
    breastfeeding and, 89, 103
    prenatal, 6, 11
vocabulary, 646. *See also*
    language; speech and sounds
    first words, 267–69, 280,
        301–2, 645, 646
    four- and five-year-old and,
        411
    helping child learn, 310
    one-year-old and, 301
    three-year-old and, 381, 383
    toilet training and, 322
    two-year-old and, 337, 342–44
vomiting, 255, 544, 555–59. *See
    also* food poisoning
    abdominal distension and, 154
    abdominal pain and, 527, 529
    appendicitis and, 531–32
    blood in diaper and, 72
    blood or bile in, 135, 541, 558
    bottle-feeding and, 130
    breastfeeding and, 88–90, 118
    causes of, 555–57
    childcare provider and, 459
    coffee-ground-like material in,
        541, 558
    coughing and, 606

    diabetes and, 633
    diarrhea and, 539–41, 559
    first month and, 196
    gastroenteritis and, 538
    gastroesophageal reflux and,
        556–57
    head injury and, 711–12
    hypertrophic pyloric stenosis
        and, 556
    ibuprofen and, 669
    infectious causes, 557–58
    meningitis and, 798
    motion sickness and, 800
    newborn, 148, 154
    nosebleeds and, 680
    one- to three-month-old and,
        221–22
    poisoning and, 713, 716
    spitting up vs., 135, 556
    treatment for, 558–59
    when to call pediatrician,
        558–59

wading pools, 333, 466, 515
Waking Up Dry (Bennett), 796
walking
    eight- to twelve-month-old
        and, 259–60, 263–65
    failure to, 297, 312, 650
    first steps, 261, 263–264, 265
    four- to six-month-old and, 248
    newborn, 63, 68
    one- to three-month-old and,
        219
    one-year-old and, 296–98, 324
    pediatrian checkups and, 84
    pregnancy and, 12
    safety and, 324, 405
    three-year-old and, 377
    two-year-old and, 340
warts, 872
washcloths, 611
wasp sting, 578–80
water, drinking, 538
    baby's need for additional, 132
    boiling, 725
    bottle and, 317
    bottled, 133, 724
    bowel movements and, 73
    chlorinated, 125
    constipation and, 536
    contaminated, 544–46,
        722–25

    CPR and, 699
    filters, 725
    fluoridated, 133, 243, 357
    formula and, 120, 125
    introducing solid foods and,
        243
    nonchlorinated, 125
    parasitic infections from, 545
    pregnancy and, 12, 654
    unfluoridated, 357
    wells and, 125, 243–44, 722,
        724–25
water bodies. *See also* drowning;
    swimming and swimming
    pools; wading pools
    mercury in, 726
    safety near, 333, 408–9,
        433–34 466, 483, 514–17
    touch supervision and, 705–6
water heater, 197, 225–26, 252,
    257, 293, 333, 404, 469,
    483, 699
weight gain
    breastfeeding and, 108–9, 113,
        117, 119, 215
    Down syndrome and, 655
    eight- to twelve-month-old
        and, 260
    first month and, 159–60, 196
    four- to seven-month-old and,
        229
    one- to three-month-old and,
        202, 215
    one-year-old and, 296, 321
    sweet beverages and, 243
    three-year-old and, 376
    two-year-old and, 339
weight loss
    breastfeeding and, 118
    diabetes and, 633
    first month and, 159
    four- to seven-month-olds and,
        255
    malabsorption and, 554
    newborn, 113, 118
well-child checkups, 27, 84, 287,
    737
    four-month-old and, 241
    one- to three-month-old and,
        219
    one-year-old and, 331
    three-year-old and, 402
    two-year-old and, 356, 371
West Nile virus, 860–61

wetting problems, 792–96. *See also* bed-wetting
  signs of, 793–94
  treatment for daytime, 794–95
wheat allergies, 255, 571
  celiac disease and, 533–34
wheelchair, 626, 651, 657
wheezing, 89, 561–64, 571–72, 576, 604, 606–7, 612
white noise, 63, 286
whooping cough (pertussis), 8–9, 450, 616–18, 821–22, *893*
whooping cough vaccine. *See* DTaP vaccine
"why" questions, 384, 414
wild animals, 518, 695
windows, 198, 334, 372, 403, 469, 479–80, 486–87

Women, Infants, and Children (WIC), 18, 111, 216
working mother
  breastfeeding and, 115, 216–17
  child's illness and, 459
  four- to seven-month-old and, 228
  one- to three-month-old and, 201–2, 215–17
  part-time work, 449
  pregnancy and chemical exposure, 6
  preschool and, 397
  sleep schedule of child and, 875
World Health Organization (WHO), 89, 125, 321
wound, infected, 862–63

X chromosome, 653
X-ray, 529, 559, 792, 810
  chest, 612, 615–16
  fractures and, 708, 710
  sinus, 677

yeast infections, 71, 114, 195
yelling, 249, 252, 310, 325, 435
YMCA, 182, 515
yogurt, 422, 543

Zika virus, 10, 654, 739, 860–61
zinc supplements, 316, 592
zippers, 340
zoo, 402, 413